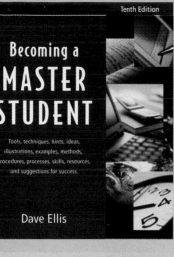

Tenth Edition

Becoming a Master Student Tenth Edition

Dave Ellis

© 2003 • 0-618-20678-7

P9-DBT-660

Students are people. They go to college, have families, work, study, and try to manage their time. *Becoming a Master Student* consistently gives students a framework for examining their lives from a self-discovery perspective, and the Tenth Edition continues this student-created, value-based approach to life and learning. Students are inspired and motivated to acquire and develop the skills needed for success in college and throughout life.

"Since reading this book, I have not only improved my academics, but also my overall time management. It has helped me in getting my priorities straight. I feel this text has been one of the most important tools for improving my overall skills."

—Joshua Furnell, student at Suffolk Community College

Some important things to note about this new edition and the enclosed chapter, *Time*:

▶ To enhance the teaching of time management and goal-setting, a number of articles have been repositioned earlier in the text.

▶ Many exercises in this chapter and throughout the text will be available online at the *Becoming a Master Student* web site. (collegesurvival.college.hmco.com/students)

▶ New coverage in this chapter includes Ways to Change a Habit and expanded information on Procrastination, plus a sidebar on cultural differences.

Read what students have to say about some of the features included in *Becoming a Master Student*:

▼ **A new feature, Student Voices, connects past students with current ones, showing how the skills within the text can be applied in real life.** (see pages 51, 173, & 274 for examples)

Student Voices

My first educational goal is to get my associate degree in Early Childhood Education at College of Menominee Nation. My second goal is to get my bachelor's degree in education. My third goal is to get a teaching job with my four-year degree. That would be a dream come true.

—ANGEL M. FOWLER,
COLLEGE OF MENOMINEE NATION,
KESHENA, WISCONSIN

"*Becoming a Master Student* helps show that even if you are of a different race and/or sex or if you are handicapped, you can still manage to do or try the task which will advance your knowledge."

—Lateria Smith, student at Catonsville Community College

Make It Easy on Yourself

A new *Course Manual for Becoming a Master Student* and HM ClassPrep CD-ROM provide detailed support for each topic related to the core text that students use.

▶ Part I, *Essentials for Planning and Instruction,* introduces teachers to the student success course and the philosophy of Becoming a Master Student, while providing guidance on how to tailor the course and create a personal philosophy statement.

▶ Part II, *Course Models and Course Content,* provides ideas and tips for lectures, exercises, and lesson plans, as well as engaging guest speakers and using videos.

▶ Part III, *Technology in the Classroom,* offers instruction on using the new HM ClassPrep CD-ROM and addresses distance and online learning.

▶ Part IV, *Diverse Classrooms and Retention Strategies,* features expanded materials for addressing a wide range of students and needs, including racial and ethnic diversity, international/ESL students, students with disabilities, and returning adults.

▶ Part V, *Assessment and Outcomes,* helps instructors create an effective evaluation procedure for measuring the usefulness of methods, adjusting the purpose to fit student needs, and judging the success of the course overall.

NEW! HM ClassPrep CD

The text-tied CD-ROM provides specific tools to use while teaching a student success course. Chapter-by-chapter materials include teaching tips, exercises, quizzes, chapter-related web links, and a bibliography for instructors to use. In addition, the following resources are included:

HOUGHTON MIFFLIN *Presents*

HMClassPrep™

Instructor Resources for

Ellis, *Becoming a Master Student*

for Windows® and Macintosh®

HOUGHTON MIFFLIN
Copyright © 2002
by Houghton Mifflin Company.
All rights reserved.
Use prescribed by
License Agreement.

0-618-23285-0

For technical assistance call 1-800-732-3223
or e-mail support@hmco.com.

Developed for Houghton Mifflin Company
by a/t media services, inc.

ABCDEFGHIJ

▶ Video clips

▶ Over 400 PowerPoint slides, 34 per chapter (also available on the *Becoming a Master Student* web site)

▶ Lecture outlines

▶ Transition guide

▶ Sample syllabi

▶ Active learning exercises

▶ Alternative examples

▶ Tenth Edition transition guide

▶ Descriptions of all book components

▶ Exercises of every chapter

▶ Customizable tests for each chapter

▶ Overview of Learning Style Inventory and video

Endless Possibilities

Take advantage of all the College Survival consultants have to offer. Every member of this unique support team has either taught or been an administrator of a student success or freshman year course. Consultants can:

▶ Assist instructors and administrators with the establishment and/or expansion of student success classes

▶ Help design or implement courses

▶ Ensure the achievement of course objectives

▶ Train faculty

Consulting services are available online, on the phone, and at training workshops and conferences. 800-528-8323
collegesurvival.college.hmco.com/instructors

Contact your sales representative—by using the rep locator on college.hmco.com/instructors—to create the full course package that best suits the needs of you and your students.

Becoming a Master Student can be combined with a multitude of supporting materials, in print, on CD-ROM, or delivered via the Internet.
▼

Supplement	For Instructor or Student	Format
Instructor's Edition	I	Print
Portfolio to Accompany *Becoming a Master Student* • Self-evaluation and reflection notebook	S	Print
Career Planning, 3/e • For programs with a career development focus	S	Print
Discovery Wheel • Personal and academic self-assessment tool	S	Print
Mastering the College Experience Telecourse • 26 half-hour videos introduce students to key concepts in *Becoming a Master Student* • License available in a broadcast, cablecast, or videocassette format	S	Videotape
Telecourse Student Guide for Mastering the College Experience • Contains overviews that summarize critical information and terms in each lesson.	S	Print
Faculty Manual for Mastering the College Experience	I	Print
Course Manual • Includes exercises to encourage classroom interaction and promote student responsibility • Offers guidance for constructing a customized course • HM ClassPrep CD-ROM provides chapter-by-chapter outlines and suggestions	I	Print CD-ROM
FREE classroom materials • 2-part exercise sheets: allow student feedback after exercises and lectures • 3-part forms: ease the process of grading for instructors and peer reviews • 3x5 cards: help improve note taking and facilitate goal-setting	I	Print
Becoming a Master Student Web Site • Instructors' area includes PowerPoint slides, video exercises, and discussion group links • Students' area includes ACE self-assessment quizzes and chapter exercises	I + S	Web
Online *Becoming a Master Student*, 2/e • Available via WebCT or Blackboard. • Online modules may be used as an Internet course or online supplement. • Modules contain topic case study and learning reflection, discovery and intention statements, practice quiz, external links, group discussions, power process case study and learning reflection, chapter topic learning tips, and a chapter test.	S	Web

Supplement	For Instructor or Student	Format
Facilitator's Manual for Online *Becoming a Master Student*	I	Web
SMARTHINKING • Real-time, text-specific tutoring available online 6 days a week. (password card required)	S	Web
PowerPoint Slides • Approximately 30 slides per chapter	I	Web

Videos
• Power Process
  • Ideas Are Tools
  • Be Here Now
  • Planning Sets You Free
  • I Create It All
  • Choose Your Conversations
  • Find a Bigger Problem
  • Employ Your Word
  • Muscle Reading
• Learning Styles Inventory
• Bias Awareness in a Multicultural World
• What Do You Want?
• Roundtable Discussion
  • Life Skills
  • Study Strategies
	S	Videotape

Houghton Mifflin College Survival Student Planner • 18-month academic planner	S	Print
Retention Management System from Noel Levitz • 194-item inventory to help predict the likelihood of a student staying in school	S	Print
Myers-Briggs Type Indicator • 93-item personality inventory provides insight on four scales: Extraversion-Introversion, Sensing-Intuition, Thinking-Feeling, and Judging-Perceiving	S	Print
Becoming a Critical Thinker, 4/e • Provides concrete and practical applications of critical thinking to everyday situations • Uses timely examples to help students connect skills to their own lives • Instructor's Resource Manual on instructor web site	S	Print
African American Master Student Profiles • Profiles of students from a wide range of fields	S	Print

Tenth Edition

Becoming a
MASTER
STUDENT

Dave Ellis

Doug Toft
Contributing Editor

Dean Mancina
Faculty Advisor

Tools, techniques, hints, ideas,
illustrations, examples, methods,
procedures, processes, skills, resources,
and suggestions for success.

Advisory Board

Mary Hale Barry
Corinthian Colleges, Inc., CA

Ray Emett
Salt Lake Community College, UT

Sandra M. Karman
The Chubb Institute, NJ

Lois Pasapane
Palm Beach Community College, FL

M. Elaine Richardson
Clemson University, SC

Dr. Karen N. Valencia
South Texas Community College, TX

Dr. Joyce Weinsheimer
University of Minnesota—Twin Cities, MN

Dr. Martha W. Williams
Valencia Community College, FL

Houghton Mifflin Company   **Boston   New York**

Editor in Chief, Humanities: Patricia A. Coryell
Associate Editor: Shani B. Fisher
Project Manager: Janet Edmonds
Editorial Assistant: Andrew Sylvester
Senior Project Editor: Rachel D'Angelo Wimberly
Editorial Assistant: May Jawdat
Senior Production/Design Coordinator: Sarah L. Ambrose
Manufacturing Manager: Florence Cadran
Marketing Manager: Barbara LeBuhn
Senior Designer: Henry Rachlin
Master Student Illustrations: Lee Christiansen

Cover credits: cover image © Stephen Gleason; Detail of an open book © Milton
Montenegro/Getty Images, Inc.; detail of an office clock © Steve Cole/Getty Images, Inc.;
pen pointing at an electronic organizer © Janis Christie/Getty Images, Inc.; laptop
computer © Tony Stone Images; Earth © Bruce Rowell/Masterfile.

College Survival
A Program of Houghton Mifflin Company
2075 Foxfield Drive, Suite 100
St. Charles, IL 60174

Excerpts from *Creating Your Future*. Copyright © 1998 by David B. Ellis. Reprinted by permission
of Houghton Mifflin Company. All rights reserved.

Excerpts from *Human Being: A Manual for Happiness, Health, Love, and Wealth* by David Ellis
and Stan Lankowitz. Reprinted by permission of Breakthrough Enterprises.

Photo and illustration credits are listed on page 391.

Printed in the U.S.A

Library of Congress Control Number: 2001133252

Student Edition ISBN: 0-618-20678-7
Instructor's Edition ISBN: 0-618-20908-5

2 3 4 5 6 7 8 9 — VH — 06 05 04 03 02

As part of Houghton Mifflin's ongoing commitment to the environment, this text has been printed on recycled paper.

For the most part, students have created this book.

The First Edition of *Becoming a Master Student* came from notes that I collected while teaching a course to students. These students ended up teaching me more than I ever imagined there was to learn about student success while I was supposed to be teaching them. Since that first edition, millions of students have used this book, and their continuing input has dramatically changed it. To all of those students of different ages and from a variety of cultures and ethnic groups, I send my heartfelt thanks.

In previous editions of this book, I listed many of the educators who have contributed significantly to the strategies and insights offered to students. Unfortunately, this list has gotten so long that I cannot list, by name, the hundreds of significant contributors. Some educators have offered an idea or two as part of an article. Others have provided the inspiration and much of the content for entire articles. Still others have offered suggestions that have totally rearranged the structure and outline of this text. Thank you all.

During the last twenty years, I have worked day to day with dozens of people who have contributed dramatically to the creation of this text. They have lent ideas, logistical support, project management, consultation, and design. To all of those people, I want you to know that this book would never have been produced without you. There are a few people out of the dozens I have worked with who have made such a difference in this book that to leave them unnamed would border on unethical. Therefore, I deeply thank and acknowledge the work of Doug Toft, Stan Lankowitz, Larry David, Jeff Swaim, Mary Maisey-Ireland, Bill Rentz, Robbie Murchison, Bill Harlan, Judith Maisey, James Anderson, Wayne Zako, Richard Kiefer, JoAnne Bangs, Leonard Running, and Shirley Wileman-Conrad.

In this book, the design and artwork are critical components of the message. For that work I appreciate the mastery of Bill Fleming, Henry Rachlin, and Walter Kopec, along with the other people who have contributed so much to the artistry of this book, including Susan Turnbull, Amy Davis, Neil Zetah, Roger Slott, Lee Christiansen, and Mike Speiser.

Along with thanking the Advisory Board members listed on the title page of this book, I also want to sincerely thank the consultants of College Survival.

Many people at Houghton Mifflin Company have provided thousands of hours of excellent and dedicated work in the creation of this book. Specifically I thank June Smith, Patricia Coryell, Shani Fisher, Janet Edmonds, Andrew Sylvester, Barbara LeBuhn, Terry Wilton, Nancy Doherty Schmitt, Rachel D'Angelo Wimberly, Sarah Ambrose, May Jawdat, Florence Cadran, Katie Huha, Tony Saizon, Diana Coe, Shawn Kendrick, Elaine Gray, and Keith Fredericks.

For their contribution to my life, and to my becoming a master student, I thank my wife, Trisha Waldron, and my best friend, Stan Lankowitz. I also treasure what I have learned from my children, Sara, Elizabeth, Snow, and Berry, and I honor the constant encouragement of my parents, Maryellen and Ken.

I know that no book and no set of ideas come from a single person, and my intention is to continue to give to others what all of the people I have mentioned here have given to me.

Dave Ellis

TABLE OF CONTENTS

Introduction

CHAPTER 1 — First Steps

CHAPTER 2 Time

CHAPTER 3 Memory

CHAPTER 4

Reading

CHAPTER 5

Notes

CHAPTER 6

Tests

CHAPTER 7

Thinking

CHAPTER 8

Communicating

CHAPTER 9

Diversity

CHAPTER 10

Resources

CHAPTER 11

Health

CHAPTER 12

What Next?

Introduction

Change and growth take place when a person has risked himself and dares to become involved with experimenting with his own life.
HERBERT OTTO

The human ability to learn and remember is virtually limitless.
SHEILA OSTRANDER & LYNN SCHROEDER

AS YOU BEGIN . . . Consider one way to ensure that this book is worthless and seven ways you can use it to succeed in school. Also do a textbook reconnaissance and discover options for getting the most from this book. You can declare what you want from your education and commit to making this book a partner in your success.

This book is worthless...

T he first edition of this book began with the sentence: *This book is worthless.* Many students thought this was a trick to get their attention. It wasn't. Others thought it was reverse psychology. It wasn't that, either. Still others thought it meant that the book was worthless if they didn't read it. It's more than that.

The book is worthless even if you read it, if reading is all you do. What was true of that first edition is true of this one. Until you take action and use the ideas in it, *Becoming a Master Student* really is worthless.

You probably won't take action and use the ideas until you are convinced that you have something to gain. The main purpose of this introduction is to persuade you to commit to spending the energy to use this book actively. Before you stiffen up and resist, the purpose of this sales pitch is not to separate you from your money. You already bought the book. Now you can get something for your money by committing yourself to take action—in other words, commit yourself to become a master student. Here's what's in it for you.

Pitch #1: You can save money now and make more later. Start

with money. Your college education is one of the most expensive things you will ever buy. Typically, it costs students $30 to $70 an hour to sit in class. Unfortunately, many students think their classes aren't even worth 50 cents an hour.

As a master student, you control the value you get out of your education, and that value

Textbook reconnaissance

Start becoming a master student this moment. Do a 15-minute "textbook reconnaissance" of this book. Here's how:

First, read the table of contents. Do it in three minutes or less. Next, look at every page in the book. Move quickly. Scan headlines. Look at pictures. Notice forms, charts, and diagrams.

A textbook reconnaissance shows you where a course is going. It gives you the big picture. That's useful because brains work best when going from the general to the specific. Getting the big picture before you start makes details easier to recall and understand later on.

Your textbook reconnaissance will work even better if, as you scan, you look for ideas you can use. When you find one, write the page number and a short description of it in the space below. The idea behind this technique is simple: It's easier to learn when you're excited, and it's easier to get excited about a course if you know it's going to be useful, interesting, or fun.

When you have found five interesting ideas, stop writing and continue your survey. Remember, look at every page, and do it quickly. And here's another useful tip for the master student: Do it now.

Page number   Description

1.

2.

3.

4.

5.

can be considerable. The joy of learning aside, college graduates make an average of over $1 million more during their lifetimes than their nondegreed peers. It pays to be a master student.

Pitch #2: You can rediscover the natural learner in you.
Joy is important too. As you become a master student, you will learn ways to learn in the most effective way possible by discovering the joyful, natural learner within you.

Children are great natural students. They quickly learn complex skills, such as language, and they have fun doing it. For them, learning is a high-energy process involving experimentation, discovery, and sometimes, broken dishes. Then comes school. For some students, drill and drudgery replace discovery and dish breaking. Learning can become a drag. You can use this book to reverse that process and rediscover what you knew as a child—that laughter and learning go hand in hand.

Sometimes learning does take effort, especially in college. As you become a master student, you will learn many ways to get the most out of that effort.

Pitch #3: You can choose from hundreds of techniques.
Becoming a Master Student is packed with hundreds of practical, nuts-and-bolts techniques. And you can begin using them immediately. For example, during your textbook reconnaissance on page 1, you practiced three powerful learning techniques in one 15-minute exercise. (If you didn't do the textbook reconnaissance, it's not too late to get your money's worth. Do it now.) If you doze in lectures, drift during tests, or dawdle on term papers, you can use the ideas in this book to become a more effective student.

Not all these ideas will work for you. That's why there are so many of them in *Becoming a Master Student*. You can experiment with the techniques. As you discover what works, you will develop a unique style of learning that you can use for the rest of your life.

Pitch #4: You get the best suggestions from thousands of students.
The concepts and techniques in this book are not here because learning theorists, educators, and psychologists say they work. They are here because tens of thousands of students from all kinds of backgrounds tried them and say they work. These are people who dreaded giving speeches, couldn't read their own notes, and couldn't remember where their ileocecal valve was. Then they figured out how to solve these problems, which was the hard part. Now you can use their ideas.

Pitch #5: You can learn about you.
The process of self-discovery is an important theme in *Becoming a Master Student*. Throughout the book you can use Discovery Statements and Intention Statements for everything from organizing your desk to choosing long-term goals. Studying for an organic chemistry quiz is a lot easier with a clean desk and a clear idea of the course's importance to you.

Pitch #6: You can use a proven product.
The first nine editions of this book were successful for hundreds of thousands of students. In schools where it was widely used, the dropout rate decreased as much as 25 percent and in some cases, 50 percent. Student feedback has been positive. In particular, students with successful histories have praised the techniques in this book.

Pitch #7: You can learn the secret of student success.
If this sales pitch still hasn't persuaded you to actively use this book, maybe it's time to reveal the secret of student success. (Provide your own drum roll here.) The secret is, there are no secrets. Perhaps the ultimate formula is to give up formulas and keep inventing.

The strategies and tactics that successful students use are well known. You have hundreds of them at your fingertips right now, in this book. Use them. Modify them. Invent new ones. You're the authority on what works for you.

However, what makes any technique work is commitment—and action. Without them, the pages of *Becoming a Master Student* are just 2.1 pounds of expensive mulch. Add your participation to the mulch, and these pages are priceless.

JOURNAL ENTRY #1

Discovery Statement

Success is a choice. Your choice. To *get* what you want, it helps to *know* what you want. That is the purpose of this Journal Entry.

Select a time and place when you know you will not be disturbed for at least 20 minutes. (The library is a good place to do this.) Relax for two or three minutes, clearing your mind. Then complete the following sentences . . . and then keep writing. Write down everything you want to get out of school. Write down everything you want your education to enable you to do after you finish school.

When you run out of things to write, stick with it just a bit longer. Be willing to experience a little discomfort. Keep writing. What you discover might be well worth the extra effort. You can begin choosing success right now by choosing a date, time, and place to complete this Journal Entry.
Write your choice here and block out the time on your calendar.

Date: _____

Time: _____

Place: _____

What I want from my education is . . .

_____

_____

_____

When I complete my education, I want to be able to . . .

_____

_____

_____

I also want . . .

_____

_____

_____

JOURNAL ENTRY #2

Discovery Statement

On a separate piece of paper, write a description of a time in your life when you learned or did something well. This situation need not be related to school. Describe the details of the situation, including the place, time, and people involved. Describe how you felt about it, how it looked to you, how it sounded. Describe the physical sensations you associate with the event. Describe your emotions also.

Get the most out of this book

1 Rip 'em out. The pages of *Becoming a Master Student* are perforated because some of the information here is too important to leave in the book and some your instructor may want to see. For example, Journal Entry #1 asks you to write some important things you want to get out of your education. To keep yourself focused, you could rip that page out and post it on your bathroom mirror or some other place where you'll see it several times a day.

You can re-insert the page by just sticking it into the spine of the book; it will hold. A piece of tape will fix it in place.

2 Skip around. You can use this book in several different ways. Read it straight through. Or pick it up, turn to any page, and find an idea you can use. Look for ideas you can use right now. For example, if you are about to choose a major or you are considering changing schools, skip directly to the articles on these topics in Chapter Twelve.

3 If it works, use it. If it doesn't, lose it. If there are sections of the book that don't apply to you at all, skip them—unless, of course, they are assigned. Then, see if you can gain value from these sections anyway. When you are committed to getting value from this book, even an idea that seems irrelevant or ineffective at first can turn out to be a powerful tool.

4 Rewrite this book. Here's an alternative strategy to the one above. If an idea doesn't work for you, rewrite it. Change the exercises to fit your needs. Create a new technique by combining several others. Create a technique out of thin air!

5 Put yourself into the book. As you read about techniques in this book, invent your own examples, starring yourself in the title role. For example, as you were reading the explanation of Exercise #1: "Textbook reconnaissance," you might have pictured yourself using this technique on your world history textbook.

Also look throughout the book for short features labeled **Student Voices**. These are quotations from students who used this book to promote their success. As you dig into the following chapters, think about what you would say if you could add your voice to this book. Look for tools and techniques that can make a huge difference in your life.

6 Yuk it up. Going to school is a big investment. The stakes are high. It's OK to be serious about that, but you don't have to go to school on the deferred-fun program. A master student celebrates learning, and one of the best ways to do that is to have a laugh now and then.

7 Own this book. Write your name and address on the first page of this book now, and don't stop there. Create a record of what you want to get out of school and how you intend to get it by completing the Journal Entries and exercises. Every time your pen touches a page, you move closer to mastery of learning.

8 Do the exercises. Action makes this book work. To get the most out of an exercise, read the instructions carefully before you begin. To get the most out of this book, do most of the exercises. More important, avoid feeling guilty if you skip some. And by the way, it's never too late to go back and do those.

These exercises invite you to write, touch, feel, move, see, search, ponder, speak, listen, recall, choose, commit, and create. You might even sing and dance. Learning often works best when it involves action.

9 Get used to a new look and tone. This book looks different from traditional textbooks. *Becoming a Master Student* presents major ideas in magazine-style articles. You will discover lots of lists, blurbs, one-liners, pictures, charts, graphs, illustrations, and even a joke or two.

The icons and key visuals in this book carry special meanings. For example, Journal Entries are introduced by a drawing of a twisted pencil, a sign of infinity, symbolizing the idea that journaling is a process that never ends. The picture of the running shoe that accompanies the exercises in this book indicates the action that makes for effective learning.

One more note: As a strategy for avoiding sexist language, this book alternates the use of feminine and masculine pronouns.

10 *Practice critical thinking.* Throughout this book are activities labeled "Practicing Critical Thinking." Look for them next to the icon of the "thinker" inside a light bulb, who's there to encourage contemplation and constant problem solving. Also note that other elements of this text promote critical thinking, including exercises and Journal Entries.

11 *Learn about learning styles.* Check out the Learning Styles Applications at the end of each chapter. These are included to increase your awareness of your preferred learning styles and to help you explore new styles. Each exercise will guide you through experiencing four specific modes of learning as applied to the content of the chapter.

12 *Enter cyberspace.* You'll see an Internet logo next to articles, exercises, and Journal Entries throughout this book. This logo indicates opportunities for you to explore the Internet as a tool for promoting your success. Many of these logos will direct you to Houghton Mifflin's College Survival/Becoming a Master Student web site: **http://collegesurvival.college.hmco.com/ students.** Visit this site regularly for articles, online exercises, and links to useful web sites.

13 *Sweat the small stuff.* Look for sidebars throughout this book—short bursts of words and pictures that are placed between longer articles. These short pieces also might offer an insight that leads you to transform your experience of higher education. Related point: Shorter chapters in this book are just as important as longer chapters.

14 *Take this book to work.* With a little tweaking in some cases, you can apply nearly all the techniques in this book to your career. **Workplace Applications** in each chapter will remind you of this fact. Use them to make seamless transition from success in school to success on the job.

EXERCISE

#2

Commitment

This book is worthless without your action. One powerful way to begin taking action is to make a commitment. Conversely, without commitment, sustained action is unlikely, and the result is a worthless book. Therefore, in the interest of saving your valuable time and energy, this exercise gives you a chance to declare your level of involvement up front. From the choices below, choose the sentence that best reflects your commitment to using this book. Write the number in the space provided at the end of the list.

1. "Well, I'm reading this book right now, aren't I?"
2. "I will skim the book and read the interesting parts."
3. "I will read the book and think about how some of the techniques might apply to me."
4. "I will read the book, think about it, and do the exercises that look interesting."
5. "I will read the book, do exercises, and complete some of the Journal Entries."
6. "I will read the book, do exercises and Journal Entries, and use some of the techniques."
7. "I will read the book, do most of the exercises and Journal Entries, and use some of the techniques."
8. "I will study this book, do most of the exercises and Journal Entries, and use some of the techniques."
9. "I will study this book, do most of the exercises and Journal Entries, and experiment vigorously with most of the suggestions in order to discover what works best for me."
10. "I promise to get value from this book, beginning with Exercise #1: 'Textbook reconnaissance,' even if I have to rewrite the sections I don't like and even if I have to invent new techniques of my own."

Enter your commitment level and today's date here:

Commitment level_____   Date_____

If you selected commitment level 1 or 2, you might consider passing this book on to a friend. If your commitment level is a 9 or 10, you are on your way to terrific success in school. If you are somewhere in between, experiment with the techniques; if you find they work, consider returning to this exercise and raising your level of commitment.

First Steps

No one can make you feel inferior without your consent.
ELEANOR ROOSEVELT

In oneself lies the whole world, and if you know how to look and learn, then the door is there and the key is in your hand. Nobody on earth can give you either that key or the door to open, except yourself.
J. KRISHNAMURTI

IN THIS CHAPTER . . . Take a First Step to lasting change: Tell the truth about your current abilities. Then set goals and align your actions by using the Discovery Wheel and Discovery and Intention Journal Entry System. Also discover and expand your learning styles, reflect on the qualities of a master student, and use a power process that can enhance the value of any idea in this book.

First Step: Truth is a key to mastery

The First Step technique is simple: Tell the truth about who you are and what you want. End of discussion. Now proceed to Chapter Two.

Well, it's not quite that simple.

The First Step is one of the most powerful tools in this book. It magnifies the power of all the other techniques. It is a key to becoming a master student.

Unfortunately, a First Step is easier to explain than it is to use. Telling the truth sounds like pie-in-the-sky moralizing, but there is nothing pie-in-the-sky or moralizing about a First Step. It is a practical, down-to-earth way to change behavior. No technique in this book has been field-tested more often or more successfully—or under tougher circumstances.

It's not easy to tell the truth about ourselves. We might have to admit that we're afraid of algebra or that we never complete term papers on time. It's tough to admit to weaknesses. For some of us, it's even harder to admit to strengths. Maybe we don't want to brag. Maybe we're attached to poor self-images. The reasons don't matter. The point is that using the First Step system in *Becoming a Master Student* means telling the truth about our positive qualities, also.

Many of us approach a frank evaluation of ourselves about as enthusiastically as we'd anticipate an audit by the IRS. There is another way to think about evaluations. If we could see them as opportunities to solve problems and take charge of our lives, we might welcome them. If we routinely experienced more happiness after evaluations, we might even greet them with hopeful excitement. It might seem natural to judge our own shortcomings and feel bad about them. Some of us believe that such feelings are necessary in order to bring about change. Others think that a healthy dose of shame is the only thing that can prevent the moral decay of our society.

There is an alternative. We can discover a way to gain skill without feeling rotten about the past. We can change the way things *are* without having to be upset about the way things *have been*. We can learn to see shame or blame as excess baggage and just set it aside. We can acknowledge and even regret our mistakes and shortcomings while accepting ourselves completely. And by doing so, we can become even more happy, healthy, loving, and wealthy in

JOURNAL ENTRY #3

Discovery Statement

Perhaps you know people who've tried to repair a car without knowing what parts they needed. Or maybe you've tried to buy clothes for someone without knowing that person's size and preferred styles. In such cases, you can be more effective when you know what the specific problem is or what the people involved truly want.

Briefly describe a time when you wanted to solve a problem but lacked specific information about the nature of that problem or had no clear idea of the outcome you desired.

_____
_____
_____
_____
_____

Now describe a time when, from your diagnosis and desired results, you were able to describe a problem accurately and solve it efficiently.

_____
_____
_____
_____
_____

Succeeding in this course—and in school—uses the same process. It begins with identifying the skills you already have, along with the new skills you want to acquire. Success also involves telling the truth about any problem you face right now and creating a plan to solve it.

Take time now to preview the Discovery Wheel exercise on page 14. Then list below several specific benefits you can gain by reading and applying the ideas in this chapter.

I discovered that I . . .

_____
_____
_____
_____

the long run. Believe it or not, we can begin working with our list of weaknesses by celebrating them.

Consider the most loving, successful, enlightened, "together" people you know. If they were totally candid with you, you'd soon hear about their mistakes and regrets. The more successful people are, the more likely they are to be willing to look at their flaws.

It might help to remember that weaknesses are often strengths carried to an extreme. The student who carefully revises her writing can make significant improvements in a paper. If she keeps revising past the due date, she could sacrifice her grade. This is just one example of how any success strategy carried too far can backfire.

Making the First Step technique work also means telling the truth about what you want. Sounds easy, you say? Many people would rather eat nails. If you don't believe it, ask three other students what they want to get out of their education. Be prepared for hemming and hawing, vague generalities, and maybe even a helping of pie-in-the-sky à la mode.

On the other hand, if one of them tells you she wants a degree in journalism with double minors in earth science and Portuguese so she can work as a reporter covering the environment in Brazil, chances are you've found a master student. The details of her vision are a clue to her mastery.

Goals are more powerful when they are specific. So are First Steps, whether they are verbal or written. For example, if you want to improve your note-taking skills, you might write, "I am an awful note taker." It would be more effective to write, "I can't read 80 percent of the notes I took in Introduction to Psychology last week, and I have no idea what was important in that class." Be just as specific about what you want. You might declare, "I want to take legible notes that help me predict what questions will be on the final exam."

By completing the exercises in this chapter, you can take a giant First Step. Your courage will be rewarded. The Discovery Wheel exercise and the rest of the exercises in this book are your First Steps to tapping resources you never imagined you had. You might even want to take a First Step in mapping out the rest of your life with a detailed career plan.

They're all First Steps—no kidding. It's just that simple. The truth has power.

JOURNAL ENTRY #4

Intention Statement

Review Exercise #1: "Textbook reconnaissance" in the Introduction. Consider the articles in this book that you thought might be valuable. Choose the one that you think might offer the most immediate, practical benefit, and skim it until you come to a specific technique you can use. Write an Intention Statement below concerning how and when you will use that technique within the next week.

For example, if you chose the article "When reading is tough," you could use any of the techniques suggested for difficult reading assignments. If you've been struggling with a tough reading assignment for a computer science course, you might use the technique of taking a break and returning to the assignment later. In that case, you could write, "I intend to put aside my textbook when I feel that I can't concentrate and come back to the assignment with fresh eyes during my study period on the following day."

I intend to . . .

_____

_____

_____

_____

_____

_____

_____

_____

If you skipped the Introduction . . .

Some people think introductions are useless clutter. The Introduction is an important part of this book. It suggests ways to get your money's worth. Please read the Introduction.

Here's what awaits you:

- **Exercise #1: "Textbook reconnaissance"**
- **This book is worthless . . .**
- **Get the most out of this book**
- **Exercise #2: "Commitment"**

Please read it now.

#3

Taking the First Step

The purpose of this exercise is to give you a chance to discover and acknowledge your own positive, as well as negative, aspects. For many students, this is the most difficult exercise in the book. To make the exercise worthwhile, do it with courage.

Some people suggest that looking at negative aspects is counter to positive thinking. Well, perhaps. Positive thinking is a great technique. So is telling the truth, especially when we see the whole picture—the negative aspects as well as the positive ones.

If you admit that you can't add or subtract and that's the truth, then you have taken a strong, positive First Step toward learning basic math. On the other hand, if you say that you are a terrible math student and that's not the truth, then you are programming yourself to accept unnecessary failure.

The point is to tell the truth. This exercise is similar to the Discovery Statements that appear in every chapter. The difference is that in this case, for reasons of confidentiality, you won't write down your discoveries in the book.

Be brave. If you approach this exercise with courage, you are likely to write down some things you wouldn't want others to read. You might even write down some truths about yourself that could get you into trouble. Do this exercise on separate sheets of paper; then hide or destroy them. Protect your privacy.

To make this exercise work, follow these three suggestions:

1. *Be specific.* It is not effective to write, "I can improve my communication skills." Of course you can. Instead, write down precisely what you can do to improve your communication skills. For example: "I can spend more time really listening while the other person is talking, instead of thinking about what I'm going to say next."

2. *Look beyond the classroom.* What goes on outside of school often has the greatest impact on your ability to be an effective student.

3. *Be courageous.* This exercise is a waste of time if done only half-heartedly. Be willing to take risks. You might open a door that reveals a part of yourself that you didn't want to admit was there. The power of this technique is that once you know what is there, you can do something about it.

Part 1

Time yourself, and for 10 minutes write as fast as you can, completing the following sentences at least 10 times with anything that comes to mind. If you get stuck, don't stop. Just write something—even if it seems crazy.

It is ineffective when I ...

It doesn't work when I ...

I could change ...

Part 2

When you have completed the first part of the exercise, review what you have written, crossing off things that don't make any sense. The sentences that remain suggest possible goals for becoming a master student.

Part 3

Here's the tough part. Time yourself, and for 10 minutes write as fast as you can, completing the following sentences with anything that comes to mind. As in Part 1, complete each sentence at least 10 times. Just keep writing, even if it sounds silly.

I am very good at ...

It is effective when I ...

Something very positive about me is ...

Part 4

Review what you have written and circle the things that you can fully celebrate. This is a good list to keep for those times when you question your own value and worth.

The Discovery and Intention

GOAL

AIRPORT

One way to become a better student is to grit your teeth and try harder. There is another way. Using familiar tools and easily learned processes, the Discovery and Intention Journal Entry system can help increase your effectiveness. Closely related to the idea of taking a First Step, this system is a way to focus your energy.

The Discovery and Intention Journal Entry system is a little like flying a plane. Airplanes are seldom exactly on course. Human and automatic pilots are always checking positions and making corrections. The resulting flight path looks like a zigzag. The plane is almost always flying in the wrong direction, but because of constant observation and course correction, it arrives at the right destination.

A similar system can be used by students. In fact, you have already used it if you completed the Journal Entries on previous pages. (If you haven't, consider doing one right now.) Most Journal Entries throughout this book are labeled as either Discovery Statements or Intention Statements—some are Discovery/Intention Statements. Each Journal Entry will contain a short set of suggestions that involve writing.

Through Discovery Statements, you can assess "where you are." These statements are a record of what you learn about yourself as a student—both strengths and weaknesses. Discovery Statements can also be declarations of what you want, descriptions of your attitudes, statements of your feelings, transcripts of your thoughts, and chronicles of your behavior.

Intention Statements can be used to alter your course. They are statements of your commitment to do a specific task, to take a certain action. An intention arises out of your choice to direct your energy toward a particular goal.

The purpose of this system is not to get you pumped up and excited to go out there and try harder.

Journal Entry System

Discovery and Intention Statements are intended to help you focus on what you want and how you intend to get it.

The Journal Entry process is a cycle. You can write Discovery Statements about where you are and where you want to go. Then you can write Intention Statements about the specific steps you will take to get there. You can then write Discovery Statements about whether you completed those steps and what you learned in the process, followed by more Intention Statements, and so on. Sometimes a statement will be long and detailed. Usually, it will be short—maybe just a line or two. With practice, the cycle can become automatic.

Don't panic when you fail to complete an intended task. Straying off course is normal. Simply make the necessary corrections. Miraculous progress might not come immediately. Do not be concerned. Stay

with the cycle. Use Discovery Statements to get a clear view of your world and what you want out of it. Then use Intention Statements to direct your actions. When you notice progress, record it.

The following statement might strike you as improbable, but it is true: It often takes the same amount of energy to get what you want in school as it takes to get what you *don't* want. Sometimes getting what you don't want takes even more effort. An airplane burns the same amount of fuel flying away from its destination as it does flying toward it. It pays to stay on course.

You can use the Discovery and Intention Journal Entry system to stay on your own course and get what you want out of school. Consider the guidelines for Discovery Statements and Intention Statements given in this chapter; then develop your own style. Once you get the hang of it, you might discover you can fly.

Deface this book

Some books should be preserved in pristine condition. This isn't one of them.

Becoming a Master Student is about learning, and learning is an active pursuit, not a passive one. Something happens when you interact with your book by writing in it. When you make notes in the margin, you can hear yourself talking with the author. When you doodle and underline, you can see the author's ideas taking shape. You can even argue with the author and come up with your own theories and explanations.

While you're at it, you can create symbols or codes that will help when reviewing the text later on, such as "Q" for questions or exclamation points for important ideas. You can also circle words to look up in a dictionary.

To complete this exercise, find something you agree with or disagree with on this page and write a short note in the margin about it. Or draw a diagram. Better yet, do both. Let creativity be your guide. Have fun.

Begin defacing now.

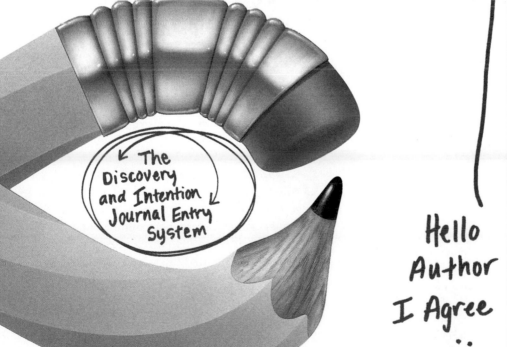

The Discovery and Intention Journal Entry System

Hello Author I Agree :)

Seven Discovery & Intention

Discovery Statements

1 Discover what you want. You can have more energy when your activities lead to what you want. Many students quit school simply because they are unclear about their goals. Writing down what you hope to achieve can make your path more clear.

2 Record the specifics. Observe your actions and record the facts. If you spent 90 minutes chatting online with a favorite cousin instead of reading your anatomy text, write about it and include the details, such as when you did it, where you did it, and how it felt.

3 Notice your inner voices and pictures. We talk to ourselves constantly in our heads, and our minds are always manufacturing pictures. When internal chatter gets in the way, write down what you are telling yourself. If this seems difficult at first, just start writing. The act of writing can trigger a flood of thoughts. Mental pictures are especially powerful. Picturing yourself flunking a test is like a rehearsal to do just that. One way to take away the power of negative images is to describe them in detail.

4 Notice physical sensations. When you approach a daunting task, such as a difficult accounting problem, notice your physical symptoms— a churning stomach, perhaps, or shallow breathing or yawning. Record your observations quickly, as soon as you make them.

Also notice how you feel when you function well. Use Discovery Statements to pinpoint exactly where and when you learn most effectively.

5 Use discomfort as a signal. When you are writing a Discovery Statement and you begin to feel uncomfortable, bored, or tired, that may be a signal that you are about to do valuable work. Stick with it. Tell yourself you can handle the discomfort just a little bit longer. You will be rewarded.

6 Suspend self-judgment. When you are discovering yourself, be gentle. If you continually judge your behaviors as "bad" or "stupid" or "galactically imbecilic," sooner or later your mind will revolt. Rather than put up with the abuse, it will quit making discoveries. For your own benefit, be kind.

7 Tell the truth. "The truth will set you free" can be viewed as a cliché. Practice telling the truth, and you might find out why the phrase is so enduring. The closer you get to the truth, the more powerful your Discovery Statements will be.

And remember, telling the truth requires courage and vigilance. Don't blame yourself when you notice that you are avoiding the truth. Just tell the truth about it.

Review the article "The Master Student" in this chapter. Then skim the master student profiles throughout this book. Choose one of the people profiled and explain how this person embodies qualities of a master student. Summarize your conclusions on a separate sheet of paper.

The **Practicing Critical Thinking** exercises that appear in every chapter incorporate ideas from Peter Facione, Dean of the College of Arts and Sciences, Santa Clara University, and creator of the California Critical Thinking Disposition Inventory. Mr. Facione provided substantial suggestions for these exercises and edited them. He can be contacted through the California Academic Press on the World Wide Web at **www.insightassessment.com/about.html**.

Adapted with permission from Critical Thinking: What It Is and Why It Counts *by Peter Facione, Millbrae, CA: The California Academic Press, 1996.*

Statement guidelines

Intention Statements

1 Make your intentions positive. Instead of writing "I will not fall asleep while studying accounting," write "I intend to stay awake when studying accounting."

Also avoid the word *try*. Trying is not doing. When we hedge our bets with *try*, we can always tell ourselves, "Well, I *tried* to stay awake." We end up fooling ourselves into thinking we succeeded.

2 Make intentions small and keepable. Give yourself opportunities to succeed. Break large goals into small, specific tasks that can be accomplished quickly. If you want to get an A in biology, ask yourself, What can I do today? You might choose to study biology for an extra hour. Make that your intention.

Experience success by choosing your intentions with care. Set goals you can accomplish.

3 Use observable criteria for success. Experiment with an idea from trainer Robert Mager, who suggests that goals be defined through behaviors that can be observed and measured.[1] Rather than writing "I intend to work harder on my history assignments," write "I intend to review my class notes, and I intend to make summary sheets of my reading." Then, when you review your progress, you can determine more precisely whether you accomplished what you intended.

4 Set timelines. Timelines can focus your attention, especially if they are used in conjunction with suggestion #2. For example, if you are assigned a term paper, break the assignment into small tasks and set a precise timeline for each one. You might write "I intend to select a topic for my paper by 9 a.m. Wednesday." Remember that you create timelines for your own benefit, not to set yourself up to feel guilty. And you can always change the timeline.

5 Be careful of intentions that depend on others. Your intention might depend on the actions of other people. If you write that you intend for your study group to complete an assignment by Monday, your success depends on the other students in the group. Make such intentions carefully; then ask for the assistance of the people they depend on.

6 Anticipate self-sabotage. Be aware of what you might do, consciously or unconsciously, to undermine your best intentions. If you intend to study differential equations at 9 p.m., notice when you sit down to watch a two-hour television movie that starts at 8 p.m.

7 Identify your rewards. Rewards that are an integral part of a goal are powerful. For example, your reward for earning a degree might be the career you've always dreamed of. External rewards, such as a movie or an afternoon in the park, are valuable, too. These rewards work best when you're willing to withhold them. If you plan to take a nap on Sunday afternoon whether or not you've finished your English assignment, the nap is not an effective reward. Another way to reward yourself is to sit quietly after you have finished your task and savor the feeling. One reason why success breeds success is that it feels good.

#5

The Discovery Wheel

An online version of this exercise is available on Houghton Mifflin's College Survival/Becoming a Master Student web site: **http://collegesurvival. college.hmco.com/students.**

The Discovery Wheel is another opportunity to tell yourself the truth about the kind of student you are and the kind of student you want to become.

This is not a test. There are no trick questions, and the answers will have meaning only for you.

Here are two suggestions to make this exercise more effective. First, think of it as the beginning of an opportunity to change. There is another Discovery Wheel at the end of this book. You will have a chance to measure your progress, so be honest about where you are now. Second, lighten up. A little laughter can make self-evaluations a lot more effective.

Here's how the Discovery Wheel works. By the end of this exercise, you will have filled in a circle similar to the one on this page. The Discovery Wheel circle is a picture of how you see yourself as a student. The closer the shading comes to the edge of the circle, the higher the evaluation. In the example to the right, the student has rated her reading skills low and her note-taking skills high.

It is dangerous, however, to think of these evaluations in terms of "higher" and "lower," if those designations reflect a negative judgment. The Discovery Wheel is not a permanent picture of who you are. It is a picture of how you view your abilities as a student today.

To begin this exercise, read the following statements and award yourself points for each one, using the point system described below. Then add up your point total for each section and shade the Discovery Wheel on page 17 to the appropriate level.

5 points
This statement is always or almost always true of me.

4 points
This statement is often true of me.

3 points
This statement is true of me about half the time.

2 points
This statement is seldom true of me.

1 point
This statement is never or almost never true of me.

1. ____1____ I start courses highly motivated and I stay that way.
2. ____2____ I have adequate support from teachers and administrators to succeed in higher education.
3. ____4____ I enjoy learning.
4. ____1____ I study even when distracted by activities of lower priority.
5. ____1____ I am satisfied with how I progress toward achieving goals.
6. ____4____ I use knowledge of learning styles to support my success in school.
7. ____5____ I am excited about courses I take.
8. ____1____ I have a clear idea of the benefits I expect to get from my education.

____19____ Total score (1) **Motivation**

1. ____1____ I set long-term goals and periodically review them.
2. ____1____ I set short-term goals to support my long-term goals.
3. ____5____ I write a plan for each day and each week.
4. ____5____ I assign priorities to what I choose to do each day.
5. ____1____ I plan review time so I don't have to cram before tests.
6. ____5____ I plan regular recreation time.
7. ____1____ I adjust my study time to meet the demands of individual courses.
8. ____2____ I have adequate time each day to accomplish what I plan.

____21____ Total score (2) **Time**

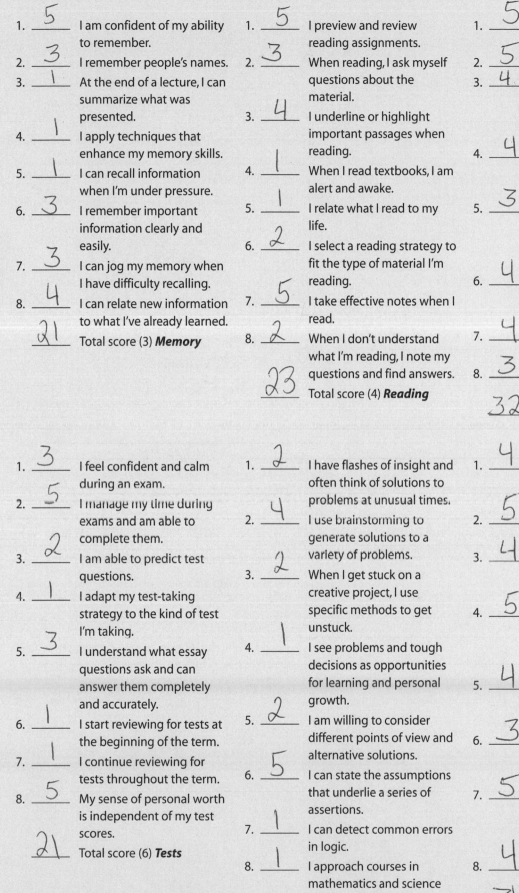

1. __5__ I am confident of my ability to remember.
2. __3__ I remember people's names.
3. __1__ At the end of a lecture, I can summarize what was presented.
4. __1__ I apply techniques that enhance my memory skills.
5. __1__ I can recall information when I'm under pressure.
6. __3__ I remember important information clearly and easily.
7. __3__ I can jog my memory when I have difficulty recalling.
8. __4__ I can relate new information to what I've already learned.
__21__ Total score (3) *Memory*

1. __5__ I preview and review reading assignments.
2. __3__ When reading, I ask myself questions about the material.
3. __4__ I underline or highlight important passages when reading.
4. __1__ When I read textbooks, I am alert and awake.
5. __1__ I relate what I read to my life.
6. __2__ I select a reading strategy to fit the type of material I'm reading.
7. __5__ I take effective notes when I read.
8. __2__ When I don't understand what I'm reading, I note my questions and find answers.
__23__ Total score (4) *Reading*

1. __5__ When I am in class, I focus my attention.
2. __5__ I take notes in class.
3. __4__ I am aware of various methods for taking notes and choose those that work best for me.
4. __4__ I distinguish important material and note key phrases in a lecture.
5. __3__ I copy down material that the instructor writes on the chalkboard or overhead projector.
6. __4__ I can put important concepts into my own words.
7. __4__ My notes are valuable for review.
8. __3__ I review class notes within 24 hours.
__32__ Total score (5) *Notes*

1. __3__ I feel confident and calm during an exam.
2. __5__ I manage my time during exams and am able to complete them.
3. __2__ I am able to predict test questions.
4. __1__ I adapt my test-taking strategy to the kind of test I'm taking.
5. __3__ I understand what essay questions ask and can answer them completely and accurately.
6. __1__ I start reviewing for tests at the beginning of the term.
7. __1__ I continue reviewing for tests throughout the term.
8. __5__ My sense of personal worth is independent of my test scores.
__21__ Total score (6) *Tests*

1. __2__ I have flashes of insight and often think of solutions to problems at unusual times.
2. __4__ I use brainstorming to generate solutions to a variety of problems.
3. __2__ When I get stuck on a creative project, I use specific methods to get unstuck.
4. __1__ I see problems and tough decisions as opportunities for learning and personal growth.
5. __2__ I am willing to consider different points of view and alternative solutions.
6. __5__ I can state the assumptions that underlie a series of assertions.
7. __1__ I can detect common errors in logic.
8. __1__ I approach courses in mathematics and science with confidence.
__18__ Total score (7) *Thinking*

1. __4__ I am candid with others about who I am, what I feel, and what I want.
2. __5__ Other people tell me that I am a good listener.
3. __4__ I can communicate my upset and anger without blaming others.
4. __5__ I have the ability to make friends and create valuable relationships in a new setting.
5. __4__ I am open to being with people I don't especially like in order to learn from them.
6. __3__ I can effectively plan and research a large writing assignment.
7. __5__ I create first drafts without criticizing my writing, then edit later for clarity, accuracy, and coherence.
8. __4__ I know ways to prepare and deliver effective speeches.
__34__ Total score (8) *Communicating*

1. __5__ I am aware of my biases and am open to understanding people from other cultures, races, and ethnic groups.

2. __5__ I build rewarding relationships with people from other backgrounds.

3. __5__ I can point out examples of discrimination and sexual harassment and effectively respond to them.

4. __5__ I am learning ways to thrive with diversity—attitudes and behaviors that will support my career success.

5. __4__ I can effectively resolve conflict with people from other cultures.

6. __4__ My writing and speaking are free of sexist expressions.

7. __5__ I can recognize bias and discrimination in the media.

8. __4__ I am aware of and interested in the changing demographics in my country and community.

__37__ Total score (9) *Diversity*

1. __1__ I have enough energy to study and still fully enjoy other areas of my life.

2. __1__ If the situation calls for it, I have enough reserve energy to put in a long day.

3. __2__ The food I eat supports my long-term health.

4. __5__ The way I eat is independent of my feelings of self-worth.

5. __5__ I exercise regularly to maintain a healthful weight.

6. __3__ My emotional health supports my ability to learn.

7. __5__ I notice changes in my physical condition and respond effectively.

8. __5__ I am in control of any alcohol or other drugs I put into my body.

__27__ Total score (11) *Health*

1. __3__ I use school-based services to support my success.

2. __3__ I know where to get help in my community for a variety of problems.

3. __3__ I am involved in extracurricular activities that align with my long-term goals and support my success in school.

4. __1__ I am confident that I will have enough money to complete the education that I want.

5. __1__ I minimize debt and repay my existing debts on time.

6. __4__ I can efficiently find information on the Internet that is useful and accurate.

7. __1__ I stay up-to-date with technology and use computers in specific ways to support my success.

8. __4__ I can effectively use libraries to find the resources and information I want.

__20__ Total score (10) *Resources*

1. __5__ I see learning as a lifelong process.

2. __1__ I relate school to what I plan to do for the rest of my life.

3. __3__ I learn by contributing to others.

4. __2__ I revise my plans as I learn, change, and grow.

5. __1__ I am clear about my purpose in life.

6. __1__ I know that I am responsible for my own education.

7. __5__ I take responsibility for the quality of my life.

8. __1__ I am willing to accept challenges even when I'm not sure how to meet them.

__19__ Total score (12) *Purpose*

Filling in your Discovery Wheel

Using the total score from each category, shade in each section of the Discovery Wheel. Use different colors, if you want. For example, you could use green to denote areas you want to work on. When you have finished, complete the following Journal Entries.

Discovery Statement

Now that you have completed your Discovery Wheel, spend a few minutes with it. Get a sense of its weight, shape, and balance. Can you imagine running your hands around it? If you could lift it, would it feel light or heavy? How would it sound if it rolled down a hill? Would it roll very far? Would it wobble? Make your observations without judging the wheel as good or bad. Simply be with the picture you have created. After you have spent a few minutes studying your Discovery Wheel, complete the following sentences on a separate sheet of paper. Don't worry if you can't think of something to write. Just put down whatever comes to mind. Remember, this is not a test.

This wheel is an accurate picture of my ability as a student because …

My self-evaluation surprises me because …

The two areas in which I am strongest are related because …

The areas in which I want to improve are …

I want to concentrate on improving these areas because …

Maybe it's your breath

The way you breathe affects the way you think, and the way you think affects the way you breathe. A good supply of oxygen to the brain is essential for focused concentration. The next time you find your mind wandering, take a short break and do the following exercise. Read all of the directions; then take a moment to practice this technique.

1. Sit up in your chair in a relaxed position, head straight and hands uncrossed in your lap.

2. Close your eyes and take 20 or 30 seconds to relax. Let go of any tension in your face, neck, and shoulders.

3. Inhale slowly, breathing deeply. Your chest will expand as your lungs fill with air.

4. When your lungs are full, pause; purse your lips as if you were about to whistle; then exhale evenly and with force through the small hole between your lips.

5. At the end of your exhalation, pause; then push out the last bit of remaining air in three short, forceful puffs.

6. Repeat this process three to five times.

7. When you have finished, sit quietly for a while, observing the rise and fall of your abdomen as you breathe normally.

Intention Statement

Select one of your discoveries from the previous Journal Entry and describe how you intend to benefit from it. Complete the statement below.

To gain some practical value from this discovery, I will …

_____

_____

_____

_____

_____

_____

_____

Learning styles
Discovering how you learn

When we learn, two things initially happen. First, we notice new information. We *perceive* and take in what's before us. Second, we make sense of the information. We *process* it in a way that helps us understand what's going on and makes the information our own. Learning styles take into account that people vary in how they naturally prefer to perceive and process information.

Knowing your preferred learning style helps you understand why some college courses might appeal to you while other aspects of the learning experience might seem dull or boring. Figuring out when to use your preferences—and when it might be helpful to include another mode of learning—can make you a more successful student.

Perceiving information. The ways that people perceive information typically range from a preference for concrete experience (CE) to a preference for abstract conceptualization (AC).

- People who favor perceiving by *concrete experience* take in information best when it seems real and present to them. They tend to sense, feel, or experience information in a way that involves them fully. Often they take an intuitive approach to noticing the information they will need to solve a problem. They typically function well in unstructured learning situations that allow them to take the initiative.

- People who favor perceiving by *abstract conceptualization* take in information best when they can think about it as a subject separate from themselves. They analyze, intellectualize, and view information from many perspectives in order to understand

Textbook reconnaissance, take two

The first chapter of a textbook usually includes key material—ideas that the author wants you to have up front. Likewise, this book is packed with articles that could benefit you right now. There just wasn't enough room to put them all in the first chapter.

While skimming the book for Exercise #1: "Textbook reconnaissance," you may have spotted the following articles in later chapters. If not, consider sampling them right now.

The seven-day antiprocrastination plan, page [50]

Seven more ways to stop procrastination, page [52]

25 ways to get the most out of now, page [54]

20 memory techniques, page [88]

Muscle reading, page [114]

The note-taking process flows, page [141]

Disarm tests, page [165]

Education's worth it—and you can pay for it, page [302]

Changing schools, page [360]

Getting the most from distance learning, page [363]

Career planning: Begin now, page [365]

their experiences. Theories help provide a framework for thinking about the information they find, and they often take a scientific approach to problems. They typically excel in well-defined, structured situations.

Processing information.
The ways that people process information typically range from a preference for active experimentation (AE) to a preference for reflective observation (RO).

- People who favor processing information by *active experimentation* prefer to jump in and start doing things immediately. Often they do not mind taking risks as they attempt to make sense of things because this helps them learn. They are results-oriented in their approach to tasks and look for practical ways to apply what they have learned.

- People who favor processing information by *reflective observation* prefer to watch and think about what is going on. Often they consider several points of view as they attempt to make sense of things and can generate many ideas about how something happens. They value patience, good judgment, and a thorough approach to understanding information.

According to David Kolb, a professor at Case Western Reserve University who developed the theory of experiential learning, learners have natural preferences about how they perceive and process information.[2] Yet they benefit most fully if they allow themselves to participate in all four components of the continuum. Successful learners:

- Involve themselves fully, openly, and without bias in new experiences (CE).

- Observe and reflect on these experiences from many perspectives (RO).

- Create concepts that integrate observations into logically sound theories (AC).

- Use these theories to make decisions and solve problems (AE).

You can use these ideas to become a well-rounded learner. First, start by understanding your natural preferences. Then balance them with activities that you consciously choose to support your learning.

Taking your Learning Style Inventory.
To help you become more aware of what you currently do to support your learning, David Kolb has developed the Learning Style Inventory (LSI), which is included on the next few pages. Completing this inventory will help you discover more about how you learn.

Step 1

Keep in mind that this is not a test. There are no right or wrong answers. Your goal is to develop a profile of your learning. Take the inventory quickly. There's no need to agonize over your responses. Recalling a recent situation whereby you learned something new at school, at work, or in your life might make it easier for you to focus and answer the questions.

Step 2

Remove the sheet of paper following page LSI-2. When you're ready to write on the inventory, press firmly so that your answers will show up on the page underneath the questions.

Step 3

Get ready to take the inventory. Note that the LSI consists of 12 sentences, each with four different endings. Read each sentence, then write a "4" next to the ending that best describes the way you currently learn. Then continue ranking the other endings with a "3," "2," or "1." This is a forced choice inventory, so you must rank each ending; no items can be left out. See the example provided at the beginning of the inventory, and then complete the 12 sentences.

- After you answer item #1, check to be sure that you wrote one "1," one "2," one "3," and one "4."

- Also check to make sure your markings are showing through onto the scoring sheet (LSI-3).

- After you have responded to the 12 items, go to the scoring page, LSI-3, which has instructions for computing your results.

Learning Style Inventory

Fill in the following blanks like this example:

A. When I learn:

    2 I am happy   **3** I am fast   **4** I am logical   **1** I am careful

REMEMBER: 4 = MOST LIKE YOU   3 = SECOND MOST LIKE YOU   2 = THIRD MOST LIKE YOU   1 = LEAST LIKE YOU.

Remove the sheet of paper following this page. Press firmly while writing.

---

1. When I learn:

____ I like to deal with my feelings.   ____ I like to think about ideas.   ____ I like to be doing things.   ____ I like to watch and listen.

---

2. I learn best when:

____ I listen and watch carefully.   ____ I rely on logical thinking.   ____ I trust my hunches and feelings.   ____ I work hard to get things done.

---

3. When I am learning:

____ I tend to reason things out.   ____ I am responsible about things.   ____ I am quiet and reserved.   ____ I have strong feelings and reactions.

---

4. I learn by:

____ feeling.   ____ doing.   ____ watching.   ____ thinking.

---

5. When I learn:

____ I am open to new experiences.   ____ I look at all sides of issues.   ____ I like to analyze things, break them down into their parts.   ____ I like to try things out.

---

6. When I am learning:

____ I am an observing person.   ____ I am an active person.   ____ I am an intuitive person.   ____ I am a logical person.

---

7. I learn best from:

____ observation.   ____ personal relationships.   ____ rational theories.   ____ a chance to try out and practice.

---

8. When I learn:

____ I like to see results from my work.   ____ I like ideas and theories.   ____ I take my time before acting.   ____ I feel personally involved in things.

---

9. I learn best when:

____ I rely on my observations.   ____ I rely on my feelings.   ____ I can try things out for myself.   ____ I rely on my ideas.

---

10. When I am learning:

____ I am a reserved person.   ____ I am an accepting person.   ____ I am a responsible person.   ____ I am a rational person.

---

11. When I learn:

____ I get involved.   ____ I like to observe.   ____ I evaluate things.   ____ I like to be active.

---

12. I learn best when:

____ I analyze ideas.   ____ I am receptive and open-minded.   ____ I am careful.   ____ I am practical.

Interpreting Your Learning Style Graph

Four modes of learning

When we're learning well, we tend to search out the answers to four key questions: Why? What? How? and, What if? Each of these questions represents a different learning mode, and learners often vary in their interest in finding the answers to these questions.

You might find yourself asking one of these questions more than the others. Or, you might ask several of these questions. Check the descriptions below and see what you think.

Mode 1: Why? Some of us want to know why we are learning things. We seek a purpose for information and a personal connection with the content. We want to know the rationale for what we're doing and how it fits in with what we already know.

Mode 2: What? Some of us crave information. When learning something, we want to know critical facts. We want to know what experts have to say about the topic. We seek a theory or model to explain what's happening.

Mode 3: How? Others hunger for an opportunity to try out what they're studying. We ask: How does this work? Does this idea make sense? How can I use this? Will it work? They want to personally apply and test theories and models.

Mode 4: What if? Some people get excited about going beyond what we're given in the classroom. We want to adapt what we're learning to a different setting or issue. We want our learning to make a difference in some area that we care about. We ask: What if we tried ...? Or, What if we combined ...?

Your preferred learning mode

When you examine the Learning Style Graph on page LSI-5, you will notice that your learning style profile (the "kite" you drew) may be primarily located in one part of that graph. This will give you an idea of your preferred learning mode. You can challenge yourself by practicing learning in the other modes as well.

Using the descriptions below and the sample graphs, identify your preferred learning mode.

Mode 1

Why? If the majority of your learning style profile is in the upper right-hand corner of the Learning Style Graph, you probably like to consider a situation from many different points of view. In this mode of learning, you determine why it is important to learn a new idea or technique.

Mode 2

What? If your learning style profile is mostly in the lower right-hand corner of the Learning Style Graph, you probably enjoy learning lots of facts and then arranging these facts in a logical and concise manner. When you are in this mode of learning, you are interested in knowing what ideas or techniques are important.

Mode 3

How? If most of your learning style profile is in the lower left-hand corner of the Learning Style Graph, you probably prefer Mode 3. In this mode, you get involved with new learning by practicing and testing it out. You want to know how ideas and techniques work. During this aspect of learning, you practice what you learn.

Mode 4

What if? If most of your learning style profile is in the upper left-hand corner of the Learning Style Graph, you probably prefer Mode 4. You like to take what you have practiced and find other uses for it. While in the aspect of learning, you ask: Where else in my life can I use this newly gained skill or information? You seek ways to relate what you have learned to other areas of your life.

Combinations

Some learning style profiles combine all four modes. The profile to the right reflects a learner who is focused primarily on gathering information—lots of information! People with this profile tend to ask for additional facts from an instructor, or they want to know where they can go to discover more about a subject.

The profile to the right indicates learners who focus more on understanding what they learn and less on gathering lots of information. People with this profile like smaller chunks of data with plenty of time to digest it. Long lectures can be difficult for these learners.

The profile to the right indicates a learner whose preferences are fairly well-balanced. People with this profile can be highly adaptable. They tend to learn no matter what the instructor does in the classroom. These people generally enjoy learning and do well in school.

CAUTION: No matter what mode you prefer, please remember that you use all four modes of learning. The goal of a master student can be to develop expertise in moving around the learning graph and balancing all four modes.

Remove this sheet before completing the Learning Style Inventory.

This page is inserted to ensure that the other writing you do in this book doesn't show through on page LSI-3.

Remove this sheet before completing the Learning Style Inventory.

This page is inserted to ensure that the other writing you do in this book doesn't show through on page LSI-3.

Scoring Your Inventory

Now fill out the Learning Style Graph (page LSI-5) and interpret your results. Please follow the next five steps.

Step 1: Add up all the numbers you gave to the items marked with brown F-shaped letters. Then write that total to the right in the blank titled, **"BROWN F"** TOTAL. Also, total all the numbers for **"TEAL W"**, **"PURPLE T"**, and **"ORANGE D"**. Write those totals to the right.

Step 2: Add the four totals to arrive at a GRAND TOTAL. This should equal 120. If you have something other than 120, go

back and re-add the colored letters; it was probably just an addition error. Now, remove this page, and continue with Step 3 on page LSI-5.

GRAND TOTAL _____

"BROWN F" TOTAL _____   **"TEAL W"** TOTAL _____

"PURPLE T" TOTAL _____   **"ORANGE D"** TOTAL _____

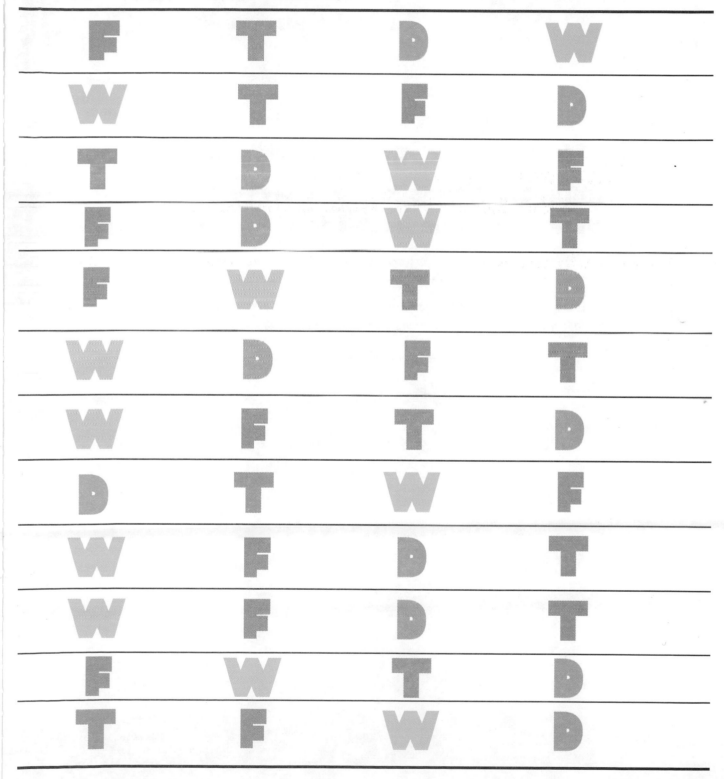

F	T	D	W
W	T	F	D
T	D	W	F
F	D	W	T
F	W	T	D
W	D	F	T
W	F	T	D
D	T	W	F
W	F	D	T
W	F	D	T
F	W	T	D
T	F	W	D

LSI-3

**Remove this page after you have
completed Steps 1 and 2 on page LSI-3.
And, then, continue with Step 3 on page LSI-5.**

*Once you have completed Step 3, discard this page so that you can more easily
compare your completed Learning Style Graph with the examples on page LSI-2.*

Learning Style Graph

Step 3: Remove the piece of paper that follows this page and then transfer your totals to the lines on the Learning Style Graph below. On the brown (F) line, find the number that corresponds to your **"BROWN F"** total from page LSI-3. Then write an X on this number. Do the same for your **"TEAL W"**, **"PURPLE T"**, and **"ORANGE D"** totals.

Step 4: Now, pressing firmly, draw four straight lines to connect the four X's and shade in the area to form a "kite." This is your learning profile. (For an example, see the illustration to the right.)

Each X that you placed on these lines indicates your preference for a different aspect of learning:

Concrete Experience ("Feeling"). The number where you put your X on this line indicates your preference for learning things that have personal meaning. The higher your score on this line, the more you like to learn things that you feel are important and relevant to you.

Reflective Observation ("Watching"). Your number on this line indicates how important it is for you to reflect on the things you are learning. If your score is high on this line, you probably find it important to watch others as they learn about a topic you are studying. You probably like to plan things out and take time to make sure that you understand a topic accurately.

Abstract Conceptualization ("Thinking"). Your number on this line indicates your preference for learning ideas, facts, and figures. If your score is high on this line, you probably like to absorb many concepts and gather lots of information on a new topic.

Active Experimentation ("Doing"). Your number on this line indicates your preference for applying ideas, using trial and error, and practicing what you learn. You enjoy hands-on activities.

Step 5: Now that you have filled out the Learning Style Graph, read page LSI-2 to further understand your preferences for learning.

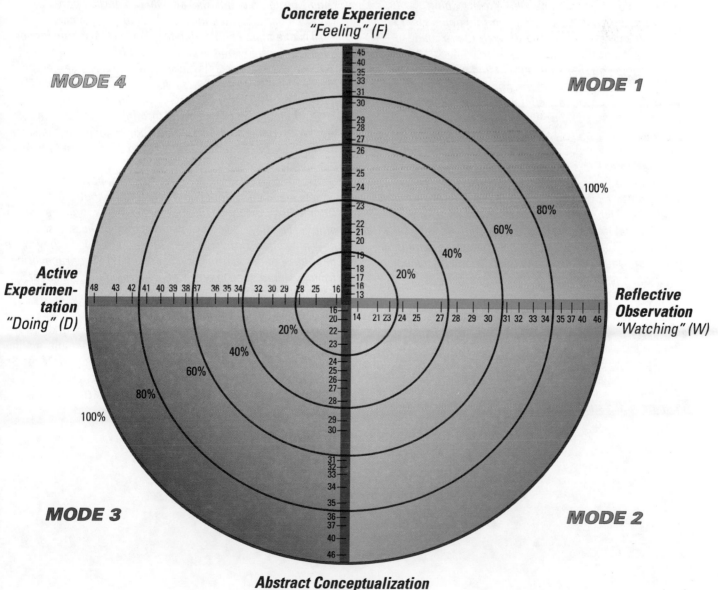

Cycle of Learning

One way to understand the four modes of learning is to see how they relate to actual examples of learning. Consider three activities: learning to ride a bicycle, learning about history, and learning to bungee jump.

Example 1:
Learning to ride a bicycle

Learning begins with developing an interest in the task (Mode 1: Why?). Why learn to ride a bike? Maybe you want to find a way to travel that's faster than walking. Or maybe you never want to pay for parking again. Learning to ride a bicycle might provide you with a quick means of affordable travel.

Riding a bicycle makes sense to you, so you want to learn whatever you need to know in order to ride a bike well (Mode 2: What?). You arrange to meet a friend who has a bike at a nearby park, and your friend explains how to balance the bicycle and what to do with your hands and feet while riding. You also watch people in the park riding their bicycles, and you note what they're doing.

After you gather this information, you decide to try out what you've learned (Mode 3: How?). You're ready to experiment and see if the information you've gathered can actually help you ride a bicycle. To find out, you get on the bicycle and see what happens. You keep trying until you figure out how to make the information work for you. Soon you're successfully riding the bicycle.

Once you've conquered the basics of riding the bicycle, you use your bike on a daily basis. You find yourself considering aspects of bike riding that you've never thought about before (Mode 4: What if?). For instance, what if you chose to use a bike as your only means of transportation? What if you rode your bike across the state during Spring break? What if you started a campaign to develop bike trails throughout your city? Riding a bike becomes more than something you just know how to do; biking becomes an important part of your life.

Example 2:
Learning about history

You're required to take an elective in history, and you decide to take a course on the History of U.S. Immigration. Your ancestors came to the U.S. as immigrants, and immigration is still taking place today. You conclude that you'll find this topic interesting (Mode 1: Why?).

Soon you're in class, and you learn that many Americans have held misconceptions and fears about immigration that persist today (Mode 2: What?).

You find yourself re-evaluating your own beliefs and assumptions about immigration. You question whether new refugees in your city are experiencing some of the same stereotyping that U.S. immigrants experienced in earlier times. You decide to become more active in your community and learn firsthand what impact immigration policies are having on your neighbors (Mode 3: How?).

You also start thinking about what it would be like to become a government attorney and devote your career to making sure that the system treats all immigrants with fairness and respect. You realize that you want to make a positive difference in the lives of people who are coming to live in the U.S. today (Mode 4: What if?).

Example 3:
Learning to bungee jump

Perhaps you've watched someone bungee jump. Many people prefer to watch this activity rather than participate. They witness a bungee jump and come to a conclusion: "This is one thing I don't need to learn!" If this is true for you, then your learning ended with Mode 1 (Why?). You chose not to move to Mode 2 (What?), which involves gathering information. For example, you don't climb up onto a platform, look over the edge, or ask how to put on ankle straps.

Other people might proceed through Mode 2 and then stop. After gathering facts about bungee jumping, they may decide they have learned enough and choose not to take the plunge.

Others might decide to make the jump, however. These people move on to action and practice—Mode 3 (How?). During the jump, they might integrate the experience with other skills they have. For example, they could add some new movement or flair to their jump. At this point they move to Mode 4 of the learning cycle (What if?). After recovering from the jump, they may start the learning cycle all over again.

These examples show how the learning cycle works. You're interested in something (Mode 1), so you gather information about it (Mode 2). You try out what you're learning (Mode 3), then you integrate it into your day-to-day life (Mode 4). You go through this cycle many times as one learning experience generates another.

Remove this sheet before completing the Learning Style Graph.

This page is inserted to ensure that the other writing you do in this book doesn't show through on page LSI-7.

Remove this sheet before completing the Learning Style Graph.

This page is inserted to ensure that the other writing you do in this book doesn't show through on page LSI-7.

Balancing Your Preferences

The chart below identifies some of the natural talents as well as challenges for people who have a strong preference for any one mode of learning. For example, if most of your "kite" is in Mode 2 of the Learning Style Graph, then look at the lower right-hand corner of this chart to see if this is an accurate description of you.

After reviewing the description of your preferred learning mode, read the sections for the other modes that start with the words "To develop." These sections explain what you do to become a more balanced learner.

Concrete Experience

MODE 4

Strengths:
Getting things done
Leadership
Risk taking

Too much of this mode can lead to:
Trivial improvements
Meaningless activity

Too little of this mode for those with other learning preferences can lead to:
Work not completed on time
Impractical plans
Not being directed to goals

To develop Mode 4 learning skills, practice:
• Committing yourself to objectives
• Seeking new opportunities
• Influencing and leading others
• Being personally involved
• Dealing with people

MODE 1

Strengths:
Imaginative ability
Understanding people
Recognizing problems
Brainstorming

Too much of this mode can lead to:
Feeling paralyzed by alternatives
Inability to make decisions

Too little of this mode for those with other preferences can lead to:
Lack of ideas
Not recognizing problems and opportunities

To develop Mode 1 learning skills, practice:
• Being sensitive to people's feelings
• Being sensitive to values
• Listening with an open mind
• Gathering information

Active Experimentation ———————————————————— **Reflective Observation**

Strengths:
Problem solving
Decision making
Deductive reasoning
Defining problems

Too much of this mode can lead to:
Solving the wrong problem
Hasty decision making

Too little of this mode for those with other learning preferences can lead to:
Lack of focus
No shifting of ideas
Scattered thoughts

To develop Mode 3 learning skills, practice:
• Creating new ways of thinking and doing
• Experimenting with new ideas
• Choosing the best solution
• Setting goals
• Making decisions

Strengths:
Planning
Creating models
Defining problems
Developing theories

Too much of this mode can lead to:
Vague ideals ("castles in the air")
Lack of practical application

Too little of this mode for those with other learning preferences can lead to:
Inability to learn from mistakes
No sound basis for work
No systematic approach

To develop Mode 2 learning skills, practice:
• Organizing information
• Building conceptual models
• Testing theories and ideas
• Analyzing quantitative data

MODE 3

MODE 2

Abstract Conceptualization

Name _____ Date _____/_____/_____

NOTE: After completing your Learning Style Inventory (page LSI-1) and filling in the Learning Style Graph (page LSI-5), be sure to read the articles "Interpreting Your Learning Style Graph" (page LSI-2) and "Cycle of Learning" (page LSI-6). Then, complete the following Journal Entry.

JOURNAL ENTRY
#7

Discovery/Intention Statement

Regarding my preferences for learning, I discovered that . . .

_____

_____

Given my preferences for learning, I intend to . . .

_____

_____

Concrete Experience
"Feeling" (F)

MODE 4

MODE 1

100%

80%

60%

40%

20%

Active Experimentation "Doing" (D)

48 43 42 41 40 39 38 37 36 35 34 32 30 29 28 25 16

Reflective Observation "Watching" (W)

20%

40%

60%

80%

100%

14 21 23 24 25 27 28 29 30 31 32 33 34 35 37 40 46

MODE 3

MODE 2

Abstract Conceptualization
"Thinking" (T)

LSI-7

USING YOUR LEARNING STYLE PROFILE TO SUCCEED IN SCHOOL

To get the most value from knowing your learning style profile, look for ways to apply this knowledge in school and at work. Consider the suggestions that follow.

Tolerate discomfort

Discomfort is a natural part of the learning process. As you participate in modes of learning that do not energize you, allow yourself to notice your struggle with a task or your lack of interest in completing it. Realize that you are balancing your learning preferences. Resist the temptation to skip a mode of learning or move too quickly through it. By tolerating discomfort and using all of the modes, you increase your chances for success.

Match activities to your learning style profile

You might want to examine your learning style profile when choosing your major and planning your career. You could focus on courses or jobs that suit your preferred modes of learning. Consulting with people who have different learning preferences can also be beneficial when you approach course work or other learning situations.

Ask for what you want

You might find that the way an instructor teaches is not always the way you prefer learning, and that teachers don't always promote all four modes of learning. Once you know your learning preferences, you can be more responsible for ensuring that your learning needs are met.

- If you have a strong preference for Mode 1, you are likely to spend time observing others and planning before taking action. You probably also enjoy working with other students. To assist yourself in school, ask questions that help you understand why it is important for you to learn about a specific topic. You might also want to make sure that you form study groups.

- If you have a strong preference for Mode 2, you are skilled in understanding theories and concepts. When in learning situations, you are likely to enjoy lectures and individual class assignments.

Chances are that you also enjoy solitary time and are not fond of working in groups. To assist yourself in school, ask questions that help you gather enough information to understand what you are learning. You might also increase your effectiveness by choosing not to concentrate equally on all of the material in a chapter, focusing primarily on specific parts of the text.

Student Voices

At first I was very angry about being left behind and was discouraged because of my learning style. In fact, I spent a lot of energy resenting my lost opportunities. Then I realized the energy I was spending on resentment could be turned into something positive. I wrote a speech and shared my experience; I addressed problems that can result from not recognizing learning styles. In the speech, I pointed out ways to identify learning style and ways to get that style met. I received a lot of good feedback from the speech, and I think it actually helped other students.

— REBECCA GULLEDGE

- If you have a strong preference for Mode 3, you probably excel at working with your hands and at laboratory stations. When in a learning situation, you are interested in knowing how things work. In addition, you probably enjoy working alone or with a small group. To assist yourself in school, ask questions that help you understand how something works and how you can experiment with these new ideas. Also allow time to practice and apply what you learn. You can conduct experiments, do projects, complete homework, create presentations, conduct research, tabulate findings, or even write a rap song that summarizes key concepts. Such activities provide an opportunity to internalize your learning through hands-on practice.

- If you have a strong preference for Mode 4, you are skilled at teaching others what you have learned and helping them see the importance of these concepts. Whether in a learning situation or in everyday life, you like to apply facts and theories. You probably enjoy carrying out plans and having new and challenging experiences. You also prefer working with others and are likely to have a large social circle. To assist yourself in school, ask questions that help you determine where else in your life you can apply what you have just learned. Also seek opportunities to demonstrate your understanding. You could coach a classmate about what you have learned, present findings from your research, report results from your experiments, demonstrate how your project works, or perform a rap song that someone else might have written.

Stay in charge of your learning

When they experience difficulty in school, some students say: "The instructor can't teach me." Or "The classroom is not conducive to the way I learn." Or "This teacher creates tests that are too hard for me." Or "In class, we never have time for questions." Or "The instructor doesn't teach to my learning style."

WORKPLACE APPLICATIONS

Bring your knowledge of learning styles to the workplace. For example, you can gear on-the-job training opportunities to your preferred modes of learning—and look for ways to experience other modes as well. Also, when working in teams, remember that your colleagues have their own learning preferences.

Such statements can become mental crutches—a set of beliefs that prevent you from taking charge of your learning. To support your self-responsibility, you could have thoughts and make statements such as: "I will discover why this information is valuable even though it isn't obvious." Or "I will find out more information and facts about this." Or "I will discover how I can experiment with this information I am learning." Or "I will discover new ways to use this information in my life." Or "I will study this information with modes of learning that are not my preferred style."

Associate with students who have different learning style profiles

If your instructor asks your class to form groups to complete an assignment, avoid joining a group in which everyone shares your preferred modes of learning. Get together with people who both complement and challenge you. This is one way you can develop skills in all four learning modes and become a more well-rounded student.

Use this book with the modes of learning in mind

The four modes of learning are part of a natural cycle. Master students learn in all four ways. If you strongly prefer one mode, then experiment with the others. *Becoming a Master Student* can help. This book is designed to move you through all four modes of learning.

- At the beginning of each chapter, you are asked to complete a Journal Entry designed to stimulate your thinking and connect the chapter content to your current life experience—to help you see why learning this material is beneficial (a Mode 1 activity).

- Next, you read articles that are filled with ideas, information, and suggestions that can help you succeed in school (a Mode 2 activity).

- You are also asked to practice new skills with exercises provided throughout each chapter (a Mode 3 activity).

- Finally, at the end of each chapter Discovery and Intention Statements and Learning Styles Applications help you look at how you can tie all of this information together and use it in your future (a Mode 4 activity).

This article and the previous one were written following the same four-mode learning cycle. In the previous article, "Discovering how you learn," the purpose and value of learning styles were reviewed (Mode 1). Then facts and theories about learning styles were discussed (Mode 2). Next, you took action and did the Learning Style Inventory (Mode 3). In this article, you are being asked to apply these concepts in your life (Mode 4).

Resources on learning styles

The Learning Style Inventory is distributed by Hay/McBer, Inc., a human resources and management consulting company located at 116 Huntington Ave., Boston, MA 02116, 1-800-729-8074, trgmcber.haygroup.com.

Experiential Learning: Experience as the Source of Learning and Development by David A. Kolb (Englewood Cliffs, NJ: Prentice-Hall, 1984). This publication explains the theory of experiential learning—with applications to education, work, and personal development—and contains information on the validity of the Learning Style Inventory.

Adaptive Style Inventory by David A. Kolb and Richard Boyatzis, distributed by Hay/McBer, Boston, MA 02116. This inventory helps assess your adaptability in different learning situations.

Learning Skills Profile by David A. Kolb and Richard Boyatzis, distributed by Hay/McBer, Boston, MA 02116. This instrument compares your learning style to your job skill demands.

The 4MAT System: Teaching to Learning Style, with Right/Left Mode Techniques by Bernice McCarthy (Barrington, IL: About Learning, 1980, 1987). The 4MAT model explains learning in terms of the ways people perceive and process information.

Myers-Briggs Type Indicator and The Keirsey Temperament Sorter. The Keirsey Temperament Sorter, by David Keirsey, is a personality test that scores results according to the Myers-Briggs Type Indicator® instrument. The MBTI®, published by Consulting Psychologists Press, is a professional instrument that may be administered only by a certified examiner.

#7

Recall an enjoyable experience

Take three minutes to remember a time when you enjoyed learning something. In the space below, make a list of the things you found enjoyable about that experience.

_____
_____
_____
_____
_____
_____
_____
_____
_____
_____
_____
_____
_____
_____
_____
_____
_____
_____
_____
_____
_____
_____
_____

Within the next 24 hours, compare your list with those of other classmates. More than likely, you'll find that your list has some items in common with theirs. This discovery echoes a principle of psychology—that learning occurs in a similar way for all of us.

At the same time, you might make a related discovery—that people prefer different aspects of learning. Some people enjoy learning things that are important in daily life. Others enjoy the process of learning for the pure pleasure of gaining knowledge and skill. Still others excel when they can take what they learn and experiment with it. Other people enjoy finding new ways to apply what they know to everyday life. And some enjoy all four modes of learning.

Claim your MULTIPLE INTELLIGENCES

People often think that being smart means the same thing as having a high IQ, and that having a high IQ leads to success in school. Psychologists are finding that IQ scores do not always foretell which students will do well in academic settings—or after they graduate.

Howard Gardner of Harvard University believes that no single measure of intelligence can tell us how smart we are. Instead, Gardner identifies the nine intelligences described below.[3] By applying Gardner's concepts, we can greatly expand our strategies for success in school, work, and relationships.

People using their **verbal/linguistic intelligence** use words effectively and learn best by speaking, writing, reading, and listening. They are likely to enjoy activities such as telling stories and doing crossword puzzles.

Those using **mathematical/logical intelligence** are good with numbers, logic, problem solving, patterns, relationships, and categories. They are generally precise, methodical, and likely to enjoy science.

When people learn visually and by organizing things spatially, they display **visual/spatial intelligence.** They think in images and pictures and understand best by seeing the subject. They enjoy charts, graphs, maps, mazes, tables, illustrations, art, models, puzzles, and costumes.

People using **bodily/kinesthetic intelligence** prefer physical activity. They enjoy activities like building things, woodworking, dancing, sewing, and crafts. They generally are coordinated and athletic, and would rather participate in games than just watch.

Those using **musical/rhythmic intelligence** enjoy musical expression through songs, rhythms, and musical instruments. They are sensitive to various kinds of sounds, remember melodies easily, and might enjoy drumming, humming, and whistling.

People using **intrapersonal intelligence** are exceptionally aware of their own feelings and values. They are generally reserved, self-motivated, and intuitive.

Evidence of **interpersonal intelligence** is seen in outgoing people. They do well with cooperative learning and are sensitive to the feelings, intentions, and motivations of others. They often make good leaders.

People using **naturalist intelligence** love the outdoors and recognize details in plants, animals, rocks, clouds, and other natural formations. These people excel in observing fine distinctions among similar items.

People using their **existentialist intelligence** enjoy asking questions such as "Why do human beings exist?" and "What is our role in the universe?" They ordinarily consider the "big picture" of humankind and excel in philosophy.

Becoming a Master Student is designed to help you develop many of these intelligences. Use the suggestions for reading, writing, speaking, thinking, and listening to promote verbal/linguistic intelligence. To promote logical/mathematical intelligence, experiment with suggestions for solving math and science problems. Use the suggestions for mind mapping and creative visualization to develop visual/spatial intelligence. To promote bodily/kinesthetic intelligence, move into action by doing the exercises throughout the text. Complete Journal Entries as a way to promote intrapersonal intelligence, and read Chapter Eight: "Communicating" for a host of ways to deepen your interpersonal intelligence.

Also use the techniques for creative thinking in Chapter Seven to invent your own ways of developing musical, naturalist, and existentialist intelligences. For example, you could write songs using lyrics based on your class notes and experiment with various kinds of background music while studying. Spend time in nature as a way to manage stress and hone your observation skills. And take courses in the liberal arts—including philosophy, religion, and the fine arts—to explore ultimate questions about human existence.

Each of us has all of these intelligences to some degree. And each of us can learn to enhance them. When we acknowledge and trust all of our intelligences, we understand and appreciate ourselves more. And we can constantly explore new ways of being smart.

 Share your strategies for promoting multiple intelligences with other students using this book, and explore their suggestions on this topic. Visit Houghton Mifflin's College Survival/Becoming a Master Student web site: **http://collegesurvival.college.hmco.com/students.**

In 1482, Leonardo da Vinci wrote a letter to a wealthy baron, applying for work. In excerpted form, he wrote,

The Master Student

IN EACH CHAPTER of this text there is an example of a person who embodies several qualities of a master student.

As you read about these people and others like them, ask yourself: How can I apply this? Look for the timeless qualities in the people you read about. Many of the strategies used by master students from another time or place are tools that you can use today.

The master students in this book were chosen because they demonstrate unusual and effective ways to learn. Remember that these are just 12 examples of master students (one for each chapter). Round out the profiles in this book with other master students you've read about or know personally.

As you meet new people, look for those who excel at learning. The master student is not a vague or remote ideal.

Rather, master students move freely among us. In fact, there's one living inside your skin.

"I can contrive various and endless means of offense and defense. . . . I have all sorts of extremely light and strong bridges adapted to be most easily carried. . . . I have methods for destroying every turret or fortress. . . . I will make covered chariots, safe and unassailable. . . . In case of need I will make big guns, mortars, and light ordnance of fine and useful forms out of the common type. . . ." And then he added, almost as an afterthought, *"In times of peace I believe I can give perfect satisfaction and to the equal of any other in architecture . . . can carry out sculpture . . . and also I can do in painting whatever may be done."*

The Mona Lisa, for example.

This book is about something that cannot be taught.

It's about becoming a master student.

A master is a person who has attained a level of skill that goes beyond technique. For a master, methods and procedures are automatic responses to the needs of the task. Work is effortless; struggle evaporates. The master carpenter is so familiar with her tools, they are part of her. To a master chef, utensils are old friends. Because these masters don't have to think about the details of the process, they bring more of themselves to their work.

Mastery can lead to flashy results—an incredible painting, for example, or a gem of a short story. In basketball, mastery might result in an unbelievable shot at the buzzer. For a musician, it might be the performance of performances, the night when everything comes together. Often the result of mastery is a sense of profound satisfaction, well-being, and timelessness. Work seems self-propelled. The master is *in* control by being *out* of control. He lets go and allows the creative process to take over. That's why after a spectacular performance, it is often said of an athlete or a performer, "He was playing out of his mind."

do to get value out of this lecture, even though it seems boring?" And she finds an answer.

Able to focus attention.
Watch a 2-year-old at play. Pay attention to his eyes. The wide-eyed look reveals an energy and a capacity for amazement that keep his attention absolutely focused in the here and now. The master student's focused attention has a childlike quality. The world, to a child, is always new. Because the master student can focus attention, to him the world is always new, too.

Willing to change.
The unknown does not frighten the master student. In fact, she welcomes it—even the unknown in herself. We all have pictures of who we think we are, and these pictures can be useful. They also can prevent learning and growth. The master student is open to changes in her environment and changes in herself.

Able to organize and sort.
The master student can take a large body of information and sift through it to discover relationships. He can play with information, organizing pieces of data by size, color, function, timeliness, and hundreds of other categories.

Competent.
Mastery of skills is important to the master student. When she learns mathematical formulas, she studies them until they become second nature. She practices until she knows them cold, then puts in a few extra minutes. She also is able to apply what she learns to new and different situations.

Joyful.
More often than not, the master student is seen with a smile on his face—sometimes a smile at nothing in particular other than amazement at the world and his experience of it.

Able to suspend judgment.
The master student has opinions and positions, and she is able to let go of them when appropriate. She realizes she is more than her thoughts. She can quiet her internal dialogue and listen to an opposing viewpoint. She doesn't let judgment get in the way of learning. Rather than approaching discussions with a "Prove it to me and then I'll believe it" attitude, she asks herself, What if this is true? and explores possibilities.

Energetic.
Notice the student with a spring in his step, the one who is enthusiastic and involved in class. When he reads, he often sits on the very edge of his chair, and he plays with the same intensity. He is a master student.

Well.
Health is important to the master student, though not necessarily in the sense of being free of illness. Rather, she values her body and treats it with respect. She tends to her emotional and spiritual health, as well as to her physical health.

Likewise, the master student is one who "learns out of her mind." Of course, that statement makes no sense. Mastery, in fact, doesn't make sense. It cannot be captured with words. It defies analysis. Mastery cannot be taught, only learned and experienced.

Examine the following list of characteristics of master students in light of your own experience. The list is not complete. It merely points in a direction. Look in that direction, and you'll begin to see the endless diversity of master students. These people are old and young, male and female. They exist in every period of history. And they come from every culture, race, and ethnic group.

Also remember to look to yourself. No one can teach us to be master students; we already *are* master students. We are natural learners by design. As students, we can discover that every day.

Following are some traits shared by master students.

Inquisitive.
The master student is curious about everything. By posing questions she can generate interest in the most mundane, humdrum situations. When she is bored during a biology lecture, she thinks to herself, "I always get bored when I listen to this instructor. Why is that? Maybe it's because he reminds me of my boring Uncle Ralph, who always tells those endless fishing stories. He even looks like Uncle Ralph. Amazing! Boredom is certainly interesting." Then she asks herself, "What can I

Self-aware. The master student is willing to evaluate himself and his behavior. He regularly tells the truth about his strengths and those aspects that could be improved.

Responsible. There is a difference between responsibility and blame, and the master student knows it well. She is willing to take responsibility for everything in her life—for events that most people would blame on others.

For example, if a master student is served cold eggs in the cafeteria, she chooses to take responsibility for getting cold eggs. This is not the same as blaming herself for cold eggs. Rather, she looks for ways to change the situation and get what she wants. She could choose to eat breakfast earlier, or she might tell someone in the kitchen that the eggs are cold and request a change. The cold eggs might continue. Even then, the master student takes responsibility and gives herself the power to choose her response to the situation.

Willing to risk. The master student often takes on projects with no guarantee of success. He is willing to participate in class dialogues at the risk of looking foolish. He is willing to tackle difficult subjects in term papers. He welcomes the risk of a challenging course.

Willing to participate. Don't look for the master student on the sidelines. She's in the game. She is a player who can be counted on. She is willing to make a commitment, and she can follow through.

A generalist. The master student is interested in everything around him. He has a broad base of knowledge in many fields and can find value that is applicable to his specialties.

Willing to accept paradox. The word *paradox* comes from two Greek words, *para* (beyond) and *doxen* (opinion). A paradox is something that is beyond opinion or, more accurately, something that might seem contradictory or absurd yet might actually have meaning.

For example, the master student can be committed to managing money and reaching her financial goals. At the same time, she can be totally detached from money, knowing that her real worth is independent of how much money she has. The master student recognizes the limitations of the mind and is at home with paradox. She can accept that ambiguity.

Courageous. The master student admits his fear and fully experiences it. For example, he will approach a tough exam as an opportunity to explore feelings of anxiety and tension related to the pressure to perform. He does not deny fear; he embraces it.

Self-directed. Rewards or punishments provided by others do not motivate the master student. Her motivation to learn comes from within.

Spontaneous. The master student is truly in the here and now. He is able to respond to the moment in fresh, surprising, and unplanned ways.

Relaxed about grades. Grades make the master student neither depressed nor euphoric. She recognizes that sometimes grades are important, and grades are not the only reason she studies. She does not measure her value as a human being by the grades she receives.

Intuitive. The master student has an inner sense that cannot be explained by logic. He has learned to trust his feelings, and he works to develop this intuitive sense.

Creative. Where others see dull details and trivia, the master student sees opportunities to create. She can gather pieces of knowledge from a wide range of subjects and put them together in a new way. The master student is creative in every aspect of her life.

Willing to be uncomfortable. The master student does not place comfort first. When discomfort is necessary to reach a goal, he is willing to experience it. He can endure personal discomfort and can look at unpleasant things with detachment.

Accepting. The master student accepts herself, the people around her, and the challenges that life offers.

Willing to laugh. The master student might laugh at any moment, and his sense of humor includes the ability to laugh at himself.

Hungry. Human beings begin life with a natural appetite for knowledge. In some people it soon gets dulled. The master student has tapped that hunger, and it gives her a desire to learn for the sake of learning.

Willing to work. Once inspired, the master student is willing to follow through with sweat. He knows that genius and creativity are the result of persistence and work. When in high gear, the master student works with the intensity of a child at play.

Caring. A master student cares about knowledge and has a passion for ideas. She also cares about people and appreciates learning from others. She flourishes in a community that values "win-win" outcomes, cooperation, and love.

The master student in you. The master student is in all of us. By design, human beings are learning machines. We have an innate ability to learn, and all of us have room to grow and improve.

It is important to understand the difference between learning and being taught. Human beings can resist being taught anything. Carl Rogers goes so far as to say that anything that can be taught to a human being is either inconsequential or just plain harmful.[4] What is important in education, Rogers asserts, is *learning*. And everyone has the ability to learn.

Unfortunately, people also learn to hide that ability. As they experience the pain that sometimes accompanies learning, they shut down. If a child experiences embarrassment in front of a group of people, he could learn to avoid similar situations. In doing so, he restricts his possibilities.

Some children "learn" that they are slow learners. If they learn it well enough, their behavior comes to match that label.

As people grow older, they sometimes accumulate a growing list of ideas to defend, a catalog of familiar experiences that discourages them from learning anything new.

Still, the master student within survives. To tap that resource, you don't need to acquire anything. You already have everything you need. Every day you can rediscover the natural learner within you.

Maslow's qualities of a self-actualizing person

Abraham Maslow was a psychologist who worked on a theory of psychological health rather than sickness. Maslow studied people whom he called "self-actualizing," which means, in part, healthy and creative.[5] He listed traits he found in self-actualizing people (ranging from Albert Einstein to anthropologist Ruth Benedict). These characteristics also describe the master student.

THE SELF-ACTUALIZING PERSON:

- is reality oriented.
- is accepting of herself and others.
- is spontaneous.
- is problem-centered rather than self-centered.
- is detached and in need of privacy.
- is independent.
- has a fresh, rather than stereotyped, appreciation of people.
- has had a mystical or spiritual experience.
- identifies with the human race as a whole.
- has a few deep, intimate relationships.
- has democratic values.
- has a philosophical rather than bitter sense of humor.
- has creative resources.
- is resistant to conformity.
- is transcendent of the environment.

JOURNAL ENTRY

#8

Discovery Statement

After reading "The Master Student," consider your own strengths and list below the qualities of a master student that you observe in yourself. This is no easy task. Most of us are competent self-critics, and we tend to discount our strong points. If you get stuck trying to complete this Journal Entry, warm up by brainstorming all of your good points on a separate sheet of paper. Remember to consider experiences both in and out of school.

The master student qualities I observe in myself include ...

_____

_____

In the space below, write a specific example of how you model one of these qualities.

_____

_____

_____

The value of higher

When you're waist-deep in reading assignments, writing papers, and studying for tests, you might well ask yourself: Is all this effort going to pay off someday? That's a fair question. It gets to a core issue—the value of getting an education beyond high school.

Reassure yourself. The potential benefits of higher education are enormous. To begin with, there are economic benefits. Over their lifetimes, college graduates on the average earn much more than high school graduates. That's just one potential payoff. Consider the others explained below.

Learn skills that apply across careers.

Jobs that involve responsibility, prestige, and higher incomes depend on self-management skills. These include knowing ways to manage time, resolve conflict, set goals, learn new skills, and control stress. Higher education is a place to learn and practice such skills.

Judging by recent trends, most of us will have multiple careers in our lifetimes. In this environment of constant change, it makes sense to learn skills that apply across careers.

Master the liberal arts.
According to one traditional model of education, there are two essential tasks for people to master—the use of language and the use of numbers. To acquire these skills, students once immersed themselves in seven subjects: grammar, rhetoric, logic, arithmetic, geometry, music, and astronomy. These subjects were called the "liberal" arts. They complemented the fine arts, such as poetry, and the practical arts, such as farming.

This model of liberal education still has something to offer. Today we master the use of language through the basic processes of communication: reading, writing, speaking, and listening. In addition, courses in mathematics and science help us understand the

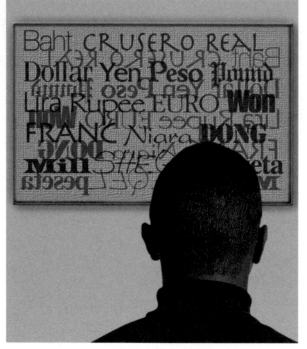

world in quantitative terms. The abilities to communicate and calculate are essential to almost every profession. Excellence at these skills has long been considered an essential characteristic of an educated person.

The word *liberal* comes from the Latin verb *libero*, which means "to free." Liberal arts are those that promote critical thinking. Studying them can free us from irrational ideas, half-truths, racism, and prejudice. The liberal arts grant us freedom to explore alternatives and create a system of personal values. These benefits are priceless, the very basis of personal fulfillment and political freedom.

Gain a broad vision.
It's been said that a large corporation is a collection of departments connected only by a plumbing system. This quip makes a point: As workers in different fields become more specialized, they run the danger of forgetting how to talk to each other.

Higher education can change that. One benefit of studying the liberal arts is the chance to gain a broad vision. Liberally educated people know something about the various kinds of problems tackled in psychology and theology, philosophy and physics, literature and mathematics. They understand how people in all of these fields arrive at conclusions and how these fields relate to each other.

Discover your values.
We do not spend all of our waking hours at our jobs. That leaves us with a decision that affects the quality of our lives: how to spend leisure time. By cultivating our interest in the arts and community affairs, the liberal arts provide us with many options for activities outside of work. These studies add a dimension to life that goes beyond having a job and paying the bills.

Practical people are those who focus on time and money. And managing these effectively calls for a clear

education

sense of values. Our values define what we commit our time and money to.

Vocational education is about how to do things that we can get paid for. Through a liberal education, we discover what's worth doing—what activities are worthy of our energy and talents. Both types of education are equally important. No matter where they've attended school, liberally educated people can state what they're willing to bet their lives on.

Discover new interests.

Taking a broad range of courses has the potential to change your direction in life. A student previously committed to a career in science might try out a drawing class and eventually switch to a degree in studio arts. Or a person who swears that she has no aptitude for technical subjects might change her major to computer science after taking an introductory computer course.

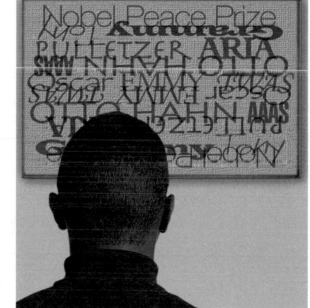

To make effective choices about your long-term goals, base those choices on a variety of academic and personal experiences. Even if you don't change majors or switch career directions, you could discover an important avocation or gain a complementary skill. For example, science majors who will eventually write for professional journals can gain value from English courses.

Hang out with the great.

Today we enjoy a huge legacy from our ancestors. The creative minds of our species have given us great works of art, systems of science, and technology that defies the imagination. Through higher education you can gain firsthand knowledge of humanity's greatest creations.

Poet Ezra Pound defined literature as "news that stays news."[6] Most of the writing in newspapers and magazines becomes dated quickly. In contrast, many of the books you read in higher education have passed the hardest test of all—time. Such works have created value for people for decades, sometimes for centuries. These creations are inexhaustible. We can return to them time after time and discover something new. These are the works we can justifiably call great. Hanging out with these works transforms us. Getting to know them exercises our minds as running exercises our bodies.

Through studying the greatest works in many fields, we raise our standards. We learn ways to distinguish what is superficial and fleeting from what is lasting and profound.

The criteria for a great novel, poem, painting, or piece of music or dance might be different for one person than for another. Differences in taste reflect the differences in our backgrounds. The point is to find those works that have enduring value—and enjoy them for a lifetime.

Join the conversation.

In ancient times—long before printing presses, televisions, and computers—people educated themselves by conversing with each other. Students in ancient Athens were often called *peripatetic* (a word that means "walking around") because they were frequently seen strolling around the city, engaged in heated philosophical debate.

Since then, the debate has deepened and broadened. The world's finest scientists and artists are voices in a conversation that spans centuries and crosses cultures. This is a conversation about the nature of truth and beauty, knowledge and compassion, good and evil—ideas that form the very basis of human society. Robert Hutchins, former president of the University of Chicago, called this the "great conversation."[7] By studying this conversation, we take on the most basic human challenges: coping with death and suffering, helping create a just global society, living with meaning and purpose.

Our greatest thinkers have left behind visible records. You'll find them in libraries, concert halls, museums, and scientific laboratories across the world. Through higher education, you gain a front-row seat for the great conversation—and an opportunity to add your own voice.

Ideas are tools

There are many ideas in this book. Don't believe any of them. Instead, think of them as tools. For example, you use a hammer for a purpose—to drive a nail.

When you use a new hammer, you might notice its shape, its weight, and its balance. You don't try to figure out whether the hammer is "right." You use it. If it works, you use it again. If it doesn't work, you get a different hammer.

This is not the attitude most people adopt when they encounter new ideas. The first thing most people do with new ideas is to measure them against old ones. If a new idea conflicts with an old one, the new one is likely to be rejected.

People have plenty of room in their lives for different kinds of hammers, but they tend to limit their capacity for different kinds of ideas. A new idea, at some level, is a threat to their very being—unlike a new hammer, which is simply a new hammer.

Most of us have a built-in desire to be right. Our ideas, we often think, represent ourselves. And when we identify with our ideas, they assume new importance in our lives. We put them on our mantels. We hang them on our walls. We wear them on our T-shirts and display them on our bumpers. We join associations of people who share our most beloved ideas. We make up rituals about them, compose songs about them, and write stories about them. We declare ourselves dedicated to these ideas.

Some ideas are worth dying for. But please note: This book does not contain any of those ideas. The ideas on these pages are strictly "hammers."

Imagine someone defending a hammer. Picture this person holding up a hammer and declaring, "I hold this hammer to be self-evident. Give me this hammer or give me death. Those other hammers are flawed. There are only two kinds of people in this world: people who believe in this hammer and people who don't."

That ridiculous picture makes a point. This book is not a manifesto. It's a toolbox, and tools are meant to be used. This viewpoint is much like one advocated by psychologist and philosopher William James. His approach to philosophy, which he called "pragmatism," emphasized the usefulness of ideas as a criterion of truth.[8] James liked to talk about the "cash value" of an idea—whether it leads to new actions and new results.

If you read about a tool in this book that doesn't sound "right" or one that sounds a little goofy, remember that the ideas here are for using, not believing. Suspend your judgment. Test the idea for yourself.

If it works, use it. If it doesn't, don't.

Ask: What if that's true?

When presented with a new idea, some of us take pride in being critical thinkers. We look for problems. We probe for weaknesses. We continue to doubt the idea until there's clear proof. Our main question seems to be "What's wrong with this idea?"

This approach can be useful at times, and it is just one approach. When we constantly look for what's wrong with new ideas, we might miss how they can be useful.

A different and potentially more powerful approach is to ask: What if that idea is true? This opens all sorts of new possibilities and variations. Rather than looking for what's wrong, we can look for what's potentially valuable. Faced with a new idea, we can stay in the inquiry, look deeper, and go further.

Keep looking for answers

The light bulb, the airplane, the computer chip, the notion of the unconscious—these and many other tools became possible when their inventors practiced the art of continually looking for additional answers.

Another way to expand your toolbox is to keep on looking for answers. Much of your education will be about finding answers to questions. Every subject you study—from algebra to history to philosophy—poses a unique set of questions. Some of the most interesting questions are those that admit many answers: How can we create a just society? How can we transmit our values to the next generation? What are the purposes of higher education? How can we prevent an environmental crisis?

Other questions are more personal: What career shall I choose? Shall I get married? Where shall I live and how shall I spend my leisure time? What shall I have, do, and be during my time on earth?

Perhaps you already have answers to these questions. Answers are wonderful, especially when they relate to our most persistent and deeply felt questions. Answers can also get in the way. Once we're convinced that we have the "right" answer, it's easy to stop looking for more answers. We then stop learning. Our range of possible actions becomes limited.

Instead of latching on to one answer, we can look for more. Instead of being content with the first or easiest

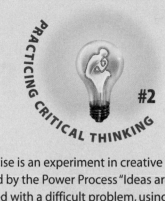

PRACTICING CRITICAL THINKING #2

This exercise is an experiment in creative thinking suggested by the Power Process "Ideas are tools." When we're faced with a difficult problem, using ideas as tools can create many possible solutions. That way, we have a bigger "tool box" of options from which to choose.

On a separate sheet of paper, describe in writing a problem that you are facing in your academic or personal life right now—anything from handling conflict with an instructor to finding a new day care provider.

Perhaps you already have a possible solution to this problem in mind. Great. Now create at least five more solutions. Whenever possible, list solutions that seem to contradict each other.

Next, write about any change in the way you see this problem after creating alternative solutions.

 If you have Internet access, connect to Houghton Mifflin's College Survival/Becoming a Master Student web site: http://collegesurvival.college.hmco.com/students. Consider posting your responses to this exercise there. And while you're there, read responses from other students who took this important step in promoting their own success.

options that come to mind, we can keep searching. Even when we're convinced that we've finally handled a problem, we can brainstorm until we find five more solutions.

When we keep looking for answers, we uncover fresh possibilities for thinking, feeling, and behaving. Like children learning to walk, we experience the joy of discovery.

A caution

A word of caution: Any tool—whether it's a hammer, a computer program, or a study technique—is designed to do a specific job. A master mechanic carries a variety of tools because no single tool works for all jobs. If you throw a tool away because it doesn't work in one situation, you won't be able to pull it out later when it's just what you need. So if an idea doesn't work for you and if you are satisfied you gave it a fair chance, don't throw it away. File it away instead. The idea might come in handy sooner than you think.

And remember, this book is not about figuring out the "right" way. Even the "ideas are tools" idea is not "right."

It's a hammer … (or maybe a saw).

WORKPLACE APPLICATIONS

The skills you learned in entering higher education can help you make the transition to a new job. For example, you can decrease unknowns by working for a company on a temporary, part-time, or contract basis. These positions can lead to an offer for full-time employment. If that happens, you'll know a lot about the company already.

master student
SUNY URRUTIA MOORE

as a student at Aims Community College in Fort Lupton-Loveland, Colorado, wrote an essay that won her a scholarship from Houghton Mifflin.

Asmall child attends a rural parochial school in a third world country in South America. In order to get to school, she has to walk a mile on a dirt road twice daily. Her supplies are a notebook, pencil, an eraser, and a yellow-brown old book borrowed from the school. The beginning of her education comes at a price. Can there be a "master student" in her?

Because education is important to her family, they make arrangements for her to finish elementary grades in a city school. To continue her education, the child attends the Superior Institute of Commerce, which is a combination of high school and business school. Throughout the seven-year program, memorization is the main strategy for learning, which awards her a "C" average grade. She could excel, but this education system doesn't teach any strategies to succeed as a student. In fact, this deficiency will carry through into later years. The small child becomes a young adult, and the small child is me, the author of this essay.

In the late 1970's, I was offered the opportunity to come to the United States of America. This was to be a radical change, which involved not only leaving my native country, Chilé, but also family and friends, a successful accounting career, and familiar surroundings. All of my possessions would be exchanged for a different country and society, unfamiliar environment, and a strange language. So I took the opportunity to move, and when I arrived in this country, I realized that I had a problem: I couldn't communicate with others! I accepted this problem and experienced the language barrier, but I did what was necessary to learn how to speak English and become fully bilingual. . . . For the last 14 years, my main focus has been taking care of my family. In addition, I have held a position as a bilingual paraprofessional for the last few years. Being willing to change, accepting the discomforts that come with it, and taking risks are qualities of the "master student." Without realizing it, I was exercising these qualities all along.

When I had the opportunity to attend college in the summer of 1999, it wasn't an easy decision to make as I had planned to spend a relaxed summer with my children. As a non-traditional student, I felt insecure, not only about my learning ability because I had been away from school for 28 years, but also because I had never learned good study skills. Besides, I would have to study in my second language. For these reasons, it took courage for me to return to school and experience something new. This is the way the "master student" would respond. . . .

The "master student" class opened up to me many strategies that I use daily. For instance, I enjoy learning actively, by reading aloud or walking as I read. I study when I'm rested and my mind is fresh and receptive. In addition, when I have the opportunity, I enjoy studying with groups. As I continue my studies toward an Associates of Arts degree with an emphasis in bilingual education, I feel confident and better equipped to meet the demands of my present and future courses.

The "master student" strategies are not only applied to studying; they are all-encompassing tools that I use for success in life. Applying time management skills has helped me set priorities. For instance, I have learned to postpone doing chores that aren't indispensable and to eliminate non-productive activities (like watching television or long phone conversations) in order to have enough time for studying or cooking nutritious meals for my family. . . .

Even though the beginning of the small child's education wasn't easy, she did the best with what she had. The young adult grasped at opportunities and was open to changes in her environment and herself. As an adult, I now eagerly pursue higher education and continue to discover the natural learner within. I will walk joyfully through the doors of opportunity and taste success.

Explain three ways that you can use knowledge of your learning styles to succeed in school.

 The purpose of the Discovery and Intention Journal Entry system is to keep you at a constant level of excitement about learning. True or False? Explain your answer.

 Our internal chatter and mental pictures can assist or hamper our success. What is one way to minimize negative images?

 Which one of the following best illustrates the suggestion to use observable criteria for success?
    (A) Work harder at math.
    (B) Create 10 flash cards covering the main points in Tuesday's lecture on the Spanish Civil War.
    (C) Find a tutor sometime this quarter.

 The guidelines for writing Discovery Statements do *not* include:
    (A) Record the specifics.
    (B) Notice your inner voices and pictures.
    (C) Notice physical sensations.
    (D) Trust expectations about what you will discover.
    (E) Use discomfort as a signal.

 List at least five guidelines for writing Intention Statements.

 According to the text, a master student is willing to accept paradox. Give an example of a paradox that is relevant to succeeding in school.

8 Give three examples of the benefits of getting an education beyond high school.

9 List the nine intelligences described in this chapter, and briefly describe how being aware of your own multiple intelligences can help you thrive in higher education.

10 According to the Power Process "Ideas are tools," if you want the ideas in this book to work, you must believe in them. True or False? Explain your answer.

JOURNAL ENTRY

#9

Discovery/Intention Statement

Review your experience of reading and doing this chapter, and complete the following sentence.

I discovered that I ...

_____

_____

_____

Now describe how and when you plan to use what you've learned from this chapter.

I intend to ...

_____

_____

_____

Name _____ Date _____/_____/_____

Even though each of us has preferred ways to learn new material, it is useful to review that material using all modes of learning. The questions below will "cycle" you through four learning modes. A similar Learning Styles Application appears at the end of every chapter in this book. Write your responses to these exercises on a separate sheet of paper. For more information about learning styles, reread the article "Learning styles: Discovering how you learn."

Mode 4 Now consider your commitment to these ideas by evaluating the amount of effort you gave to learning each one. Use the following priority scale.
A = I gave my best effort to learn this idea.
B = I made a reasonable effort to learn this idea.
C = I could do more to learn this idea.

Finally, go beyond the classroom. Describe ways to use these ideas that can make your work life or personal relationships more rewarding.

Mode 1 Write a short paragraph explaining (1) ways you have applied any of the following ideas (or related ideas) in your life prior to reading this chapter and (2) how further mastering these ideas could make a positive difference in your education.
• Telling the truth about your current abilities
• Writing a journal focused on self-discovery and intention
• Claiming your multiple intelligences
• Considering ideas as tools

Mode 3 Using the 15 items you just listed, rank them from (1) most important idea I taught myself to (15) least important idea I taught myself. After you have ranked them, write an Intention Statement describing how you plan to put each idea into practice.

Mode 2 After reviewing the above topics, list 15 new ideas or suggestions you've learned from this chapter. Include those that you already know about but have never used.

BIBLIOGRAPHY

INTERNET RESOURCES

ENDNOTES

1 Robert Mager, *Preparing Instructional Objectives* (Belmont, CA: Fearon, 1975).

2 David A. Kolb, *Experiential Learning: Experience as the Source of Learning and Development* (Englewood Cliffs, NJ: Prentice-Hall, 1984).

3 Howard Gardner, *Frames of Mind: The Theory of Multiple Intelligences* (New York: Basic Books, 1993).

4 Carl Rogers, *Freedom to Learn* (Columbus, OH: Merrill, 1969).

5 Abraham Maslow, *The Further Reaches of Human Nature* (New York: Viking, 1971).

6 Ezra Pound, *The ABC of Reading* (New York: New Directions, 1934).

7 Robert Hutchins, "The Great Conversation: The Substance of a Liberal Education," *Great Books of the Western World, vol. 1* (Chicago: Encyclopædia Britannica, 1952).

8 William James, *Pragmatism and Other Essays* (New York: Washington Square, 1963).

ADDITIONAL READING

James, William. *Talks to Teachers on Psychology and to Students on Some of Life's Ideals.* New York: Norton, 1983.

Kolb, David A. *Experiential Learning: Experience as the Source of Learning and Development.* Englewood Cliffs, NJ: Prentice-Hall, 1984.

Light, Richard J. *Making the Most of College: Students Speak Their Minds.* Cambridge, MA: Harvard University Press, 2001.

About College Life
collegelife.miningco.com/

About Learning/4MAT
http://aboutlearning.com/

Becoming a Master Student home page
collegesurvival.college.hmco.com/students/ellis2/index.html

Consulting Psychologists Press/Myers-Briggs Type Indicator®
http://www.cpp-db.com/

CHAPTER 2

Time

Even if you are on the right track, you'll get run over if you just sit there.
WILL ROGERS

Dost thou love life, then do not squander time, for that's the stuff life is made of.
BENJAMIN FRANKLIN

IN THIS CHAPTER . . . Move from "I don't have enough time" to "I've got the time for what matters." Monitor the ways you use time now and then discover the freedom in planning. Overcome procrastination, use 25 ways to get the most from each hour, and create motivation. Also change habits and develop the capacity to be here now—a way to create value in each moment.

You've got the time

The words *time management* can call forth images of restriction and control. You might visualize a prune-faced Scrooge hunched over your shoulder, stopwatch in hand, telling you what to do every minute.

Bad news.

Good news: You do have enough time for the things you want to do. All it takes is learning a few ways to manage time.

Time is an equal opportunity resource. All of us, regardless of gender, race, creed, or national origin, have exactly the same number of hours in a week. True, some of us have enough money to delegate tasks or hire others to do them for us. Yet no matter how newsworthy we are, no matter how rich or poor, we get 168 hours to spend each week—no more, no less.

Time is also an unusual commodity. It cannot be saved. You can't stockpile time like wood for the stove or food for the winter. It can't be seen, felt, touched, tasted, or smelled. You can't sense time directly. Even brilliant scientists and philosophers find it hard to describe.

Because time is so elusive, it is easy to ignore. That doesn't bother time at all. Time is perfectly content to remain hidden until you are nearly out of it. And when you are out of it, you are out of it.

Time is a nonrenewable resource. If you are out of wood, you can chop some more. If you're out of money, you can earn a little extra. If you're out of love, there is still hope. If you're out of health, it can often be restored. But when you're out of time, that's it. When this minute is gone, it's gone.

Time seems to pass at varying speeds. Sometimes it crawls and sometimes it's faster than a speeding bullet. On Friday afternoons, classroom clocks can creep. After you've worked a 10-hour day, reading the last few pages of an economics assignment can turn minutes into hours. A year in school can stretch out to an eternity. At the other end of the spectrum, time flies. There are moments when you are so absorbed in what you're doing that hours disappear like magic.

You can manage this commodity so you won't waste it or feel regretful about how you spent it.

Approach time as if you are in control. Sometimes it seems that your friends control your time, that your boss controls your time, that your teachers or your parents or your kids or somebody else controls your time. Maybe that is not true. When you say you don't have enough

time, you might really be saying that you are not spending the time you do have in the way that you want.

Time management gives you a chance to spend your most valuable resource in the way you choose. Start by observing how you use time. The next exercise offers an opportunity to do this.

10

Discovery Statement

List five times during the past year when you rushed to finish a project or when you did not find time for an activity that was important to you.

_____

_____

_____

_____

_____

_____

_____

_____

_____

Now preview this chapter. Look for five ideas that could help you avoid such situations in the future. List those suggestions here, along with their related page numbers.

Strategy　　　　　　　　　　Page number

_____

_____

_____

_____

_____

_____

_____

_____

_____

#8

The Time Monitor/Time Plan process

An online version of this exercise and the Time Management Plan are available at Houghton Mifflin's College Survival/Becoming a Master Student web site: **http://collegesurvival.college.hmco. com/students.**

The purpose of this exercise is to transform time into a knowable and predictable resource. You can do this by repeating a two-phase cycle of monitoring and planning.

This exercise takes place over two weeks. During the first week, you can monitor your activities to get a detailed picture of how you spend your time. Then you can plan the second week thoughtfully. Monitor your time during the second week, compare it to your plan, and discover what changes you want to make in the following week's plan.

Monitor your time in 15-minute intervals, 24 hours a day, for seven days. Record how much time you spend sleeping, eating, studying, attending lectures, traveling to and from class, working, watching television, listening to music, taking care of the kids, running errands—everything.

If this sounds crazy, hang on for a minute. This exercise is not about keeping track of the rest of your life in 15-minute intervals. It is an opportunity to become conscious of how you spend your time, your life. Use the Time Monitor/Time Plan process only for as long as it is helpful to you.

When you know how your time is spent, you can find ways to adjust and manage it so that you spend your life doing the things that are most important to you. Monitoring your time is a critical first step toward putting you in control of your life.

Some students choose to track their time on 3x5 cards, calendars, campus planners, or software designed for this purpose. You might even develop your own form for monitoring your time.

1. Get to know the Time Monitor/ Time Plan

Look at the Time Monitor/Time Plan on page 41. Note that each day has two columns, one labeled "monitor" and the other labeled "plan." During the first week, use only the "monitor" column. After that, use both columns simultaneously to continue the monitor-plan process.

To become familiar with the form, look at the example on page 41. When you begin an activity, write it down next to the time you begin and put a line just above that spot. Round off to the nearest 15 minutes. If, for example, you begin eating at 8:06, enter your starting time as 8:00. Over time, it will probably even out. In any case, you will be close enough to realize the benefits of this exercise. (Note that you can use the blank spaces in the "monitor" and "plan" columns to cover most of the day.)

On Monday, the student in this example got up at 6:45 a.m., showered, and got dressed. He finished this activity and began breakfast at 7:15. He put this new activity in at the time he began and drew a line just above it. He ate from 7:15 to 7:45. It took him 15 minutes to walk to class (7:45 to 8:00), and he attended classes from 8:00 to 11:00.

Keep your Time Monitor/Time Plan with you every minute you are awake for one week. Take a few moments every two or three hours to record what you've done. Or enter a note each time you change activities.

Here's an eye-opener for many students. If you think you already have a good idea of how you manage time, then predict how many hours you will spend in each category of activity listed in the form on page 42. (Four categories are already provided; you can add more at any time.) Do this before your first week of monitoring. Write your predictions in the margin to the left of each category. After monitoring your time for one week, see how accurate your predictions were.

2. Remember to use your Time Monitor/Time Plan

It might be easy to forget to fill out your Time Monitor/Time Plan. One way to remember is to create a visual reminder for yourself. You can use this technique for any activity you want to remember.

Relax for a moment, close your eyes, and imagine that you see your Time Monitor/Time Plan. Imagine that it has arms and legs and is as big as a person. Picture the form sitting at your desk at home, in your car, in one of your classrooms, or in your favorite chair. Visualize it sitting wherever you're likely to sit. When you sit down, the picture of the Time Monitor/Time Plan will get squashed.

You can make this image more effective by adding sound effects. The Time Monitor/Time Plan might scream, "Get off me!" Or since time can be related to money, you might associate the Time Monitor/Time Plan with the sound of an old-fashioned cash register. Imagine that every time you sit down, a cash register rings.

3. Evaluate the Time Monitor/Time Plan

After you've monitored your time for one week, group your activities together by categories. The form on page 42 includes the categories "sleep," "class," "study," and "meals." Another category, "grooming," might include showering, putting on makeup, brushing teeth, getting dressed. "Travel" can include walking, driving, taking the bus, and riding your bike. Other categories could be "exercise," "entertainment," "work," "television," "domestic," and "children."

Write in the categories that work for you, and then add up how much time you spent in each of your categories. Put the totals in the "monitored" column

MONDAY __ / 12		
MONITOR		PLAN
	Get up	
	Shower	
7:00		7:00
	Breakfast	7:15
	↓	7:30
	Walk to	7:45
8:00	class	8:00
		8:15
	Econ I	8:30
		8:45
9:00		9:00
		9:15
		9:30
		9:45
10:00	Bio I	10:00
		10:15
		10:30
		10:45
11:00	Study	11:00
		11:15
		11:30
		11:45
12:00	Lunch	12:00
		12:15
		12:30
		12:45
1:00	Eng. Lit.	1:00
		1:15
		1:30
		1:45
2:00	Coffeehouse	2:00
		2:15
		2:30
		2:45
3:00		3:00
		3:15
		3:30
		3:45
4:00	Study	4:00
		4:15
		4:30
		4:45
5:00	Dinner	5:00
		5:15
		5:30
		5:45
6:00		6:00
		6:15
	Babysit	6:30
		6:45
7:00		7:00

TUESDAY __ / 13		
MONITOR		PLAN
	Sleep	
7:00		7:00
		7:15
		7:30
	Shower	7:45
8:00	Dress	8:00
	Eat	8:15
		8:30
		8:45
9:00	Art	9:00
	Apprec.	9:15
	Project	9:30
		9:45
10:00		10:00
		10:15
		10:30
		10:45
11:00	Data	11:00
	process	11:15
		11:30
		11:45
12:00		12:00
		12:15
		12:30
		12:45
1:00	Lunch	1:00
		1:15
		1:30
		1:45
2:00	Work	2:00
	on book	2:15
	report	2:30
		2:45
3:00	Art	3:00
	Apprec.	3:15
		3:30
		3:45
4:00		4:00
		4:15
		4:30
		4:45
5:00	Dinner	5:00
		5:15
		5:30
		5:45
6:00	Letter to	6:00
	Uncle Jim	6:15
		6:30
		6:45
7:00		7:00

on page 42. Make sure the grand total of all categories is 168 hours.

Now take a minute and let these numbers sink in. Compare your totals to your predictions and notice your reactions. You might be surprised. You might feel disappointed or even angry about where your time goes. Use those feelings as motivation to plan your time differently. Go back to the "planned" column and choose how much time you want to spend on various daily activities. As you do so, allow yourself to have fun. Approach planning in the spirit of adventure. Think of yourself as an artist who's creating a new life.

In several months you might want to take another detailed look at how you spend your life. You can expand the two-phase cycle of monitoring and planning to include a third phase: evaluating. Combine this with planning your time, following the suggestions in this chapter. You can use a continuous cycle: monitor, evaluate, plan; monitor, evaluate, plan. When you make it a habit, this cycle can help you get the full benefits of time management for the rest of your life. Then time management becomes more than a technique. It's transformed into a habit, a constant awareness of how you spend your lifetime.

WEEK OF ___/___/___		
CATEGORY	MONITORED	PLANNED
Sleep		
Class		
Study		
Meals		

MONDAY ___/___/___		TUESDAY ___/___/___		WEDNESDAY ___/___/___	
MONITOR	PLAN	MONITOR	PLAN	MONITOR	PLAN
7:00	7:00	7:00	7:00	7:00	7:00
	7:15		7:15		7:15
	7:30		7:30		7:30
	7:45		7:45		7:45
8:00	8:00	8:00	8:00	8:00	8:00
	8:15		8:15		8:15
	8:30		8:30		8:30
	8:45		8:45		8:45
9:00	9:00	9:00	9:00	9:00	9:00
	9:15		9:15		9:15
	9:30		9:30		9:30
	9:45		9:45		9:45
10:00	10:00	10:00	10:00	10:00	10:00
	10:15		10:15		10:15
	10:30		10:30		10:30
	10:45		10:45		10:45
11:00	11:00	11:00	11:00	11:00	11:00
	11:15		11:15		11:15
	11:30		11:30		11:30
	11:45		11:45		11:45
12:00	12:00	12:00	12:00	12:00	12:00
	12:15		12:15		12:15
	12:30		12:30		12:30
	12:45		12:45		12:45
1:00	1:00	1:00	1:00	1:00	1:00
	1:15		1:15		1:15
	1:30		1:30		1:30
	1:45		1:45		1:45
2:00	2:00	2:00	2:00	2:00	2:00
	2:15		2:15		2:15
	2:30		2:30		2:30
	2:45		2:45		2:45
3:00	3:00	3:00	3:00	3:00	3:00
	3:15		3:15		3:15
	3:30		3:30		3:30
	3:45		3:45		3:45
4:00	4:00	4:00	4:00	4:00	4:00
	4:15		4:15		4:15
	4:30		4:30		4:30
	4:45		4:45		4:45
5:00	5:00	5:00	5:00	5:00	5:00
	5:15		5:15		5:15
	5:30		5:30		5:30
	5:45		5:45		5:45
6:00	6:00	6:00	6:00	6:00	6:00
	6:15		6:15		6:15
	6:30		6:30		6:30
	6:45		6:45		6:45
7:00	7:00	7:00	7:00	7:00	7:00
	7:15		7:15		7:15
	7:30		7:30		7:30
	7:45		7:45		7:45
8:00	8:00	8:00	8:00	8:00	8:00
	8:15		8:15		8:15
	8:30		8:30		8:30
	8:45		8:45		8:45
9:00	9:00	9:00	9:00	9:00	9:00
	9:15		9:15		9:15
	9:30		9:30		9:30
	9:45		9:45		9:45
10:00	10:00	10:00	10:00	10:00	10:00
	10:15		10:15		10:15
	10:30		10:30		10:30
	10:45		10:45		10:45
11:00	11:00	11:00	11:00	11:00	11:00
	11:15		11:15		11:15
	11:30		11:30		11:30
	11:45		11:45		11:45
12:00	12:00	12:00	12:00	12:00	12:00

THURSDAY ___/___/___

MONITOR	PLAN
7:00	7:00
	7:15
	7:30
	7:45
8:00	8:00
	8:15
	8:30
	8:45
9:00	9:00
	9:15
	9:30
	9:45
10:00	10:00
	10:15
	10:30
	10:45
11:00	11:00
	11:15
	11:30
	11:45
12:00	12:00
	12:15
	12:30
	12:45
1:00	1:00
	1:15
	1:30
	1:45
2:00	2:00
	2:15
	2:30
	2:45
3:00	3:00
	3:15
	3:30
	3:45
4:00	4:00
	4:15
	4:30
	4:45
5:00	5:00
	5:15
	5:30
	5:45
6:00	6:00
	6:15
	6:30
	6:45
7:00	7:00
	7:15
	7:30
	7:45
8:00	8:00
	8:15
	8:30
	8:45
9:00	9:00
	9:15
	9:30
	9:45
10:00	10:00
	10:15
	10:30
	10:45
11:00	11:00
	11:15
	11:30
	11:45
12:00	12:00

FRIDAY ___/___/___

MONITOR	PLAN
7:00	7:00
	7:15
	7:30
	7:45
8:00	8:00
	8:15
	8:30
	8:45
9:00	9:00
	9:15
	9:30
	9:45
10:00	10:00
	10:15
	10:30
	10:45
11:00	11:00
	11:15
	11:30
	11:45
12:00	12:00
	12:15
	12:30
	12:45
1:00	1:00
	1:15
	1:30
	1:45
2:00	2:00
	2:15
	2:30
	2:45
3:00	3:00
	3:15
	3:30
	3:45
4:00	4:00
	4:15
	4:30
	4:45
5:00	5:00
	5:15
	5:30
	5:45
6:00	6:00
	6:15
	6:30
	6:45
7:00	7:00
	7:15
	7:30
	7:45
8:00	8:00
	8:15
	8:30
	8:45
9:00	9:00
	9:15
	9:30
	9:45
10:00	10:00
	10:15
	10:30
	10:45
11:00	11:00
	11:15
	11:30
	11:45
12:00	12:00

SATURDAY ___/___/___

MONITOR	PLAN

SUNDAY ___/___/___

MONITOR	PLAN

JOURNAL ENTRY

#11

Discovery Statement

After one week of monitoring my time, I discovered that . . .

_____

_____

_____

I want to spend more time on . . .

_____

_____

_____

I want to spend less time on . . .

_____

_____

_____

I was surprised that I spent so much time on . . .

_____

_____

_____

I was surprised that I spent so little time on . . .

_____

_____

_____

I had strong feelings about my use of time when (describe the feeling and the situation) . . .

_____

_____

The ABC daily to-do's
(or working your A's off)

NE of the most effective ways to stay on track and actually get things done is to use a daily to-do list. While the Time Monitor/Time Plan is a general picture of the week, your daily to-do list itemizes specific tasks you want to complete within 24 hours. Keep the list with you at all times, crossing off activities when you finish them and adding new ones when you think of them.

The advantage of keeping a daily list is that you don't have to remember what to do next. It's on the list. A typical day in the life of a student is full of separate, often unrelated tasks—reading, attending lectures, reviewing notes, working at a job, writing papers, researching special projects, running errands. It's easy to forget an important task on a busy day. When that task is written down, you don't have to rely on your memory.

Write out your daily to-do list the night before. That way, when your day begins, so will you. List everything you want to accomplish on a sheet of paper or a daily planning calendar, or in a special notebook. You can also use 3x5 cards. Cards work well because you can slip them into your pocket.

Rate each task by priority. One way to do this comes from an excellent book, *Take Control of Your Time and Life,* by Alan Lakein: Simply label each task A, B, or C.[1]

A's on your list are those things that are most important. These are assignments that are coming due or jobs that need to be done immediately. Also included are activities that lead directly to your long-, mid-, or short-term goals.

The B tasks on your list are important, but less so than the A's. B's might someday become A's. For the present, these tasks are important, but are not as urgent as A's. They can be postponed, if necessary.

C's do not require immediate attention. C priorities include activities such as "shop for a new blender" and "research genealogy on the Internet." C's are often small, easy jobs with no set timeline.

NCE you've labeled the tasks on your list, schedule time for all of the A's. The B's and C's can be done randomly during the day when you are in between tasks and are not yet ready to start the next A.

When you use the ABC priority method, you might experience an ailment common to students: C fever. This is the uncontrollable urge to drop that A task and begin crossing C's off your to-do list. If your history paper is due tomorrow, you might feel compelled to vacuum the rug, call your third cousin in Tulsa, and make a trip to the store for shoelaces. The reason C fever is so common is that A tasks are usually more difficult or time-consuming to achieve, with a higher risk of failure.

If you notice symptoms of C fever, ask: Does this job really need to be done now? Do I really need to alphabetize my tape collection, or might I better use this time to study for tomorrow's data processing exam?

Use your to-do list to keep yourself on task, working on your A's. Don't panic or berate yourself when you realize that in the last six hours, you have completed 11 C's and not a single A. Calmly return to the A's.

As you complete tasks, cross them off your list. Crossing off tasks can be fun—a visible reward for your diligence—and can also foster a sense of accomplishment.

Another option is to put each to-do activity on its own 3x5 card. This allows you to easily sort jobs by priority or time on task.

At the end of the day, evaluate your performance. Look for A priorities you didn't complete. Look for tasks that repeatedly turn up as B's or C's on your list and never seem to get done. Consider changing these to A's or dropping them altogether. Similarly, you might consider changing an A that didn't get done to a B or C priority.

Develop your own style. You might find that grouping tasks by categories such as "errands" or "reading assignments" works best. Be creative.

And be willing to admit mistakes. You might at first rank some tasks as A's only to realize later that they are actually C's. Some of the C's that lurk at the bottom of your list day after day might really be A's. When you keep a daily to-do list, you can adjust these priorities *before* they become problems.

OTE: The ABC system is not the only way to rank items on your to-do list. Some people prefer the "80-20" system. This is based on the idea that 80 percent of the value of any to-do list comes from only 20 percent of the tasks on that list. So on a to-do list of 10 items, find the two that will contribute most to your life, and complete those tasks without fail.

Another option is to rank items as "yes," "no," or "maybe." Do all of the tasks marked "yes." Ignore those marked "no." And put all of the "maybe's" on the shelf for later. You can come back to the "maybe's" at a future point and rank them as "yes" or "no."

Keep in mind the power of planning a whole week or even two weeks in advance. Planning in this way can make it easier to put activities in context—to see how your daily goals relate to your long-term goals. Weekly planning can also free you from feeling that you have to polish off your whole to-do list in one day. Instead, you can spread tasks out over the whole week.

In any case, make starting your own to-do list an A priority.

Strategies for scheduling

Schedule fixed blocks of time first.
Start with class time and work time, for instance.
These time periods are usually determined in
advance. Other activities must be scheduled around
them. Then schedule essential daily activities such as
sleeping and eating. No matter what else you do, you
will sleep and eat. Be realistic about how much time
you need for these functions.

Include time for errands. The time
we spend buying toothpaste, paying bills, and doing
laundry is easy to overlook. These little errands can
destroy a tight schedule and make us feel rushed and
harried all week. Plan for them and remember to
allow for travel time between locations.

Schedule time for fun. Fun is important.
Brains that are constantly stimulated by new ideas
and new challenges need time off to digest them. Take
time to browse aimlessly through the library, stroll
with no destination, ride a bike, or do other things you
enjoy. Recreation deserves a place in your priorities.
It's important to "waste" time once in a while.

Set realistic goals. Don't set yourself up for
failure by telling yourself you can do a four-hour job
in two hours. There are only 168 hours in a week. If
you schedule 169 hours, you've already lost before you
begin.

Allow flexibility in your schedule.
Recognize that unexpected things will happen and
plan for the unexpected. Leave some holes in your
schedule; build in blocks of unplanned time. Consider
setting aside time each week marked "flex time" or
"open time." These are hours to use for emergencies,
spontaneous activities, catching up, or seizing new
opportunities.

**Study two hours for every hour
in class.** In higher education, it's standard advice
to allow two hours of study time for every hour spent
in class. Students making the transition from high
school to college are often unaware that more is
expected of them.

If you are taking 15 credit hours, plan to spend
30 hours a week studying. The benefits of following
this advice will be apparent at exam time.

This guideline is just that—a guideline, not an
absolute rule. Consider what's best for you. If you do
the Time Monitor/Time Plan exercise in this chapter,
note how many hours you actually spend studying for
each hour of class. Then ask how your schedule is
working. You might want to allow more study time
for some subjects.

Also keep in mind that the "two hours for one"
rule doesn't distinguish between focused time and
unfocused time. In one four-hour block of study time,
it's possible to use up two hours for phone calls,
breaks, daydreaming, and doodling. When it comes to
scheduling time, quality counts as much as quantity.

**Avoid scheduling marathon
study sessions.** When possible, study in
shorter sessions. Three three-hour sessions are usually
far more productive than one nine-hour session. In
a nine- or 10-hour study marathon, the percentage
of time actually spent on a task can be depressingly
small. With 10 hours of study ahead of you, the
temptation is to tell yourself, "Well, it's going to be
a long day. No sense rushing into it. Better sharpen
about a dozen of these pencils and change the light
bulbs." In a nine-hour sitting you might spend only
six or seven hours studying, whereas three shorter
sessions will likely yield much more productive time.
When you do study in long sessions, stop and rest for
a few minutes every hour. Give your brain a chance
to take a break.

If you must study in a large block of time, work
on several subjects and avoid studying similar topics
back-to-back. For example, if you plan to study
sociology, psychology, and computer science,
sandwich computer science in between psychology
and sociology.

Set clear starting and stopping times.

Tasks often expand to fill the time we allot for them. "It always takes me an hour just to settle into a reading assignment" might become a self-fulfilling prophecy.

Try planning a certain amount of time for a reading assignment—set a timer, and stick to it. Students often find that they can decrease study time by forcing themselves to read faster. This can usually be done without sacrificing comprehension.

The same principle can apply to other tasks. Some people find they can get up 15 minutes earlier in the morning and still feel alert throughout the day. Plan 45 minutes for a trip to the grocery store instead of one hour. Over the course of a year, those extra minutes can add up to hours.

Feeling rushed or sacrificing quality is not the goal here. The point is to push ourselves a little and discover what our time requirements really are.

Plan for the unexpected.

The best-laid plans can be foiled by the unexpected. Children and day care providers get sick. Cars break down in winter. Subway trains run late. The electric power shuts off, silencing alarm clocks.

That's when it pays to have a backup plan. You can find someone to care for your children when the babysitter gets the flu. You can plan an alternative way to get to work. You can set the alarm on your watch as well as the one on your nightstand. Giving such items five minutes of careful thought today can save you hours in the future.

Involve others when appropriate.

Sometimes the activities we schedule depend on gaining information, assistance, or direct participation from other people. If we neglect to inform them of our plans or forget to ask for their cooperation at the outset—surprise! Our schedules can crash.

Statements such as these often follow the breakdown: "I just assumed you were going to pick up the kids from school on Tuesday." "I'm working overtime this week and hoped that you'd take over the cooking for a while."

When you schedule a task that depends on another person's involvement, let that person know—the sooner, the better.

Back up to a bigger picture.

When scheduling activities for the day or week, take some time to lift your eyes to the horizon. Step back for a few minutes and consider your longer-range goals—what you want to accomplish in the next six months, the next year, the next five years, and beyond. Ask whether any of the activities you've scheduled actually contribute to those goals. If they do, great. If not, ask whether you can delete other items from your calendar to make room for goal-related activities.

You can make this kind of adjustment to your schedule even when your goals are not precisely defined. You might suddenly sense that this is the time in your life to start a new relationship, take a long trip, or move to a new house. Pay attention to these intuitions; allow space in your daily and weekly schedules to explore and act on your dreams.

Aim to free up at least one hour each day for doing something you love instead of saving it for a more "reasonable" or "convenient" time.

"Filter" tasks before scheduling them.

To trim the "fat" from your schedule, ask some questions before you add an activity to your calendar or to-do list. For example: What do I need to accomplish before I can schedule this item? If I choose never to do this item, could I live with the consequences? What would be the consequences if I put off this task for a month? Six months? One year?

Consider technology carefully.

Today you can choose from a constantly expanding line of digital devices for planning. These range from software for your desktop computer (such as *Microsoft Scheduler/Outlook* or *Hallmark Connections*) to hand-held tools such as the Palm Pilot™. If you already use a computer for many daily tasks, you might enjoy experimenting with this emerging technology. Keep some possible disadvantages in mind, including the cost of these items. For scheduling, it's tough to beat good old-fashioned—and inexpensive—pencil and paper.

For updates on useful technology for planning, visit Houghton Mifflin's College Survival/Becoming a Master Student web site: **http://collegesurvival.college.hmco. com/students**.

THE SEVEN-DAY ANTIPROCRASTINATION PLAN

Listed here are seven strategies you can use
to reduce or eliminate many styles of procrastination.
The suggestions are tied to the days of the week to help you remember them.
Use this list to remind yourself that each day of your life
presents an opportunity to stop the cycle of procrastination.

1 MONDAY

Make it meaningful. What is important about the task you've been putting off? List all the benefits of completing it. Look at it in relation to your short-, mid-, or long-term goals. Be specific about the rewards for getting it done, including how you will feel when the task is completed. To remember this strategy, keep in mind that it starts with the letter M, like the word Monday.

2 TUESDAY

Take it apart. Break big jobs into a series of small ones you can do in 15 minutes or less. If a long reading assignment intimidates you, divide it into two-page or three-page sections. Make a list of the sections and cross them off as you complete them so you can see your progress. This strategy starts with the letter T, so mentally tie it to Tuesday.

3 WEDNESDAY

Write an intention statement. For example, if you can't get started on a term paper, you might write, "I intend to write a list of at least 10 possible topics by 9 p.m. I will reward myself with an hour of guilt-free recreational reading." Write your intention on a 3x5 card and carry it with you, or post it in your study area where you can see it often. In your memory, file the first word in this strategy—write—with Wednesday.

4 THURSDAY

Tell everyone. Publicly announce your intention to get a task done. Tell a friend you intend to learn 10 irregular French verbs by Saturday. Tell your spouse, roommate, parents, and children. Include anyone who will ask whether you've completed the assignment or who will suggest ways to get it done. Make the world your support group. Associate tell with Thursday.

5 FRIDAY

Find a reward. Construct rewards to yourself carefully. Be willing to withhold them if you do not complete the task. Don't pick a movie as a reward for studying biology if you plan to go to the movie anyway. And when you legitimately reap your reward, notice how it feels. Remember that Friday is a fine day to find a reward. (Of course, you can find a reward on any day of the week. Rhyming Friday with fine day is just a memory trick.)

6 SATURDAY

Settle it now. Do it now. The minute you notice yourself procrastinating, plunge into the task. Imagine yourself at a cold mountain lake, poised to dive. Gradual immersion would be slow torture. It's often less painful to leap. Then be sure to savor the feeling of having the task behind you. Link settle with Saturday.

7 SUNDAY

Say no. When you keep pushing a task into a low-priority category, re-examine your purpose for doing it at all. If you realize that you really don't intend to do something, quit telling yourself that you will. That's procrastinating. Just say NO! Then you're not procrastinating. You don't have to carry around the baggage of an undone task. Sunday—the last day of this seven-day plan—is a great day to finally let go and just say no.

> **Student Voices**
>
> Making lists has been one of my favorite tools to stay on track and prioritize. Not much gives me more pleasure than to cross off duties one by one and to see the number of items left to do shrink to nothing, or what can be put off until another time.
>
> —Laurie Murray

7 MORE WAYS TO STOP PROCRASTINATION

Perhaps you didn't get around to using the seven-day antiprocrastination plan. Well, there's plenty more where that plan came from. Consider seven more suggestions.

Observe your procrastination.   Instead of rushing to fix your procrastination problem, take your time. Get to know your problem well. Avoid judgments. Just be a scientist and record the facts. Write Discovery Statements about the specific ways you procrastinate and the direct results. Find out if procrastination keeps you from getting what you want. Clearly seeing the cost of procrastination can help you kick the habit.

Discover your procrastination style.   Psychologist Linda Sapadin identifies different styles of procrastination.[2] For example, *dreamers* have big goals that they seldom translate into specific plans. *Worriers* focus on the "worst case" scenario and are likely to talk more about problems than about solutions. *Defiers* resist new tasks or promise to do them and don't follow through. *Overdoers* create extra work for themselves by refusing to delegate tasks and neglecting to set priorities.

Awareness of procrastination styles is a key to changing your behavior. For example, if you exhibit the characteristics of an overdoer, then say no to new projects. Also ask for help in getting your current projects done.

Look for self-defeating beliefs.   Certain thoughts fuel procrastination and keep you from experiencing the rewards in life that you deserve. Psychologists Jane Burka and Lenora Yuen[3] list these examples:

> *I must be perfect.*
>
> *Everything I do should go easily and without effort.*
>
> *It's safer to do nothing than to take a risk and fail.*
>
> *If it's not done right, it's not worth doing at all.*
>
> *If I do well this time, I must always do well.*
>
> *If I succeed, someone will get hurt.*

If you find such beliefs running through your mind, write them down. Getting a belief out of your head and onto paper can rob that belief of its power. Also write a more effective belief that you want to adopt. For example: "Even if I don't complete this task perfectly, it's good enough for now and I can still learn from my mistakes."

WORKPLACE APPLICATIONS

Use a lifeline to chart your career path for decades into the future. See the following example.

May 2007	Graduate with a teaching degree
August 2008	Begin teaching high school physics
September 2015	Begin saving 5 percent of income to fund a personal sabbatical
September 2019	Return to school for a graduate degree in school administration
September 2021	Begin career as a high school principal
September 2025	Take a one-year sabbatical to live and work part-time in New Zealand
September 2026	Return to job as a high school principal
January 2029	Begin a home-based consulting business, advising teachers and principals about ways to avoid job burnout

Trick yourself into getting started.
Practice being a con artist—and your own unwitting target. If you have a 50-page chapter to read, grab the book and say to yourself, "I'm not really going to read this chapter right now. I'm just going to flip through the pages and scan the headings for ten minutes." If you have a paper due next week, say, "I'm not really going to outline this paper today. I'll just spend five minutes writing anything that comes into my head about the assigned topic."

Tricks like these can get you started at a task you've been dreading. Once you get started, you might find it easy to keep going.

Let feelings follow action.
If you put off exercising until you feel energetic, you might wait for months. Instead, get moving now and watch your feelings change. After five minutes of brisk walking, you might be in the mood for a 20-minute run. This principle—action generates motivation—can apply to any task that's been delegated to the back burner.

Choose to work under pressure.
Sometimes people thrive under pressure. As one writer put it, "I don't do my *best* work because of a tight timeline. I do my *only* work with a tight timeline." Used selectively, this strategy might also work for you.

Put yourself in control. You might consciously choose to work with a timeline staring you in the face. If you do, then schedule a big block of time right before your project is due. Until then, enjoy!

Take it easy.
You can find shelves full of books with techniques for overcoming procrastination. Resist the temptation to use all of these techniques at once. You could feel overwhelmed, give up, and sink back into the cycle of procrastination.

Instead, make one small, simple change in behavior—today. Tomorrow, make the change again. Take it day by day until the new behavior becomes a habit. One day you might wake up and discover that procrastination is part of your past.

EXERCISE

#9

Create a lifeline

An online version of this exercise is available at Houghton Mifflin's College Survival/Becoming a Master Student web site: **http://collegesurvival.college. hmco.com/students.**

On a large sheet of paper, draw a horizontal line. This line will represent your lifetime. Now add key events in your life to this line in chronological order. Examples are birth, first day at school, graduation from high school, and enrollment in higher education.

Now extend the lifeline into the future. Write down key events you would like to see occur in one year, five years, and 10 years or more from now. Choose events that align with your core values. Work quickly in the spirit of a brainstorm. This is not a final plan.

Afterward, take a few minutes to review your lifeline. Select one key event for the future and list any actions you could take in the next month to bring yourself closer to that goal. Do the same with other key events on your lifeline. You now have the rudiments of a comprehensive plan for your life.

Finally, extend your lifeline another 50 years beyond the year when you would reach age 100. Describe in detail what changes in the world you'd like to see as a result of the goals you attained in your lifetime.

25

ways to get the
most out of now

The following time-management techniques are about when to study, where to study, ways to handle the rest of the world, and things you can ask yourself when you get stuck. As you read, underline, circle, or otherwise note the suggestions you think will be helpful. Pick two or three techniques to use now. When they become habits, come back to this article and select a couple more.

When to study

1. Study difficult (or "boring") subjects first. If your chemistry problems put you to sleep, get to them first, while you are fresh. We tend to give top priority to what we enjoy studying, yet the courses we find most difficult often require the most creative energy. Save your favorite subjects for later. If you find yourself avoiding a particular subject, get up an hour earlier to study it before breakfast. With that chore out of the way, the rest of the day can be a breeze.

Continually being late with course assignments indicates a trouble area. Further action is required. Clarify your intentions about the course by writing down your feelings in a journal, talking with an instructor, or asking for help from a friend or counselor. Consistently avoiding study tasks can also be a signal to re-examine your major or course program.

2. Be aware of your best time of day.
Many people learn best in daylight hours. If this is true for you, schedule study time for your most difficult subjects before nightfall.

Unless you grew up on a farm, the idea of being conscious at 4 a.m. might seem ridiculous. Yet many successful business people begin the day at 5 a.m. or earlier. Athletes and yogis use this time, too. Some writers complete their best work before 9 a.m.

For others, the same benefits are experienced by staying up late. They flourish after midnight. If you aren't convinced, then experiment. When you're in a time crunch, get up early or stay up late. You might even see a sunrise.

3. Use waiting time.
Five minutes waiting for a subway, 20 minutes waiting for the dentist, 10 minutes in between classes—waiting time adds up fast. Have short study tasks ready to do during these periods. For example, you can carry 3x5 cards with facts, formulas, or definitions and pull them out anywhere.

A tape recorder can help you use commuting time to your advantage. Make tape cassettes of yourself reading your notes. Then play these tapes in a car stereo as you drive, or listen through your headphones as you ride on the bus or subway.

Where to study

4. Use a regular study area.
Your body and your mind know where you are. Using the same place to study, day after day, helps train your responses. When you arrive at that particular place, you can focus your attention more quickly.

5. Study where you'll be alert.
In bed, your body gets a signal. For most students, that signal is more likely to be "Time to sleep!" than "Time to study!" Just as you train your body to be alert at your desk, you also train it to slow down near your bed. For that reason, don't study where you sleep.

Easy chairs and sofas are also dangerous places to study. Learning requires energy. Give your body a message that energy is needed. Put yourself in a situation that supports this message.

Some schools offer empty classrooms as places to study. Many students report finding themselves studying effectively in a classroom setting.

6. Use a library.
Libraries are designed for learning. The lighting is perfect. The noise level is low. A wealth of material is available. Entering a library is a signal to focus the mind and get to work. Many students can get more done in a shorter time frame at the library than anywhere else. Experiment for yourself.

Student Voices

I am a person who can be easily distracted, and the library has the fewest distractions for me. My home has the most distractions, with TV, food, people coming over, and my cat begging for attention. I know that if I really want to learn, I need to make a trip to the library.

— JAMES HEAD

Ways to handle the rest of the world

7. Pay attention to your attention. Breaks in concentration are often caused by internal interruptions. Your own thoughts jump in to divert you from your studies. When this happens, notice these thoughts and let them go.

Perhaps the thought of getting something else done is distracting you. One option is to handle that other task now and study later. Or write yourself a note about it, or schedule a specific time to do it.

8. Agree with living mates about study time. This includes roommates, spouses, and children. Make the rules clear, and be sure to follow them yourself. Explicit agreements—even written contracts—work well. One student always wears a colorful hat when she wants to study. When her husband and children see the hat, they respect her wish to be left alone.

9. Get off the phone. The telephone is the ultimate interrupter. People who wouldn't think of distracting you might call at the worst times because they can't see that you are studying. You don't have to be a telephone victim. If a simple "I can't talk, I'm studying" doesn't work, use dead silence. It's a conversation killer. Or short-circuit the whole problem: Unplug the phone. Other solutions include getting an answering machine and studying at the library.

10. Learn to say "no." This is a timesaver and a valuable life skill for everyone. Some people feel it is rude to refuse a request. But saying no can be done effectively and courteously. Others want you to succeed as a student. When you tell them that you can't do what they ask because you are busy educating yourself, most people will understand.

11. Hang a "do not disturb" sign on your door. Many hotels will give you a free sign, for the advertising. Or you can create a sign yourself. They work. Using signs can relieve you of making a decision about cutting off each interruption—a timesaver in itself.

12. Get ready the night before. Completing a few simple tasks just before you go to bed can help you get in gear the next day. If you need to make some phone calls first thing in the morning, look up those numbers, write them on 3x5 cards, and set them near the phone. If you need to drive to a new location, make note of the address and put it next to your car keys. If you plan to spend the next afternoon writing a paper, get your materials together: dictionary, notes, outline, paper, and pencil (or disks and computer). Pack your lunch or gas up the car. Organize your diaper bag, briefcase, or backpack.

13. Call ahead. We often think of talking on the telephone as a prime time-waster. Used wisely, the telephone can actually help manage time. Before you go shopping, call the store to see if it carries the items you're looking for. If you're driving, call for directions to your destination. A few seconds on the phone can save hours in wasted trips and wrong turns.

14. Avoid noise distractions. To promote concentration, avoid studying in front of the television and turn off the radio. Many students insist that they study better with background noise, and this might be true. Some students report good results with carefully selected and controlled music. For many others, silence is the best form of music to study by.

At times noise levels might be out of your control. A neighbor or roommate might decide to find out how far he can turn up his CD player before the walls crumble.

Meanwhile, your ability to concentrate on the principles of sociology goes down the drain. To avoid this scenario, schedule study sessions during periods when your living environment is usually quiet. If you live in a residence hall, ask if study rooms are available. Or go somewhere else where it's quiet, such as the library. Some students have even found refuge in quiet restaurants, Laundromats, and places of worship.

15. Notice how others misuse your time. Be aware of repeat offenders. Ask yourself if there are certain friends or relatives who consistently interrupt your study time. If avoiding the interrupter is impractical, send a clear message. Sometimes others don't realize that they are breaking your concentration. You can give them a gentle yet firm reminder. If this doesn't work, there are ways to make your message more effective. For more ideas, see the Communicating chapter.

Things you can ask yourself when you get stuck

16. Ask: What is one task I can accomplish toward achieving my goal? This is a helpful technique to use when faced with big, imposing jobs. Pick out one small accomplishment, preferably one you can complete in about five minutes; then do it. The satisfaction of getting one thing done can spur you on to get one more thing done. Meanwhile, the job gets smaller.

17. Ask: Am I being too hard on myself? If you are feeling frustrated with a reading assignment, notice that your attention wanders repeatedly, or fall behind on math problems that are due tomorrow, take a minute to listen to the messages you are giving yourself. Are you scolding yourself too harshly? Lighten up. Allow yourself to feel a little foolish and then get on with the task at hand. Don't add to the problem by berating yourself.

Worrying about the future is another way people beat themselves up: How will I ever get all this done? What if every paper I'm assigned turns out to be this hard? If I can't do the simple calculations now, how will I ever pass the final? Instead of promoting learning, such questions fuel anxiety.

Labeling and generalizing weaknesses are other ways people are hard on themselves. Being objective and specific will help eliminate this form of self-punishment and will likely generate new possibilities. An alternative to saying "I'm terrible in algebra" is to say "I don't understand factoring equations." This rewording suggests a plan to improve.

18. Ask: Is this a piano? Carpenters who construct rough frames for buildings have a saying they use when they bend a nail or accidentally hack a chunk out of a two-by-four: "Well, this ain't no piano." It means

Keep going?

Some people keep going, even when they get stuck or fail again and again. To such people belongs the world. Consider the hapless politician who compiled this record:

• Failed in business, 1831

• Defeated for legislature, 1832

• Second failure in business, 1833

• Suffered nervous breakdown, 1836

• Defeated for Speaker, 1838

• Defeated for Elector, 1840

• Defeated for Congress, 1843

• Defeated for Senate, 1855

• Defeated for Vice President, 1856

• Defeated for Senate, 1858

• Elected President, 1860

Who was the fool who kept on going in spite of so many failures?

Answer: The fool was Abraham Lincoln.

that perfection is not necessary. Ask yourself if what you are doing needs to be perfect. You don't have to apply the same standards of grammar to lecture notes that you apply to a term paper. If you can complete a job 95 percent perfectly in two hours and 100 percent perfectly in four hours, ask yourself whether the additional 5 percent improvement is worth doubling the amount of time you spend.

Sometimes it *is* a piano. A tiny miscalculation can ruin an entire lab experiment. A misstep in solving a complex math problem can negate hours of work. Computers are notorious for turning little errors into nightmares. Accept lower standards only when appropriate.

A related suggestion is to weed out low-priority tasks. The to-do list for a large project can include dozens of items, not all of which are equally important. Some can be done later on, while others could be skipped altogether, if time is short.

Apply this idea when you study. In a long reading assignment, look for pages you can skim or skip. When it's appropriate, read chapter summaries or article abstracts. When reviewing your notes, look for material that might not be covered on a test and decide whether you want to study it.

19. Ask: Would I pay myself for what I'm doing right now?

If you were employed as a student, would you be earning your wages? Ask yourself this question when you notice that you've taken your third snack break in 30 minutes. Most students are, in fact, employed as students. They are investing in their own productivity and paying a big price for the privilege of being a student. Sometimes they don't realize what doing a mediocre job might cost them.

20. Ask: Can I do just one more thing?

Ask yourself this question at the end of a long day. Almost always you will have enough energy to do just one more short task. The overall increase in your productivity might surprise you.

21. Ask: Am I making time for things that are important but not urgent?

If we spend most of our time putting out fires, we can feel drained and frustrated. According to Stephen R. Covey,[4] this happens when we forget to take time for things that are not urgent but are truly important. Examples include exercising regularly, reading, praying or meditating, spending quality time alone or with family and friends, traveling, and cooking nutritious meals. Each of these can contribute directly to a long-term goal or life mission. Yet when schedules get tight, we often forgo these things, waiting for that elusive day when we'll "finally have more time."

That day won't come until we choose to make time for what's truly important. Knowing this, we can use some of the suggestions in this chapter to free up more time.

Remember cultural differences

There are as many different styles for managing time as there are people. These styles vary across cultures.

In the United States and England, for example, business meetings typically start on time. That's also true in Scandinavian countries such as Norway and Sweden. However, travelers to Panama might find that meetings start about a half-hour late. And people who complain about late meetings while doing business in Mexico might be considered rude.

Cultural differences can get even more pronounced. In her book *Freedom and Culture,* anthropologist Dorothy Lee writes about a group of people in the Trobriand Islands east of New Guinea.[5] Their language has no verb tenses—no distinction between past, present, and future. The Trobrianders celebrate each event as an end in itself, not as a means to achieve some future goal. In this culture, the whole concept of time management would have little meaning.

When you study or work with people of different races and ethnic backgrounds, look for differences in their approach to time. A behavior that you might view as rude or careless—such as showing up late for appointments—could simply result from seeing the world in a different way.

22. Ask: Can I delegate this?

Instead of slogging through complicated tasks alone, you can draw on the talents and energy of other people. Busy executives know the value of delegating tasks to coworkers. Without delegation, many projects would flounder or die.

You can apply the same principle. Instead of doing all the housework or cooking by yourself, for example, you can assign some of the tasks to family members or roommates. Rather than making a trip to the library to look up a simple fact, you can call and ask a library assistant to research it for you. Instead of driving across town to deliver a package, you can hire a delivery service to do so. All of these tactics can free up extra hours for studying.

It's not practical to delegate certain study tasks, such as writing term papers or completing reading assignments. However, you can still draw on the ideas of others in completing such tasks. For instance, form a writing group to edit and critique papers, brainstorm topics or titles, and develop lists of sources.

If you're absent from a class, find a classmate to summarize the lecture, discussion, and any assignments due. Presidents depend on briefings. You can use this technique, too.

23. Ask: How did I just waste time?

Notice when time passes and you haven't accomplished what you had planned to do. Take a minute to review your actions and note the specific ways you wasted time. We operate by habit and tend to waste time in the same ways over and over again. When you are aware of things you do that drain your time, you are more likely to catch yourself in the act next time. Observing one small quirk might save you hours. But keep this in mind: Noting how you waste time is not the same as feeling guilty about it. The point is not to blame yourself but to increase your skill. That means getting specific information about how you use time.

24. Ask: Could I find the time if I really wanted to?

Often the way people speak rules out the option of finding more time. An alternative is to speak about time with more possibility.

The next time you're tempted to say "I just don't have time," pause for a minute. Question the truth of this statement. Could you find four more hours this week for studying? Suppose that someone offered to pay you $10,000 to find those four hours. Suppose, too, that you will get paid only if you don't lose sleep, call in sick for work, or sacrifice anything important to you. Could you find the time if vast sums of money were involved?

Remember that when it comes to school, vast sums of money *are* involved.

25. Ask: Am I willing to promise it?

This might be the most powerful time-management idea of all. If you want to find time for a task, promise yourself—and others—that you'll get it done.

To make this technique work, do more than say that you'll try or that you'll give it your best shot. Take an oath, as you would in court. Give your word.

One way to accomplish big things in life is to make big promises. There's little reward in promising what's safe or predictable. No athlete promises to place seventh in the Olympic games. Chances are that if we're not making large promises, we're not stretching ourselves.

The point of making a promise is not to chain ourselves to a rigid schedule or to impossible expectations. We can also promise to reach goals without unbearable stress. We can keep schedules flexible and carry out our plans with ease, joy, and satisfaction.

At times we can go too far. Some promises are truly beyond us, and we might break them. However, failing to keep a promise is just that—failing to keep a promise. A broken promise is not the worst disaster in the world.

Promises can work magic. When our word is on the line, it's possible to discover reserves of time and energy we didn't know existed. Promises can push us to exceed our expectations.

Time management for right-brained people

or what to do if making to-do lists is not your style

Ask some people about managing time, and a dreaded image appears in their minds. They see a person with a 50-item to-do list clutching a calendar chock full of appointments. They imagine a robot who values cold efficiency, compulsively accounts for every minute, and is too rushed to develop personal relationships. Often this image is what's behind the comment "Yeah, there are some good ideas in those time-management books, but I'll never get around to using them. Too much work."

These stereotypes about time management hold a kernel of truth. Sometimes people who pride themselves on efficiency are merely keeping busy. In their rush to check items off their to-do lists, they might be fussing over things that don't need doing—insignificant tasks that create little or no value in the first place. If this is one of your fears, relax. The point of managing time is not to overload your schedule with extra obligations. Instead, the aim is to get the important things done and still have time to be human. An effective time manager is productive and relaxed at the same time.

Personal style enters the picture, too. Many of the suggestions in this chapter appeal to "left-brained" people—those who thrive on making lists, scheduling events, and handling details. These suggestions might not work for people who like to see wholes and think visually. Remember that the strategies discussed in this chapter represent just one set of options for managing time.

The trick is to discover what works for you. Do give time-management strategies a fair chance. Some might be suitable, with a few modifications. Instead of writing a conventional to-do list, for instance, you can plot your day on a mind map. (Mind maps are explained in the Notes chapter.) Or write to-do's, one per 3x5 card, in any order in which tasks occur to you. Later you can edit, sort, and rank the cards, choosing which items to act on.

Strictly speaking, time cannot be managed. Time is a mystery, an abstract concept that cannot be captured in words. The minutes, hours, days, and years march on whether we manage anything or not. What we *can* do is manage ourselves in respect to time. A few basic principles can do that as well as a truckload of cold-blooded techniques.

Know your values. Begin by managing time from a bigger picture. Instead of thinking in terms of minutes or hours, view your life as a whole. Consider what that expanse of time is all about.

As a thought-provoking exercise, write your own obituary. Describe the way you want to be remembered. List the contributions you intend to make during your lifetime. If this is too spooky, write a short mission statement for your life—a paragraph that describes your values and the kind of life you want to lead. Periodically during the day, stop to ask if what you're doing is contributing to those goals.

Do less. Managing time is as much about dropping worthless activities as about adding new and useful ones. The idea is to weed out those actions that deliver little reward.

Decide right now to eliminate activities with a low payoff. When you add a new item to your schedule, consider dropping a current one.

Slow down. Sometimes it's useful to hurry, such as when you're late for a meeting or about to miss a train. At other times, haste is a choice that serves no real purpose. If you're speeding through the day like a launched missile, consider what would happen if you got to your next destination a little bit later than planned. Rushing to stay a step ahead might not be worth the added strain.

Remember people. Few people on their deathbed ever say, "I wish I'd spent more time at the office." They're more likely to say, "I wish I'd spent more time with my family and friends." The pace of daily life can lead us to neglect the people we cherish.

Efficiency is a concept that applies to things—not people. When it comes to maintaining and nurturing relationships, we can often benefit from loosening up our schedules. We can allow extra time for conflict management, spontaneous visits, and free-ranging conversations.

Focus on outcomes.

You might feel guilty when you occasionally stray from your schedule and spend two hours napping or watching soap operas. But if you're regularly meeting your goals and leading a fulfilling life, there's probably no harm done. When managing time, the overall goal of personal effectiveness counts more than the means used to achieve it. This can be true even when your time-management style differs from that recommended by experts.

Likewise, there are many methods for planning your time. Some people prefer a written action plan that carefully details each step leading to a long-range goal. Others just note the due date for accomplishing a goal and periodically assess their progress. Either strategy can work.

Visualizing the desired outcome can be as important as having a detailed action plan. Here's an experiment. Write a list of goals you plan to accomplish over the next six months. Then create a vivid mental picture of yourself attaining them and enjoying the resulting benefits.

Visualize this image several times in the next few weeks. File the list away, making a note on your calendar to review it in six months. At that time, note how many of your goals you have actually accomplished.

Handle it now.

A backlog of unfinished tasks can result from postponing decisions or procrastinating. An alternative is to handle the task or decision immediately. Answer that letter now. Make that phone call as soon as it occurs to you.

You can also save time by graciously saying no immediately to projects that you don't want to take on. Saying "I'll think about doing that and get back to you later" might mean that you'll have to take more time to say no later.

Buy less.

Before you purchase an item, ask how much time it will take to locate, assemble, use, repair, and maintain it. You might be able to free up hours by doing without. If the product comes with a 400-page manual or 20 hours of training, beware. Before rushing to the store to add another possession to your life, see if you can reuse or adapt something you already own.

Forget about time.

Schedule "downtime"—a period when you're accountable to no one else and have nothing to accomplish—into every day. This is time to do nothing, free of guilt. Even a few minutes spent in this way can yield a sense of renewal.

Also experiment with decreasing your awareness of time. Leave your watch off for a few hours each day. Spend time in an area that's free of clocks. Notice how often you glance at your watch, and make a conscious effort to do that less often.

If you still want some sense of time, then use alternatives to the almighty, unforgiving clock. Measure your day with a sundial, hourglass, or egg timer. Or synchronize your activities with the rhythms of nature, for example, by rising at dawn. You can also plan activities to harmonize with the rhythms of your body. Schedule your most demanding tasks for times when you're normally most alert. Eat when you're hungry, not according to the clock. Toss out schedules when it's appropriate. Sometimes the best-laid plans are best laid to rest.

Take time to retreat from time. Create a sanctuary, a haven, a safe place in your life that's free from any hint of schedules, lists, or accomplishments. One of the most effective ways to manage time is periodically to forget about it.

10

Planning
sets you free

One kind of self-direction has the power to lift the quality of your life almost immediately: planning. When you plan, you are the equal of the greatest sculptor, painter, or playwright. More than creating a work of art, you are designing a life. Seeing it this way can draw you into the passion, energy, and excitement of planning.

Planning allows you to glimpse new possibilities. More than that, it brings possibilities into the arena of action. Planning is the art of transforming dreams into realities, thoughts into deeds, the ideal into the real.

When you plan, you can create freedom. This contradicts the common notion of planning: "Me? Plan? No way. I don't want to be uptight. I don't want to be restrained. I don't want to lose my spontaneity. I don't want to be some tense person who never gets to have any fun. I want to be free. I want to be me."

Great. Then plan.

"No, no," goes the reply. "If I plan, I'll be trapped. I won't be able to let loose and have a good time. I won't be able to get what I want in life. I'll be boxed in by this plan."

Planning
sets you free

Actually, rather than a restraint, planning is a way to freedom, to living life to the fullest. One path to feeling calm, peaceful, fun-loving, joyful, and powerful is to have a plan. When we are uptight, worried, and hassled—when we're not feeling free—we often have no plan.

Planning increases our freedom in the following ways.

You set the plan

One freedom in planning stems from the simple fact that you set the plan. The course and direction are yours.

Often, particularly at work or in school, people do not feel this way. They feel that the plan is coming from someone else—their employer, supervisor, or teacher.

Consider that this view is inaccurate. If we look ahead into the future, we can choose to see any circumstance as part of a plan for our whole lives. Even when we don't like aspects of a job, for example, working provides income and helps us develop useful skills for the next job. When we plan far enough in advance, a job no longer has to feel limiting.

You can change the plan

Another freedom in planning is the freedom to make changes. An effective plan is flexible, not carved in stone.

Tell people that you have a 20-year plan for your career. They might ask, "Well, if the economy changes, would you consider changing your plan?" "Yes," you reply. "I change it every year." Then comes the laughter:

"Well, it really isn't a 20-year plan if you change it every year. It's actually a one-year plan."

In reality, we can change our plans frequently and still preserve the advantages of long-range planning. Those advantages come from choosing our overall direction and taking charge of our lives.

You choose how to achieve the plan

Planning increases freedom when it creates choices. Suppose you take a new job and with it comes a detailed agenda of goals to achieve in one year. You might say, "I didn't choose these goals. There are things in this plan I don't like. But I like the rest of the job, even though these goals come with it. I guess I'll just have to put up with them."

Even when others select the goals, you can decide whether to accept them. You can also choose your own unique way to attain any goal.

It's easy to start depending on other people not only for goals but also for ways to achieve them. We start looking to others for direction, something a lot of companies promote when they "manage" people. There's little freedom in that—little creativity or choice. If we're without a plan, we allow others to make our choices for us. We can easily become victims of our circumstances. Planning allows us to choose, from

moment to moment and on our own, ways to accomplish a goal.

When there's a plan, there's a chance

Few architects propose a building project without a blueprint. Few entrepreneurs get venture capital without a sound business plan. And few film producers begin shooting a movie without a script. Instead, these people first create a vision of the future, a plan to achieve a projected outcome. The rationale for creating this vision is to avoid wasting precious time, money, effort, and talent.

It's amazing that so many people have no vision for something as vital as their own lives and then end up living "lives of quiet desperation." Creating your future through planning is a way to avoid that fate.

Planning to meet a goal doesn't ensure accomplishment, but it does boost the odds of success. Your clearly defined goals and carefully chosen action plans increase the probability that you'll achieve what you want.

By making it more likely that we'll reach our goals, planning offers a significant source of freedom. We have a goal. We've laid out the necessary actions in logical sequence. And we've decided on a timeline to perform each action. Now the goal seems possible, whereas before it had seemed impossible.

Much of what people undertake at school, at work, in relationships, and at home is simply "digging in"— frantic action with no plan. "Sure, we might never reach the goal," they say, "but at least we're out there trying." In this statement we hear a loss of hope. Planning can replace despair with a purpose and a timeline.

Writing down what you want exponentially increases your chances of getting it. When you clearly define a goal, your mind and body start to operate more consistently in ways to achieve your dreams.

Planning frees you from constant decisions

When you plan, you set aside a time for choosing. That is when you look, decide, commit, promise, and set a direction. In effect, you say, "This is my life, my month, my week, my day. I'll take some time to be responsible for it."

Remember that we don't need to spend all of our time planning. Planning by itself is totally ineffective. Nothing in our lives will change until there is action. The value of planning is that it promotes action. After we plan, we are free to act. We're released from the dilemma of always wondering what's supposed to happen next.

When we operate without a plan, we might change our minds often: "Hmmm. . . . That chocolate cake smells great. Maybe I'll have a piece— but maybe I shouldn't. It's a lot of calories. I don't know. . . ." That debate takes up a lot of time and energy.

But suppose you plan to stop eating chocolate cake. What's more, you write down this plan. You speak about this plan to friends, even commit yourself to it in their presence. Temptation still occurs: "Gee, that cake smells great." But then you remember: "Wait. I don't have to make this decision now. I'll just follow my plan and avoid chocolate cake."

Planning makes adjustments easier

With a plan, you are free to handle unexpected change. You've got a timetable, and your actions for the day are ranked in order of importance. If something happens that calls for a change in the agenda, there's no need to panic. In fact, having a written plan makes adjustments easier.

Suppose you are scheduled to give a talk in your speech class next week. Suddenly you find out there was a misprint in the course schedule. You're supposed to speak two days from now, not seven. Without a plan, you would face a lengthy mental process, a whole series of questions: What will I do now? When will I have time to get that speech done? How will this affect the rest of my schedule?

With a plan, things are different. You might say, "I don't have to worry about this. I've done my plan for the week, and I know I have free time tomorrow night between 7 and 10 p.m. I can finish the speech then."

Planning enables us to respond to crises or opportunities. With a plan, we can take initiative rather than merely react to events. When we plan, we *give* our time to things instead of allowing things to *take* our time.

Planning is about creating our own experience. When we plan, our lives do not just "happen" to us. Instead, they flow from choices we've consciously made for ourselves. This self-direction is a fundamental freedom in planning—and one of the most valued freedoms of all.

Gearing up:
Using a long-term planner

Planning a day or a week at a time is a powerful practice. Seeing how your days and weeks fit into a larger picture can yield even more benefits. One way to begin long-term planning is to get an overview of your quarter or semester. Using a quarter, semester, or yearly calendar helps you remember upcoming goals and commitments. On this calendar you can enter test dates, lab sessions, due dates for assignments, days classes will be canceled, and other items that extend beyond the next week or two. Also list interim due dates, such as when you plan to complete the first draft of a term paper. Then, when planning your day or week, scan this calendar to refresh your memory.

Many office supply stores carry academic planners that cover an entire school year. You can also be creative and make your own. A big roll of newsprint pinned to a bulletin board or taped to a wall will do nicely.

Use your academic or yearly planner to mark significant events, such as:

- birthdays, anniversaries, and other special occasions. Include a "tickler" note well ahead of time to remind yourself to pick up cards or gifts
- medical and dental checkups, car maintenance schedules, meetings, luncheons, and other appointments

- concerts, plays, television and radio programs you want to enjoy
- due dates for major bills—insurance, taxes, car registration, credit card and installment loan payments, medical expenses, interest charges, and charitable contributions. Use your calendar to keep track of the amounts you pay
- trips, vacations, and holidays

Consider keeping your long-term planner for years to come. It can be as revealing and as fun to read as a personal journal. This calendar is a snapshot of your life. It says a lot about who you are—and who you can be.

WORKPLACE APPLICATIONS

Use a long-term planner to manage major projects at work. Besides scheduling a due date for the final product, set interim due dates—what you'll produce at key points leading up to that final date. Example: You're planning to launch a new in-house training program in one year. Set individual due dates for finishing each major component of the program, such as manuals, web sites, and videos.

Week of	Monday	Tuesday	Wednesday	Thursday	Friday	Saturday	Sunday
9/5							
9/12		English quiz					
9/19			English paper due		Speech #1		
9/26	Chemistry test					Skiing at the lake	
10/3		English quiz			Speech #2		
10/10			Geography project due				
10/17				---No classes---			

Name _____

LONG-TERM PLANNER: ___/___/___ to ___/___/___

Week of	Monday	Tuesday	Wednesday	Thursday	Friday	Saturday	Sunday
__/__							
__/__							
__/__							
__/__							
__/__							
__/__							
__/__							
__/__							
__/__							
__/__							
__/__							
__/__							
__/__							
__/__							
__/__							
__/__							
__/__							
__/__							
__/__							
__/__							
__/__							
__/__							
__/__							
__/__							
__/__							
__/__							
__/__							
__/__							
__/__							
__/__							

LONG-TERM PLANNER: ___/___/___ to ___/___/___

Week of	Monday	Tuesday	Wednesday	Thursday	Friday	Saturday	Sunday
__/__							
__/__							
__/__							
__/__							
__/__							
__/__							
__/__							
__/__							
__/__							
__/__							
__/__							
__/__							
__/__							
__/__							
__/__							
__/__							
__/__							
__/__							
__/__							
__/__							
__/__							
__/__							
__/__							
__/__							
__/__							
__/__							
__/__							
__/__							
__/__							
__/__							

MASTER
STUDENT

Strategies for long-term planning

Use the following suggestions for long-term planning. These strategies can help you plan anything in your life, from getting an education or managing money to finding a job or developing new relationships.

Keep in mind that there's really no "right" way to do long-term planning. The main thing is to immerse yourself in the process of planning. Then you can see for yourself the benefits it brings. Begin by planning to plan—setting aside time to put down your goals in writing. From there you can launch your future.

State your goals effectively.
Goals are specific changes you'd like to bring about in yourself or your environment. To help make your goals happen, state them as results you can measure. Think in detail about how things will be different once your goals are attained. List the specific changes in what you'd see, feel, touch, taste, hear, be, do, or have.

Suppose that one of your goals is to become a better student by studying harder. You're headed in a powerful direction; now go for the specifics. Translate that goal into a concrete action, such as "I will study two hours for every hour I'm in class." Measurable goals make clear what actions are needed and what results are expected.

Remember the difference between measurements and values.
In planning, it's possible to get the intended results yet still miss the purpose. Say that you want to learn Spanish. One way to state that goal in measurable terms is to write, "I will sign up for a Spanish course and attend at least 98 percent of the class meetings." However, merely showing up for class every time does not guarantee completing the assigned work—or enjoying Spanish.

Ideals, values, emotions, and other nonmeasurable factors are the "fuel" for our plans. Often they're what inspired us in the first place. "I want to be a better student," "I want to become a more loving person," or "I want to enjoy music"—none of these is stated as a measurable goal. Yet it's useful to keep such values in mind. They help us remember the purpose of our planning.

Work backward, from the future to the present.
When you plan, consider working from the general to the specific. Short-range goals are often easier to plan when they flow naturally from long-range objectives.

To apply this idea, start planning as far in the future as you can and work backward to the present. The specific length of time doesn't matter. For some people, long-range might mean starting out at 10, 20, or even 50 years from now. For others, imagining three years ahead might feel like reaching into the distant future. Any of these alternatives is fine.

Once you have stated your long-range goals, work backward until you get to a one-day plan. Suppose your 30-year goal is to retire and maintain your present standard of living. Ask yourself: In order to accomplish that goal, what needs to be in place in 20 years? To get to that point, what is needed in 10 years? In one year? In one month? In one week? With the answers to such questions, you can make an informed choice about what step to take today.

Write out your plan. Writing uncovers holes in a plan—gaps in logic, hidden assumptions, contradictions, and other forms of fuzzy thinking. Writing a plan down keeps it specific and powerful.

You can also use other media to shape your plans. For example, make a drawing that represents where you want to be in 20 years. Draw yourself, the people you want in your life, and the things you want to be, have, and do. Capturing your plans in a painting, a sculpture, or a collage can also help shape your future.

Be willing to act—even if the plan is not complete. Many careers, successful businesses, and enduring social changes have begun with the most simple intention or sketchy plan. One African American woman, Rosa Parks, sparked the civil rights movement by refusing to sit at the back of a bus. Albert Schweitzer first considered doing medical relief work in Africa when he saw a magazine article about the needs of people in the Belgian Congo.

Complete, detailed plans are powerful. At the same time, taking action on an incomplete plan is one way to fill in the gaps. An unfinished plan is no excuse for missing a rewarding experience or for ignoring a worthy idea.

Just open your mouth and talk planning. Conversations about planning can bring our intentions into focus. We can even start talking about a plan before we really have one.

In planning, you don't have to go it alone. You can talk to others about your dreams, wishes, fantasies, and goals. You can speak of your desire to take charge of your learning, your life, and your career. The more you speak about your goals, the more real they become. Your plan might start out as a hazy ideal. That's fine. By speaking about it with others, you can fill in the details.

Look boldly for things to change. To create new goals, open up your thinking about what aspects of your life can be changed and what cannot. Be willing to put every facet of your life on the table.

It's fascinating to note the areas that are off-limits when people set goals. Money, sex, spirituality, career, marriage, and other topics can easily fall into the category "I'll just have to live with this."

For example, you might think that you have to live with the face you have now. Maybe not. There are ways to change your face even without plastic surgery. Physical therapists tell us that there are dozens of muscles in the face. Learning to relax them and bring more of them under conscious control will change the way you look. Even something as simple as a smile can go a long way toward changing your appearance.

When creating your future by setting goals, consider the whole range of your experience. Staying open-minded can lead to a future you've never dreamed possible.

Look for what's missing in your life. Goals usually arise from a sense of what's missing in our lives. Goal setting is fueled by unresolved problems, incomplete projects, relationships we want to develop, and careers we still want to pursue. When nothing's missing, goals can seem irrelevant. Affluent people rarely set a goal of eating three meals a day.

To create the life of your dreams, release negative judgments about what's missing from your life. Forgive yourself for not attaining some of the things you want. Instead of talking about your shortcomings or deficiencies, talk about your potential. The person with a bulging belly and weak knees can honestly say, "There's a lot of potential in this body!"

Maintain what you love about your life.

Not all goals need to spring from a sense of need. You can also make it a goal to maintain things that you already have or to keep doing the effective things that you already do. If you exercise vigorously three times each week, you can set a goal to keep exercising. If you already have a loving relationship with your spouse, you can set a goal to nurture that relationship for the rest of your life.

Create a vision for the ages.

Think of long-term planning as "visioning." This process can include goals that we want to achieve 10, 20, or even 50 years from now. Visions that extend beyond our lives are especially powerful. A plan might even include goals to be accomplished several centuries from now. Such plans allow us to contribute to a project that extends well beyond our years. Throughout history, people have conceived projects compelling enough to inspire action over many generations. The pyramids built in ancient Egypt are an example. They were conceived by pharaohs whose vision for these structures was so stunning that their descendants chose to continue the work for decades.

Another example of a multigenerational project is taking place in the Black Hills of South Dakota. In 1938, the sculptor Korczak Ziolkowski envisioned a monument to the Indian chief Crazy Horse that would be carved from a mountain larger than Mount Rushmore and would stand taller than the Washington Monument.

As Ziolkowski saw it, this monument and a related educational center would testify to the Native American way of life. Ziolkowski died in 1982. Today his work is continued by his family and other people inspired by his original vision.

Take time to create multigenerational goals. Describe your own "pyramids"—projects so important that others might be moved to continue them after you die. These projects could involve physical creations. They could also be organizations, such as Mothers Against Drunk Driving, or enterprises, such as a family farm.

Describe ideas for a multigenerational project that you could launch. Express your ideas in writing, visual art, music, or any other appropriate medium. Create a vision that could survive you for lifetimes.

Remember to remember.

A key part of making any plan work is simply remembering the plan. Yet this can be a challenge. In the midst of an active life, we can easily lose sight of our goals.

To get around this, include your goals on a monthly calendar or daily to-do list. Post notes on your refrigerator. Write your goals on 3x5 cards and tape them to your desk or bathroom mirror, or tack them to a wall. Think of these as flash cards for the future. Do whatever it takes to keep the vision alive.

Student Voices

My first educational goal is to get my associate degree in Early Childhood Education at College of Menominee Nation. My second goal is to get my bachelor's degree in education. My third goal is to get a teaching job with my four-year degree. That would be a dream come true.

— ANGEL M. FOWLER

#3

Divide and conquer your goals

An online version of this exercise is available at Houghton Mifflin's College Survival/Becoming a Master Student web site: **http://collegesurvival.college.hmco.com/students.**

This exercise offers a chance for you to use two essential thinking skills—the ability to generate and the ability to evaluate. You will translate a broad goal into specific, concrete behaviors, making the goal as real as a chain saw.

Many of us have vague, idealized notions of what we want out of life. These notions float among the clouds in our heads. They are wonderful, fuzzy, safe thoughts such as "I want to be a good person," "I want to be financially secure," or "I want to be happy." Such goals are great possible beginnings for more tangible plans. Left in a generalized form, these goals can leave us confused about how to use them in choosing what to do this weekend.

In contrast, there is nothing vague or fuzzy about chain saws. You can see them, feel them, and hear them. They have a clear function.

Goals can be every bit as real and useful—if you make them real. One way to make goals effective is to examine them up close. Find out what they look like; listen to what they sound like. Pick them up and feel how heavy they are. That's what this exercise is about. It's a chance to inspect the switches, valves, joints, cogs, and fastenings of one of your long-term goals. You will do this by choosing a long-term goal and breaking it into smaller segments until you have taken it completely apart.

Disassembled, a goal might look different to you. When you look at it closely, a goal you thought you wanted might not be something you want after all. Or you might discover you want to choose a new path to a goal you are sure you want. Perhaps you will also see how your education relates to your long-term goal.

For this exercise, you will use a pen, extra paper, and a watch with a second hand. (A digital watch with a built-in stopwatch is even better.) Timing is an important part of the brainstorming process, so follow the stated time limits. This entire exercise takes about an hour.

Part one: Long-term goals

Long-term goals represent major targets in your life. These goals can take five to 20 years to achieve. In some cases, they will take a lifetime. They can include goals in education, careers, personal relationships, travel, financial security—whatever is important to you. Consider the answers to the following questions as you create your long-term goals: What do you want to accomplish in your life? Do you want your life to make a statement? What is it?

Brainstorm

Begin with an eight-minute brainstorm. For eight minutes write down everything you think you want in your life. Write as fast as you can and write whatever comes into your head. Leave no thought out. Don't worry about accuracy. The object of a brainstorm is to generate as many ideas as possible. Use a separate sheet of paper for this part of the exercise.

Evaluate

After you have finished brainstorming, spend the next six minutes looking over your list. Analyze what you wrote. Read the list out loud. If something is missing, add it. Look for common themes or relationships between goals. Then select three long-term goals that are important to you—goals that will take many years to achieve. Write these goals in the space provided.

Long-term goal:

_____

_____

_____

_____

Long-term goal:

_____

_____

_____

_____

Long-term goal:

_____

_____

_____

_____

Before you go on, take a minute to reflect on the process you've used so far. What criteria did you use to select your top three goals? For example, list some of the core values (such as love, wealth, or happiness) underlying these goals.

Part two: Mid-term goals

Mid-term goals are objectives you can accomplish in one to five years. They include goals such as completing a course of education or achieving a specific career level. These goals usually support your long-term goals.

Brainstorm

Read out loud the three long-term goals you selected in Part One. Choose one of them. Then brainstorm a list of goals you might achieve in the next one to five years that would lead to the accomplishment of that one long-term goal. These are mid-term goals. Spend eight minutes on this brainstorm. Remember, neatness doesn't count. Go for quantity.

Evaluate

Analyze your brainstorm of mid-term goals. Then select three that you estimate to be most important in meeting the long-term goal you picked. Allow yourself five minutes for this part of the exercise. Write your selections in the space provided.

Mid-term goal:

_____
_____
_____

Mid-term goal:

_____
_____
_____

Mid-term goal:

_____
_____
_____

Again, pause for reflection before going on to the next part of this exercise. Why do you see these three goals as more important than the other mid-term goals you generated? Write about your reasons for selecting these three goals.

Part three: Short-term goals

Short-term goals are the ones you can accomplish in a year or less. These goals are specific achievements, such as completing a particular course or group of courses. A financial goal probably would include an exact dollar amount. Whatever your short-term goals are, they will require action now or in the near future.

Brainstorm

Review your list of mid-term goals and select one. In another eight-minute brainstorm, generate a list of short-term goals—those you can accomplish in a year or less that will lead to the attainment of that mid-term goal. Write down everything that comes to mind. Do not evaluate or judge these ideas yet. For now, the more ideas you write down, the better.

Evaluate

Analyze your list of short-term goals. The most effective brainstorms are conducted by suspending judgment, so you might find some bizarre ideas on your list. That's fine. Now is the time to cross them out. Next evaluate your remaining short-term goals to determine which ones you can accomplish and are willing to accomplish. Select three and write them in the space provided.

Short-term goal:

_____

Short-term goal:

_____

Short-term goal:

_____

Part four: Next steps

Take a few minutes to reflect on all of the goals you selected in this exercise. Look for relationships between them. For example, goals could fall in the same category (career or health). Or they could fall in a time sequence, such as goals to be accomplished in one year, five years, and 10 years.

Also think about what accomplishing these goals can mean to you. Think about how the process of choosing them felt.

To make this process even more powerful, write a list of small, achievable steps you can take to accomplish each short-term goal. Make these steps specific enough to include a timeline. Then return to this list of steps in a few weeks and note your progress.

The more you practice, the more effective you can be at choosing goals that have meaning for you. You can repeat this exercise, using the other long-term goals you generated or creating new ones. By using this "divide and conquer" process, you can make long-term goals real in the here and now.

Ways to change a habit

When people talk about how difficult it is to change a behavior they don't like, they often resort to an explanation: "Well, that's just my nature." Often what's implied by this statement is "And because it's my nature, don't expect me to change."

Instead of talking about human nature, we can talk about habits. Thinking about ourselves as creatures of habit instead of as creatures defined by our nature gives us power. Then we are not faced with the monumental task of changing our very nature. Rather, we can take on the doable job of changing our habits. And by changing our habits, we can achieve more of our goals.

Success in school and in life is largely a matter of cultivating effective habits. The new habit that you choose does not have to make headlines. It can be one simple, small change in behavior.

After interviewing hundreds of people, psychologists James Prochaska, John Norcross, and Carlo DiClemente identified stages that people typically go through when adopting a new behavior.[6] These stages take people from *contemplating* a change and making a clear

determination to change to taking *action* and *maintaining* the new habit. Following are ways to help yourself move successfully through each stage.

Tell the truth

Telling the truth about any habit—from chewing our fingernails to cheating on tests—frees us. Without taking this step, our efforts to change might be as ineffective as rearranging the deck chairs on the *Titanic.* Telling the truth allows us to see what's actually sinking the ship.

When we admit what's really going on in our lives, our defenses are down. We're open to help from others. The support we need to change the habit has an opportunity to enter.

Choose and commit to a new behavior

It often helps to choose a new habit to replace an old one. First, commit to practice the new habit. Tell key people in your life about your commitment to change. Make a plan for when and how. Answer questions such as these: When will I apply the new habit? Where will I be? Who will be with me? What will I be seeing, hearing, touching, saying, or doing? How, exactly, will I think, speak, or act differently?

Take the student who always snacks when she studies. Each time she sits down to read, she positions a bag of potato chips within easy reach. For her, opening a book is a cue to start chewing. Snacking is especially easy given the place she chooses to study: the kitchen. She chooses to change this habit by studying at a desk in her bedroom instead of at the kitchen table. And every time she feels the urge to bite into a potato chip, she decides to drink from a glass of water instead.

Affirm your intention

You can pave the way for a new behavior by clearing a mental path for it. See yourself carrying out your plan. Before you apply the new behavior, rehearse it in your mind. Mentally picture what actions you will take and in what order.

Say that you plan to improve your handwriting when taking notes. Imagine yourself in class with a blank notebook poised before you. See yourself taking up a finely crafted pen. Notice how comfortable it feels in your hand. See yourself writing clearly and legibly. You can even picture how you will make individual letters—the *e*'s, *i*'s, and *r*'s. Then, when class is over, see yourself reviewing your notes and taking pleasure in how easy they are to read.

Such scenes are more vivid if you include all of your senses. Round out your mental picture by adding sounds, textures, and colors.

You can act as if your intention is already a reality, as if the new habit is already a part of you. Be the change you want to see—today. In some cases, this might be enough to change the old habit completely.

Start with a small change

You can sometimes rearrange a whole pattern of behaviors by changing one small habit. If you have a habit of being late for class, and if you want to change that pattern, then be on time for one class. As soon as you change the old pattern by getting ready and going on time to one class, you'll likely find yourself arriving at all of your classes on time. You might even start arriving everywhere else on time.

If you know that you are usually nervous, you don't have to change how you react in all situations at all times. Just change your nervous behavior in one setting. Like magic, watch the rest of your nervousness lessen or even disappear. The joy of this process is watching one small change of habit ripple through your whole life.

Get feedback and support

This is a crucial step and a place where many plans for change break down. It's easy to practice your new behavior with great enthusiasm for a few days. After the initial rush of excitement, however, things can get a little tougher. We begin to find excuses for slipping back into an old habit: "One more cigarette won't hurt." "I can get back to my diet tomorrow." "It's been a tough day. I deserve this beer."

One way to get feedback is to bring other people into the picture. Ask others to remind you that you are changing your habit. If you want to stop an old behavior, such as cramming for tests, then it often works to tell everyone you know that you intend to stop. When you want to start a new behavior, though, consider telling

only a few people—those who truly support your efforts. Starting new habits might call for the more focused, long-lasting support that close friends or family members can give.

Support from others can be as simple as a quick phone call: "Hi. Have you started that outline for your research paper yet?" Or it can be as formal as a support group that meets once weekly to review everyone's goals and action plans.

You are probably the most effective source for your own support and feedback. You know yourself better than anyone else and can design a system to monitor your behavior. You can create your own charts or diagrams to track your behavior or you can write about your progress in your journal. Figure out a way to monitor your progress.

Practice, practice, practice . . . without reproach

Psychologists such as B. F. Skinner define learning as a stable change in behavior that comes as a result of practice.[7] This idea is key to changing habits. Act on your intention. If you fail or forget, let go of any self-judgment. Just keep practicing the new habit and allow whatever time it takes to make a change.

Accept the feelings of discomfort that might come with a new habit. Keep practicing the new behavior, even if it feels unnatural. Trust the process. You will grow into the new behavior. Keep practicing until it becomes as natural as breathing. However, if this new habit doesn't work, simply note what happened (without guilt or blame), select a new behavior, and begin this cycle of steps again.

Going back to square one doesn't mean you've failed. Even when you don't get the results you want from a new behavior, you learn something valuable in the process. Once you understand ways to change one habit, you understand ways to change many habits.

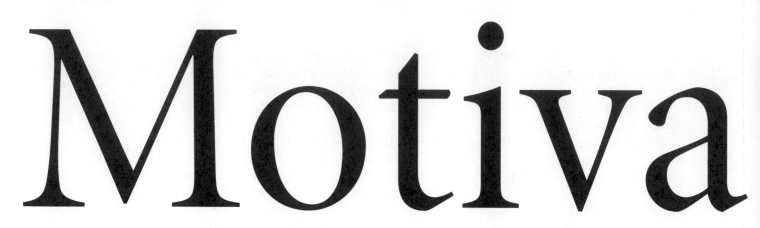

Motiva

The terms *self-discipline, willpower,* and *motivation* are often used to describe something missing in ourselves. Time after time we invoke these words to explain another person's success—or our own shortcomings: "If I were more motivated, I'd get more involved in school." "Of course she got an A. She has self-discipline." "If I had more willpower, I'd lose weight."

We can stop assuming that we lack certain valuable personality traits. Instead, we can say that we're already motivated and disciplined, lacking only certain skills that come with practice. Perhaps what we call motivation is just a habit. The following suggestions offer ways to develop that habit.

Promise it

Motivation can come simply from being clear about your goals and acting on them. Say that you want to start a study group. You can commit yourself to inviting people and setting a time and place to meet. Promise your classmates that you'll do this, and ask them to hold you accountable. Self-discipline, willpower, motivation—none of these mysterious characteristics needs to get in your way. Just make a promise and keep your word.

Befriend your discomfort

Sometimes keeping your word means doing a task you'd rather put off. The mere thought of doing laundry, reading a chapter in a statistics book, or proofreading a term paper can lead to discomfort. In the face of such discomfort, we can procrastinate. Or we can use this barrier as a means to get the job done.

Begin by investigating the discomfort. Notice the thoughts running through your head and speak them out loud: "I'd rather walk on a bed of coals than do this." "This is the last thing I want to do right now."

Also observe what's happening with your body. For example, are you breathing faster or slower than usual? Is your breathing shallow or deep? Are your shoulders tight? Do you feel any tension in your stomach?

Once you're in contact with your mind and body, stay with the discomfort a few minutes. Don't judge it as good or bad. Accepting the thoughts and body sensations robs them of power. They might still be there, but in time they can stop being a barrier for you.

Discomfort can be a gift—an opportunity to do valuable work on yourself. On the other side of discomfort lies mastery.

Change your mind—and your body

You can also get past discomfort by planting new thoughts in your mind or changing your physical stance. For example, instead of slumping in a chair, sit up straight or stand up. You can also get physically active by taking a short walk. Notice what happens to your discomfort.

Work with thoughts, also. Replace "I can't stand this" with "I'll feel great when this is done" or "Doing this will help me get something I want."

Sweeten the task

Sometimes it's just one aspect of a task that holds us back. We can stop procrastinating merely by changing that aspect. If distaste for our physical environment keeps us from studying, we can change that environment. Reading about social psychology might seem like a yawner when we're alone in a dark corner of the house. Moving to a cheery, well-lit library can sweeten the task.

Talk about how bad it is

One way to get past negative attitudes is to take them to an extreme. When faced with an unpleasant task, launch into a no-holds-barred gripe session. Pull out all the stops: "There's no way I can start my income taxes now. This is terrible beyond words, an absolute disaster. This is a catastrophe of global proportions. . . ."

Griping taken this far can restore perspective. It shows how self-talk can turn inconveniences into crises.

tio n or "I'm just not in the mood"

Turn up the pressure

Sometimes motivation is a luxury. Pretend that the due date for your project has been moved up one month, one week, or one day. Raising the stress level slightly can spur you into action. Then the issue of motivation seems beside the point, and meeting the due date moves to the forefront.

Turn down the pressure

The mere thought of starting a huge task can induce anxiety. To get past this feeling, turn down the pressure by taking "baby steps." Divide a large project into small tasks. In 30 minutes or less you could preview a book, create a rough outline for a paper, or solve two or three math problems. Careful planning can help you discover many such steps to make a big job doable.

Ask for support

Other people can become your allies in overcoming procrastination. For example, form a support group and declare what you intend to accomplish before each meeting. Then ask members to hold you accountable. If you want to begin exercising regularly, ask another person to walk with you three times weekly. People in support groups ranging from Alcoholics Anonymous to Weight Watchers know the power of this strategy.

Adopt a model

One strategy for succeeding at any task is to hang around the masters. Find someone you consider successful and spend time with her. Observe this person and use her as a model for your own behavior. You can "try on" this person's actions and attitudes. Look for tools that feel right for you.

Compare the payoffs to the costs

Behaviors such as cramming for exams or neglecting exercise have payoffs. Cramming might give us more time that's free of commitments. Neglecting exercise can give us more time to sleep.

One way to let go of such unwanted behaviors is first to celebrate them—even embrace them. We can openly acknowledge the payoffs.

Celebration can be especially powerful when we follow it up with the next step—determining the costs. For example, skipping a reading assignment can give you time to go to the movies. However, you might be unprepared for class and have twice as much to read next week.

Maybe there is another way to get the payoff (going to the movies) without paying the cost (skipping the reading assignment). With some thoughtful weekly planning, you might choose to give up a few hours of television and end up with enough time to read *and* go to the movies.

Comparing the costs and benefits of any behavior can fuel our motivation. We can choose new behaviors because they align with what we want most.

Do it later

At times, it's effective to save a task for later. For example, writing a résumé can wait until you've taken the time to analyze your job skills and write career goals. This is not a lack of motivation—it's planning.

When you do choose to do it later, turn this decision into a promise. Estimate how long the task will take and schedule a specific date and time for it on your calendar.

Heed the message

Sometimes lack of motivation carries a message that's worth heeding. An example is the student who majors in accounting but seizes every chance to be with children. His chronic reluctance to read accounting textbooks might not be a problem. Instead, it might reveal his desire to major in elementary education. His original career choice might have come from the belief that "real men don't teach kindergarten." In such cases, lack of motivation signals a deeper wisdom trying to get through.

Be here now

If this Power Process were advertised on late-night television, some people might even buy it. The ad might sound like this:

Being right here, right now is such a simple idea.

It seems obvious. Where else can you be but where you are? When else can you be there but when you are there?

The answer is that you can be somewhere else at any time—in your head. It's common for our thoughts to distract us from where we've chosen to be. When we let this happen, we lose the benefits of focusing our attention on what's important to us in the present moment.

To "be here now" means to do what you're doing when you're doing it and to be where you are when you're there. Students consistently report that focusing attention on the here and now is one of the most powerful tools in this book.

Leaving the here and now

We all have a voice in our head that hardly ever shuts up. If you don't believe it, conduct this experiment: Close your eyes for 10 seconds and pay attention to what is going on in your head. Please do this right now. Notice something?

Perhaps your voice was saying, "Forget it. I'm in a hurry." Another might have said, "I wonder when 10 seconds is up." Another could have been saying, "What little voice? I don't hear any little voice." That's the voice.

This voice can take you anywhere at any time—especially when you are studying. When the voice takes you away, you might appear to be studying, but your brain is at the beach.

All of us have experienced this voice, as well as the absence of it. When the voice is silent, time no longer seems to exist. We forget worries, aches, pains, reasons, excuses, and justifications. We fully experience the here and now. Life is magic.

There are many benefits of such a state of consciousness. It is easier to discover the world around us when we are not chattering away to ourselves about how we think it ought to be, has been, or will be. Letting go of inner voices and pictures—being totally in the moment—is a powerful tool.

Do not expect to be rid of daydreams entirely. That is neither possible nor desirable. Inner voices serve a purpose. They enable us to analyze, predict, classify, and understand events out there in the "real" world.

Your stream of consciousness serves a purpose. When you are working on a term paper, your inner voices might suggest ideas. When you are listening to your sociology instructor, your inner voices can alert you to possible test questions. When you're about to jump out of an airplane, they could remind you to take a parachute. The trick is to consciously choose when to be with your inner voices and when to let them go.

Returning to the here and now

A powerful step toward returning to the here and now is to notice when we leave it. Our mind has a mind of its own, and it seems to fight back when we try to control it too much. The thoughts in our mind seem to want to live. If you doubt this, for the next 10 seconds do not, under any circumstances, think of a pink elephant. Please begin not thinking about one now.

Persistent image, isn't it? Most ideas are this insistent when we try to deny them or force them out of our consciousness.

For example, during class you might notice yourself thinking about a test you took the previous day, or a party planned for the weekend, or the DVD player you want.

Instead of trying to force a stray thought out of your head—a futile enterprise—simply notice it. Accept it. Tell yourself, "There's that thought again." Then gently return your attention to the task at hand. That thought, or another, will come back. Your mind will drift. Simply notice again where your thoughts take you and gently bring yourself back to the here and now.

Another way to return to the here and now is to notice your physical sensations. Notice the way the room looks or smells. Notice the temperature and how the chair feels. Once you've regained control of your attention by becoming aware of your physical surroundings, you can more easily take the next step and bring your full attention back to your present task.

We can often immediately improve our effectiveness—and our enjoyment—by fully entering into each of our activities, doing one thing at a time.

For example, take something as simple as peeling and eating an orange. Carefully notice the color, shape, and surface of the orange. Hold it close to your nose and savor the pungent, sweet smell. Then slowly peel the orange and see if you can hear every subtle sound that results. Next take one piece of the orange and place it in your mouth. Notice the feel of the fruit on your tongue. Chew the piece slowly, letting the delicious juice bathe your taste buds. Notice each individual sensation of pleasure that ripples through your body as you sample this delicious treat.

"Be here now" can turn the act of eating an orange into a rich experience. Imagine what can happen when you bring this quality of attention to almost everything that you do.

Choose when to be here now

Remember that no suggestion is absolute—including the suggestion to do one thing at a time with full, focused attention. Sometimes choosing to do two or more things at once is useful, even necessary. For example, you might study while doing laundry. You might ask your children to quiz you with flash cards while you fix dinner.

The key to this Power Process is to *choose*. When you choose, you overcome distractions and stay in charge of your attention.

Experiment with noticing your inner voices. Let go of the ones that prevent you from focusing on learning. Practice the process. Be here now, moment by moment.

The here and now in your future

You also can use this Power Process to keep yourself pointed toward your goals. In fact, one of the best ways to get what you want in the future is to realize that you do not have a future. The only time you have is right now.

The problem with this idea is that some students might think: "No future, huh? Terrific! Party time!" Being in the here and now, however, is not the same as living for today and forgetting about tomorrow.

Nor is the "be here now" idea a call to abandon goals. Goals are merely tools we create to direct our actions right now. They are useful only in the present. Goals, like our ideas of the past and future, are creations of our minds. The only time they are real is in the here and now.

The power of this idea lies in a simple but frequently overlooked fact: The only time to do anything is now. You can think about doing something next Wednesday. You can write about doing something next Wednesday. You can daydream, discuss, ruminate, speculate, and fantasize about what you will do next Wednesday.

But you can't do anything on Wednesday until it is Wednesday.

Sometimes students think of goals as things that exist in the misty future. And it's easy to postpone action on things in the misty future, especially when everyone else is going to a not-so-misty party.

However, the word *goal* comes from the Anglo-Saxon *gaelan*, which means "to hinder or impede," as in the case of a boundary. That's what a goal does. It restricts, in a positive way, our activity in the here and now. It channels our energy into actions that are more likely to get us what we really want. That's what goals are for. And they are useful only when they are directing action in the here and now.

The idea behind this Power Process is simple. When you plan for the future, plan for the future. When you listen to a lecture, listen to a lecture. When you read this book, read this book. And when you choose to daydream, daydream. Do what you're doing when you're doing it.

Be where you are when you're there. Be here now . . . and now . . . and now.

master student
MALCOLM X

(1925–1965) martyred militant, emerged from the heart of the ghetto to fight against racial segregation and oppression. At the peak of his power, his fears of assassination came true.

Many who today hear me somewhere in person, or on television, or those who read something I've said, will think I went to school far beyond the eighth grade. This impression is due entirely to my prison studies. It had really begun back in the Charlestown Prison, when Bimbi first made me feel envy of his stock of knowledge. Bimbi had always taken charge of any conversation he was in, and I had tried to emulate him.

But every book I picked up had few sentences which didn't contain anywhere from one to nearly all of the words that might as well have been in Chinese. When I just skipped those words, of course, I really ended up with little idea of what the book said. So I had come to the Norfolk Prison Colony still going through only book-reading motions. . . . I saw that the best thing I could do was to get hold of a dictionary—to study, to learn some words. I was lucky enough to reason also that I should try to improve my penmanship. It was sad. I couldn't even write in a straight line. It was both ideas together that moved me to request a dictionary along with some tablets and pencils from the Norfolk Prison Colony school.

I spent two days just riffling uncertainly through the dictionary's pages. I'd never realized so many words existed! I didn't know which words I needed to learn. Finally, just to start some kind of action, I began copying.

In my slow, painstaking, ragged handwriting, I copied into my tablet everything printed on that first page, down to the punctuation marks. I believe it took me a day. Then, aloud, I read, back to myself, everything I'd written on the tablet. Over and over, aloud, to myself, I read my own handwriting. I woke up the next morning thinking about those words—immensely proud to realize that not only had I written so much at one time, but I'd written words that I never knew were in the world. Moreover, with a little effort I also could remember what many of these words meant. . . . I was so fascinated that I went on—I copied the dictionary's next page. And the same experience came when I studied that. With every succeeding page, I also learned of people and places and events from history. Actually the dictionary is like a miniature encyclopedia. Finally the dictionary's A section had filled a whole tablet— and I went on into the B's. That was the way I started copying what eventually became the entire dictionary. . . . I suppose it was inevitable that as my word base

broadened, I could for the first time pick up a book and read and now begin to understand what the book was saying. Anyone who has read a great deal can imagine the new world that opened. Let me tell you something: From then until I left that prison, in every free moment I had, if I was not reading in the library, I was reading on my bunk. You couldn't have gotten me out of books with a wedge. Between Mr. Muhammad's teachings, my correspondence, my visitors—usually Ella and Reginald— and my reading of books, months passed without my even thinking about being imprisoned. In fact, up to then, I never had been so truly free in my life. . . . Not long ago, an English writer telephoned me from London, asking questions. One was, "What's your alma mater?" I told him, "Books."

From *The Autobiography of Malcolm X* by Malcolm X and Alex Haley. Copyright © 1964 by Alex Haley and Malcolm X. Copyright © 1965 by Alex Haley and Betty Shabazz. Used by permission of Random House, Inc.

For more information on Malcolm X's unusual learning strategies, visit Houghton Mifflin's College Survival/Becoming a Master Student web site: **http://collegesurvival.college.hmco. com/students.**

What are at least three ways you can control interruptions when you study?

 It is effective to leave holes in your schedule to allow for the unexpected. True or False? Explain your answer.

 Suppose that after you choose where to focus your attention, your mind wanders. The Power Process "Be here now" suggests that one of the most effective ways to bring your focus back to the here and now is to:
    (A) Slap your cheek and shout "Attention" as loudly as you can.
    (B) Notice that your thoughts have wandered and gently bring them back
    (C) Sleep.
    (D) Concentrate as hard as you can to force distracting thoughts out of your head.
    (E) Ignore physical sensations.

 What are at least five of the 25 ways to get the most out of now?

 In time-management terms, what is meant by "This ain't no piano"?

 Define "C fever" as it applies to the ABC priority method.

 Scheduling marathon study sessions once in a while is generally an effective strategy. True or False? Explain your answer.

8 Describe at least three strategies for overcoming procrastination.

 9 What two ideas, taken together, led Malcolm X to request a dictionary along with some tablets and pencils from the Norfolk Prison Colony school?

 10 "Working your A's off" refers to:

(A) A strategy for organizing your study area.

(B) Using a dictionary when reading unfamiliar material.

(C) The importance of your physical exercise program.

(D) Accomplishing the top-priority items on your to-do list.

(E) A strategy for being here now.

JOURNAL ENTRY

#12

Discovery/Intention Statement

While reading this chapter, what did you discover about the way you manage time?

I discovered that . . .

_____

_____

Pick two strategies for working with time and write a one-sentence Intention Statement about how you plan to use each one in the next 72 hours.

With regard to strategy one, I intend to . . .

_____

_____

With regard to strategy two, I intend to . . .

_____

_____

Mode 4 *Think again about the planning strategy you used. Is there any way you could modify this strategy to make it work better for you? Describe what specific changes you would make in applying this technique.*

Mode 1 *List five benefits that you could experience by mastering the Power Process "Be here now." Think of specific ways that applying this Power Process to your course work could promote your success in school.*

Mode 3 *Choose one of the strategies mentioned in this chapter for planning your time. Experiment with it for the next week. Then describe how well it worked for you.*

Mode 2 *Review the reading "25 ways to get the most out of now." On a separate sheet of paper, list each of those strategies and rank them using the ABC priority method. Assign an A to those strategies you're most likely to use.*

BIBLIOGRAPHY

ENDNOTES

1 Alan Lakein, *Take Control of Your Time and Life* (New York: New American Library, 1973).

2 Linda Sapadin, *It's About Time—The Six Styles of Procrastination and How to Overcome Them* (New York: Penguin, 1997).

3 Jane B. Burka and Lenora R. Yuen, *Procrastination: Why You Do It, What to Do About It* (Reading, MA: Addison-Wesley, 1983).

4 Stephen R. Covey, *The Seven Habits of Highly Effective People: Restoring the Character Ethic* (New York: Simon & Schuster, 1989).

5 Dorothy Lee, *Freedom and Culture* (Englewood Cliffs, NJ: Prentice-Hall, 1959).

6 James O. Prochaska, John C. Norcross, and Carlo C. DiClemente, *Changing for Good* (New York: Avon, 1994).

7 B. F. Skinner, *Science and Human Behavior* (Boston: Free Press, 1965).

ADDITIONAL READING

Covey, Stephen R. *First Things First.* New York: Simon & Schuster, 1994.

Ellis, Dave. *Creating Your Future: Five Steps to the Life of Your Dreams.* Boston: Houghton Mifflin, 1998.

Keyes, Ralph. *Timelock: How Life Got So Hectic and What You Can Do About It.* New York: HarperCollins, 1991.

Scharf-Hunt, Diana, and Pam Hait. *Studying Smart: Time Management for College Students.* New York: HarperPerennial, 1990.

Winston, Stephanie. *Getting Organized.* New York: Warner, 1978.

INTERNET RESOURCES

LifePlan Shareware
www.mindtools.com/lifeplan.html

Mind Tools—Time Management Skills
www.psychwww.com/mtsite/page5.html

Online Personal Calendars, such as:
calendar.yahoo.com/

Self-Improvement Online—Time Management, Procrastination
www.selfgrowth.com
www.ucc.vt.edu/lynch/TimeManagement.htm

CHAPTER 3 Memory

The art of true memory is the art of attention.
SAMUEL JOHNSON

Memory is the mother of imagination, reason and skill. . . . This is the companion, this is the tutor, the poet, the library with which you travel.
MARK VAN DOREN

IN THIS CHAPTER . . . Move from "I never remember" to "I never forget." On the way, explore the memory jungle. Experiment with 20 memory techniques, strategies for remembering names, and tools for tapping into your "secret brain." Also move through obstacles by learning to love your problems, and read some success stories that began as notable failures.

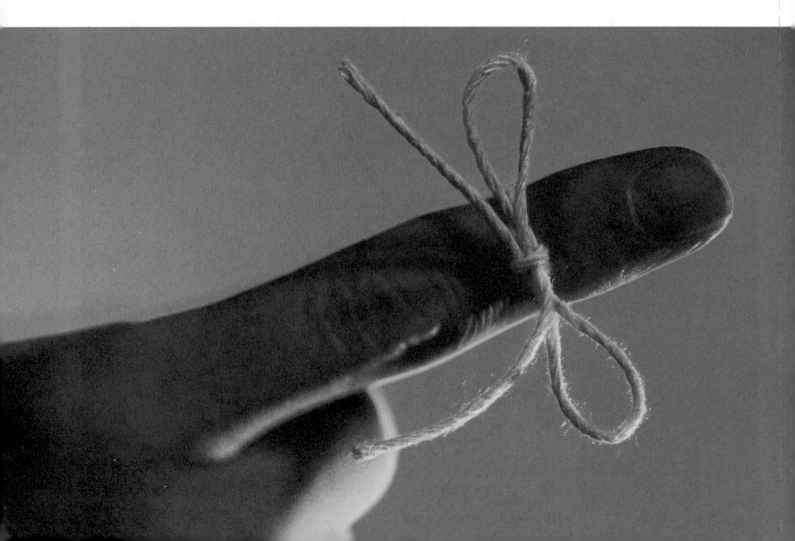

You never forget

One key to using your memory more effectively is to realize that—short of injury, disease, or death—your brain never loses anything. Once a thought or perception has been stored in your memory, it stays there for the rest of your life. What we call forgetting is either the inability to recall stored information or the failure to store information in the first place.

For example, during certain kinds of brain surgery, the patient remains conscious. Surgeon Wilder Penfield found that when sections of the brain are stimulated with a mild electrical current, the patient will often remember events of her childhood with absolute clarity.[1] She can recall details she thought were long forgotten, such as the smell of her father's starched shirts or the feel of sunlight warming her face through the window of her first-grade classroom.

People under hypnosis have reported similar experiences. Some have been able to recall events that took place shortly after their birth. Working with police, hypnotists have helped witnesses of crimes remember vital information, such as license plate numbers.

Once information is stored in our memory, it's possible that it is never forgotten. Sometimes, however, we do have difficulty recalling a piece of information. The data might still be in our heads. We simply can't find it.

Just as often, when we think we have forgotten something, the truth is that we never stored it in our memory in the first place.

JOURNAL ENTRY #13

Discovery Statement

Describe three situations in which you could be more effective by improving your memory skills.

_____

_____

_____

_____

_____

_____

_____

_____

Now preview this chapter and list five useful memory strategies you can use immediately. Also note the page numbers where these strategies are explained.

Strategy   Page number

_____

_____

_____

_____

_____

_____

_____

The memory jungle

Think of your memory as a vast, overgrown jungle. This memory jungle is thick with wild plants, exotic shrubs, twisted trees, and creeping vines. It spreads over thousands of square miles—dense, tangled, forbidding. Imagine that the jungle is bounded on all sides by towering mountains.

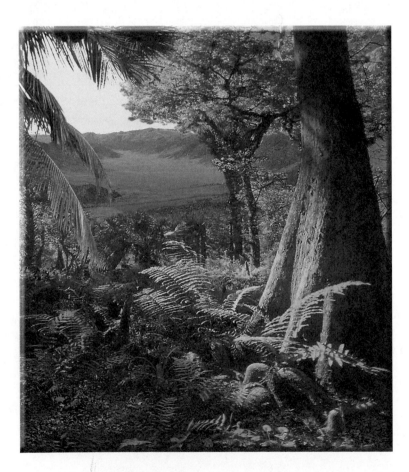

There is only one entrance to the jungle, a small meadow that is reached by a narrow pass through the mountains.

In the jungle there are animals, millions of them. The animals represent all of the information in your memory. Imagine that every thought, picture, or perception you ever had is represented by an animal in this jungle. Every single event ever perceived by any of your five senses—sight, touch, hearing, smell, or taste—has also passed through the meadow and entered the jungle. Some of the thought animals, such as the color of your seventh-grade teacher's eyes, are well hidden. Other thoughts, such as your cell phone number or the position of the reverse gear in your car, are easier to find.

There are two rules of the memory jungle. Each thought animal must pass through the meadow at the entrance to the jungle. And once an animal enters the jungle, it never leaves.

The meadow represents short-term memory. You use this kind of memory when you look up a telephone number and hold it in your memory long enough to make a call. Short-term memory appears to have a limited capacity (the meadow is small) and disappears fast (animals pass through the meadow quickly).

The jungle itself represents long-term memory. This is the kind of memory that allows us to recall information from day to day, week to week, and year to year. Remember that thought animals never leave the long-term memory jungle.

The following visualizations can help you recall useful concepts about memory.

Visualization #1: A well-worn path

Imagine what happens as a thought, in this case we'll call it a deer, bounds across short-term memory and into the jungle. The deer leaves a trail of broken twigs and hoof prints that you can follow. Brain research suggests that thoughts can wear paths in the memory.[2] These paths are called *neural traces*. The more well-worn the neural trace, the easier it is to retrieve (find) the thought. In other words, the more often the deer retraces the path, the clearer the path becomes. The more often you recall information, and the more often you put the same information into your memory, the easier it is to find.

When you buy a new car, for example, the first few times you try to find reverse, you have to think for a moment. After you have found reverse gear every day for a week, the path is worn into your memory. After a year, the path is so well-worn that when you dream about driving your car backward, you even dream the correct motion for putting the gear in reverse.

Visualization #2: A herd of thoughts

The second picture you can use to your advantage is the picture of many animals gathering at a clearing—like thoughts gathering at a central location in the memory. It is easier to retrieve thoughts that are grouped together, just as it is easier to find a herd of animals than it is to find a single deer.

Pieces of information are easier to recall if you can associate them with similar information. For example, you can more readily remember a particular player's batting average if you can associate it with other baseball statistics.

Visualization #3: Turning your back

Imagine releasing the deer into the jungle, turning your back on it, and counting to 10. When you turn around, the deer is gone. This is exactly what happens to most of the information you receive.

Generally, we can recall only 50 percent of the material we have just read. Within 24 hours, most of us can recall only about 20 percent. This means that 80 percent of the material has not been stored and is wandering around, lost in the memory jungle.

The remedy is simple: Review quickly. Do not take your eyes off the thought animal as it crosses the short-

term memory meadow, and review it soon after it enters the long-term memory jungle. Wear a path in your memory immediately.

Visualization #4: You are directing the animal traffic

The fourth picture is one with you in it. You are standing at the entrance to the short-term memory meadow, directing herds of thought animals as they file through the pass, across the meadow, and into your long-term memory. You are taking an active role in the learning process. You are paying attention. You are doing more than sitting on a rock and watching the animals file past into your brain. You become part of the process, and as you do, you take control of your memory.

To experience an online version of these visualizations, visit Houghton Mifflin's College Survival/Becoming a Master Student web site: **http://collegesurvival.college.hmco.com/students.**

20 memory techniques

Experiment with these techniques to make a flexible, custom-made memory system that fits your style of learning. The 20 techniques are divided into four categories, each of which represents a general principle for improving memory.

Briefly, the categories are:

1. *Organize it.* Organized information is easier to find.

2. *Use your body.* Learning is an active process; get all of your senses involved.

3. *Use your brain.* Work *with* your memory, not *against* it.

4. *Recall it.* This is easier when you use the other principles to store information.

The first three categories, which include techniques #1 through #16, are about storing information effectively. Most memory battles are won or lost here.

To get the most out of this article, first survey the following techniques by reading each heading. Then read the techniques. Next, skim them again, looking for the ones you like best.

Mark those and use them.

Organize it

1 Learn from the general to the specific.
Imagine looking at a new painting this way: Blindfold yourself, put a magnifying glass up to your eye, and move your face to within inches of the painting. Now yank the blindfold off and begin studying the painting, one square inch at a time. Chances are, even after you finish looking at the painting this way, you won't know what it is.

Unfortunately, many students approach new courses and textbooks just this way. They feel driven to jump right in and tackle the details before they get the big picture.

Here is a different approach. Before you begin your next reading assignment, skim it for the general idea. You can use the same techniques you learned in Exercise #1: "Textbook reconnaissance" on page 1.

You can also use this technique at the beginning of a course. Ask someone who has already taken it to quickly review it with you. Do a textbook reconnaissance of the reading assignments for the entire course. This technique works best at the beginning of a term, but it's never too late to use it.

If you're lost, step back and look at the big picture. The details might make more sense.

2 Make it meaningful.
A skydiver will not become bored learning how to pack her parachute. Her reward for learning the skill is too important. Know what you want from your education, then look for connections between what you want and what you are studying. If you're bogged down in quadratic equations, stand back for a minute. Think about how that math course relates to your goal of becoming an electrical engineer.

When information helps you get something you want, it's easier to remember. That is one reason why it pays to be specific about what you want.

3 **Create associations.** The data already stored in your memory is arranged according to a scheme that makes sense to you. When you introduce new data, you can recall it more effectively if you store it near similar or related data.

Say you are introduced to someone named Margarita. One way to remember her name would be to visualize another person you know named Margarita. When you see the new Margarita again, your mind is more likely to associate her with the Margarita you already know.

Use your body

4 **Learn it once, actively.** According to an old saying, we remember 90 percent of what we do, 75 percent of what we see, and 20 percent of what we hear.

These percentages might not be scientifically provable, but the idea behind them is sound. Action is a great memory enhancer. You can test this theory by studying your assignments with the same energy that you bring to the dance floor or the basketball court.

This technique illustrates the practical advantage of knowing about learning styles. In Chapter One, the article "Learning styles—Discovering how you learn" explains four aspects of learning: concrete experience, abstract conceptualization, active experimentation, and reflective observation. Many courses in higher education lean heavily toward abstract conceptualization, that is, lectures, papers, and textbooks. Such courses might not give you the chance to act on ideas, experiment with them, and test them in situations outside the classroom.

So create those opportunities yourself. For example, your introductory psychology book probably offers some theories about how people remember information. Choose one of those theories and test it on yourself. See if you can turn that theory into a new memory technique.

Your English teacher might tell you that one quality of effective writing is clear organization. To test this idea, examine the texts you come in contact with daily—newspapers, popular magazines, web sites, and textbooks. Look for examples of clear organization *and* unclear organization. Then write Intention Statements about ways to organize your own writing more clearly.

Your sociology class might include a discussion about how groups of people resolve conflict. See if you can apply any of these ideas to resolving conflict in your own family. Then write Discovery Statements about your experiences.

The point behind each of these examples is the same: To remember an idea, go beyond thinking about it. *Do* something with it.

You can use simple, direct methods to infuse your learning with action. When you sit at your desk, sit up straight. Sit on the edge of your chair, as if you were about to spring out of it and sprint across the room.

Also experiment with standing up when you study. It's harder to fall asleep in this position. Some people insist that their brains work better when they stand.

Pace back and forth and gesture as you recite material out loud. Use your hands. Get your whole body involved in studying.

These techniques are also great ways to battle boredom. Boredom puts memory to sleep. Wake it up by using your arms and legs as well as your eyes, ears, and voice.

Learning can be deceptive. Most learning, especially in higher education, takes place in a passive setting. Students are seated, quiet, and subdued.

Don't be fooled. Learning takes energy. When you learn effectively, you are burning calories, even if you are sitting at a desk reading a textbook.

5 **Relax.** When you're relaxed, you absorb new information quickly and recall it with greater ease and accuracy.

Part of this is common sense. Students who can't recall information under the stress of a final exam can often recite the same facts later when they are relaxed.

Relaxing might seem to contradict the idea of active learning in technique #4, but it doesn't. Being relaxed is not the same as being drowsy, zoned out, or asleep. Relaxation is a state of alertness, free of tension, during which your mind can play with new information, rolling it around and creating associations with it, and apply many of the other memory techniques. You can be active *and* relaxed.

Many books, tapes, and seminars are available to teach you ways to relax. Courses in accelerated and "whole mind" learning also teach relaxation techniques. In addition, relaxation exercises are included in this book. Experiment with these exercises and apply them as you study.

"Mellowing out" might do more than lower your blood pressure. It might help you succeed in school.

6 _Create pictures._ Draw diagrams. Make cartoons. Use these images to connect facts and illustrate relationships. Associations within and among abstract concepts can be "seen" and recalled more easily when they are visualized. The key is to use your imagination.

For example, Boyle's law states that at a constant temperature, the volume of a confined ideal gas varies inversely with its pressure. Simply put, cutting the volume in half doubles the pressure. To remember this concept, you might picture someone "doubled over" using a bicycle pump. As she increases the pressure in the pump by decreasing the volume in the pump cylinder, she seems to be getting angrier. By the time she has doubled the pressure (and halved the volume) she is boiling ("Boyle-ing") mad.

Another reason to create pictures is that visual information is associated with a different part of the brain than the part that processes verbal information. When you create a picture of a concept, you are anchoring the information in a second part of your brain. This increases your chances of recalling that information.

To visualize abstract relationships effectively, create an action-oriented image, such as the person using the pump. Make the picture vivid, too. The person's face could be bright red. And involve all of your senses. Imagine how the cold metal of the pump would feel and how the person would grunt as she struggled with it. (Most of us would have to struggle. It would take incredible strength to double the pressure in a bicycle pump, not to mention a darn sturdy pump.)

7 _Recite and repeat._ When you repeat something out loud, you anchor the concept in two different senses. First, you get the physical sensation in your throat, tongue, and lips when voicing the concept. Second, you hear it. The combined result is synergistic, just as it is when you create pictures. That is, the effect of using two different senses is greater than the sum of their individual effects.

The "out loud" part is important. Reciting silently, in your head, can be useful—in the library, for example—but it is not as effective as making noise. Your mind can trick itself into thinking it knows something when it doesn't. Your ears are harder to fool.

The repetition part is important, too. Repetition is the most common memory device because it works. Repetition blazes a trail through the pathways of your brain, making the information easier to find. Repeat a concept out loud until you know it, then say it five more times.

Recitation works best when you recite concepts in your own words. For example, if you want to remember that the acceleration of a falling body due to gravity at sea level equals 32 feet per second per second, you might say, "Gravity makes an object accelerate 32 feet per second faster for each second that it's in the air at sea level." Putting it in your own words forces you to think about it.

Have some fun with this technique. Recite by writing a song about what you're learning. Sing it in the shower. Use any style you want ("Country, jazz, rock, or rap; when you sing out loud, learning's a snap!").

Or imitate someone. Imagine your textbook being read by Bill Cosby, Madonna, or Clint Eastwood ("Go ahead, punk. Make my density equal mass over volume").

Recite and repeat.

It's a technique you can use anywhere.

8 _Write it down._ This technique is obvious, yet easy to forget. Writing a note to yourself helps you remember an idea, even if you never look at the note again.

You can extend this technique by writing it down not just once, but many times. Let go of the old image of being in elementary school and being forced to write "I will not throw paper wads" 100 times on the chalkboard after school. Used with items that you choose to remember, repetitive writing is a powerful technique.

Writing engages a different kind of memory than speaking. Writing prompts us to be more logical, coherent, and complete. Written reviews reveal gaps in knowledge that oral reviews miss, just as oral reviews reveal gaps that written reviews miss.

Another advantage of written reviews is that they more closely match the way you're asked to remember materials in school. During your academic career, you'll probably take far more written exams than oral exams. Writing can be an effective way to prepare for such tests.

Finally, writing is physical. Your arm, your hand, and your fingers join in. Remember, you remember what you do.

Use your brain

9 _Reduce interference._ Turn off the music when you study. Find a quiet place that is free from distractions. If there's a party at your house, go to the library. If you have a strong attraction to food, don't torment yourself by studying next to the refrigerator.

Two hours of studying in front of the television might be worth 10 minutes of studying where it is quiet. If you have two hours in which to study _and_ watch television, it's probably better to study for an hour and then watch television for an hour. Doing one activity at a time increases your ability to remember.

10 *Overlearn.* One way to fight mental fuzziness is to learn more than you need to know about a subject simply to pass a test. Another option is to pick a subject apart, to examine it, add to it, and go over it until it becomes second nature.

This technique is especially effective for problem solving. Do the assigned problems, then do more problems. Find another text and work similar problems. Make up your own problems and work those. When you pretest yourself in this way, the potential rewards are speed, accuracy, and greater confidence at exam time.

11 *Escape the short-term memory trap.* Short-term memory is different from the kind of memory you'll need during exam week. For example, most of us can look at an unfamiliar seven-digit phone number once and remember it long enough to dial it. See if you can recall that number the next day.

Short-term memory can fade after a few minutes, and it rarely lasts more than several hours. A short review within minutes or hours of a study session can move material from short-term memory into long-term memory. That quick minireview can save you hours of study time when exams roll around.

12 *Use daylight.* Study your most difficult subjects during daylight hours. Many people can concentrate more effectively during the day. The early morning hours can be especially productive, even for people who hate to get up with the sun.

13 *Distribute learning.* As an alternative to marathon study sessions, experiment with shorter, spaced-out sessions. You might find that you can get far more done in three two-hour sessions than in one six-hour session.

For example, when you are studying for your American history exam, study for an hour or two and then wash the dishes. While you are washing the dishes, part of your mind will be reviewing what you studied. Return to American history for a while, then call a friend. Even when you are deep in conversation, part of your mind will be reviewing history.

You can get more done if you take regular breaks. You can even use the breaks as minirewards. After a productive study session, give yourself permission to log on and check your email, listen to a song, or play 10 minutes of hide-and-seek with your kids.

There is an exception to this idea. When you are engrossed in a textbook and cannot put it down, when you are consumed by an idea for a term paper and cannot

think of anything else—keep going. The master student within you has taken over. Enjoy the ride.

14 *Be aware of attitudes.* People who think history is boring tend to have trouble remembering dates and historical events. People who believe math is difficult often have a hard time recalling mathematical equations and formulas. All of us can forget information that contradicts our opinions.

Being aware of attitudes is not the same as fighting them or struggling to give them up. Simply acknowledge them. Notice them. Your awareness can deflate an attitude that is blocking your memory.

One way to befriend a self-defeating attitude about a subject is to relate it to something you are interested in. For example, consider a person who is fanatical about cars. She can rebuild a motor in a weekend and has a good time doing so. From this apparently specialized interest, she can explore a wide realm of knowledge. She can relate the workings of an engine to principles of physics, math, and chemistry. Computerized parts in newer cars can lead her to the study of data processing. She can research how cars have changed our cities and helped create suburbs, a topic that includes urban planning, sociology, business, economics, psychology, and history.

We remember what we find interesting. If you think a subject is boring, remember that everything is related to everything else. Look for connections that relate to your own interests.

15 *Choose what not to store in memory.* We can adopt an "information diet." Just as we choose to avoid certain foods in our diet, we can choose not to retain certain kinds of information in our memory.

Decide what's essential to remember from a reading assignment or lecture. Extract the core concepts. Ask what you'll be tested on, as well as what you want to remember. Then apply memory techniques to those ideas.

16 *Combine memory techniques.* All of these memory techniques work even better in combination. Choose two or three techniques to use on a particular assignment, and experiment for yourself.

For example, after you take a few minutes to get an overview of a reading assignment (#1), you could draw a quick picture to represent the main point (#6). Or you could overlearn that math formula (#10) by singing a jingle about it (#7) all the way to work. If you have an attitude that math is difficult, you could acknowledge that (#14); then you could distribute your study time in short, easy-to-handle sessions (#13). Combining memory techniques involves combining sight, sound, and touch when you study. The effect is synergistic.

Recall it

17 *Remember something else.* When you are stuck and can't remember something that you're sure you know, remember something else that is related to it.

If you can't remember your great-aunt's name, remember your great-uncle's name. During an economics exam, if you can't remember anything about the aggregate demand curve, recall what you do know about the aggregate supply curve. If you cannot recall specific facts, remember the example that the instructor used during her lecture. Information is stored in the same area of the brain as similar information. You can unblock your recall by stimulating that area of your memory.

You can take this technique one step further with a process that psychologists call *elaboration*.[3] The key is to ask questions that prompt you to create more associations. For example, when you meet someone new, ask yourself: What are the distinctive features of this person's face? Does she remind me of someone else?

A brainstorm is a good memory jog. If you are stumped when taking a test, start writing down lots of answers to related questions, and—pop!—the answer you need is likely to appear.

18 *Notice when you do remember.* Everyone has a different memory style. Some people are best at recalling information they've read. Others have an easier time remembering what they've heard, seen, or done.

To develop your memory, notice when you recall information easily and ask yourself what memory techniques you're using naturally. Also notice when it's difficult to recall information. Be a reporter. Get the facts and then adjust your learning techniques. And remember to congratulate yourself when you remember.

19 *Use it before you lose it.* Even information stored in long-term memory becomes difficult to recall when we don't use it regularly. The pathways to the stored information become faint with disuse. For example, you can probably remember your current phone number. What was your phone number 10 years ago?

This points to a powerful memory technique. To remember something, access it a lot. Read it, write it, speak it, listen to it, apply it—find some way to make contact with the material regularly. Each time you do so, you widen the neural pathway to the material and make it easier to recall the next time.

Another way to contact the material is to teach it. Teaching demands mastery. When you explain the function of the pancreas to a fellow student, you discover quickly whether you really understand the pancreas.

Study groups are especially effective because they put you on stage. The friendly pressure of knowing you'll teach the group helps focus your attention.

20 *And remember, you never forget.* You might not believe that an idea or thought never leaves your memory. That's OK. In fact, it doesn't matter whether you agree with the idea or not. It can work for you anyway.

Test the concept. Adopt an attitude that says, "I never forget anything. I might have difficulty recalling something from my memory, but I never really forget it. I will find out where I stored it." The intention to remember can be more powerful than any memory technique.

Many people use the flip side of this technique and get the opposite results. "I never remember anything," they say over and over again. "I've always had a poor memory. I'm such a scatterbrain." That kind of negative self-talk is self-fulfilling.

An alternative is to speak more positively, or at least more accurately. Instead of saying, "I don't remember," you can say, "It will come to me." The latter statement implies that the information you want is stored in your mind and that you can retrieve it—just not right now.

We can also use affirmations that support us as we develop our memories. Possibilities include "I recall information easily and accurately," "At any time I choose, I will be able to recall key facts and ideas," and "My memory serves me well."

Or even "I never forget!"

Set a trap for your
memory

When you want to remind yourself to do something, link that activity to another event that you know will take place.

The key is to "trap" your memory by picking events that are certain to occur.

Say you're walking to class and suddenly remember that your accounting assignment is due tomorrow. Switch your watch to the opposite wrist. Now you're "trapped." Every time you glance at your wrist and remember that you have switched your watch, it becomes a reminder that you were supposed to remember something else. (You can do the same with a ring.)

If you empty your pockets every night, put an unusual item in your pocket to remind yourself to do something before you go to bed. For example, to remember to call your younger sister on her birthday, pick an object from the playpen—a teething toy, perhaps—and put it in your pocket. That evening, when you empty your pocket and find the teething toy, you're more likely to make the call.

Everyday rituals such as feeding a pet, reaching for car keys, and unlacing shoes are seldom forgotten. Tie a triple knot in your shoelace as a reminder to set the alarm for your early morning study group meeting.

You can even use imaginary traps. To remember to write a check for the phone bill, picture your phone hanging on the front door. In your mind, create the feeling of reaching for the doorknob and grabbing the phone instead. When you get home and reach to open the front door, the image is apt to return to you.

Link two activities together, and make the association unusual.

Remembering your car keys . . . or anything else

Pick something you frequently forget. Some people chronically lose their car keys or forget to write down checks in their check register. Others let anniversaries and birthdays slip by.

Pick your forgettable item or task. Then design a strategy for remembering it. You are on your own, and you are your own best expert. Use any of the techniques from this chapter, research other techniques, or design your own from scratch. Describe your technique and the results on a separate sheet of paper.

In this exercise, as in most of the exercises in this book, a failure is also a success. If you failed, you have at least succeeded in discovering a technique that didn't work for you this time. Don't be concerned with whether your technique will work. Design it; then find out. If it doesn't work, use another method.

Give your "*secret brain*" a chance

Sometimes the way you combine studying with other activities can affect how well you remember information. For example, memory technique #11, "Escape the short-term memory trap," suggests reviewing or reflecting on material shortly after you learn it. This is one way to avoid what psychologists call *retroactive inhibition*, something that can happen when a new, unrelated activity interferes with previous learning. Reviewing prevents such a conflict and allows your brain to store information more effectively in your long-term memory. This kind of learning takes place at a level below conscious awareness. Consider the following scenarios.

Scenario #1

You've just left your evening psychology class after a fascinating lecture on Sigmund Freud's theory of dreams. You want to make it home in time to tuck your children in bed, so you hurry out of class. In five minutes you're cruising down the highway. You decide to flip on the radio as you drive. Doesn't matter what station, just something to help you unwind. After all, it's been a long day—nine hours at the office and three in class. You deserve a break. Later, just before going to sleep, you decide to sneak in a few pages of that mystery novel you've wanted to finish. After you find out who poisoned the butler, you settle in for a well-deserved rest.

Scenario #2

Instead of driving yourself home after your "session with Sigmund," you have arranged to car-pool with a classmate. On the way home, you talk about the lecture. The discussion ignites into a debate as you and your friend take opposite stands on a key point of Freud's theory. After you arrive home, you take some time to check in with your children and talk about the day. Later, just before going to sleep, you mull over the conversation and make a mental note to write down your dreams in the morning. You decide to let the mystery novel wait until tomorrow night.

In the morning, you write down your dreams and explain last night's lecture to your children at breakfast. While you slept, your brain was not only manufacturing dreams but also storing the key points of Freud's theory— something that will come in handy for the mid-term exam. In short, you expended the same amount of energy, had the same amount of fun, and saved yourself hours of review time later in the term. Nice work.

NOTABLE FAILURES

PART ONE

Creative and imaginative people are often not recognized by their contemporaries. Even more often, their abilities are not recognized by their teachers or employers. History is full of examples.

Einstein was four years old before he could speak and seven before he could read. **Isaac Newton** did poorly in grade school. **Beethoven's** music teacher once said of him, "As a composer he is hopeless."

When **Thomas Edison** was a boy, his teachers told him he was too stupid to learn anything. **F. W. Woolworth** got a job in a dry goods store when he was 21, but his employers would not let him wait on customers because he "didn't have enough sense."

A newspaper editor fired **Walt Disney,** claiming that he had "no good ideas." **Caruso's** music teacher told him, "You can't sing. You have no voice at all." The director of the Imperial Opera in Vienna told **Madame Schumann-Heink** that she would never be a singer and advised her to buy a sewing machine. **Leo Tolstoy** flunked out of college. **Wernher von Braun** flunked ninth-grade algebra. **Admiral Richard E. Byrd** had been retired from the navy as "unfit for service" until he flew over both Poles.

Louis Pasteur was rated as "mediocre" in chemistry when he attended the Royal College. **Abraham Lincoln** entered the Black Hawk War as a captain and came out as a private. **Louisa May Alcott** was told by an editor that she could never write anything that would have popular appeal. **Fred Waring** was once rejected for high school chorus. **Winston Churchill** failed the sixth grade.

"Humbling Cases for Career Counselors" by Dr. Milton E. Larson from Phi Delta Kappan, *February 1973 issue, Volume LIV, No. 6, p. 374, © 1973. Reprinted by permission.*

PRACTICING CRITICAL THINKING #4

One key to memory is focused attention and observation. Apply this idea by carefully observing an educational building in your city or town or a classroom in your school. From your observation, infer the educational philosophy of the person who designed this physical space.

For example, consider the layout of a large classroom with a podium in front for one speaker and seats for several hundred members of an audience. This design could flow from the following assumptions:

- Lectures are an ideal way to convey information and ideas.

- Large class sizes can be just as effective as small class sizes.

- One person at a time should do most of the talking, and the other people should be listening.

- Students should listen primarily to the speaker at the front of the room, not to other students.

On a separate piece of paper, describe the classroom or educational building you've chosen to observe, along with your inferences. What did the person who designed this structure think about how education is supposed to happen?

JOURNAL ENTRY #14

Discovery Statement

Take a minute to reflect on the memory techniques in this chapter. You already use some of these techniques without being conscious of them. In the space below, list at least three techniques you have used in the past and describe how you used them.

Remembering names

One powerful way to immediately practice memory techniques is to use them to remember names.

Recite and repeat in conversation.
When you hear a person's name, repeat it. Immediately say it to yourself several times without moving your lips. You could also repeat the name out loud in a way that does not sound forced or artificial: "I'm pleased to meet you, Maria."

Ask the other person to recite and repeat.
You can let other people help you remember their names. After you've been introduced to someone, ask that person to spell the name and pronounce it correctly for you. Most people will be flattered by the effort you're making to learn their names.

Visualize.
After the conversation, construct a brief visual image of the person. For a memorable image, make it unusual. Imagine the name painted in hot pink fluorescent letters on the person's forehead.

Admit you don't know.
Admitting that you can't remember someone's name can actually put people at ease. Most of them will sympathize if you say, "I'm working to remember names better. Yours is right on the tip of my tongue. What is it again?" (By the way, that's exactly what psychologists call that feeling—the "tip of the tongue" phenomenon.)

Introduce yourself again.
Most of the time we assume introductions are one-shot affairs. If we miss a name the first time around, our hopes for remembering it are dashed. Instead of giving up, introduce yourself again: "Hello, again. We met earlier. I'm Jesse, and please tell me your name again."

Use associations.
Link each person you meet with one characteristic that you find interesting or unusual. For example, you could make a mental note: "Vicki Cheng—long, black hair" or "James Washington—horn-rimmed glasses." To reinforce your associations, write them on 3×5 cards as soon as you can.

Limit the number of new names you learn at one time.
Occasionally, we find ourselves in situations where we're introduced to many people at the same time: "Dad, these are all the people in my Boy Scout troop." "Let's take a tour so you can meet all 32 people in this department."

When meeting a group of people, concentrate on remembering just two or three names. Free yourself from feeling obligated to remember everyone. Few of the people in mass introductions expect you to remember their names. Another way to avoid memory overload is to limit yourself to learning just first names. Last names can come later.

Ask for photos.
In some cases, you might be able to get photos of all the people you meet. For example, a small business where you apply for a job might have a brochure with pictures of all the employees. Ask for individual or group photos and write in the names if they're not included. You can use these photos as "flash cards" as you drill yourself on names.

Go early.
Consider going early to conventions, parties, and classes. Sometimes just a few people show up on time at these occasions. That's fewer names for you to remember. And as more people arrive, you can overhear them being introduced to others—an automatic review for you.

Make it a game.
In situations where many people are new to one another, consider pairing up with another person and staging a contest. Challenge each other to remember as many new names as possible. Then choose an "award"—such as a movie ticket or free meal—for the person who wins.

WORKPLACE APPLICATIONS

Remembering names is a big plus when meeting new people in job settings and when making future job contacts. Read "Remembering names" for ways to master this important social skill.

MNEMONIC devices

It's pronounced *ne-mon´-ik*. It's a trick that can increase your ability to recall everything, from speeches to grocery lists. Some entertainers use mnemonic devices to perform "impossible" feats of memory, such as recalling the names of everyone in a large audience after hearing them just once. Waiters using this technique to take orders can then serve food correctly without the aid of pad and pencil. Using mnemonic devices, speakers can go for hours without looking at their notes. The possibilities for students are endless.

There is a catch. Mnemonic devices have three serious limitations. First, they don't always help you understand or digest material. Instead of encouraging critical thinking skills, mnemonics rely only on rote memorization. Second, the mnemonic device itself is sometimes complicated to learn and time-consuming to develop. It might take more energy to create such a device than to memorize something by using a more traditional memory technique, such as repetition. Third, mnemonic devices can be forgotten. Recalling a mnemonic device might be as hard as recalling the material itself.

In spite of their limitations, mnemonic devices are powerful. There are four general categories: new words, creative sentences, rhymes and songs, and special systems, including the loci and peg systems.

MNEMONIC devices (continued)

New words.

Acronyms are words created from the initial letters of a series of words. Examples include NASA (**N**ational **A**eronautics and **S**pace **A**dministration), radar (**ra**dio **d**etecting **a**nd **r**anging), scuba (**s**elf-**c**ontained **u**nderwater **b**reathing **a**pparatus), and laser (**l**ight **a**mplification by **s**timulated **e**mission of **r**adiation). You can make up your own acronyms to recall series of facts. A common mnemonic acronym is Roy G. Biv, which has helped thousands of students remember the colors of the visible spectrum (**r**ed, **o**range, **y**ellow, **g**reen, **b**lue, **i**ndigo, and **v**iolet). IPMAT helps biology students remember the stages of cell division (**i**nterphase, **p**rophase, **m**etaphase, **a**naphase, and **t**elophase).

Creative sentences.

Acrostics are sentences that help you remember a series of letters that stand for something. For example, the first letters of the words in the sentence "Every good boy does fine" (E, G, B, D, and F) are the music notes of the lines of the treble clef staff.

Rhymes and songs.

Madison Avenue advertising executives spend billions of dollars a year on commercials designed to burn their messages into your memory. Coca-Cola's song, "It's the Real Thing," practically stands for Coca-Cola, despite the fact that the soda contains artificial ingredients.

Rhymes have been used for centuries to teach children basic facts: "In fourteen hundred and ninety-two, Columbus sailed the ocean blue" or "Thirty days hath September. . . ."

Systems—loci and peg.

Use the *loci system* to create visual associations with familiar locations. It can also help you remember things in a particular order.

The loci system is an old one. Ancient Greek orators used it to remember long speeches. For example, if an orator's position was that road taxes must be raised to pay for school equipment, his loci visualizations might have looked like the following.

First, as he walks in the door of his house, he imagines a large *porpoise* jumping through a hoop. This reminds him to begin by telling the audience the *purpose* of his speech. Next, he visualizes his living room floor covered with paving stones, forming a road leading into the kitchen. In the kitchen, he pictures dozens of school children sitting on the floor because they have no desks.

Now it's the day of the big speech. The Greek politician is nervous. He is perspiring, and his toga sticks to his body. He stands up to give his speech, and his mind goes blank. "No problem," he thinks to himself. "I am so nervous that I can hardly remember my name. But I *can* remember the rooms in my house. Let's see, I'm walking in the front door and—wow! I see the porpoise. Oh, yeah, that reminds me to talk about the purpose of my speech."

Unusual associations are the easiest to remember. This system can also be adapted to locations in your body. You can visually link things you want to remember with places under your skin. The shopping list is remembered when you recall the visualizations of a loaf of bread stuck in your brain cavity, a large can of frozen orange juice squeezed into your larynx, a bunch of broccoli tucked under your collar bone, etc.

The *peg system* employs key words represented by numbers. For example, 1 = bun, 2 = shoe, 3 = tree, 4 = door, 5 = hive, 6 = sticks, 7 = heaven, 8 = gate, 9 = wine, and 10 = hen. In order for this system to be effective, these peg words need to be learned well.

You might use the peg system to remember that the speed of light is 186,000 miles per second. Imagine a hamburger bun (1) entering a gate (8) made of sticks (6). Since we tend to remember pictures longer than we do words, it might be easier to recall this weird scene than the numbers 1, 8, and 6 in order.

Q: *How can a bun crashing through a gate of sticks help you remember the speed of light?*

A: *With the peg system, bun = 1, gate = 8, sticks = 6 (the speed of light is 186,000 miles per second).*

EXERCISE

Be a poet

Construct your own mnemonic device for remembering some of the memory techniques in this chapter. Make up a poem, jingle, acronym, or acrostic, or use another mnemonic system. Describe your mnemonic device in the space below.

_____

_____

_____

_____

_____

_____

EXERCISE

Master review schedule

This exercise will give you an opportunity to step back and look at your review habits. The more difficult it is for you to find time for review, the greater the benefit of this exercise.

Your basic tool is a one-month calendar. Use it to block out specific times to review key subjects. (See the example on pages 101–102.) Mark the appropriate dates of the month in the upper left-hand corner of every square. Then schedule weekly review periods for each subject.

You might want to copy this form onto both sides of a sheet of paper. Or make several copies of this form and tape them together so that you can see several months at a glance. If you already use a monthly or weekly planner, use it to schedule your review time.

Schedule at least two major review periods for each course. The length of these review periods could range from two to five hours, depending on your needs. Use your imagination and skill to create extra review time.

Besides scheduling review time, you can use your calendar to record assignments, log day-to-day changes in your health or moods, list the places you visit while you are on vacation, or note each day that you practice a new habit.

You can download a blank monthly calendar on Houghton Mifflin's College Survival/Becoming a Master Student web site: http://collegesurvival.college.hmco.com/students.

NOTABLE FAILURES

PART TWO

People often fail—or at least are told they are failures—many times before they reach their goals. Consider the following examples.

Albert Einstein's parents thought he was retarded. He spoke haltingly until age 9, and after that he answered questions only after laboring in thought about them. He was advised by a teacher to drop out of high school: "You'll never amount to anything, Einstein."

Charles Darwin's father said to his son, "You will be a disgrace to yourself and all your family." (Darwin did poorly in school.)

Henry Ford barely made it through high school.

Sir Isaac Newton did poorly in school and was allowed to continue only because he failed at running the family farm.

Pablo Picasso was pulled out of school at age 10 because he was doing so poorly. A tutor hired by Pablo's father gave up on Pablo.

Giacomo Puccini's first music teacher said that Puccini had no talent for music. Later Puccini composed some of the world's greatest operas.

The machines of the world's greatest inventor, **Leonardo da Vinci,** were never built, and many wouldn't have worked anyway.

Clarence Darrow became a legend in the courtroom as he lost case after case.

Edwin Land's attempts at instant movies (Polarvision) failed completely. He described his efforts as trying to use an impossible chemistry and a nonexistent technology to make an unmanufacturable product for which there was no discernible demand.

After the success of the show *South Pacific*, composer **Oscar Hammerstein** put an ad in *Variety* that listed over a dozen of his failures. At the bottom of the ad, he repeated the credo of show business, "I did it before, and I can do it again."

Asked once about how he felt when his team lost a game, **Joe Paterno,** coach of the Penn State University football team, replied that losing was probably good for them since that was how the players learned what they were doing wrong.

R. Buckminster Fuller built his geodesic domes by starting with a deliberately failed dome and making

it "a little stronger and a little stronger . . . a little piece of wood here and a little piece of wood there, and suddenly it stood up."

Igor Stravinsky said, "I have learned throughout my life as a composer chiefly through my mistakes and pursuits of false assumptions, not by my exposure to the founts of wisdom and knowledge."

Charles Goodyear bungled an experiment and discovered vulcanized rubber.

Before gaining an international reputation as a painter, **Paul Gauguin** was a failed stockbroker.

The game MONOPOLY® was developed by **Charles Darrow,** an unemployed heating engineer. Darrow presented his first version of the game to a toy company in 1935. That company originally rejected the game for containing 52 "fundamental errors." Today the game is so successful that its publisher, Parker Brothers, prints more than $40 billion of MONOPOLY® money each year. That's twice the amount of real money printed annually by the U.S. mint.

Robert Pirsig's best-selling book, *Zen and the Art of Motorcycle Maintenance*, was rejected by 121 publishers.

Spike Lee applied for graduate study at the top film schools in the country, including the University of Southern California and the University of California at Los Angeles. Due to his scores on the Graduate Record Exam, both schools turned Lee down.

Jaime Escalante is a nationally known educator and the subject of the film *Stand and Deliver*. When he first tried to get a teaching job in California, the state refused to accept his teaching credentials from Bolivia.

Before **Alan Page** became the first African American to sit on the Minnesota Supreme Court, he played in the American Football League. Seeking a career change, he entered law school. After three weeks he dropped out and did not enroll again for another eight years.

Before the career planning book *What Color Is Your Parachute?* became a perennial best-seller, author **Richard Nelson Bolles** got laid off from a job and ended up broke. One Friday in 1971, his cash reserves included only the $5.18 in his pocket. Bolles sold two copies of his book that day and was able to survive through the weekend. Today, *What Color Is Your Parachute?* sells nearly 20,000 copies every month.

Monday	Tuesday	Wednesday	Thursday	Friday	Saturday	Sunday

Name _____

Month _____

Name ———

Month ———

Monday	Tuesday	Wednesday	Thursday	Friday	Saturday	Sunday

Calendar 1 (top, partially visible)

	Tuesday	Wednesday	Thursday	Friday	Saturday
English Lit - MacBeth	2 Biology Review 2 hours	3 Research for Psych paper	4 Biology Review 2hrs / Psych Research / Flute lesson 6pm	5 Algebra Review 2 hrs / Biology Test Ch. 1-8	6 Caitlin's Party!
8 Algebra Test Ch. 8-12 / ⚠ Need longer review next time!	9 1st draft of Psych paper 3 hrs.	10 FREE DAY! NO HOMEWORK YAY! ☺	11 Government Read Ch. 5 / Flute lesson 6pm	12 Mom's Birthday	13 Tennis Tournament
15 Algebra Ch. 13 - worksheet due Wed.	16 2nd draft of Psych paper 3 hours	17 Get class assignments for next week	18 Psych Rough Draft to Ms Hinzman.	19 Make-Up Biology lab 2-4pm	20 Psych Paper due Monday - 3 hr. editing and rewrite
22 Band trip to Washington, D.C. Arriv...	23 Rehearsal	24 ...	26 Rehearsal	27 Rehearsal / Cherry Blossom Festival Parade WE TOOK FIRST!!	28 HO...

Calendar 2 — Name: STEVE — Month: APRIL

Monday	Tuesday	Wednesday	Thursday	Friday	Saturday	Sunday
			1 • WORK 7:00-4:00 / • Algebra - 4:00-7:00 / • Euro. Hist-7:00-10:00 / • Alg. homework 11:00→?	2 • WORK 7:00-4:00 / • Alg. Lab-4:00-7:00 / • Euro. Hist-7:00-10:00 / • Geology review 11:00→	3 • soccer game 9:00-11:00 / • Kids Fishing / ★ Alg. review / ★ Geol. review 4:00-10:00	4 • Church 8:00-10:00 / • picnic all day long !! / ★ Alg. review / ★ Geol. review 7:00-11:00
5 WORK 7:00-4:00 / ★Alg. quiz-4-7 / ★Hist - 7-10 / ★Geol - read ch. 8 10:00-12:00	6 WORK 7:00-4:00 / ★Algebra - 4-7 / ★Geology 7-10 / ★Hist - read CH 6-7 10:00-1:00	7 WORK 7:00-4:00 / ★Algebra - 4-7 / ★Geology - 7-10 / ★Alg. homework 10:00-12:00	8 WORK 7:00-4:00 / ★Algebra - 4-7 / ★Hist - 7-10 / ★Alg. homework 10:00-12:00 / ★Hist review	9 WORK 7:00-4:00 / ★Algebra Lab 4-7 / ★Hist - 7-10 TEST	10 soccer 8:00-10:00 / ★xard work / • Birthday Party @ 5:00 / • read Hist/Geol	11 • church 7:00-10:00 / ★read/review / • Alg. - 7-9 / • Hist. - 9-10 / • Geol - 10-11
12 WORK 7:00-4:00 / ★Alg. quiz - 4-7 / ★Hist - 7-10 / ★Geol - read CH 9 10:00-12:00	13 WORK 7:00-4:00 / ★Algebra - 4-7 / ★Geology - 7-10 / ★Hist - read CH 8-9 10:00-1:00	14 WORK 7:00-4:00 / ★Algebra - 4-7 / ★Geology - 7-10 / ★Hist - read CH 9-10 10:00-1:00	15 WORK 7:00-4:00 / ★Algebra - 4-7 / ★History 7-10 / ★Geol - read/review 10:00-12:00 (LAB)	16 WORK 7:00-4:00 / ★Algebra Lab 4-7 / ★Hist - 7-10	17 soccer game 8:00-12:00 / • xard work / • bike/hike / read	18 church 8:00-10:00 / ★read review / • Alg - 7-9 / • Hist - 9-10 / • Geol - 10-11
19 WORK 7:00-4:00 / ★Alg. quiz - 4-7 / ★Hist - 7-10 / ★Geol - read CH 10-11 10:00-1:00	20 WORK 7:00-4:00 / ★Algebra - 4-7 / ★Geology - 7-10 / ★Hist - read CH 10 10:00-12:00	21 WORK 7:00-4:00 / ★Algebra - 4-7 / ★Geology - 7-10 / ★Alg - review for Test 10:00-12:00	22 WORK 7:00-4:00 / ★Algebra - 4-7 TEST / ★Hist 7-10 / ★Geol - read/review 10:00-12:00	23 WORK 7:00-4:00 / ★Algebra Lab 4-7 / ★Hist - 7-10	24 soccer game 7:00-11:00 / • review & organize notes for finals	25 church 8:00-10:00 / FINALS REVIEW / • Geol - 12:00-3:00 / • Alg - 3:30-7:00 / • Hist - 8:00-12:00 / • AlgLab - 12:00-1:00
26 WORK 7:00-4:00 / ★Alg. quiz - 4-7 / ★Hist - 7-10 / ★Geol - review for test/final 10:00-12:00	27 WORK 7:00-4:00 / ★Algebra - 4-7 / ★Geology - 7-10 / ★Hist - review for test/final 10:00→?	28 WORK 7:00-4:00 / ★Algebra - 4-7 / ★Geology - 7-10 FINAL	29 WORK 7:00-4:00 / ★Algebra 4-7 FINAL / ★Hist - 7-10 FINAL	30 WORK 7:00-4:00 / ★Algebra Lab 4-7 FINAL		

(left margin: FINALS)

Calendar 3 — Name: Holly — Month: October

	Tuesday					
5 library w/sarah / CPR class 6-10	6 Biology review 10am / Calc I quiz	7 Psych exam / Fight w/ Matt boys are dumb! :^(	8 Biology review 10am / CPR class 6-10	... to Springfield this w...		
12 Ethics quiz / library w/sarah	13 Biology exam / Philosophy review 1-4pm	14 Tiffany's Bday! / rescheduled Hooray! / congrat 1pm!	15 Calc I section review / philosophy review w/molly 1-4 am	16 Dinner w/Mike	17 Harney Peak Hike very fun!	
19 10 am mtg w/Dr. Taft re: advisory committee / lunch w/Mike / World History study group 2-4	20 Calc I section final / philosophy final	21 Spring intern app. due today! / world History study group 2-4	22 Pick up seafoam dress gas! Final fittings 3pm	23 Breanna + Ed's wedding (home this weekend)	24	
26 Ethics mid-term / world history review!	27 senator Jackson speech + rally 6pm	28 world History mid-term	29 English lit term paper due today!	30 Apple orchard / pumpkin picking	31 Halloween party @ Jen's	

(left margin bottom: ...os com ...rm Paper ...e!!)

Love your problems (and experience your barriers)

We all have problems and barriers that block our progress or prevent us from moving into new areas.

Often, the way we respond to our problems puts boundaries on our experiences. We place limitations on what we allow ourselves to be, do, and have.

Our problems might include fear of speaking in front of a group, anxiety about math problems, or reluctance to sound ridiculous when learning a foreign language. We might have a barrier about looking silly when trying something new. Some of us even have anxiety about being successful.

Problems often work like barriers. When we bump up against one of our problems, we usually turn away and start walking along a different path. And all of a sudden—bump!—we've struck another barrier. And we turn away again. As we continue to bump into problems and turn away from them, our lives stay inside the same old boundaries. Inside these boundaries, we are unlikely to have new adventures. We are unlikely to improve or to make much progress.

The word *problem* is a wonderful word coming from the ancient Greek word *proballein,* which means "to throw forward." In other words, problems are there to provide an opportunity for us to gain new skills. If we respond to problems by loving them instead of resisting them, we can expand the boundaries in which we live our lives. When approached with acceptance, and even love, problems can "throw" us forward.

Three ways to handle a barrier

It's natural to have barriers, but sometimes they limit our experience so much that we get bored, angry, or frustrated with life. When this happens, consider the following three ways of dealing with a barrier. One way is to pretend it doesn't exist. Avoid it, deny it, lie about it. It's like turning your head the other way, putting on a fake grin, and saying, "See, there's really no problem at all. Everything is fine. Oh, that problem. That's not a problem—it's not really there."

In addition to making us look foolish, this approach leaves the barrier intact, and we keep bumping into it. We deny the barrier and might not even be aware that we're bumping into it. For example, a student who has a barrier about math might subconsciously avoid enriching experiences that include math.

A second approach is to fight the barrier, to struggle against it. This usually makes the barrier grow. It increases the barrier's magnitude. A person who is obsessed with weight might constantly worry about being fat. She might struggle with it every day, trying diet after diet. And the more she struggles, the bigger the problem gets.

The third alternative is to love the barrier. Accept it. Totally experience it. Tell the truth about it. Describe it in detail. When you do this, the barrier loses its power. You can literally love it to death.

The word *love* might sound like an overstatement. In this Power Process, the word means to accept your problems, to allow and permit them. When we fight a problem, it grows bigger. The more we struggle against it, the stronger it seems to become. When we accept the fact that we have a problem, we are more likely to find effective ways to deal with it.

Suppose one of your barriers is being afraid of speaking in front of a group. You can use any of these three approaches.

First, you can get up in front of the group and pretend that you're not afraid. You can fake a smile, not admitting to yourself or the group that you have any concerns about speaking—even though your legs have turned to rubber bands and your mind to jelly. The problem is that everyone in the room, including you, will know you're scared when your hands start shaking, your voice cracks, and you forget what you were going to say.

The second way to approach this barrier is to fight it. You can tell yourself, "I'm not going to be scared," and then try to keep your knees from knocking. Generally, this doesn't work. In fact, your knee-knocking might get worse.

The third approach is to go to the front of the room, look out into the audience, and say to yourself, "I am scared. I notice that my knees are shaking and my mouth feels dry, and I'm having a rush of thoughts about what might happen if I say the wrong thing. Yup, I'm scared, and that's OK. As a matter of fact, it's just part of me, so I accept it and I'm not going to try to fight it. I'm going to give this speech even though I'm scared."

You might not actually eliminate the fear; however, your barrier about the fear—which is what inhibits you—might disappear. And you might discover that if you examine the fear, love it, accept it, and totally experience it, the fear itself also disappears.

Applying this process

Applying this process is easier if you remember two ideas. First, loving a problem is not necessarily the same as enjoying it. Love in this sense means total and unconditional acceptance.

Second, unconditional acceptance is not the same as unconditional surrender. Accepting a problem does not mean escaping from it or giving up on finding a solution. Rather, this process involves freeing ourselves from the grip of the problem by diving *into* the problem headfirst and getting to know it in detail.

When people first hear about this Power Process, they often think it means to be resigned to the problem. Actually, loving a problem does not stop us from acting.

Loving a problem does not keep us mired in it. In fact, fully accepting and admitting the problem usually assists us in taking effective action—and might help us free ourselves of the problem once and for all.

Love your pain

When we totally experience pain, it often diminishes and sometimes it disappears. This strategy can work with emotions and even with physical pain.

Make it your aim to love the pain, that is, to fully accept the pain and know all the details about it. Most pain has a wavelike quality. It rises, reaches a peak of intensity, and then subsides for a while. See if you can watch the waves as they come and go.

When you are willing to love your problems, you drain them of much of their energy and claim more energy for yourself.

Love your enemies

All of us remember times when we behaved in ways that we regret. Even though these behaviors are part of our past, they don't define who we are. At any given moment, we are capable of behaving in many different ways. We have a history of behaviors, and that history does not have to determine how we behave in the future. Separating ourselves from our behaviors helps us forgive and love ourselves.

We can do the same with others. When a child misbehaves, for example, we can deal with the inappropriate behavior while unconditionally loving the child.

We can even do the same with someone we consider an enemy. The idea of loving someone who is threatening us can be disarming. Remember that you can practice loving while taking whatever actions are appropriate in any given situation. If you are physically attacked, for example, you can defend yourself against the attacking behavior while you practice loving the attacker. If you are

WORKPLACE APPLICATIONS

When applying for jobs, present yourself as someone who can solve a company problem. During a job interview, for example, you might say, "I've found it difficult to order products from your web site. Five people have told me the same thing. I have a list of ideas that could solve this problem." Then explain one item from your list.

emotionally attacked, a hostile response will likely only generate even more hostility. By loving your enemy and responding with grace and dignity, you increase the chances of diminishing the antagonism while inviting productive communication.

A primary advantage of loving your enemy is that it benefits you. Research indicates that highly charged and sustained negative emotions can inflict damage to a person's physical and mental well-being. When facing an enemy, you can practice reversing those negative emotional reactions and at the same time promote your own health.

Cultivate humor

Love and laughter are allies. It's hard to resist or struggle with a problem while we are laughing at it. Humor helps us put troubling circumstances into perspective. When we can genuinely laugh at our problems, they lose power over us and it's easier to love them.

Problems that appear serious today will often seem a bit silly and even funny a few years from now, such as noticing spinach in your teeth after you get home from a first date, having your computer crash after you've worked for days on an important project and forgot to back it up, or misunderstanding a message and showing up two hours late for an important interview.

You don't have to wait weeks, months, or years before you start laughing about such problems. As long as you're going to laugh anyway, why wait? Start now. The sooner you can enjoy the humor in your problems, the sooner you can face them effectively, solve them, and even love them.

Student Voices

I am now 37 years old and have returned to college. I am very apprehensive about this experience. However, I am not trying to conquer my fear. My fear has become my friend. When I embraced my fear it was a moment of enlightenment. I thought I would appear foolish, old, and unsuccessful. By recognizing these feelings and taking away their powers over me, they become harmless. They also became the fuel for my drive for success.

— RICHARD HERBERT

JOURNAL ENTRY #15

Discovery Statement

On a separate sheet of paper, describe one or two barriers that have kept you from getting what you want in school. First, read about barriers as discussed in the Power Process "Love your problems" in this chapter. If you have trouble identifying a barrier, review the exercise "Taking the First Step" that you completed in Chapter One.

JOURNAL ENTRY #16

Intention Statement

Complete the following Intention Statement on a separate sheet of paper. It is in three parts.

1. Describe how you could set up circumstances that would allow you to experience a barrier you identified in the previous Journal Entry. What could you do to put yourself right up against the barrier?

To experience the barrier, I could ...

Also, I could ...

2. Brainstorm a list of possible benefits or rewards you would enjoy if you let yourself experience away the barrier (let it disappear). Do this on 3×5 cards or on the sheet of paper.

3. This is for the courageous. Pick just one circumstance that you intend to set up in order to experience the barrier you have been writing about. This can be your opportunity to learn to love your barrier and deal with it. Choose a circumstance that you can arrange within the next three days. For example, if your barrier is fear of speaking in front of a group, the circumstance you arrange could be to ask a question in class or to give a speech.

I intend to ...

#13

PRACTICING CRITICAL THINKING #5

Move from problems to solutions

Most of us spend a great deal of time thinking and talking about problems and little time, if any, thinking and talking about solutions. This exercise gives you a chance to define some of the problems you're currently experiencing and then to start solving them.

In the space below, describe at least three problems that could interfere with your success as a student. The problems might be related to courses, teachers, personal relationships, finances, or anything else that might get in the way of your being successful.

My problem is that ...

_____

_____

My problem is that ...

_____

_____

_____

My problem is that ...

_____

_____

_____

Next, brainstorm at least three possible solutions to at least one of those problems. If you can't think of anything, just begin to write and see what happens. You might invent new and powerful solutions.

I could solve my problem by ...

_____

_____

I could solve my problem by ...

_____

_____

I could solve my problem by ...

_____

_____

_____

Videotape a television debate or discussion that involves a panel of experts on a given topic. When you play back the program, stop the tape after a question to one of the experts and predict how that person will respond to the question. Also describe what you think would be an effective response from the expert. Start the tape again so that you can observe the expert's actual response and then evaluate that response.

As you do this exercise, stay alert for errors in reasoning, claims that are presented without evidence, unsystematic thinking, bias, jumping to conclusions, or stereotypes.

Write your observations on a separate sheet of paper.

 Now go to Houghton Mifflin's College Survival/Becoming a Master Student web site: **http://collegesurvival.college.hmco.com/students.**

Look for links to discussion groups with other students and share your responses to this exercise. By reviewing other students' postings, you could discover many more possible solutions to your own problems. While you're there, offer some possible solutions to the problems that others have posted.

master student
FRED SMITH

a graduate of Yale, is the founder and CEO of Federal Express Corporation.

Frederick W. Smith may have a common last name, but he is a most uncommon man. What other American business leader of today had a revolutionary idea and converted it into a company that, starting from scratch and with heavy early losses, passed the $500 million revenue mark and had a 10 percent net profit margin in a few years?

What other American business leader with so brilliant an idea first wrote it out in a college paper that was graded C? Or says that the people with the greatest impact on him have been a poorly educated sergeant whom he led in combat and a science professor who liked to buzz a university stadium in a fighter plane?

Fred Smith is chairman and chief executive officer of Memphis-based Federal Express Corporation, an air cargo firm that specializes in overnight delivery door-to-door, using its own planes.

To put it another way, Fred Smith is Federal Express.

Smith got his revolutionary idea in the 60's while majoring in economics and political science at Yale. Technological change had opened a radically new transportation market, he decided. . . .

"Steamboats and trains were the logistics arm of the Industrial Revolution's first stage," he says. "Trucks became a good logistics arm later—and still are because of their flexibility. But moving the parts and pieces to support the Electronics Age requires very fast transportation over long distances. I became convinced that a different type of system was going to be a major part of the national economy. . . ."

Smith spelled it out in an overdue economics paper. To cut cost and time, packages from all over the country would be flown to a central point, there to be distributed and flown out again to their destinations—a hub-and-spokes pattern, his company calls it today. The flying would be late at night when air lanes were empty. Equipment and documents from anywhere in the U.S. could be delivered anywhere in the U.S. the next day. . . .

For the benefit of business history, it would be nice to have that college paper today. But who saves college papers, particularly those done in one night and branded mediocre?

He says one reason he was no scholastic superstar was that many courses he had to take didn't interest him. Other things did. He and two faculty members resurrected a long-dormant flying club at Yale. One of his cohorts was Professor Norwood Russell Hansen.

"Russ taught the psychology of science—how science was developed," Smith says. "I was a friend of his, not one of his students. He had a big impact on me because of his outlook on life. He was a great singer and a pianist of virtual concert talent. He rode a motorcycle, and he had a World War II fighter plane that he flew all over the place. He buzzed Yale Bowl from time to time. He marched to the beat of a different drummer. . . ."

Will Smith be successful in future undertakings? Says Arthur C. Bass, vice chairman: "A few years ago, some of us used to let off steam in the afternoon playing basketball on a court behind an apartment house. It was amazing—no matter who had the ball and no matter where Fred was on the court, if Fred's side needed to score to win, he would get the ball and make the winning basket. That's the way he is in the business world."

"A Business Visionary Who Really Delivered" by Henry Altman, from Nation's Business, *November 1981. Reprinted by permission of* Nation's Business, *November 1981. Copyright ©1981, U.S. Chamber of Commerce.*

For more biographical information on Fred Smith, visit Houghton Mifflin's College Survival/Becoming a Master Student web site: **http://collegesurvival.college.hmco. com/students.**

Name _____ Date _____/_____/_____

 Explain how the "recite and repeat" memory technique leads to synergy.

 Give a specific example of "setting a trap" for your memory.

 Describe a visualization that can help you remember Boyle's law.

 Define *acronym* and give an example.

 Memorization on a deep level can take place if you:
    (A) Repeat the idea.
    (B) Repeat the idea.
    (C) Repeat the idea.
    (D) All of the above.

 Mnemonic devices are tricks that can increase your ability to:
    (A) Distribute your learning.
    (B) Manage your time.
    (C) Check your tire pressure.
    (D) Understand or digest material.
    (E) Recall information.

 Briefly describe at least three memory techniques.

There are four general categories of mnemonic devices given in the text. Explain two of them.

 Briefly describe two ideas that can help you unconditionally accept a problem you're having right now.

 Explain a strategy that can help transfer information from your short-term memory into your long-term memory.

JOURNAL ENTRY

#17

Discovery/Intention Statement

After reading and doing this chapter, summarize what you have learned about your current memory skills.

I discovered that I …

_____

_____

_____

    Pick three memory techniques and write a short Intention Statement about how you will use them in the next week.

I intend to …

_____

_____

_____

LEARNING STYLES APPLICATION   CHAPTER 3

Mode 4 *Return once more to your top five memory techniques. Now describe how you could apply each technique in an area of your life other than school.*

Mode 1 *Write a short paragraph describing the way you feel when you want to remember something but have trouble doing so. Think of three specific incidents in which you experienced this problem. Examples are trying to remember someone's name or a fact you needed in order to answer a test question.*

Mode 3 *For each of the five techniques you just listed, describe a specific way you could apply that technique while attending class or studying.*

Mode 2 *List and explain the five most useful memory techniques you learned from this chapter. Choose the techniques that are likely to work best for you.*

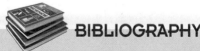

BIBLIOGRAPHY

ENDNOTES

1 Wilder Penfield, "Consciousness, Memory and Man's Conditioned Reflexes," in Karl Pribram, ed., *On the Biology of Learning* (New York: Harcourt Brace Jovanovich, 1969).

2 H. Hyden, "Biochemical Aspects of Learning and Memory," in Karl Pribram, ed., *On the Biology of Learning* (New York: Harcourt Brace Jovanovich, 1969).

3 Daniel L. Schacter, *The Seven Sins of Memory: How the Mind Forgets and Remembers* (Boston: Houghton Mifflin, 2001), p. 34.

ADDITIONAL READING

Brown, Alan C. *Maximizing Memory Power.* New York: Wiley, 1986.

Higbee, Kenneth L. *Your Memory: How It Works and How to Improve It.* Englewood Cliffs, NJ: Prentice-Hall, 1996.

Lucas, Jerry, and Harry Lorayne. *The Memory Book.* New York: Ballantine Books, 1975.

Schacter, Daniel L. *Searching for Memory: The Brain, the Mind, and the Past.* New York: HarperCollins, 1997.

INTERNET RESOURCES

MemoryTalk.com
www.memorytalk.com/index.html

Mind Tools—Memory Techniques and Mnemonics
www.psychwww.com/mtsite/memory.html

SelfGrowth.com
www.selfgrowth.com/selfimprovgroup.html

Reading

IN THIS CHAPTER . . . Expand your mental endurance with Muscle Reading. Weigh in with tools for reading faster, increasing comprehension, and building your vocabulary. You do these things even when reading is tough, learning English as a second language, or reading with children underfoot. Support these changes by noticing your mental pictures and letting go of any that block your success.

Muscle Reading

Picture yourself sitting at a desk, a book in your hands. Your eyes are open, and it looks as if you're reading. Suddenly your head jerks up. You blink. You realize your eyes have been scanning the page for 10 minutes, and you can't remember a single thing you have read.

Or picture this: You've had a hard day. You were up at 6 a.m. to get the kids ready for school. A coworker called in sick, and you missed your lunch trying to do your job and his. You picked up the kids, then had to shop for dinner. Dinner was late, of course, and the kids were grumpy.

Finally, you get to your books at 8 p.m., and you begin plodding through something called "the equity method of accounting for common stock investments." You tell yourself, "I am preparing for the future," as you claw your way through two paragraphs and begin the third.

Suddenly, everything in the room looks different. Your head is resting on your elbow, which is resting on the equity method of accounting. The clock reads 11:00 p.m. Say good-bye to three hours.

Sometimes the only difference between a sleeping pill and a textbook is that the textbook doesn't have a warning on the label about operating heavy machinery.

Muscle Reading is a technique you can use to avoid mental minivacations and reduce the number of unscheduled naps during study time, even after a hard day. More than that, Muscle Reading is a way to decrease effort and struggle by increasing energy and skill. Once you learn this technique, you can actually spend less time on your reading and get more out of it.

This is not to say that Muscle Reading will make your education a breeze. Muscle Reading might even look like more work at first. Effective textbook reading is an active, energy-consuming, sit-on-the-edge-of-your-seat business. That's why this strategy is called Muscle Reading.

Discovery Statement

Think about how reading skills relate to your educational goals. Preview this chapter and review your Discovery Wheel, especially the section on reading. Then list below what you want to learn from this chapter.

I want to learn …

_____
_____
_____
_____

JOURNAL ENTRY

#19

Discovery Statement

Take 10 minutes to read as much as you can of the articles on Muscle Reading that follow in this chapter. Then close the book and, on a separate sheet of paper, write a summary of what you read.

Next, compare your summary to the original text. Was your summary complete and accurate? Did you encounter any problems in reading this material, such as words you didn't understand or paragraphs you paused to reread? Sum up your reading experience by completing this statement:

I discovered that I …

_____
_____
_____
_____

Now list some specific reading skills you want to gain by working through this chapter.

_____
_____
_____
_____
_____

How MUSCLE READING works

Muscle Reading is a three-phase technique you can use to extract the ideas and information you want.

- Phase one includes things to do *before you read*.
- Phase two takes place *while you read*.
- Phase three includes steps you can take *after you read*.

Each of the three phases has three steps.

Phase one—before you read:

Step 1: Preview

Step 2: Outline

Step 3: Question

Phase two—while you read:

Step 4: Read

Step 5: Underline

Step 6: Answer

Phase three—after you read:

Step 7: Recite

Step 8: Review

Step 9: Review again

A nine-step reading strategy might seem cumbersome and unnecessary for a two-page reading assignment. It is. Keep in mind that Muscle Reading is not an all-or-nothing package. Use it appropriately. You can choose what steps to apply as you read.

To assist your recall of all nine steps, memorize these short sentences:

Pry out questions.

Root up answers.

Recite, review, and review again.

These sentences are an acrostic. The first letter of each word stands for one of the nine steps listed above:

PREVIEW

Take a moment to invent images for each of those sentences.

For *phase one*, visualize or feel yourself prying questions out of a text. These are questions you want answered based on your brief survey of the assignment. Make a mental picture of yourself scanning the territory, spotting a question, and reaching into the text to pry it out. Hear yourself saying, "I've got it. Here's my question."

Then for *phase two*, root up the answers to your questions. Get your muscles involved. Flex. Feel your fingertips digging into the text to root up the answers to your questions.

Finally, you enter *phase three*. Hear your voice reciting what you have learned. Hear yourself making a speech about the material. Hear yourself singing it.

To jog your memory, write the first letters of the Muscle Reading acrostic in a margin or at the top of your notes. Then check off the steps you intend to follow. Or write the Muscle Reading steps on 3×5 cards and use them for bookmarks.

Muscle Reading could take a little time to learn. At first, you might feel it's slowing you down. That's natural. Mastery comes with time and practice.

Phase one:
BEFORE YOU READ

Step 1: Preview   Before you begin, survey the entire assignment. You might want to refer to Exercise #1: "Textbook reconnaissance," which guided you through a survey of this book. Previewing in this way can significantly increase your comprehension of reading material.

If you are starting a new book, look over the table of contents and flip through the text page by page. If you're going to read one chapter, flip through the pages of that chapter. Even if your assignment is merely a few pages in a book, you can benefit from a brief preview of the table of contents.

Keep the preview short. If the entire reading assignment will take less than an hour, your preview might take five minutes. Previewing is also a way to get yourself started when an assignment looks too big to handle. It is an easy way to step into the material.

Keep an eye out for summary statements. If the assignment is long or complex, read the summary first. Many textbooks have summaries in the introductions or at the end of each chapter.

Read all of the chapter headings and subheadings. Like the headlines in a newspaper, these are usually printed in larger, bolder type. Often headings are brief summaries in themselves.

When previewing, look for familiar concepts or facts. These items can help link new information to previously learned material. Look for ideas that spark your imagination or curiosity. Ask yourself how the material can relate to your long-term goals. Inspect drawings, diagrams, charts, tables, graphs, and photographs.

You don't have to memorize what you preview to get value from this step. Previewing sets the stage for incoming information by warming up a space in your mental storage area.

Step 2: Outline

With complex material, take time to understand the structure of what you are about to read. Outlining actively organizes your thoughts about the assignment and can make complex information easier to understand.

If your textbook provides chapter outlines, spend some time studying them. When an outline is not provided, sketch a brief one in the margin of your book or at the beginning of your notes on a separate sheet of paper. Later, as you read and take notes, you can add to your outline.

Headings in the text can serve as major and minor entries in your outline. (For example, the heading for this article is "Phase one: Before you read," and subheadings throughout the article list the three steps in this phase.) When you outline, feel free to rewrite headings so that they are more meaningful to you.

The amount of time you spend on this step will vary according to the nature of the material. For some assignments (fiction and poetry, for example), you can skip this step altogether. For others, a 10-second mental outline is all that you might need.

Step 3: Question

Before you begin a careful reading, determine what you want from an assignment. It might help to write down a list of questions.

Questions might come from a course syllabus or as a result of your preview. Or you can turn chapter headings and subheadings into questions. For example, if a heading is "Transference and suggestion," you can ask yourself, What are transference and suggestion? How does transference relate to suggestion? Make up a quiz as if you were teaching this subject to your classmates.

If you can't answer your questions, ask yourself if you understood the terms and concepts in the reading material or if you asked the right questions. If you didn't understand the terms and concepts, ask for help from your instructor or a classmate. If you think you did not ask the right questions, try revising them and then answering them.

Have fun with this technique. Make the questions playful or creative. You don't need to answer every question that you ask. The purpose of making up questions is to get your brain involved in the assignment. Take your unanswered questions to class, where they can be springboards for class discussions.

Demand your money's worth from your textbook. If you do not understand a concept, write specific questions about it. The more detailed your questions, the more powerful this technique becomes.

READ

Phase two:
WHILE YOU READ

Step 4: Read At last! You have previewed the assignment, organized it in your mind, and formulated questions. Now you are ready to begin reading.

Before you dive into the first paragraph, take a few moments to reflect on what you already know about this subject. Do this even if you think you know nothing. This technique prepares your brain to accept the information that follows.

As you read, be conscious of where you are and what you are doing. Use the Power Process "Be here now." When you notice your attention wandering, gently bring it back to the present.

One way to stay focused is to avoid marathon reading sessions. Schedule breaks and set a reasonable goal for the entire session. Then reward yourself with an enjoyable activity for 5 or 10 minutes every hour or two.

For difficult reading, set shorter goals. Read for a half-hour and then take a break. Most students find that shorter periods of reading distributed throughout the day and week can be more effective than long sessions.

You can use the following four techniques to stay focused as you read.

First, visualize the material. Form mental pictures of the concepts as they are presented. If you read that a voucher system can help control cash disbursements, picture a voucher handing out dollar bills.

Second, read it out loud. This works especially well with complicated material. Some of us remember better and understand more quickly when we hear an idea.

Third, get a "feel" for the subject. For example, let's say you are reading about a microorganism—a paramecium—in your biology text. Imagine what it would feel like to run your finger around the long, cigar-shaped body of the organism. Imagine feeling the large fold of its gullet on one side and the hairy little cilia as they wiggle in your hand.

Fourth, remember that a goal of your reading is to answer the questions you listed during phase one.

A final note: It's easy to fool yourself about reading. Having an open book in your hand and moving your eyes across a page doesn't mean you are reading effectively. Reading textbooks takes energy, even if you do it sitting down. There's a story about corporate presidents—that they usually wear out the front of their chairs first. Approach your reading assignment like a company president. Sit up. Keep your spine straight. Use the edge of your chair. And avoid reading in bed—except for fun.

Step 5: Underline Deface your books. Use them up. Have fun writing and coloring in them. Indulge yourself as you never could with your grade-school books.

The purpose of making marks in a text is to create signals for reviewing. Underlining or highlighting can save lots of time when you study for tests.

Underlining offers a secondary benefit. When you read with a pen or pencil in your hand, you involve your kinesthetic sense—your sense of touch and motion. Being physical with your books can help build strong neural pathways in your memory.

Avoid underlining or highlighting too soon. Wait until you complete a chapter or section to make sure you know what is important. Then mark up the text. Sometimes, underlining after you read each paragraph works best.

Underlining with a pen can sometimes make the important parts harder to read. As an alternative, some people use colored highlighters. You can still use a pen for making notes in the margins and circling important sections.

Underline or highlight sparingly, usually less than 10 percent of the text. If you mark up too much on a page, you defeat the purpose—to flag the most important material for review.

Try underlining the answers to the questions you created during the first phase of the Muscle Reading process using a different colored highlighter or pen.

Write in the margins of your texts. Write summary statements and questions. Mark passages that you don't understand. If you find a list or series of elements in a paragraph, you can circle and number them.

Step 6: Answer   As you read, get the answers to your questions and write them down. Fill in your outline. Write down new questions and note when you don't find the answers you were looking for. Use these notes to ask questions in class, or when you see your instructor privately.

When you read, create an image of yourself as a person in search of the answers. You are a detective, watching for every clue, sitting erect in your straight-backed chair, demanding that your textbook give you what you want—the answers.

Phase three:
AFTER YOU READ

Step 7: Recite   Talk to yourself about what you've read. Or talk to someone else. When you finish reading an assignment, make a speech about it. A classic study suggests that you can profitably devote up to 80 percent of your study time to active reciting.[1]

One way to get yourself to recite is to look at each underlined point. Note what you marked, then put the book down and start talking out loud. Explain as much as you can about that particular point.

To make this technique more effective, do it in front of a mirror. It might seem silly, but the benefits can be enormous. Reap them at exam time.

Friends are even better than mirrors. Form a group and practice teaching each other what you have read. One of the best ways to learn anything is to teach it to someone else.

In addition, talk about your reading whenever you can. Tell friends and family members what you're learning from your textbooks.

RECITE   REVIEW

NOT ONCE

Talking about your reading reinforces a valuable skill—the ability to summarize. To practice this skill, pick one chapter (or one section of a chapter) from any of your textbooks. State the main topic covered in this chapter. Then state the main points that the author makes about this topic.

For example, the main topic up to this point in this chapter is Muscle Reading. The main point about this topic is that Muscle Reading includes three phases—steps to take before you read, while you read, and after you read. For a more detailed summary, you could name each of the nine steps.

Note: The "topic-point" method does not work so well when you want to summarize short stories, novels, plays, and other works of fiction. In these cases, focus on *action*. In most stories, the main character confronts a major problem and takes a series of actions to solve it. Describe that problem and talk about the character's key actions—the turning points in the story.

Step 8: Review
Plan to do your first complete review within 24 hours of reading the material. Sound the trumpets! This is critical: A review within 24 hours moves information from your short-term memory to your long-term memory. It can save you hours later on.

Review within one day. If you read the material on Wednesday, review it on Thursday. During this review, look over your notes and clear up anything you don't understand. Recite some of the main points again.

This review can be short. You might spend as little as 15 minutes reviewing a difficult, two-hour reading assignment. Investing time now can save you hours later when studying for exams.

Step 9: Review again
The final step in Muscle Reading is the weekly or monthly review. This step can be very short—perhaps only four or five minutes per assignment. Simply go over your notes. Read the highlighted parts of your text. Recite one or two of the more complicated points.

The purpose of these reviews is to keep the neural pathways to the information open and to make them more distinct. That way, the information can be easier to recall. You can accomplish these short reviews anytime, anywhere, if you are prepared.

Conduct a five-minute review while you are waiting for a bus to arrive, for your socks to dry, or for the water to boil. Three-by-five cards are a handy review tool. Write down formulas, concepts, and facts on cards and carry them with you. These short review periods can be effortless and fun.

Sometimes longer review periods are appropriate. For example, if you found an assignment difficult, consider rereading it. Start over, as if you had never seen the material. Sometimes a second reading will provide you with surprising insights.

Decades ago, psychologists identified the primacy-recency effect, which suggests that we most easily remember the first and last items in any presentation.[2] Previewing and reviewing your reading is a powerful way to put this theory to work for you.

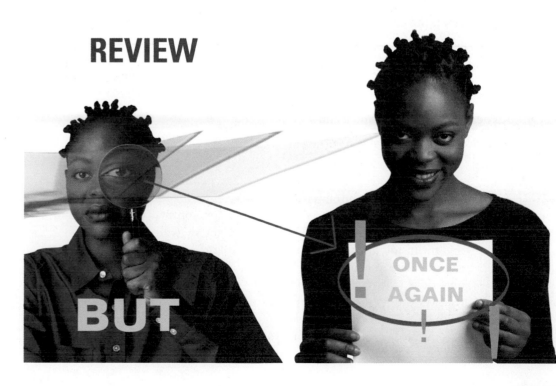

REVIEW

BUT

ONCE AGAIN

Read with a dictionary in your lap

Malcolm X demonstrated one way to improve vocabulary. While in prison, he read and copied the entire dictionary. Few of us have such a single-minded sense of purpose with regard to vocabulary building. Yet we all share the ability and desire to learn.

You can use that natural ability to strengthen your vocabulary by concentrating on words that interest you. Look up unfamiliar words. Pay special attention to words that arouse your curiosity.

You can regularly use two kinds of dictionaries: the desk dictionary and the unabridged dictionary. A desk dictionary is the one you use several times a day. Keep this book within reach (maybe in your lap) so you can look up unfamiliar words. You can find a large, unabridged dictionary in the library or bookstore. It provides more complete information about words and definitions not included in your desk dictionary, and you'll find a history of each word. Both kinds of dictionaries are available on CD-ROM for personal computers.

Construct a word stack.

When you come across an unfamiliar word, write it down on a 3×5 card. Below the word, copy the sentence in which it was used. You can look up each word immediately, or you can accumulate a stack of these cards and look the words up later. Write the definition on the back of the 3×5 card, adding the diacritical marks that tell you how to pronounce the word.

To expand your vocabulary and find the history behind the words, you can take your stack of cards to an unabridged dictionary. As you find related words in the dictionary, add them to your stack. These cards become a portable study aid that you can review in your spare moments.

Learn—even when your dictionary is across town.

When you are listening to a lecture and hear an unfamiliar word or when you are reading on the bus and encounter a word you don't know, you can still build your word stack. Pull out a 3×5 card and write down the word and its sentence. Later, you can look up the definition and write it on the back of the card.

Use more options for learning words.

There are other strategies for dealing with new words. One is to guess the meaning of the words from context. To do this, reread the sentences that surround the new word and see if they point to a logical meaning. Or simply circle or highlight the word and continue reading. When you're done, you can look up all unfamiliar words at one time.

Another suggestion is to divide an unfamiliar word into syllables and look for familiar parts. This works well if you make it a point to learn common prefixes (beginning syllables) and suffixes (ending syllables). For example, the suffix *-tude* usually refers to a condition or state of being. Knowing this makes it easier to conclude that *habitude* refers to a usual way of doing something and that *similitude* means being similar or having a quality of resemblance.

The Universal Law of Reading

First corollary:
To read effectively, always sit in a canoe
and wear a face mask, snorkel, and flippers.

Second corollary:
Don't believe everything you read.

#14

It's hard to know what's going on ... until you have the big picture

Read the following paragraph and then summarize it in one sentence.

"With hocked gems financing him, he defied all scornful laughter that tried to prevent his scheme. 'Your eyes deceive,' they said. 'It is like a table, not an egg.' Now three sturdy sisters sought truth. As they forged along, sometimes through calm vastness, yet more often over turbulent peaks and valleys, their days became weeks as many doubters spread fearful rumors about the edge. At last, from nowhere winged creatures appeared, signifying the journey's end."

Summarize this paragraph.

_____

_____

_____

Most people have difficulty knowing what in the world the previous paragraph is about. If it was part of a reading assignment about Christopher Columbus that you had previewed, then it would make more sense. Read it again while thinking about the famous world traveler.

Reading *fast*

One way to read faster is to read faster. This might sound like double talk, but it is a serious suggestion. The fact is, you can probably read faster—without any loss in comprehension—simply by making a conscious effort to do so. Your comprehension might even improve.

Experiment with the "just do it" method right now. Read the rest of this article as fast as you can. After you finish, come back and reread the same paragraphs at your usual rate. Note how much you remember from your first sprint through. You might be surprised to find how well you comprehend material even at dramatically increased speeds. Build on that success by experimenting with the following guidelines.

Get your body ready.

Gear up for reading faster. Get off the couch. Sit up straight at a desk or table, on the edge of your chair, with your feet flat on the floor. If you're feeling adventurous, read standing up.

Set a time limit.

When you read, use a clock or a digital watch with a built-in stopwatch to time yourself. You are not aiming to set speed records, so be realistic. For example, set a goal to read two or three sections of a chapter in an hour, using all the steps of Muscle Reading. If that works, set a goal of 50 minutes for reading two or three sections. Test your limits. The idea is to give yourself a gentle push, increasing your reading speed without sacrificing comprehension.

Relax.

It's not only possible to read fast when you're relaxed, it's easier. Relaxation promotes concentration. And remember, relaxation is not the same as sleep. You can be relaxed *and* alert at the same time.

Move your eyes faster.

When we read, our eyes leap across the page in short bursts called *saccades* (pronounced să-käds´). A saccade is also a sharp jerk on the reins of a horse—a violent pull to stop the animal quickly. Our eyes stop like that, too, in pauses called *fixations.*

Although we experience the illusion of continuously scanning each line, our eyes actually take in groups of words, usually about three at a time. For more than 90 percent of reading time, our eyes are at a dead stop, in those fixations.

One way to decrease saccades is to follow your finger as you read. The faster your finger moves, the faster your eyes move. You can also use a pen, pencil, or 3×5 card as a guide.

Your eyes can move faster if they take in more words with each burst— for example, six instead of three. To practice taking in more words between fixations, find a newspaper

with narrow columns. Then read down one column at a time and fixate only once per line.

A related technique to try during class time is to find a reading partner to observe your eye movements as you read. Ask your partner to count the number of fixations you make before your eyes sweep back to the left side of the page to begin another line. Figure out the average number of fixations per line and the average number of words per line. From these two numbers you can determine how many words you're taking in between fixations. For example, if you fixate twice per line and the average number of words per line is eight, then you are reading about four words at a time.

When using either of these techniques, simply make a conscious effort to fixate less. You might feel a little uncomfortable at first. That's normal. Just practice often, for short periods of time.

Notice and release ineffective habits.

Our eyes make *regressions.* That is, they back up and reread words. You can reduce regressions by paying attention to them. Use the handy 3×5 card to cover words and lines that you have read. You can then note how often you stop and move the card back to reread the text. Don't be discouraged if you stop often at first. Being aware of it helps you regress less frequently.

Also notice *vocalizing*. Obviously, you're more likely to read faster if you don't read out loud or move your lips. You can also increase your speed if you don't subvocalize—that is, if you don't mentally "hear" the words as you read them. To stop doing it, just be aware of it.

When you first attempt to release regression and vocalizing, choose simpler reading material. That way, you can pay closer attention to your reading habits. Gradually work your way up to more complex material.

If you're pressed for time, skim.
When you're in a hurry, experiment by skimming the assignment instead of reading the whole thing. Read the headings, subheadings, lists, charts, graphs, and summary paragraphs. Summaries are especially important. They are usually found at the beginning or end of a chapter or section.

Stay flexible.
Remember that speed isn't everything. Skillful readers vary their reading rate according to their purpose and the nature of the material. An advanced text in analytic geometry usually calls for a different reading rate than the Sunday comics.

You also can use different reading rates on the same material. For example, you might first sprint through an assignment for the key words and ideas, then return to the difficult parts for a slower and more thorough reading.

Explore more resources.
You can find many books about speed-reading. Ask a librarian to help you find a few. Using them can be a lot of fun. For more possibilities, including courses and workshops, go to your favorite search engine on the Internet and key in the word "speed-reading."

In your research, you might discover people who offer to take you beyond speed-reading. According to some teachers, you can learn to flip through a book and "mentally photograph" each page—hundreds or even thousands of words at once. To prepare for this feat, you first do relaxation exercises to release tension while remaining alert. In this state, you can process vast quantities of information at a level other than your conscious mind.

You might find these ideas controversial. Approach them in the spirit of the Power Process "Ideas are tools." Also remember that you can use more conventional reading techniques at any time.

One word of caution: Courses and workshops range from cheap to expensive. Before you lay out any money, check the instructor's credentials and talk to people who've taken the course. Also find out whether the instructor offers free "sampler sessions" and whether you can cancel at some point in the course for a full refund.

Finally, remember the first rule of reading fast: Just do it!

Relax
Eye strain can be the result of continuous stress. You can take a break from your reading and use this exercise to release tension.

1. Sit on a chair or lie down and take a few moments to breathe deeply.

2. Close your eyes, place your palms over your eyes, and visualize a perfect field of black.

3. Continue to be aware of the blackness for two or three minutes while you breathe deeply.

4. Now remove your hands from your eyes and open your eyes slowly.

5. Relax for a minute more, then continue reading.

WORKPLACE APPLICATIONS

Apply the techniques for reading faster to documents that you read at work. Keep in mind that you don't have to "get it all" the first time you read a document. Experiment with making several quick passes through the material. For example, make your first pass a quick preview. Then go for a second pass, reading the first sentence of each paragraph or the first and last paragraphs in each chapter. For your third pass, read the material paragraph by paragraph, sentence by sentence.

When reading is tough

Sometimes ordinary reading methods are not enough. Many students get bogged down in a murky reading assignment. If you are ever up to your neck in textbook alligators, you can use the following techniques to drain the swamp.

1 Read it again. Difficult material—such as the technical writing in science texts—is often easier the second time around. If you read an assignment and are completely lost, do not despair. Admit your confusion. Sleep on it. When you return to the assignment, regard it with fresh eyes.

2 Look for essential words. If you are stuck on a paragraph, mentally cross out all the adjectives and adverbs and read the sentence without them. Find the important words. These will usually be verbs and nouns.

3 Hold a minireview. Pause briefly to summarize what you've read so far, verbally or in writing. Stop at the end of a paragraph and recite, in your own words, what you have just read. Jot down some notes or create a short outline or summary.

4 Read it out loud. Make noise. Read a passage out loud several times, each time using a different inflection and emphasizing a different part of the sentence. Be creative. Imagine that you are the author talking.

5 Use your instructor. Admit when you are stuck and make an appointment with your instructor. Most teachers welcome the opportunity to work individually with students. Be specific about your confusion. Point out the paragraph that you found toughest to understand.

6 Stand up. Changing positions periodically can combat fatigue. Experiment with standing as you read, especially if you get stuck on a tough passage and decide to read it out loud.

7 Find a tutor. Many schools provide free tutoring services. If tutoring services are not provided by your school, other students who have completed the course can assist you.

8 Use another text. Find a similar text in the library. Sometimes a concept is easier to understand if it is expressed another way. Children's books, especially children's encyclopedias, can provide useful overviews of baffling subjects.

9 Pretend you understand, then explain it. We often understand more than we think we do. Pretend the material is clear as a bell and explain it to another person or even yourself. Write your explanation down. You might be amazed by what you know.

10 Ask: What's going on here? When you feel stuck, stop reading for a moment and diagnose what's happening. At these stop points, mark your place in the margin of the page with a penciled *S* for "Stuck." Seeing a pattern to your marks over several pages might indicate a question you want to answer before reading further. Or you might discover a reading habit you'd like to change.

PRACTICING CRITICAL THINKING

#6

Read an editorial in a newspaper or magazine. Analyze this editorial by taking notes in a three-column format on a separate sheet of paper. Use the first column for listing major points, the second for supporting points, and the third for key facts or statistics that support the major or minor points. For example:

Major point
The "female condom" has not yet been proved effective as a method of birth control.

Supporting point
Few studies exist on this method.

Key fact
One of the few studies showed a 26 percent failure rate for the female condom.

Ask another person to do this exercise with you. Then compare and discuss your notes. In the space below, describe how your opinions on this issue were modified in light of the reasons and evidence presented.

_____
_____
_____
_____
_____
_____

JOURNAL ENTRY

#20

Discovery Statement

Now that you have read about Muscle Reading, review your assessment of your reading skills in the Discovery Wheel on page [17]. Do you still think your evaluation was accurate? What new insights do you have about the way you read textbooks? Are you a more effective reader than you thought? Less effective? Record your observations below.

_____
_____
_____
_____
_____
_____

English as a second language

Englisch lesen als zweite Sprache

En lisant l'anglais comme une deuxième langue

Leer el inglés como segunda lengua

The English language is full of exceptions to the rules. For this reason, it is probably more difficult to learn than many other languages. Contrary to the rules of phonetics, for example, words in English are often not spelled the way they sound. Even trying to spell the word *phonetics* using phonetics can get you into trouble.

Whatever your native language, consider using the following suggestions as you master English. Also note that many of these suggestions can apply to learning any language.

Give it time
Reading English slowly can aid comprehension. Accept how fast you read right now, even as you seek to increase your speed. As you practice, both your reading speed and comprehension can improve. There are no instant pills to take. Learning English takes time.

Use Muscle Reading
Many of the Muscle Reading techniques apply to those who are reading English as a second language. For example, read some assignments more than once. The first time through, look for major ideas and be aware of the general content. The next time through, fill in more of the details.

Get at word meanings
As suggested in a previous article, have a dictionary handy. Before looking up an unfamiliar word, see if you can figure out its meaning from the context. If someone says, "It will probably be cold at the football game, so be sure to bring a warm XXXXX," you would probably not show up with a calculator or a fishing pole.

Practice speaking English
Look for times when you can practice speaking English. Asking questions or making comments in class is an effective way to practice. By doing so, you can become more involved and increase your understanding of the course content. Another way to practice is to repeat out loud what you have just read.

The more you practice English, the faster you can learn. Relying on translations or spending much of your time speaking your native language could slow your progress.

Practice writing in English
Writing in English, which involves spelling and a more precise use of grammar, might be more difficult than either reading or speaking. Get extra practice by writing grocery lists, to-do lists, notes to friends, appointments on calendars, and entries in your personal journal.

Think in English
Thinking in English is a variation of speaking it. The next time you want to explore some future project or remember the trip you took last summer, think about it in English. Some students are pleasantly surprised when they even start dreaming in English.

Learn academic English
Formal, academic English might vary greatly from your own English dialect. Consider approaching academic English as a foreign language, even if English is your native tongue. The techniques that help you learn French or Spanish can also help you master the English you use in school.

Celebrate your gains
Acknowledge yourself and celebrate when you make small gains. Your English skills might not improve 100 percent all at once. However, one hundred small gains of 1 percent each could accomplish the same thing. Lots of little learnings can amount to major shifts in your English proficiency.

Use school services
Many schools have ESL (English as a Second Language) programs that offer a variety of services, such as tutoring, as well as courses and workshops on learning English. Ask your advisor or counseling office.

Reading with children underfoot

It is possible to combine effective study time _and_ quality time with children. The following suggestions come mostly from students who are also parents. The specific strategies you use will depend on your schedule and the ages of your children.

Attend to your children first.
When you first come home from school, keep your books out of sight. Spend 10 minutes with your children before you settle in to study. Give them hugs and ask about their day. Then explain that you have some work to do. Your children might reward you with 30 minutes of quiet time. A short time of full, focused attention from a parent can be more satisfying than longer periods of partial attention.

Of course, this suggestion won't work with the youngest children. If your children are infants or toddlers, schedule sessions of concentrated study for when they are asleep.

Use "pockets" of time.
See if you can arrange study time at school before you come home. If you arrive at school 15 minutes earlier and stay 15 minutes later, you can squeeze in an extra half-hour of study time that day. Also look for opportunities to study in between classes.

Before you shuttle children to soccer games or dance classes, throw a book in the car. While your children are warming up for the game or changing clothes, steal another 15 minutes to read.

Plan special activities for your child.
Find a regular playmate for your child. Some children can pair off with close friends and safely retreat to their rooms for hours of private play. You can check on them occasionally and still get lots of reading done.

Another option is to take your children to a public playground. While they swing, slide, and dig in the sand, you can dig into your textbooks. Lots of physical activity will tire out your children in constructive ways. If they go to bed a little early, that's extra time for you to read.

After you set up appropriate activities for your children, don't attend to them every second, even if you're nearby as they play. Obviously, you want to break up fights, stop unsafe activity, and handle emergencies. Short of such incidents, you're free to read.

Use television creatively.
Another option is to use television as a babysitter—when you can control the programming. Rent a videotape for your child to watch as you study. If you're concerned about your child becoming a "couch potato," select educational programs that keep his mind active.

See if your child can use headphones while watching television. That way, the house stays quiet while you study.

Allow for interruptions.
It's possible that you'll be interrupted even if you set up special activities for your child in advance. If so, schedule the kind of studying that can be interrupted. You could, for instance, write out or review flash cards with key terms and definitions. Save the tasks that require sustained attention for other times.

Plan study breaks with children.
Another option is to take 10 minutes each hour that you study to be with your children. View this not as an interruption but as a study break.

Or schedule time to be with your children when you've finished studying. Let your children in on the plan: "I'll be done reading at 7:30. That gives us a whole hour to play before you go to bed."

Many children love visible reminders that "their time" is approaching. An oven timer works well for this purpose. Set it for 15 minutes of quiet time. Follow that with five minutes of show-and-tell, storybooks, or another activity with your child. Then set the timer for another 15 minutes of studying, another break, and so on.

Develop a routine.
Many young children are lovers of routine. They often feel more comfortable when they know what to expect. You can use this to your benefit. One option is to develop a regular time for studying: "From 4 p.m. to 5 p.m. each afternoon is time for me to do my homework." Let your child know this schedule; then enforce it.

Bargain with children. Reward them for keeping the schedule. In return for quiet time, give your child an extra allowance or special treat. Children might enjoy gaining "credits" for this purpose. Each time they give you an hour of quiet time for studying, make an entry on a chart, put a star on their bulletin board, or give them a "coupon." Let children know that after they've accumulated a certain number of entries, stars, or coupons, they can cash in for a big reward—a movie or a trip to the zoo.

Ask other adults for help.
This suggestion for studying with children is a message repeated throughout the book: Enlist other people in your success.

Getting help can be as simple as asking your spouse, partner, neighbor, or a fellow student to take care of the children while you study. Offer to trade childcare with a neighbor: You will take his kids and yours for two hours on Thursday night if he'll take them for two hours on Saturday morning. Some parents start blockwide baby-sitting co-ops based on the same idea.

Find community activities and services.
Ask if your school provides a day care service. In some cases, these services are available to students at a reduced cost. Community agencies such as the YMCA might offer similar programs.

You can also find special events that appeal to children. Storytelling hours at the library are one example. While your child is being entertained or supervised, you can stay close by. Use the time to read a chapter or review class notes.

Make it a game.
Reading a chemistry textbook with a 3-year-old in the same room is not as preposterous as it sounds. The secret is to involve your child. For instance, use this time to recite. Make funny faces as you say the properties of the transition elements in the periodic table. Talk in a weird voice as you repeat Faraday's laws. Draw pictures and make up an exciting story about the process of titration.

Read out loud to your children, or use them as an audience for a speech. If you invent rhymes, poems, or songs to help you remember formulas or dates, teach them to your children. Be playful. Kids are attracted to energy and enthusiasm.

Whenever possible, involve family members in tasks related to reading. Older children can help you with research tasks—finding books at the library, looking up news articles, even helping with typing.

When you can't read everything, just read something.
One objection to reading with children nearby is "I just can't concentrate. There's no way I can get it all done while children are around."

That's OK. Even if you can't absorb an entire chapter while the kids are running past your desk, you can skim the chapter. Or you could just read the introduction and summary. When you can't get it *all* done, just get *something* done. Caution: If you always read this way, your education might be compromised. Supplement this strategy with others so that you can get all of your reading done.

Discover more ways that students read effectively with children underfoot. Visit Houghton Mifflin's College Survival/Becoming a Master Student web site: **http://collegesurvival.college.hmco.com/students.**

Catalog reconnaissance

Look at every page in your school catalog—quickly. (If your school posts its catalog only on a web site, then go to that web site.) Notice what is new, interesting, or puzzling. Locate the description for your major program and note the courses you are required to take for graduation. Find out more about courses that are new to you. If you see that you have to take macroeconomics to graduate, find out how that differs from microeconomics and accounting.

Locate the major program that is most different from yours. Look through the courses students in that major are required to take. Pick out a course that looks interesting, even though it is different from anything you ever thought you'd take. Find out more about that course.

Notice your pictures and let them go

One of the brain's primary jobs is to manufacture images. We use mental pictures to make predictions about the world, and we base much of our behavior on those predictions.

When a cook adds chopped onions, mushrooms, and garlic to a spaghetti sauce, he has a picture of how the sauce will taste and measures each ingredient according to that picture. When an artist is creating a painting or sculpture, he has a mental picture of the finished piece. Novelists often have mental images of the characters that they're about to bring to life. Many parents have a picture about what they want their children to become.

These kinds of pictures and many more have a profound influence on us. Our pictures direct our thinking, our conversations, and our actions—all of which help create our immediate circumstances. That's amazing, considering that we often operate with little, if any, conscious knowledge of our pictures.

Just about any time we feel a need, we conjure up a picture of what will satisfy that need. A baby feels hunger pangs and starts to cry. Within seconds, his mother appears and he is satisfied. The baby stores a mental picture of his mother feeding him. He connects that picture with stopping the hunger pangs. Voilà! Now he knows how to solve the hunger problem. The picture goes on file.

According to psychologist William Glasser, our minds function like a huge photo album.[3] Its pages include pictures of all the ways we've satisfied needs in the past. Whenever we feel dissatisfied, we mentally search the album for a picture of how to make the dissatisfaction go away. With that picture firmly in mind, we act in ways to make the world outside our heads match the pictures inside.

Remember that pictures are not strictly visual images. They can involve any of the senses. When you buy a CD, you have a picture of how it will sound. When you buy a sweater, you have a picture of how it will feel.

A problem with pictures

The pictures we make in our heads are survival mechanisms. Without them, we couldn't get from one end of town to the other. We couldn't feed or clothe ourselves. Without a picture of a socket, we couldn't screw in a light bulb.

Pictures can also get in our way. Take the case of a student who plans to attend a school he hasn't visited. He chose this school for its strong curriculum and good academic standing, but his brain didn't stop there. In his mind, the campus has historic buildings with ivy-covered walls and tree-lined avenues. The professors, he imagines, will be as articulate as Bill Moyers and as entertaining as Oprah Winfrey. His roommate will be his best friend. The cafeteria will be a cozy nook serving delicate quiche and fragrant teas. He will gather there with fellow students for hours of stimulating, intellectual conversation. The library will have every book; the computer lab, every new piece of technology.

The school turns out to be four gray buildings downtown, next to the bus station. The first class he attends is taught by an overweight, balding professor, who is wearing a purple-and-orange bird of paradise tie and has a bad case of the sniffles. The cafeteria is a nondescript hall with machine food, and the student's apartment is barely large enough to accommodate his roommate's tuba. This hypothetical student gets depressed. He begins to think about dropping out of school.

The problem with pictures is that they sometimes prevent us from seeing what is really there. That happened to the student in this story. His pictures prevented him from noticing that his school is in the heart of a culturally vital city—close to theaters, museums, government offices, clubs, and all kinds of stores. The professor with the weird tie is not only an expert in his field, but is also a superior teacher. The school cafeteria is skimpy because it can't compete with the variety of inexpensive restaurants in the area. There might even be hope for a tuba-playing roommate.

Anger and disappointment are often the results of our pictures. We set up expectations of events before they occur, which can lead to disappointment. Sometimes we don't even realize that we have the expectation. The next time you discover you are angry, disappointed, or frustrated, look to see which of your pictures aren't being fulfilled.

Take charge of your pictures

Having pictures is unavoidable. Letting these pictures run our lives is avoidable. Some techniques for dealing with pictures are so simple and effortless, they might seem silly.

One way to deal with pictures is to notice them. Be aware of them. Just open up your mental photo album and notice how the pictures there influence your thoughts, feelings, and actions. Just becoming aware of your pictures and how they affect you can be a huge step toward dealing with them effectively.

When you notice that pictures are getting in your way, then, in the most gentle manner possible, let your pictures go. Let them drift away like wisps of smoke picked up by a gentle wind.

Pictures are persistent. They come back over and over. Notice them again and let them go again. At first, a picture might return repeatedly and insistently. Pictures are like independent beings. They want to live. If you can see the picture as a thought independent from you, you will likely find it easier to let it go.

You are more than your pictures. Many images and words will pop into your head in the course of a lifetime. You do not have to identify with these pictures. You can let pictures go without giving up yourself.

If your pictures are interfering with your education, visualize them scurrying around inside your head. See yourself tying them to a brightly colored helium balloon and letting them go. Let them float away again and again.

Sometimes we can let go of old pictures and replace them with new ones. We stored all those pictures in the first place. We can replace them. Our student's new picture of a great education can include the skimpy cafeteria, the professor with the weird tie, and the roommate with the tuba.

Noticing pictures—a way to embrace diversity

One way to succeed in a diverse classroom or work site is to shine a light on our pictures of people from other races and ethnic groups. We can test those pictures through action—by interacting with people of other cultures. It's easy to believe that certain groups of people are lazy, perpetually late, or rude as long as we never deal directly with individuals from those groups. Inaccurate pictures tend to die when people from different cultures study together, work together, and live together.

One picture that many of us can shed is the one that says, "I have no pictures about people from other cultures." Even people with the best of intentions can carry around subtle biases and stereotypes. By admitting this possibility, we can look inward even more deeply and replace our pictures with more fair and compassionate ones. Whenever we notice an inaccurate picture about a person of color and let it go, we strike a blow against racism and take a step toward embracing diversity.

We can take charge of the images that float through our minds. We don't have to be ruled by an album of antique pictures. Instead, we can stay aware of our pictures and keep looking for new ones.

And when those new pictures no longer serve us, we can also let them go.

PRACTICING CRITICAL THINKING #7

One of the suggested strategies for understanding difficult reading material is to read another publication on the same subject. This is one example of critical thinking skills—explaining and assessing alternative views on an issue.

Apply this strategy now. Find and read a newspaper or magazine article that's relevant to one of your current reading assignments. Now summarize and compare the viewpoints on the subject presented by both authors. List the major questions addressed along with the answers that are offered. Look for points of disagreement and agreement.

Also consider the methods the authors use to reach their conclusions and the evidence they present. Determine if one author's viewpoint is more reasonable, given all of the suitable evidence. In the space below, write a paragraph that states and supports your conclusion.

_____
_____
_____
_____
_____
_____
_____
_____
_____
_____
_____
_____
_____
_____
_____
_____
_____
_____
_____
_____
_____
_____
_____
_____
_____

Student Voices

I always pictured the master student with Scotch-taped glasses, an array of pens in the shirt pocket, and with a copy of the latest *Popular Mechanics* or the *Wall Street Journal* under his arm. Equipped with a sky-high IQ and supportive parents, he would be bound to find his way into the NASA space program or the Supreme Court. . . . Where do we find this inspired, determined and persistent student? We do not have to look too far. Every single student has the potential to become a master in his or her quest. Feel free to join us on a trip worthwhile. You don't even have to wear Scotch-taped glasses.

— MALTE STRAUSS

HELEN KELLER

(1880–1968) Author and lecturer. Illness left her blind and deaf at the age of 19 months.

The morning after my teacher came she led me into her room and gave me a doll. The little blind children at the Perkins Institution had sent it and Laura Bridgman had dressed it; but I did not know this until afterward. When I had played with it a little while, Miss Sullivan slowly spelled into my hand the word "d-o-l-l." I was at once interested in this finger play and tried to imitate it. When I finally succeeded in making the letters correctly I was flushed with childish pleasure and pride. Running downstairs to my mother I held up my hand and made the letters for doll. I did not know that I was spelling a word or even that words existed; I was simply making my fingers go in monkey-like imitation. In the days that followed I learned to spell in this uncomprehending way a great many words, among them *pin, hat, cup,* and a few verbs like *sit, stand,* and *walk.* But my teacher had been with me several weeks before I understood that everything has a name.

One day, while I was playing with my new doll, Miss Sullivan put my big rag doll into my lap also, spelled "d-o-l-l" and tried to make me understand that "d-o-l-l" applied to both. Earlier in the day we had had a tussle over the words "m-u-g" and "w-a-t-e-r." Miss Sullivan had tried to impress it upon me that "m-u-g" is mug and that "w-a-t-e-r" is water, but I persisted in confounding the two. In despair she had dropped the subject for the time, only to renew it at the first opportunity.

I became impatient at her repeated attempts and, seizing the new doll, I dashed it upon the floor. I was keenly delighted when I felt the fragments of the broken doll at my feet. Neither sorrow nor regret followed my passionate outburst. I had not loved the doll. In the still, dark world in which I lived there was no strong sentiment or tenderness. I felt my teacher sweep the fragments to one side of the hearth, and I had a sense of satisfaction that the cause of my discomfort was removed. She brought me my hat, and I knew I was going out into the warm sunshine. This thought, if a wordless sensation may be called a thought, made me hop and skip with pleasure.

We walked down the path to the well house, attracted by the fragrance of honeysuckle with which it was covered. Someone was drawing water and my teacher placed my hand under the spout. As the cool stream gushed over one hand she spelled into the other the word *water,* first slowly, then rapidly. I stood still, my whole attention fixed upon the motions of her fingers. Suddenly I felt a misty consciousness as of something forgotten—a thrill of returning to thought; and somehow the mystery of language was revealed to me. I knew then that "w-a-t-e-r" meant the wonderful cool something that was flowing over my hand. That living word awakened my soul, it gave it light, hope, joy, set it free! There were barriers still, it is true, but barriers that could in time be swept away.

I left the well house eager to learn. Everything had a name, and each name gave birth to a new thought. As we returned to the house, every object which I touched seemed to quiver with life. That was because I saw everything with the strange, new sight that had come to me.

From The Story of My Life *by Helen Keller, 22–24, 1905.*

For more biographical information about Helen Keller, visit Houghton Mifflin's College Survival/Becoming a Master Student web site: **http://collegesurvival.college.hmco.com/ students.**

1 What is an acrostic that can help you remember the nine steps of Muscle Reading?

 2 You must complete all nine steps of Muscle Reading to get the most out of any reading assignment. True or False? Explain your answer.

 3 Describe at least three strategies you can use to preview a reading assignment.

 4 What is one benefit of outlining a reading assignment?

 5 Define the terms *prefix* and *suffix,* and explain how they can assist you in learning the meanings of new words.

 6 To get the most benefit from marking a book, underline at least 25 percent of the text. True or False? Explain your answer.

 7 Explain at least three techniques you can use when reading is tough.

8 Mental pictures are strictly visual images. True or False? Explain your answer.

 9 Define the "topic-point" method of summarizing.

 10 List at least three techniques for increasing your reading speed.

JOURNAL ENTRY

#21

Discovery/Intention Statement

Review what you learned about your reading habits in this chapter and complete the following sentence.

I discovered that I . . .

_____

_____

_____

Quickly review this chapter and choose three techniques that you will put into practice.

I intend to . . .

_____

_____

_____

LEARNING STYLES APPLICATION   CHAPTER 4

Mode 4 *Create your own procedure for effective reading. Consider how you would adapt or modify the steps of Muscle Reading. List and describe each step of your procedure.*

Mode 1 *List current reading assignments that you could use to practice the nine steps of Muscle Reading.*

Mode 3 *Take the list you made for Mode 2 and rank each idea's potential usefulness to you. Assign a 1 to the most useful idea and a 10 to the least useful one. Then describe how you will practice the top three ideas on your list.*

Mode 2 *List 10 new ideas or suggestions for reading that you learned from this chapter.*

 BIBLIOGRAPHY

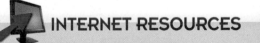 **INTERNET RESOURCES**

ENDNOTES

1 G. S. Gates, "Recitation as a factor in memorizing," *Archives of Psychology,* No. 40, 1917.

2 R. Rosnow and E. Robinson, eds., *Experiments in Persuasion* (New York: Academic Press, 1967).

3 William Glasser, *Take Effective Control of Your Life* (New York: Harper & Row, 1984).

ADDITIONAL READING

Adler, Mortimer, and Charles Van Doren. *How to Read a Book.* New York: Touchstone, 1972.

Barzun, Jacques, and Henry F. Graff. *The Modern Researcher.* New York: Harcourt Brace Jovanovich, 1977.

Birkerts, Sven. *The Gutenberg Elegies: The Fate of Reading in an Electronic Age.* New York: Ballantine, 1994.

Gilbart, Helen W. *Pathways: A Guide to Reading and Study Skills.* Boston: Houghton Mifflin, 1982.

McCutcheon, Randall. *Can You Find It? Twenty-Five Library Scavenger Hunts to Sharpen Your Research Skills.* Minneapolis: Free Spirit, 1991.

Pauk, Walter. *How to Study in College.* Boston: Houghton Mifflin, 1997.

Rial, Arlyne. *Speed Reading Made Easy.* Garden City, NY: Doubleday, 1985.

Soukhanov, Anne H., ed. *The American Heritage Dictionary of the English Language.* Boston: Houghton Mifflin, 1992.

Wurman, Richard Saul. *Information Anxiety.* New York: Doubleday, 1989.

The American Heritage® Dictionary, 4th Edition
education.yahoo.com/reference/dictionary/

Internet Resources for Reading/Study Skills
www.lsc.cc.mn.us/programs/read/internet.html

Mind Tools — Improving Reading Skills
www.psychwww.com/mtsite/page3.html

National Coalition for Campus Children's Centers
www.campuschildren.org/index.html

CHAPTER 5 Notes

This is what learning is. You suddenly understand something you've understood all your life, but in a new way.
DORIS LESSING

I write to understand as much as to be understood.
ELIE WIESEL

IN THIS CHAPTER . . . Make your notes more powerful by experimenting with new ways to observe, record, and review. Take effective notes on reading, keep up when instructors talk fast, and improve your handwriting. Also use the art of journal writing to take notes on your life. And discover "I create it all"—a way to maximize your choices even when circumstances seem to drag you down.

The note-taking process flows

One way to understand note taking is to realize that taking notes is the least important part of the process.

Effective note taking consists of three parts: observing, recording, and reviewing. First, you observe an event—most often a statement by the instructor. Then you record your observations of that event—that is, you "take notes." Finally, you review what you have recorded.

Each part of the process is essential, and each depends on the others. Your observations determine what you record. What you record determines what you review. Less obviously, how well you review can determine how effective your next observations will be. For example, if you review your notes on the Sino-Japanese War of 1894, the next day's lecture on the Boxer Rebellion of 1900 will make more sense.

Certainly, legible and speedy handwriting is also useful in taking notes. A knowledge of outlining is handy, too. A nifty pen, a new notebook, even a fancy tape recorder or a laptop computer are all great note-taking devices.

And they're all worthless—unless you participate as an energetic observer in class and regularly review your notes after class. If you take those two steps, you can turn even the most disorganized chicken scratches into a powerful tool.

JOURNAL ENTRY

#22

Discovery Statement

Recall a recent incident in which you had difficulty taking notes. Perhaps you were listening to an instructor who talked fast, or you got confused and stopped taking notes altogether. Describe the incident here.

_____
_____
_____
_____
_____
_____
_____
_____
_____
_____
_____
_____

Now preview this chapter for five suggestions that you can use right away to take better notes. Sum up each of those strategies in a few words and note page numbers where you can find out more about each suggestion.

Strategy   Page number

_____
_____
_____
_____
_____
_____
_____
_____
_____
_____
_____

Observe
The note-taking process flows

OBSERVE.

Sherlock Holmes, a fictional master detective and student of the obvious, could track down a villain by observing the wrinkles in his hat and the mud on his shoes. In real life, a doctor can save a life by observing a mole—one a patient has always had—that suddenly deserves medical attention.

An accountant can save a client thousands of dollars by observing the details of a spreadsheet. A student can save hours of study time by observing that she gets twice as much done at a particular time of day.

Keen observers see facts and relationships. They know ways to focus their attention on the details, then tap their creative energy to discover patterns. To sharpen your classroom observation skills, experiment with the following techniques and continue to use those that you find most valuable.

Set the stage

1 *Complete outside assignments.* Nothing is more discouraging (or boring) than sitting through a lecture about the relationship of the Le Chatelier principle to the principle of kinetics if you have never heard of Le Chatelier or kinetics.

Instructors usually assume that students complete assignments, and they construct their lectures accordingly. The more familiar you are with a subject, the more easily you can absorb important information during class lectures.

2 *Bring the right materials.* A good pen does not make you a good observer, but the lack of a pen or a notebook can be distracting enough to take the fine edge off your concentration. Make sure you have a pen, pencil, notebook, and any other materials you will need. Bring your textbook to class, especially if the lectures relate closely to the text.

If you are consistently unprepared for class, that might be a message about your intentions concerning the course. Find out if it is. The next time you're in a frantic scramble to borrow pen and paper 37 seconds before class begins, notice the cost. Use the borrowed pen and paper to write a Discovery Statement about your lack of preparation. Consider whether you intend to be successful in the class.

3 *Sit front and center.* Students who get as close as possible to the front and center of the classroom often do better on tests for several reasons. The closer you sit to the lecturer, the harder it is to fall asleep. The closer you sit to the front, the fewer interesting, or distracting, heads there are to watch between you and the instructor. Material on the board is easier to read from up front. Also, the instructor can see you more easily when you have a question.

Instructors are usually not trained as actors or performers. Some can project their energy to a large audience; many cannot. A professor who sounds boring from the back of the room might sound more interesting if you're closer. Get close to the energy.

Sitting up front is a way to commit yourself to getting what you want out of school. One reason students gravitate to the back of the classroom is that they think the instructor is less likely to call on them. Sitting in back can signal a lack of commitment. When you sit in front, you are declaring your willingness to take a risk and participate.

4 **Conduct a short preclass review.** Arrive early, then put your brain in gear by reviewing your notes from the previous class. Scan your reading assignment. Look at the sections you have underlined. Review assigned problems and exercises. Note questions you intend to ask.

5 **Clarify your intentions.** Write a short Intention Statement about what you plan to get from the class. Describe your intended level of participation or the quality of attention you will bring to the subject. Be specific. If you found previous class notes to be inadequate, write down things you intend to do to make your notes from this class session more useful.

"Be here now" in class

6 **Accept your wandering mind.** The techniques in the Power Process "Be here now" can be especially useful when your head soars into the clouds. Don't fight daydreaming. When you notice your mind wandering, look at this as an opportunity to refocus your attention. If you notice that your attention is wandering from thermodynamics to beach parties, let go of the beach.

7 **Notice your writing.** When you discover yourself slipping into a fantasyland, notice how your pen feels in your hand. Notice how your notes look. Paying attention to the act of writing can bring you back to the here and now.

You also can use writing more directly to clear your mind of distracting thoughts. Pause for a few seconds and write those thoughts down. If you're distracted by thoughts of errands you want to run after class, list them on a 3×5 card and stick it in your pocket. Or simply put a symbol, such as an arrow or asterisk, in your notes to mark the places where your mind started to wander. Once your distractions are out of your mind and safely stored on paper, you can gently return your attention to taking notes.

8 **Be with the instructor.** In your mind, put yourself right up front with the instructor. Imagine that you and the instructor are the only ones in the room and the lecture is a personal conversation with you. Pay attention to the instructor's body language and facial expressions. Look the instructor in the eye.

9 **Notice your environment.** When you become aware of yourself daydreaming, bring yourself back to class by paying attention to the temperature in the room, the feel of your chair, or the quality of light coming through the window. Run your hand along the surface of your desk. Listen to the chalk on the blackboard or the sound of the teacher's voice. Be in that environment. Once your attention is back in the room, you can focus on what's happening in class.

10 **Postpone debate.** When you hear something you disagree with, note your disagreement and let it go. Don't allow your internal dialogue to drown out subsequent material. If your disagreement is persistent and strong, make note of this and then move on. Internal debate can prevent you from absorbing new information. It is OK to absorb information you don't agree with. Just absorb it with the mental tag "I don't agree with this and my instructor says. . . ."

11 **Let go of judgments about lecture styles.** Human beings are judgment machines. We evaluate everything, especially other people. If another person's eyebrows are too close together (or too far apart), if she walks a certain way or combs her hair a certain way, we instantly make up a story about her. We do this so quickly that the process is usually not a conscious one.

Don't let your attitude about an instructor's lecture style, habits, or appearance get in the way of your education. You can decrease the power of your judgments if you pay attention to them and let them go.

You can even let go of judgments about rambling, unorganized lectures. Turn them to your advantage. Take the initiative and organize the material yourself. While taking notes, separate the key points from the examples and supporting evidence. Note the places where you got confused and make a list of questions to ask.

12 **Participate in class activities.** Ask questions. Volunteer for demonstrations. Join in class discussions. Be willing to take a risk or look foolish, if that's what it takes for you to learn. Chances are, the question you think is "dumb" is also on the minds of several of your classmates.

13 **Relate the class to your goals.** If you have trouble staying awake in a particular class, write at the top of your notes how that class relates to a specific goal. Note the reward or payoff for reaching that goal.

14 **Think critically about what you hear.** This might seem contrary to #10: "Postpone debate." It's not. You might choose not to think critically about the instructor's ideas during the lecture. That's fine. Do it later, as you review and edit your notes. This is a time to list questions or write down your agreements and disagreements.

Watch for clues

15 ***Be alert to repetition.*** When an instructor repeats a phrase or an idea, make a note of it. Repetition is a signal that the instructor thinks the information is important.

16 ***Listen for introductory, concluding, and transition words and phrases.*** These include phrases such as "the following three factors," "in conclusion," "the most important consideration," "in addition to," "on the other hand." These phrases and others signal relationships, definitions, new subjects, conclusions, cause and effect, and examples. They reveal the structure of the lecture. You can use these phrases to organize your notes.

17 ***Watch the board or overhead projector.*** If an instructor takes time to write something down, consider that a signal that the material is important. Copy all diagrams and drawings, equations, names, places, dates, statistics, and definitions.

18 ***Watch the instructor's eyes.*** If an instructor glances at her notes and then makes a point, it is probably a signal that the information is especially important. Anything she reads from her notes is a potential test question.

19 ***Highlight the obvious clues.*** Instructors will often tell students point-blank that certain information is likely to appear on an exam. Make stars or other special marks in your notes next to this information. Instructors are not trying to hide what's important.

20 ***Notice the instructor's interest level.*** If the instructor is excited about a topic, it is more likely to appear on an exam. Pay attention when she seems more animated than usual.

JOURNAL ENTRY #23

Discovery Statement

Think back on the last few lectures you have attended and also recall some of your previous lecture classes. How do you currently observe (listen to) lectures? What specific behaviors do you have as you sit and listen? How are these behaviors different from those in the past? Write your responses in the space below.

_____

_____

_____

_____

_____

_____

_____

EXERCISE #17

The in-class oxygenator

If you become sleepy in class, the problem might be lack of oxygen. You can run through the following process in 30 seconds.

1. Straighten your spine. Put both feet on the floor, uncross your arms and legs, sit up straight, and hold your head up high.

2. Take a deep breath, and while you're holding it, tense the muscles in your body. Start with the muscles in your feet, then in your legs, thighs, stomach, chest, shoulders, neck, jaw, forehead, arms, and hands. Hold these muscles tense while counting to five, and then relax and exhale.

3. Next, breathe deeply three times. Inhale slowly, using your abdomen as well as your chest. Pause momentarily at the top of the breath, and then exhale completely. When you have exhaled as much as you can, force out more air by contracting the muscles of your abdomen.

4. Repeat step #2.

   Once you've activated all of your muscles and filled your body with oxygen, you are ready to return your attention to the task at hand. Practice this exercise now by completing all four steps twice. Then make a mental note to use this exercise the next time you get drowsy in class or when studying. With a little practice, you can do it subtly. Your instructor and classmates won't even notice.

Record

The note-taking process flows

RECORD.

The format and structure of your notes are more important than how fast you write or how elegant your handwriting is. The following techniques can improve the effectiveness of your notes.

1 Use the Cornell format of note taking.

In his writings on student success, Walter Pauk suggests a note-taking system he calls the Cornell format.[1] It works like this: On each page of your notes, draw a vertical line, top to bottom, 1 1/2 inches from the left edge of the paper. Write your notes to the right of the line. Reserve the area to the left of the line for key word clues and sample questions. Fill in the left-hand column when you review your notes.

Metal Conductive	Hard, shiny, malleable (roll into sheets), ductile (pulled into wires). Conducts electric current & heat. 3 or fewer electrons in outer level so good conductors because electrons can move thru.
Metallic Bond	Outer electrons distributed as common electric cloud. Electrons shared equally by all ions which explains properties (conductive, malleable, ductile) → ions slide by each other & can be displaced w/o shattering.
Alkali Metals	Soft metals. Most reactive – kept under oil so won't react directly w/oxygen or H_2O. Forms compound by ionic bonding. Can identify alkalis by flame test. Electrons gain energy when heated. When cooling, lose energy as light. Ex: Ca = red, Cu = green, K = blue

2 Create mind maps.

This system, developed by Tony Buzan,[2] can be used in conjunction with the Cornell system. In some circumstances, you might want to use mind maps exclusively.

To understand mind maps, first review the features of traditional note taking. Roman numeral and capital letter outlines contain main topics that are followed by minor topics, which, in turn, are subdivided further. They organize a subject in a sequential, linear way.

Such organization doesn't reflect some other aspects of brain function. This point has been made in the discussions about "left brain" and "right brain" activities. People often use the term *right brain* when referring to creative, pattern-making, visual, intuitive brain activity. They use the term *left brain* when talking about the orderly, logical, step-by-step characteristics of thought. Writing teacher Gabrielle Rico uses another metaphor. She refers to the left-brain mode as our "sign mind" (concerned with words) and the right-brain mode as our "design mind" (concerned with visuals).[3]

A mind map uses both kinds of brain functions. Mind maps can contain lists and sequences and show relationships. They also provide a picture of a subject. Mind maps are visual patterns that can serve as a framework for recall. They work on both verbal and nonverbal levels.

One benefit of mind maps is that they quickly, vividly, and accurately show the relationships between ideas. Also, mind mapping helps you think from general to specific. By choosing a main topic, you focus first on the big picture, then zero in on subordinate ideas. And by using only key words, you can condense a large subject into a small area on a mind map. You can review more quickly by looking at the key words on a mind map than by reading notes word for word. The sample mind map on page 147 illustrates these points.

As you build a mind map on paper, you are also constructing a map in your mind. When you are finished, the picture of the map enters your memory. You could throw away your paper mind map and still retain most of the benefits of making it.

The following guidelines can assist you in creating mind maps.

Give yourself plenty of room. Use blank paper that measures at least 11 by 17 inches. If that's not available, turn regular notebook paper on its side so that you take notes in a horizontal (instead of vertical) format. Another option is to find software that allows you to draw flow charts or diagrams. Then you can generate mind maps on a computer.

Determine the main concept of the lecture. Write that concept in the center of the page and circle it, underline it, or highlight it in some way. Record concepts related to the main concept on lines radiating from the center.

Use key words only. Aim for one word per line. Though this might seem awkward at first, it prompts you to summarize and reduce ideas to their essence. That's fewer words for you to write now and fewer to review when it's time to prepare for tests. (Using shorthand symbols and abbreviations can help.) Key words are usually nouns and verbs that carry the bulk of the speaker's ideas. Choose words rich in associations and those that can help you re-create the lecture.

Jazz it up. Use color to organize your mind map. If there are three main subjects covered in the lecture, you can record each subject in a different color. Add symbols and other images.

Create links. One mind map doesn't have to include all of the ideas in a book or an article. Instead, you can link mind maps. For example, draw a mind map that sums up the five key points in a chapter; then make a separate, more detailed mind map for each of those key points. Within each mind map, include references to the other mind maps. This helps in seeing the relationships among many ideas.

Some students pin several mind maps next to each other on a bulletin board or tape them to a wall. This gives a dramatic, and effective, look at the big picture.

Combine formats. Mind maps can be used along with Cornell format notes in a number of ways. You can divide your note paper in half, reserving one half for mind maps and the other for information more suited to the traditional paragraph method: equations, long explanations, and word-for-word definitions. You can incorporate a mind map into your paragraph-style notes wherever you feel one is appropriate. Mind maps are also useful for summarizing notes taken in the Cornell format.

Another way to use mind maps is to modify the Cornell format by drawing a line down the center of the page and using the left-hand side for mind mapping and the right-hand side for more linear information, such as lists, graphs, and paragraphs.

3 Write notes in outline form. You can use a standard Roman numeral outline or a free form, indented outline to organize the information in a lecture.

The outline form illustrates major points and supporting ideas. The main advantage to taking notes in outline form is that it can totally occupy your attention. You are not only recording ideas but also organizing them. That can be an advantage if material is presented in a disorganized way.

4 Write notes in paragraphs. When it is difficult to follow the organization of a lecture or to put information into outline form, create a series of informal paragraphs. These paragraphs will contain few complete sentences. Reserve complete sentences for precise definitions, direct quotations, and important points that the instructor emphasizes by repetition or other signals—such as the phrase "This is an important point." For other material, apply the suggestions in technique #5: "Use key words."

Write related thoughts in a paragraph, leaving a space when the lecturer moves on to another point. That way, you can go back and add information that the instructor offers later. When you review your notes, you can reorganize them and create an outline.

5 Use key words. An easy way to sort the extraneous material from the important points is to take notes using key words. Key words or phrases contain

the essence of communication. They include technical terms, names, numbers, equations, and words of degree: *most, least, faster,* etc.

Key words evoke images and associations with other words and ideas. They trigger your memory. That makes them powerful review tools.

One key word can initiate the recall of a whole cluster of ideas. A few key words can form a chain from which you can reconstruct an entire lecture.

To see how key words work, take yourself to an imaginary classroom. You are now in the middle of an anatomy lecture. Picture what the room looks like, what it feels like, how it smells. You hear the instructor say:

> *OK, what happens when we look directly over our heads and see a piano falling out of the sky? How do we take that signal and translate it into the action of getting out of the way? The first thing that happens is that a stimulus is generated in the neurons—receptor neurons—of the eye. Light reflected from the piano reaches our eyes. In other words, we see the piano. The receptor neurons in the eye transmit that sensory signal, the sight of the piano, to the body's nervous system. That's all they can do, pass on information. So we've got a sensory signal coming into the nervous system. But the neurons that initiate movement in our legs are effector neurons. The information from the sensory neurons must be transmitted to effector neurons or we will get squashed by the piano. There must be some kind of interconnection between receptor and effector neurons. What happens between the two? What is the connection?*

Key words you might note in this example include *stimulus, generated, receptor neurons, transmit, sensory signals, nervous system, effector neurons,* and *connection.* You could reduce the instructor's 148 words to these 12 key words. With a few transitional words, your notes might look like this:

Stimulus (piano) generated in receptor neurons (eye). Sensory signals transmitted by nervous system to effector neurons (legs). What connects receptor to effector?

Note the last key word of the lecture, *connection.* This word is part of the instructor's question and leads to the next point in the lecture. Be alert for questions like this. They can help you organize your notes, and they are often clues for test questions.

6 Use pictures and diagrams. Make relationships visual. Copy all diagrams from the board and invent your own. This technique can be used anytime, with or without mind mapping. A drawing of a piano falling on someone who is looking up, for example, might be used to demonstrate the relationship of receptor neurons to effector neurons. Label the eyes "receptor" and the feet "effector." This picture implies that the sight of the piano must be translated into a motor response. By connecting the explanation of the process with the unusual picture of the piano falling, you can link the elements of the process together.

7 Copy material from the board. Record all formulas, diagrams, and problems. Copy dates, numbers, names, places, and other facts. If it's on the board, put it in your notes. You can even use your own signal or code to flag that material. If it appears on the board, it can appear on a test.

8 Use a three-ring binder. Three-ring binders have several advantages over other kinds of notebooks. First, pages can be removed and spread out when you review. This way, you can get the whole picture of a lecture. Second, the three-ring binder format allows you to insert handouts right into your notes. Third, you can insert your own out-of-class notes in the correct order. Fourth, you can easily make additions, corrections, and revisions.

9 Use only one side of a piece of paper. When you use one side of a page, you can review and organize all your notes by spreading them out side by side. Most students find the benefit well worth the cost of the paper. Perhaps you're concerned about the environmental impact of consuming more paper. If so, you can use the blank side of old notes and use recycled paper.

10 Use 3×5 cards. As an alternative to using notebook paper, use 3×5 cards to take lecture notes. Copy each new concept onto a separate 3×5 card. Later, you can organize these cards in an outline form and use them as pocket flash cards.

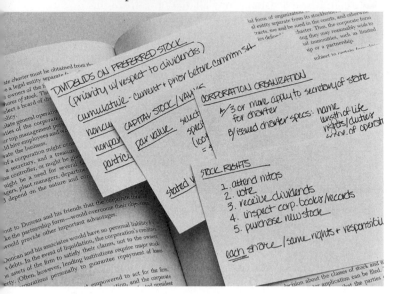

11 Keep your own thoughts separate. For the most part, avoid making editorial comments in your lecture notes. The danger is that when you return to your notes, you might mistake your own idea for that of the instructor. If you want to make a comment—either a question to ask later or a strong disagreement—clearly label it as your own. Pick a symbol or code and use it in every class.

12 Use an "I'm lost" signal. No matter how attentive and alert you are, you might get lost and confused in a lecture. If it is inappropriate to ask a question, record in your notes that you were lost. Invent your own signal—for example, a circled question mark. When you write down your code for "I'm lost," leave space for the explanation or clarification that you will get later. The space will also be a signal that you missed something. Later, you can call your instructor or ask to see a fellow student's notes. As long as you are honest with yourself when you don't understand, you can stay on top of the course.

13 Label, number, and date all notes. Develop the habit of labeling and dating your notes at the beginning of each class. Number the page, too. Sometimes the sequence of material in a lecture is important. Write your name and phone number in each notebook in case you lose it. Class notes become more and more valuable as a term or semester progresses.

14 Use standard abbreviations. Be consistent with your abbreviations. If you make up your own abbreviations or symbols, write a key explaining them in your notes.

Avoid vague abbreviations. When you use an abbreviation such as *comm.* for *committee*, you run the risk of not being able to remember whether you meant *committee, commission, common, commit, community, communicate,* or *communist.*

One way to abbreviate is to leave out vowels. For example, *talk* becomes *tlk, said* becomes *sd, American* becomes *Amrcn.*

WARNING: Abbreviations can be hazardous to your academic health. If you use inconsistent or vague abbreviations, there will be a price to pay in confusion later on. One way to avoid that is to write out abbreviated terms during pauses in a lecture, when the meaning of your shorthand is still fresh in your short-term memory.

15 Leave blank space. Notes tightly crammed into every corner of the page are hard to read and difficult to use for review. Give your eyes a break by leaving plenty of space.

Later, when you review, you can use the blank space in your notes to clarify points, write questions, or add other material. Instructors often return to material covered earlier in the lecture. If you leave adequate space, you can add information.

16 Use tape recorders effectively. There are persuasive arguments for *not* using a tape recorder. Here are the main ones.

When you tape a lecture, there is a strong temptation to daydream. After all, you can always listen to the lecture again later on. Unfortunately, if you let the recorder do all the work, you are skipping a valuable part of the learning process. Your active participation in class can turn a lecture into a valuable study session.

There are more potential problems. Listening to tape-recorded lectures can take a lot of time—more time than reviewing written notes. Tape recorders can't answer the questions you didn't ask in class. Also, tape recorders malfunction. In fact, the unscientific Hypothesis of Recording Glitches states that the tendency of tape recorders to malfunction is directly proportional to the importance of the material.

With those warnings in mind, some students use a tape recorder effectively. For example, you can use recordings as backups to written notes. (Check with your instructor first. Some prefer not to be taped.) Turn the recorder on, then take notes as if it weren't there.

Recordings can be especially useful if an instructor speaks fast.

You could also record yourself after class, reading your written notes. Teaching the class to yourself is a powerful review tool. Instead of taping all of your notes, for example, you might record only the key facts or concepts.

You can have fun, too. As you tape, speak in funny voices. Do imitations of your teachers or favorite actors. Add background music. Make these tapes enjoyable for listening. You can use the recordings you make or the backup recordings from class to review while you drive, wash dishes, or exercise.

Some tape recorders have a feature called compressed speech. This speeds up the voice on the tape, which can save you listening time.

Knowing the pitfalls of tape recorders, experiment for yourself. Then adopt a strategy that works for you.

17 Use complete sentences when material is important. Sometimes key
words aren't enough. When an instructor repeats a sentence word for word, she might be sending you a signal. Technical definitions are often worded precisely because even a slightly different wording will change the intended meaning, rendering the definitions useless or incorrect.

18 Take notes in different colors. You can
use colors as highly visible organizers. For example, you can signal important points with red. Or use one color of ink for notes about the text and another color for lecture notes. Notes that are visually pleasing can be easier to review.

19 Use graphic signals. The following ideas
can be used with any note-taking format, including mind maps.

- Use brackets, parentheses, circles, and squares to group information that belongs together.
- Use stars, arrows, and underlining to indicate important points. Flag the most important points with double stars, double arrows, or double underlines.
- Use arrows and connecting lines to link related groups and to replace words such as *leads to*, *becomes*, and *produces*.
- Use equal signs and greater- and less-than signs to indicate compared quantities.
- Use question marks for their obvious purpose. Double question marks can signal tough questions or especially confusing points.

To avoid creating confusion with graphic symbols, use them carefully and consistently. Write a "dictionary" of your symbols in the front of your notebooks, such as the one shown below.

20 Record effectively when learning
online. While in school, you might log lots of computer time. Your courses might require you to receive and send email messages, visit web sites, and take part in interactive chat room sessions with teachers and other students. You might even sign up for classes that take place entirely online.

When it comes to taking notes, an online course presents opportunities—and potential problems.

One opportunity is that students can print out anything that appears on a computer screen. This includes articles, email messages, chat room sessions, and more.

One potential problem: Students might skip taking notes altogether. ("I can just print out everything!") They would miss the chance to internalize a new idea by restating it in their own words—a requirement for taking notes in a traditional classroom.

Result: Material would pass from computer to printer without ever intersecting a student's brain.

To prevent this problem, find ways to actively engage with online course material. Talk about what you're learning (and consider running a tape recorder at the same time). Write summaries of online articles and chat room sessions. Also write Discovery and Intention Statements to capture key insights from the course and ways you plan to apply them.

Of course, it's fine to print out materials. Then you can treat your printouts like a textbook and apply the steps of Muscle Reading explained in this book.

Review
The note-taking process flows

YES!

REVIEW.

Think of reviewing as an integral part of note taking rather than as an added task. To make information useful, make it available to your recall.

1 *Review within 24 hours.* In the last chapter, when you read the suggestion to review what you've read within 24 hours, you were asked to sound the trumpet. Well, if you have one, get it out and sound it again. This might be the most powerful note-taking technique you can use. It can save you hours of review time later in the term.

Many students are surprised that they can remember the content of a lecture in the minutes and hours after class. They are even more surprised by how well they can read even the sloppiest of notes.

Unfortunately, short-term memory deteriorates quickly. The good news: If you get back to your notes for a quick review soon enough, you can move that information from short-term to long-term memory. And you can do it in just a few minutes—often 10 minutes or less.

The sooner you review your notes, the better, especially if the class was difficult. In fact, you can start reviewing during class. When your instructor pauses to set up the overhead projector or erase the board, scan your notes. Dot the *i*'s, cross the *t*'s, and write out unclear abbreviations. Another way to use this technique is to get to your next class as quickly as you can. Then use the four or five minutes before the lecture begins to review the notes you just took in the previous class.

If you do not get to your notes immediately after class, you can still benefit by reviewing later in the day. A review right before you go to sleep can also be valuable.

Think of the day's unreviewed notes as leaky faucets, constantly dripping, losing precious information until you shut them off with a quick review. Remember, it's possible to forget up to 80 percent of the material within 24 hours—unless you review.

2 *Edit notes.* During your first review, fix words that are illegible. Write out abbreviated words that might be unclear to you later. Make sure you can read everything. If you can't read something or don't understand something you can read, then mark it, and make a note to ask your instructor or another student. Check to see that your notes are labeled with the date and class and that the pages are numbered. You can edit with a different colored pen or pencil if you want to distinguish between what you wrote in class and what you filled in later.

3 *Fill in key words in the left-hand column.* This task is important if you are to get the full benefit of using the Cornell format. Using the key word principles described earlier in this chapter, go through your notes and write key words or phrases in the left-hand column.

These key words will speed the review process later. As you read your notes and focus on extracting key concepts, your understanding of the lecture is further reinforced.

4 *Use your key words as cues to recite.* With a blank sheet of paper, cover your notes, leaving only the key words in the left-hand margin showing. Take each key word in order and recite as much as you can about the point. Then uncover your notes and look for any important points you missed.

5 *Conduct short weekly review periods.* Once a week, review all your notes again. The review sessions don't need to take a lot of time. Even a 20-minute weekly review period is valuable. Some students find that a weekend review, say on Sunday afternoon, helps them stay in continuous touch with the material. Scheduling regular review sessions on your calendar helps develop the habit.

As you review, step back to see the larger picture. In addition to reciting or repeating the material to yourself, ask questions about it: Does this relate to my goals? How does this compare to information I already know, in this field or another? Will I be tested on this material? What will I do with this material? How can I associate it with something that deeply interests me? Am I unclear on any points? If so, what exactly is the question I want to ask?

6 *Consider typing up your notes.* Some students type clean copies of their handwritten notes using a computer. The argument for doing so is threefold. First, typed notes are easier to read. They also take up less space. In addition, the process of typing them forces you to review the material.

Yet another alternative is to bypass handwriting altogether and take notes in class on a laptop computer. Possible drawbacks: Laptops are more expensive than PCs, and computer errors can wipe out your notes.

Experiment with typing notes and see what works for you. For example, you might type up only portions of notes—summaries or outlines.

7 Create mind map summaries.

Mind mapping is an excellent way to make summary sheets. After making your map, look at your original notes and fill in anything you missed. This system is fun to use. It's quick, and it gives your brain a hook on which to fasten the material.

Data Processing

comp = computer
tech = technology
chgs = changes
dev = developed
mach = machine

machines are useful — Save labor
Science + tech = Social value
1642 Pascal calculating machine
Scientific revolution 1543–1687

History of Computers

Hollerith – EAMS
WWI – Mark I mechan/relay
1951 1st comp
Eckert – mauchly
WWI Edvack
18,000 vactubes
American ingenuity

1804 Jaquard
industrial revolution
punch cards

Television note taking

You can use evening news broadcasts to practice listening for key words, writing quickly, focusing your attention, and reviewing. As with other skills, the more you practice note taking, the better you become.

The next time you watch the news, have pen and paper at hand. During the commercials, review and revise your notes. At the end of the broadcast, spend five minutes reviewing all of your notes. Create a mind map of a few news stories, then re-create the news of the day for a friend.

This exercise will help you develop an ear for key words. Since you can't ask questions or request that the speaker slow down, you train yourself to stay totally in the moment. If you get behind, relax, leave a space, and return your attention to the broadcast.

Don't be discouraged if you miss a lot the first time around. Do this exercise several times and observe how your mind works.

If you find it too difficult to take notes during a fast-paced television news show, check your local broadcast schedule for a news documentary. These are often slower paced. Another option is to videotape a program and then take notes. You can stop the tape at any point to check your notes.

You can also ask a friend to do the same exercise, and then compare notes the next day.

Discovery Statement

Think about the way you have conducted reviews of your notes in the past. Respond to the following statements by checking "Always," "Often," "Sometimes," "Seldom," or "Never" after each.

I review my notes immediately after class.
__Always __Often __Sometimes __Seldom __Never

I conduct weekly reviews of my notes.
__Always __Often __Sometimes __Seldom __Never

I make summary sheets of my notes.
__Always __Often __Sometimes __Seldom __Never

I edit my notes within 24 hours.
__Always __Often __Sometimes __Seldom __Never

Before class, I conduct a brief review of the notes I took in the previous class.
__Always __Often __Sometimes __Seldom __Never

Improving your handwriting

Many people are resigned to writing illegibly for the rest of their lives. They feel that they have no control over their handwriting. Yet everyone's handwriting does change. Your signature when you're on top of the world is not the same as when you are down in the dumps. Handwriting also changes as you mature. If you unconsciously change your handwriting, you can change it consciously. The prerequisite for improving your handwriting is simply a desire to change.

If you want to write more legibly, here are some possibilities.

Use the First Step technique. Take a First Step by telling the truth about the problem. Admit it, then acknowledge your desire to improve.

The problem, by the way, is not bad handwriting; it's the impact of the handwriting. The problem is usually expressed as "I can't read my notes and therefore I have difficulty studying." Or "The people I work with are getting upset because they can't read what I write."

Use creative visualizations. Find a quiet spot to sit, then relax your whole body, close your eyes, and see yourself writing clearly. Feel the pen as it moves over the page, and picture neat, legible letters as you write them.

Keep your eye on the ballpoint. Watch the way you write. Don't "try" to change. Focus all of your attention on the tip of the pen, right where it meets the paper. When you do this, let go of judgments or evaluations about how you write. By focusing your attention on the tip of your pen, you are giving your brain something to do, thereby letting your body do the writing.

Demonstrate your excellence. At least once a day, write something down as clearly as you can. Write it as if it were going to appear on the front page of the *New York Times*. You can program your body to write clearly.

Revise sloppy writing immediately. Use an erasable pen or pencil. When you write something sloppily, fix it immediately. At first, you might find yourself rewriting almost everything. This technique can help you learn to write legibly.

Practice with the best materials. When you put a quality pen to fancy paper, there is incentive to produce clean, crisp, pleasing lines. Practice with these fine materials by writing notes to people you care about.

Take a calligraphy course. Improve your hand-eye coordination with calligraphy. The practice you get working with a calligraphy pen might improve your overall writing.

Dot all i's and cross all t's. The time you spend dotting and crossing will eliminate time spent scratching your head.

Ensure that holes exist. Leave holes in your a's, e's, and o's. If you don't, they can easily be mistaken for i's.

Notice problem letters. Go through your notes and circle letters that you have difficulty deciphering. Practice writing these letters.

When understanding is critical, print. When an important idea must be letter perfect, print it. Printing will stand out from your other notes. And you can read printing faster when you review.

Be willing to slow down ... some. Weigh the costs and benefits of writing more slowly as a way to improve your handwriting. If you cannot read what you write, then speed is of little use. On the other hand, writing too slowly and carefully when taking notes can result in missing the main points of a lecture. One possible solution is to write less. Take fewer notes; write down only what's essential. Learning to take notes efficiently could allow you to improve your handwriting and spend less time writing and more time learning.

Appreciate the value of legible writing. Notice how you feel when your own handwriting works well for you. Write a Discovery Statement when you become aware that you have improved your handwriting, and list the benefits of the improvement.

Consider the impact of handwriting

Step one

Imagine for a moment that you are the teacher for the student success course at your school. Following is a Discovery Statement submitted by one of your students:

> I discovered that I prefer using the Cornell system when taking notes in my psychology class.
>
> I also discovered that creating a mind map works better for notes on philosophy course.

Describe below your first impressions of this student's handwriting. List any assumptions you made about:

- The student's level of interest in the class.

- The amount of time the student put into the assignment.

- This student's feelings about you as a teacher.

   Also note any feelings you have about the student, based on this piece of writing.

_____

_____

_____

Step two

Bring yourself back to your current role as a person taking a student success course. On a separate sheet of paper, copy the above Discovery Statement in your own handwriting.

Step three

Now consider your handwriting. In the space below, list the assumptions your instructor might make about you and your commitment to this class. Follow up with an Intention Statement about any changes you want to make in your handwriting.

_____

_____

_____

_____

_____

_____

20

Apply a process

"Love your problems" was the Power Process presented in Chapter Three. Write down how you can apply the idea of loving your problems to the task of note taking.

_____

_____

_____

_____

_____

_____

Create your instructor

There are as many definitions of a "poor" instructor as there are students. For some students, "poor" means "boring," "rude," or "insensitive." Or maybe it's an instructor who never remembers what day it is, blows her nose every five minutes, and wears a cologne that could kill a hamster at 30 paces.

Faced with such facts, you have some choices. One is to label the instructor a "dud," "dweeb," "geek," or "airhead," and let it go at that. When you choose this solution, you get to endure class, complain to other students, and wait for a miracle. This choice puts you at the mercy of circumstance. It gives your instructor responsibility for the quality of your education, not to mention responsibility for giving you value for your money.

There is another option. You do not have to give away your power. Instead, you can take responsibility for your education. Use any of the following techniques to change the way you experience your instructors. In effect, you can "create your instructor."

Research the instructor. There are formal and informal sources of information you can turn to before you register for class. One is the school catalog. Alumni magazines or newsletters or the school newspaper might run articles on teachers. In some schools, students circulate informal evaluations of instructors. Also talk to students who have taken courses from the instructor.

Or introduce yourself to the instructor. Visit her during office hours and ask about the course. This can help you get the flavor of the class and clues to her teaching style.

Show interest in class. Students give teachers moment-by-moment feedback in class. That feedback comes through posture, eye contact, responses to questions, and participation in class discussions. If you find a class boring, re-create the instructor through a massive display of interest. Ask lots of questions. Show enthusiasm through nonverbal language—sit up straight, make eye contact, take detailed notes. Your enthusiasm might enliven your instructor. If not, you are still creating a more enjoyable class for yourself.

Take responsibility for your attitude. Maybe your instructor reminds you of someone you don't like—your annoying Aunt Edna, a rude store clerk, or the fifth-grade teacher who kept you after school. Your attitudes are in your own head and beyond the instructor's control.

An instructor's beliefs about politics, religion, or feminism are not related to teaching ability. Likewise, using a formal or informal lecture style does not indicate knowledge of subject matter. Being aware of such things can help you let go of negative judgments.

Get to know the instructor better. You might be missing the strong points of an instructor you don't like. Meet with your instructor during office hours. Ask questions that weren't answered in class. Teachers who seem boring in class can be fascinating in person. Prepare to notice your pictures and let them go.

Open up to diversity. Sometimes students can create their instructors by letting go of pictures about different races and ethnic groups. According to one picture, a Hispanic person cannot teach English literature. According to other pictures, a white teacher cannot have anything valid to say about African music; a teacher in a wheelchair cannot command the attention of 100 people in a lecture hall; and a male instructor cannot speak credibly about feminism. All of those pictures can clash with reality. Releasing them can open up new opportunities for understanding and appreciation.

Separate liking from learning.

If you're dissatisfied with your instructor, your assessment is probably valid. Don't assume that you are wrong for disliking her. Instructors who know a lot about their specialty might not be skilled teachers.

Even in this situation, you can still create value. The idea is to accept your feelings and take responsibility for what you learn. Remember that you don't have to like an instructor to learn from one.

One strategy is to focus on content instead of form. Form is the way something is organized or presented. If you sit through a three-hour class irritated at the sound of an instructor's voice, you're focusing on the form of her presentation. When you put aside your concern about her voice and rivet your attention on the points she's making, you're focusing on content.

Personal preferences can get in the way, too. That happens when you don't like an instructor's clothes, hairstyle, political views, or mannerisms. If you see this happening, notice your response without judgment. Then gently return your attention to the class content.

Form your own opinion about each instructor.

Students talk about teachers, and you might hear conflicting reports. The same instructor could be described as a riveting speaker or completely lacking charisma. Decide for yourself.

Seek alternatives.

You might feel more comfortable with another teacher's style or way of organizing course materials. Consider changing teachers, asking another teacher for help outside class, or attending an additional section taught by a different instructor. You can also learn from other students, courses, tutors, study groups, books, and tapes. You can be a master student, even when you have teachers you don't like. Your education is your own creation.

Avoid excuses.

Instructors know them all. Most teachers can see a snow job coming before the first flake hits the ground. Accept responsibility for your own mistakes, and avoid thinking you can fool the professor. When you treat instructors honestly, you are more likely to be treated as a responsible adult in return.

Submit professional work.

Prepare papers and projects as if you were submitting them to an employer. Pay attention to form. Imagine that a promotion and raise will be determined by your work. Instructors often grade hundreds of papers during a term. Your neat, orderly, well-organized paper can lift an instructor's spirits after a long night of deciphering gibberish.

Arrive early for class.

You can visit with your instructor and get to know her better. You can review notes and prepare for class. Being on time demonstrates your commitment and interest.

Accept criticism.

Learn from your teachers' comments about your work. It is a teacher's job to give feedback. Don't take it personally.

Use conference time effectively.

Instructors are usually happy to answer questions about class content. To get the most out of conference time, be prepared to ask those questions. Bring your notes, text, and any other materials you might need. During this session you can also address more difficult subjects, such as grades, attendance policies, lecture styles, term papers, or personality conflicts.

Instead of trying to solve a serious problem in the few minutes before or after class, set up a separate meeting. The instructor might feel uncomfortable discussing the problem in front of the other students. The communication techniques suggested in this chapter can help make your conference time more effective.

Use course evaluations.

In many classes you'll have an opportunity to evaluate the instructor. When you're asked to do so, respond honestly. Write about the aspects of the class that did not work well for you. Offer specific ideas for improvement. Also note what did work well. Formal evaluations often come late in the course, after final tests and assignments. This might lead students to gloss over evaluations or give only vague feedback. If you want your feedback to make a difference, treat this evaluation as you would an assignment.

Take further steps, if appropriate.

Sometimes severe conflict develops between students and instructors. Feedback from students might not be enough to reach a resolution. In such cases, you might decide to file a complaint or ask for help from a third party, such as an administrator.

If you do, be prepared to document your case in writing. When talking about the instructor, offer details. Describe specific actions that created problems for the class. Stick to the facts—events that other class members can verify. Your school might have a set of established grievance procedures to use in these cases. Before you act, understand what the policies are. You are a consumer of education. You have a right and a responsibility to complain if you think you have been treated unfairly.

Get to the bones of your book with concept maps

Concept mapping, a tool pioneered by Joseph Novak and D. Bob Gowin, is a way to make the main ideas in a book leap off the page.[4] In creating a concept map, you reduce an author's message to its essence—its bare bones. This visual device helps display how a text is organized. Concept maps also promote critical thinking by revealing gaps in logic. Like mind maps (explained earlier in this chapter), concept maps let you form multiple connections between ideas. People who view mind maps as too unstructured or messy might find concept maps more appealing.

To create a concept map, follow four steps:

1. **List the key concepts in the text.** Aim to express each concept in three words or less. Most concept words are nouns, including terms and proper names.

   At this point, you can list the concepts in any order. For ease in ranking the concepts later, write each one on a single 3×5 card.

2. **Rank the concepts so that they flow from general to specific.** On a large sheet of paper, write the main concept at the top of the page. Place the most specific concepts near the bottom. Arrange the rest of the concepts in appropriate positions throughout the middle of the page. Circle each concept.

3. **Draw lines that connect the concepts.** On these connecting lines, add words that describe the relationship between the concepts. Again, limit yourself to the fewest words needed to make an accurate link. Linking words are often verbs, verb phrases, or prepositions.

4. **Finally, review your map.** Look for any concepts that are repeated in several places on the map. You can avoid these repetitions by adding more links between concepts. Also look for accurate linking words and missing concepts.

Below is a sample concept map.

 To see sample concept maps based on selected articles in this book, visit Houghton Mifflin's College Survival/Becoming a Master Student web site: **http://collegesurvival.college.hmco.com/students.**

JOURNAL ENTRY

#25

Discovery/Intention Statement

Of the classes in which you are presently enrolled, pick the one you find the least interesting. In the space below, write down all of the ways *you* make the class uninteresting (or less interesting than other classes).

_____

_____

_____

Now write down three ways you can re-create this class as interesting.

_____

_____

_____

  Share your responses to this Journal Entry with other students and see what they have to say. Visit Houghton Mifflin's College Survival/Becoming a Master Student web site: **http://collegesurvival.college.hmco.com/students.**

When your instructor talks fast

1 Take more time to prepare for class. Familiarity with a subject increases your ability to pick up on key points. If an instructor lectures quickly or is difficult to understand, conduct a thorough preview of the material to be covered.

2 Be willing to make choices. When an instructor talks fast, focus your attention on key points. Instead of trying to write everything down, choose what you think is important. Occasionally, you will make a wrong choice and neglect an important point. Worse things could happen. Stay with the lecture, write down key words, and revise your notes immediately after class.

3 Exchange photocopies of notes with classmates. Your fellow students might write down something you missed. At the same time, your notes might help them. Exchanging photocopies can fill in the gaps.

4 Leave large empty spaces in your notes. Leave plenty of room for filling in information you missed. Use a symbol that signals you've missed something, so you can remember to come back to it.

5 See the instructor after class. Take your class notes with you and show the instructor what you missed.

6 Use a tape recorder. Taping a lecture gives you a chance to hear it again whenever you choose. Some tape recorders allow you to vary the speed of the tape. With this feature, you can perform magic and actually slow down the instructor's speech.

7 Before class, take notes on your reading assignment. You can take detailed notes on the text before class. Leave plenty of blank space. Take these notes with you to class and simply add your lecture notes to them.

8 Go to the lecture again. Many classes are taught in multiple sections. That gives you the chance to hear a lecture at least twice—once in your regular class and again in another section of the class.

9 Learn shorthand. Some note-taking systems, known as shorthand, are specifically designed for getting ideas down fast. Books and courses are available to help you learn these systems. You can also devise your own shorthand. Invent one- or two-letter symbols for common words and phrases.

10 Ask questions—even if you're totally lost. Many instructors allow a question session. This is the time to ask about the points you missed.

There might be times when you feel so lost that you can't formulate a question. That's OK. One option is to report this fact to the instructor. She can often guide you to a clear question. Another option is to ask a related question. Often this will lead you to the question you really want to ask.

11 Ask the instructor to slow down. This is the most obvious solution. If asking the instructor to slow down doesn't work, ask her to repeat what you missed.

PRACTICING CRITICAL THINKING #8

Use a concept map as a tool to interpret and assess a piece of writing. First, list the key concepts from a chapter (or section of a chapter) in a textbook you're reading. Then connect these concepts with linking words, using the format described in the box "Get to the bones of your book with concept maps."

Now take a few minutes to evaluate the author's presentation. Pay special attention to the links between concepts. Are they accurate? Do they reflect false assumptions or logical fallacies? Write down your evaluation on a separate sheet of paper.

WORKPLACE APPLICATIONS

When taking notes during fast-paced meetings and conference calls, use suggestions from the article "When your instructor talks fast." Immediately after the call or meeting, review and edit your notes. Flag items that require follow-up action.

Taking notes on
The art of journal writing

If you've been writing Discovery and Intention Statements as you use *Becoming a Master Student,* you've already practiced the art of journal writing. You can continue this practice well beyond this course—for a lifetime, in fact.

Journal writing provides many benefits. To begin with, it offers a chance to hone writing skills and reflect on course work. In addition, journals promote self-awareness. Through journal writing we discover patterns in our lives. Our experiences take on the form of a story, with a beginning, middle, and end. We learn to step back from the daily hustle, spot recurring problems, and invent solutions.

Keeping a journal is a low-cost activity with a high return on investment. Begin with a pencil and a ream of the cheapest paper you can find. As your budget allows, you might wish to work with fancy pens and high-quality paper. You can also key in journal entries on a computer.

Just jump in and start

One thing that stops people from keeping a journal is writer's block. To get past this problem, do a free writing exercise: Set a timer and write for five minutes without stopping to revise. Just keep your hand moving and write anything that pops into your head. Put yourself on automatic pilot until the words start happening on their own.

There are many other ways to get started. Write letters—including those you don't plan to send. The person you're writing the letter to can be famous or obscure, near or far, dead or alive. This can be a useful way to deal with anger or grief.

Also use leading sentences to jump-start your writing. For example, many Journal Entries in this book start with "I discovered that I . . ." or "I intend to. . . ." Invent your own lead-ins.

Feel free to dream wildly. Create a compelling future. Include the details—what you want to have, do, and be five, 10, or 50 years from now. Write as if you've already attained your long-term goals. After this kind of brainstorm, focus on one goal and write an action plan to achieve it.

Make lists

For example, write down the five most influential people in your life and what they've taught you. If you're a parent, list the three most important skills you want to teach your children.

Keep a list of your favorite quotations. Record notable things that you and your friends say. In addition, list new words and their definitions. Writing them down helps these words become part of your working vocabulary.

You can make lists of any persons you've harmed and note how you plan to make amends. Listing resentments can rob them of their power and move you toward forgiveness.

Also make a list of what you've received from others. Record your thanks to people from whom you have benefited. You could end up with "an attitude of gratitude."

You know what's going on in your life better than anyone else. Create lists that serve your own purposes.

Use a journal for critical thinking

There's a saying about note taking: Words that go directly from the instructor's mouth to the student's paper—without ever entering the student's mind.

your journey

You can avoid this fate by writing in a journal. Here is a chance for you to stretch out mentally. Reflect on the significance of your courses. Draw on your own experiences for examples of the ideas you're studying. Speculate about how you might apply what you're learning in class.

One technique recommended by writing teachers Richard Solly and Roseann Lloyd is to imagine that you're sitting face to face with the author of your textbook.[5] Write what you would say to this person. Argue. Debate. Note questions you'd want to ask this person and then pose them in class.

Play with learning styles

Journals don't have to be limited to note paper. Draw. Paint. Create a collage or sculpture. Visualizing through art is a powerful way to remember your experiences. Write a piece of music. Dictate your journal entries into a tape recorder. Use a journal to take risks and explore new learning styles.

If you're shy about doing any of this, remember that no one else has to see the results. Your journal is in safe hands—your own.

Reread your journal

Use journals periodically to get in touch with an old friend—yourself. Rereading a journal entry can transport you across the years and alter your emotional state in seconds. Reading about times when you excelled at work, school, or relationships can rekindle your zest for life.

To aid in locating important entries, create an index or a table of contents for your journal notebook. If you use a computer for journal writing, see if your word processing software can do this automatically.

Use a journal to manage stress

Much stress has its source in negative self-talk—nagging voices in our heads that make dire predictions for the future and undermine our abilities: "This is the worst thing that could ever happen to me" or "I never finish what I start."

Getting these disempowering ideas outside your head and onto paper is one way to defuse them. Begin by listing any irrational, self-defeating beliefs you have. Then write down more reasonable, empowering beliefs and Intention Statements.

Use a journal to increase writing skills

Writing in a journal can sharpen your powers of observation. To begin with, list as many details as you can about a person or an object in your environment. Make your description as complete, vivid, and detailed as you can.

Try your hand at fiction too. Create characters for plays or novels. Write poems, short stories, or articles that you might submit for publication.

Review your journal for writing topics. Perhaps you've already written something that could become the basis for a research paper.

Use a journal for personal growth

Visualizations and affirmations can begin on the pages of your journal. Also write about your fears, hopes, dreams, and ambitions. In this way, a journal becomes a trusted confidant who always respects your safety and privacy. Here is a counselor who's available anyplace, anytime—for free.

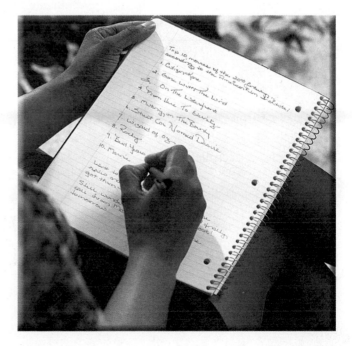

Taking notes while reading

Taking notes while reading requires the same skills that apply to class notes: observing, recording, and reviewing. Just remember that there are two kinds of notes that apply to reading: review notes and research notes.

Review notes will look like the notes you take in class. Sometimes you will want more extensive notes than you can write in a margin of your text. You can't underline or make notes in library books, so make separate notes when you use these sources.

Mind map summaries of textbook material are particularly useful for review. You can also outline material from the text or take notes in paragraph form. Single out a particularly difficult section of a text and make separate notes. Or make mind map summaries of overlapping lecture and text material. Use the left-hand column for key words and questions, just as you do in your class notes.

Research notes

Research notes—those you make for papers and speeches—follow a different format. Creating papers and speeches is a special challenge, and the way you take notes can help you face those challenges.

Use the mighty 3×5 card. There are two kinds of research cards: source cards and information cards. Source cards identify where information is found. For example, a source card on a book will show the title, author, date and place of publication, and publisher. Source cards are also written for magazine articles, interviews, tapes, or any other research material.

When you write source cards, give each source a code—either the initials of the author, a number, or a combination of numbers and letters.

The beauty of using source cards is that you are creating your bibliography as you do the research. When you are done, simply alphabetize the cards by author and—voilà!—instant bibliography.

Write the actual notes on information cards. At the top of each information card, write the code for the source from which you got the information. Also include the page number your notes are based on.

Most important, remember to write only one piece of information on each information card. You can then sort your cards and use them to construct an outline of the paper.

Another option is to take notes using a computer. This offers the same advantage as 3×5 cards—ease of rearranging text and pictures—while enabling you to print out copies to exchange with other students.

Thinking about notes

Whether you are making review notes or research notes, use your own words as much as possible. When you do so, you are thinking about what you are reading. If you do quote your source word for word, put that material within quotation marks.

Close the book after reading an assignment and quickly write down a summary of the material. This writing can be loose, without any structure or format. The important thing is to do it right away, while the material is still fresh in your mind.

Special cases

The style of your notes can vary according to the material. If you are assigned a short story or poem, read the entire work once without taking any notes. On your first reading, enjoy the piece. When you finish, write down your immediate impressions. Then go over the piece and make brief notes on characters, images, symbols, settings, plot, point of view, or other aspects of the work.

Normally, you would ask yourself questions *before* you read an assignment. When you read fiction or poetry, however, ask yourself questions *after* you have read the piece. Then reread (or skim it if it's long) to get answers. Your notes can reflect this question-and-answer process.

When you read scientific or other technical material, copy important formulas and write down data that might appear on an exam. Re-create important diagrams and draw your own visual representations of concepts.

WORKPLACE APPLICATIONS

When compiling a sales report or creating a meeting summary, it is important to keep track of all sources and information. Before you begin, plan your strategy. Look over material quickly and write out a plan of action. Take notes as you read; pull out important information that will help you draw conclusions. Organize the information so that the most important material in your spreadsheet or chart stands out.

POWER PROCESS
I create it all

This is a powerful tool in times of trouble. In a crisis, "I create it all" can lead the way to solutions. "I create it all" means treating experiences, events, and circumstances in your life as if you created them.

For example, when your dog tracks fresh tar on the white carpet, when your political science teacher is a crushing bore, when your spouse dents the car, when your test on Latin American literature focuses on an author you've never read—it's time for a Power Process. Tell yourself, "I created it all."

"Baloney!" you shout. "I didn't let the dog in, that teacher really is a bore, I wasn't even in the car, and nobody told me to read Gabriel García Márquez. I didn't create these disasters."

Good points. Obviously, "I create it all" is one of the most unusual and bizarre suggestions in this book. It certainly is not an idea to be easily believed. In fact, believing it can get you into trouble. "I create it all" is strictly a practical idea. Use it when it works. Don't when it doesn't.

Keeping that caution in mind, consider how powerful this Power Process can be. It is really about the difference between two distinct positions in life: being a victim or being self-responsible.

A victim of circumstances is controlled by outside forces. We've all felt like victims at one time or another. When tar-footed dogs tromped on the white carpets of our lives, we felt helpless. In contrast, we can take responsibility. *Responsibility* is the important word. It does not mean "blame." Far from it. Responsibility is "response-

ability." It is the ability to choose a response.

Practicing resignation

If we don't take responsibility, we acknowledge that the power to determine what happens in our lives rests outside ourselves. When we feel as if we don't have control of our lives, we feel resigned. The opposite of practicing "I create it all" is practicing resignation.

There is a phenomenon called "learned resignation." An interesting experiment with dogs demonstrates how learned resignation works.

A dog is put in a caged pen with a metal floor that can be electrified. When the cage door is left open and the dog is given a mild shock, she runs out of the cage to escape the discomfort. Then the dog is put back into the cage, the door is shut and locked, and a mild shock is given again. The dog runs around, looking for an escape. When she doesn't find one, she just lies down, sits, or stands there, and quits trying to find a way out. She has no control over her circumstance and is learning to be resigned.

Now, here comes the interesting part. After the dog has consistently quit trying to escape the shock, the door is opened and the dog is led in and out several times. Then the dog is left in the cage, the door is left open, and the shock is administered once again. Now the dog doesn't even try to escape, even though the escape possibility is right in front of her. The dog continues to endure the shock. She has learned to be resigned.

A variety of this phenomenon can occur in human beings as well. When we consistently give control of our lives over to other people and to circumstances, we run the risk of learning to give up. We might develop the habit of being resigned, even with abundant opportunity all around us.

Applying this process

Many students approach grades from the position of being victims. When the student who sees the world this way gets an F, she reacts something like this:

"Oh, no!" (Slaps forehead.)

"Rats!" (Slaps forehead again.) (Students who get lots of F's often have flat foreheads.)

"Another F! That teacher couldn't teach her way out of a wet paper bag. She can't teach English for anything. And that textbook—what a bore! How could I read it with a houseful of kids making noise all the time? And then friends came over and wanted to party, and. . . ."

The problem with this viewpoint is that in looking for excuses, the student is robbing herself of the power to get anything other than an F. She's giving all of her power to a bad teacher, a boring textbook, noisy children, and friends.

There is another way, called "taking responsibility." You can recognize that you choose your grades by choosing your actions. Then you are the source, rather than the result, of the grades you get. The student who got an F could react like this:

"Another F. Oh, shoot, well, hmmm. . . . How did I choose this F? What did I do to create it?"

Now, that's power. By asking, "How did I contribute to this outcome?" you give yourself a measure of control. You are no longer the victim. This student might continue by saying, "Well, let's see. I didn't review my notes after class. That might have done it." Or "I studied in the same room with my children while they watched TV. Then I went out with my friends the night before the test. Well, that

probably helped me fulfill some of the requirements for getting an F."

The point is this: When the F is the result of your kids, your roommate, the book, or the teacher, you probably can't do anything about it. However, if you chose the F, you can choose differently next time. You are in charge.

Choosing our thoughts

There are times when we don't create it all. We do not create earthquakes, floods, avalanches, or monsoons. Yet if we look closely, we discover that we *do* create a larger part of our circumstances than most of us are willing to admit.

For example, we can choose our thoughts. And thoughts can control our perceptions by screening information from our senses. We can never be aware of every single thing in our environment. If we could, we'd go crazy from sensory overload. Instead, our brains filter out most sensory inputs. This filtering colors the way we think about the world.

Imagine for a moment that the universe is whole and complete. It is filled with everything you would ever want, including happiness, love, and material wealth. When you adopt this viewpoint, your brain will look for sensory input that supports this idea.

Now take the opposite view. Imagine that happiness, love, and wealth are scarce. Now your brain has a different mission. You will tend to see the news stories about poverty, hate, suicide, drug addiction, or unemployment. You could easily miss the stories of people who recovered from addiction, rose out of poverty, or resolved conflict.

Many people have no experience of abundance or happiness. Maybe their thoughts limit what they see. By choosing new thoughts, they might see the same circumstances in new ways.

Choosing our behaviors

Moment by moment we make choices about what we will do and where we will go. The results of these choices are where we are in life. A whole school of psychology called control theory is based on this point, and psychiatrist William Glasser has written extensively about it.[6]

All those choices help create our current circumstances—even those circumstances that are not "our fault." After a car accident, we tell ourselves: "It just happened. That car came out of nowhere and hit me." We forget that driving five miles per hour slower and paying closer attention might have allowed us to miss the driver who was "to blame."

Some cautions

The presence of blame is a warning that "I create it all" is being misused. "I create it all" is not about blaming yourself or others.

And it is not designed to be applied to other people. For example, if someone tells you about an aspect of your behavior that she finds annoying, this is not the time to reply, "Get off my back. *You* create it all." Remember, the power in this idea is seeing how *you* create it yourself, not how someone else did.

Feeling guilty is another warning signal. Guilt actually involves the same dynamic as blaming. If you are feeling guilty, you have just shifted the blame from another person to yourself.

Another caution is that this Power Process is not a religion. Acting as if you "create it all" does not mean denying God. It is simply a way to expand the choices you already have.

This Power Process is easy to deny. Tell your friends about it, and they're likely to say, "What about world hunger? I didn't cause that. What about people who get cancer? Did they create that?"

These are good arguments, and they miss the point. Victims of rape, abuse, incest, and other violence can still use "I create it all" to choose their response to the people and events that violated them.

Some people approach world hunger, imprisonment, and even cancer with this attitude: "Pretend for a moment that I am responsible for this. What will I do about it?" These people see problems in a new way, and they find choices that other people miss.

"I create it all" is not always about disaster. It also works when life is going great. We often give credit to others for our good fortune when it's actually time to pat ourselves on the back. By choosing our behavior and thoughts, we can create A's, interesting classes, enjoyable relationships, material wealth, and contributions to a better world.

How people use this process

Throughout history, people have used this Power Process, even if they didn't call it by the same name. Viktor Frankl, a psychiatrist and a survivor of Nazi concentration camps, created courage and dignity out of horror and humiliation. Reflecting on his experiences at Auschwitz and other camps, he wrote, "Everything can be taken from a man but one thing: the last of the human freedoms—to choose one's own attitude in any given set of circumstances, to choose one's own way."[7]

Writer W. E. B. Du Bois created an enduring book—*The Souls of Black Folk*—out of the experience of racial discrimination in America.[8]

Thousands of people are living productive lives and creating positive experiences out of a circumstance called cancer.

Whenever tar-footed dogs are getting in the way of your education, remember this Power Process. When you use it, you instantly open up a world of choices. You give yourself power.

EXERCISE

#21

They made me do it

Write down some of the activities you have completed in the last 24 hours, from making the bed to going to class. List these activities in one of the following columns as activities you chose to do, or as activities that you were required to do by someone else. If there was a particular person who requested that you do something, write that person's name after the activity.

Activities I chose   Activities others chose for me

_____

_____

_____

_____

Of the activities others chose for you, which ones were truly consistent with your values and purposes? If you discover you did some things that you didn't want to do, consider not doing them in the future. On a separate sheet of paper, write how you feel about a specific activity and why you don't want to do it again. Consider communicating this message to the person who "made" you do the activity.

master student
RAUL JULIA

received four Tony nominations for performances on Broadway. He was also active in the Hunger Project.

I've always known I was an actor. I acted in my first play when I was five years old. The play was in Spanish and I was the devil competing with a student, a farmer, and a hunter to capture the heart of a fair maiden. During the opening performance, I remember choosing to let go and risk being foolish. I fell to the floor and started rolling all over the stage like I was having a fit. No control. Everyone was stunned because this was not in the script. Suddenly I got up and started saying my lines. I've been acting and taking risks ever since.

I am committed to acting. Many years ago I had to choose between doing what I loved—acting—or going into my father's restaurant business in Puerto Rico. Choosing an acting career was a financial risk and besides, being a successful actor in the United States was as unlikely as being a prince in a fairy tale. I chose to do what I loved, no matter what. What's the point of doing anything you don't love? It's not worth it.

I love acting and I'm very excited about making movies. And there's more to it. It's called The Hunger Project. Getting in touch with my work in The Hunger Project carries me through.

I was attracted to The Hunger Project in 1977, when for the first time in my life, I realized that we could actually end hunger on the planet.

I feel I have a responsibility beyond myself and my family to others who are starving. I have the good fortune to be able to feed my family. I imagine myself looking for work, not finding any, and not being able to provide food. This is happening right now for many people. All that is needed to end this tragedy is the commitment of people like you and me.

My commitment to end hunger inspires my acting. When I'm tired, disgusted, bored, or just don't feel like it, I remember that the more successful I become, the more of a difference I can make. Since I am now committed to something more than self-gratification, my work becomes finer. I am still learning and growing, of course, and contribution brings a different quality to my work.

Many of my high school Jesuit teachers had been tortured while they were imprisoned in China. The General of the Jesuit Order had been at Hiroshima when they dropped the bomb. The primary thing I learned from the Spanish Jesuits is that a hero is someone who goes beyond himself to make a difference for other people.

Going beyond yourself includes going beyond your cultural

background. It is best to educate yourself about your background, be proud of who you are, and be accurate and knowledgeable when you communicate about it. Once you are knowledgeable and proud of your culture, you can go beyond yourself and become whatever you want to be. Transcending your background allows you to be free and proud.

I don't go around waving a flag saying that I am "Mr. Puerto Rico." I have that background and I am proud of it. I love Puerto Rico, I love my culture, and I love my background. But before anything else, I am a human being. My cultural heritage is in the background. I am first a human being who happened to be born into that background. If we see it that way, we can appreciate the diversity and, at the same time, enjoy our heritage even more. Then we don't need to use it as a shield in competition or as a prejudicial label.

The planet is small enough. It is time to put all that cultural and nationalistic kind of flag-waving in the background. It is now time for everyone on the planet to be human beings together.

For more biographical information about Raul Julia, visit Houghton Mifflin's College Survival/Becoming a Master Student web site: **http://collegesurvival.college. hmco.com/students.**

Quiz

1 What are the three major steps in effective note taking as explained in this chapter? Describe each step in one sentence.

2 Techniques you can use to "set the stage" for note taking do *not* include:

    (A) Complete outside assignments.
    (B) Bring the right materials.
    (C) Set aside questions in order to concentrate.
    (D) Conduct a short preclass review.
    (E) Sit front and center.

3 What is an advantage of sitting to the front and center of the classroom?

4 The ways instructors behave sometimes indicate that the material they are presenting is important. Describe at least three ways.

5 An effective method to postpone debate during a lecture is to ignore your own opinions and passively record the instructor's words. True or False? Explain your answer.

6 When using the Cornell system of note taking:

    (A) Write the main point on a line or in a box, circle, or any other shape.
    (B) Use only Roman numerals in an outline form.
    (C) Copy each new concept on a separate 3×5 card.
    (D) Remember that it doesn't work when used along with a mind map format.
    (E) Draw a vertical line about 1 1/2 inches from the left edge of the paper.

7 Explain how key words can be used. Then select and write down at least five key words from this chapter.

8 Reviewing within 24 hours assists short-term memory only. Long-term memory requires reviews over a longer period of time. True or False? Explain your answer.

9 Compare and contrast source cards and information cards. How are they alike? How are they different?

10 Briefly explain one of the cautions given regarding the use of the Power Process "I create it all."

JOURNAL ENTRY

#26

Discovery/Intention Statement

Quickly review this chapter and summarize what you learned about your note-taking skills.

I discovered that I ...

_____

_____

_____

Write an Intention Statement declaring how you will use two techniques from this chapter.

I intend to ...

_____

_____

_____

LEARNING STYLES APPLICATION   CHAPTER 5

Mode 4 *Create an original technique for taking notes. Think about how you could modify or combine several of the methods mentioned in this chapter.*

Mode 1 *Imagine that you've just been assigned to give a 20-minute talk with lots of facts on global warming. You have only 24 hours to prepare your presentation. Review the options for taking notes explained in this chapter and choose those you think would be most effective to use in this situation.*

Mode 3 *Keep in mind that you do not have to use one particular style of taking notes for all your classes. List possible situations in which you could use each of the major note-taking methods described in this chapter.*

Mode 2 *Compare and contrast the various methods of note taking mentioned in this chapter, including mind maps, the Cornell system, and 3×5 cards. On a separate sheet of paper, list the distinctive benefits and features of each method. How are the methods alike? How do they differ?*

BIBLIOGRAPHY

ENDNOTES

1 Walter Pauk, *How to Study in College* (Boston: Houghton Mifflin, 1997).

2 Tony Buzan, *Use Both Sides of Your Brain* (New York: Dutton, 1991).

3 Gabrielle Rico, *Writing the Natural Way* (Los Angeles: J. P. Tarcher, 1983).

4 Joseph Novak and D. Bob Gowin, *Learning How to Learn* (New York: Cambridge University Press, 1984).

5 Richard Solly and Roseann Lloyd, *Journey Notes: Writing for Recovery and Spiritual Growth* (Center City, MN: Hazelden, 1989).

6 William Glasser, *Take Effective Control of Your Life* (New York: Harper & Row, 1984).

7 Viktor Frankl, *Man's Search for Meaning* (New York: Simon & Schuster, 1970).

8 W. E. B. Du Bois, *The Souls of Black Folk* (New York: Bantam, 1989).

ADDITIONAL READING

Buzan, Tony. *Make the Most of Your Mind.* New York: Simon & Schuster, 1977.

Corey, Gerald. *I Never Knew I Had a Choice.* Monterey, CA: Brooks-Cole, 1982.

Glasser, William. *Schools Without Failure.* New York: Harper & Row, 1968.

Hill, Napolean. *Think and Grow Rich.* New York: Fawcett, 1996.

INTERNET RESOURCES

Improving Note Taking with Concept Maps
www.psychwww.com/mtsite/mindmaps.html

Internet Resources for Reading/Study Skills
www.lsc.cc.mn.us/programs/read/internet.html

Note Taking Skills
http://www.sas.calpoly.edu/asc/ssl/notetaking.systems.html

Researching and Documenting Sources
http://.owl.english.purdue.edu/handouts/research/index.htm

Rules to Improve Your Note Taking Skills
http://www.drake.edu/provost/acadsuccess/notebook12-0.html

Tests

IN THIS CHAPTER . . . Disarm fears of failing with techniques to use before a test and during a test. Also harness the power of cooperative learning by studying with other people. Learn to let go of anxiety about tests—or anything else. Even if you get an "F," see it as feedback—not failure. In fact, you can find reasons to celebrate mistakes and even have some fun during finals. It's all easier when you learn to detach.

Disarm tests

On the surface, tests don't look dangerous, yet sometimes we treat them as if they were land mines. Suppose a stranger walks up to you on the street and asks, "Does a finite abelian P-group have a basis?" Will you break out in a cold sweat? Will your muscles tense up? Will your breathing become shallow?

Probably not. Even if you have never heard of a finite abelian P-group, you are likely to remain coolly detached. However, if you find the same question on a test and if you have never heard of a finite abelian P-group, then your hands might get clammy.

Grades (A to F) are what we use to give power to tests. And there are lots of misconceptions about what grades are. Grades are not a measure of intelligence. Grades don't measure creativity. They are not an indication of your ability to contribute to society. Grades are simply a measure of how well you do on tests.

Some people think that a test score measures what a student accomplished in a course. This is false. A test score is a measure of what a student scored on a test. If you are anxious about a test and blank out, then the grade cannot measure what you learned. The reverse is also true: If you are good at taking tests and a lucky guesser, the score won't be an accurate reflection of what you've learned.

Grades are not a measure of self-worth. Yet we tend to give test scores the power to determine how we feel about ourselves. Common thoughts include "If I fail a test, I am a failure" or "If I do badly on a test, I am a bad person." The truth is that if you do badly on a test, you are a person who did badly on a test. That's all.

Carrying around misconceptions about tests and grades can put undue pressure on your performance. It's like balancing on a railroad track. Many people can walk along the rail and stay balanced for long periods. Yet the task seems entirely different if the rail is placed between two buildings, 52 stories up.

It is easier to do well on exams if you don't exaggerate the pressure on yourself. Don't give the test some magical power over your own worth as a human being. Academic tests are not a matter of life and death. Even scoring low on important tests—entrance tests for college or medical school, law boards, CPA exams—usually means only a delay.

Whether a risk is real or imaginary, it can reach the point where it becomes paralyzing. The way to deal with tests is to keep the risk in perspective. Keep the railroad track on the ground.

JOURNAL ENTRY #27

Discovery Statement

Mentally re-create a time when you had difficulty taking a test. Do anything that helps you re-experience this event. You could draw a picture of yourself in this situation, list some of the questions you had difficulty answering, or describe the feelings you had after finding out your score on the test. Describe that experience here.

_____

_____

_____

_____

_____

_____

_____

_____

_____

_____

_____

Now preview this chapter, looking for three strategies that could prevent such incidents from happening again. List those strategies below and note the page numbers where you can find out more about each strategy.

Strategy   Page number

_____

_____

_____

_____

_____

_____

_____

_____

What to do before the test

Manage review time

A key to successful test preparation is managing review time. The biggest benefit of early review is that facts have time to roam around in your head. A lot of learning takes place when you are not consciously studying. Your brain has time to create relationships that can show up when you need them—like during a test. Use short daily review sessions to prepare the way for major review sessions. Reviewing with a group often generates new insights and questions.

Daily reviews. Daily reviews include the short pre- and post-class reviews of lecture notes. Research indicates that this is an effective tool for moving ideas from short-term to long-term memory. Also conduct brief daily reviews when you read. Before reading a new assignment, scan your notes and the sections you underlined in the previous assignment. Use the time you spend waiting for the bus or doing the laundry to conduct short reviews.

Concentrate daily reviews on two kinds of material: material you have just learned, either in class or in your reading, and material that involves simple memorization (equations, formulas, dates, definitions).

Conduct short daily reviews several times throughout the day. To make sure you do, include them on your daily to-do list. Write down reminders, such as "5 min. review of biology" or "10 min. review of economics," and give yourself the satisfaction of crossing them off your list.

Begin to review on the first day of class. The first day, in fact, is important. Most instructors outline the whole course at that time. You can start reviewing within seconds after learning. During a lull in class, go over the notes you just took. Then immediately after class, review your notes again.

Weekly reviews. Weekly reviews are longer—about an hour per subject. They are also more structured than short daily reviews. When a subject is complex, the brain requires time to dig into the material. Avoid skipping from subject to subject too quickly. Review each subject at least once a week. Weekly sessions include reviews of assigned reading and lecture notes. Look over any mind map summaries or flash cards you have created. You can also practice working on sample problems.

Major reviews. Major reviews are usually conducted the week before finals or other major exams. They integrate concepts and deepen understanding of the material presented throughout the term. These are longer review periods—two to five hours at a stretch, punctuated by sufficient breaks. Remember that the effectiveness of your review begins to drop after an hour or so unless you give yourself a short rest.

After a certain point, short breaks every hour might not be enough to refresh you. That's when it's time to quit. Learn your limits by being conscious of the quality of your concentration. During long sessions, study the most difficult subjects when you are the most alert: at the beginning of the session. Your commitment to review is your most powerful ally. Create a system of rewards for time spent reviewing. Use the Intention Statements in this chapter or invent your own to draw detailed plans for review time.

Create review tools

Checklists, mind map summaries, and flash cards take the guesswork and much of the worry out of studying. They divide a big job into smaller parts. When you use these review tools, your confidence can increase and you can probably sleep better at night.

Study checklists. Study checklists are used the way a pilot uses a preflight checklist. Pilots go through a standard routine before they take off. They physically mark off each item: test flaps, check magnetos, check fuel tanks, adjust instruments, check rudder. They use a written list to be absolutely certain they don't miss anything. Once they are in the air, it's too late, and the consequences of failing to check the fuel tanks could be drastic. Taking an exam is like flying a plane. Once the test begins, it's too late to memorize that one equation you forgot to include in your review.

Make a list for each subject. List reading assignments by chapters or page numbers. List dates of lecture notes. Write down various types of problems you will need to solve. Write down other skills you must master. Include major ideas, definitions, theories, formulas, and equations. For math and science tests, choose some problems and do them over again as a way to review for the test.

A study checklist is not a review sheet; it is a to-do list. Checklists contain the briefest possible description of each item to study.

Begin keeping a study checklist the very first day of class. Add to it as the term progresses. When you conduct your final review, check items off the list as you review them.

Mind map summary sheets.

There are several ways to make a mind map as you study for tests. Start by creating a map totally from memory. You might be surprised by how much you already know. Mind maps release floods of information from the brain because the mind works by association. Each idea is linked to many other ideas. You think of one and other associations come to mind.

Let the associations flow. If one seems to go someplace else, simply start another branch on your map. After you have gone as far as you can using recall alone, go over your notes and text and fill in the rest of the map.

Another way to create a mind map summary is to go through your notes and pick out key words. Then, without looking at your notes, create a mind map of everything you can recall about each key word. Finally, go back to your notes and fill in material you left out. You can also start a mind map with underlined sections from your text.

Make mind maps for small, detailed topics as well as for broad ones. You can mind map a whole course or a single lecture or a single point from a lecture.

Flash cards.
Three-by-five flash cards are like portable test questions.

Take them with you everywhere and use them anytime. On one side of the cards, write the questions. On the other, write the answers. It's that simple.

Use flash cards for formulas, definitions, theories, key words from your notes, axioms, dates, foreign language phrases, hypotheses, and sample problems. Create flash cards regularly as the term progresses. Buy an inexpensive card file to keep your flash cards arranged by subject.

Carry a pack of flash cards with you whenever you think you might have a spare minute to review them.

Plan a strategy

Knowing what is going to be on a test doesn't require highly sophisticated technology or any code breaking. Some instructors even hand out lists of questions to be used as study guides for a test. Even if they don't, the following strategies can help you predict most of the test questions.

Do a dry run.
One of the most effective ways to prepare for a test is to practice the tasks you'll actually do on it. Write up your own questions and take this "test" several times before the actual exam. Say that the test will include mainly true/false or short-answer questions. Brainstorm a list of such questions—a mock test—and do a dry run.

Also predict the level of questions. Some are likely to draw on rote memorization, while others might require application or analysis. You might type up this "test" so that it looks like the real thing.

Ask the instructor what to expect.
One great source of information about the test is your instructor. Ask him what to expect. What topics will be emphasized? What kinds of questions will be included? How can you best allocate your review time? The instructor might decline to give you any of this information. More often,

instructors will answer some or all of your questions about the test.

Get copies of old exams.
Copies of previous exams for the class might be available from the instructor, the instructor's department, the library, or the counseling office. Old tests can help you plan a review strategy. One caution: If you rely on old tests exclusively, you might gloss over material the instructor has added since the last test. Check your school's policy about making past tests available to students. Some might not allow it.

As you begin

Prepare yourself for the test by arriving early. That often leaves time to do a relaxation exercise. While you're waiting for the test to begin and talking with classmates, avoid the question "How much did you study for this test?" This question might only fuel the anxiety that you didn't study enough.

Pay particular attention to verbal directions given as a test is distributed. Then scan the whole test immediately. Evaluate the importance of each section. Notice how many points each part of the test is worth and estimate how much time you will need for each section, using its point value as your guide. For example, don't budget 20 percent of your time for a section that is worth only 10 percent of the points.

Read the directions slowly. Then reread them. It can be agonizing to discover that you lost points on a test merely because you failed to follow the directions. When the directions are confusing, ask to have them clarified.

Jot down memory aids, formulas, equations, facts, or other material you know you'll need and might forget. Do this in the margins. If you use a separate sheet of paper, you might appear to be cheating.

Now you are ready to begin the test.

Cooperative learning
Studying with people

Education often looks like competition. We compete for entrance to school, for grades when we're in school, and for jobs when we leave school. In that climate, it's easy to overlook the power of cooperation.

Consider the idea that competition is not necessary for success in school. In some cases, competition actually works *against* success. It is often stressful. It can strain relationships. We can often get more done by sharing our skills and resources than by working alone.

As social animals, humans draw strength from groups. Study groups can feed you this strength, while supplying you with energy. In addition to offering camaraderie, study groups can elevate your spirits on days when you just don't feel like working at your education. You might be more likely to keep an appointment to study with a group than to study by yourself. If you skip a solo study session, no one else would know. If you declare your intention to study with others who are depending on you, your intention gains strength. In addition to drawing strength from the group, you can support others when their spirits are low.

Almost every job is accomplished by the combined efforts of many people. For example, manufacturing a single car calls for the contribution of designers, welders, painters, electricians, marketing executives, computer programmers, and many others. Jobs in today's economy call for teamwork—the ability to function well in groups. That's a skill you can start developing by studying with others.

Study groups are especially important if going to school has thrown you into a new culture. Joining a study group with people you already know can ease the transition. Promote your success in school by refusing to go it alone.

To multiply the benefits you get from study groups, seek out people of other cultures, races, and ethnic groups. You can get a whole new perspective on the world, along with some valued new friends. You can also get practice working on a diverse team—an important asset in today's job market.

Form a study group

Look for dedicated students. Find people you are comfortable with and who share some of your academic goals.

You can include people who face academic or personal challenges similar to your own. For example, if you are divorced and have two toddlers at home, you might look for other single parents who have returned to school.

To get the benefit of other perspectives, also include people who face challenges that are different from your own. Studying with friends is fine, but if your common interests are beer and jokes, beware of getting together for schoolwork.

Look for students who pay attention, ask questions, and take notes during class, and invite them to join your group. Choose people with similar educational goals but different backgrounds and methods of learning. Each of you can gain by seeing the material from a new perspective.

Ask two or three people to get together for a snack and talk about group goals, meeting times, and other logistics. You don't have to make an immediate commitment.

Limit groups to five or six people. Larger groups can be unwieldy. Test the group first by planning a one-time session. If that session works, plan another. After a few successful sessions, you can schedule regular meetings.

Another way to form a study group is to post a note on a bulletin board asking interested students to contact you. Or pass around a sign-up sheet before class. The advantage of these methods is that you don't have to face rejection. The disadvantages are that they take more time and you have less control over who applies to join the group.

Conduct a study group

There are many ways to conduct a study group. Begin with the following suggestions and see what works.

Test each other by asking questions. Group members can agree to bring four or five sample test questions to each meeting. Then you can all take the test made up from these questions.

Practice teaching each other. Teaching is a great way to learn something. Turn the material you're studying into a list of topics, and assign a specific topic to each person, who will then teach it to the group. When you teach something, you naturally assume a teacher's attitude—"I know this"—as opposed to a student's attitude—"I still have to learn this." The vocalization involved in teaching further reinforces the concepts.

Compare notes. Make sure that you all heard the same thing in class and that you all recorded the important information. Ask others to help explain material in your notes that is confusing to you.

Brainstorm test questions. Set aside five or 10 minutes of each study session to use brainstorming techniques (described in this book as a technique for creative thinking) to create test questions. You can add these to the "Test questions" section of your notebook.

Set an agenda for each meeting. Select activities from this article, or create other activities to do as a group. Set approximate time limits for each agenda item and determine a quitting time. Finally, end each meeting with assignments for each member.

Work in groups of three at a computer to review a course. Choose one person to operate the keyboard. Another person can dictate summaries of lectures and assigned readings. The third person can act as fact checker, consulting textbooks, lecture notes, and class handouts.

Create wall-sized mind maps or concept maps to summarize a textbook or series of lectures. Work on large sheets of butcher paper, or tape together pieces of construction paper. When doing a mind map, assign one "branch" of the mind map to each member of the study group. Use a different colored pen or marker for each branch. (For more information on concept maps and mind maps, see Chapter Five.)

Pair off to do "book reports." One person can summarize an assigned reading. The other person can act as an interviewer on a talk show, posing questions and asking for further clarification.

Ask members of your group to prepare and deliver full-length lectures on different topics of a course. Volunteer to lecture on the topic that you know least about, and come prepared to answer questions from other group members.

Ask for group support in personal areas. Other people might have insight into problems such as transportation, childcare, finances, and time scheduling. Study groups can provide personal support for getting what you want from school.

JOURNAL ENTRY

#28

Intention Statement

I intend to form a study group. I will take steps to get the group organized.

I intend to set up the first group meeting by … (date)

_____

_____

_____

_____

My reward for fulfilling this intention will be …

_____

_____

_____

_____

What to do during the test

In general

It's time to begin. If necessary, allow yourself a minute or two of "panic" time. Notice any tension you feel, and apply one of the techniques explained in "Let go of test anxiety" later in this chapter.

Answer the easiest, shortest questions first. This gives you the experience of success. It also stimulates associations and prepares you for more difficult questions.

Next answer multiple choice, true/false, and fill-in-the-blank questions. Then proceed to short-answer and essay questions. Use memory techniques, if you're stuck.

Pace yourself and watch the time. If you can't think of an answer, move on. Follow your time plan.

Leave plenty of space in between answers to essay questions. This allows you to go back and add more information in the extra space, if there's time.

Look for answers in other test questions. A term, name, date, or other fact that escapes you might appear in the test itself. You can also use other questions to stimulate your memory.

In quick-answer questions (multiple choice, true/false), your first instinct is usually best. If you think your first answer is wrong because you misread the question, do change your answer.

Multiple choice questions

Check the directions to see if the questions call for more than one answer. Answer each question in your head before you look at the possible answers. If you can come up with the answer before you look at the choices, you can eliminate the possibility of being confused by those choices.

Be sure to read all answers to multiple choice questions before selecting one. Sometimes two answers will be similar and only one will be correct.

If you have no clue as to what the answer is and if incorrect answers are not deducted from your score, use the following guidelines to guess.

1 If two answers are similar, except for one or two words, choose one of these answers.

2 If two answers have similar-sounding or similar-looking words (*intermediate, intermittent*), choose one of these answers.

3 If the answer calls for a sentence completion, eliminate the answers that would not form grammatically correct sentences.

4 If two quantities are almost the same, choose one of them.

5 If answers cover a wide range (4.5, 66.7, 88.7, 90.1, 5000.11), choose one in the middle of the range.

6 If there is no penalty for guessing and none of the above techniques works, close your eyes and go for it.

Note: None of these suggestions for guessing is meant to take the place of studying for the test.

True/false questions

Answer true/false questions quickly. Often these questions are not worth many points individually.

Read carefully. Sometimes one word can make a statement inaccurate. If any part of a true/false statement is false, the entire statement is false.

Look for qualifiers like *all, most, sometimes, never,* or *rarely.* These are the key words upon which the question depends. Absolute qualifiers such as *always* or *never* generally indicate a false statement.

Machine-graded tests

To do well on these tests, make sure that the answer you mark corresponds to the question you are answering. Check the test booklet against the answer sheet whenever you switch sections and whenever you come to the top of a column. Watch for stray marks; they can look like answers.

Open-book tests

When studying for an open-book test, write down any formulas you will need on a separate sheet of paper. Place Post-It® notes on important pages (containing tables, for instance) so you don't have to waste time flipping through the book. You could also use paper clips. If you plan to use your notes, number them and write a short table of contents.

Prepare thoroughly for open-book exams. They are usually the most difficult tests.

Short-answer/fill-in-the-blank tests

These questions often ask for definitions or short descriptions. Concentrate on key words and facts. Be brief.

Overlearning material can really pay off. When you know a subject backward and forward, you can answer this type of question almost as fast as you can write.

Essay questions

As in objective tests, managing your time is important. Note how many questions you have to answer and monitor your progress during the test period. Writing shorter answers and completing all of the questions on an essay test will almost always yield a better score than leaving some questions blank.

Find out what the question is asking—precisely. If a question asks that you *compare* Gestalt and Reichian therapies, no matter how eloquently you *explain* them, you are on a one-way trip to No Credit City. For more ideas on this point, see the article "Words to watch for in essay questions."

Before you write, make a quick outline. There are three reasons for doing this. First, you might be able to write faster. Second, you're less likely to leave out important facts. Third, if you don't have time to finish your answer, your outline could win you some points.

When you start to write, get to the point. Forget introductions. General statements such as "There are many interesting facets to this difficult question" can cause acute irritation for teachers grading dozens of tests.

One way to get to the point is to include part of the question in your answer. Suppose the question is "Discuss how increasing the city police budget might or might not contribute to a decrease in street crime." Your first sentence might be "An increase in police expenditures

will not have a significant effect on street crime for the following reasons." Your position is clear. You are on your way to an answer.

When you expand your answer with supporting ideas and facts, start out with the most solid points. Don't try for drama by saving the best for last.

Some final points in regard to style

1 **Write legibly.** Grading essay questions is in large part a subjective process. Sloppy, difficult-to-read handwriting might actually lower your grade.

2 **Be brief.** Avoid filler sentences that say nothing, such as "The question certainly bears careful deliberation in order to take into account all the many interesting facts pertaining to this important period in the history of our great nation." Write as if you expect the person grading your test to be tired, bored, and overworked. Even a well-rested instructor doesn't like to wade through a swamp of murky writing in order to spot an occasional lonely insight.

3 **Use a pen.** Many instructors will require this because pencil is difficult to read. Consider using an erasable pen so that you can make corrections without cross-outs.

Hint: If you're left-handed, you can put a blank 3×5 card under your left hand so you don't smear the ink as you write.

4 **Write on one side of the page only.** If you write on both sides of the page, writing will show through and obscure the writing on the other side. If necessary, use the blank side to add points you missed. Leave a generous left-hand margin and plenty of space between your answers in case you want to add to them later.

Finally, if you have time, review your answers for grammar and spelling errors, clarity, and legibility.

F is for feedback, not failure

Sometimes when students get an F on an assignment, they interpret that letter as a message: "You are a failure." That interpretation is not accurate.

Getting an F means only that you failed a test—not that you failed your life.

From now on, imagine that the letter *F* when used as a grade represents another word: *feedback.* An F is an indication that you didn't understand the material well enough—it's a message to do something differently before the next test or assignment. If you interpret F as *failure,* you don't get to change anything. But if you interpret F as *feedback,* you can change your thinking and behavior in ways that promote your success.

Read a short published essay. Imagine that you are an English teacher, and give the essay a letter grade or numerical score. In the space below, state your criteria—your bases for assigning the grade—and justify the grade you gave.

Now reflect on the criteria you just used. A grade can measure achievement toward an absolute standard. Or it can measure a student's development from a starting point. Write about which of these criteria you would use (or any others) and when you would apply them.

_____

_____

_____

_____

_____

_____

_____

_____

_____

_____

_____

_____

_____

_____

_____

_____

_____

_____

_____

_____

_____

_____

_____

_____

_____

_____

Words to watch for in
ESSAY
QUESTIONS

The following words are commonly found in essay test questions. Understanding them is essential to success on such questions. If you want to do well on essay tests, study this page thoroughly. Know these words backwards and forwards. To heighten your awareness of them, underline the words when you see them in a test question.

Analyze: Break into separate parts and discuss, examine, or interpret each part. Then give your opinion.

Compare: Examine two or more things. Identify similarities and differences.

Contrast: Show differences. Set in opposition.

Criticize: Make judgments. Evaluate comparative worth. Criticism often involves analysis.

Define: Give the meaning, usually one that is specific to the course or subject. Explain the exact meaning. Definitions are usually short.

Describe: Give a detailed account. Make a picture with words. List characteristics, qualities, and parts.

Discuss: Consider and debate or argue the pros and cons of an issue. Write about any conflict. Compare and contrast.

Explain: Make an idea clear. Show logically how a concept is developed. Give the reasons for an event.

Prove: Support with facts (especially facts presented in class or in the text).

Relate: Show the connections between ideas or events. Provide a larger context.

State: Explain precisely.

Summarize: Give a brief, condensed account. Include conclusions. Avoid unnecessary details.

Trace: Show the order of events or the progress of a subject or event.

If any of these terms is still unclear to you, go to your unabridged dictionary. Thorough knowledge of these words helps you answer essay questions in ways that best demonstrate your understanding of the course content.

Review these key words and other helpful vocabulary by using the online flashcards on the Becoming a Master Student web site at **http://collegesurvival.college.hmco.com/students.**

INTEGRITY in test taking
The costs of cheating (even if you don't get caught)

Cheating on tests can be a tempting choice. One benefit is that we might get a good grade without having to study. Instead of studying, we could spend more time watching TV, partying, sleeping, or doing anything that seems more fun. Another benefit is that we could avoid the risk of doing poorly on a test—which could happen even if we *do* study.

But before you rush out to make cheating a habit, remember that it also carries costs. Here are some to consider.

We learn less. While we might think that some courses offer little or no value, it is more likely that we can create value from any course. If we look deeply enough, we can discover some idea or acquire some skill to prepare us for future courses or a career after graduation.

We lose money. Getting an education costs a lot of money. Cheating sabotages our purchase. We pay full tuition without getting full value for it.

Fear of getting caught promotes stress. When we're fully aware of our emotions about cheating, we might discover intense stress. Even if we're not fully aware of our emotions, we're likely to feel some level of discomfort about getting caught.

Violating our values promotes stress. Even if we don't get caught cheating, we can feel stress about violating our own ethical standards. Stress can compromise our physical health and overall quality of life.

Cheating on tests can make it easier to violate our integrity again. Human beings become comfortable with behaviors that they repeat. Cheating is no exception.

Think about the first time you drove a car. You might have felt excited—even a little frightened. Now driving is probably second nature, and you don't give it much thought. Repeated experience with driving creates familiarity, which lessens the intense feelings you had during your first time at the wheel.

We can experience the same process with almost any behavior. Cheating once will make it easier to cheat again. And if we become comfortable with compromising our integrity in one area of life, we might find it easier to compromise in other areas.

Cheating lowers our self-concept. Whether or not we are fully aware of it, cheating sends us the message that we are not smart enough or not responsible enough to make it on our own. We deny ourselves the celebration and satisfaction of authentic success.

An effective alternative to cheating is to become a master student. Ways to do this are described on every page of this book.

Have some FUN!

Contrary to popular belief, finals week does not have to be a drag.

In fact, if you have used techniques in this chapter, exam week can be fun. By planning ahead, you will have done most of your studying long before finals arrive. You can feel confident and relaxed.

When you are well prepared for tests, you can even use fun as a technique to enhance your performance. The day before a final, go for a run or play a game of basketball. Take in a movie or a concert. Watch TV. A relaxed brain is a more effective brain. If you have studied for a test, your mind will continue to prepare itself even while you're at the movies.

Get plenty of rest, too. There's no need to cram until 3 a.m. when you have used the techniques in this chapter.

On the day of the big test, you can wake up refreshed, have a good breakfast, and walk into the exam room with a smile on your face. You can also leave with a smile on your face, knowing that you are going to have a fun week. It's your reward for studying regularly throughout the term.

If this kind of exam week sounds inviting, you can begin preparing for it right now.

Ways to predict
test questions

Predicting test questions can do more than get you a better grade on a test. It can keep you focused on the purpose of a course and can help you design your learning strategy. It can be fun, too.

First, get organized. Have a separate section in your notebook labeled "Test questions." Add several questions to this section after every lecture and assignment.

You also can create your own code or graphic signal—such as a *T!* in a circle—to flag possible test questions in your notes.

The format of a test can help you predict questions. Ask your instructor to describe the test—how long it will be and what kind of questions to expect (essay, multiple choice). Do this early in the term so you can be alert for possible test questions throughout the course.

During lectures you can watch for test questions by observing what an instructor says and how he says it. Instructors give clues. For example, they might repeat important points several times, write them on the board, or return to them in subsequent classes.

Instructors might use certain gestures when making critical points. They might pause, look at notes, or read passages word for word.

Also pay attention to questions the instructor poses to students, and note questions that other students ask.

When material from reading assignments is also covered extensively in class, it is likely to be on a test.

See the article "Words to watch for in essay questions." Use it as a guide to turn the key words in your notes into questions.

Put yourself in your instructor's shoes. What information would you want students to take away from this course? What kinds of questions would you ask? Make practice test questions and then answer them.

Save all quizzes, papers, lab sheets, and graded material of any kind. Quiz questions have a way of appearing, in slightly altered form, on final exams. If copies of previous exams are available, use them to predict test questions.

For science courses and other courses involving problem solving, work on sample problems using different variables.

You can also brainstorm test questions with other students. This is a great activity for study groups.

Finally, be on the lookout for these words: *This material will be on the test.*

I. (Bones) - living organs, weight
   A. Marrow - in center nerves + blood .
      1. Red
         a. in flat bones bones
         b. produces red .
      2. Yellow - mostly -
         a. in center of l
         b. might make -
            great blood b
            diseases
   B. Haversian canals - bones (for oxygen
   C. Periostium - protect bone
   D. Composed of:
      1. Minerals, organi
         a. Calcium + pho
            calcium phos,
            calcium carbo
         b. Hardness dep
            mineral
      2. Embryo - skelet
      (T) Ossification - fo

Let go of test anxiety

If you freeze during tests and flub questions when you know the answers, you might be suffering from test anxiety. A little tension before a test is good. That tingly, butterflies-in-the-stomach feeling you get from extra adrenaline can sharpen your awareness and keep you alert. You can enjoy the benefits of a little tension while you stay confident and relaxed. Sometimes, however, tension is persistent and extreme. It causes loss of sleep, appetite, and sometimes even hair. That kind of tension is damaging. It is a symptom of test anxiety, and it can prevent you from doing your best on exams.

TEST CHANGED TO TODAY

Other symptoms include nervousness, fear, dread, irritability, and a sense of hopelessness. Boredom also can be a symptom of test anxiety. Frequent yawning immediately before a test is a common reaction. Yawning looks like boredom, and it is often a sign of tension. It means oxygen is not getting to the brain because the body is tense. A yawn is one way the body increases its supply of oxygen.

You might experience headaches, an inability to concentrate, or a craving for food. For some people, test anxiety makes asthma or high blood pressure worse. During an exam, symptoms can include confusion, panic, mental blocks, fainting, sweaty palms, and nausea.

Symptoms after a test include the following.

Mock indifference: "I answered all the multiple choice questions as 'none of the above' because I was bored."

Guilt: "Why didn't I study more?"

Anger: "The teacher never wanted me to pass this stupid course anyway."

Blame: "If only the textbook weren't so dull."

Depression: "After that test, I don't see any point in staying in school."

Test anxiety can be serious—students have committed suicide over test scores. This anxiety can also be managed.

Test anxiety has two components, mental and physical. The mental component of stress includes all of your thoughts and worries about tests. The physical component includes bodily sensations and tension.

The following techniques can help you deal with the mental and physical components of stress in any situation, from test anxiety to stage fright.

Dealing with thoughts

1 Yell "Stop!" When you notice that your mind is consumed with worries and fears, that your thoughts are spinning out of control, mentally yell "Stop!" If you're in a situation that allows it, yell it out loud.

This action is likely to bring your focus back to the present moment and allow you to redirect your thoughts. Once you've broken the cycle of worry, you can use any of the following techniques.

2 Daydream. When you fill your mind with pleasant thoughts, there is no room left for anxiety. If you notice yourself worrying about an upcoming test, substitute your visions of doom with images of something you like to do. Daydream about being with a special friend or walking alone in a favorite place.

3 Visualize success. Most of us live up—or down—to our own expectations. If you spend a lot of time mentally rehearsing how it will be to fail a test, your chances of doing so increase.

Once you've stopped the cycle of worry, take time to rehearse what it will be like to succeed. Be specific. Create detailed pictures, actions, and even sounds as part of your visualization. You might be able to visit the room where you will take the test. If so, mentally rehearse while you are actually in this room.

4 Focus. Focus your attention on a specific object. Examine details of a painting, study the branches on a tree, or observe the face of your watch (right down to the tiny scratches in the glass). During an exam, take a few seconds to listen to the sounds of concentration—the squeaking of chairs, the scratching of pencils, the muted coughs. Touch the surface of your desk and notice the texture. Concentrate all of your attention on one point. Don't leave room in your mind for anxiety-related thoughts.

5 Praise yourself. Talk to yourself in a positive way. Many of us take the first opportunity to say, "Way to go, dummy! You don't even know the answer to the first question on the test." We wouldn't dream of treating a friend that way, yet we do this to ourselves.

An alternative is to give yourself some encouragement. Treat yourself as if you were your own best friend. Consider telling yourself, "I am very relaxed. I am doing a great job on this test."

6 Consider the worst. Rather than trying to put a stop to your worrying, consider the very worst thing that could happen. Take your fear to the limit of absurdity.

Imagine the catastrophic problems that might occur if you were to fail the test. You might say to yourself, "Well, if I fail this test, I might fail the course, lose my financial aid, and get kicked out of school. Then I won't be able to get a job, so the bank will repossess my car, and I'll start drinking. . . ." Keep going until you see the absurdity of your predictions. After you stop chuckling, you can backtrack to discover a reasonable level of concern. Your worry about failing the entire course if you fail the test might be justified. At that point ask yourself, Can I live with that? Unless you are taking a test in parachute packing and the final question involves jumping out of a plane, the answer will almost always be yes. (If the answer is no, use another technique. In fact, use several other techniques.)

The cold facts are hardly ever as bad as our worst fears. Shine a light on your fears, and they become more manageable.

7 Zoom out. When you're in the middle of a test or another situation where you feel distressed, zoom out. Think the way film directors do when they dolly a camera out and away from an action scene. In your mind, imagine that you're floating away and viewing the situation as a detached outside observer.

If you're extremely distressed, let your imagination take you even farther. See yourself rising above the scene so that your whole community, city, nation, or planet is within view.

From this larger viewpoint, ask yourself whether this situation is worth worrying about. This is not a license to belittle or avoid problems; it is permission to gain some perspective.

Another option is to zoom out in time. Imagine yourself one week, one month, one year, one decade, or one century from today. Assess how much the current situation will matter when that time comes.

Dealing with the physical sensations of anxiety

1 Breathe. You can calm physical sensations within your body by focusing your attention on your breathing. Concentrate on the air going in and out of your lungs. Experience it as it passes through your nose and mouth.

Do this for two to five minutes. If you notice that you are taking short, shallow breaths, begin to take longer and deeper breaths. Fill your lungs so that your chest expands, then release all the air. Imagine yourself standing on the tip of your nose. Watch the breath pass in and out as if your nose were a huge ventilation shaft for an underground mine.

2 Scan your body. Simple awareness is an effective technique to reduce the tension in your body.

Sit comfortably and close your eyes. Focus your attention on the muscles in your feet and notice if they are relaxed. Tell the muscles in your feet that they can relax.

Move up to your ankles and repeat the procedure. Next go to your calves and thighs and buttocks, telling each group of muscles to relax.

Do the same for your lower back, diaphragm, chest, upper back, neck, shoulders, jaw, face, upper arms, lower arms, fingers, and scalp.

3 Tense and relax. If you are aware of a particularly tense part of your body or if you discover tension when you're scanning your body, you can release this with the tense-relax method.

To do this, find a muscle that is tense and make it even more tense. If your shoulders are tense, pull them back, arch your back, and tense your shoulder muscles even more tightly; then relax. The net result is that you can be aware of the relaxation and allow yourself to relax more.

You can use the same process with your legs, arms, abdomen, chest, face, and neck. Clench your fists, tighten your jaw, straighten your legs, and tense your abdomen all at once. Then relax and pay close attention to the sensations of relaxation. By paying attention, you can learn to re-create these sensations whenever you choose.

4 *Use guided imagery.* Relax completely and take a quick fantasy trip. Close your eyes, free your body of tensions, and imagine yourself in a beautiful, peaceful, natural setting. Create as much of the scene as you can. Be specific. Use all of your senses.

For example, you might imagine yourself at a beach. Hear the surf rolling in and the sea gulls calling to each other. Feel the sun on your face and the hot sand between your toes. Smell the sea breeze. Taste the salty mist from the surf. Notice the ships on the horizon and the rolling sand dunes. Use all of your senses to create a vivid imaginary trip.

Some people find that a mountain scene or a lush meadow scene works well. You can take yourself to a place you've never been or re-create an experience out of your past. Find a place that works for you and practice getting there. When you become proficient, you can return to it quickly for trips that might last only a few seconds.

With practice you can even use this technique while you are taking a test.

5 *Describe it.* Focus your attention on your anxiety. If you are feeling nauseated or if you have a headache, then concentrate on that feeling. Describe it to yourself. Tell yourself how large it is, where it is located in your body, what color it is, what shape it is, what texture it is, how much water it might hold if it had volume, and how heavy it is.

6 *Be with it.* As you describe anxiety in detail, don't resist it. If you can completely experience a physical sensation, it will often disappear. People suffering from severe and chronic pain have used this technique successfully.

7 *Exercise aerobically.* This is one technique that won't work in the classroom or while you're taking a test. Yet it is an excellent way to reduce body tension.

Do some kind of exercise that will get your heart beating at twice your normal rate and keep it beating at that rate for 15 or 20 minutes. Aerobic exercises include rapid walking, jogging, swimming, bicycling, basketball, and anything else that elevates your heart rate and keeps it elevated.

8 *Get help.* When these techniques don't work, when anxiety is serious, get help. If you become withdrawn, have frequent thoughts about death or suicide, get depressed and stay depressed for more than a few days, or have prolonged feelings of hopelessness, see a counselor.

Depression and anxiety are common among students. Suicide is the second leading cause of death among young adults between the ages of 15 and 25. This is tragic and unnecessary. Many schools have counselors available. If not, the student health service or another office can refer you to community agencies that provide free or inexpensive counseling. You can also get emergency assistance over the phone. Most phone books contain listings for suicide prevention hot lines and other emergency services.

Twenty things I like to do

One way to relieve tension is to mentally yell "Stop!" and substitute a pleasant image (daydream) for the stressful thoughts and emotions you are experiencing.

In order to create a supply of pleasant images to recall during times of stress, conduct an eight-minute brainstorm about things you like to do. Your goal is to generate at least 20 ideas. Time yourself and write as fast as you can on a separate sheet of paper.

When you have completed your list, study it. Pick out two activities that seem especially pleasant, and elaborate on them by creating a mind map. Write down all of the memories you have about that activity.

You can use these images to calm yourself in stressful situations.

Student Voices

Perhaps the most frightening nightmare I have is taking a test. Although receiving a grade is a measure of how well I did and not a measure of my intelligence, the fear persists. In this dream, though, my favorite tool, the checklist, came to my hand. The items I had to review were popping to attention like little soldiers as I marked them off. I could daydream the day of the test and gently let my anxiety disappear in a gentle puff of wind. I could savor the reward I promise myself no matter the consequences of the test.

— CHARLES R. MCINTYRE

#29

Discovery Statement

On a separate sheet of paper, do a timed, four-minute brainstorm of all the reasons, rationalizations, justifications, and excuses you have used to avoid studying. Be creative. Then review your list, pick the three you use most, and write them down in the space below.

_____
_____
_____
_____
_____
_____
_____
_____

JOURNAL ENTRY

#30

Intention Statement

Pick one of the reasons for avoiding studying that you listed in the previous Journal Entry. Write an Intention Statement about what you will do to begin eliminating that excuse. Make this Intention Statement one that you can keep, with a timeline and a reward.

I intend to …

_____
_____
_____
_____
_____
_____
_____
_____
_____
_____

EXERCISE

#23

Rehearse for success

Sit up in a chair, legs and arms uncrossed. Close your eyes, let go of all thoughts, and focus on your breathing for a minute or two.

Then relax various parts of your body, beginning with your feet. Relax your toes, your ankles. Move up to your calves and thighs. Relax your buttocks. Relax the muscles of your lower back, abdomen, and chest. Relax your hands, arms, and shoulders. Relax your neck, jaw, eyelids, and scalp.

When you are completely relaxed, imagine yourself in an exam room. It's the day of the test. Visualize taking the test successfully. The key is detail. See the test being handed out. Notice your surroundings. Hear the other students shift in their seats. Feel the desk, the pen in your hand, and the exam in front of you. See yourself looking over the exam calmly and confidently. You discover that you know all of the answers.

Stay with this image for a few minutes. Next, imagine yourself writing quickly. Watch yourself turn in the test with confidence. Finally, imagine receiving the test grade. It is an A. Savor the feeling.

As soon as you realize you are feeling anxious about an upcoming test, begin using this technique. The more you do this visualization, the better it can work.

 For an online version of this exercise, visit Houghton Mifflin's College Survival/Becoming a Master Student web site: **http://collegesurvival.college. hmco.com/students.**

Overcoming math and science anxiety

$$\sum_{n=1}^{\infty} (-1)^n \frac{|\sin(n)|}{n}$$

$$f(x,y) = \begin{cases} \dfrac{x \cos x}{\sin x} \\ 1 \end{cases}$$

When they open books about math or science, some capable students break out in a cold sweat. This is a symptom of two conditions that can undermine students' confidence—math anxiety and science anxiety.

If you want to improve your math or science skills, you're in distinguished company. Albert Einstein felt he needed to learn more math to work out his general theory of relativity, so he asked a friend, mathematician Marcel Grossman, to teach him. It took several years. You won't need that long.

Think of the benefits of overcoming math and science anxiety. Many more courses, majors, jobs, and careers could open up for you. Knowing these subjects can also put you at ease in everyday situations: calculating the tip for a waiter, planning your finances, working with a spreadsheet on a computer. Speaking the languages of math and science can also help you feel at home in a world driven by technology.

Many schools offer courses in overcoming math and science anxiety. It can pay to check them out. The following suggestions just might start you on the road to enjoying science and mathematics.

Notice your pictures about math and science.
Sometimes what keeps people from succeeding at math and science is their mental picture of scientists and mathematicians. Often that picture includes a man dressed in a faded plaid shirt, baggy pants, and wingtip shoes. He's got a calculator on his belt and six pencils jammed in his shirt pocket.

Such pictures are far from the truth. Succeeding in math and science won't turn you into a nerd. Not only can you enjoy school more, you'll find that your friends and family will still like you.

Our mental pictures about math and science can be funny. At the same time, they can have serious effects. For many years, science and math were viewed especially as fields for white males. This picture excluded women and people of color. Promoting success in these subjects for all students is a key step in overcoming racism and sexism.

Look out for shaky assumptions.
Sheila Tobias, author of several books on overcoming math anxiety, points out that people often make faulty assumptions about how math and science are learned.[1] These assumptions can include:

- Math calls only for logic, not imagination.
- There's only one right way to do a science experiment or solve a math problem.
- There is a magic secret to doing well in math or science.

These ideas can be easily refuted. To begin with, mathematicians and scientists regularly talk about the importance of creativity and imagination in their work. They sometimes find it hard to explain how they arrive at a particular hypothesis or conclusion. And as far as we know, the only secret they count on is hard work.

Get your self-talk out in the open and change it.
When students fear math and science, they often say negative things to themselves about their abilities in these subjects. Many times this self-talk includes statements such as:

- "I'll never be fast enough at solving math problems."
- "I'm one of those people who can't function in a science lab."
- "I'm good with words, so I can't be good with numbers."

Faced with this kind of self-talk, you can take three steps.

1 *Get a clear picture of such statements.* When negative thoughts come to mind, speak them out loud or write them down. By getting self-doubt out in the open, it's easier to refute it.

2 *Next, do some critical thinking about these statements.* Look for the hidden assumptions they contain. Acknowledge what is accurate about them and also what's false.

Negative self-statements are usually based on scant evidence. They can often be reduced to two simple ideas: "Everybody else is better at math and science than I am" and "Since I don't understand it right now, I'll never understand it." Both of these statements are illogical. Many people lack confidence in their math and science skills. To verify this, just ask other students. Also ask about ways they deal with the confusion. Remember that you can overcome negative self-statements when they trouble you in other courses. If you can learn a rap song or sketch the outline of a tree, you can do mathematics and science.

3 *Start some new self-talk.* Use self-statements that affirm your ability to succeed in math and science.

- "When learning about math or science, I proceed with patience and confidence."
- "Any confusion I feel now will be resolved."
- "I learn math and science without comparing myself to others."
- "I ask whatever questions are needed to aid my understanding."
- "I am fundamentally OK as a person, even if I make errors in math and science."
- "I can succeed in math and science."

Notice your body sensations.
Math or science anxiety is seldom just a "head trip." It registers in our bodies, too. Examples can include a tight feeling in the chest, sweaty palms, drowsiness, or a mild headache.

Let those sensations come to the surface. Instead of repressing them, open up to them. Doing so often decreases their urgency.

Make your text an A priority.
In a history, an English, or an economics class, the teacher might refer to some of the required readings only in passing. In contrast, math and science courses are often text-driven—that is, class activities closely follow the format and content of the book. This makes it doubly important to complete your reading assignments.

Master one concept before going on to the next, and stay current with your reading.

Read slowly when appropriate.
It's ineffective to breeze through a math or science book as you would the newspaper. To get the most out of your text, be willing to read each sentence slowly and reread it as needed. A single paragraph might merit 15 or 20 minutes of sustained attention.

Read chapters and sections in order, as they're laid out in the text. To strengthen your understanding of the main concepts, study all tables, charts, graphs, case studies, and sample problems. From time to time, stop, close your book, and mentally reconstruct the steps of an experiment or a mathematical proof.

Read actively.
Science is not only a body of knowledge, it is an activity. To get the most out of your math and science texts, read with paper and pencil in hand. Work out examples and copy diagrams, formulas, and equations. Understand each step used in solving a problem or testing a hypothesis. STUDY DIAGRAMS, CHARTS, AND OTHER ILLUSTRATIONS CAREFULLY. They are important learning tools and are often a source for test questions.

Examples are particularly important. When reading texts in other courses, you might skim over examples to focus on major concepts. Math and science call for close attention to detail. In some cases, the examples included in the text are the main points.

Participate actively in class.
Success in math and science depends on your active involvement. Attending class regularly, completing homework assignments, speaking up when you have a question, and seeking extra help can be crucial. Some students bemoan that they'll never be any good in math and science and then behave in a way that confirms that belief. Get around this mental trap by giving to math and science at least the same amount of time that you give to other courses. If you want to succeed, make daily contact with these subjects.

Learn from specific to general.
A powerful way to learn material in some courses is to get an overview of the main topic before focusing on the details. You might want to use

the opposite strategy when studying math and science. Learning these subjects often means comprehending one limited concept before going on to the next one. Through an orderly process of cumulative knowledge, the big picture gradually comes into view. Jumping to general conclusions too soon might be confusing or inaccurate.

Remind yourself of the big picture.

Pause occasionally to get an overview of the branch of science or math you're studying. What's it all about? What basic problems is the discipline trying to solve? How is this knowledge applied in daily life?

For example, much of calculus has to do with finding the areas of "funny shapes"—shapes other than circles that have curves. Physics studies how matter and energy interact. Physics and calculus are used by many people, including architects, engineers, and space scientists.

Ask questions fearlessly. In any

subject, learning is enhanced when we ask questions. And there are no dumb questions. To master math and science, ask whatever questions will aid your understanding. Students come to higher education with widely varying backgrounds in these subjects. Your questions might not be the same as those of other people in your class. Go ahead and ask.

One barrier to asking questions is the thought: Will the teacher and other students think I'm stupid or ill-prepared if I ask this? What if they laugh or roll their eyes? This will usually not happen. If it does, remember your reasons for going to school. Your purpose is not to impress the teacher or other students but to learn. And sometimes learning means admitting ignorance.

Remember that part of the instructor's responsibility is to offer help to students who seek it. If the jump to the big picture looks like you are crossing a void, remember that teachers and tutors are there to help you reach the other side.

Take a First Step about your
current knowledge. Math and science

are cumulative. Concepts tend to build upon each other in sequential order. If you struggled with algebra, for example, you will probably have trouble with trigonometry or calculus.

To ensure that you have an adequate base of knowledge, tell the truth about your current level of knowledge and skill. Before you register for a

math or science course, seek out the assigned texts for the class. Look at the kind of material that's covered in early chapters. If that material seems new or difficult for you, see the instructor and express any concerns you have. Ask for suggestions on ways to prepare for the course.

Remember that it's OK to continue your study of math and science from your current level of ability—whatever that level might be.

Remember what you've learned.

Applying strategies that you've already learned in this book will help you in math and science. Use chapter summaries and introductory outlines to organize your learning. Review your notes frequently to transfer information into your long-term memory. Develop a strategy and schedule that works best for you, and make a date with yourself to study.

Use lab sessions to your
advantage. Laboratory work is crucial to

many science classes. To get the most out of these sessions, prepare. Know in advance what procedures you'll be doing and what materials you'll need. If possible, visit the lab before your assigned time and get to know the territory. Find out where materials are stored and where to dispose of chemicals or specimens. Bring your lab notebook and worksheets to class to record and summarize your findings.

If you're not planning to become a scientist, the main point is to understand the process of science—how scientists observe, collect data, and arrive at conclusions. This is more important than the result of any one experiment.

Use cooperative learning. Math

and science are often seen as solitary endeavors in which students either sink or swim on their own. This does not have to be your experience. Instead of going it alone, harness the power of cooperative learning. Study math and science with others. That way you can learn about different approaches to reaching solutions.

By studying with others and creating an environment where it's OK to make mistakes, you can overcome a variety of fears. From the first day of a math or science course, be on the lookout for potential study group members. You can start to associate math and science with the fun of group interaction.

JOURNAL ENTRY

#31

Discovery Statement

Most of us can recall a time when learning became associated with anxiety. For many of us, this happened early with math and science.

One step toward getting past this anxiety is to write a math or science autobiography. Recall specific experiences in which you first felt stress over these subjects. Where were you? How old were you? What were you thinking and feeling? Who else was with you? What did those people say or do?

Describe one of these experiences in the space below.

_____

_____

_____

_____

Now recall any incidents in your life that gave you positive feelings about math or science. Again, describe one of these incidents in detail. Use the space below.

_____

_____

_____

_____

_____

_____

Now sum up the significant discoveries you made while describing these two sets of experiences.

I discovered that my biggest barrier in math or science is …

_____

_____

_____

I discovered that the most satisfying aspect of doing math and science is …

_____

_____

_____

JOURNAL ENTRY

#32

Intention Statement

List three actions you can take to overcome any anxiety you feel about math or science. Then schedule a specific time for taking each action.

Action 1: I intend to …

_____

_____

_____

_____

Action 2: I intend to …

_____

_____

_____

_____

_____

Action 3: I intend to …

_____

_____

_____

_____

WORKPLACE APPLICATIONS

The same techniques that help you manage test anxiety can help you manage stress at work. Apply these techniques while interviewing for a job, making a presentation, doing a performance review, or carrying out any task that raises your anxiety level.

Taking Math & Science tests

1 Translate problems into English. Putting problems into words aids your understanding. When you study equations and formulas, put those into words, too. The words help you see a variety of applications for each formula. For example, $c^2 = a^2 + b^2$ can be translated as "the square of the hypotenuse of a right triangle is equal to the sum of the squares of the other two sides."

2 Perform opposite operations. If a problem involves multiplication, check your work by division; add, then subtract; factor, then multiply; find the square root, then the square; differentiate, then integrate.

3 Use time drills. Practice working problems fast. Time yourself. Exchange problems with a friend and time each other. You can also do this in a study group.

4 Analyze before you compute. Set up the problem before you begin to solve it. When a problem is worth a lot of points, read it twice, slowly. Examine it carefully. When you take the time to analyze a problem, you can often discover computational shortcuts.

5 Make a picture. When you are stuck, draw an elaborate colored picture or a diagram. Sometimes a visual representation will clear a blocked mind. (Making pictures is also an excellent study and review tool in math and science.)

6 Estimate first. Estimating is a good way to double-check your work. Doing this first can help you notice when your computations go awry, allowing you to correct the error quickly.

7 Check your work systematically. When you check your work, ask yourself: Did I read the problem correctly? Did I use the correct formula or equation? Is my arithmetic correct? Is my answer in the proper form?

Ask yourself whether your answer makes sense. Are the units correct? Is your answer consistent with the parameters of the question?

Avoid the temptation to change an answer in the last few minutes—unless you're certain that the answer is wrong. In a last-minute rush to finish the test, it's easier to choose the wrong answer.

8 Review formulas. Right before the test, review any formulas you'll need to use. Then write them down in the margins of the test or on the back of the test paper. Check with your instructor before the day of the test to make sure he will allow you to write formulas or prompts on the test form or your answer sheet.

Discovery Statement

Explore your feelings about tests. Complete the following sentences.

As exam time gets closer, one thing I notice that I do is ...

_____

_____

When it comes to taking tests, I have trouble ...

_____

_____

The night before a test, I usually feel ...

_____

_____

The morning of a test, I usually feel ...

_____

_____

During a test, I usually feel ...

_____

_____

After a test, I usually feel ...

_____

_____

When I get a test score, I usually feel ...

_____

_____

For an online version of this exercise, visit Houghton Mifflin's
College Survival/Becoming a Master Student web site: **http://collegesurvival.college.hmco.com/students.**

PRACTICING CRITICAL THINKING

#10

Create a short multiple choice test on a topic in a course you're taking right now. Ask several people from the class to take this exam. Then, as a group, discuss the answers to each question. Ask group members to reveal the answer they chose for each question and their reasons for choosing that answer. After the discussion, have members retake the test. If their answers have changed, ask them to explain why they revised their thinking.

How to Cram

(handwritten: 25% learn 75% review)

First, know the limitations of cramming and be aware of its costs. Cramming won't work if you neglected all of the reading assignments, or if you skipped most of the lectures—and daydreamed through the rest.

The more courses you have to cram for, the less effective cramming will be.

Cramming is not the same as learning. When you rely on cramming, you cheat yourself of a true education for one basic reason: You won't remember what you cram.

This point is especially important to recognize if you cram for mid-term exams. Some students think they are actually learning the material that they cram into their heads. They will be unpleasantly surprised during finals.

Cramming is also more work. It takes longer to learn material when you do it under pressure. You can't learn the same quantity of material in less time when you cram. You can learn *some* of the material, with less comprehension and little or no long-term retention.

The purpose of cramming, therefore, is only to make the best of the situation. Cram to get by in a course so that you can do better next time. Cramming might help raise a grade, if you have been reasonably attentive in class, have taken fair notes, and have read or skimmed most of the material for the course.

Those are the limitations and costs of cramming. Here is a six-step cramming process.

1 Make choices.
Don't try to learn it all when you cram. You can't. Instead, pick out a few of the most important elements of the course and learn those backwards, forwards, and upside down.

For example, you can devote most of your attention to the topic sentences, tables, and charts in a long reading assignment instead of reading the whole assignment. A useful guideline is to spend 25 percent of cramming time learning new material and 75 percent of cramming time drilling yourself on that material.

2 Make a plan.
Cramming is always done when time is short. That is all the more reason to take a few minutes to create a plan. Choose what you want to study (step #1), determine how much time you have, and set timelines for yourself. It's easy to panic and jump right in. Making a plan can save you time and allow you to work faster. *(handwritten: set timelines)*

3 Use mind map review sheets and flash cards.
Condense the material you have chosen to learn onto mind maps. Choose several elements of the mind maps to put on 3×5 flash cards. Practice re-creating the mind maps, complete with illustrations. Drill yourself with the flash cards.

4 Recite ad nauseam.
The key to cramming is repetitive recitation. Recitation can burn facts into your brain like no other study method. Go over your material again and again and again. One option is to tape-record yourself while you recite. Then play the tape as you fall asleep and as you get up in the morning.

5 Relax.
Because you do not learn material well when you cram, you are more likely to freeze and forget it under the pressure of an exam. Relaxation techniques can be used to reduce test anxiety, both before and during the test.

6 Don't "should" on yourself. *(handwritten: no guilt)*
One word to avoid during the cramming process is "should." For example, you could start your cramming session by telling yourself you should have studied earlier, you should have read the assignments, and you should have been more conscientious. By the time you open your book, you might feel too guilty and depressed to continue.

Consider this approach. Tell yourself it would have been more effective to study earlier and more often. Remind yourself that you will have an opportunity to do so next time. Give yourself permission to be the fallible human being you are.

In short, lighten up. Our brains work better when we aren't criticizing ourselves.

8 reasons to celebrate mistakes

Most of us are haunted by the fear of failure. We dread the thought of making mistakes or being held responsible for a major breakdown. We shudder at the missteps that could cost us grades, careers, money, or even relationships.

It's possible to take an entirely different attitude toward mistakes. Rather than fearing them, we could actually celebrate them. We could revel in our redundancies, frolic in our failures, and glory in our goof-ups. We could marvel at our mistakes and bark with loud laughter when we "blow it."

A creative environment is one in which failure is not fatal. Businesses, striving to be on the cutting edge of competition, desperately seek innovative changes. They know that innovation requires risk taking, despite the chance of failure.

This is not idle talk. There are places where people actually celebrate mistakes. Management consultant Tom Peters gives these examples in an issue of the *Executive Excellence* newsletter:

- One marketing director at Pizza Hut ended up with $5 million in unused sunglasses when a sales promotion scheme backfired. (The sunglasses were specifically designed for viewing the movie *Back to the Future, Part 2.*) He was promoted soon afterward, and the company's profits still increased 36 percent that year.

- The chief executive officer of Temps & Co., a temporary services firm, opens some meetings by asking managers to describe their biggest mistakes. The person with the "best" mistake gets a $100 prize. One of the winning mistakes was typing a social security number in the place of the dollar amount and cutting a multimillion-dollar paycheck.

- At its First Annual Doobie Awards, the Public Broadcasting System honored prominent mistakes made by its members. Nominees included an executive whose "improved" time sheets required three sign-offs instead of one. "It's a way of not taking ourselves too seriously," said one recipient of the award. "It gets a message across. . . . That it's okay to try and fail."

Eight solid reasons for celebrating mistakes

1 Celebration allows us to notice the mistake. Celebrating mistakes gets them out into the open. Mistakes that are hidden cannot be corrected. It's only when we shine a light on a mistake and examine it that we can fix it. This is the opposite of covering up mistakes or blaming others for them. Hiding mistakes takes a lot of energy—energy that could be channeled into correcting errors.

2 Mistakes are valuable feedback. A manager of a major corporation once made a mistake that cost his company $100,000. He predicted that he would be fired when his boss found out. Instead, his boss responded, "Fire you? I can't afford to do that. I just spent $100,000 training you." Mistakes are part of the learning process. Not only are mistakes usually more interesting than most successes—they're often more instructive.

3 Mistakes demonstrate that we're taking risks. People who play it safe make few mistakes. Making mistakes is evidence that we're stretching to the limit of our abilities—growing, risking, and learning. Fear of making mistakes can paralyze us into inaction. Celebrating mistakes helps us move into gear and get things done.

4 Celebrating mistakes reminds us that it's OK to make them. When we celebrate, we remind ourselves that the person who made the mistake is not bad—just human. This is not a recommendation that you purposely set out to make mistakes. Mistakes are not an end in themselves. Rather, their value lies in what we learn from them. When we make a mistake, we can admit it and correct it.

5 Celebrating mistakes includes everyone. It reminds us that the exclusive club named the Perfect Performance Society has no members. All of us make mistakes. When we notice them, we can work together. Blaming others or the system prevents the cooperative efforts that can improve our circumstances.

6 Mistakes occur only when we aim at a clear goal. We can express concern about missing a target only if the target is there in the first place. If there's no target or purpose, then there's no concern about missing it. Making a mistake affirms something of great value—that we have a plan.

7 Mistakes happen only when we're committed to making things work. Systems work when people are willing to be held accountable. Openly admitting mistakes promotes accountability. Imagine a school where there's no concern about quality and effectiveness. Teachers usually come to class late. Residence halls are never cleaned, and scholarship checks are always late. The administration is in chronic debt, students seldom pay tuition on time, and no one cares. In this school, the word *mistake* would have little meaning. Mistakes become apparent only when people are committed to improving the quality of an institution. Mistakes go hand in hand with a commitment to quality.

8 Celebrating mistakes cuts the problem down to size. On top of the mistake itself, there is often a layer of regret, worry, and desperation about having made the mistake in the first place. Not only do people have a problem with the consequences of the mistake, they have a problem with themselves for making a mistake in the first place. When we celebrate mistakes, we eliminate that layer of concern. When our anxiety about making a mistake is behind us, we can get down to the business of correcting the mistake.

WORKPLACE APPLICATIONS

Celebrating mistakes offers a way to enhance your job skills. Recall a mistake you made at work and then do some journal writing about it. In a Discovery Statement, describe what you did to create a result you didn't want. ("I discovered that I tend to underestimate the number of hours projects take.") Then write an Intention Statement describing something you can do differently in the future. ("I intend to keep track of my actual hours on each project so that I can give more accurate estimates.")

EXERCISE

#24

Master mind map (part one)

On a separate sheet of paper, create a mind map of the first six chapters of this book. Use a large sheet of paper for this purpose. Create your map without reviewing. (Don't even look up chapter titles.) The purpose of this exercise is to demonstrate to yourself how much material you retain. You might be surprised by the results.

After creating your master mind map, go back through the text and review each chapter, spending no more than 10 minutes per chapter. Then, based on this review, revise your mind map to make it more accurate and complete.

See some sample mind maps on Houghton Mifflin's College Survival/Becoming a Master Student web site: **http://collegesurvival.college.hmco.com/students.**

Detach

This Power Process helps you release the powerful, natural student within you. It is especially useful whenever negative emotions are getting in the way of your education.

Attachments are addictions. When we are attached to something, we think we cannot live without it, just as a drug addict feels he cannot live without drugs. We believe our well-being depends on maintaining our attachments.

We can be attached to just about anything—expectations, ideas, objects, self-perceptions, people, results, rewards. The list is endless.

One person, for example, might be so attached to his car that he takes an accident as a personal attack. Pity the poor unfortunate who backs into this person's car. He might as well back into the owner himself.

Another person might be attached to his job. His identity and sense of well-being depend on it. He could become suicidally depressed if he gets fired.

We can be addicted to our emotions as well as to our thoughts. We can identify with our anger so strongly that we are unwilling to let it go. We can also be addicted to our pessimism and reluctant to give it up. Rather than perceive these emotions as liabilities, we can see them as indications that it's time to practice detachment.

Most of us are addicted, to some extent, to our identities. We are Americans, veterans, high achievers, Elks, bowlers, loyal friends, Episcopalians, business owners, humanitarians, devoted parents, dancers, hockey fans, or birdwatchers. If we are attached to these roles, they can dictate who we think we are.

When these identities are threatened, we might fight for them as if we were defending our lives. The more addicted we are to an identity, the harder we fight to keep it. It's like a drowning man—the more he resists drowning, the more he literally becomes "attached" to his would-be rescuer, grasping and grabbing, until they both sink.

Ways to recognize an attachment

When we are attached and things don't go our way, we might feel irritated, angry, jealous, confused, fatigued, bored, frightened, or resentful.

Suppose you are attached to getting an A on your physics test. You feel as though your success in life depends on getting an A. It's not just that you want an A. You *need* an A. During the exam, the thought "I must get an A" is in the back of your mind as you begin to work a problem. And the problem is difficult. The first time you read it, you have no idea how to solve it. The second time around, you aren't even sure what it's asking. The more you struggle to understand it, the more confused you get. To top it all off, this problem is worth 40 percent of your score.

As the clock ticks away, you work harder, getting more stuck, while that voice in your head gets louder: "I must get an A. I MUST get an A. I MUST GET AN A!"

At this point, your hands begin to sweat and shake. Your heart is pounding. You feel nauseated. You can't concentrate. You flail about for the answer as if you were drowning. You look up at the clock, sickened by the inexorable sweep of the second hand. You are doomed. Now is a time to detach.

Ways to use this process

Detachment can be challenging. In times of stress, it might seem like the most difficult thing in the world to do. You can practice a variety of strategies to help you move toward detachment:

Practice observer consciousness. This is the quiet state above and beyond your usual thoughts, the place where you can be aware of being aware. It's a tranquil spot, apart from your emotions. From here, you can observe yourself objectively, as if you were someone else. Pay attention to your emotions and physical sensations. If you are confused and feeling stuck, tell yourself, "Here I am, confused and stuck." If your palms are sweaty and your stomach is one big knot, admit it.

Practice perspective. Put current circumstances into a broader perspective. View personal issues within the larger context of your community, your nation, or your planet. You will likely see them from a different point of view. Imagine the impact your present problems will have 20 or even 100 years from now.

Take a moment to consider the worst that could happen. During that physics exam, notice your attachment to getting an A. Realize that even flunking the test will not ruin your life. Seeing this helps you put the test in perspective.

Practice breathing. Calm your mind and body with breathing or relaxation techniques.

It might be easier to practice these techniques when you're not feeling strong emotions. Notice your thoughts, behaviors, and feelings during neutral activities such as watching television.

Practice detaching. The key is to let go of automatic emotional reactions when you don't get what you want.

Rewrite the equation

To further understand this notion of detaching, we can borrow an idea from mathematics. An equation is a set of symbols joined by an equal sign (=) that forms a true statement. Examples are $2 \times 2 = 4$ and $a + b = c$.

Equations also work with words. In fact, our self-image can be thought of as a collection of equations. For example, the thought "I am capable" can be written as the equation $I = capable$. "My happiness depends on my car" can be written as $happiness = car$. The statement "My well-being depends on my job" becomes $well\text{-}being = job$.

Each equation is a tip-off to an attachment. When we're upset, a closer look often reveals that one of our attachments is threatened. The person who believes that his happiness is equal to his current job will probably be devastated if his company downsizes and he's laid off.

Once we discover a hidden equation, we can rewrite it. In the process, we can watch our upsets disappear. The person who gets laid off can change his equation to *my happiness = my happiness.* In other words, his happiness does not have to depend on any particular job.

People can rewrite equations under the most extreme circumstances. A man dying from lung cancer spent his last days celebrating his long life. One day his son asked him how he was feeling.

"Oh, I'm great," said the man with cancer. "Your mom and I have been having a wonderful time just rejoicing in the life that we have gotten to live together."

"Oh, I'm glad you're doing well," said the man's son. "The prednisone you have been taking must have kicked in again and helped your breathing."

"Well, not exactly. Actually, my body is in terrible shape, and my breathing has been a struggle these last few days. I guess what I'm saying is that my body is not working well at all, but I'm still great."

The dying man rewrote the equation $I = my\ body.$ He knew that he had a body and that he was more than his body. This man lived this Power Process and gave his son—the author of this book—an unforgettable lesson about detachment.

Some cautions

Giving up an addiction to being an A student does not mean giving up being an A student. And giving up an addiction to a job doesn't mean getting rid of the job. It means not investing your entire well-being in the grade or the job. Keep your desires and goals alive and healthy while detaching from the compulsion to reach them.

Notice also that detachment is different from denial. Denial implies running away from whatever you find unpleasant. In contrast, detachment includes accepting your emotions and knowing the details of them—down to every thought and physical sensation involved. It's OK to be angry or sad. Once you accept and fully experience your emotions, you can more easily move beyond them.

Being detached is not the same as being apathetic. We can be 100 percent detached and 100 percent involved at the same time. In fact, our commitment toward achieving a particular result is usually enhanced by being detached from it.

Detach and succeed

When we are detached, we perform better. When we think everything is at stake, the results might suffer. Without anxiety and the need to get an A on the physics test, we are more likely to recognize the problem and remember the solution.

This Power Process is useful when you notice that attachments are keeping you from getting what you want. Behind your attachments is a master student. By detaching, you release that master student. Detach.

master student
BARBARA JORDAN

(1936–1996) the first African American to become a state senator in Texas and the first African American to enter Congress since the Reconstruction.

So I was at Boston University in this new and strange and different world, and it occurred to me that if I was going to succeed at this strange new adventure, I would have to read longer and more thoroughly than my colleagues at law school had to read. I felt that in order to compensate for what I had missed in earlier years, I would have to work harder, and study longer, than anybody else. . . . I did my reading not in the law library, but in a library at my graduate dorm, upstairs where it was very quiet, because apparently nobody else studied there. So I would go there at night after dinner. I would load my books under my arm and go to the library, and I would read until the wee hours of the morning and then go to bed. . . .

I was always delighted when I would get called upon to recite in class. But the professors did not call on the "ladies" very much. There were certain favored people who always got called on, and then on some rare occasions a professor would come in and would announce: "We're going to have Ladies Day today." And he would call on the ladies. We were just tolerated. We weren't considered really top drawer when it came to the study of law.

At some time in the spring, Bill Gibson, who was dating my new roommate, Norma Walker, organized a black study group, as we blacks had to form our own. This was because we were not invited into any of the other study groups. There were six or seven in our group—Bill, and Issie, and I think Maynard Jackson—and we would just gather and talk it out and hear ourselves do that. One thing I learned was that you had to talk out the issues, the facts, the cases, the decisions, the process. You couldn't just read the cases and study alone in your library as I had been doing; and you couldn't get it all in the classroom. But once you had talked it out in the study group, it flowed more easily and made a lot more sense. . . .

Finally I felt I was really learning things, really going to school. I felt that I was getting educated, whatever that was. I became familiar with the process of thinking. I learned to think things out and reach conclusions and defend what I had said.

In the past I had got along by spouting off. Whether you talked about debates or oratory, you dealt with speechifying. But I could no longer orate and let that pass for reasoning because there was not any demand for an orator in Boston University Law School. You had to think and read and understand and reason. I had learned at twenty-one that you couldn't just say a thing is so because it might not be so, and somebody brighter, smarter, and more thoughtful would come out and tell you it wasn't so. Then, if you still thought it was, you had to prove it. Well, that was a new thing for me. I cannot, I really cannot describe what that did to my insides and to my head. I thought: I'm being educated finally.

From Barbara Jordan, a Self-Portrait *by Barbara Jordan and Shelby Hearon. Reprinted by permission of The Wendy Weil Agency, Inc. Copyright © 1978, 1979 by Shelby Hearon and Barbara Jordan.*

For more information on the strategies that Barbara Jordan used to succeed in school and in her career, visit Houghton Mifflin's College Survival/Becoming a Master Student web site: http://collegesurvival.college.hmco.com/students.

Name _____ Date _____/_____/_____

 1 Preparing for tests can include creating review tools. What are at least two of these tools?

 2 When answering multiple choice questions, it is better to read all of the possible answers before answering the question in your head. True or False? Explain your answer.

 3 The presence of absolute qualifiers, such as *always* or *never*, generally indicates a false statement. True or False? Explain your answer.

 4 When answering an essay question, which of the following techniques is least effective?
   (A) Before you write your answer, make a quick outline.
   (B) Try for drama by saving the best points for last.
   (C) Find out precisely what the question is asking by knowing standard essay question words.
   (D) Include part of the question in your answer.
   (E) Avoid filler sentences that say nothing.

 5 Grades are:
   (A) A measure of creativity.
   (B) An indication of your ability to contribute to society.
   (C) A measure of intelligence.
   (D) A measure of test performance.
   (E) C and D.

 6 How does *detachment* differ from *denial*?

Quiz
C O N T I N U E D

 7 Choose one technique for taking math and science tests and explain how it, or some variation of it, could apply to taking a test in another subject.

 8 What are at least three benefits of participating in a study group?

 9 Describe at least three techniques for dealing with the thoughts connected to test anxiety.

10 Describe at least three techniques for dealing with the physical feelings connected to test anxiety.

JOURNAL ENTRY

#34

Discovery/Intention Statement

Review what you learned in this chapter and complete the following sentence.

In reading and doing this chapter, I discovered that I ...

_____

_____

Write about your intention to use one of the stress-management techniques and test-taking strategies from this chapter.

I intend to ...

_____

_____

LEARNING STYLES APPLICATION CHAPTER 6

Mode 4 *Explain how the suggestions given in this chapter for managing test anxiety could help you manage any stress you're currently experiencing. Think about ways to use these suggestions outside your schoolwork.*

Mode 1 *Write a short paragraph explaining ways in which you are already effectively using any of the techniques in this chapter.*

Mode 3 *Of the 10 new suggestions you just listed, choose five that you will actually use. Describe when or where you could use each technique.*

Mode 2 *List 10 new suggestions for reviewing course material or taking tests that you gained from reading this chapter.*

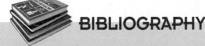
BIBLIOGRAPHY

ENDNOTE

1 Sheila Tobias, *Succeed with Math: Every Student's Guide to Conquering Math Anxiety* (New York: College Board, 1995).

ADDITIONAL READING

Kogelman, Stanley, and Joseph Warren. *Mind over Math.* New York: Dial Press, 1978.

Mallow, Jeffry V. *Science Anxiety: Fear of Science and How to Overcome It.* New York: Thomond, 1986.

McCarthy, Michael J. *Mastering the Information Age.* Los Angeles: J. P. Tarcher, 1991.

Pauk, Walter. *How to Study in College.* Seventh Edition. Boston: Houghton Mifflin, 2001.

INTERNET RESOURCES

Academic Skills Center—Dartmouth University
www.dartmouth.edu/~acskills/success/study.html

Study Guides and Test Taking Strategies
www.eop.mu.edu/study

Test Taking Strategies
www.d.umn.edu/student/loon/acad/strat/test_take.html

Web Sites for College Study Strategies—110 links
alc.stcloudstate.edu/Counseling/CLASSES/110/links.htm

Thinking

I always wanted to be somebody, but I should've been more specific.
LILY TOMLIN

Creativity was in each one of us as a small child. In children it is universal. Among adults it is almost nonexistent. The great question is: What has happened to this enormous and universal human capacity?
TILLIE OLSEN

IN THIS CHAPTER . . . Play with techniques for creative thinking and take steps toward becoming a critical thinker. The journey includes ways to uncover assumptions, spot logical fallacies, solve problems, and make decisions. Apply your skills to practical issues such as choosing a major and solving math and science problems. By then you'll be ready to find a bigger problem—one that's worthy of your time and talents.

Critical thinking: A survival skill

Society depends on persuasion. Advertisers want us to spend money. Political candidates want us to "buy" their stands on the issues. Teachers want us to agree that their classes are vital to our success. Parents want us to accept their values. Authors want us to read their books. Broadcasters want us to spend our time in front of the radio or television, consuming their programs and not those of the competition. The business of persuasion impacts upon all of us.

A typical American sees thousands of television commercials each year. And that's just one medium of communication. Add to that the writers and speakers who enter our lives through radio shows, magazines, books, billboards, brochures, Internet sites, and fundraising appeals—all with a product, service, cause, or opinion for us to embrace.

This leaves us with hundreds of choices about what to buy, where to go, and who to be. It's easy to lose our heads in the crosscurrent of competing ideas—unless we develop skills in critical thinking. When we think critically, we can make choices with open eyes.

Uses of critical thinking

Critical thinking underlies reading, writing, speaking, and listening. These are the basic elements of communication—a process that occupies most of our waking hours.

Critical thinking also plays an important part in social change. Consider that the institutions in any society—courts, governments, schools, businesses—are the products of a certain way of thinking. Any organization draws its life from certain assumptions about the way things should be done. Before the institution can change, those assumptions need to be loosened up or reinvented. In many ways, the real location of an institution is inside our heads.

Critical thinking also helps us uncover bias and prejudice. This is a first step toward communicating with people of other races, ethnic backgrounds, and cultures.

Crises occur when our thinking fails to keep pace with reality. An example is the ecological crisis, which sprang from the assumption that people could pollute the earth, air, and water without long-term consequences. Consider how different our world would be if our leaders had

Discovery Statement

Describe a time when you felt stuck in your thinking, unable to choose among several different solutions to a problem or several stands on a key issue in your life. List below the specific time, place, and circumstances involved.

_____

_____

_____

_____

_____

_____

_____

_____

_____

_____

Now scan this chapter for useful ideas or techniques on decision making, problem solving, and critical thinking. Note below any strategies that look especially promising to you.

I discovered that I might be able to improve my thinking skills by…

_____

_____

_____

_____

_____

_____

_____

_____

_____

_____

_____

thought like the first female chief of the Cherokees. Asked about the best advice her elders had given her, she said, "Look forward. Turn what has been done into a better path. If you are a leader, think about the impact of your decision on seven generations into the future."

Novelist Ernest Hemingway once said that anyone who wants to be a great writer must have a built-in, shockproof "crap" detector. That inelegant comment points to a basic truth: As critical thinkers, we are constantly on the lookout for thinking that's inaccurate, sloppy, or misleading.

Critical thinking is a skill that will never go out of style. Throughout history, half-truths, faulty assumptions, and other nonsense have at one time been commonly accepted as true. Examples include:

- Illness results from an imbalance in the four vital fluids: blood, phlegm, water, and bile.

- Caucasians are inherently more intelligent than people of other races.

- Women are incapable of voting intelligently.

- We will never invent anything smaller than a transistor. (That was before the computer chip.)

- Computer technology will usher in the age of the paperless office.

In response to such ideas rose the critical thinkers of history. These men and women courageously pointed out that—metaphorically speaking—the emperor had no clothes.

Critical thinking is a path to freedom from half-truths and deception. You have the right to question what you see, hear, and read. Acquiring this ability is one of the major goals of a liberal education.

Critical thinking as thorough thinking

For some people, the term *critical thinking* has negative connotations. If you prefer, use the words *thorough thinking* instead. Both terms point to the same array of activities: sorting out conflicting claims, weighing the evidence, letting go of personal biases, and arriving at reasonable views. This adds up to an ongoing conversation, a constant process, not a product.

We live in a society that seems to value quick answers and certainty. This is often at odds with effective thinking. Thorough thinking is the ability to examine and re-examine ideas that might seem obvious. Such thinking takes time and the willingness to say three subversive words: "I don't know."

Thorough thinking is also the willingness to change our point of view as we continue to examine a problem. This calls for courage and detachment. Just ask anyone who has given up a cherished point of view in light of new evidence.

Skilled students are thorough thinkers. They distinguish between opinion and fact. They ask powerful questions. They make detailed observations. They uncover assumptions and define their terms. They make assertions carefully, basing them on sound logic and solid evidence. Almost everything that we call *knowledge* is a result of these activities. This means that critical thinking and learning are intimately linked.

It's been said that human beings are rational creatures. Yet no one is born a thorough thinker. This is a learned skill. Use the suggestions in this chapter to claim the vast, latent thinking powers that are your birthright.

Finding "aha!"
Creativity fuels critical thinking

The first half of this book is about the nuts and bolts of education. It offers suggestions for ways to tell the truth about your skills as a student and ways to set goals to improve them. Also included are guidelines for managing your time, making your memory more effective, improving your reading skills, taking useful notes, and prospering during exams. Those techniques are about the business of acquiring knowledge.

The point of education is not just to have knowledge. The point is to use original thinking to create new knowledge—not in a mechanical way, like a computer, but in imaginative and innovative ways. That's the primary agenda for the second half of this book.

Begin with creative thinking, a powerful starting point for critical thinking.

Central to creative thinking is something called the "aha!" experience. Nineteenth-century poet Emily Dickinson described the aha! this way: "If I feel physically as if the top of my head were taken off, I know that is poetry." Aha! is the burst of creative energy heralded by the arrival of a new, original idea. It is the sudden emergence of a new pattern, a previously undetected relationship, or an unusual combination of familiar elements. It is an exhilarating experience.

Aha! does not always result in a timeless poem or a Nobel Prize. It can be inspired by anything from playing a new riff on a guitar to discovering why your car's fuel pump doesn't work. A nurse might notice a patient's symptom that everyone else missed. That's an aha! An accountant might discover a tax break for a client. That's an aha! A teacher might invent a way to reach a difficult student. Aha!

School is a natural breeding ground for aha!s. Term papers, speeches, math problems, science projects, even tests—all of these can inspire aha!, especially in the hands of skilled students.

The flip side of aha! is following through. The creative process is both fun *and* work. It is effortless and uncomfortable. It's the result of luck and persistence. It involves spontaneity and step-by-step procedures.

Many people overlook the follow-up to creative thinking—critical thinking. The latter step involves molding and shaping a rough-cut idea into a polished creation. Employers in all fields are desperately seeking those rare people who can find aha! and do something with it. The necessary skills include the ability to spot assumptions, weigh evidence, separate fact from opinion, organize thoughts, and avoid errors in logic. You'll find more details on each of these topics throughout this chapter. All this can be demanding work. Just as often, it can be energizing and fun.

Use this chapter to discover the joy of aha! through creative thinking. Follow it up with skills in critical thinking, and you have a combination that can supercharge your success in school.

Tangram

A tangram is an ancient Chinese puzzle game that stimulates the "play instinct" so critical to creative thinking. The cat figure above was created by rearranging seven sections of a square. Hundreds of images can be devised in this manner. Playing with tangrams allows us to see relationships we didn't notice before.

The rules of the game are simple: Use these seven pieces to create something that wasn't there before. Be sure to use all seven. You might start by mixing up the pieces and seeing whether you can put them back together to form a square. Make your own tangram by cutting pieces like those above out of poster board. When you come up with a pattern you like, trace around the outside edges of it and see if a friend can discover how you did it.

Techniques for *creative* thinking

Use the following techniques to generate ideas about everything, whether you're studying math problems, remodeling a house, or writing a bestseller. With practice, you can set the stage for creative leaps, jump with style, and land on your feet with brand-new ideas in hand.

Conduct a brainstorm.

Brainstorming is a technique for finding solutions, creating plans, and discovering new ideas. When you are stuck on a problem, brainstorming can break the logjam.

For example, if you run out of money two days before payday every week, you can brainstorm ways to make your money last longer. You can brainstorm ways to pay for your education. You can brainstorm ways to find a job.

The purpose of brainstorming is to generate as many solutions as possible. Sometimes the craziest, most outlandish ideas, while unworkable in themselves, can lead to new ways to solve problems. Use the following steps to try out the brainstorming process.

First, state the issue or problem precisely by writing it down. For example, you might write, "Methods and techniques I can use to get more information about multinational trade organizations in Central Africa."

Next, set a time limit for your brainstorming session. Use a clock to time it to the minute. Digital sports watches with built-in stopwatches work well. Experiment with various lengths of time. Both short and long brainstorms can be powerful.

Before you begin, sit quietly for a few seconds to collect your thoughts. Then start timing and write as fast as you can.

Write down everything. Accept every idea. If it pops into your head, put it down on paper. Quantity, not quality, is the goal. Avoid making judgments and evaluations during the brainstorming session.

After the session, review, evaluate, and edit. Toss out any truly nutty ideas, but not before you give them a chance.

For example, during your brainstorm on Central African trade organizations, you might have written "Go to Central Africa and ask someone about them." Impossible? Perhaps your school would give you a semester of independent study to research the subject. A trade organization might offer a scholarship to pay for the trip. You could also "visit" Central Africa via a web site, or communicate directly with a trade organization by email.

Brainstorms often produce solutions that look wacky at first and can later bring about surprising, life-changing results. Stay open to possibilities.

Here are some other tips for brainstorming sessions.

Let go of the need for a particular solution. Brainstorming sessions can reveal new ways of thinking about old problems.

Relax. Creativity is enhanced by a state of relaxed alertness. If you are tense or anxious, use some of the relaxation techniques described in this text. (Start with "Let go of test anxiety" in the Tests chapter.)

Set a quota or goal for the number of solutions you want to generate. Goals give your subconscious mind something to aim for.

Use 3 × 5 cards or a computer to record each solution. When you review your session, you can arrange solutions in patterns to look for relationships. Or you can arrange them in order of priority.

Brainstorm with others. This is a powerful technique. Group brainstorms can take on lives of their own. Ask one member of the group to write down solutions. Feed off the ideas of others, and remember to avoid evaluating or judging anyone's idea during the brainstorm.

Multiply brainstorms. Pick one item from your first brainstorm and conduct another brainstorm about that idea.

Be wild and crazy. If you get stuck, think of an outlandish idea and write it down. One crazy idea can unleash a flood of other, more workable solutions.

 Focus and let go. Focusing and letting go are alternating parts of the same process. Intense focus taps the resources of your conscious mind. Letting go gives your subconscious mind time to work. When you focus for intense periods and then let go for a while, the conscious and subconscious parts of your brain work in harmony. In doing so, they can produce the highest-quality results.

Focusing attention means being in the here and now. To focus your attention on a project, notice when you pay attention and when your mind starts to wander. And involve all of your senses.

For example, if you are having difficulty writing a paper at a computer, practice focusing by listening to the sounds as you type. Notice the feel of the keys as you strike them. When you know the sights, sounds, and sensations you associate with being truly in focus, you'll be able to repeat the experience and focus on your paper more easily.

You can use your body to focus your concentration. Some people concentrate better lying down. Others focus more easily if they stand or pace back and forth. Still others need to have something in their hands. Experiment. Notice what works for you and use it.

Be willing to recognize conflict, tension, and discomfort. Notice them and fully accept them, rather than fighting against them. Look for the specific thoughts and body sensations that make up the discomfort. Allow them to come fully into your awareness, and then let them pass.

You might not be focused all of the time. Periods of inspiration might last only seconds. Be gentle with yourself when you notice that your concentration has lapsed.

In fact, that might be a time to let go. "Letting go" means not forcing yourself to be creative.

Practice focusing for short periods at first, then give yourself a break. Phone a friend. Get up and take a walk around the room or around your block. Take a few minutes to look out your window. Listen to some music or, better yet, sing a few songs to yourself.

You also can break up periods of focused concentration with stretches, sit-ups, or pushups. Use relaxation and breathing exercises. Muscle tension and the lack of oxygen can inhibit self-expression.

Movies, music, walks in the park, and other pleasant activities stir the creative soup that's simmering in your brain.

Take a nap when you are tired. Thomas Edison took frequent naps. Then the light bulb clicked on.

Cultivate creative serendipity. The word *serendipity* comes from a story by Horace Walpole, "The Three Princes of Serendip." The princes had a knack for making lucky discoveries. Serendipity is that knack. This is more than luck. It is the ability to see something valuable that you weren't looking for. History is full of serendipitous people.

Edward Jenner noticed "by accident" that milkmaids seldom got smallpox. The result was his discovery that mild cases of cowpox immunized them. Penicillin was also discovered "by accident." Alexander Fleming was growing bacteria in a laboratory petri dish. A spore of *Penicillium notatum,* a kind of mold, blew in the window and landed in the dish, killing the bacteria. Fleming isolated the active ingredient. A few years later, during World War II, it saved thousands of lives. Had Fleming not been alert to the possibility, the discovery might never have been made. You can train yourself in the art of serendipity. First, keep your eyes open. You might find a solution to an accounting problem in a Saturday morning cartoon. You might discover a term paper subject at the corner convenience store.

Multiply your contacts with the world. Resolve to meet new people. Join a study or discussion group. Read. Go to plays, concerts, art shows, lectures, and movies. Watch television programs you normally wouldn't watch. Use idea files and play with data, as described below.

Finally, expect discoveries. One secret of "luck" is being prepared to recognize it when you see it.

Keep idea files.
We all have ideas. People who are viewed as creative are those who treat their ideas with care. That means recognizing them, recording them, and following up on them.

One way to keep track of ideas is to write them down on 3×5 cards. Invent your own categories and number the cards so you can cross-reference them. For example, if you have an idea about making a new kind of bookshelf, you might file a card under "Remodeling." A second card might also be filed under "Marketable Ideas." On the first card, you can write down your ideas, and on the second, you can write "See card #321—Remodeling."

Include in your files powerful quotations, random insights, notes on your reading, and useful ideas you encounter in class. Collect jokes, too.

Keep a journal. Journals don't have to be exclusively about your own thoughts and feelings. You can record observations about the world around you, conversations with friends, important or offbeat ideas—anything.

To fuel your creativity, read voraciously, including newspapers and magazines. Keep a clip file of interesting articles. Explore beyond mainstream journalism. There are hundreds of low-circulation specialty magazines and Internet sites that cover almost any subject you can imagine.

Keep letter-sized files of important correspondence, magazine and news articles, and other material. You can also create idea files on a computer using word processing, outlining, or database software.

Safeguard your ideas, even if you're pressed for time. Jotting down four or five words is enough to capture the essence of an idea. You can write down one quotation in a minute or two. And if you carry 3×5 cards in a pocket or purse, you can record ideas while standing in line or sitting in a waiting room.

Review your files regularly. Some amusing thought that came to you in November might be the perfect solution to a problem in March.

Collect and play with data.
Look from all sides at the data you collect. Switch your attention from one aspect to another. Examine each fact, and avoid getting stuck on one particular part of a problem.

Turn a problem upside down by picking a solution first and then working backward. Ask other people to look at the data. Solicit opinions.

Living with the problem invites a solution. Write down data, possible solutions, or a formulation of the problem on 3×5 cards and carry them with you. Look at them before you go to bed at night. Review them when you are waiting for the bus. Make them part of your life and think about them frequently.

Look for the obvious solutions or the obvious "truths" about the problem, then toss them out! Ask yourself: Well, I know X is true, but if X were *not* true, what would happen? Or ask the reverse: If that *were* true, what would follow next?

Put unrelated facts next to each other and invent a relationship between them, even if it seems absurd at first. In *The Act of Creation,* novelist Arthur Koestler says that finding a context in which to combine opposites is the essence of creativity.[1]

Make imaginary pictures with the data. Condense it. Categorize it. Put it in chronological order. Put it in alphabetical order.

Put it in random order. Order it from most to least complex. Reverse all of those orders. Look for opposites.

It has been said that there are no new ideas—only new ways to combine old ideas. Creativity is the ability to discover those new combinations.

Create while you sleep.

A part of our mind works as we sleep. You've experienced this directly if you've ever fallen asleep with a problem on your mind and awakened the next morning with a solution. For some of us, the solution appears in a dream or just before falling asleep or waking up.

You can experiment with this process. Ask yourself a question as you fall asleep. Keep pencil and paper or a tape recorder near your bed. The moment you wake up, begin writing or speaking and see if an answer to your question emerges.

Many of us have awakened from a dream with a great idea, only to fall asleep and lose it forever. To capture your ideas, keep a notebook by your bed at all times. Put the notebook where you can find it easily.

There is a story about how Benjamin Franklin used this suggestion. Late in the evenings, as he was becoming drowsy, he would sit in his rocking chair with a rock in his right hand and a metal bucket on the floor beneath the rock. The moment he fell asleep, the rock would fall from his grip into the bottom of the bucket, making a loud noise that awakened him. Having placed a pen and paper nearby, he immediately wrote down what he was thinking. Experience taught him that his thoughts at this moment were often insightful and creative.

Refine ideas and follow through.

Many of us ignore this part of the creative process. How many great moneymaking schemes have we had that we never pursued? How many good ideas have we had for short stories that we never wrote? How many times have we said to ourselves, "You know, what they ought to do is attach two handles to one of those things, paint it orange, and sell it to police departments. They'd make a fortune." And we never realize that we are "they."

Genius resides in the follow-through—the application of perspiration to inspiration. One powerful tool you can use to follow through is the Discovery and Intention Journal Entry system. Write your idea in a Discovery Statement and then write what you intend to do about it in an Intention Statement. Use the guidelines listed in Chapter One. You also can use the writing techniques in the Communicating chapter as a guide for refining your ideas.

Another way to refine an idea is to simplify it. And if that doesn't work, mess it up. Make it more complex.

Finally, keep a separate file in your idea file for your own inspirations. Return to it regularly to see if there is anything you can use. Today's defunct term paper idea could be next year's A in speech class.

Create success strategies.

Use creative thinking techniques to go beyond the pages of this book and create your own ways to succeed in school. Read other books on success. Interview successful people. Reflect on any of your current behaviors that help you do well in school. Change any habits that fail to serve you.

If you created a study group with people from one of your classes, set aside time to talk about ways to succeed in any class. Challenge each other to practice your powers of invention. Test any new strategies you create and report to the group on how well they're working for you.

Trust the process.

Learn to trust the creative process—even when no answers are in sight. Often we are reluctant to look at problems if no immediate solution is at hand. We grow impatient and tend to avoid frustration by giving up. Most of us do this to some degree with personal problems. If we are having difficulty with a relationship and don't see a quick resolution, we deny that the problem exists rather than face it.

Trust that a solution will show up. Frustration and a feeling of being stuck are often signals that a solution is imminent.

Sometimes solutions break through in a giant AHA! More often they come in a series of little aha!s. Be aware of what your aha!s look, feel, and sound like. That sets the stage for even more flights of creative thinking.

Becoming a critical thinker

Critical thinking is a path to intellectual adventure. Though there are dozens of possible approaches, the process can be boiled down to concrete steps. This article offers some starting points for your journey.

Think of the following suggestions as a toolbox for critical thinking. For other handy implements, see *Becoming a Critical Thinker* by Vincent Ryan Ruggiero.

Be willing to say "I don't know."

Some of the most profound thinkers have practiced the art of critical thinking by using two magic phrases: "I don't know" and "I'm not sure yet."

Those are words many people do not like to hear. We live in times when people are criticized for changing their minds. Our society rewards quick answers and quotable sound bites. We're under considerable pressure to utter the truth in 15 seconds or less.

In such a society, it is courageous and unusual to take the time to pause, to look, to examine, to be thoughtful, to consider many points of view—and to not know. When a society adopts half-truths in a blind rush for certainty, a willingness to embrace uncertainty can move us forward.

Define your terms.

Imagine two people arguing about whether an employer should limit health care benefits to members of a family. To one person, the word *family* means a mother, father, and children; to the other person, the word *family* applies to any long-term, supportive relationship between people who live together. Chances are, the debate will go nowhere until these people realize that they're defining the same word in different ways.

Conflicts of opinion can be resolved—or at least clarified—when we define our key terms up front. This is especially true with abstract, emotion-laden terms such as *freedom, peace, progress,* or *justice.* Blood has been shed over the meaning of these words. It pays for us to define them with care.

Practice tolerance.

Having opinions about issues is natural. When we stop taking positions on things, we've probably stopped breathing. The problem occurs when we become so attached to our current opinions that we refuse to consider other options.

One path to critical thinking is tolerance for a wide range of

opinions. Consider ideas that are widely accepted today in Western cultures—for example, civil liberties for people of color and the right of women to vote. These ideas were once considered dangerous. Ideas that seem outlandish today might become widely accepted a century, a decade, or even a year from now. Remembering this can help us practice tolerance for differing opinions today.

Understand before criticizing.

Critical thinkers take the time to understand an idea before agreeing or disagreeing with it. This principle is central to many professions. Physicians diagnose before they prescribe. Lawyers brief themselves on the opposing counsel's case. Effective teachers find out what students already know before guiding them to new ideas. Skilled salespeople determine what a customer's needs are before they present a product. Polished debaters can sum up the viewpoints they disagree with—often better than the people who support those ideas.

Effective understanding calls for listening without judgment. To enter another person's world, sum up her viewpoint in your own words. If you're conversing with that person, keep revising your summary until she agrees that you've stated her position accurately. If you're reading an article, write a short summary of it. Then scan the article again, checking to see if your summary is on target.

Watch for hot spots.

Many people have mental "hot spots"— topics that provoke strong opinions and feelings. Examples are abortion, homosexuality, gun control, and the death penalty.

To become more skilled at critical thinking, notice your own particular hot spots. Make a clear intention to accept your feelings about these topics and to continue using critical thinking techniques.

One way to cool down our hot spots is to remember that we can change or even give up our current opinions without giving up ourselves.

That's a key message behind "Ideas are tools" and "Detach." These Power Processes remind us that human beings are much more than the sum of their current opinions.

Consider the source.

Look again at that article on the problems of manufacturing cars powered by natural gas; it might have been written by an executive from an oil company. Check out the expert who disputes the connection between smoking and lung cancer; that "expert" might be the president of a tobacco company.

This is not to say that we should dismiss the ideas of people who have a vested interest in stating their opinions. Rather, we can take their self-interest into account as we consider their ideas.

Seek out alternative views.

Imagine Karl Marx, Cesar Chavez, and Donald Trump assembled in one room to choose the most desirable economic system. Picture Mahatma Gandhi, Winnie Mandela, and General George Patton lecturing at a UN conference on conflict resolution. Visualize Fidel Castro, George W. Bush, and Mother Teresa in a discussion about distributing the world's resources equitably. When seeking out alternative points of view, let such events unfold in your mind.

Dozens of viewpoints exist on every critical issue—ways to reduce crime, end world hunger, prevent war, educate our children, and countless others. In fact, few

problems allow for any permanent solution. Each generation produces new answers, based on current conditions. Our search for answers is a conversation that spans centuries. On each question, many voices are waiting to be heard.

You can take advantage of this diversity by seeking out alternative views with an open mind. When talking to another person, be willing to walk away with a new point of view—even if it's the one you brought to the table. After thinking thoroughly, you can adopt new perspectives or hold your current viewpoints in a different way.

Ask questions.

Stripped to its essence, critical thinking means asking and answering questions. If you want to practice this skill, get into the habit of asking powerful questions.

In *How to Read a Book,* Mortimer Adler and Charles Van Doren list four questions that sum up the task of thinking about another person's ideas.[2]

1 *What is the writing or speech about as a whole?* To answer this question, state the basic theme in one sentence. Then list the major and minor topics covered.

2 *What is being said in detail?* List the main terms, assertions, arguments. Also state what problems the writer or speaker is trying to solve.

3 *Is it true?* Examine the author's logic and evidence. Look for missing information, faulty information, incomplete analysis, and errors in reasoning. Also determine which problems the writer or speaker truly solved and which remain unsolved.

4 *What of it?* After answering the first three questions, prepare to change your thinking or behavior as a result of encountering new ideas.

These four questions apply not only to reading but also to any other intellectual activity. They get to the heart of critical thinking.

Look for at least three answers.
When asking questions, we can let go of the temptation to settle for just a single answer. Once you have come up with an answer, say to yourself, "Yes, that is one answer. Now what's another?"

Using this approach can sustain honest inquiry, fuel creativity, and lead to conceptual breakthroughs.

Be prepared: The world is complicated, and critical thinking is a complex business. Some of your answers might contradict others. Resist the temptation to have all of your ideas in a neat, orderly bundle.

Lay your cards on the table.
Science and uncritical thinking differ in many ways. Uncritical thinkers shield themselves from new information and ideas. In contrast, scientists constantly look for facts that contradict their theories. In fact, science never proves anything once and for all. Scientific theories are tentative and subject to change. Scientists routinely practice critical thinking.

We can follow their example. When talking or writing, we can put all of our ideas on the table for open inquiry. We can allow others to

Student Voices

A Master Student practices critical thinking. . . . She does not always accept the first answer as the only answer, and constantly questions what is put before her. I am determined to get every ounce of information, to glean and hold onto it, use it, and mature my thinking.

—LYNN LINEBERGER

fully examine our opinions and beliefs. When doing so, we make room for new ideas that might have the capacity to alter our lives.

Write about it.
Thoughts can move randomly at blinding speed. Writing slows that process down. Gaps in logic that slip by us in thought or speech are often exposed when we commit the same ideas to paper. Writing down our thoughts allows us to see differing points of view more clearly—and therefore to think more thoroughly. Writing is an unparalleled way to practice precise, accurate thinking.

Accept your changing perspectives.
Over the years, you might notice that your outlook on significant issues has changed. Consider your opinions regarding your own particular hot spots.

Compare your current stand on these issues to the stand you took five years ago or ten years ago. Also look at your current goals in all areas of your life and compare them to the goals you had in the past. You'll probably see some evolution in your perspectives and plans—perhaps even a complete change of heart on some issues or a change in the direction of your life.

In addition to changes in the *content* of your thinking, you'll also notice changes in your *process* of thinking. Along with shifting viewpoints come modifications in the way you *arrive* at those viewpoints. These changes might accelerate during your years in higher education.

Researcher William Perry found that students in higher education move through stages of intellectual development.[3] Students in earlier stages tend to think there is only one correct viewpoint on each issue, and they look to their instructors to reveal that truth. Later, students acknowledge a variety of opinions on issues and construct their own viewpoints.

In their book *Women's Ways of Knowing*, Mary Field Belenky and her

The purpose of this exercise is to explore how your feelings can inhibit your ability to think objectively.

For each of us there are issues that trigger strong emotional reactions. For some people, these topics could include gay and lesbian rights, capital punishment, the destruction of the environment, or biological engineering. Your own list could include these topics or others.

Create your list in a two-column format on a separate sheet of paper. In one column, write a word or short phrase summarizing each issue. In the other column, describe the way you typically respond when each issue comes up in conversation or writing.

Now describe what you can do to remain more objective when one of your "hot button" issues comes up.

_____

_____

_____

_____

_____

_____

colleagues explain a set of different thinking processes.[4] These processes range from *silence*, by which people see themselves as being mindless and dependent on authority, to *constructed knowledge*, by which people create their own ideas from a variety of sources.

Using ideas from these researchers, you can monitor changes in your thinking processes. Distinguish between opinions that you accept from authorities and opinions that are based on your own use of logic and search for evidence. Also look for opinions that result from objective procedures (following instructions or applying a method) and personal sources (using intuition or instinctive knowledge).

Remember that the process of becoming a critical thinker will take you through a variety of stages. Give yourself time, and celebrate your growing mastery.

Combine perspectives.

One humorist compared finding the truth to painting a barn door by throwing open cans of paint at it. Few people who throw at the door miss it entirely. Yet no one can really cover the whole door in one toss.

People who express a viewpoint are seeking truth. Yet almost no reasonable person claims to cover the whole barn door—to have the Whole Truth about anything. Instead, each viewpoint is one approach among many possible approaches. If you don't think that any one opinion is complete, then it's up to you to combine the perspectives on the issue. In doing so, you can choose an original viewpoint. This, like composing a song or painting a picture, is a creative act and an exhilarating exercise in critical thinking.

Create on your feet

A popular trend in executive offices these days are "stand-up" desks—raised desks at which you stand rather than sit. Standing has advantages over sitting for long periods. You stay more alert and creative when you're on your feet.

One theory is that our problem-solving ability improves when we stand. Increased heart rate and blood flow to the brain could be key factors.

Standing is great for easing lower-back pain, too. Sitting aggravates the spine and its supporting muscles.

You can join the ranks of some influential people who spend their days standing, rather than sitting, on the job. They claim to get more done and are more comfortable doing it.

The list of stand-up advocates includes Robert Birk, former chairman of Merrill Lynch & Co.; George Shinn, former chairman and chief executive officer of First Boston Corp.; and C. Peter McColough, former chairman of Xerox, along with Xerox's president and at least one vice president. The list also includes Secretary of State Colin Powell.

This is a technique with tradition. Thomas Jefferson used a stand-up desk, upon which he wrote the Declaration of Independence. Donald Rumsfeld, U.S. Secretary of Defense, used one at his private business and uses one in the White House. Winston Churchill, Ernest Hemingway, and Virginia Woolf were all fond of standing while working.

Experiment with this idea. Consider setting your desk up on blocks or putting a box on top of your desk so that you can stand while writing, preparing speeches, or studying. Discover whether this approach works for you.

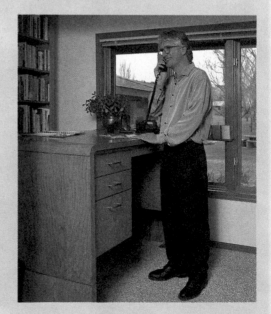

Uncovering assumptions

Consider the following argument:

Orca whales mate for life.
Orca whales travel in family groups.
Science has revealed that Orca whales are intelligent.
Therefore, Orca whales should be saved from extinction.

One idea underlies this line of thought:

Any animal that displays significant human characteristics deserves special protection.

Whether or not you agree with this argument, consider for a moment the process of making assumptions. Assumptions are assertions that guide our thinking and behavior. Often these assertions are unconscious. People can remain unaware of their most basic and far-reaching assumptions—the very ideas that shape their lives.

Spotting assumptions can be tricky, since they are usually unstated and offered without evidence. And scores of assumptions can be held at the same time. Those assumptions might even contradict each other, resulting in muddled thinking and confused behavior. This makes uncovering assumptions a feat worthy of the greatest detective.

Letting assumptions remain in our subconscious can erect barriers to our success. Take the person who says, "I don't worry about saving money for the future. I think life is meant to be enjoyed today—not later." This statement rests on at least two assumptions: *saving money is not enjoyable*, and *we can enjoy ourselves only when we're spending money.*

It would be no surprise to find out that this person runs out of money near the end of each month and depends on cash advances from high-interest credit cards. She is shielding herself from some ideas that could erase her debt: Saving money can be a source of satisfaction, and many enjoyable activities cost nothing.

The stakes in uncovering assumptions are high. Prejudice thrives on the beliefs that certain people are inferior or dangerous due to their skin color, ethnic background, or sexual preference. Those beliefs have led to flawed assumptions such as *mixing the blood of the races will lead to genetically inferior offspring* and *racial integration of the armed forces will lead to the destruction of morale.*

When we remain ignorant of our assumptions, we also make it easier for people with hidden agendas to do our thinking for us. Demagogues and unethical advertisers know that unchallenged assumptions are potent tools for influencing our attitudes and behavior.

Take this claim from an advertisement: "Successful students have large vocabularies, so sign up today for our seminar on word power!" Embedded in this sentence are several assumptions. One is that a cause-and-effect relationship exists between a large vocabulary and success in school. Another is that a large vocabulary is the single or most important factor in that success. This claim also assumes that the advertiser's seminar is the best way to develop your vocabulary. In reality, none of these assumptions might be true.

Assertions and opinions flow from our assumptions. Heated conflict and hard feelings often result when people argue on the level of opinions—forgetting that the real conflict lies at the level of their assumptions.

An example is the question about whether the government should fund public works programs that create jobs during a recession. People who advocate such programs often assume that creating such jobs is an appropriate task for the federal government. On the other hand, people who argue against such programs might assume that the government has no business interfering with the free workings of the economy. There's little hope of resolving this conflict of opinion unless we deal with something more basic: our assumptions about the proper role of government.

You can follow a three-step method for testing the validity of any viewpoint. First, look for the assumptions—the assertions implied by that viewpoint. Second, write down these assumptions. Third, see if you can find any exceptions to them. This technique helps detect many errors in logic.

Working with assumptions

Read several issues of any widely circulated magazine. After doing so, note the basic assumptions that flow between the lines. Sum up the editors' values—their assumptions about what's important in life. For example, articles in *People* magazine might be based on the assumption that happiness is being rich and well known. List the assumptions you discovered below.

_____

_____

_____

_____

_____

_____

_____

_____

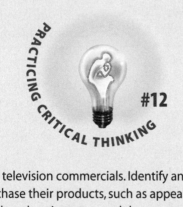

Gather several print advertisements or taped television commercials. Identify any techniques that the advertisers are using to persuade you to purchase their products, such as appealing to emotions or playing on fears. In the space below, briefly describe the advertisements and the assumptions that they are based on.

_____

_____

_____

_____

_____

Do the techniques work as well on you now that you've noticed them? Explain.

_____

_____

_____

_____

_____

_____

Ways to fool yourself

Six common mistakes in logic

1 Jump to conclusions. Jumping to conclusions is the only exercise that some lazy thinkers get. This fallacy involves drawing conclusions without sufficient evidence. Take the bank officer who hears about a student failing to pay back an education loan. After that, the officer turns down all loan applications from students. This person has formed a rigid opinion on the basis of hearsay. Jumping to conclusions—also called *hasty generalization*—is at work here.

2 Attack the person. This mistake in logic is common at election time. An example is the candidate who claims that her opponent has failed to attend church regularly during the campaign. People who indulge in personal attacks are attempting an intellectual sleight of hand to divert our attention from the truly relevant issues.

3 Appeal to an authority. A professional athlete endorses a brand of breakfast cereal. A famous musician features a soft drink company's product in a rock video. The promotional brochure for an advertising agency lists all of the large companies that have used its services.

In each case, the people involved are trying to win your confidence—and your dollars—by citing authorities. The underlying assumption is usually this: *Famous people and organizations buy our product. Therefore, you should buy it too.* Or *You should accept this idea merely because someone who's well known says it's true.*

Appealing to authority is usually a substitute for producing real evidence. It invites sloppy thinking. When our only evidence for a viewpoint is an appeal to authority, it's time to think more thoroughly.

4 Point to a false cause. The fact that one event follows another does not necessarily mean that the two events have a cause-and-effect relationship. All we can actually say is that the events might be correlated. For example, as children's vocabularies improve, they can get more cavities. This does not mean that cavities are the result of an improved vocabulary! Instead, the increase in cavities is due to other factors, such as physical maturation and changes in diet or personal care.

5 Think in all-or-nothing terms. Consider these statements: *Doctors are greedy. . . . You can't trust politicians. . . . Students these days are just in school to get high-paying jobs; they lack idealism. . . . Homeless people don't want to work.*

These opinions imply the word *all.* They gloss over individual differences, claiming that all members of a group are exactly alike. They also ignore key facts, for instance, that some doctors volunteer their time at free medical clinics and that many homeless people are children who are too young to work. All-or-nothing thinking is one of the most common errors in logic.

6 Base arguments on emotion. The politician who ends every campaign speech with flag waving and slides of his mother eating apple pie is staking his future on appeals to emotion. Get past the fluff and see if you can uncover any worthwhile ideas.

Gaining skill at
decision making and

Our lives are largely a result of the decisions we make—and the actions that follow from those decisions. By making new decisions, we can create new results in our lives and find new ways to solve problems. A folksy saying sums it up: "If you always do what you've always done, you'll always get what you've always gotten."

We are making decisions all of the time, whether we realize it or not. Even avoiding decisions is a form of decision making. The student who puts off studying for a test until the last minute might really be saying, "I've decided this course is not important" or "I've decided not to give this course much time."

When people refuse to make decisions, they leave their lives to chance. Philosopher Walter Kaufman calls this *decidophobia*—the fear of making decisions.[5] He defines *autonomy* as "making with open eyes the decisions that give shape to one's life."

By strengthening our decision-making skills, we can take charge of our lives and find solutions to our problems. Decide right now to apply some of the following suggestions, and you can take your overall decision making to new heights of effectiveness.

Recognize decisions.
Decisions are more than wishes or desires. There's a world of difference between "I wish I could be a better student" and "I will take more powerful notes, read with greater retention, and review my class notes daily." Decisions are specific and lead to focused action.

When we decide, we narrow down. We give up actions that are inconsistent with our decision. Deciding to eat fruit instead of ice cream for dessert rules out the next trip to the ice cream store.

Clarify your values.
When you know specifically what you want from life, making decisions becomes easier. This is especially true when you define your values precisely and put them in writing. Saying that you value education is fine. Now give that declaration some teeth. Note that you value continuous learning as a chance to upgrade your career skills, for instance. That can make registering for next quarter's classes much easier.

Base your decisions on a life plan.
The value of having a long-term plan for our lives is that it provides a basis for many of our year-to-year and week-to-week decisions. When we're clear about what we want to accomplish in five years, 10 years, or even 50 years, it's easier to make a meaningful to-do list for today.

Gather information.
Powerful decisions flow from the quality of the information we have on hand. Many times failure results when we lack the facts needed to make an informed decision.

Use time as an ally.
Sometimes we face dilemmas—situations in which any course of action leads to undesirable consequences. In such cases, consider putting a decision on hold. Wait it out. Do nothing until the circumstances change, making one alternative clearly preferable to another, or until an effective solution announces itself.

Use intuition.
Some decisions seem to make themselves. A solution pops into our mind and we gain newfound clarity. Suddenly we realize what we've truly wanted all along.

Using intuition is not the same as forgetting about the decision or refusing to make it. Intuitive decisions usually arrive after we've gathered the relevant facts and faced a problem for some time.

Act on your decision.
Action is a clue to a true decision. Once we actually make a decision, we usually follow it with action. There comes a time to move from the realm of reflection and commitment to the arena of action. What we gain is valuable feedback about the results of our decisions—and the opportunity to make even more decisions.

problem solving

Practice four problem-solving steps.

Decision making and problem solving involve similar thinking skills. You can approach problem solving as a process with four P's: Define the *problem,* generate *possibilities,* create a *plan,* and *perform* your plan.

1 Define the problem.

This step paves the way for the remaining three. Once we define a problem, we're well on the way to no longer having a problem. A clear definition of the problem often suggests appropriate ways to solve it.

To define a problem effectively, understand what a problem is—a mismatch between what you want and what you have. Problem solving is all about reducing the gap between these two factors.

Start with what you have. Tell the truth about what's present in your life right now, without shame or blame. For example: "I often get sleepy while reading my physics assignments, and after closing the book I cannot remember what I just read."

Next, describe in detail what you want. Go for specifics: "I want to remain alert as I read about physics. I also want to accurately summarize each chapter I read."

One more point: When we define a problem in limiting ways, our solutions merely generate new problems. As Einstein said, "The world we have made is a result of the level of thinking we have done thus far. We cannot solve problems at the same level at which we created them."

This idea has many applications to success in school. An example is the student who struggles with note taking. The problem, she thinks, is that her notes are too sketchy. The logical solution, she decides, is to take *more* notes, and her new goal is to write down almost everything her instructors say. No matter how fast and furiously she writes, she cannot capture all of the instructors' comments.

Consider what happens when this student defines the problem in a new way. After more thought, she decides that her dilemma is not the *quantity* of her notes but their *quality.* She adopts a new format for taking notes, dividing her note paper into two columns. In the right-hand column she writes down only the main points of each lecture. And in the left-hand column she notes two or three supporting details for each point.

While doing so, she makes the joyous discovery that there are usually just three or four core ideas to remember from each lecture. She originally thought the solution was to take more notes. What really worked was taking notes in a new way.

2 Generate possibilities.

Now put on your creative thinking hat. Open up. Brainstorm as many possible solutions to the problem as you can. The article "Techniques for *creative* thinking" in this chapter offers many suggestions for doing this.

3 Create a plan.

After rereading your problem definition and list of possible solutions, choose the solutions that seem most workable. Think about what specific actions will reduce the gap between what you have and what you want. To make your plan even more powerful, put it in writing. Use the guidelines for Intention Statements in Chapter One.

4 Perform your plan.

The final step gets you off your chair and out into the world. Now you actually *do* what you have planned. Though this step doesn't take long to explain, it's as significant as the others. Ultimately, your skill in solving problems lies in what you do. Through the quality of your actions, you become the architect of your own success.

Student Voices

One of the more general but crucial attributes of a master student is the ability to think critically. This is an important quality in all areas of life because our choices dictate our direction for better or for worse. A master student is a well-rounded, mature individual who has attained wisdom from an accumulation of life experiences. Successful choices are a result of solving a problem, looking at pros and cons, making the decision or choice, and checking how you feel about (and how others will be affected by) this conclusion. This takes concerted effort, but a master student uses this inquisitive, analytical, and open-minded process to gain self-confidence and maturity.

—KRISTINE RUGGLES

"But I don't know what I want to do"

Choosing a major

One decision that troubles many students in higher education is the choice of an academic major. It's easy to put off this decision when we view it as an irrevocable choice that determines our future. Instead, we can look at choosing a major as the start of a continuing path toward self-knowledge.

When choosing a major, you can benefit from staying undecided for a while. This important decision is not one that is usually made on the spur of the moment. Choosing a major calls for gathering facts, weighing alternatives, and allowing unhurried time for wondering, pondering, doodling, and daydreaming. The following ideas can help bring your options into focus.

Know thyself

Choosing a major can be more effective when you begin from a basis of self-knowledge. The exercises and Journal Entries in this book are a starting place toward gaining that knowledge. After reviewing what you wrote, do any of them again with an eye as to how the insights they afford might bear on your choice of major.

Ask others

Other people might have valuable suggestions about a choice of major for you. Ask key people in your life for their ideas and listen with an open mind. Whether or not you choose to follow up on their suggestions is a decision that you alone will make.

Plan your life

Your choice of a major can fall into place once you clarify the overall direction of your life. Consider your values—the personal qualities you consider to be most important in living effectively. Also decide what you want to accomplish in five years, 10 years, or even 50 years from today. After that, choosing your courses for next quarter might seem like a piece of cake.

Plan your career

There are many excellent materials that can assist you in planning your career. For an overview of the topic and an immediate chance to put ideas on paper, see the article "Career planning: Begin now" in the last chapter of this book. Also distinguish between careers that require specific majors and those that do not.

Consider further schooling

With some specific ideas for your life and career plans in hand, think about the possible need for an advanced degree in your field. Such degrees are required for many careers, such as medicine, counseling, law, and college teaching.

Draw on other resources

Remember that people commonly work in fields with little or no direct relationship to their major. Other experiences besides courses in your major can be tools for defining your skills and interests. Examples are part-time jobs, internships, work-study programs, and extracurricular activities.

Do some research

When the only tool you have for choosing a major is a few course listings in your school catalog, trying to decide on a major can seem like a pretty academic affair. Instead, go beyond the printed page. Talk to some people. Visit with instructors who teach the courses in a given major. Ask them about required course work and career options in the field. Also ask for the names of students taking courses in a given major and sit in with them on some of those classes. In addition, contact students who've graduated and are working in the field.

Choose a complementary minor

You can add flexibility to your academic program through your choice of a minor. That course of study can complement or contrast with your choice of a major. The student who wants to be a minister could opt for a minor in English; all of those courses in composition can help in writing sermons. Or the student with a major in psychology might choose a minor in business administration, with the idea of managing a counseling service some day.

Invent a major

When choosing a major, you might not need to limit yourself to those listed in your course catalog. Many schools now have flexible programs that allow for independent study. Through such programs you might be able to combine two existing majors, or invent one of your own. Some people even graduate without a conventional major, creating instead a focus in the humanities or liberal arts studies.

Just choose

Chances are, you probably are close to knowing what your major's going to be. To verify this, you can do a short, playful experiment. Search your school's catalog for a list of available majors. Now cross out all of those majors that you already know are not right for you. You will probably eliminate well over half the list. Next, scan the remaining majors. Pretend that you have to choose a major today. Write down the first three ideas that come to mind.

Choose again

Changing majors is a natural result of getting to know yourself and your school's educational program better. Consider that you're likely to change jobs—as well as careers—several times in your life. As you discover more about your passions and potentials while in school, let your choice of a major reflect that ongoing quest.

MAJORS FOR THE TAKING

The variety of majors available in higher education is staggering. Many schools also allow for double majors, individually designed majors, interdepartmental majors, and minors in various areas. Knowing this, you can create a course of study that matches your skills, interests, and passions.

Take a glance through the school catalogs in your local library, or visit their sites on the World Wide Web. You'll find schools offering majors such as these:

Agribusiness	Kinesiology
Agronomy	Liberal studies
Airway science	Machine shop welding
Architectural drafting	Medical records services
Audiology	Music therapy
Botany	Office management
Building construction technology	Paralegal studies
Ceramics	Pet-assisted therapy facilitation
Classical languages	Petroleum land management
Climatology	Recreational leadership
Criminal justice	Respiratory therapy
Cytotechnology	Retail management
Dance	Sculpture
Dietetics	Substance abuse counseling
Equestrian studies	Theology
Exercise and sport science	Third World studies
Fashion design and merchandising	Transportation technologies
Film studies	Upholstery
Forestry	Urban affairs
Hospitality and tourism services	Water utilities operation
Human ecology	Wildlife fisheries
	Zoological sciences

WORKPLACE APPLICATIONS

One way to generate a burst of creativity followed by critical thinking is to take an idea that seems obvious and state its opposite. Then see if you can find evidence to support the opposite idea.

This principle has been used with great success in business. An example comes from Jan Carlzon, president of the Scandinavian Airline SAS and author of *Moments of Truth*. Carlzon questioned an "obvious" truth—that upper management in any company should make most of the decisions. He went for the opposite idea and allowed rank-and-file employees to make daily decisions that directly affected customers.

If a customer got bumped from a flight, an SAS counter clerk could decide on the spot whether to pay the customer's hotel bill for the night or find the customer an alternate flight on a competitor's airline. After implementing this policy, SAS's business grew dramatically.

Solving math and science problems

Solving problems is a key part of reading textbooks about math and science. You can approach math and science problems the way rock climbers approach mountains. The first part of the process is devoted to preparations you make before you get to the rock. The second part is devoted to techniques used on the rock (problem) itself.

To the uninitiated, rock climbing looks dangerous. For the unprepared, it is. A novice might come to a difficult place in a climb and panic. When a climber freezes, she is truly stuck. Experienced climbers figure out strategies in advance for as many situations as possible. With preparation and training, the sport takes on a different cast. Sometimes students get stuck, panic, and freeze when working on problems. Use the following suggestions to avoid that. Experiment with these techniques as you work through textbooks in math and science. You can also use them on tests.

Before you get to the rock

1 Review. Review problems you've solved before. Look over assigned problems and more. Make up your own variations on these problems. Work with a classmate and make up problems for each other to solve. The more problems you review, the more comfortable you're likely to feel solving new ones. Set clear goals for practice and write Intention Statements about meeting those goals. Find out if practice problems or previous tests are on file in the library.

2 Classify problems by type. Make a list of the different kinds of problems and note the elements of each. After classifying problems by type or category, you can isolate those that you find the most difficult. Practice them more often, and get help if you need it.

3 Know your terminology. Mathematicians and scientists often borrow words from plain English and assign new meanings to them. For example, the word *work* is usually thought of as referring to a job. For the physicist, *work* means *force multiplied by distance*. To ensure that you understand the terminology used in a problem, see if you can restate the problem in your own words. Translate equations into English sentences. Use 3×5 flash cards to study special terms.

4 Understand formulas. Some students memorize the problems and answers discussed in class—without learning the formulas or general principles behind the problems. This kind of rote learning doesn't allow them to apply the principles or formulas to new problems. One solution is to practice a variety of problems to understand ways to arrive at those answers.

You might be asked to memorize some formulas for convenience. If you understand the basic concepts behind these formulas, it is easier to recall them accurately. More importantly, you will probably be able to re-create the formulas if your recall falters. Understanding is preferable to memorization.

5 Learn the metric system. The metric system is based on divisions and multiples of tens. It's easy to learn, but it takes practice. The metric system is a great example of the benefit of applying a logical thought process to a problem.

6 Use summary sheets. Groups of terms and formulas can be easier to recall if you list them on a sheet of paper or put them on 3×5 cards. Mind map summary sheets allow you to see how various kinds of problems relate to one another. Creating a structure on which you can hang data helps your recall.

7 When practicing, time yourself. Sometimes speed counts. Notice how fast you can work problems. This gives you an idea of how much time to allot for different types of problems. Remember that it is always important to practice before taking tests.

8 Use creative visualizations. Before you begin a problem-solving session, take a minute to relax, breathe deeply, and prepare yourself for the task ahead. Use the techniques described on pages 215 and 216 to see yourself solving problems successfully. A calm attitude is important. Visualize preparing for a test, taking the test, and solving the problems with ease.

On the rock

1 Survey the territory thoroughly. Read the problem at least twice before you begin. Read slowly. Be sure you understand what is being asked.

Let go of the expectation that you'll find the solution right away. You might make several attempts at solving the problem before you find a solution that works.

2 Sort the facts. Survey the problem for all of the givens. Determine the principles and relationships involved. Look for what is to be proved or what is to be discovered. Write these down.

3 Set up the problem. Before you begin to compute, determine the strategies you will use to arrive at solutions. When solving equations, carry out the algebra as far as you can before plugging in the actual numbers.

Remember that solving a math or science problem is like putting together a puzzle. You might work around the edges for a while and try many pieces before finding one that fits.

4 Cancel and combine. When you set up a problem logically, you can take shortcuts. For example, if the same term appears in both dividend and divisor, they will cancel each other out.

5 Draw a picture. Make a diagram. A visual approach to math and science problems might work best for you. Pictures help keep the facts straight. They can show relationships more effectively than words.

To keep on track, record your facts in tables. Consider using three columns labeled "What I already know," "What I want to find out," and "What connects the two." This third column is the place to record a formula that can help you solve the problem.

6 Read the problem out loud. Sometimes the sound of your voice will jar loose the solution to a problem. Talk yourself through the solution. Read equations out loud.

7 Play with possibilities. There's usually not one "right" way to solve a problem. Several approaches or formulas might work, though one might be more efficient than another. Be willing to think about the problem from several angles or to proceed by trial and error.

8 Notice when you're in deep water. It's tempting to shy away from difficult problems. Unfortunately, the more you do this, the more difficult the problems become. Math and science courses present wonderful opportunities to use the First Step technique explained in Chapter One. When you feel that you're beginning to get into trouble, write a precise Discovery Statement about the problem. Then write an Intention Statement about what you will do to solve the problem.

9 Check results. Work problems backwards, then forwards. Start at both ends and work toward the middle to check your work.

Take a minute to make sure you kept the units of measurement clear. Say that you're calculating the velocity of an object. If you're measuring distance in meters and time in seconds, then the final velocity should be in meters per second.

Another way to check your work is to estimate the answer before you compute it. Then ask yourself if your answer to the problem seems in the ballpark when compared to the estimate.

10 Savor the solution. Savor the times when you're getting correct answers to most of the problems in the textbook. Relish the times when you feel relaxed and confident as you work, or when the problems seem easy. Then remember these times if you feel math or science anxiety.

POWER PROCESS
Find a bigger problem

Most of the time we view problems as barriers. They are a source of inconvenience and annoyance. They get in our way and prevent us from having happy and productive lives. When we see problems in this way, our goal becomes to eliminate problems.

This point of view might be flawed. It is impossible to live a life without problems. Besides, they serve a purpose. They are opportunities to participate in life. Problems stimulate us and pull us forward.

When problems are seen in this way, the goal becomes not to eliminate them, but to find the problems that are worthy of us. Worthy problems are those that draw on our talents, move us toward our purpose, and increase our skills. The challenge is to tackle those problems that provide the greatest benefits for others and ourselves. Viewed in this way, problems give meaning to our lives.

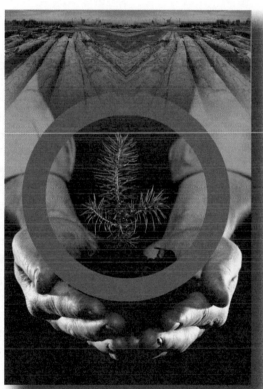

Problems fill the available space

Problems seem to follow the same law of physics that gases do: They expand to fill whatever space is available. If your only problem for the entire day is to write a follow-up letter to a job interview, you can spend the whole day finding paper and pen, thinking about what you're going to say, writing the letter, finding an envelope and stamp, going to the post office—and then thinking about all of the things you forgot to say.

If, on that same day, you also need to go food shopping, the problem of the letter shrinks to make room for a trip to the grocery. If you also want to buy a car, it's amazing how quickly and easily the letter and the grocery shopping tasks are finished. One way to handle little problems is to find bigger ones. Remember that the smaller problems still need

to be solved. The goal is to do it with less time and energy.

Bigger problems are plentiful

Bigger problems are not in short supply. Consider world hunger. Every minute of every day, people die because they don't have enough to eat. Also consider nuclear war, which threatens to end life on the planet. Child abuse, environmental pollution, human rights violations, drug abuse, street crime, energy shortages, poverty, and wars throughout the world await your attention and involvement. You can make a contribution.

Play full out

Considering bigger problems does not have to be depressing. In fact, it can be energizing—a reason for getting up in the morning. Taking on a huge project is a tool for creating passion and purpose.

Some people spend vast amounts of time in activities they consider boring: their jobs, their hobbies, their relationships. They find themselves going through the motions, doing the same walk-on part day after day without passion or intensity. Writer Henry David Thoreau described this kind of existence as "lives of quiet desperation."

The suggestion to play full out holds another possibility: We can spend much of our time fully focused and involved. We can experience efficiency and enthusiasm as natural parts of our daily routines. Energy and vitality can accompany most of our activities.

When we take on a big problem, we play full out. We do justice to our potentials. We then love what we do and do what we love. We're awake, alert, and engaged. Playing full out means living our lives as if our lives depended on it.

You can make a difference

Perhaps a little voice in your mind is saying, "That's crazy. I can't do anything about global problems" or "Everyone knows that hunger has always been around and always will be, and there is nothing anyone can do about it." These thoughts prevent you from taking on bigger problems.

Realize that you *can* make a difference. Your thoughts and actions can change the quality of life on the planet.

This is your life. It's your school, your city, your country, and your world. Own it. Inhabit it. Treat it with the same care that you would a prized possession.

One way to find problems that are worthy of your talents and energies is to take on bigger ones. Take responsibility for problems that are bigger than you are sure you can handle. Then notice how your other problems dwindle in importance—or even vanish.

Asking questions

Thinking is born of questions. Questions open up areas of knowledge that might otherwise remain unexplored. Questions wake people up and lead them to investigate more closely issues and assumptions that had previously gone unchallenged. Questions promote curiosity, create new distinctions, and multiply possibilities. Besides, teachers love them. One of the best ways to develop your relationship with a teacher is to ask a question.

Questions are also great ways to improve relationships with friends and coworkers. When you ask a question, you bring a huge gift to people—an invitation for them to speak their brilliance and an offer to listen to their answers.

Students often say, "I don't know what to ask." If you have ever been at a loss for what to ask, here are some ways to construct powerful questions about any subject you study in school, or about any area of your life that you choose to examine.

Write something you're sure of and put a question mark after it. Perhaps one of the things you know for certain about your educational plans is that you would never take a course in philosophy. In that case, you can write, "I don't take philosophy courses?" That suggests another question: "In what ways would taking a philosophy course serve my success in school?" Taking such a course can promote your skills in both critical thinking and writing. Powerful questions can encourage us to look at tried-and-true "facts" in new ways.

Ask about what's missing. Another way to invent useful questions is to notice what's missing from your life and then ask how to supply it. For example, if you want to take better notes, you can write, "What's missing is skill in note taking. How can I gain more skill in taking notes?" Or "What's missing is time. How do I create time in my day to actually do the things that I say I want to do?"

Just let your pen start moving. Sometimes you can access a deeper level of knowledge by taking out your pen, putting it on a piece of paper, and writing down questions—even before you know *what* to write. Don't think. Just watch the paper and notice what appears. The results might be surprising.

Pretend to be someone else. Another way to invent questions is first to think of someone you greatly respect. Then pretend you're that person and ask the questions you think *she* would ask.

Ask what else you want to know. Many times you can quickly generate questions by simply asking yourself, What else do I want to know? Ask this question immediately after you read a paragraph in a book or listen to someone speak.

Begin a general question, then brainstorm endings. Beginning a general question and brainstorming a long list of endings can help you invent a question that you've never asked before. For instance:

What can I do when . . . ? What can I do when an instructor calls on me in class and I have no idea what to say? What can I do when a teacher doesn't show up for class on time? What can I do when I feel overwhelmed with assignments?

How can I . . . ? How can I get just the kind of courses that I want? How can I expand my career options? How can I become much more effective as a student, starting today?

When do I . . . ? When do I decide on a major? When do I transfer to another class? When do I meet with an instructor to discuss an upcoming term paper?

Start from the assumption that you are brilliant, and begin asking questions that can help you unlock your brilliance.

Fix-the-world brainstorm

This exercise works best with four to six people. Pick a major world problem such as hunger, nuclear proliferation, poverty, terrorism, overpopulation, or pollution. Then conduct a 10-minute brainstorm on the steps an individual could take to contribute to solving the problem. Use the brainstorming techniques explained earlier in this book. Remember not to evaluate or judge the solutions during the process. The purpose of a brainstorm is to generate a flow of ideas.

After the brainstorming session, discuss the process and the solutions that it generated. Did you feel any energy from the group? Were any new or exciting ideas created? Are any of the ideas worth pursuing? On a separate sheet of paper, write Discovery and Intention Statements about these ideas.

Translating goals into action

Choose one long-range goal—any personal project or social change you'd like to see. Examples are learning to scuba dive, eating a more healthful diet, studying to be an astronaut, improving health care for chronically ill children, inventing energy-saving technology, increasing the effectiveness of American schools, or becoming a better parent. List your goal on a separate sheet of paper.

Next, ask yourself: What specific actions are needed in the short term to meet my long-range goal? List those actions. Finally, translate any action you just listed into steps you could complete in less than one hour or could start in the next 24 hours.

WORKPLACE APPLICATIONS

After reading the Power Process "Find a bigger problem," consider the merits of the opposite strategy—"Find a smaller problem." If this idea seems to conflict with the message of the Power Process, remember that the strategies in this book are not true or false, good or bad. Rather, different problems can call for different strategies. Sometimes the opposite approach can create the result you desire.

You might feel overwhelmed when faced with an important problem, such as choosing a career, finding a new job, or managing a year-long project at work. One response is to give up—to quit. Another is to resign yourself to drudgery and dive into the project with a deep sigh, always feeling a monumental weight on your shoulders.

"Find a smaller problem" offers an alternative. It works this way: Divide a huge project into many small jobs. Rather than worry about the project as a whole, turn your full attention to a small, specific task until it is complete. Do the same with the next small task, and the next. Just handle the details, one after another, until the project is finished.

Example: Instead of searching through the help wanted listings in dozens of newspapers and trade journals to find a new job, just focus on calling one of your contacts—a person who might know of an opening in your field. Then focus all of your attention on calling another contact, then another one, and so on.

Another name for this strategy is "divide and conquer." It's based on the idea that excellence means handling the details with exquisite care.

The role of planning is critical. "Find a smaller problem" is not a suggestion to fill your days with busywork. If we plan effectively, the small jobs we do are critical to the success of the bigger project.

master student
ISABEL ALLENDE

novelist, learned firsthand about censorship when her uncle Salvador Allende, president of Chile, was overthrown by a military coup in 1973.

I *have lived skirting violence, escaping it with very much luck.* People very close and dear to me have suffered prison, torture, death, and exile. . . . I felt a visceral terror in Chile. It is difficult to talk about that. It is difficult to understand fear if you have not lived it. It is something transforms us, takes us over completely. At the beginning, after the military coup of 1973, many people did not realize what was happening because we were not used to repression. Our country was an old democracy; we didn't know what a dictatorship was and even presumptuously scoffed at the "Banana Republics" where puppet tyrants ruled. We never imagined that could happen in Chile. The press was censored. Only rumors circulated; rumors about the tortured, the disappeared, the dead. Soon my job as a journalist allowed me to get closer to the sources of information, and that was how I was able to learn about the new reality better than others. . . . At the beginning, soon

after the military coup, it was possible for me to be in solidarity before all that pain, that injustice. There was space to move because the repression took a while to become efficient. I gave asylum to a few people. I had a very primitive vehicle, a Citroën painted with huge flowers in different colors. Sometimes I would pick up someone being persecuted by the authorities, hide him for a few days, and as soon as I could I would show him to an embassy where he would usually have to jump the fence to get in. I didn't realize the danger to which I was exposing myself. . . .

The solutions lie within the men and women who live in this world. It was experience that better made me understand the power of love, especially those months in Chile under the dictatorship. Love is an extraordinary force, capable of confronting violence. For every one torturer, there are a thousand people ready to risk their lives in order to save another. For every soldier who shoots in a neighborhood, there are a thousand *compañeros* who help and protect each other. Most people feel solidarity toward others; that becomes clear in crisis situations. There are moments in the history of a country, a society, sometimes of an entire continent or of humanity itself, when the forces of evil seem to triumph. Evil

carries with it a great shamelessness, great impudence. When someone acts in an evil manner, they do it boldly; that is why it is so obvious. Kindness, on the other hand, is discreet and tender, but no less effective. Just like in the movies, I believe that the good guys are going to win. I have no doubt about it. When I travel, especially in the United States, the young people talk to me about their disillusionment. They feel anguish about their world, about their history. They feel that they cannot control anything, that they are prey to a nuclear catastrophe, that we will all be blown up into little pieces and that no one can do anything about it. . . . When I listen to them, I feel like crying, shaking them, shouting at them that the lack of hope is the worst trap. I believe that I can change the world and I try to do that every moment of my life.

For more biographical information on Isabel Allende, visit Houghton Mifflin's College Survival/Becoming a Master Student web site: **http://collegesurvival.college. hmco.com/students.**

1 List and briefly describe three techniques for creative thinking.

 2 Explain what is meant in this chapter by *aha!*

 3 Define *serendipity* and give an example.

 4 Explain the connection that the text makes between critical thinking and social change.

 5 Define the word *dilemma*. Then explain one strategy for responding to dilemmas.

 6 According to the text, critical thinking and thorough thinking are two distinct and different activities. True or False? Explain your answer.

 7 Define *all-or-nothing thinking* and give an example.

8 Explain the suggestion "watch for hot spots" and describe its connection to critical thinking.

 9 Name at least one fallacy involved in this statement: "Everyone who's ever visited this school has agreed that it's the best in the state."

10 List the four suggested steps for problem solving and give an example of each step.

JOURNAL ENTRY

#36

Discovery/Intention Statement

Write a short statement about your current level of skill in creative and critical thinking.

I discovered that I...

_____
_____
_____
_____

Now choose three suggestions from this chapter to use during the next week. Along with each suggestion, note a possible benefit that could come from applying the suggestion.

I intend to ...

_____
_____
_____
_____

LEARNING STYLES APPLICATION   CHAPTER 7

Mode 4 *After experimenting with the two techniques you chose, evaluate how well they worked for you. Then describe any ways you could modify these techniques to make them work more effectively.*

Mode 1 *Describe a major decision you face in your life right now. Examples are decisions about what courses to take next quarter or what career you will choose. Describe how you have made such decisions in the past. List techniques that worked well for you, along with those that did not.*

Mode 3 *From the list of suggestions you made for Mode 2, choose two that you will definitely apply. Describe how you will use each technique.*

Mode 2 *List five specific suggestions from this chapter that could help you think through your options and make the decision you listed for Mode 1.*

BIBLIOGRAPHY

ENDNOTES

1 Arthur Koestler, *The Act of Creation* (New York: Dell, 1964).

2 Mortimer J. Adler and Charles Van Doren, *How to Read a Book* (New York: Simon & Schuster, 1987).

3 William Perry, *Forms of Intellectual and Ethical Development in the College Years* (New York: Holt, Rinehart and Winston, 1970).

4 Mary Field Belenky et al., *Women's Ways of Knowing: The Development of Self, Voice, and Mind* (New York: Basic Books, 1997).

5 Walter J. Kaufman, *From Decidophobia to Autonomy: Without Guilt and Justice* (New York: Delta, 1975).

ADDITIONAL READING

Facione, Peter. *Critical Thinking: What It Is and Why It Counts.* Millbrae, CA: California Academic Press, 1996.

LeBoeuf, Michael. *Imagineering: How to Profit from Your Creative Powers.* New York: Berkley, 1990.

Pirsig, Robert. *Zen and the Art of Motorcycle Maintenance.* New York: Perennial Classics, 2000.

Ruggiero, Vincent Ryan. *Becoming a Critical Thinker,* 4/e. Boston: Houghton Mifflin, 2002.

INTERNET RESOURCES

Critical Thinking—Essays, Articles, Commentary, and Book Chapters
www.wvu.edu/~lawfac/jelkins/thinking.html

Critical Thinking on the Web
www.philosophy.unimelb.edu.au/reason/critical/

Evaluating Web Pages
www.lib.berkeley.edu/TeachingLib/Guides/Internet/Evaluate.html

Resources for Independent Thinking
www.rit.org/links/links.html

Communicating

Listening means trying to see the problem the way the speaker sees it—which means not sympathy, which is feeling for him, but empathy, which is feeling with him.
S. I. HAYAKAWA

You have two ears and one mouth. Remember to use them in more or less that proportion.
PAULA BERN

IN THIS CHAPTER . . . Look for ways to prevent misunderstanding and to move toward loving relationships. Start by listening more effectively when other people send messages to you. Then consider suggestions for sending your own messages. Experiment with the fine arts of managing conflict, accepting constructive criticism, complaining effectively, and offering compliments. Expand your communication skills with a three-phase process for writing and by delivering speeches. Also consider the power of making and keeping agreements. You can employ your word in ways that maximize your freedom and choice.

The communication loop

Communication is often garbled when we try to send and receive messages at the same time.

One effective way to improve your ability to communicate is to be aware of when you are the receiver and when you are the sender. If you are receiving (listening), then just receive. Avoid switching into the sending (talking) mode. When you are sending, stick with it until you are finished.

If the other person is trying to send a message when you want to be the sender, you have at least three choices: Stop sending and be the receiver, stop sending and leave, or ask the other person to stop sending so that you can send. It is ineffective to try to send and receive at the same time.

This becomes clear when we look at what happens in a conversation. When we talk, we put thoughts into words. Words are a code for what we experience. This is called *encoding*. The person who receives the message takes our words and translates them into his own experience. This is called *decoding*.

A conversation between two people is like a communication between two telegraph operators. One encodes a message and sends it over the wire. The operator at the other end receives the coded signal, decodes it, evaluates it, and sends back another coded message. The first operator decodes this message and sends another. The cycle continues. The messages look like this:

```
1 ..—..—.·-     3 —.—..— OPERATOR 1
2 —.-..—..       4 ..—... . OPERATOR 2
```

In this encoding-decoding loop we continually switch roles. One minute we send, the next we receive. When both operators send at the same time, neither knows what the other one sent. Neither can reply. Communication works best when each of us has the opportunity to send a complete message, sufficient time to comprehend, and plenty of time to respond.

There are other problems in communication. As psychotherapist Virginia Satir reminds us, only a small percentage of communication is verbal.[1] All of us send messages with our bodies and with the tone of our voices. Throw in a few other factors, such as a hot room or background noise, and it's a wonder we communicate at all.

Another problem is that the message sent is often not the message received. This process of continually encoding and decoding words can result in the simplest message

being muddled. For some, the word *chair* conjures up the image of an overstuffed rocking recliner. Others visualize a metal folding chair. And some people think of the person who "chairs" a meeting. If simple things like this can be misunderstood, it's easy to see how more complex ideas can wreak havoc on communication. For example, a "good teacher" can mean someone who is smart, entertaining, easy, challenging, creative—or a hundred other things.

Communicating effectively means getting on the same wavelength. Even then, it helps to keep checking with each other to make sure we are talking about the same thing.

These difficulties are never fully overcome. They can be partially alleviated by using effective communication techniques and by having a sincere intention to understand one another. An earlier chapter in this book suggested techniques for one key communication skill—reading. Use this chapter to master the related skills of speaking, listening, and writing.

JOURNAL ENTRY #37

Discovery Statement

Describe a time when you experienced an emotionally charged conflict with another person. Were you able to resolve this dispute effectively? If so, list below the strategies you used. Also list any different outcomes you would like to achieve the next time you experience conflict with another person.

_____

_____

_____

_____

Now scan this chapter for ideas that can help you get your feelings across more skillfully in such situations. List several ideas here.

_____

_____

_____

_____

_____

_____

Andre ✓

Meet the Lorenz Attractor. This owl-like diagram demonstrates orderly feedback structures in what were once presumed to be chaotic systems. Scientists think that feedback loops such as this have the potential to explain everything from the weather to traffic jams—and, yes, even the complexities of human communication.

The communication loop
Listening

You observe a person in a conversation who is not talking. Is he listening? Maybe. Maybe not. He might be preparing his response or daydreaming. Listening is not easy. Doing it effectively requires concentration and energy.

It's worth it. Listening well promotes success in school: more powerful notes, more productive study groups, better relationships with students and instructors. A skilled listener is appreciated by friends, family, and business associates. The best salespeople and managers are the best listeners. People love a good listener. Through skilled listening, you gain more than respect. You gain insight into other people. You learn about the world and about yourself.

To be a good listener, choose to listen. Once you've made this choice, you can use the following techniques to be a more effective listener. These ideas are especially useful in times of high emotional tension.

This idea is not an absolute. While maintaining eye contact is important in some cultures, people from other cultures are uncomfortable with sustained eye contact. Some individuals learn primarily by hearing; they can listen more effectively by turning off the visual input once in a while. Keep in mind the differences among people.

3 Display openness.
You can communicate openness by means of your facial expression and body position. Uncross your arms and legs. Sit up straight. Face the other person and remove any physical barriers between you, such as a pile of books.

4 Listen without response.
This doesn't mean that you should never respond. It means wait. When listening to another person, we often interrupt with our own stories, opinions, suggestions, and inappropriate comments, as in the following dialogue:

"Oh, I'm so excited. I just found out that I am nominated to be in *Who's Who in American Musicians*."

Nonverbal listening

Much of listening is nonverbal. Here are five guidelines for effective nonverbal listening.

1 Be quiet.
Silence is more than staying quiet while someone is speaking. Allowing several seconds to pass before you begin to talk gives the speaker time to catch his breath or gather his thoughts. He might want to continue. Someone who talks nonstop might fear he will lose the floor if he pauses.

If the message being sent is complete, this short break gives you time to form your response and helps you avoid the biggest barrier to listening—listening with your answer running. If you make up a response before the person is finished, you might miss the end of the message—which is often the main point.

Pausing for several seconds might be inappropriate. Ignore this suggestion completely when someone asks in a panic where to find the nearest phone to call the fire department.

2 Maintain eye contact.
Look at the other person while he speaks. Doing so demonstrates your attentiveness and helps keep your mind from wandering. Your eyes also let you "listen" to body language and behavior. When some of us remove our glasses, not only do we fail to see—we fail to listen.

"Yeah, that's neat. My Uncle Elmer got into *Who's Who in American Veterinarians.* He sure has an interesting job. One time I went along when he was treating a cow."

Watch your nonverbal responses, too. A look of "Good grief!" from you can keep the other person from finishing his message.

5 Send acknowledgments.

It is important to periodically let the speaker know that you are still there. Your words or nonverbal gestures of acknowledgment let the speaker know that you are interested and that you are with him and his message. These include "Umhum," "OK," "Yes," and head nods.

These acknowledgments do not imply your agreement. When people tell you what they don't like about you, your head nod doesn't mean that you agree. It just indicates that you are listening.

Verbal listening

Sometimes speaking promotes listening.

1 Feed back meaning.

Paraphrase the communication. This does not mean parroting what another person says. Instead, briefly summarize. Feed back what you see as the essence of that person's message: "Let me see if I understood what you said . . ." or "What I'm hearing you say is... ."

(Psychotherapist Carl Rogers referred to this technique as *reflection.*)[2] Often, the other person will say, "No, that's not what I meant. What I said was. . . ."

There will be no doubt when you get it right. The sender will say, "Yeah, that's it," and either continue with another message or stop sending when he knows you understand.

If you don't understand the message, be persistent. Be concise. This is not a time to stop the other person by talking on and on about what you think you heard.

2 Listen beyond words.

Be aware of nonverbal messages and behavior. You might point out that the speaker's body language seems to be the exact opposite of his words. For example: "I noticed you said you are excited, but you look bored."

Keep in mind that the same nonverbal behavior can have different meanings, depending on the listener's cultural background. Someone who looks bored might simply be listening in a different way.

The idea is to listen not only to the words, but also to the emotion behind the words. Sometimes that emotional message is more important than the verbal content.

3 Take care of yourself.

People seek good listeners, and there are times when you don't want

to listen. You might be distracted with your own concerns. Be honest. Don't pretend to listen. You can say, "What you're saying is important, and I'm pressed for time right now. Can we set aside another time to talk about this?" It's OK *not* to listen.

4 Listen for requests and intentions.

"This class is a waste of my time." "Our instructor talks too fast." An effective way to listen to such complaints is to look for the request hidden in them.

"This class is a waste of my time" can be heard as "Please tell me what I'll gain if I participate actively in class." "The instructor talks too fast" can be asking "What strategies can I use to take notes when the instructor covers material rapidly?" We can even transform complaints into intentions. Take this complaint: "The parking lot by the dorms is so dark at night that I'm afraid to go to my car." This complaint can result in having a light installed in the parking lot.

Viewing complaints as requests gives us more choices. Rather than responding with defensiveness ("What does he know anyway?"), resignation ("It's always been this way and always will be"), or indifference ("It's not my job"), we can decide whether to grant the request (do what will alleviate the other's difficulty) or help the person translate his own complaint into an action plan.

The communication loop
Sending

We have been talking with people for years, and we usually manage to get our messages across. There are times, though, when we don't. Often, these times are emotionally charged. Sometimes we feel wonderful or rotten or sad or scared, and we want to express it. Emotions can get in the way of the message. Described below are four techniques for delivering a message through tears, laughter, fist pounding, or hugging. They are: Replace "You" messages with "I" messages, avoid questions that aren't really questions, notice nonverbal messages, and notice barriers to communication.

The "I's" have it! It can be difficult to disagree with someone without his becoming angry or your becoming upset. When conflict occurs, we often make statements about the other person, or "You" messages:

"You are rude."

"You make me mad."

"You must be crazy."

"You don't love me anymore."

This kind of communication results in defensiveness. The responses might be:

"I am not rude."

"I don't care."

"No, *you* are crazy."

"No, *you* don't love *me!*"

"You" messages are hard to listen to. They label, judge, blame, and assume things that might or might not be true. They demand rebuttal. Even praise can sometimes be an ineffective "You" message. "You" messages don't work.

When communication is emotionally charged, psychologist Thomas Gordon suggests that you consider limiting your statements to descriptions about yourself.[3] Replace "You" messages with "I" messages.

"You are rude" might become "I feel upset."

"You make me mad" could be "I feel angry."

"You must be crazy" can be "I don't understand."

"You don't love me anymore" could become "I'm afraid we're drifting apart."

Suppose a friend asks you to pick him up at the airport. You drive 20 miles and wait for the plane. No friend. You decide your friend missed his plane, so you wait three hours for the next flight. No friend. Perplexed and worried, you drive home. The next day, you see your friend downtown.

"What happened?" you ask.

"Oh, I caught an earlier flight."

"You are a rude person," you reply.

Look for the facts, the observable behavior. Everyone will agree that your friend asked you to pick him up, that he did take an earlier flight, and that you did not receive a call from him. But the idea that he is rude is not a fact—it's a judgment.

He might go on to say, "I called your home and no one answered. My mom had a stroke and was rushed to Valley View. I caught the earliest flight I could get." Your judgment no longer fits.

When you saw your friend, you might have said, "I waited and waited at the airport. I was worried about you. I didn't get a call. I feel angry and hurt. I don't want to waste my time. Next time, you can call me when your flight arrives, and I'll be happy to pick you up."

"I" messages don't judge, blame, criticize, or insult. They don't invite the other person to counterattack with more of the same. "I" messages are also more accurate. They report our own thoughts and feelings.

At first, "I" messages might feel uncomfortable or seem forced. That's

Five ways to say "I"

An "I" message can include any or all of the following five parts. Be careful when including the last two, since they can contain hidden judgments or threats.

1. **Observations.** Describe the facts—the indisputable, observable realities. Talk about what you—or anyone else—can see, hear, smell, taste, or touch. Avoid judgments, interpretations, or opinions. Instead of saying, "You're a slob," say, "Last night's lasagna pan was still on the stove this morning."

2. **Feelings.** Describe your own feelings. It is easier to listen to "I feel frustrated" than to "You never help me." Stating how you feel about another's actions can be valuable feedback for that person.

3. **Wants.** You are far more likely to get what you want if you *say* what you want. If someone doesn't know what you want, he doesn't have a chance to help you get it. Ask clearly. Avoid demanding or using the word *need*. Most people like to feel helpful, not obligated. Instead of saying, "Do the dishes when it's your turn, or else!" say, "I want to divide the housework fairly."

4. **Thoughts.** Communicate your thoughts, and use caution. Beginning your statement with the word "I" doesn't qualify it as an "I" message." I think you are a slob" is a "You" judgment in disguise. Instead, say, "I'd have more time to study if I didn't have to clean up so often."

5. **Intentions.** The last part of an "I" message is a statement about what you intend to do. Have a plan that doesn't depend on the other person. For example, instead of "From now on we're going to split the dishwashing evenly," you could say, "I intend to do my share of the housework and leave the rest.

OK. Use the five ways to say "I" explained above.

Questions are not always questions.

You've heard these "questions" before. A parent asks, "Don't you want to look nice?" Translation: "I wish you'd cut your hair, lose the blue jeans, and put on a tie." Or how about this question from a spouse: "Honey, wouldn't you love to go to an exciting hockey game tonight?" Translation: "I've already bought tickets."

We use questions that aren't questions to sneak our opinions and requests into conversations. "Doesn't it upset you?" means "It upsets me," and "Shouldn't we hang the picture over here?" means "I want to hang the picture over here."

Communication improves when we say, "I'm upset," and "Let's hang the picture over here."

Notice nonverbal messages.

How you say something can be more important than what you say. Your tone of voice and your gestures can support, modify, or contradict your words. Your posture, the way you dress, how often you shower, and even the poster hanging on your wall can negate your words before you say them.

Most nonverbal behavior is unconscious. We can learn to be aware of it. Then we can choose our nonverbal messages. The key is to be clear about our intention and purpose. When we know what we want to say and are committed to getting it across, our inflections, gestures, and words work together and send a unified message.

Notice barriers to sending your message.

Sometimes fear stops us from sending messages. We are afraid of other people's reactions, sometimes justifiably. Being truthful doesn't mean being insensitive to the impact our messages have on others. Tact is a virtue; letting fear prevent communication is not.

Assumptions can also be used as excuses for not sending messages. "He already knows this," we tell ourselves.

Predictions of failure can be barriers to sending, too. "He won't listen," we tell ourselves. That statement might be inaccurate. Perhaps the other person senses that we're angry and listens in a guarded way. Or perhaps he is listening and sending nonverbal messages we don't understand.

Or we might predict, "He'll never do anything about it even if I tell him." Again, making assumptions can defeat your message before you send it.

It's easy to make excuses for not communicating. If you have fear or some other concern about sending a message, be aware of it. Don't expect the concern to go away. Realize that you can communicate even with your concerns. You can choose to make them a part of the message: "I am going to tell you how I feel, and I'm afraid that you will think it's stupid."

Talking to someone when you don't want to could be a matter of educational survival. A short talk with an advisor, a teacher, a friend, or a family member might solve a problem that could jeopardize your education.

Thanks!

JOURNAL ENTRY #38

Discovery/Intention Statement

Think about one of your relationships for a few minutes. It might involve a parent, sibling, spouse, child, friend, hairdresser, etc. In the space below, write down some things that are not working in the relationship. What bugs you? What do you find irritating or unsatisfying?

I discovered that ...

_____
_____
_____
_____
_____
_____
_____
_____

Now think for a moment about what you want from this relationship. More attention? Less nagging? More openness, trust, security, money, or freedom? Choose a suggestion from this chapter, and describe how you could use it to make the relationship work.

I intend to ...

_____
_____
_____
_____
_____
_____
_____
_____

WRITING WELL PAYS

Learning to write well pays. Writing effectively can help you express yourself powerfully and persuasively. Writing helps you organize information and adapt your ideas to different audiences. It can also help you give clear instructions—a task that occupies much of your waking time. By becoming a skilled writer, you can become a better thinker, speaker, reader, and listener.

Good writing is a marketable skill. To verify this, flip through the "Help Wanted" section in a large Sunday newspaper. Note how many job descriptions call for good writing skills.

Writing is also a powerful way to learn. Professional writers report that one of the joys of their craft is the repeated opportunity to explore new fields. They constantly learn new subjects by researching and writing about them. They know that you can literally write your way into a subject—that is, as you write about a subject, you are also learning more about that subject. Through writing, you can get a much clearer picture of what you know, what you don't know, and where to look for the missing pieces.

Writing is an essential skill in the age of information. Computers have made it possible to store and retrieve data on a vast scale. Today the human race mass-produces information. This barrage of information is not always helpful. It's possible to get lost in stacks of computer printouts, professional journals, newspapers, magazines, and books.

Writing can help. When you write, you not only gather information; you also assess it. You sift through the data, play with it, and sort it out. You look for relationships among facts and choose ideas that are useful to you. Through writing, you turn data into insight.

The fine art of conflict management

Becky

Conflict management is one of the most practical skills you'll ever learn. Following are several strategies that can help. To bring these ideas to life, think of ways to apply them to a current conflict in your life.

State the problem openly.
Using "I" messages as explained earlier in this chapter, state the problem. Tell people what you observe, feel, think, want, and intend to do. Allow the other person in a particular conflict to do the same. You might have different perceptions. This is the time to define the conflict clearly. It's hard to fix something before everyone agrees on what's broken.

We can move toward agreement more quickly by laying all of our cards on the table. People are often reluctant to communicate all of their concerns. This very reluctance holds some problems in place.

Focus on solutions.
After stating the problem, dream up as many solutions as you can. Be outrageous. Don't evaluate them. Quantity, not quality, is the key. If you get stuck, restate the problem and continue brainstorming.

Next, evaluate the solutions you brainstormed. Discard the unacceptable ones. Talk about which solutions will work and how difficult they will be to implement. You might hit upon a totally new solution.

Choose one solution that is most acceptable to everyone involved and implement it. Agree on who is going to do what by when. Then keep your agreements.

Finally, evaluate the effectiveness of your solution. If it works, pat yourselves on the back. If not, make changes or implement a new solution.

Understand all points of view.
If you want to defuse tension or defensiveness, set aside your opinions for a moment. Take the time to understand the other points of view. Sum up those viewpoints in words that the other parties can accept. When people feel that they've been heard, they're often more willing to listen.

Step back from the conflict.

Instead of trading personal attacks during a conflict, step back. Defuse the situation by approaching it in a neutral way. Define the conflict as a problem to be solved, not as a contest to be won. Detach. Give up being "right" and aim for being effective instead.

Let it get worse before it gets better.

Sometimes a conflict needs to escalate so that everyone is truly aware of it. Many of us are reluctant to allow this to happen. That's understandable—and it can prevent us from getting to the bottom of the problem.

Often it is not necessary for a conflict to get worse. Yet being willing to allow this possibility gives us freedom to clear the air.

Just speak.

When we're locked in combat with someone, it's tempting to hold back—to say only a fraction of what we're thinking or feeling. This can be one more way to keep the conflict alive.

An alternative is to "empty our buckets"—to let the words and the feelings flow without editing. In this case, we don't worry about making a perfect "I" statement. We just say the first things that come to mind. This is one way to get all of our cards on the table.

Commit to the relationship.

The thorniest conflicts usually arise between people who genuinely care for each other. It's hard to be in conflict when the relationship doesn't matter to us.

Begin by affirming your commitment to the other person: "I care about you, and I want this relationship to last. So I'm willing to do whatever it takes to resolve this problem." Also ask the other person for a similar commitment.

You might be unsure of your commitment to the relationship. If so, postpone any further communication for now. Take some time to be alone and consider the value of this relationship to you. People engaged in conflict often stop seeing each other. Many times we increase the odds of solving the problem when we stay in a relationship.

Back up to common ground.

Conflict heightens the differences between people. When this happens, it's easy for them to forget how much they still agree with each other. As a first step in managing conflict, back up to common ground. List all of the points on which you are *not* in conflict: "I know that we disagree about how much to spend on a new car, but we do agree that the old one needs to be replaced." Often, such comments put the problem in perspective and pave the way for a solution.

Listen for the request in the complaint.

People complain to us when they want something different from us. And when we take the complaint at face value, we might feel blamed or put down.

Go deeper. Listen for the request that's behind the complaint. If a friend complains that you always interrupt him, take it as a request: "Please let me finish what I'm saying before you speak." This makes it easier to respond to the request—not to the accusation or the anger.

Slow down the communication.

In times of great conflict, people often talk all at once. Words fly like speeding bullets, and no one is really listening. Such discussions generate a lot of heat and little light. Chances for resolving the conflict take a nosedive.

When this happens, choose either to listen or to talk—not both at the same time. Just send your message. Or just receive the other person's message. Usually, this slows down the pace, clears the smoke, and allows everyone to become more levelheaded.

To slow down the communication even more, take a break. Depending upon the level of conflict, that might mean anything from a few minutes to a few days.

A related suggestion is to do something nonthreatening together. Share an activity with others that's not a source of conflict.

Be a complete listener.

In times of conflict, we often say one thing and mean another. So before responding to what the other person says, use active listening. Check to see if you have correctly received that person's message: "What I'm hearing you say is. . . . Did I get it correctly?"

Listening completely can also include asking for more discussion. Often, people will stop short of their true message. Encourage them to continue by asking for it: "Anything else that you want to say about that? Is something more on your mind right now?"

Get to the point—then elaborate.

Sometimes people in conflict build up to their main points cautiously. This technique works well for actors on a stage who want to add drama to a scene. It doesn't work so well for the rest of us, especially when we're in conflict.

Making your listener wait in suspense while you saunter up to your message can lead to problems: During the interval, the listener might become impatient and more irritable. Or he could imagine something far worse than what you actually intend to say. As an alternative, get to your point right away. When that's done, there is usually the opportunity to provide supporting details.

Recap your message.
As we send messages in times of conflict, we might talk for a long time. Sometimes people under emotional stress can't take it all in. And even if they get our whole message, they might not understand which of our points is most important.

You can follow that homespun advice given to professional speakers: First, tell 'em what you're going to say. Then tell 'em. Then tell 'em what you've told 'em.

Before you yield the floor to someone else, review your main messages and repeat your key requests.

Use a mediator.
Even an untrained mediator—someone who's not a party to the conflict—can do much to decrease tension. Mediators can help all those involved get their points of view across. In this case, the mediator's role is not to give advice but to keep the discussion on track and moving toward a solution.

Allow for cultural differences.
People respond to conflict in different ways, depending on their cultural background. Some stand close, speak loudly, and make direct eye contact. Other people avert their eyes, mute their voices, and increase physical distance.

Even small gestures carry different meanings across cultures. For example, people in the United States sometimes make an "OK" sign by curling the thumb and index finger of one hand into a circular shape. In other countries, this gesture is considered obscene.

When it seems to you that other people are sidestepping or escalating a conflict, consider whether your reaction is based on cultural bias.

Apologize or ask for forgiveness.
Conflict often arises from our own errors. We don't usually do these things on purpose. They're just mistakes.

Others might move quickly to end the conflict when we acknowledge this fact, apologize, and ask for forgiveness. This is "spending face"—an alternative to the age-old habit of "saving face." We can simply admit that we are less than perfect and own up to our goof-ups.

Write a letter and send it.
What can be difficult to say to another person face to face might be effectively communicated in writing. When people in conflict write letters to each other, they automatically apply many of the suggestions in this article. Letter writing is a way to slow down the communication and ensure that only one person at a time is sending a message.

One drawback: It's possible for people to misunderstand what you say in a letter. To avoid further problems, make clear what you are not saying: "I am saying that I want to be alone for a few days. I am not saying that I want you to stay away forever." Saying what you are not saying is often useful in face-to-face communication as well.

Before you send your letter, put yourself in the shoes of the person who will receive it. Imagine how your comments could be misinterpreted. Then rewrite your letter, correcting any areas that are open to misinterpretation.

Write a letter and don't send it.
Sometimes we feel compelled to blame other people or speak to them angrily. This is likely to fan the flames instead of resolve the conflict.

If this happens, consider a way to get the problem off your chest and the upset out of your system—without beating up the other person: Write the nastiest, meanest letter you can imagine. Let all of your frustration, anger, and venom flow onto the page. Be as mean and blaming as you can. When your pen has cooled off, see if there is anything else you want to add.

Then take the letter and destroy it. Your writing has served its purpose. Chances are that you've calmed down and are ready for some skilled conflict management.

Permit the emotion.
Crying is OK. Being upset is all right. Feeling angry is often appropriate. Allowing other people to see the strength of our feelings can go a long way in

WORKPLACE APPLICATIONS

Bring to mind a coworker with whom you are currently in conflict. Then reread the article "The fine art of conflict management" and choose three suggestions for resolving this conflict. As you read, visualize the suggestions working for you.

clearing up the conflict. Emotion is part of life and an important part of any communication.

Just allow the full range of your feelings. Often what's on the far side of anger is love. When we clear out the resentment and hostility, we might find genuine compassion taking its place.

Videotape the disagreement.

This is an option for the brave—those who really want feedback on their conflict management skills. With the agreement of all parties involved, set up a camera and videotape your conversation. Later, play back the tape and review your side of the conversation. Look for any ways that you perpetuated the upset. Spot anything you did or said to move the problem toward a solution.

In the midst of a raging argument, when emotions run high, it's almost impossible to see ourselves objectively. Let the video camera be your unbiased observer.

Agree to disagree.

Sometimes we say all we have to say. We do all of the problem solving we can do. We get all points of view across. And the conflict remains, staring us right in the face.

What's left is to recognize that honest disagreement is a fact of life. We can peacefully coexist with other people—and respect them—even though we don't agree on fundamental issues. Conflict can be accepted even when it is not resolved.

Do nothing.

Sometimes we worsen a conflict by insisting that it be solved immediately. It can be wise to sit tight and wait things out. Some conflicts resolve themselves with the passage of time.

See the conflict within you.

Sometimes the conflict we see in the outside world has its source in the world behind our eyeballs. A cofounder of Alcoholics Anonymous put it this way: "It is a spiritual axiom that every time we are disturbed, no matter what the cause, there is something awry with us."

It's been said that nobody else can hurt us as much as our own thoughts can. When we're angry or upset, we can take a minute to look inside. Perhaps we were ready to take offense, waiting to pounce on something the other person said. Perhaps, without realizing it, we did something to create the conflict. Or maybe the other person is simply saying what we know to be true—and don't want to admit.

When these things happen, we can shine a light on ourselves. A simple spot check on our own thinking might help the conflict disappear—right before our eyes.

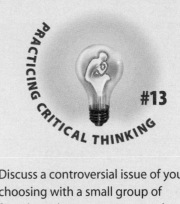

PRACTICING CRITICAL THINKING #13

Discuss a controversial issue of your choosing with a small group of friends or classmates. At several points in your discussion, stop to evaluate your group's critical thinking. Answer the following questions:

- Are we staying open to opposing ideas—even if we initially disagree with them?

- Are we asking for evidence for each key assertion?

- Are we adequately summarizing one another's point of view before we analyze it?

- Are we foreseeing the possible consequences of taking a particular stand on any issue?

- Are we considering more than one solution to problems?

- Are we willing to change our stands on issues or suspend judgment when appropriate?

- Are we being systematic as we consider the issues?

You deserve compliments

For some people, compliments are more difficult to accept than criticisms. Here are some hints for handling compliments.

1. Accept the compliment. We sometimes respond to praise with "Oh, it's really nothing" or "This old thing? I've had it for years." This type of response undermines both you and the person who sent the compliment.

2. Choose another time to deliver your own compliments. Automatically returning a compliment can appear suspiciously polite and insincere.

3. Let the compliment stand. "Do you really think so?" questions the integrity of the message. It can also sound as if we're fishing for more compliments. Accepting compliments is not the same as being conceited. You are worthy and capable. Allow people to acknowledge that.

EXERCISE

#28

Write an "I" message

First, pick something about school that irritates you. Then pretend that you are talking to the person who is associated with this irritation. In the space below, write down what you would say to this person as a "You" message.

_____

_____

_____

_____

Now write the same complaint as an "I" message. Include at least the first three elements suggested in "Five ways to say 'I.'"

_____

_____

_____

_____

JOURNAL ENTRY

#39

Discovery Statement

Recall a writing assignment that you were asked to complete this term. Evaluate the process you used to complete the writing, listing below anything you would do differently for your next writing project. (For example, you might want to avoid a last-minute timeline crunch or use your research time more effectively.)

_____

_____

_____

_____

Now preview the remaining articles in this chapter for any strategies that can help you gain your desired outcomes. List at least five strategies here, along with their related page numbers.

Strategy	Page number	Strategy	Page number
_____	_____	_____	_____
_____	_____	_____	_____
_____	_____	_____	_____

Sometimes relationships work exceptionally well; sometimes they don't. Of all of the factors that affect relationships, the biggest is communication (the topic of this chapter). Here's a list of other actions that can benefit your relationships.

Do tell the truth. Life is complicated when you don't. For example, if you think a friend is addicted to drugs, telling him so in a supportive, nonjudgmental way is a sign of friendship. Psychotherapist Sidney Jourard referred to such openness and honesty as *transparency* and wrote eloquently about how it can heal and deepen relationships.[4]

Do support others. Encourage fellow students to reach their goals and be successful. Respect their study time. Helping them to stay focused can help you as well.

Don't pry. Being a good listener is invitation enough for fellow students to share their problems, feelings, and personal goals.

Don't borrow—too much. Borrowing a book or a tennis racket might seem like a small thing. Yet these requests can become a sore point in a relationship. Some people have difficulty saying no and resent lending things. Consider keeping borrowing to a minimum.

Do divide chores. Whether it's a class project or a household chore, do your part. Frustrations result when people can't come to an agreement on a fair division of work—or fail to live up to such an agreement.

Don't gripe. There is a difference between griping and sharing problems. Gripers usually don't seek solutions. They just want everyone to know how unhappy they are. Sharing a problem is an appropriate way of starting the search for a solution.

Relationships can work

Do write a letter. Sometimes it's not easy to express viewpoints face to face, so write a letter. Even if you never send it, you've rehearsed what you want to say.

Do get involved. Being involved in extracurricular activities is a great way to meet people with common interests. If you commute and have little time for these activities, study at the library, eat at the cafeteria, or relax at the student union. You might be surprised at how many friends you can make.

Don't brag. Other students are turned off by constant references to how much money you have, how great your girlfriend is, how numerous your social successes are,

or how much status your family enjoys. There is a difference between sharing excitement and being obnoxious.

Do detach. Allow others to accept responsibility for their problems. Pitying them, getting upset along with them, or assuming responsibility for solving their problems is not helpful.

Do allow people to be upset. Trying to joke people out of their anger by discounting their frustration or minimizing their disappointment invalidates their feelings. You can best support them by allowing them to experience their emotions.

Do ask for help. One of the central messages of this book is that you are not alone. You can draw on the talent, strength, and wisdom of other people. People often respond to a genuine request for help.

Do share yourself. When we brood on negative thoughts and refuse to speak them out loud, we lose perspective. And when we keep joys to ourselves, we diminish our satisfaction. A solution is to share regularly what we think and feel. Imagine a community in which people freely and lovingly speak their minds—without fear or defensiveness. That can be your community.

Don't preach. This piece of advice might seem funny at the end of a list of do's and don't's. Sometimes people ask for advice. It's OK to share your values and opinions. It's *not* OK to pretend that you know what's best for someone else. Respect the differences between peoples and don't try to reform the world.

Relationships change, and the changes can be painful. Be prepared. Forget about buying broken heart insurance. We are too high a risk. In fact, any time we choose to care about another person, we risk a painful, but rarely fatal, broken heart.

Relationships grow and die. Lovers and spouses leave. Children grow up and move away. Parents die. We might even surpass the people we once looked to as models; that's a kind of loss, too. All of these events can lead to pain.

Pain is a part of living and can be dealt with in ways that help us learn. When an important relationship ends and you feel bad, allow yourself to experience that feeling. It is appropriate to be miserable when you are. It's normal to cry and express your feelings. It is also possible to go to class, study, work, eat, sleep, get your laundry done, and feel miserable at the same time.

Sometimes emotional pain is intense. If you feel absolutely rotten, useless, ugly, and unlovable, look in the mirror and tell yourself over and over again how rotten, useless, ugly, and unlovable you are. It might be hard to berate yourself for very long and keep a straight face. (Apply this suggestion with care.)

One option is to throw a pity party and talk about how rotten things have been going for you. Be prepared for your depressed mood to change quickly.

If you are determined to feel sorry for yourself, go all the way. Increase your misery by studying a few extra hours. It could go like this: You get some extra studying done and start feeling like a good student. Maybe you are more worthwhile than you thought. You fight it, but you can't help feeling pleased with yourself. The pain

Relationships change

subsides. Feeling good about yourself has an interesting side effect: Usually others start feeling good about you, too.

Another way to work through this kind of pain is to do something. Do anything. Exercise. Mop the kitchen floor, clean out your dresser drawers, iron your shirts. This sounds ridiculous, but it works.

Remember that your purpose is not to avoid pain, but to see it from a more balanced viewpoint. Japanese psychiatrist Morita Masatake, a contemporary of Sigmund Freud, based his whole approach toward treatment on this insight: We can face our emotional pain directly and still take constructive action. One of Masatake's favorite suggestions for people who felt depressed was that they tend a garden.

Do things with other people. Include old friends. Make new friends. Talking to people is a way of healing.

You can also use the Power Processes when you feel pain. Tell the truth about your feelings and fully experience them. Embrace this barrier and "be here now" with it. Surrender to your negative feelings. Yes, it can be difficult to practice the Power Processes at times like this. And when your practice becomes this intense, it can yield the most learning.

Writing about your feelings and what you're learning through the pain can also bring perspective. Your journal is one friend who is on call 24 hours each day, every day of the year. You can approach this friend in any mood and say anything at all. Now that's unconditional acceptance.

If you feel severely depressed and stay that way, talk to someone. If friends and family members can't help, then remember that most schools and communities have counselors available. Take action. Depression can affect your health, and it can be alleviated. Emotional pain does not last forever. Often it ends in a matter of weeks. One case disappeared in four hours and 12 minutes.

There's no need to let a broken heart stop your life. Though you can find abundant advice on the subject, just remember a simple and powerful idea: "This, too, shall pass."

1. Go to the source. Start with the person who is most directly involved with the problem.

2. Present the facts without blaming anyone. Your complaint will carry more weight if you document the facts. Keep track of names and dates. Note what actions were promised and what results actually occurred.

3. Go up the ladder to people with more responsibility. If you don't get satisfaction at the first level, go to that person's direct supervisor. Requesting a supervisor's name will often get results. Write a letter to the company president.

Seven steps to effective complaints

Sometimes skill in relationship building means making a complaint. Whining, blaming, pouting, kicking, and spitting usually don't get results. Here are some guidelines for complaining effectively.

Criticism really can be constructive.

Although receiving criticism is rarely fun, it is often educational. Here are some ways to get the most value from it.

Avoid finding fault. When your mind is occupied with finding fault in others, you aren't open to hearing constructive comments about yourself.

Take it seriously. Some people laugh or joke in order to

4. Ask for commitments. When you find someone who is willing to solve your problem, get him to say exactly what he is going to do and when.

5. Use available support. There are dozens of groups, as well as government agencies, willing to get involved in resolving complaints. Contact consumer groups of the Better Business Bureau. Trade associations can sometimes help. Ask city council members, county commissioners, state legislators, and senators and representatives. All of them want your vote, so they usually are eager to help.

cover up their anger or embarrassment at being criticized. A humorous reaction on your part can be mistaken for a lack of concern.

6. Take legal action, if necessary. Small-claims court is relatively inexpensive, and you don't have to hire a lawyer. These courts can handle cases involving small amounts of money (usually up to $1,000 or $2,000). Legal aid offices can sometimes answer questions.

React to criticism with acceptance. Most people don't enjoy pointing out another's faults. Denial, argument, or joking makes it more difficult for them to give honest feedback. You can disagree with criticism and still accept it calmly.

Keep it in perspective. Avoid blowing the criticism out of proportion. The purpose of criticism is to generate positive change and self-improvement. There's no need to overreact to it.

Listen without defensiveness. You can't hear the criticism if you're busy framing your rebuttal.

7. Don't give up. Assume that others are on your team. Many people are out there to help you. State what you intend to do and ask for their partnership.

V.I.P.'s (Very Important Persons)

Step 1   Under the column below titled "Name," write the names of at least seven people who have positively influenced your life. They might be relatives, friends, teachers, or perhaps persons you have never met. (Complete each step before moving on.)

Step 2   In the next column, rate your gratitude for this person's influence (from 1 to 5, with 1 being a little grateful and 5 being extremely grateful).

Step 3   In the third column, rate how fully you have communicated your appreciation to this person (again, 1 to 5, with 1 being not communicated and 5 being fully communicated).

Step 4   In the final column, put a U beside the persons with whom you have unfinished business (such as an important communication that you have not taken the opportunity to send).

Name	Grateful (1-5)	Communicated(1-5)	U
1.			
2.			
3.			
4.			
5.			
6.			
7.			

Step 5   Now select two persons with U's beside their names and write them a letter. Express the love, tenderness, and joy you feel toward them. Tell them exactly how they have helped change your life and how glad you are that they did.

Step 6   You also have an impact on others. Make a list of people whose lives you have influenced. Consider sharing with these people why you enjoy being part of their lives.

1.

2.

3.

4.

5.

6.

Phase 1: Getting ready to write
Creating something from nothing

This chapter outlines a three-phase process for writing any paper or speech:

1. Getting ready to write

2. Writing the first draft

3. Revising your draft

Even though this article lays out a step-by-step process of preparing to write, remember that writing is highly personal. You might go through the steps in a different order or find yourself working on several at once.

Step 1: List and schedule writing tasks

You can divide the ultimate goal—a finished paper—into smaller steps that you can tackle right away. Estimate how long it will take to complete each step. Start with the date your paper is due and work backward to the present. Say that the due date is December 1 and you have about three months to write the paper. List November 20 as your targeted completion date, plan what you want to get done by November 1, then list what you want to get done by October 1.

Step 2: Generate ideas for a topic

Brainstorm with a group.
There's no need to create in isolation. Forget the myth of the lonely, frustrated artist rehashing ideas alone in a dark Paris cafe. You can harness the natural creative power of a group to assist you. For ideas about ways to brainstorm, see the Thinking chapter.

Speak it.
To get ideas flowing, start talking. Admit your confusion or lack of a clear idea. Then just speak. By putting your thoughts into words, you'll start thinking more clearly. Novelist E. M. Forster said, "Speak before you think is creation's motto."

Use free writing.
Free writing, a technique championed by writing teacher Peter Elbow, sends a depth probe into your creative mind.[5] This is one way to bypass your internal censors, those little voices in your head that constantly say, "That sentence wasn't very good. Why don't you stop this before you get hurt?"

There's only one rule in free writing: Write without stopping. Set a time limit—say, 10 minutes—and keep your pencil in motion or your fingers dancing across the keyboard the whole time.

> "Speak before you think."
> –E.M. Forster

Give yourself permission to keep writing, even if you don't think it's very good, even if you want to stop and rewrite. There's no need to worry about spelling, punctuation, or grammar. It's OK if you stray from the initial subject. Just keep writing and let the ideas flow. Experiment with free writing as soon as your instructor assigns a paper.

Step 3: Refine initial ideas

Select a topic and working title. It's easy to put off writing if you have a hard time choosing a topic. However, it is almost impossible to make a wrong choice at this stage. Just choose any subject. You can choose again later.

Using your instructor's guidelines for the paper or speech, sit down and make a list of topics that interest you. Write as many of these as you can think of in two minutes. Then choose one. If you can't, use scissors to cut your list into single items, put them in a box, and pull one out. To avoid getting stuck on this step, set a precise timeline for yourself: "I will choose a topic by 4 p.m. on Wednesday."

The most common pitfall is selecting a topic that's too broad. "Harriet Tubman" is not a useful topic for your American history paper. Instead, consider "Harriet Tubman's activities as a Union spy during the Civil War." Your topic statement can function as a working title.

Write a thesis statement. Clarify what you want to say by summarizing it in one concise sentence. This sentence is called a thesis statement, and it refines your working title. It also helps in making a preliminary outline.

You might write a thesis statement such as "Harriet Tubman's activities with the Underground Railroad led to a relationship with the Union army during the Civil War." A statement that's clear and to the point can make your paper easier to write. Remember that it's OK to rewrite your thesis statement as you learn more about your topic.

A thesis statement is different from a topic statement. Like newspaper headlines, a thesis statement makes an assertion or describes an action. It is expressed in a complete sentence, including a verb. "Diversity" is a topic. "Cultural diversity is valuable" is a thesis statement.

Step 4: Consider your purpose

Effective writing flows from a purpose. Discuss the purpose of your assignment with your instructor. Also think about how you'd like your reader or listener to change after considering your ideas. Do you want him to think differently, to feel differently, or to take a certain action?

Your writing strategy is greatly affected by how you answer these questions. If you want someone to think differently, make your writing clear and logical. Support your assertions with evidence. If you want someone to feel differently, consider crafting a story. Write about a character your audience can empathize with, and tell how he resolves a basic problem. And if your purpose is to move the reader into action, explain exactly what steps to take and offer solid benefits for doing so.

To clarify your purpose, state it in one sentence. For example: "The purpose of this paper is to define the term *master student* in such a clear and convincing way that I win a scholarship from Houghton Mifflin."

Step 5: Do initial research

At this stage, the objective of your research is not to uncover specific facts about your topic. That comes later. First, you want to gain an overview of the subject. Discover the structure of your topic—its major divisions or branches. Say that you want to persuade the reader to vote for a certain candidate. You must first learn enough about this person to summarize his background and state his stands on key issues.

Step 6: Outline

An outline is a kind of map. When you follow a map, you avoid getting lost. Likewise, an outline keeps you from wandering off the topic.

To start an outline, gather a stack of 3×5 cards and brainstorm ideas you want to include in your paper. Write one phrase or sentence per card.

Then experiment with the cards. Group them into separate stacks, each stack representing one major category. After that, arrange the stacks in order. Finally, arrange the cards within each stack in a logical order. Rearrange them until you discover an organization that you like.

If you write on a computer, consider using outlining software. These programs allow you to record and rearrange ideas on the screen, much like the way you'd create and shuffle 3×5 cards.

After you write the first draft of your outline, test it. Make sure that each word in your outline relates directly to your statement of purpose.

Step 7: Do in-depth research

You can find information about research skills in the chapters on Reading and Notes. Following are added suggestions.

Use 3x5 cards.

If 3×5 cards haven't found their way into your life by now, joy awaits you. These cards work wonders when conducting research. Just write down one idea per card. This makes it easy to organize—and reorganize—your ideas.

Organizing research cards as you create them saves time. Use rubber bands to keep source cards separate from information cards and to maintain general categories.

You can also save time in two other ways. First, copy all of the information correctly. Always include the source code and page number on information cards. Second, write legibly, using the same format for all of your cards.

In addition to source cards and information cards, generate idea cards. If you have a thought while you are researching, write it down on a card. Label these cards clearly as your own ideas.

An alternative to 3×5 cards is a computer outlining or database program. Some word processing packages also include features that can be used for note taking.

Sense the time to begin writing.

A common mistake that beginning writers make is to hold their noses, close their eyes, and jump into the writing process with both feet and few facts. Avoid this temptation by gathering more information than you think you can use.

You can begin writing even before your research is complete. The act of writing creates ideas and reveals holes in research.

Finding a natural place to begin is one signal to begin writing. This is not to say that the skies will suddenly open up and your completed paper, flanked by trumpeting angels, will appear before your eyes. You might instead get a strong sense of how to write just one small section of your paper. When this happens, write.

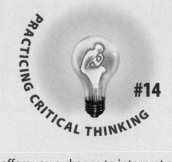

PRACTICING CRITICAL THINKING #14

The following exercise offers you a chance to interpret and categorize different views on an issue. This exercise can be done with any number of people. When more people take part, you are more likely to gain a wider range of opinions.

Select a topic—for example, the United States' and Britain's 1998 air strikes on Iraq. Ask everyone to spend five minutes writing down their opinions about this issue. Ask them to recall articles they read, reports they heard, or experiences they had during this incident. Each opinion can be recorded on one 3×5 card. Examples might include:

- This incident shows that sustained international conflict cannot be managed by diplomacy alone.

- The United States and Britain should have acted more decisively and sooner to help resolve this conflict.

- Any agreement reached between the parties in this conflict is likely to unravel within a few years.

Write as many opinions as you can in five minutes. Whenever possible, include reasons and evidence for your opinions. All of your thoughts about the issue are important.

Now spread all of the 3×5 cards out on a desk or on the floor. Ask everyone to take 10 minutes in order to walk around and read what other people have written. Whenever you find an opinion that intrigues you or leads you to think about the issue in a new way, write that opinion on a 3×5 card.

After reviewing all of the opinions, reasons, and evidence, return to your own cards and pick up the ones you still agree with after reading everyone else's cards. Now you have in hand the cards that reflect your current opinion about this issue.

After this process, you might have decided that some of your former opinions have little value. They remain on the floor. You could also decide that other opinions need substantial change.

At this point, review the stack of cards you now hold in your hands. These cards represent your considered opinion about the topic. You might have only the cards you initially wrote (no changes in your opinions about the topic), or a combination of your own and others' opinions (some change in your thoughts about the topic), or completely new cards (a total shift in your opinion about the topic).

Keep in mind that opinions on any topic are subject to change in light of further reasoning and new evidence. This is often the result of high-quality critical thinking. Change might occur when you discover new information, see the topic from a new vantage point, have new experiences in life, or attach greater significance to something than you did before.

On a separate sheet of paper, write a Discovery Statement about what you learned about yourself through this exercise. Describe any qualities of a critical thinker that you displayed. Also list the critical thinking qualities or skills you used.

Phase 2: Writing the first draft
Getting down to it

If you've followed the steps in the previous article, you've already done much of the hard work. Now you can relax into writing your first draft.

First, gather your notes that you have arranged to follow your outline. Then write about the ideas in your notes. Write in paragraphs, one idea per paragraph. If you have organized your notes logically, related facts will appear close to each other. As you complete this task, keep the following suggestions in mind.

FIRST DRAFT

Remember that the first draft is not for keeps.
You can save quality for later, when you revise. Your goal at this point is simply to generate lots of material.

Don't worry about grammar, punctuation, or spelling as you write your first draft. Write as if you were explaining the subject to a friend. Let words flow. The very act of writing will release creative energy. It's perfectly all right to crank out a draft that you heavily rewrite or even throw away. The purpose of a first draft is merely to have something to work with—period. For most of us, that's a heck of a lot better than facing a blank page. You will revise this rough draft several times, so don't worry if the first draft seems rough or choppy.

Write freely.
Many writers prefer to get their first draft down quickly. Their advice is to just keep writing, much as in free writing. You can pause occasionally to glance at your notes and outline. The idea is to avoid stopping to edit your work. You can save that for the next step.

Another option is to write a first draft without referring back to your notes and outline. If you've immersed yourself in the topic, chances are that much of the information is already bubbling up near the surface of your mind anyway. Later, when you edit, you can go back to your notes and correct any errors.

Keep in mind that there's no obligation to write straight through, following your outline from beginning to end. Some professional writers prefer to write the last chapter of a novel or the last scene of a play first. With the ending firmly in mind, they can then guide the reader through all of the incidents that lead up to it. You might feel more comfortable with certain aspects of your topic than with others. Dive in where you feel most comfortable.

Be yourself.
As you write, let go of the urge to sound "official" or "scholarly." Write not to the teacher, but to an intelligent student or someone you care about. Visualize this person and choose the three or four most important things you'd say to him about the topic. This helps you avoid the temptation to write merely to impress. Write the way you speak.

The other side of this coin is that we can't really write the way we speak.

The spoken word is accompanied by facial expressions and gestures, as well as changes in voice tone, pitch, and volume. Slang expressions used in everyday speech are not appropriate in academic writing. Compensate for elements peculiar to the spoken language by being clear and concise and by providing smooth, logical transitions from subject to subject.

Let your inner writer take over.
There might be times during a first draft when ideas come to you without effort. It might feel as if thoughts are flowing from head to hand without conscious effort on your part. This is a natural "high" similar to states that accomplished athletes, musicians, and artists have reported. Writer Natalie Goldberg says that in such moments you are in touch with your "inner writer."[6] Such "peak experiences" can yield moments of pure joy. Often, those moments come just after a period of feeling stuck. Welcome getting stuck. A breakthrough is not far behind.

Ease into it.
Some people find that it works well to forget the word *writing.* Instead, they ease into the task with activities that help generate ideas. You can free-associate, cluster, meditate, daydream, doodle, draw diagrams, visualize the event you want to describe, talk into a tape recorder—anything that gets you started.

Make writing a habit.
Inspiration is not part of the working vocabulary for many professional writers. Instead of waiting for inspiration to strike, they simply make a habit of writing at a certain time each day. You can use the same strategy. Schedule a block of time to write your first draft. The very act of writing can breed inspiration.

Respect your deep mind.
Part of the process of writing takes place outside our awareness. There's nothing mysterious about this. Many creative people report that ideas come to them while they're doing something totally unrelated to writing. Often this happens after they've been grappling with a question and have reached a point where they feel stuck. It's like the composer who said, "There I was, sitting and eating a sandwich, and all of a sudden this darn tune pops into my head." You can trust your deep mind. It's writing while you eat, sleep, and brush your teeth.

Get physical.
Writing is physical, like jogging or playing tennis. You can move your body in ways that are in tune with the flow of your ideas. While working on the first draft, take breaks. Go for a walk. Speak or sing your ideas out loud. From time to time, practice relaxation techniques and breathe deeply.

Use affirmations and visualizations.
Write with the idea that the finished paper or speech is inside you, waiting to be released. Affirmations and visualizations can help you with this. Imagine what your finished paper will look like. Construct a detailed mental picture of the title page and major sections of the paper. See a clean, typed copy, and imagine how it will feel to hold the paper and flip through the pages.

Then support your writing by sprinkling your self-talk with statements that affirm your abilities. For example: "I express myself clearly and persuasively." "I am using an effective process to write my paper." "I will be pleased with the results."

Hide it in your drawer for a while.
Schedule time for rewrites before you begin, and schedule at least one day between revisions so that you can let the material sit. On Tuesday night, you might think your writing sings the song of beautiful language. On Wednesday, you will see that those same words, such as the phrase "sings the song of beautiful language," belong in the trash basket.

Ideally, a student will revise a paper two or three times, make a clean copy of those revisions, then let the last revised draft sit for at least three or four days. The brain needs that time to disengage itself from the project. Obvious grammatical mistakes, awkward constructions, and lapses in logic are hidden from us when we are in the middle of the creative process. Give yourself time to step back, and then go over the paper one last time before starting the third phase of the writing process.

StudentVoices

Education is a process of learning to read, write, and compute, and the result of this process is a Master Student who is capable of solving problems and who is able to think independently. What is important is not information itself, but knowing how to use that information to function in life. Furthermore, study skills and successful endeavors improve with repetition in the same way skills in sports improve with practice.

— BELLE ROYLES

Phase 3: Revising your draft
Polishing your creation

One definition of a writer is anyone who rewrites. Some people who write for a living will rewrite a piece seven, eight, or even more times. Ernest Hemingway rewrote the last page of *A Farewell to Arms* 39 times before he was satisfied with it. When asked what the most difficult part of this process was, he simply said, "Getting the words right."

People who rewrite care. They care about the reader. They care about precise language and careful thinking. And they care about themselves. They know that the act of rewriting teaches them more about the topic than almost any other step in the process.

There's a difference in pace between writing a first draft and revising it. Keep in mind the saying "Write in haste, revise at leisure." When you edit and revise, slow down and take a magnifying glass to your work. One guideline is to allow 50 percent of writing time for planning, research, and writing the first draft. Then give the remaining 50 percent to revising.

An effective way to revise your paper is to read it out loud. The eyes tend to fill in the blanks in our own writing. The combination of voice and ears forces us to pay attention to the details.

Another revision technique is to have a friend revise your paper. This is never a substitute for your own revision, but a friend can often see mistakes you miss. Remember that when other people criticize or edit your work, they're not attacking you. They're just commenting on your paper. With a little practice, you can actually learn to welcome feedback.

Reading out loud and having a friend edit your paper are techniques that can help you in each step of rewriting.

Step 1: Cut

Writer Theodore Cheney suggests that an efficient way to begin revising is to cut the passages that don't contribute to your purpose.[7] Right now it might not pay to polish individual words, phrases, and sentences—especially if you decide later that you don't need them. To save time, decide now what words you want to keep and what you want to let go.

Look for excess baggage. Avoid at all costs and at all times the really, really terrible mistake of using way too many unnecessary words, a mistake that some student writers often make when they sit down to write papers for the various courses in which they participate at the fine institutions of higher learning that they are fortunate to attend. (Example: The previous sentence could be edited to "Avoid unnecessary words.")

Approach your rough draft as if it were a chunk of granite from which you will chisel the final product. In the end, much of your first draft will be lying on the floor. What is left will be the clean, clear, polished product.

Sometimes the revisions are painful. Sooner or later, every writer invents a phrase that is truly clever but makes no contribution to the purpose of the paper. Grit your teeth and let it go.

Note: For maximum efficiency, make the larger cuts first—sections, chapters, pages. Then go for the smaller cuts—paragraphs, sentences, phrases, words.

Keep in mind that cutting a passage means just for now, for this

☐ Avoid ~~at all costs and at all times the really, really terrible mistake of~~ using ~~way too many~~ unnecessary words, ~~a mistake that some student writers often make when they sit down to write papers for the various courses in which they participate at the fine institutions of higher learning which they are fortunate to attend.~~

paper, for this assignment. You might want to keep a file of deleted phrases or sentences and save it for future use.

Step 2: Paste

In deleting passages, you've probably removed some of the original transitions and connecting ideas from your draft. The next task is to rearrange what's left of your paper so that it flows logically. Look for consistency within paragraphs and effective transitions from paragraph to paragraph and from section to section.

If your draft doesn't hang together, then reorder your ideas. Imagine yourself with a pair of scissors and a glue stick. You're going to cut the paper into scraps—one scrap for each point. Then you're going to paste these points down in a new, more logical order.

Step 3: Fix

Now it's time to look at individual words and phrases.

In general, rely on nouns and verbs. Using too many adjectives and adverbs weakens your message and adds unnecessary bulk to your writing. Write about the details, and be specific. Also, use the active rather than the passive voice.

Instead of writing in the passive voice:
A project was initiated.

You can make it active by writing:
The research team began a project.

Instead of writing verbosely:
After making a timely arrival and perspicaciously observing the unfolding events, I emerged totally and gloriously victorious.

You can write as Julius Caesar did:
I came, I saw, I conquered.

Instead of writing vaguely:
The speaker made effective use of the television medium, asking in no uncertain terms that we change our belief systems.

You can write specifically:
The reformed criminal stared straight into the television camera and shouted, "Take a good look at what you're doing! Will it get you what you really want?"

Also define any terms that the reader might not know and put them into plain English whenever you can.

Step 4: Prepare

In a sense, any paper is a sales effort. If you hand in a paper with wrinkled jeans, its hair tangled and unwashed and its shoes untied, your instructor is less likely to buy it. To avoid this situation, present a paper that uses an acceptable format for margin widths, endnotes, title pages, and other details.

If you used the Internet or another computer resource as part of your research, then follow an accepted form for citing such material in endnotes and bibliographies. Ask your instructor for specific instructions, or use the following examples as guidelines.

Citing a page from the World Wide Web:
> Pritzker, Edward J. An Early Fragment from Indian Buddhist Texts. Online. Ingress Communications. Available: http://www.ingress.com/~asta nart/pritzker/pritzker.html. Accessed 8 June 1995.

Citing material from a CD-ROM:
> Oxford English Dictionary on Compact Disc. 2nd ed. CD-ROM. Oxford: Oxford University Press, 1992.

Citing material from an email message:
> Stanley Thomas (thomas@usinternet.com). 19 September 1998. Email to Lee Chang (Chang@mho.net).

If you "cut and paste" material from a web page directly into your paper, be sure to place that material in quotation marks and cite the source. And before referencing an email message, verify the sender's identity. Remember that someone sending an email can pretend to be someone else.

Use quality paper for your final version. For an even more professional appearance, bind your paper with a paper or plastic cover.

Step 5: Proofread

Read over your paper with an eye for spelling and grammar. Many dictionaries include useful summaries of grammar principles. Another resource is the Grammar Hotline at 1-805-378-1494.

As you ease down the homestretch, read your revised paper one more time. This time, go for the big picture and look for:

- A clear thesis statement.
- Sentences that introduce your topic, guide the reader through the major sections of your paper, and summarize your conclusions.
- Details—such as quotations, examples, and statistics—that support your conclusions.
- Lean sentences that have been purged of needless words.
- Plenty of action verbs and concrete, specific nouns.

When you're through proofreading, take a minute to savor the result. You've just witnessed something of a miracle—the mind attaining clarity and resolution. That's the aha! in writing.

PRACTICING CRITICAL THINKING

#15

Choose a subject about which you have some detailed or advanced knowledge. Explain a topic in that field for someone who knows nothing about it. Put your explanation in writing.

Next, field-test your explanation. Present it to a sample member of your chosen audience, perhaps a relative or friend. Based on your field test, describe how you could revise your presentation to make it more effective. Summarize your ideas in the space below. Also reflect on what it means to say that your presentation is "effective."

_____

_____

_____

_____

_____

_____

_____

_____

_____

JOURNAL ENTRY

#40

Discovery Statement

This Journal Entry is for people who avoid writing. As with any anxiety, you can approach writing anxiety by accepting it fully. Realize that it's OK to feel anxious about writing. Others have shared this feeling, and many people have worked with it successfully.

Begin by telling the truth. Describe exactly what happens when you start to write. What thoughts or images run through your mind? Do you feel any tension or discomfort in your body? Where? Let the thoughts and images come to the surface without resistance. Complete the following statement.

When I begin to write, I discover that I ...

_____

_____

_____

_____

_____

Giving credit where credit is due:
Avoiding the high cost of
plagiarism

There's a branch of law known as *intellectual property*. This field is based on the idea that original works, such as speeches, publications, and artistic creations, are not free for the taking. Anyone who borrows from these works is obligated to acknowledge the work's creator. This is the purpose behind copyrights, patents, and trademarks.

Using another person's words without giving proper credit is called *plagiarism*. This is a real concern for anyone who writes, including students. Plagiarism can have big-time consequences, ranging from a failing grade to expulsion from school.

To avoid plagiarism when writing a research paper, be careful as you take notes. If you use a direct quote from another writer or speaker, put that person's words in quotation marks. Also note the details about the source of the quotation: publication title, publisher, date, and page number. Many instructors will ask you to add endnotes to your paper that include this information. If you use index cards to take notes, include source information on each card with a quotation.

Instead of using a direct quote, you might choose to paraphrase an author's words. Credit paraphrases in the same way that you credit direct quotes.

Keep in mind that paraphrasing does not mean copying a passage word for word and then rearranging or deleting a few phrases to disguise the fact. Consider this paragraph:

Higher education also offers you the chance to learn how to learn. In fact, that's the subject of this book. Employers value the person who is a "quick study" when it comes to learning a new job. That makes your ability to learn a marketable skill.

Following is an improper paraphrase of that passage:

With higher education comes the chance to learn how to learn. Employers value the person who is a "quick study" when it comes to learning a new job. That makes your ability to learn a marketable skill.

A better paraphrase of the same passage would be:

The author notes that when we learn how to learn, we gain a skill that is valued by employers.

Out of a concern for avoiding plagiarism, some students go overboard in crediting their sources. You do not need to credit wording that's wholly your own. Nor do you need to credit general ideas. For example, the suggestion that people use a to-do list to plan their time is a general idea. When you use your own words to describe to-do lists, there's no need to credit a source. But if you borrow someone else's wording to explain this idea, do give credit.

Writing and delivering
Speeches

Polishing your speaking skills can help you think on your feet and communicate clearly. These are skills that you will use during school and in any career you choose.

Organizing your speech. Some people tune out during a speech. Just think of all the times you have listened to instructors, lecturers, politicians, and others. Think of all the wonderful daydreams you have had during their speeches. Your audiences are like you.

The way you plan and present your speech can determine the number of audience members who stay with you until the end.

Writing a speech is similar to writing a paper. In both cases, you consider your purpose and ways to organize your ideas. Speeches are usually organized in three main parts: the introduction, the main body, and the conclusion.

Introduction. The introduction sets the stage for your audience. This is the time you make clear where you are taking them. Avoid rambling speeches with no clear organization. They put audiences to sleep. The following introduction, for example, tells exactly what is coming. The speech has three distinct parts, each in logical order.

Cock fighting is a cruel sport. I intend to describe exactly what happens to the birds, tell you who is doing this, and show you how you can stop this inhumane practice.

To make an effective speech, be precise about your purpose. Speeches can inform, persuade, motivate, or entertain. Choose what you want to do, and let your audience know what your intentions are.

Since the choice is yours, talk about things that hold your interest. Include your personal experiences. Start with a bang! Compare the following two introductions to speeches on the subject of world hunger.

Example number one:

I'm very honored to be here with you today. I intend to talk about malnutrition and starvation.

First, I want to outline the extent of these problems, then I will discuss some basic assumptions concerning world hunger, and I will propose some solutions.

You can almost hear the snores from the audience.

Example number two:

More people have died from hunger in the past five years than have been killed in all the wars, revolutions, and murders in the past 150 years. Yet there is enough food to go around. I'm honored to be with you today to discuss the problem. . . .

Though some members of an audience begin to drift during a speech, most people pay attention to the first few seconds of any speech. So the beginning sentences of your speech are the place to highlight your main points. One practical note: Before you begin, be sure you have the audience's attention. If people are still filing into the room or adjusting seats, they're not ready to listen.

Main body. The main body of the speech is the content—70 to 90 percent of most speeches. In the main body, you will develop your ideas in much the same way that you develop a written paper.

In speeches, transitions are especially important. Give your audience a signal when you change points: "On the other hand, until the public realizes what is happening to children in these countries . . ." or "The second reason hunger persists is. . . ."

In long speeches, recap from time to time and preview what's to come. Use facts, descriptions, expert opinions, and, statistics, to hold your audience's attention.

Conclusion. At the end of the speech, summarize your points and draw your conclusion. You started with a bang; now finish with drama. The first and last parts of a speech are the most important. Make it clear to your audience when you've reached the end. Avoid endings such as "This is the end of my speech". A simple standby is "So in conclusion, I want to reiterate three points: First. . . ." When you are finished, stop talking.

Using notes. Some professional speakers recommend writing key words on a few 3×5 cards. They make it easy to keep your speech in order. Number the cards so that if you drop them, you can quickly put them in order again. As you finish the information on each card, move it to the back of the pile. Write information clearly and in letters large enough to be seen from a distance.

The disadvantage of the 3×5 card system is that it involves a lot of card shuffling. Some speakers prefer to use standard outlined notes. Another option is mind mapping. Even an hour-long speech can be mapped on one sheet of paper. You can also use memory techniques to memorize the outline of your speech.

Ways to practice. The key to successful public speaking is practice. When you practice, do so in a loud voice. Your voice sounds different when you talk loudly, and this can be unnerving. Get used to it early.

If possible, practice in the room in which you will deliver your speech. Hear what your voice sounds like over a sound system. If you can't practice your speech in the actual room, at least visit the site ahead of time. Also make sure that the materials you will need for your speech, including audiovisual aids, will be available when you want them.

Record your speech and listen to it. Better yet, videotape your presentation. Many schools have video equipment available for students' use.

When practicing, listen for repeated phrases: *you know, kind of, really,* plus any little *uh*'s, *umm*'s, and *ah*'s. To get rid of these tell yourself that you intend to notice every time they pop up in your daily speech. When you hear them, tell yourself that you don't use those words anymore. Also ask someone else to monitor your speech for these phrases. Eventually, they are likely to disappear.

Practice your speech in front of friends or while looking in the mirror. Speaking before one or two friends builds confidence; it can be even more demanding than talking in front of a large group.

Use stress reduction techniques before and during your speech. Practice them ahead of time. Then, before you speak, visualize yourself in the room, successfully giving the speech.

When you practice your speech, avoid delivering it word for word, as if you were reading a script. Know your material and present the information in a way that is most natural for you. Diligent practice relieves you of having to rely heavily on your notes.

One more note about getting ready: If you want to get your message across, dress appropriately.

Delivering the speech. For some beginners, the biggest problem in delivering a speech is nervousness. If this is your concern, make it easier on yourself by knowing your material inside and out.

Nervousness is common. You can deal with it by noticing it. Tell yourself, "Yes, my hands are clammy. I notice that my stomach is slightly upset. My face feels numb." Allow these symptoms to exist. Experience them fully. When you do, those symptoms often become less persistent. Use the Power Process "Love your problems."

Also use the Power Process "Be here now." Be totally in the present moment. Notice how the room feels. Notice the temperature and lighting. See the audience. Look at them. Make eye contact. Notice all of your thoughts about how you feel and then gently release them.

Another technique is to look at your audience and imagine everyone dressed as clowns. Chances are that if you lighten up and enjoy your presentation, so will they.

When you speak, talk loudly enough to be heard. To help yourself project, avoid leaning over your notes or the podium. Also maintain eye contact. When you look at people, they become less frightening. Remember that it is easier to listen to someone who looks at you. Find a few friendly faces around the room and imagine that you are talking to them individually. If you notice a side conversation in the room, continue speaking and look directly at the people who are chatting. You will usually regain their attention.

You can increase the impact of words by keeping track of the time during your speech. Better to end early than run late. The conclusion of your speech is what is likely to be remembered, and you might lose this opportunity if people are looking at the clock. Use audiovisual aids, flip charts, and other props whenever possible.

Only a fraction of our communication is verbal. Be aware of what your body is telling your audience. Contrived or staged gestures will look dishonest. Be natural. If you don't know what to do with your hands, notice that. Then don't do anything with them.

Pause when appropriate. Beginners sometimes feel that they have to fill every moment with the sound of their voice.

After you speak. Review and reflect upon your performance: Did you finish on time? Did you cover all of the points you intended to cover? Was the audience attentive? Did you handle any nervousness effectively?

Welcome evaluation from others. Most of us find it difficult to hear criticism about our speaking. Be aware of resisting such criticism, and then let go of your resistance. Listening to feedback will increase your skill.

Employ your word

When you speak and give your word, you are creating—literally. Your speaking brings life to your values and purpose. In large part, others know who you are by the words you speak and the agreements you make. You can learn who you are by observing which commitments you choose to make and which ones you choose to avoid.

Your word makes things happen

Circumstances, events, and attitudes fall into place. The resources needed to accomplish whatever was promised become available. When you give your word, all this comes about.

The person you are right now is, for the most part, a result of the choices and agreements you've made in your life up to this point. Your future is largely determined by the choices and agreements you will make from this point on. By making and keeping agreements, you employ your word to create your future.

The world works by agreement

There are six billion people on planet Earth. We live on different continents, in different nations, and communicate in different languages. We have diverse political ideologies and subscribe to various social and moral codes.

This complex planetary network is held together by people keeping their word. Agreements minimize confusion, prevent social turmoil, and keep order. Projects are finished, goods are exchanged, and treaties are made. People, organizations, and nations know what to expect when agreements are kept. When people keep their word, the world works. Agreements are the foundation of many things that we often take for granted. Words, our basic tool of communication, work only because we agree about their meanings. A pencil is a pencil only because everyone agrees to call a thin, wood-covered column of graphite a pencil. We could just as easily call them ziddles. Then you might hear someone say, "Do you have an extra ziddle? I forgot mine."

Money exists only by agreement. If we leave a $100 MONOPOLY® bill (play money) on a park bench next to a real $100 bill (backed by the United States Treasury), one is more likely to disappear than the other. The only important difference between the two pieces of paper is that everyone agrees that one can be exchanged for goods and services and the other cannot. Shopkeepers will sell merchandise for the "real" $100 bill because they trust a continuing agreement.

Relationships work by agreement

Relationships are built on agreements. They begin with our most intimate personal contacts and move through all levels of families, organizations, communities, and nations.

When we break a promise to be faithful to a spouse, to help a friend move to a new apartment, or to pay a bill on time, relationships are strained and the consequences can be painful. When we keep our word, relationships are more likely to be satisfying and harmonious. Expectations of trust and accountability develop. Others are more likely to keep their promises to us.

Perhaps our most important relationship is the one we have with ourselves. Trusting ourselves to keep our word is enlivening. As we experience success, our self-confidence increases.

When we commit to complete a class assignment and then keep our word, our understanding of the subject improves. So does our grade. We experience satisfaction and success. If we break our word, we create a gap in our learning, a lower grade, and possibly negative feelings.

Ways to make and keep agreements

Being cautious about making agreements can improve the quality of our lives. Making only those promises that we fully intend to keep improves the likelihood of reaching our goals. We can ask ourselves what level of commitment we have to a particular promise.

At the same time, if we are willing to take risks, we can open new doors and increase our possibilities for success. The only way to ensure that we keep all of our agreements is either to make none or to make only those that are absolutely guaranteed. In either case, we are probably cheating ourselves. Some of the most powerful promises we can make are those that we have no idea how to keep. We can stretch ourselves and set goals that are both high and realistic.

If we break an agreement, we can choose to be gentle with ourselves. We can be courageous, quickly admit our mistake to the people involved, and consider ways to deal with the consequences.

Examining our agreements can improve our effectiveness. Perhaps we took on too much—or too little. Perhaps we did not use all of the resources that were available to us—or we used too many. Perhaps we did not fully understand what we were promising. When we learn from both our mistakes and our successes, we can become more effective at employing our word.

Move up the ladder of powerful speaking

The words used to talk about whether or not something will happen fall into several different levels. We can think of each level as one rung on a ladder—the ladder of powerful speaking. As we move up the ladder, our speaking becomes more effective.

- The lowest rung on the ladder is *obligation*. Words used at this level include *I should, he ought to, someone better, they need to, I must,* and *I had to*. Speaking this way implies that people and circumstances other than ourselves are in control of our lives. When we live at the level of obligation, we often feel passive and helpless to change anything.

Note: When we move to the next rung, we leave behind obligation and advance to self-responsibility. All of the rungs to come work together to reinforce this characteristic.

- The next rung up is *possibility*. At this level, we examine new options. We play with new ideas, possible solutions, and alternative courses of action. As we do, we learn that we can make choices that dramatically affect the quality of our lives. We are not the victims of circumstance. Phrases that signal this level include *I might, I could, I'll consider, I hope to,* and *maybe*.

- From possibility we can move to another rung—*preference*. Here we begin the process of choice. The words *I prefer* signal that we're moving toward one set of possibilities over another, perhaps setting the stage for eventual action.

- Above preference is a rung called *passion*. Again, certain words signal this level: *I want to, I'm really excited to do that, I can't wait*. Possibility and passion are both exciting places to be. Even at these levels, though, we're still far from action. Many of us want to achieve lots of things and have no specific plan for doing so.

- Action comes with the next rung—*planning*. When people use phrases such as *I intend to, my goal is to, I plan to,* and *I'll try like mad to,* they're at the level of planning. The Intention Statements you write in this book are examples of planning.

- The highest rung on the ladder is *promising*. This is where the power of your word really comes into play. At this level, it's common to use phrases such as these: *I will, I promise to, I am committed, you can count on it*. This is where we bridge from possibility and planning to action. Promising brings with it all of the rewards of employing your word.

master student
GREG LOUGANIS

four-time Olympic Gold Medal diving champion, published his autobiography in 1995 to tell his story of facing challenges of fear and discrimination regarding his Samoan heritage, dyslexia, substance abuse, sexual orientation, domestic violence, and living with AIDS.

Going into 1980, Ron and I talked about what we thought was possible for me at the upcoming Olympics in Moscow. Ron wasn't someone who talked about expectations, but based on how well I'd been doing at competitions, he thought it was possible for me to win both 3-meter springboard and 10-meter platform at the Olympic trials and at the Moscow Games. Ron didn't *expect* me to do it, but he thought it was possible, and we both thought it was something we could work toward. It was a goal to reach for...

It didn't matter how much effort I made in preparing for the Olympics, because history intervened and there was no 1980 Olympics for the U. S. Olympic team. The Soviet Union invaded Afghanistan in December 1979, and President Carter demonstrated the U. S. government's displeasure by deciding to boycott the Moscow Olympics.

Despite the boycott, we still had the Olympic trials. At first it was like we were just going through the motions. The trials were held at the end of June, in Austin, Texas, at the

Texas Swimming Center at the University of Texas. Fifty-three of the top men and women divers from around the country came to compete.

Success in diving is never guaranteed. All it takes is one mistake, and you can blow your entire lead. I had to concentrate from my first dive to my last.

In the springboard competition, I was happiest with my seventh dive of the final round, a reverse two-and-a-half pike, which is a difficult dive. I got six 10's and a 9.5, an almost-perfect score. My total score at the end of the final round was 940 points, 28 points ahead of the second-place finisher. Then on platform I finished 65 points ahead of the next diver. I scored several 10's in that round despite the fact that I cut my palm on a pipe at the bottom of the 18-foot pool on my first dive.

When you dive off the 10-meter platform, you're going at 32 miles per hour when you hit the water, and your hands hit the water first. So with a cut palm, it really hurt. But by that point in my career, I didn't let a minor injury get in the way of a good dive.

Ron once told me that I dove with more pain and suffering and sickness than any diver he had ever had. A lot of my injuries were just routine, sprains and stomach viruses, but sometimes I did klutzy things. One time I sat down on a glass when I was in a boat and cut my butt. That

doesn't sound like anything big, but when you're in the middle of a dive and you're pulling your legs up to your chest, the stitches hurt like crazy.

A week later, I was diving on springboard and I slipped going up the ladder and gashed and bruised my leg right on the spot where I had to grab my leg and squeeze hard during the dive. Each time I dove I wanted to scream.

Another time, I had some warts on my hands and feet that I needed to have removed. I don't know why I decided to do it ten days before the nationals. That doesn't sound like such a big deal, but when I hit the water from the 10-meter platform, the pain brought tears to my eyes.

One time I almost didn't get through it. At the national championships in Indianapolis in 1986, I caught a stomach virus. I was very sick, but I did a few dives, went into the bathroom, threw up, and came back out and did a few more dives. I don't know how, but I won.

I may cry easily, but I never give up.

From Breaking the Surface *by Greg Louganis with Eric Marcus. Copyright © 1995 by Greg Louganis. Reprinted by permission of Random House, Inc.*

For more biographical information about Greg Louganis, visit Houghton Mifflin's College Survival/Becoming a Master Student web site: http://collegesurvival.college.hmco.com/students.

1 What is the difference between *encoding* and *decoding* as explained in this chapter?

 2 One suggested guideline for nonverbal listening is to respond frequently to the speaker. True or False? Explain your answer.

 3 The suggested techniques for verbal listening include which of the following?
   (A) Parrot exactly what another person says.
   (B) Pay attention to the speaker's words and not the emotions behind the words.
   (C) Always put your own concerns aside in order to listen attentively.
   (D) Look for the requests hidden in complaints.

 4 Reword the following complaint as a request: "You always interrupt when I talk!"

 5 List the five parts of an "I" message (the five ways to say "I").

 6 The fact that a disagreement is getting worse means that there's little hope for conflict resolution. True or False? Explain your answer.

 7 Which of the following is an effective thesis statement? Explain your answer.
   (A) Two types of thinking.
   (B) Critical thinking and creative thinking go hand in hand.
   (C) The relationship between critical thinking and creative thinking.

8 Define *plagiarism* and explain ways to avoid it.

 9 Describe at least three techniques for practicing and delivering a speech.

 10 What characteristic distinguishes the top five rungs of the ladder of powerful speaking from the bottom rung?

JOURNAL ENTRY

#41

Discovery/Intention Statement

Review what you learned in this chapter about listening and describe your current level of skill as a listener.

I discovered that…

_____

_____

_____

Now choose a suggestion from this chapter that could immediately apply to one of your current relationships. Describe how you will supply this suggestion.

I intend to…

_____

_____

_____

LEARNING STYLES APPLICATION   CHAPTER 8

Mode 4 Explain how you will approach conflict management differently, having read this chapter and having applied several of its ideas.

Mode 1 Think of a conflict you are experiencing right now with an important person in your life. (If you cannot think of one, recall a conflict you've experienced in the past.) Do you think that any of the ideas in this chapter could help you resolve this conflict? Explain your answer.

Mode 3 From the five suggestions you listed for Mode 2, choose two that you will definitely commit to using. Describe when and where you plan to use each suggestion.

Mode 2 After reviewing this chapter, choose five specific suggestions that could help you resolve the conflict you listed for Mode 1.

BIBLIOGRAPHY

INTERNET RESOURCES

ENDNOTES

1 Virginia Satir, *Peoplemaking* (Palo Alto, CA: Science and Behavior, 1972).

2 Carl Rogers, *On Becoming a Person* (Boston: Houghton Mifflin, 1961).

3 Thomas Gordon, *Parent Effectiveness Training: The Tested New Way to Raise Responsible Children* (New York: New American Library, 1975).

4 Sidney Jourard, *The Transparent Self* (New York: Van Nostrand, 1971).

5 Peter Elbow, *Writing with Power: Techniques for Mastering the Writing Process* (New York: Oxford University Press, 1981).

6 Natalie Goldberg, *Writing Down the Bones: Freeing the Writer Within* (Boston: Shambhala, 1992).

7 Theodore Cheney, *Getting the Words Right: How to Revise, Edit and Rewrite* (Cincinnati, OH: Writer's Digest, 1983).

ADDITIONAL READING

Deida, David. *The Way of the Superior Man.* Austin, TX: Plexus, 1997.

Gibaldi, Joseph. *MLA Handbook for Writers of Research Papers.* New York: Modern Language Association, 1999.

Pennebaker, James W. *Opening Up: The Healing Power of Confiding in Others.* New York: Morrow, 1990.

Strunk, William, Jr., and E. B. White. *The Elements of Style.* New York: Macmillan, 1979.

Ueland, Brenda. *If You Want to Write: A Book About Art, Independence and Spirit.* St. Paul, MN: Graywolf, 1987.

Advanced Public Speaking Institute
http://www.public-speaking.org/

A Guide for Writing Research Papers based on MLA
http://webster.commnet.edu/mla.htm

LEO: Literacy Education Online
http://leo.stcloudstate.edu/

Public Speaking Resource Center
http://college.hmco.com/communication/resources/students/public.html

Yahoo! Links-Writing
dir.yahoo.com/Social_Science/Communications/Writing/

Diversity

Candor is a compliment; it implies equality. It's how true friends talk.
PEGGY NOONAN

We don't see things as they are; we see things as we are.
ANÄIS NIN

IN THIS CHAPTER . . . Take your skills at living with diversity to a new level by communicating across cultures and dealing with sexism and sexual harassment. If you're returning to school after a long absence, you can learn the art of re-entry. Also increase your effectiveness by adapting to the culture of higher education, becoming a leader, and choosing your conversations and your community.

Living with diversity

Those of us who can study, work, and live with people from other cultures, economic classes, and races can enjoy more success at school, on the job, and in our neighborhoods. Sharing in this success means learning new ways to think, speak, and act. Learning about diversity opens up a myriad of possibilities—an education in itself. At first, this can seem frightening, frustrating, or even painful. It can also be exciting, enriching, and affirming.

Our classrooms, offices, and factories will become a "rainbow coalition" of people from many different cultures, socioeconomic backgrounds, and races. The people called "minorities" in this country are already a numerical majority across the world. According to the world population profile from the U.S. Bureau of the Census, China and India account for almost two of every five people on earth. The more developed countries make up only 20 percent of the world's population, and the population of the United States makes up less than 5 percent of our global village.

By the year 2056, the "average" United States resident will list his or her ancestry as African, Asian, Hispanic, or Arabic—not white European. In many city school systems, Caucasian students are already in the minority. This is not the result of government policy or pressure from special interest groups. It simply is a fact—one for which some people feel ill-prepared.

The cultures of the world meet daily. Several forces are shrinking our globe. One is the growth of a world economy. Another is the "electronic village" forged across nations by newspapers, radios, televisions, telephones, fax machines, and computers.

We have an opportunity to benefit from this change instead of merely reacting to it. At one time, only sociologists and futurists talked about the meeting of cultures. Now all of us can enter this conversation. We can value cultural diversity and learn how to thrive with it.

JOURNAL ENTRY #42

Discovery Statement

Brainstorm some possible benefits you could gain by getting along more effectively with people of other races or ethnic groups. Write your ideas on a separate sheet of paper.

Next, preview this chapter for any ideas or techniques that could help you attain these benefits. Briefly sum up those ideas below.

_____

_____

_____

_____

_____

_____

_____

_____

_____

_____

_____

_____

_____

JOURNAL ENTRY #43

Discovery Statement

On a separate sheet of paper, describe an incident in which you were discriminated against because you differed in some way from the other people involved. This could be any kind of difference, such as hair length, style of clothing, political affiliation, religion, skin color, sexual orientation, age, gender, economic status, or accent. How would you have liked the other people to have responded to you?

Now describe an incident in which someone you know experienced a similar kind of discrimination. Scan this chapter for ideas that could help you respond more effectively to such discrimination and list those ideas below.

Describe a time you may have discriminated against someone, or treated someone differently, because of a difference.

Diversity is real—

We have always lived with people of different races and cultures. Many of us come from families who immigrated to the United States or Canada just two or three generations ago. The things we eat, the tools we use, and the words we speak are a cultural tapestry woven by many different peoples.

Think about a common daily routine. A typical American citizen awakens in a bed (an invention from the Near East). After dressing in clothes (often designed in Italy), she eats breakfast on plates (made in China), eats a banana (grown in Honduras), and brews coffee (shipped from Nicaragua). After breakfast, she reads the morning newspaper (printed by a process invented in Germany on paper, which was first made in China). Then she flips on a tape player (made in Japan) and listens to music (possibly performed by a band from Cuba).

Multiculturalism refers to racial and ethnic diversity—and many other kinds of diversity as well. As anthropologist Dorothy Lee reminds us, culture is simply one society's solutions to perennial human problems, such as how to worship, celebrate, resolve conflict, work, think, and learn.[1] Culture is a set of learned behaviors—a broader concept than race, which refers to the biological makeup of people.

From this standpoint, we can speak of the culture of large corporations or the culture of the fine arts. There are the cultures of men and women; heterosexual, homosexual,

and bisexual people; and older and younger people. There are differences between urban and rural dwellers, between people who are able-bodied and those with disabilities, and between people from two-parent families and people from single-parent families. There are social classes based on differences in standards of living. And diversity in religion is a factor, too. This can be especially difficult to accept, since many of us identify strongly with our religious faith.

In some respects, culture can be compared to an iceberg. Only parts of any given culture—such as language patterns or distinctive apparel—exist on a visible level. Just as most of an iceberg lies under water and out of sight, many aspects of culture lie beneath our conscious awareness. This invisible realm includes assumptions about the meanings of beauty and friendship, the concepts of sin and justice, approaches to problem solving, interpretations of eye contact and body language, and patterns of supervisor and employee relationships.

People can differ in countless ways—race, gender, ethnic group, sexual orientation, and more. The suggestions offered in this chapter can help you respond effectively to the many kinds of diversity you'll encounter. Higher education could be your chance to develop an attitude of tolerance, open-mindedness, and respect for individual differences.

Discrimination is also real.
The ability to live with diversity is now more critical than ever. Racism, homophobia, and other forms of discrimination still exist, even on campuses. According to the FBI, a total of 7,876 hate crimes took place in the United States during 1999. Of those crimes, 6,535 were based on the victim's race, national origin, or religion; another 1,317 were based on sexual orientation. Nearly 10 percent of these crimes took place in college and other school settings.

Of course, discrimination can be far more subtle than hate crime. Imagine how you would respond to the following situations:

- Members of a sociology class are debating the merits of reforming the state's welfare system. The instructor calls on a student from a reservation and says, "Tell us. What's

and valuable

the Native American perspective on this issue anyway?" Here the student is being typecast as a spokesperson for her entire ethnic group.

- Students in a mass media communications class are learning to think critically about television programs. They're talking about a situation comedy set in an urban high-rise apartment building with mostly African American residents. "Man, they really whitewashed that show," says one student. "It's mostly about inner-city black people, but they didn't show anybody on welfare, doing drugs, or joining gangs." The student's comment perpetuates common racial stereotypes.

- On the first day of the term, students taking English composition enter a class taught by a professor from Puerto Rico. One of the students asks the professor, "Am I in the right class? Maybe there's been a mistake. I thought this was supposed to be an English class, not a Spanish class." The student assumed that only Caucasian people can be qualified to teach English courses.

Forrest Toms of Training Research and Development defines racism as "prejudice plus power"—the power to define reality, to enshrine one set of biases. The operating assumption behind racism is that differences mean deficits.

When racism lives, we all lose—even those groups with social and political power. We lose the ability to make friends and to function effectively on teams. We crush human potential. People without the skills to bridge cultures are already at a disadvantage.

Higher education offers a chance to change this. Academic environments can become cultural laboratories—places for you to meet people of other races and cultures in an atmosphere of tolerance. People who create alliances outside their immediate group are preparing to succeed in both school and work.

Diversity is valuable.
Synergy is the idea that the whole is more than the sum of its parts. Consider some examples: A symphony orchestra consists of many different instruments; when played together, their effect is multiplied many times. A football team has members with different specialties, but together they can win a league championship.

Diversity in a society offers another example of synergy. It takes no more energy to believe that differences enrich us than it does to believe that differences endanger us. Embracing diversity adds value to any organization and can be far more exciting than just meeting the minimum requirements for affirmative action.

Today we are waking up not only to the *fact* of diversity but also to the *value* of diversity. Biologists tell us that diversity of animal species benefits our ecology. The same idea applies to the human species. Through education our goal can be to see that we are part of a complex world—that our culture is different from, not better than, others. Knowing this, we can stop saying, "This is the way to work, learn, relate to others, and view the world." Instead, we can say, "Here is the way I have been doing it. I would also like to see your way."

Accepting diversity does not mean ignoring the differences among cultures so that we all become part of a faceless "melting pot." Instead, we can become more like a mosaic—a piece of art in which each element maintains its individuality and blends with others to form a harmonious whole.

Learning to live with diversity is a process of returning to "beginner's mind"—a place where we question our biases and assumptions. This is a magical place, a place of new beginnings and options. It takes courage to dwell in beginner's mind—courage to go outside the confines of our own culture and world-view. It can feel uncomfortable at first. Yet there are lasting rewards to gain.

As you read the following articles, look to yourself. This chapter aims to help you examine your own biases. With knowledge about your prejudices, you can go beyond them. You can discover ways to communicate across cultures.

Each idea in this chapter is merely a starting point. When it comes to overcoming the long history of prejudice and discrimination, there are no quick, easy answers. Continue to experiment and see what works for you. As you read, constantly ask: How can I use this material to live and work more effectively in a multicultural world? The answers could change your life.

Student Voices
A master student tries on other people's skin, and it is not judgmental. We are all different and a master student accepts that diversity.

— LYNN LINEBERGER

Communicating with people of other cultures is a learned skill—a habit. According to management consultant Stephen R. Covey, a habit is the point at which desire, knowledge, and skill meet.[2] Desire is about wanting to do something. Knowledge is understanding what to do. And skill is the ability to do it.

Desire, knowledge, and skill are equally important for bridging gaps in cultural understanding. This article speaks to the first two factors—*desire* and *knowledge*—and also provides suggestions for gaining *skill*.

Desire to communicate.

When our actions are grounded in a sincere desire to understand others, we can be much more effective. Knowing techniques for communicating across cultures is valuable. At the same time, this cannot take the place of the sincere desire and commitment to create understanding. If you truly value cultural diversity, you can discover and create ways to build bridges between people.

Communicating

Know about other cultures.

Back up your desire with knowledge. People from different cultures read differently, write differently, think differently, eat differently, and learn differently than you. Knowing this, you can be more effective with your classmates, coworkers, and neighbors.

Cultures also differ in a variety of dimensions. One of the most important dimensions is *style*. We can also speak of learning styles, communication styles, relationship styles, and other styles.

James Anderson, dean of the Division of Undergraduate Studies at North Carolina State University, speaks of the relationship between analytical and relational styles.[3] Most of our schools favor students with an analytical style. These students learn abstract concepts easily and are adept at reading, writing, and discussing ideas. They can learn parts of a subject even if they don't have a view of the whole. Often these students are self-directed, and their performance is not affected by the opinions of others.

A bias toward the analytical style tends to exclude students with a relational style—students who learn by getting the big picture of a subject before the details. They learn better initially by speaking, listening, and doing rather than by reading or writing. These students prefer to learn about subjects that relate to their concerns or are presented in a lively, humorous way. In addition, they are influenced by the opinions of people they value and respect. All of these things point to a unique learning style.

Differing styles exist in every aspect of life—family structure, religion, relationships with authority, and more. Native Americans might avoid conflict and seek mediators. People from certain Asian cultures might feel that it's rude to ask questions. Knowing about such differences can help avoid misunderstandings.

Today there is a wealth of material about cultural diversity. The greater our knowledge of other cultures, the easier it is for us to be tolerant. The more we explore our differences, the more we can discover our similarities.

Begin with an intention to increase your sensitivity toward other cultures. Be willing to ask questions and share ideas with all kinds of people. Just get the conversation started. You can learn something valuable from anyone when you reach out.

Develop skills.

With the desire to communicate and gain knowledge of other cultures, you can develop specific skills on three levels. The first is personal—becoming aware of your own biases. The second is interpersonal—forming alliances with people of other races and cultures. The third is institutional—pointing out the discrimination and racism that you observe in organizations. Be an advocate for change.

Be active.

Learning implies activity. Learning ways to communicate across cultures is no exception. It's ineffective to assume that this skill will come to you merely by sharing the same classroom with people from other races and ethnic groups. It's not the responsibility of others to raise your cultural awareness. That job is yours, and it calls for energy.

across cultures

Think critically.

Communicating across cultures is closely linked to critical thinking. To embrace diversity, we can learn to avoid errors of perception, judgment, and premature reaction. (Many of these are explained further by Vincent Ryan Ruggiero in the book *Becoming a Critical Thinker.*)

Stereotypes offer examples of poor critical thinking. When we hear statements such as "Black people depend on welfare," we can shift our thinking skills into high gear. We can ask for evidence and uncover accurate

information—for example, the fact that most black people do not depend on welfare.

Within stereotypes we can sometimes find a kernel of truth. An example is the statement "Women are highly emotional." True, some women focus on emotional responses as they learn. And so do some men. When we make statements about a whole group of people based on attributes of a few of its members, we put on the blinders of prejudice. One path to escape stereotypes is critical thinking.

Look for common ground.

Some goals cross culture lines. Most people want health, physical safety, economic security, and education.

Most students want to succeed in school and prepare for a career. They often share the same teachers. They have access to many of the same resources at school. They meet in the classroom, on the athletic field, and at cultural events. To promote cultural understanding, we can become aware of and celebrate our differences. We can also return to our common ground.

Practice looking for common ground. You can cultivate friends from other cultures. Do this through volunteering, serving on committees, or joining study groups—any activity in which people from other cultures are also involved. Then your understanding of other people unfolds in a natural, spontaneous way.

The trick is to keep a balance, to honor the differences among people while remembering what we have in common.

Assume differences in meaning.

Each day we can make an intention to act and speak with the awareness that cultures differ. One option is to look for several possible meanings of our words and actions.

Assume that differences in meaning exist, even if you don't know what they are. After first speaking to someone from another culture, don't assume that you've been understood or that you fully understand the other person. The same action can have different meanings at different times, even for members of the same

knowledge

culture. Check it out. Verify what you think you have heard. Listen to see if what you spoke is what the other person received.

If you're speaking to someone who doesn't understand English well, keep the following ideas in mind:

- Speak slowly and distinctly.
- To clarify your statement, don't repeat individual words over and over again. Restate your entire message in simple, direct language. Avoid slang.
- Use gestures to accompany your words.

skill

- Since English courses for non-native speakers often emphasize written English, write down what you're saying. Print your message in capitalized block letters.
- Stay calm and avoid sending nonverbal messages that you're frustrated.

Look for individuals, not group representatives.
Sometimes the way we speak glosses over differences among individuals and reinforces stereotypes. For example, a student worried about her grade in math expresses concern over "all those Asian students who are skewing the class curve." Or a Caucasian music major assumes that her African American classmate knows a lot about jazz. We can avoid such errors by seeing people as individuals—not spokespersons for an entire group.

Get inside another culture.
You might find yourself fascinated by one particular culture. Consider learning as much about it as possible. Immerse yourself in that culture. Read novels, see plays, go to concerts, listen to music, look at art, take courses, learn the language. Find opportunities to speak with members of that culture. Your knowledge will be an opening to new conversations.

Celebrate your own culture.
Learning about other cultures does not mean abandoning your own. You could gain new appreciation for it. You might even find out that members of your ethnic group have suffered discrimination—for example, that Irish people once lived in ghettos in the United Kingdom. In the process, you can gain new insight into the experiences of other people.

Find a translator, mediator, or model.
People who move with ease in two or more cultures can help us greatly.

Diane de Anda, a professor at the University of California, Los Angeles, speaks of three kinds of people who can communicate across cultures. She calls them *translators, mediators,* and *models.*[4]

A translator is someone who is truly bicultural—a person who relates skillfully to people in a mainstream culture and people from a contrasting culture. This person can share her own experiences in overcoming discrimination, learning another language or dialect, and coping with stress. She can point out differences in meaning between cultures and help resolve conflict.

Mediators are people who belong to the dominant or mainstream culture. Unlike translators, they might not be bicultural. However, mediators value diversity and are committed to cultural understanding. Often they are teachers, counselors, tutors, mentors, or social workers.

Models are members of a culture who are positive examples. They are students from any racial or cultural group who participate in class and demonstrate effective study habits. Models can also include entertainers, athletes, and community leaders.

Your school might have people who serve these functions, even if they're not labeled translators, mediators, or models. Some schools have mentor or "bridge" programs that pair new students with teachers of the same race or culture. Students in these programs get coaching in study skills and life skills; they also develop friendships with a possible role model. Ask your student counseling service about such programs.

Develop support systems.
Many students find that their social adjustment affects their academic performance. Students with strong support systems—such as families, friends, churches, self-help groups, and mentors—are using a powerful strategy for success in

school. As an exercise, list the support systems that you rely on right now. Also list new support systems you could develop.

Support systems can help you bridge culture gaps. With a strong base of support in your own group, you can feel more confident in meeting people outside that group.

Ask for help.

If you're unsure about how well you're communicating, ask questions: "I don't know how to make this idea clear for you. How might I communicate better?" "When you look away from me during our conversation, I feel uneasy. Is there something else we need to talk about?" "When you don't ask questions, I wonder if I am being clear. Do you want any more explanation?" Questions such as these can get cultural differences out in the open in a constructive way.

Remember diversity when managing conflict.

While in school or on the job, you might come into conflict with a person from another culture. Conflict is challenging enough to manage when it occurs between members of the same culture. When conflict gets enmeshed with cultural differences, the situation can become even more difficult.

Fortunately, many of the guidelines offered in the Communicating chapter about managing conflict apply across cultures. Also keep the following suggestions in mind:

- *Keep your temper in check.* People from other cultures might shrink from displays of sudden, negative emotion—for example, shouting or pointing.
- *Deliver your criticisms in private.* People in many Asian and Middle

Eastern cultures place value on "saving face" in public.

- *Give the other person space.* Standing too close can be seen as a gesture of intimidation.
- *Address people as equals.* For example, don't offer the other person a chair so that she can sit while you stand and talk.
- *Stick to the point.* When feeling angry or afraid, you might talk more than usual. A person from another culture—especially one who's learning your language—might find it hard to take in everything you're saying. Pause from time to time so that others can ask clarifying questions.
- *Focus on actions, not personalities.* People are less likely to feel personally attacked when you request specific changes in behavior. "Please show up for work right at 9 a.m." is often more effective than "You're irresponsible."
- *Be patient.* This guideline applies especially when you're a manager or supervisor. People from other cultures might find it difficult to speak candidly with someone they view as an authority figure. Encourage others to speak. Allowing periods of silence might help.
- *Take time to comment when others do well.* However, avoid excessive compliments. People from other cultures might be uncomfortable with public praise and even question your sincerity.

Change the institution.

None of us are individuals living in isolation. We live in systems that can be racist. As a student, you might see people of color ignored in class. You might see people of a certain ethnic group passed over in job hiring or underrepresented in school organizations. And you might see gay and lesbian students ridiculed or even threatened with violence. One way to stop these actions is to point them out.

Federal civil rights laws, as well as the written policies of most schools, ban racial and ethnic discrimination. If your school receives federal aid, it must set up procedures that protect students against such discrimination. Find out what those procedures are and use them, if necessary.

Throughout recent history, much social change has been fueled by students. When it comes to ending discrimination, you are in an environment where you can make a difference. Run for student government. Write for school publications. Speak at rallies. Express your viewpoint. This is training for citizenship in a multicultural world.

Reap the rewards.

The price we pay for failure to understand other cultures is fear and bigotry—the assumption that one group has the right to define all others. Attitudes such as these cannot withstand the light of knowledge, compassion, and common values.

WORKPLACE APPLICATIONS

When you work with people from other cultures, look for common ground in values related to employment that you share. Possibilities include the desire to gain recognition, win a promotion, provide financial security for a family—or simply to have fun.

The art of reentry
Going back to school as an older student

If you're returning to school after a long break from the classroom, there's no reason to feel out of place. Returning adults and other nontraditional students are already a majority in some schools.

Being an older student puts you on strong footing. With a rich store of life experience on which to draw, you can ask meaningful questions and more easily make connections between course work and daily life. Many instructors will especially enjoy working with you.

Following are some suggestions for returning adult students. Even if you don't fit into this category, you can look for ways to apply these ideas.

Ease into it.   If you're new to higher education, consider easing into it. You can choose to attend school part-time before making a full-time commitment.

Plan your week.   Many older students report that their number one problem is time. One solution is to plan your week. By planning a week at a time instead of just one day ahead, you get a bigger picture of your roles as student, employee, and family member. For more suggestions on managing time, see the Time chapter.

Delegate tasks.   Consider hiring others to do some of your household work or errands. Yes, this costs money. It's also an investment in your education and future earning power.

If you have children, delegate some of the chores to them. Or start a meal co-op in your neighborhood. Cook dinner for yourself and someone else one night each week. In return, ask that person to furnish you with a meal on another night. A similar strategy can apply to childcare and other household tasks.

Add 15 minutes to your day.   If you're pressed for time, get up 15 minutes earlier or stay up 15 minutes later. Chances are, the lost sleep won't affect your alertness during the day. You can use the extra time to scan a reading assignment or outline a paper. Stretching each day by just 15 minutes yields 91 extra hours in a year. That's time you can use to promote your success in school.

Get to know younger students.
You share a central goal with younger students: succeeding in school. It's easier to get past the generation gap when you remember this. Consider pooling resources with younger students. Share notes, form study groups, or edit each other's term papers.

Get to know other returning students.   Introduce yourself to other older students. Being in the same classroom gives you an immediate bond. You can exchange work and home phone numbers, and build a network of mutual support. Some students adopt a buddy system, pairing up with another student in each class to complete assignments and prepare for tests.

Find common ground with instructors.   Many of your teachers might be juggling academic careers, work schedules, and family lives, too. Finding common ground gives you one more way to break the ice with instructors.

Enlist your employer's support.
Employers often promote continuing education. Further education can increase your skills either in a specific subject or in working with people. That makes you a more valuable employee or consultant.

Let your employer in on your educational plans. Point out how the skills you gain in class will help you meet work objectives. Offer informal "seminars" at work to share what you're learning in school.

Get extra mileage out of your current tasks.
You can look for specific ways to merge your work and school lives. Some schools will offer academic credit for work and life experience. Your company might reimburse its employees for some tuition costs or even grant time off to attend classes.

Experiment with combining tasks. For example, when you're assigned a research paper, choose a topic that relates to your current job tasks.

Look for childcare.
For some students, returning to class means looking for childcare outside the home. Many schools offer childcare facilities at reduced rates for students.

Review your subjects before you start classes.
Say that you're registered for trigonometry and you haven't taken a math class since high school. Consider brushing up on the subject before classes begin. Also talk with future instructors about ways to prepare for their classes.

Prepare for an academic environment.
If you're used to an efficient corporate setting, school life might present some frustrations. A lack of advanced computer systems might slow down your class registration. Faculty members might take a little longer to return your calls or respond to letters, especially during holiday and summer breaks. Knowing the rhythm of academic life can help you plan around these possibilities.

Be willing to let go of old images about how to study.
Rather than returning to study habits from previous school experiences, many older students find it more effective to view their school assignments exactly as they would view a project at work. They use the same tactics in the library as on the job, which often helps them learn more actively.

"Publish" your schedule.
After you plan your study and class sessions for the week, post your schedule in a place where others who live with you will see it. You can treat this as a game. Make your schedule look like an "official" document. Laminate a daily calendar, fill in your schedule with a magic marker, and post this in a high-traffic area in your house. Designate open slots in your schedule where others can sign up for "appointments" to see you. If you use an online calendar, print out copies to put in your school binder or on your refrigerator door, mirror, or closet.

Share your educational plans.
The fact that you're in school will affect the key relationships in your life. Committing yourself to attending classes and studying on your own time might prompt feelings of guilt about taking time away from others. You can prevent problems by discussing these issues ahead of time. Another strategy is to actively involve your spouse, partner, children, or close friends in your schooling. Offer to give them a tour of the school and introduce them to your instructors.

Take this a step further and ask the key people in your life for help. Ask them to think of ways that they can support your success in school and to commit to those actions. Make your own education a joint mission that benefits all of you.

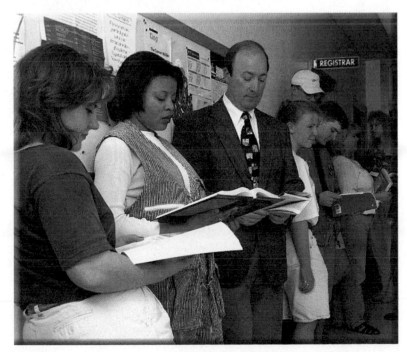

Adapting to the culture of higher education

You share one thing in common with other students at your vocational school, college, or university: Entering higher education represents a change in your life. You've joined a new culture with its own set of rules, both spoken and unspoken. The skills you practice in making this transition can apply to any transition in life—whether it's beginning a new relationship or relocating to a new community.

Begin by taking a First Step about your reactions to entering higher education. It's OK to feel anxious, isolated, homesick, or worried about doing well academically. Such emotions are common among first-time students.

One of the few constants in life is the fact of change. All of the cells in your body will regenerate many times during your life. The thoughts, feelings, and behaviors that make up your sense of self are also in flux. That's especially true as you enter a new environment. This fact of change can work in your favor. Chances are that any initial discomfort you feel about academic life will wane over time.

For more help in making the transition to higher education, consider the following.

Understand that higher education differs from high school.
Even if you attended high school many years ago, you might find it useful to review some basic differences between secondary and post-secondary education. Unlike high school, higher education is optional. If you've gone to public schools all your life, you've probably never had tuition payments to worry about. With higher education that changes, too.

Higher education presents you with more choices—where to attend school, how to structure your time, what to study, and with whom to associate. You might experience new academic standards as well.

Often there are fewer tests in higher education than in high school, and the grading might be tougher. You'll probably find that teachers expect you to study more than you did in high school. At the same time, your instructors might give you less guidance about what or how to study.

Watch for differences in teaching styles. Instructors at colleges, universities, and vocational schools are often steeped in their subject matter. Many did not take courses in how to teach. They might not be as engaging as some of your high school teachers. And some professors are more interested in research than in teaching. Once you understand such differences, you can better accept and work with them.

Balance work and school schedules.
Full-time students can find that working too many hours outside class compromises their success in school. This is especially true during their first year of higher education. As you coordinate your work and study schedules, consider the limits on your energy and time. Also create "buffer zones" in your schedule—pockets of unplanned time that you can use for unforeseen events.

Decrease the unknowns. Before classes begin, get a map of the school property and walk through your first day's schedule, perhaps with a classmate or friend. Visit your instructors in their offices and introduce yourself. Anything you can do to get familiar with the new routine will help.

Seek stability zones. Not all the facets of your life have to change at the same time. Balance change in one area with stability in another. While in school, keep in contact with family members and old friends. Maintain long-term relationships, including relationships with key places, such as your childhood home. Postpone other major changes for now.

Form support systems. With higher education might come a kind of culture shock and the thought "I don't know who I am anymore." To deal with this, build support systems into your life. Cultivate new friendships, including those with members of other races and cultures. School activities, student services, and study groups are ways to get support. Student services include career planning and placement, counseling services, financial aid, student ombudspersons, language clubs, and programs for minority students.

Remember earlier transitions. Recall times in the past when you coped with major change. Write Discovery Statements describing those experiences in detail. List any strategies you used to make those transitions effectively. You've weathered major change before, and you can do it again.

Work with your academic advisor. Meet with your academic advisor regularly. This person has a big picture of all the resources available at the school and how they can benefit you. Your school might offer peer advisory programs as well.

Even when you work with an advisor, you're still in charge of your education. Don't be afraid to change advisors when that seems appropriate.

Take the initiative in meeting new people. Promise yourself to meet one new person each week, and write an Intention Statement describing specific ways to do this. Introduce yourself to classmates. Prime times to do that are just before and after class. Realize that most of the people in this new world of higher education are waiting to be welcomed. You can help them and help yourself at the same time.

Choose an issue that allows for several different viewpoints—for example, gun control, legal rights for homosexual couples, or human cloning. Then form the strongest possible arguments for at least two points of view regarding this issue. Include a viewpoint that's different from your current one. On a separate piece of paper, summarize each point of view in one sentence.

Now examine your two sets of arguments. What impact did this exercise have on your own thoughts about this issue? In a short paragraph, describe your conclusions.

Find a short editorial in your local newspaper. Then, on a separate sheet of paper, rewrite the editorial twice based on the following criteria about the source of truth:

• To be true, any point of view must be consistent with my own cultural or religious traditions.

• To be true, any point of view must be consistent with the findings of science.

Review both of your rewritten editorials. If the act of writing changed your viewpoint on this issue, describe that change on a separate piece of paper. Perhaps you can create a point of view that satisfies both of the criteria mentioned above. If so, summarize that viewpoint in a sentence or two as well.

Dealing with sexism and

Sexism and sexual harassment are real. They are terms for events that occur at vocational schools, colleges, and universities throughout the world. Nearly all of these incidents are illegal or against school policies.

In the United States, women make up the majority of first-year students in higher education. Yet until the early nineteenth century, they were banned from colleges and universities. Today women in higher education still encounter bias based on gender.

This bias can take many forms. For example, instructors might gloss over the contributions of women. Students in philosophy class might never hear of a woman named Hypatia, an ancient Greek philosopher and mathematician. Those majoring in computer science might never learn about Grace Hopper, who developed a computer language named COBOL. And your art history textbook might not mention the Mexican painter Frida Kahlo or the American painter Georgia O'Keeffe.

Though men can be subjects of sexism and sexual harassment, women are more likely to experience this form of discrimination. Even the most well-intentioned people might behave in ways that hurt or discount women. Sexism takes place when:

- Instructors use only masculine pronouns—*he, his,* and *him*—to refer to both men and women.

- Career counselors hint that careers in mathematics and science are not appropriate for women.

- Students pay more attention to feedback from a male teacher than from a female teacher.

- Women are not called on in class, their comments are ignored, or they are overly praised for answering the simplest questions.

- Examples given in a textbook or lecture assign women only to traditionally "female" roles—wife, mother, day care provider, elementary school teacher, nurse, and the like.

- People assume that middle-aged women who return to school have too many family commitments to study adequately or do well in their classes.

Many kinds of behavior—both verbal and physical—fall under the title of sexual harassment. This kind of discrimination involves unwelcome sexual conduct. Examples of such conduct in a school setting are:

- Sexual touching or advances.
- Any other unwanted touch.
- Unwanted verbal intimacy.
- Sexual graffiti.
- Displaying or distributing sexually explicit materials.
- Sexual gestures and jokes.
- Pressure for sexual favors.
- Talking about personal sexual activity.
- Spreading rumors about someone's sexual activity or rating someone's sexual performance.

Sexual Harassment: It's Not Academic, a pamphlet from the U.S. Department of Education, quotes a woman who experienced sexual harassment in higher education: "The financial officer made it clear that I could get the money I needed if I slept with him."

That's an example of *quid pro quo harassment.* This legal term applies when students believe that an educational decision depends on submitting to unwelcome sexual conduct. *Hostile environment harassment* takes place when such incidents are severe, persistent, or pervasive.

The feminist movement has raised our awareness about discrimination against women. We can now respond to sexism and sexual harassment in the places we live, work, and go to school. Specific strategies follow.

Point out sexist language and behavior

When you see examples of sexism, point them out. Your message can be more effective if you use "I" messages instead of personal attacks, as explained in the Communicating chapter. Indicate the specific statements and behaviors that you consider sexist.

For example, you could rephrase a sexist comment so that it targets another group, such as Jews or African Americans. People might spot anti-Semitism or racism more readily than sexism.

Keep in mind that men can also be subjected to sexism, ranging from antagonistic humor to exclusion from jobs that have traditionally been done by women.

sexual harassment

Observe your own language and behavior

Looking for sexist behavior in others is effective. Detecting it in yourself can be just as powerful. Write a Discovery Statement about specific comments that could be interpreted as sexist. Then notice if you say any of these things. Also ask people you know to point out occasions when you use similar statements. Follow up with an Intention Statement that describes how you plan to change your speaking or behavior.

You can also write Discovery Statements about the current level of intimacy (physical and verbal) in any of your relationships at home, work, or school. Be sure that any increase in the level of intimacy is mutually agreed upon.

Encourage support for women

Through networks, women can work to overcome the effects of sexism. Strategies include study groups for women, women's job networks, and professional organizations, such as Women in Communications. Other examples are counseling services and health centers for women, family planning agencies, and rape prevention centers. Check your school catalog and library to see if any of these services are available at your school.

If your school does not have the women's networks you want, you can help form them. Sponsor a one-day or one-week conference on women's issues. Create a discussion or reading group for the women in your class, department, residence hall, union, or neighborhood.

Set limits

Women, value yourselves. Recognize your right to an education without the distraction of inappropriate and invasive behavior. Trust your judgment about when your privacy or your rights are being violated. Decide now what kind of sexual comments and actions you're uncomfortable with—and refuse to put up with them.

If you are sexually harassed, take action

Some key federal legislation protects the rights of women. One is Title VII of the Civil Rights Act of 1964. Guidelines for interpreting this law offer the following definition of harassment.

Unwelcome sexual advances, requests for sexual favors, and other verbal or physical conduct of a sexual nature constitute sexual harassment when:

1. *Submission to this conduct becomes a condition of employment.*

2. *Women's response to such conduct is used as a basis for employment decisions.*

3. *This conduct interferes with work performance or creates an offensive work environment.*

The law also states that schools must take action to prevent sexual harassment.

Another relevant law is Title IX of the Education Amendments of 1972. This act bans discrimination against students and employees on the basis of gender. It applies to any educational program receiving federal funds.

If you believe that you've been sexually harassed, report the incident to a school official. This person can be a teacher, administrator, or campus security officer. Check to see if your school has someone specially designated to handle your complaint, such as an affirmative action officer or Title IX coordinator.

You can also file a complaint with the Office of Civil Rights (OCR), a federal agency that makes sure schools comply with Title IX. In your complaint, include your name, address, and daytime phone number, along with the date of the incident and a description of it. Do this within 180 days of the incident. You can contact the OCR at 1-800-421-3481 or go to the agency's web site at **http://bcol01.ed.gov/CFAPPS/OCR/contactus.cfm.**

Your community and school might also offer resources to protect against sexual discrimination. Examples are public interest law firms, legal aid societies, and unions that employ lawyers to represent students.

Seven steps to nonsexist writing

Picture a country that is dominated by women. The vast majority of people in positions of power are female. This includes executives, administrators, managers, police officers, judges, physicians, and lawyers. Ninety-nine percent of this country's elected officials are women. In fact, the country has never had a male president. In the country's 200-year history, only two men have sat on the Supreme Court. Most of the announcers on radio and television are female. And during marriage ceremonies, it's the custom for a minister (almost always a woman) to say, "I now pronounce you woman and husband."

Now imagine that you're reading a popular book about the history of this society. You might find a passage like this one:

> The story of this country is a tale of uncommon courage. We can remember the women who fought to free our country from colonial domination and the women who drafted its constitution. Our proud foremothers guided the country from infancy into the splendor of full-fledged womanhood. And the spirit of this country is still unshakable, thanks to the women who guide it now.

Men reading these words might feel excluded—and for good reason. Judging from the way this passage was written, it's hard to imagine that men even exist.

Now return to our world. You're likely to find examples of a similar problem—only this time, it's women who are being left out.

The lesson is clear: Use language that includes both women and men. Carrying out this suggestion can be tricky, even when we have the best of intentions. Following are some tools you can use to create writing that's gender fair—without twisting yourself into verbal knots.

1 Use gender-neutral terms. Instead of writing *policeman* or *chairman*, for example, use *police officer* or *chairperson*. In many cases there's no need to identify the gender or marital status of a person. This allows us to dispose of expressions such as *female driver, little woman,* and *lady doctor.*

2 Use examples that include both men and women. Good writing thrives on examples and illustrations. As you search for details to support the main points in your papers, include the stories and accomplishments of women as well as men.

3 Alternate pronoun gender. In an attempt to be gender fair, some writers make a point of mentioning both sexes whenever they refer to gender. Another method is to alternate the gender of pronouns throughout a text. Still another option is to alternate masculine and female pronouns in even- and odd-numbered chapters—the strategy used in this book.

4 Switch to plural. With this strategy, a sentence such as *The writer has many tools at his disposal* becomes *Writers have many tools at their disposal.*

5 Avoid words that imply sexist stereotypes. Included here are terms such as *tomboy, sissy, office boy, advertising man, man-eater, mama's boy, old lady,* and *powder puff.*

6 Use parallel names. When referring to men and women, use first and last names consistently. In the same paper, for instance, avoid the phrase *President George W. Bush and his wife.* An alternative is to mention the First Lady's full name: *Laura Welch Bush.*

7 Visualize a world of sexual equality. Our writing is a direct reflection of the way we perceive the world. As we make a habit of recognizing women in roles of leadership, our writing can reflect this shift in viewpoint. That's a powerful step toward gender-fair writing.

PEOPLE AT WORK

We are all leaders

No matter our station in life, at some point most of us become leaders.

Many people mistakenly think that leaders are only those with formal titles such as *supervisor* or *manager*. In fact, some leaders have no such titles. Some have never supervised others. Like Mahatma Gandhi, some people change the face of the world without ever reaching a formal leadership position.

While many of us will never become so well known, we all have the capacity to make significant changes in the world around us. Through our actions and words we constantly influence what happens in our classrooms, offices, communities, and families. We are conscious leaders, even if sometimes we are unconscious of that fact.

To become more effective leaders, we can understand the many ways we influence others. The following strategies can have a positive impact on our relationships with our children, parents, friends, schools, employers, and employees. They can help us relate to our politicians, our places of worship, our cities, our states, and our planet.

Own your leadership

Let go of the reluctance that many of us feel toward assuming leadership. It's impossible to escape leadership. Every time you speak, you lead others in some small or large way. Every time you take action, you lead others through your example. Every time you ask someone to do something, you are in essence leading that person. Leadership becomes more effective when it is consciously applied.

Be willing to be uncomfortable

Leaders often are not appreciated or even liked. They can feel isolated, cut off from their colleagues. This can sometimes lead to self-doubt and even fear.

Leadership is a courageous act. Before you take on a leadership role, be aware that you might experience such feelings. Also remember that none of them needs to stop you from leading.

Allow huge mistakes

The more important and influential you are, the more likely your mistakes will have huge consequences. The chief financial officer for a large company can make a mistake that costs thousands or even millions of dollars. A physician's error could cost a life. As commander in chief of the armed forces, the president of a country can make a decision that costs thousands of lives.

At the same time, these people are in a position to make huge changes for the better—to save thousands of dollars or lives through their power, skill, and influence.

People in leadership positions can become paralyzed and ineffective if they fear making a mistake. It's necessary for them to act even when information is incomplete or when they know a catastrophic mistake is a possible outcome.

Take on big projects

Leaders make promises. And effective leaders make big promises. These words—"I will do it; you can count on me"—distinguish a leader.

Look around your world to see what needs to be done and then take it on. Consider taking on the biggest

project you can think of—ending world hunger, eliminating nuclear weapons, wiping out poverty, promoting universal literacy. Think about how you'd spend your life if you knew that you could make a difference in these overwhelming problems. Then take the actions you considered. See what a difference they make for you and others.

Tackle projects that stretch you to your limits—projects that are worthy of your time and talents.

Provide feedback

An effective leader is a mirror to others. Share what you see. Talk with others about what they are doing effectively—and what they are doing ineffectively.

Keep in mind that people might not enjoy your feedback. Some would probably rather not hear it at all.

Two things can help. One is to let people know up front that if they sign on to work with you, they can expect feedback. Also give your feedback with skill. Use "I" messages as explained in the Communicating chapter. Back up any criticisms with specific observations and facts. And when people complete a task with exceptional skill, point that out, too.

Paint a vision

Help others see the big picture, the ultimate purpose of a project. Speak a lot about the end result and the potential value of what you're doing.

There's a biblical saying: "Without vision, the people perish." Long-term goals usually involve many intermediate steps. Unless we're

reminded of the purpose for those day-to-day actions, our work can feel like a grind. Leadership is the art of helping others lift their eyes to the horizon—keeping them in touch with the ultimate value and purpose of a project. Keeping the vision alive helps their spirits soar again.

Model your values

"Be the change you want to see" is a useful motto for leaders. Perhaps you want to see integrity, focused attention, and productivity in the people around you. Begin by modeling these qualities yourself.

It's easy to excite others about a goal when you are enthusiastic yourself. Having fun while being productive is contagious. If you bring these qualities to a project, others might follow suit.

Make requests— lots of them

An effective leader is a request machine. Making requests—both large and small—is an act of respect. When we ask a lot from others, we demonstrate our respect for them and our confidence in their abilities.

At first, some people might get angry when we make requests of them. Over time, many will see that requests are compliments, opportunities to expand their skills. Ask a lot from others, and they might appreciate you for it.

Follow up

What we don't inspect, people don't respect. When other people agree to do a job for you, follow up to see how it is going. This can be done in a way that communicates your respect and interest—not your fear that the project might flounder. When you display a genuine interest in other people and their work, they are more likely to view you as a partner in achieving a shared goal.

Focus on the problem, not the person

Sometimes projects do not go as planned. Big mistakes occur. If this happens, focus on the project and the mistakes—not the personal faults of your colleagues. People do not make mistakes on purpose. If they did, we would call them "on-purposes," not mistakes. Most people will join you in solving a problem if your focus is on the problem, not on what they did wrong.

Acknowledge others

Express genuine appreciation for the energy and creativity that others have put into their work. Take the time to be interested in what they have done and to care about the results they have accomplished. Thank and acknowledge them with your eyes, your words, and the tone of your voice.

Share credit

As a leader, constantly give away the praise and acknowledgment that you receive. When you're congratulated for your performance, pass it on to others. Share the credit with the group.

When you're a leader, the results you achieve depend on the efforts of many others. Acknowledging that fact often is more than telling the truth—it's essential if you want to continue to count on their support in the future.

Delegate

Ask a coworker or classmate to take on a job that you'd like to see done. Ask the same of your family or friends. Delegate tasks to the mayor of your town, the governor of your state, and the leaders of your country.

Take on projects that are important to you. Then find people who can lead the effort. You can do this even when you have no formal role as a leader.

Communicate assertively— not aggressively

Aggressive behavior is generally ineffective. People who act aggressively are domineering. They often get what they want by putting down other people or using strong-arm methods. When they win, other people lose.

Assertive behavior is a sign of a healthy, strong leader. Assertive people are confident and respectful of others as well as themselves. They ask directly for what they want without feeling embarrassed or inadequate. When they fail to get what they want, their self-esteem does not suffer.

Many people don't act assertively for fear they will appear aggressive. However, passive behavior—neither assertive nor aggressive—can get us nowhere. By remaining quiet and submissive, we allow others to infringe on our rights. When others run our lives, we fail to have the lives we want. The alternative is to ask for what we want, appropriately and assertively.

Listen

Sometimes it seems that effective leaders talk a lot. Chances are, they also listen a lot. As a leader, be aware of what other people are thinking, feeling, and wanting. Listen fully to the concerns and joys of others. Before you criticize their views or make personal judgments, take the time to understand what's going on inside them.

This is not merely a personal favor to the people you work with. The more you know about your coworkers or classmates, the more effectively you can lead them.

Practice

Leadership is an acquired skill. No one is born knowing how to make requests, give feedback, create budgets, do long-range planning, or delegate tasks. We learn these things over time, with practice, by seeing what works and what does not.

At times, leadership is a matter of trial and error and flying by the seat of our pants. As a leader, you might sometimes feel that you don't know what you're doing. That's OK. A powerful course of action can be discovered in mid-stream. We can *act* as leaders even when we don't *feel* like leaders. As a process of constant learning, leadership calls for all of the skills of master students.

Look for areas in which you can make a difference and experiment with these strategies. Right now there's something worth doing that calls for your leadership. Take action now and others will join you.

WORKPLACE APPLICATIONS

We often see delegation as a tool that's available only to those above us in the chain of command. Actually, delegating up or across an organization can be the most effective.

Consider delegating a project to your boss. That is, ask her to take on a job that you would like to see accomplished. This may be a job that you cannot do, given your position in the company.

44

Discovery/Intention Statement

There are things we think about telling people, but don't. Examine your relationships and complete the following statements.

I discovered that I am not communicating about ...

_____

with ...

_____

I discovered that I am not communicating about ...

_____

with ...

_____

I discovered that I am not communicating about ...

_____

with ...

_____

I discovered that I am not communicating about ...

_____

with ...

_____

Now choose one idea from this chapter that can open communication with these people in these areas. Describe below how you will use this idea.

I intend to ...

_____
_____
_____

Finally, scan this chapter for ideas that can help you get your feelings across more skillfully in such situations. List several ideas here.

_____
_____
_____

Choose your conversations and your community

Certain things are real for us because we can see them, touch them, hear them, smell them, or taste them. Books, pencils, tables, chairs, food, other people—all are real in this sense. Much of the time they enter our lives in a straightforward, uncomplicated way.

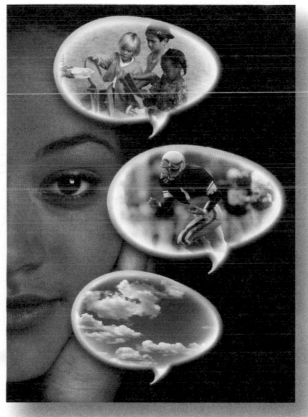

Many other aspects of our lives, however, do not have this kind of reality. None of us can point to a purpose, for example. Nor would a purpose step up and introduce itself or buy you lunch. The same is true about other abstract concepts, such as quality, intelligence, love, trust, human rights, or student success.

Such ideas are created by our words. They don't really exist until we begin talking about them. According to communication theorist Lee Thayer, these concepts come alive for us only to the degree that we define them, discuss them, question them, debate them, read about them, and write about them.[5] We create and sustain these ideas by staying in conversations about them. Through our words, we make them so. And, as S. I. Hayakawa's study of general semantics reminds us, the ideas we create through conversation translate into our actions.[6]

Keep in mind that conversations can exist in many forms. One involves people talking out loud to each other. At other times, the conversation takes place inside our heads, and we call it thinking. We are even having a conversation when we read a magazine or book, watch television or a movie, or write a letter or a report.

Conversations shape our lives

All this has three implications that wind their way through every aspect of our lives. One is that conversations exercise incredible power over what we think, feel, and do. We become our conversations. They shape our attitudes, our decisions, our opinions, our emotions, and our actions. Each of these is primarily the result of what we say over and over again, to ourselves and to others. If you want clues as to what a person will be like tomorrow, listen to what she's talking about today.

Conversation is constant

This leads to a second discovery. Given that conversations are so powerful, it's amazing that few people act on this fact. Most of us swim in a constant sea of conversations, almost none of which we carefully and thoughtfully choose.

Consider how this works. It begins when we pick up the morning paper. The articles on the front page invite us to a conversation about current events. Often the headlines speak of war, famine, unemployment figures, and other species of disaster. The advertisements start up a conversation about fantastic products for us to buy. They talk about hundreds of ways for us to part with our money.

That's not all. If we flip on the radio or television, or if we surf the Web, millions of other conversations await us. Thanks to modern digital technology, many of these conversations take place in CD-quality sound, high-resolution images, and living color 24 hours each day.

Something happens when we tune in to conversation in any of its forms. We give someone else permission to dramatically influence our thoughts—the conversation in our heads. When we watch a movie, scenes from that movie become the images in our minds. When we read a book, passages from that book become the voice in our heads. It's possible to let this happen dozens of times each day without realizing it.

You have a choice

The real power of this process lies in a third discovery: We can choose our conversations. Certain conversations create real value for us. They give us fuel for reaching our goals. Others distract us from what we want. They might even create lasting unhappiness and frustration.

We can choose more of the conversations that exhilarate and sustain us. Sometimes we can't control the outward circumstances of our lives. Yet no matter what happens, we can retain the right to choose our conversations.

Suppose that you meet with an instructor to ask about some guidelines for writing a term paper. She launches into a tirade about your writing skills and lack of preparation for higher education. This presents you with several options. One is to talk about what a jerk the instructor is and give up on the idea of learning to write well. Another option is to refocus the conversation on what you can do to improve your writing skills, such as working with a writing tutor or taking a basic composition class. These two sets of conversations will have vastly different consequences for your success in school.

The conversations we have are dramatically influenced by the people we associate with. If you want to change your attitudes about almost anything—prejudice, politics, religion, humor—then choose your conversations by choosing your community. Spend time with people who speak about and live consistently with the attitudes you value. Use conversations to change habits. Use conversations to create new options in your life.

A big part of this Power Process is choosing *not* to participate in certain conversations. Sometimes we find ourselves in conversations that are not empowering—gripe sessions, gossip, and the like. That's a time for us to switch the conversation channel. It can be as simple as excusing ourselves and walking away. Sometimes we can redirect the conversation by posing a new question or introducing a new topic. At other times we can choose to stop reading certain books or cease watching some television programs. We might choose not to be with certain people. We might leave a job, seek a new place to live, or withdraw from certain projects.

Some conversations are about antagonism. Instead of resolving conflict, they fan the flames of prejudice, half-truths, and misunderstanding. We can begin taking charge of these conversations by noticing where they start and how they continue.

You can take charge of the conversation inside your head, too. If that conversation is not consistent with your goals and values, just pick up a pencil. Write a letter to a friend, or to yourself. Write a Discovery Statement about the movie inside your head, and then start writing a new script with dialogue that empowers you.

Three ways to choose conversations

Before choosing whether to participate in a particular conversation, we can pay attention to several characteristics of that conversation: *time frame, topic,* and *attitude.* When we choose conversations that are more balanced within each of these areas, our lives will be more balanced as well.

First, we can notice the *time frame* of the conversation—whether it is about the past, the present, or the future. Most people focus much of their conversation on the past. Often they are blaming ("If she wasn't such a jerk, I wouldn't be in this mess"), justifying ("I would have been on time, but between my crazy kids and the crazy traffic, I had a terrible morning"), or regretting ("If only I had bought that land before they started to develop it").

Conversations about the past can be fun and valuable. They can help us learn from our mistakes, celebrate our successes, grieve over our losses, and enjoy fond memories. The problem arises when our conversations are out of balance. When the majority of our conversations are about what has already happened, then both our thoughts and our actions become predominantly influenced by the past. With so much focus and attention on what has gone before, our future could become little more than a repetitive variation of the past.

An alternative is to balance our conversations, making a conscious effort to include the present and the future, as well as the past. Shifting conversations to the present offers many benefits. Much of our pleasure comes from paying attention to what we're doing in the present moment—enjoying great food, performing well in sports, or becoming lost in captivating music. As we engage in conversations about what is currently happening around us, we enhance the richness and quality of our lives.

Benefits also come from conversations about the future. These conversations help us create the most wonderful life possible. Instead of worrying, we can use our planning skills to make our vision of the future a reality.

In looking for ways to balance our conversations, we can select among four *topics:* things, others, self, or "us." Most conversations fall into one of these categories. Like the time frame of conversations, the topics of most conversations are unbalanced. Most people talk about things (cars, houses, trips, football games, weather) and others (politicians, actors, neighbors, kids, coworkers) far more than they talk about themselves or about their relationships.

Of course, there is no problem in having conversations about things and others. But when we talk mostly about things and others, we neglect the rich intimacy that comes from revealing ourselves to another person. When we choose our conversations thoughtfully, we can share our heartfelt desires, fears, joys, and celebrations. We can also choose to talk about the quality of our relationships and how they can be improved.

Depending on our *attitude,* we can choose conversations that dwell on problems, or we can choose conversations that focus on finding solutions. Most people's conversations are out of balance in this area. They spend about 90 percent of their time complaining and talking about what is not working. And they spend only about 10 percent of their time looking for solutions and celebrating what *is* working.

We can reverse these percentages. We can spend about 10 percent of our conversation space looking at and defining problems. Then we can invest the rest of our time discussing solutions, exploring new possibilities, discovering exciting new passions and potentials, and achieving amazing results.

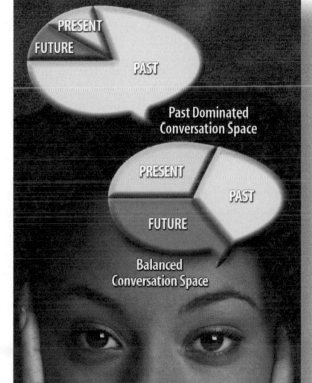

PRESENT
FUTURE
PAST

Past Dominated
Conversation Space

PRESENT
PAST
FUTURE

Balanced
Conversation Space

Conversations promote success

All of this can apply to succeeding in school. Excelling in higher education means allowing plenty of time for the conversations that start in class and continue in our textbooks and notes. You can extend those conversations by visiting the instructor during office hours, talking to classmates, and forming study groups. You can read other books and engage in other conversations that support your work in school.

Right now you're holding a conversation about student success. This conversation has a big red cover that features the words *Becoming a Master Student*. Its chapters invite you to 12 subconversations that can make a real difference in what you get in exchange for your hard-earned tuition money.

When we choose our conversations, we discover a tool of unsurpassed power. This tool has the capacity to remake our thoughts—and thus our lives. It's as simple as choosing the next article you read or the next topic you discuss with a friend.

Begin applying this Power Process today. Start choosing your conversations and watch what happens.

JOURNAL ENTRY

#45

Discovery Statement

In the space below, list two conversations you've had today and summarize their content. Now reflect on those conversations. Determine whether they were in line with your values and goals. Write down your ideas.

_____

_____

_____

_____

_____

_____

_____

_____

_____

_____

_____

_____

_____

_____

_____

_____

_____

_____

_____

_____

PRACTICING CRITICAL THINKING #18

In the space below, write down the first words that come to mind when you hear the terms listed below. Do this now.

musician _____
_____

Eskimo _____
_____

homeless people _____
_____

mathematicians _____
_____

football players _____
_____

Rhodes scholars _____
_____

Next, exchange lists with a friend. Discuss any evidence of stereotypes or bias in the responses. Write down your conclusions on a separate sheet of paper. What counts as evidence of bias? Why? Write a brief response.

_____
_____
_____
_____
_____
_____
_____
_____
_____
_____
_____
_____
_____
_____
_____
_____
_____

master student
RON BROWN

(1941–1996) first African American secretary of commerce and first African American chairman of the Democratic National Committee, died in a plane crash in Bosnia while on a diplomatic mission.

Ron Brown was born in Washington, D.C., to William and Gloria Brown, both graduates of Howard University. The family moved to New York City when he was relatively young. His father managed the legendary Hotel Theresa in Harlem. Here, Ron encountered the social, artistic, political, and powerful elite of the African-American community. He encountered people who ran the race of life brilliantly, daring to be first in what they did. They were people like Jackie Robinson, the first African American to play professional baseball; W. E. B. Du Bois, one of the first African Americans to receive a Ph.D. from Harvard; Duke Ellington, one of the first African Americans to own and lead an internationally acclaimed big band; Ralph Ellison, one of the first widely successful African American writers; Adam Clayton Powell, the first African-American congressman from Harlem. . . . Often as he peered out of the twelfth floor window of the Hotel Theresa, and observed the hustle and bustle of 125th St. below, he realized how easy it was to get lost in the superficial crowd of everyday life. He realized that the view from the top was a little better than the view from the bottom and that the Hotel

Theresa with its legendary reputation and world famous clientele was simply his personal tutoring ground, training him to see above and beyond the crowded streets of New York City.

From the many heated discussions that Ron was involved in at the Hotel Theresa, Ron developed an agile mind and a disciplined tongue. He became almost invincible in his ability to present sound and convincing arguments. In this black cultural Mecca, he studied how creative, artistic, and powerful African-American people behaved. He learned early that hard work, commitment, and perseverance characterized people of position and power. He learned the importance of appearance, preparation, and personal influence in the race called life as he listened intensely to guests' lively stories and daring escapades of world travel.

With this strong sense of self and the willingness to seek different academic and cultural experiences, he got himself accepted by Middlebury College in rural Vermont. This was significant, in that Middlebury was the first college known to have graduated an African American (Alexander L. Twight, in 1823). At Middlebury, far from the blacktop boulevards and the high-rise tenements of Harlem, Ron really began to excel. He was the first black initiated into the Middlebury chapter of the national, all-white fraternity Sigma Phi Epsilon, which eventually lost its national charter because of his induction. . . .

Hard work and relentless self-discipline helped make him the first

black chairman of the Democratic National Committee. For his uncompromising and productive efforts, he was selected by President Clinton to a cabinet-level position as the first African-American Secretary of Commerce.

Paramount in Ronald Harmon Brown's strategies for success was knowing how to solicit trust from himself. He learned early to accept himself for who he was and what he could or couldn't do. Knowing his own strengths and weaknesses, he never shortchanged himself. He learned self-reliance by preparing for every area of his life. He was confident in his ability to lead, orchestrate, mediate, and guide. He knew the importance of building lasting relationships. . . .

He was a man who learned not to get in his own way. So often we can become a greater hindrance to ourselves, more than racism, sexism, or any other kind of "ism." A healthy and confident attitude about our gifts, talents, and skills will certainly enable us to achieve our dreams.

Ron Brown's life shouts to each of us, "Be your own best cheerleader. Root for a winner. Be that winner yourself."

Osborne Robinson, Jr., African American Master Student Profiles. *Copyright © 1998 by Houghton Mifflin Company. Reprinted with permission.*

**For more biographical information on Ron Brown, visit Houghton Mifflin's College Survival/Becoming a Master Student web site:
http://collegesurvival.college.hmco.com/students.**

Quiz

1. Racial, ethnic, and other kinds of diversity have become key factors in our lives only in the last decade or two. True or False? Explain your answer.

2. Define the term *culture* and give some examples of different cultures.

3. List five strategies for communicating across cultures.

4. Give two examples of sexist behavior that could take place in higher education.

5. Define the terms *translator, mediator,* and *model* as explained in this chapter and give one example of each term.

6. Whether you are a traditional or a nontraditional student, describe at least three suggestions for older students returning to school that you could use.

7. Explain three strategies for taking charge of the conversations in your life.

Quiz
CONTINUED

 8 Describe at least three ways to create "gender-fair" writing.

 9 Rewrite the following sentence so that it is gender neutral: "Any writer can benefit from honing his skill at observing people."

 10 Few of us get the chance to be leaders. True or False? Explain your answer.

JOURNAL ENTRY

#46

Discovery/Intention Statement

After reviewing this chapter, describe what you have learned about the way you relate to people who are different from you.

I discovered that I ...

_____

_____

_____

Now choose two suggestions for communicating across cultures and describe how you will use them to promote your success in school.

I intend to ...

_____

_____

_____

LEARNING STYLES APPLICATION   CHAPTER 9

Mode 4 List three specific actions you can take to begin conversations that promote your success in school and after you graduate. For ideas, review the Power Process "Choose your conversations and your community."

Mode 1 Brainstorm a list of the most valuable suggestions you gained from this chapter on the following topics:
- Exploring your potential biases and lack of knowledge about other cultures.
- Building relationships with people from other cultures.

Mode 3 List three ways to respond effectively to the examples you listed in Mode 2.

Mode 2 On a separate sheet of paper, describe any examples of discrimination, sexism, or sexual harassment you've personally witnessed.

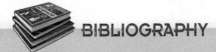

BIBLIOGRAPHY

ENDNOTES

1 Dorothy Lee, *Freedom and Culture* (Englewood Cliffs, NJ: Prentice-Hall, 1959).

2 Stephen R. Covey, *The Seven Habits of Highly Effective People: Restoring the Character Ethic* (New York: Simon & Schuster, 1989).

3 James Anderson, personal communication, 1990.

4 Diane de Anda, *Bicultural Socialization: Factors Affecting the Minority Experience* (Washington, DC: National Association of Social Workers, 1984).

5 Lee Thayer, "Communication—Sine Qua Non of the Behavioral Sciences," in David L. Arm, ed., *Vistas in Science* (Albuquerque, NM: University of New Mexico, 1968).

6 S. I. Hayakawa, *Language in Thought and Action* (New York: Harcourt Brace Jovanovich, 1972).

ADDITIONAL READING

Beckham, Barry, ed. *The Black Student's Guide to Colleges.* New York: Madison Books UPA, 1996.

Dumond, Val. *The Elements of Nonsexist Usage.* New York: Prentice-Hall, 1990.

Hurtado, Sylvia, et al. *Enacting Diverse Learning Environments: Improving the Climate for Racial/Ethnic Diversity in Higher Education.* Ashe-Eric Higher Education Reports, 1999.

Thiederman, Sondra. *Profiting in America's Multicultural Marketplace—How to Do Business Across Cultural Lines.* New York: Lexington Books, 1992.

INTERNET RESOURCES

American Civil Liberties Union
www.aclu.org

Association for Non-Traditional Students in Higher Education
www.antshe.org/

Diversity Web
www.diversityweb.org/

National Organization for Women
www.now.org

Parents and Friends of Lesbians and Gays
www.pflag.org

Race, Gender, and Affirmative Action
www-personal.umich.edu/%7Eeandersn/biblio.htm

Sexual Harassment: It's Not Academic
http://www.ed.gov/offices/OCR/docs/ocrshpam.html

Tolerance.org
www.tolerance.org

Resources

Every problem has a gift for you in its hands.
RICHARD BACH

Develop a plan of control over your spending. Then you will make progress toward the kind of living which means the most to you.
SYLVIA PORTER

Not I, but the city teaches.
SOCRATES

IN THIS CHAPTER . . . Connect to resources at your school and in your community that can help you succeed. Manage financial resources with ways to increase the money that comes into your life and decrease the money that flows out. Access digital resources by getting connected to cyberspace, finding what you want on the Internet, and using computers to manage information and ideas. As you stay up-to-date with technology, avoid the pitfalls of wasting time with your computer and of computer "addiction." Also approach the library as a resource full of buried treasure—a place with the latest information technology as well as print and audiovisual resources.

Supercharge your education

A supercharger increases the air supply to an internal combustion engine. The difference in power can be dramatic.

You can make just as powerful a difference in your education by using all of the resources available to students. In this case, your "air supply" includes people, organizations, libraries, school and community services, publications, extracurricular activities, and the Internet.

Some of those people and organizations are sources of "green energy"—money that you can use to finance your education and achieve your long-term goals. Money produces a lot of unnecessary conflict. And it doesn't seem to matter how much money a person has. People who earn $10,000 a year might say they never have enough. People who earn $150,000 a year might say the same thing. Use the suggestions in this chapter to handle money worries, no matter what your income level.

Of all resources, people are the most important. You can isolate yourself, study hard, and get a good education. If you establish relationships with teachers, staff members, fellow students, and employers, then you can get a great education.

School can be a frightening place for new students. People of diverse cultures, older students, commuters, and people with disabilities can feel excluded. School and community organizations and services offer chances for students to network and break through barriers of isolation.

Unfortunately, resources at many schools go largely unused. Few students take the time to learn about them. These students are content to feed an adequate air supply to their education, and that's fine. Another option is to pour on the oxygen by actively searching your school and community for resources you can use to meet your goals.

When you enrolled for classes, you also signed up for a world of available services and support. All of them can help you succeed in school, and many are free. In addition, communities of almost any size have resources to offer. Whether you live in a town of 500 people or a city of 500,000, treasures await you. Start uncovering them today.

Discovery Statement

Recall a problem you've recently experienced with money—for example, struggling to meet the minimum monthly payment on a credit card, or not having enough money in your checking account to buy something you really want. Briefly describe that problem here.

I discovered that I ...

I have so many financial problems right now it's unbelievable! I can't make any of my ends meet. I can't make all my monthly payments. And I keep dipping into my TIAA CREF mutual fund that Dad left me 4 years ago. When am I going to quit doing that? How did I get myself into such a fix? I simply must lower my expenses. I cannot increase my income right now because I'm teaching as much as I possibly can.

Now scan this chapter for possible resources you could use to solve this problem. Keep an eye out for campus, community, and Internet resources that might be available to you. List several suggestions here.

Connect to
school resources

Academic advisors can help you with selecting courses, choosing majors, career planning, and adjusting in general to the culture of higher education.

Alumni organizations can be good sources of information about the pitfalls and benefits of being a student at your school.

Arts resources can include museums, art galleries, observatories, and special libraries.

Athletic centers and *gymnasiums* often open weight rooms, swimming pools, indoor tracks, basketball courts, and racquet-sport courts to students.

Car-pooling maps can provide information on getting across town or across the country—and offer a way to meet new friends.

Chapels are usually open to students of any religion.

Childcare is sometimes provided at a reasonable cost through the early childhood education department.

Computer labs where students can go 24 hours a day to work on projects and use the Internet are often free.

Counseling centers help students deal with the emotional pressures of school life, usually for free or at low cost.

The *financial aid office* helps students with loans, scholarships, and grants.

Job placement offices can help you find part-time employment while you are in school and a job after you graduate.

The *registrar* handles information about transcripts, grades, changing majors, transferring credits, and dropping or adding classes.

The *school catalog* offers course descriptions, requirements for graduation, and information on everything from school history to grading practices.

The *school newspaper* provides information about school policies, activities, and services. You can advertise in it for a job, a roommate, or a ride to Dubuque. Larger schools also might have their own radio and television stations.

School security can tell you what's safe and what's not. They can also provide information about parking, bicycle regulations, and traffic rules. Some school security agencies will provide safe escort at night for female students.

Student government can assist you to develop skills in leadership and teamwork. Many employers value this kind of experience.

Student health clinics often provide free or inexpensive treatment of minor problems. Many offer information about alcohol and drug abuse and addiction.

Student organizations offer you an opportunity to explore fraternities, sororities, service clubs, veterans' organizations, religious groups, sports clubs, political groups, and programs for special populations. The last includes women's centers, multicultural student centers, and organizations for international students, disabled students, and gay and lesbian students.

Student unions are hubs for social activities, special programs, and free entertainment. Clubs and organizations often meet there, too.

Tutoring can help, even if you think you are hopelessly stuck in a course. It is usually free and is available through academic departments or counseling centers.

These are just a few examples. Check your school catalog, newspaper, and web site for the specific resources available to you. Your school fees pay for them, so use them.

Connect to community resources

Chambers of commerce provide information about local attractions, organizations, clubs, activities, museums, galleries, libraries, and businesses.

Childcare is provided by both public organizations (such as schools) and private organizations (such as girls' clubs and boys' clubs).

Churches and synagogues have members happy to welcome fellow worshippers who are away from home.

Community education classes are usually offered by local school districts. Use them to learn about anything from tax planning to ballroom dancing.

Consumer credit counseling can help even if you've really blown your budget. It's usually free. Remember, no matter how bad your financial picture, you are probably in better shape than most governments.

Governments (city, county, state, and federal) often have programs for students. Check the government listings in your local telephone directory.

Hot lines can save your life during a crisis. Professionals or trained volunteers are often available for help 24 hours a day.

Legal aid services provide free or inexpensive assistance to low-income people.

Local newspapers list community events and free services. Reading a local newspaper also helps you get a feel for a new city.

Local residents of your community are likely to know the best restaurants, the most fascinating secondhand stores, and the safest hiking spots close to town.

Money is sometimes available in a real emergency from the Salvation Army, the Red Cross, local churches, or a county relief agency.

Outside counseling can assist you with a problem when you can't get help at school. Look for job service offices, rehabilitation offices, veterans' outreach programs, church agencies, social service agencies, and area mental health clinics.

Political parties always want volunteers. Working for a candidate you believe in is one way to learn organizational skills, meet people, and make a difference in the world.

Public health centers provide inexpensive or free medical care.

Public transportation (buses, trains, trolleys, subways, and the occasional horse-drawn carriage) offers money-saving alternatives to owning a car.

Recreation departments of the city or county, YWCAs, YMCAs, and other organizations provide free or inexpensive ways to exercise and have fun.

Specialty clubs and organizations promote everything from public speaking (Toastmasters) to conservation (the Sierra Club).

Support groups exist for people with almost any problem, from drug addiction to cancer.

Resources such as these can go unused—even by the people who pay taxes to support them. Taking advantage of community resources and letting others know about them is an act of service.

societies

age clubs

counseling programs

ent government

ssional organizations for

udents in medicine, law,

usiness, journalism, etc.

ty basketball

dent newspaper or yearbook

munity service programs

dy groups

port groups

nd volleyball

hnic music groups

arching bands

toring programs

ork-study

mpus film societies

oncert bands

ance ensembles

rawing and painting clubs

Jazz bands and combos

opera companies

Pottery studios

Chamber music groups

Theater groups

Swimming lessons

Programs and services for

   students of color

Golf team

Fraternities and sororities

Football

Orchestras

Political action groups

Reap the benefits
Extracurricular activities

Many students in higher education are busier than they've ever been before. Often that's due to the variety of extracurricular activities available to them: athletics, fraternities, sororities, student newspapers, debate teams, study groups, political action groups, and many more.

With this kind of involvement comes potential benefits. People involved in extracurricular activities are often excellent students. Such activities help them bridge the worlds inside and outside the classroom. Through student organizations they develop new skills, explore possible careers, build contacts for jobs, and add experiences to their résumés. They make new friends among both students and faculty, work with people from other cultures, and sharpen their skills at conflict resolution.

Getting involved in such organizations comes with some risks as well. When students don't balance extracurricular activities with class work, their success in school can suffer. They can also compromise their health through losing sleep, neglecting exercise, skipping meals, or relying on fast food. These costs are easier to avoid if you keep a few suggestions in mind:

- **Enter any commitment outside class consciously,** with your eyes open. Decide up front how many hours each week or month you can devote to a student

organization. Leave room in your schedule for relaxing and for unplanned events.

- **Learn new skills** in managing your time. Chapter Two is teeming with ideas.

- **Make commitments** from the biggest possible picture of your time. Write down three or four of the biggest goals you'd like to achieve in your lifetime. Then choose extracurricular activities that directly support those goals.

- **Notice when your actions** fail to match your promises. You might agree to show up for meetings and consistently find yourself forgetting them or showing up late. If that happens, write a Discovery Statement about the way you're using time. Follow that with an Intention Statement about ways to keep your agreements—or consider renegotiating your agreements.

- **Say no to activities** that fail to create value for you. Avoid joining groups only because you feel guilty or obligated to do so.

- **Check out the rules** before joining any student organization. Ask about dues and attendance requirements.

- **Do a trial run** and attend one or two meetings of an organization before you decide to join. Explain that you're in the process of making a decision and want to find out what the group is about before you make a full commitment.

Students with disabilities: Ask for what you want

Equal opportunity for people with disabilities is the law. In the United States, both the Civil Rights Act of 1964 and the Rehabilitation Act of 1973 offer legal protection. The Americans with Disabilities Act of 1990 extends earlier legislation.

It used to be that students with disabilities faced a restricted set of choices in school. For instance, many had trouble majoring in subjects that call for using technical equipment—engineering, science, or medicine. New technology, such as computers and calculators operated with voice commands, can change that. Students with disabilities can now choose from any course or major offered in higher education.

Even the most well-intentioned instructors can forget about promoting learning for people with disabilities. To protect your rights, speak up. Ask for what you want. Begin with the suggestions in the Communicating chapter for being assertive, using "I" messages, and listening actively. All of them can help you succeed in school. So can the following.

Use available resources. A wealth of resources already exists to support your success in school. To begin with, check into services offered by your state. Departments of rehabilitation often provide funds for education or can help you find that money. State commissions on disabilities can guide you to services. In addition, the Job Accommodation Network (1-800-526-7234) offers help in placing employees with learning or physical disabilities.

Also find out about services at your school. Libraries might furnish books in Braille or on audiotapes for the visually impaired. Many counseling and student health centers target certain services to people with disabilities, including learning disabilities. Some schools offer disability resource centers. Other services to ask about include:

- Permits that allow you to park a car closer to classrooms.
- Note-taking services.
- Lecture transcriptions.
- Textbook-reading services and textbooks on tape.
- Sign language interpreters.
- Help in selecting courses and registering for classes.
- Assistants for laboratory courses in science.
- Shuttle buses for transportation between classes.
- Closed captioning for instructional television programs.
- TTY/TDD devices for students with hearing impairments.
- Assistance with taking tests.

Speak assertively.

Tell instructors when it's appropriate to consider your disability. If you use a wheelchair, for example, ask for appropriate transportation on field trips. If you have a visual disability, request that instructors speak as they write on the chalkboard. Also ask them to use high-contrast colors and to write legibly.

Plan ahead.

Meet with your counselor or advisor to design an educational plan—one that takes your disability into account. A key part of this plan is choosing instructors. Ask for recommendations before registering for classes. Interview prospective instructors and sit in on their classes. Express an interest in the class, ask to see a course outline, and discuss any adjustments that could help you complete the course. Some of the services you request might take extra time to deliver. Allow for possible delays as you plan your schedule.

Use empowering words.

Changing just a few words can make the difference between asking for what you want and apologizing for it. When people refer to disabilities, you might hear words such as *special treatment*, *accommodation*, and *adaptation*. Experiment with using *adjustment* and *alternative* instead. The difference between these terms is equality. Asking for an adjustment in an assignment is asking for the right to produce equal work—not for special treatment that "waters down" the assignment.

Ask for appropriate treatment.

Many instructors will be eager to help you. At times they might go overboard. For example, a student who has trouble writing by hand might ask to complete in-class writing assignments on a computer. "OK," the teacher replies, "and take a little extra time. For you, there's no rush."

For some students this is a welcome response. For others, there is no need for an extended timeline. They can say, "Thank you for thinking of me. I'd prefer to finish the assignment in the time frame allotted for the rest of the class."

Take care of yourself.

Many students with chronic illnesses or disabilities find that rest breaks are essential. If this is true for you, write such breaks into your daily or weekly plan. A related suggestion is to treat yourself with respect. If your health changes in a way that you don't like, avoid berating yourself. Even when you do not choose the conditions in your life, you can choose your attitude toward those conditions.

It's important to accept compliments and periodically review your accomplishments in school. Fill yourself with affirmation. As you educate yourself, you are attaining mastery.

Student Voices

Before I was diagnosed with dyslexia, I was constantly frustrated whenever I had to take a test. I was never able to complete my exams because I didn't read or write as quickly as the other students in my class. When I discussed this problem with my advisor, he recommended I talk to a counselor in the learning assistance center. Now, I take my tests at the learning center and have additional time to accommodate for my disability.

—IRENE CHO

The source of money problems

Most money problems result from spending more than is available. It's that simple, even though often we do everything we can to make the problem much more complicated.

The solution also is simple: *Don't spend more than you have.* If you are spending more money than you have, increase your income, decrease your spending, or do both. This idea has never won a Nobel Prize in economics, but you won't go broke applying it.

There is a big payoff in making money management seem more complicated than it really is. If we don't understand money, then we don't have to be responsible for it. After all, if we don't know how to change a flat tire, we don't have to be the one responsible for fixing it. If we never learn to cook, then someone else can take on the responsibility for making dinner.

It works the same way with money. If we never learn how to manage money, we have an excuse for not facing the truth about it. The responsibility belongs to someone or something else.

That no longer applies when you admit a basic truth about money: It doesn't work to spend more than you have. This principle does not require that you live like a miser, pinching pennies and saving used dental floss. On the contrary, mastering money is more likely to bring you prosperity. The fact is, most students can afford school, including many who drop out because they couldn't handle their money.

Three steps to financial independence

- Tell the truth about how much money you have and how much you spend.
- Make a commitment to spend no more than you have.
- Begin saving money.

If you do these three things consistently, most of your money worries will be over. You could even have an experience of financial independence. This does not necessarily mean having all of the money you could ever desire. Instead, financial independence can mean freedom from money worries by living within your means.

Telling the truth, living within your means, and saving are three steps that you can begin now. Soon you can be controlling money, instead of letting money control you.

(and a simple solution . . .)

Increase money in

For many of us, making more money is the most appealing way to fix a broken budget. After all, if we increase the amount of money coming in, we can still enjoy the benefits of spending it.

This approach is reasonable, and at the same time it has a potential problem. When our income increases, most of us continue to spend more than we make. Our money problems persist, even at higher incomes. You can avoid this dilemma by managing your expenses no matter how much money you make. (See the next article.)

There are several ways to increase your income while you go to school. One of the most obvious ways is to get a job (or another job) that pays more. You can also get scholarships and grants. You can borrow money, inherit it, or receive it as a gift. You can sell property, collect income from investments, or use your savings.

Other ways to increase your money supply include lotteries and theft. These alternatives are risky and could easily distract you from your life as a student.

Start by making money the old-fashioned way: Earn it.

Work while you're in school.

If you work while you go to school, you can earn more than money. Working helps you gain experience, establish references, and expand your contacts in the community. Getting a work-study job or an internship can help you land a paying job after graduation.

Regular income, even at minimum wage, can make a big difference. Look at your monthly budget to see how it would be affected if you worked just 15 hours a week (times 4 weeks a month) for only $7 an hour.

A job also will demonstrate your work patterns. Future employers won't expect you to have been in the president's Cabinet, but they would like to know that you can get along with coworkers and get to work on time.

Many students work full-time or part-time jobs. Work and school don't have to conflict, especially if you plan your time, delegate household tasks, and ask for your employer's support.

Find a job.

To get the most out of your job search, take some time to define what you want. Describe your dream job—the work you would do if you had no money worries. Then brainstorm ways to find or create that job. Asking other people to help you create your brainstorm can enable you to see more options and make your dream a reality.

Next, make a list of your work skills. To get a full picture of your abilities, include both content skills and transferable skills. *Content skills* qualify you for a specific job. For example, having a knowledge of accounting principles qualifies you to work as an accountant. *Transferable skills* can apply to many jobs, even in different fields. Examples are writing, speaking, planning, learning, budgeting, and leading meetings. Many people forget about transferable skills and shortchange themselves when they write a résumé. Be creative and explore your skills in all areas.

With your list of skills in hand, go to the library or a career counselor and find out which jobs call for your skills. On most campuses, there is a person in the financial aid office whose job is to help students find work while they're in school. Find that person. Often students fail to appreciate the vast range of jobs that are available. Doing some research can greatly multiply your job options.

Most jobs are never advertised. In fact, your best source of information about new jobs is people—friends, relatives, coworkers, and fellow students. Ask around. Tell everyone you want a job. In particular, tell people who might be able to create a job for you. Many jobs are created on the spot when a person with potential simply shows up and asks.

Make a list of several places that you would like to work. Include places that have advertised job openings and those that haven't. Then go to each place on your list and tell someone that you would like a job. This will yield more results than depending on the want ads alone.

The people you speak to might say that there isn't a job available, or that the job is filled. That's OK. Ask to see the person in charge of hiring and tell him you want to work. He will probably say he doesn't have a job available. No problem. Ask to fill out an application or leave a résumé to be considered for future job openings. Then ask when you can check back.

Now he sees you as more than an application in a file. You are a living, breathing, motivated human being. The next time you meet, you won't be strangers. Remember to check back, the sooner the better.

Job hunting is like prospecting for gold. You dig a lot of holes and uncover a lot of rocks before you succeed. Eventually, you will find work.

Before you start your search, set a quota. Tell yourself you will continue the search until you have spoken to at least 100 people, or some other number you can live with.

After two or three interviews you might get tired of hearing people say, "We don't have an opening" or "We've already filled that job." At this point, consider your quota—the number chosen before you had your first few rejections. If you ask enough people, someone will say, "Yes!" Each time you hear "No," silently thank the person for putting you one "no" closer to a "yes."

Consider creating your own job or becoming self-employed. You could offer any service from lawn mowing to computer consulting.

Self-created jobs can blossom into amazing careers. For example, David Filo and Jerry Yang started making lists of their favorite sites on the World Wide Web while they were graduate students. They went on to create Yahoo!, an Internet search directory and one of today's most influential web sites.

Find another job.
First, determine whether you really want to change jobs. Make a list of the benefits of your present job. ("It pays $7 an hour. It's close to where I live. I can study on the job.") Then list the disadvantages. ("I have to wear a chicken suit. The boss is grouchy. It pays $7 an hour.")

If the disadvantages outweigh the benefits, start looking for another job. You have an income now, so you won't be tempted to take the first job you find. And once you have compared the advantages and disadvantages of your current job, you will have a more accurate picture of the next job you are seeking.

You can use the same techniques to find a new job that you used to find the old one. You can also use contacts that you have developed while working at your current job. You might even find a better job within the same company. That is one reason it pays to do your best, even in a job you don't like.

Keep your job in perspective.
If your job is in your career field, great. If it is meaningful and contributes to society, great. If the job involves working with people you love and respect, fantastic. If not—well, remember that almost any job can support you in reaching your educational goals.

It's also easy to let a job eat up time and energy that you need for your education. You can avoid this by managing your time effectively.

To get started, choose several time-management techniques from Chapter Two. Then decide how you will use them. You're more likely to avoid conflict between work and school if you write long-term plans, keep a semester or quarterly calendar, create a weekly plan, and prioritize your to-do lists.

This might sound like a lot of work, but it will probably take you only a few minutes a day, and it can save you hours.

Decrease money out

Learning ways to control your expenses is a powerful tool for managing money, and it is usually much easier than increasing your income.

There are many ways to decrease the amount of money you spend. Consider the ideas that follow and invent more of your own.

Redefine money.
Start by understanding money in a new way. According to authors Joe Dominguez and Vicki Robin, money is what we accept in exchange for our life energy—our time, passion, and effort.[1] When you take on this view of money, you might naturally find yourself spending less without sacrifice or self-discipline.

Dominguez and Robin suggest that you calculate your real hourly wage as a way to measure how you spend your life energy. This wage is the amount you're paid for each hour you work, *minus* work-related expenses such as transportation and childcare. This real hourly wage then gives you a way to see how many hours you have to work to buy something new. If you find out that a new CD player will cost 50 hours of your life energy, you might reconsider how important the player is to you.

Create a budget.
Budgeting is a type of planning. Like other forms of planning, budgeting creates freedom. When you have a budget and stick to it, you can relax. You can be confident. You don't have to worry about whether you can pay your bills. When you budget, you're more assured of having money for major expenses such as trips, tuition, or unexpected emergencies.

Budgeting is easy, once you acquire the habit. The basic idea is to project how much money is coming in and how much is going out. Budgets are most useful when you set up two: one for the next month and one that is long-range—for a year or more.

A monthly budget will include recurring income and expense items—such as paychecks, food costs, and housing—that vary little from one month to the next. It also will list unusual income and expenses, such as tuition payments that you make only a few times per year.

A long-range budget shows the big picture. It helps you make realistic choices about how to make or spend money now with an eye to having the funds you need beyond the next month.

Monitor money out.
Discovering how much you really spend can help decrease money out. Each month, review your checkbook, receipts, and other financial records. You can also write down each cash purchase you make on a 3×5 card or track your expenses with computer software.

Sort your expenses into major categories such as food, entertainment, tuition, housing, etc. At the end of the month, total up how much you spend in each category. You might be surprised at how much you spend in nonessential categories, such as fast food and impulse purchases. Once you know the actual amount, you might find yourself decreasing these expenses effortlessly.

Spend on purpose.
Monitoring expenses allows us to make choices about money that are consistent with our life purpose and

long-term goals. For example, someone might say that he values health. If he discovers that he spends $200 per month on alcoholic beverages, he might conclude that there's a contradiction between his values and his behavior. He can then redefine his values, change his spending habits, or both.

Look to the big-ticket items.
Your choices about which car to buy and where to live can save you tens of thousands of dollars. When you look for places to cut expenses, look to the items that cost the most. That's where you can have a big impact on your budget.

Look to the small-ticket items.
Doing small jobs yourself—such as changing the oil for your car—and taking advantage of sales promotions can save you hundreds of dollars over the course of a year.

Decreasing the money you spend on very small purchases can make the difference between a balanced budget and uncomfortable debt. That three-dollar cappuccino is tasty, but the amount that some of us spend on such treats over the course of a year could give anyone the jitters. To save money and promote health, you could substitute herbal tea for coffee and increase the amount of plain water you drink.

Use the telephone.
Find out in advance if a store has what you want at the right price. You can save time, gasoline, and money.

Do comparison shopping.
Prices vary dramatically on big-ticket items such as cars, clothes, and housing. Shop around or wait for sales. Waiting for sales is a way to control impulse buying. Almost everything goes on sale sooner or later. If you plan to buy a big-ticket item, such as a computer or car, leave your checkbook at home when you first go shopping. Look at all of the possibilities, then go home and make your decision when you don't feel pressured. Shop at secondhand stores, outlets, or garage sales.

One of the biggest expenses you will have as a student is college tuition. This also is an area that is open to comparison shopping. If you are looking ahead to graduate school or are considering transferring to another undergraduate program, compare the course offerings, credentials of instructors, and tuition expenses of possible schools. Some of the smaller, less expensive colleges and universities offer educational opportunities on a par with schools that have a higher profile.

Be aware of quality.
The cheapest product is not always the least expensive over the long run. Sometimes a slightly more expensive item is the best buy because it will last longer. Keep in mind that there is no correlation between the value of something and the amount of money spent to advertise it. Inspect your purchases carefully to see if they are well made.

Use coupons.
Newspapers and magazines carry clip-out coupons that offer discounted prices. Beware of misleading coupons—ones that advertise widgets for $11.95 when down the street, you can buy generic widgets for $8.95.

Cook for yourself.
This one simple idea could save many a sinking budget. Instead of eating out, head to the grocery store. Let nutrition and value be your guides. Fresh fruits and vegetables and whole grains are not only better for you than processed food—they also cost less. Cooking for yourself doesn't take much time if you plan in advance.

Plan your wardrobe.
Stick to one or two color schemes. Find items that you can mix and match with other items. That fuschia jacket looks fantastic in the store, but what can you wear with it? And when?

Shop for next year's clothes at end-of-season sales. If you do decide to go along with the latest fad, buy cheap. The style might go out of fashion before the item wears out.

Conserve energy.
To save money on utilities bills, turn out the lights. Keep windows and doors closed in winter. Avoid loss of cool air in summer. When you wash dishes or take a bath in winter, leave the hot water in the sink or tub until it is cool. The heat is exchanged in the room rather than warming the sewer for half a block. In cool weather, dress warmly and keep the house at 68 degrees or less. In hot weather, take cool showers and baths. Set the air conditioning at 74 degrees or above.

Keep your housing costs reasonable.
Sometimes a place a little farther from your school or a smaller house will be much less expensive. You can keep your housing costs down by finding a roommate. Also look for opportunities to house-sit rather than paying rent. Some homeowners will even pay a responsible person to live in their house when they are away.

Be a good tenant. Pay your rent on time and treat rental property with respect. Landlords appreciate good tenants and will often give a break in future rent or deposit refunds to someone they trust. Offer to do repairs or maintenance in exchange for reduced rent. Ask the owner of each place you rent for a favorable reference.

Pay cash.
To avoid interest charges, deal in cash. If you don't have the cash, don't buy. Buying on credit makes it more difficult to monitor spending. You can easily bust next month's budget with this month's credit purchases.

Fix things yourself. Many repair or service jobs are easy when you take the time to look into them. Ask friends for help. It's cheaper (and more fun) to buy a friend lunch or treat him to a movie than to pay a repair shop.

Notice what you spend on "fun." Blowing your money on fun is fun. It is also a sure-fire way to ruin your budget.

When you spend money on entertainment, ask yourself what the benefits will be and whether you could get the same benefits for less money. You can read or borrow magazines for free at the library. Most libraries also loan music tapes, CDs, and videotapes at no expense. Meeting your friends at a bar can be less fun than meeting at a friend's house, where there is no cover charge.

Free entertainment is everywhere. However, it usually isn't advertised, so you'll have to search it out. Look in your school and local newspapers for listings of events, such as poetry readings at libraries or concerts at places of worship, many of which are free and open to the public.

Use public transportation or car pools. Aside from tuition, a car can be the biggest financial burden in a student's budget. The purchase price is often only the tip of the iceberg. Be sure to consider the cost of parking, insurance, repairs, gas, oil changes, maintenance, and tires. When you add up all of those items, you might find it makes more sense to take the bus or a cab instead.

Postpone purchases. When you are ready to buy something, wait a week, even if the salesperson pressures you. What seems like a necessity today might not even cross your mind the day after tomorrow. If this seems like a hardship, give yourself a small reward for waiting, and write yourself a reminder note to reconsider the purchase in a week.

FREE FUN

Sometimes it seems that the only way to have fun is to spend money. Not true. Aside from free entertainment available through your school and your community, your imagination is the only limit on free fun. Many of these ideas might seem crazy. Pick a few that sound like fun and experiment. Add your own ideas.

- Exercise
- Visit a pet store
- Take a candlelight bath
- Grow a beard
- Start a club
- Write a letter—a continuing story or mirror-readable-only letter
- Play board games
- Hold an egg toss
- Have a massage
- Reread old letters and journals
- Climb trees
- Paint scenes on your windows
- Write a poem
- Give a haircut
- Learn to juggle
- Adopt a grandparent, little brother, or sister
- Bicycle
- Play cards
- Throw a popcorn-and-television-movie party
- Window-shop

- Arm-wrestle
- Donate blood
- Go puddle stomping
- Make yourself breakfast in bed
- Hike
- Watch sunrises or sunsets
- Skip
- Kiss
- Build a snowman
- Call a friend (not long distance)
- Floss your teeth
- Have a pillow fight
- Plan a slumber party
- Sleep outside
- Read
- Watch birds
- Dress up
- Look at old photographs
- Draw
- Make wildflower garlands
- Toast marshmallows
- Listen to music
- Dance

- Watch people
- Whittle
- Whistle
- Stretch
- Take a nap
- Fill a friend's car with balloons
- Have a goofy scavenger hunt
- Peel an orange, keeping the peel in one piece
- Stargaze
- Short sheet the beds
- Skip stones
- Play tag
- Weed a garden
- Wash and wax your car
- Scratch a back
- Go fishing
- Fly a kite
- Throw a house-cleaning party
- Go to the library to read or listen to tapes
- Start a comedy improvisation group
- Get involved in a political issue
- Join intramural sports
- Set a new record (best out of 100) in basketball free throws
- Walk
- Build a snow sculpture

Take charge of your credit card

A credit card is compact and convenient. That piece of plastic seems to promise peace of mind. Low on cash this month? Just whip out your card, slide it across the counter, and relax. Your worries are over—that is, until you get the bill.

Credit cards often come with a hefty interest rate, sometimes as high as 20 percent. That's one-fifth of your credit card bill. Imagine working five days a week and getting paid for only four: You'd lose one-fifth of your income. Likewise, when people rely on high-interest credit cards to get by from month to month, they lose one-fifth of their monthly payments to interest charges.

In a 2000 survey by Nellie Mae, a student loan corporation, 78 percent of undergraduate students had credit cards. Their average credit card debt was $2,748. Suppose that a student with this debt used a card with an 18 percent annual percentage rate. Also suppose that he pays only the minimum balance due each month. He'll be making payments for 15 years and will pay an additional $2,748 in interest fees.

Credit cards do offer potential benefits. Getting a card is one way to establish a credit record. Many cards offer rewards, such as frequent flier miles and car rental discounts. Your monthly statement also offers a way to keep track of your expenses.

Used wisely, credit cards can help us become conscious of what we spend. Used unwisely, they can leave us with a load of debt that takes decades to repay. That load can seriously delay other goals—paying off student loans, financing a new car, buying a home, or saving for retirement.

Use the following three steps to take control of your credit cards before they take control of you. Write these steps on a 3×5 card and don't leave home without it.

Do a First Step about money

See your credit card usage as an opportunity to take a financial First Step. If you rely on credit cards to make ends meet every month, tell the truth about that. If you typically charge up to the maximum limit and pay just the minimum balance due each month, tell the truth about that, too.

Write Discovery Statements focusing on what doesn't work—and what does work—about the way you use credit cards. Follow up with Intention Statements regarding steps you can take to use your cards differently. Then take action. Your bank account will directly benefit.

Scrutinize credit card offers

Beware of cards offering low interest rates. These rates are often only temporary. After a few months, they could double or triple. Also look for annual fees and other charges buried in the fine print.

To simplify your financial life and take charge of your credit, consider using only one card. Choose one with no annual fee and the lowest interest rate. Don't be swayed by offers of free T-shirts or coffee mugs. Consider the bottom line and be selective.

Pay off the balance each month

Keep track of how much you spend with credit cards each month. Then save an equal amount in cash. That way, you can pay off the card balance each month and avoid interest charges. Following this suggestion alone might transform your financial life.

If you do accumulate a large credit card balance, ask your bank about a "bill-payer" loan with a lower interest rate. You can use this loan to pay off your credit cards. Then promise yourself never to accumulate credit card debt again.

Money for the future

The benefits of taking control of your money are cumulative. The more you plan and take appropriate action today, the fewer money worries you will have tomorrow.

Start saving now. You don't have to wait until you finish school to begin saving for the future. You can begin now, even if you are in debt and living on a diet of macaroni. Saving now helps you establish a habit that will really pay off in the future.

You can save for short-term goals (a new winter coat), mid-term goals (a down payment on a car next year), or long-term goals (a down payment on a house in several years). You also can put money aside for emergencies. One guideline for economic freedom is to have savings equal to at least six months of living expenses. Build this nest egg first. Then save for major, long-term expenses, such as a child's education or your retirement. Remember that your living expenses might increase as you get older, and that calls for a bigger nest egg.

Savings can include liquid investments, such as insured savings accounts, certificates of deposit, and savings bonds. (The word *liquid* means that you can turn these investments into cash immediately when you need to.) See your banker or an independent certified financial planner for advice on ways to save. In general, avoid getting investment advice from someone who has something to sell, such as a stockbroker or a realtor.

Saving is one of the most effective ways to take control of your money. To reach your goals, save at least 10 percent of your monthly take-home pay. If you can save more, that's even better.

Invest after you have a cushion. Investing is risky. Invest only after you have that nest egg—enough savings in the bank to meet your expenses for three to six months, even if you lose your job.

If you do have money to invest, consider something safe, such as Treasury securities (bills, notes, and bonds backed by the federal government), bonds, no-load mutual funds, or blue chip stocks.

Sensible investing requires extensive homework. Avoid taking a friend's advice on how to invest your hard-earned money. Risk only the money that you can afford to lose. Keep the grocery money in savings.

Even a small amount of money set aside each month can grow rapidly. The sooner you begin to invest, the more opportunity your money has to grow. Time allows you to take advantage of the power of compound interest. The more time you give it, the greater the advantage.

Consider the following comparison. Person A invests $2,000 per year for seven years. He starts when he is 22 years old and makes his last investment when he is 28. Person B invests $2,000 per year for 33 years. He starts at age 29 and makes his last investment when he is 61. Say that both receive a 10 percent return and their interest is compounded monthly. When each is 62 years old, person A will have invested $14,000 and have a total of $628,329. Person B will have invested $66,000 and have a total of $600,082.

An investment of $14,000 made early in life could return more money than an investment of $66,000 made later in life.

Save on insurance. Buy health, auto, and life insurance with high deductibles to save on premiums. Once you have insured your health or your life, it's usually possible to stay insured, even if you develop a major illness. For that reason, insuring yourself now is a wise investment for the future.

There are basically two kinds of life insurance: term and whole life. Term insurance is less expensive. It pays when you die, and that's it. Whole life is more expensive. It pays when you die, yet it also accumulates money during your lifetime and serves as a savings and investment plan. Under a typical whole life policy, you could collect a pension when you retire in addition to having your life insured.

You might get a higher return on your money if you buy the lower-priced term insurance and invest the extra dollars in something other than insurance. This is not always true, however. Some new policies, called *universal life*, combine features of term and whole life insurance. All insurance policies are not alike, so shop with more than one agent before you decide. Ask questions about anything you don't understand. If the agent can't answer your questions satisfactorily, then get another agent.

Shop around for insurance. Benefits, premiums, exclusions, and terms vary considerably from policy to policy, so study each one carefully. Also ask for safe driver, nonsmoker, or good student discounts.

Be careful with contracts.

Before you sign anything, read the fine print. If you are confused, ask questions and keep asking until you are no longer confused.

Be leery of someone who says, "Oh, this is just the standard lease arrangement. I wouldn't try to pull the wool over your eyes. You look too smart for that."

After you sign a contract or a lease, read the entire document again. If you think you have signed something that you will regret, back out quickly and get your release in writing. Purchase contracts in many states are breakable if you act quickly. For example, you might be allowed to back out of a purchase agreement within three days with no penalty.

If you can't get out, get legal help immediately. If you have little money, inquire at any attorney's office or look in the phone book for a legal aid office. Legal aid attorneys offer free or low-cost assistance to people who meet certain income guidelines.

Be particularly careful of long-term purchase agreements. That beautiful cookware might cost you only 72 cents a day, but if you have to make payments for three years, it will cost you $788.

Use credit wisely.

A good credit rating is a worthy objective. If you don't already have one, you can begin to establish a credit rating now. Borrow a small amount of money and pay it back on time. Consider borrowing for the next major purchase you make. Start now to demonstrate that you can be trusted to make all of your payments, and that you will make them on time.

Utility companies also influence your credit rating. Pay your telephone, gas, electric, and water bills on time. Avoid the temptation to let big companies wait for their money. Develop a credit rating that will support your borrowing large amounts of money if you need it.

Explore "budget plans" for monthly payments that might otherwise fluctuate, such as those for heating your home. These plans average your yearly expenses so that you pay about the same amount each month, making it easier to budget monthly.

Before you borrow money to buy a car or some other big-ticket item, know what that item will be worth *after* you buy it. A new $20,000 car might be worth only $15,000 the minute you drive it off the lot. To maintain your net worth, don't borrow any more than $15,000 to buy the car.

if you're in trouble.

You can aim to handle money problems in a way that protects a good credit rating. If you get in over your financial head, get specific data. Find out exactly how much money you earn and spend each month. If you can't pay your bills in full, be honest with creditors. Many will let you pay off a large debt in small installments.

Also consider credit counseling. Most cities have agencies with professional advisors who can help you straighten out your financial problems. If you're divorced and having serious trouble collecting child support, contact the Association for Children for Enforcement of Support at 1-800-537-7072.

JOURNAL ENTRY

#48

Discovery Statement

On a separate sheet of paper, write a one-sentence statement of your purpose for taking part in higher education. Allow yourself to write many drafts of this mission statement, and review it periodically as you continue your education.

You might find it difficult to express this statement in one sentence. If so, write a paragraph or more. Then look for the sentence that seems most charged with energy for you. The following are some possible examples:

• My purpose for being in school is to gain skills that I can use to contribute to others.

• My purpose for being in school is to live an abundant life that is filled with happiness, health, love, and wealth.

• My purpose for being in school is to enjoy myself by making lasting friendships and following the lead of my interests.

Education's worth it . . .

A college education is one of the most durable and worthwhile investments you can make. It's also one of the safest investments possible. When you are clear about what you want, education is usually a way to get it.

Education is a unique purchase—one of the few things you can buy that will last your lifetime. It can't rust, corrode, break down, or wear out. Education can't be stolen, burned, repossessed, or destroyed. Education is a purchase that becomes a permanent part of you. Once you have it, no one can take it away.

Think about all of the services and resources that your tuition money buys: Academic advising to help you choose classes and select a major. Access to the student health center and counseling services. Career planning and job placement offices that you can visit even after you graduate. Athletic, arts, and entertainment events at a central location. A student center where you can meet people and socialize. If you live in, you get a place to stay with meals provided, all for less than the cost of an average hotel room. And, by the way, you also get to attend classes.

When you consider how much nonstudents would have to pay for such an array of services, you can see that higher education is a bargain.

Investing money in your abilities is also one of the safest investments you can make over the long term. Money invested in land, gold, oil, or stocks can easily be lost. Over a lifetime, a college graduate can expect to earn about $1 million more on average than a person whose education stops with high school. Education also pays off in job promotions and career satisfaction.

The list of possible benefits continues. Higher education has been suggested as the source of everything from better health to happier marriages. With higher education, you can:

- Grasp world events with more ease.
- Have more economic and social opportunities.
- Be better equipped to become a parent.
- Learn ways to acquire new job skills, pursue new interests, and thrive on change.
- Enjoy increased flexibility on the job (with tight supervision less likely).
- Receive improved retirement benefits.
- Have greater travel opportunities.

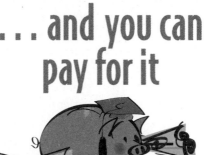

. . . and you can pay for it

- Improve the likelihood that your children will further their education.

In short, education is a good deal. It is worth investing in again and again as circumstances change and you update your skills. There are many ways to pay for school. The kind of help you get depends on your financial need. In general, financial need equals the cost of your schooling minus what you can reasonably be expected to pay.

Receiving financial aid has little to do with "being poor." Your prospects for aid depend greatly on the costs of the school you attend. Do not assume that your application for financial aid will be rejected.

Financial aid includes money you don't pay back (grants and scholarships), money you do pay back (loans), and work-study programs that land you a job while you're in school. Most students receive a package that includes several of these elements.

A plan for paying for your entire education makes completing your degree work a more realistic possibility. Create a master plan—a long-term budget listing how much you need to complete your education and where you plan to get the money.

When you know precisely how much you need, ask for help. Every school has someone to assist with this. You can also get help from publications in financial aid offices and most public and academic libraries.

Once you've lined up financial aid, keep it flowing. Find out the requirements for keeping your loans, grants, and scholarships. Also get to know someone in the financial aid office at your school and chat with that person at least once each year. Ask about new programs and changes to existing programs.

Remember that many financial aid packages are contingent on your making "satisfactory academic progress"—that is, doing well in school. Besides helping you earn more money in the future, being a successful student can help you keep the money flowing even while you're in school.

 In applying for financial aid, you'll probably use a form called the Free Application for Federal Student Aid (FAFSA). You can access this form on the World Wide Web at **www.fafsa.ed.gov/.**

Education by the hour

Determine exactly what it costs you to go to school. Fill in the blanks. Use totals for a semester, quarter, or whatever term system your school uses.

Note: Include only the costs that relate directly to going to school. For example, under "Transportation" list only the amount that you pay for gas to drive back and forth to school—not the total amount you spend on gas for a semester.

Tuition	$_____
Books	$_____
Fees	$_____
Transportation	$_____
Clothing	$_____
Food	$_____
Housing	$_____
Entertainment	$_____
Other (such as insurance, medical, childcare)	$_____
Subtotal	$_____
Salary you could earn per term if you weren't in school	$_____
Total (A)	$_____

Now figure out how many classes you attend in one term. This is the number of your scheduled class periods per week multiplied by the number of weeks in your school term. Put that figure below:

Total (B) _____

Divide the **Total (B)** into the **Total (A)** and put that amount here: $_____

This is what it costs you to go to one class one time.

Discovery/Intention Statement

After completing the exercise "Education by the hour," describe below what you have learned about the cost of your education.

I discovered that I ...

_____
_____
_____
_____
_____
_____
_____
_____
_____
_____

Now that you are aware of the cost of your education, describe how you will use this knowledge.

I intend to ...

_____
_____
_____
_____
_____
_____
_____
_____
_____
_____
_____
_____

StudentVoices

The *Education by the Hour* exercise made me realize that school is costing me a lot and everything counts when I don't attend class or do an assignment. I couldn't believe how much of my money I was wasting for not attending only one of my classes.

— LUZ LOPEZ

Seventeen places to find money

The most frequent reason students give for dropping out of school is "I can't afford it."

For most students, that statement might be inaccurate. Maybe a more accurate statement would be: "Given the value that I think I will get from going to school, I don't think it is worth the trouble to find the money." If the lack of money seems to be stopping you from continuing your formal education, look first to see if you really want to continue. Check to see if "lack of money" might be a convenient excuse for discontinuing something that you don't find valuable.

After telling the truth about your desires concerning education, you might find that you don't really want to be in school. If so, leave. Drop out. Take a break. Go and do what you really want to do. On the other hand, when you examine your deep desires, you could discover that you really do want to go to school. If so, there are lots of places that you can find the money.

There's an old saying that knowledge is power. When it comes to financial aid, knowledge is money. Millions of dollars are waiting to flow into the hands of people who want to take part in higher education. But the funds are available only when students know ways to find them. Some ideas are listed below.

1. Pell Grants are financed by the federal government and do not have to be repaid.

2. Supplemental Educational Opportunity Grants (SEOG) are designed to complement other forms of financial aid.

3. Work-study arranges for jobs at the school or in the community. Your hours of work will be based on your class schedules and your academic progress.

4. Perkins Loans are long-term loans based on financial need and have low interest rates.

5. Federal loan programs offer low-interest loans from banks and credit unions. Ask about Stafford Loans, Supplemental Loans, Consolidation Loans, Ford Direct Student Loans, and the PLUS program (Parent Loans for Undergraduate Students).

6. Scholarships are available through most schools for outstanding performance in athletics, academics, or the arts. Also inquire at fraternal, service, educational, and social organizations, and at credit unions.

7. The Veterans Administration has money available for some veterans and their dependents.

8. Active military personnel can take advantage of various financial aid programs by contacting their local personnel office.

9. Company assistance programs, provided by employers, might offer financial aid for employees to attend school while working.

10. Social security payments are available up to age 18 for unmarried students with a deceased parent or a parent who is disabled or drawing social security benefits.

11. State governments often provide grants and other forms of aid.

12. The U.S. Bureau of Indian Affairs has financial aid available for some Native American students.

13. Relatives will often provide financial help for a dedicated student.

14. Personal savings comprise the bulk of money spent on higher education.

15. Employment is another way students can get additional money. Working in a job related to your future career field can supplement your education as well as your finances.

16. The local branch of your state employment office provides information about government programs that are set up to train the unemployed. Ask about the JTPA (Job Training Partnership Act) and WIN (Work Incentive) programs.

17. Selling something might be a last resort, but it is an option. Consider the money you have tied up in a car, horse, piano, house, or hobby.

Note: Programs listed in this article change constantly. In some cases, money is limited and application deadlines are critical. Be sure to get the most current information from the financial aid office at your school.

We live like royalty

"But I really don't have enough money. You don't know what it's like to get by on what I make."

Suggesting that money worries are unnecessary upsets some people. That's not the intention of this article. The point is this: Frustration about not having enough money will not get us more money, nor will it help us spend less.

"I don't have enough" can have several meanings. One is "I don't have enough money to meet my obligations." Another is "I want to have the things that people with more money have." Both kinds of upset are usually unnecessary.

If you want to eliminate money worries, keep experimenting with the ideas in this chapter on handling money problems. This book is also full of ideas on handling frustrations in general. The Power Processes can be applied to your relationship with money. You can ease the frustration by being here now, detaching, surrendering, letting go of your pictures of how much money you ought to have, loving your frustration to death, or looking at how you create your money woes. This is sometimes hard work, requiring the courage to look inward, and the potential rewards are enormous.

You can also consider alternatives to "I don't have enough." Some of those alternatives include:

"I have money I haven't even spent yet."

"I deserve money and have as much as I need."

"I am rich."

"I live like royalty."

These thoughts, when repeated constantly, can change how you feel about money. They can open you up to new possibilities for making and saving money. Consequently, these thoughts can affect how much money you actually have.

Some of us don't say to ourselves, "I live like royalty." We don't see the riches we possess. We truly do "create it all" by our selective perceptions, only we are choosing to create scarcity.

Step back in time just 300 years and imagine how a king or queen might have lived. These ruling monarchs would have enough to eat. Several times a year, they would have a feast. In their food would be spices from the four corners of the earth. These people would eat until they were stuffed. And after a meal, they could summon entertainment with the snap of a finger.

Transportation was no problem. Horses were always ready and a driver would chauffeur the king or queen from kingdom to kingdom.

Dress was lavish. Monarchs wore the finest cloth. The king and queen got new clothes at least once a year and never had to wear anything that was full of holes.

Their house was a castle. It was clean and dry, and had warm fireplaces in many rooms. The inhabitants were safe from nature and relatively safe from intruders.

In short, these people lived a royal existence. And they didn't have it nearly as good as most people in North America today.

Connect to cyberspace

The Internet is a complex of computer networks used by people across the world. Connecting to this network gives you access to millions of pages of text, animation, audio clips, video clips, and more. Through this connection you can expand your experience of diversity with a few clicks on a computer mouse. You can link to people across the world and explore a vast array of cultures and countries. They're just about all present in cyberspace.

Choosing hardware and software

To enter this multimedia world, you'll need some computer hardware (equipment) and software (programs that allow you to use the equipment). Equipment usually includes a keyboard, a CPU (central processing unit), a monitor (the "screen"), a printer, and a modem (a device that sends data over telephone or cable lines). Laptop computers combine the keyboard, CPU, and monitor into one portable unit.

You might also use a scanner (which transfers text and images from paper to a computer disk) and a CD drive that allows you to access data on compact discs and write (save) data on them.

When shopping for a computer, remember the "five S's": storage, software, speed, sight, and savings.

Storage. Personal computers store data in two ways. One is random access memory (RAM) or primary storage, which is the amount of data the computer can instantly manage without accessing its secondary storage. Secondary storage is the hard disk, which stores data permanently.

When it comes to storage, more is usually better. Having more RAM will help you fly faster on the Internet. And having a lot of hard disk space will allow you to store more software and more of the documents that you create or download from the Internet.

Software. Next, think about the basic software for your computer—its operating system. The operating system is also called a *platform*.

In personal computers, the most popular platforms are Windows and Macintosh. (Computers with the Windows platform are called *PCs*.) These two platforms are different, and transferring data between them can be tricky. A reasonable option is to choose the platform most likely to be used by people in your major.

Word processing software handles many writing and other basic tasks. And you'll need specific software to browse the Internet. Netscape Communicator and Microsoft Internet Explorer are two widely used browsers.

Speed. A computer's speed is determined by the kind of chip that powers its processor. Go for the fastest chip you can afford. Chip speed is often rated in megahertz. The higher the megahertz, the faster the computer.

You'll use a telephone or cable modem to connect to the Internet. Again, get the fastest connection you can afford. This will save you time when you access the Internet.

Sight. If you have any dollars left, channel them into getting the best monitor you can afford. Look for a monitor that delivers high resolution images in millions of colors, and go for a monitor that will be easy on your eyes. If you find yourself spending hours at the computer to finish a paper or create a presentation, you'll be thankful you spent money on a quality monitor.

Savings. Overall, personal computer prices are falling, even as these computers offer more speed, storage, and other goodies. But read ads carefully: Package prices might not include everything you need. Scout out student discounts. Find out if your school gives grants or loans to fund computer purchases.

Also determine whether your computer purchase is tax-deductible. It might be if you're attending school to maintain your current job.

Remember that there are plenty of alternatives to buying a new computer. One is to buy used equipment that you can upgrade if you choose. Another is to scout out computers that you can use for free or at low cost. Check for a student computer lab on your campus or at a public library.

Accessing the Internet

Currently there are several ways for you to access the Internet. One option is an Internet service provider (ISP) that offers basic Internet access to individuals for a flat monthly fee. Look for them in your local phone directory.

Commercial online services such as America Online offer another option. Such services offer Internet access plus additional online features of their own.

Before signing up for any service, ask whether you pay a flat monthly fee or a per-hour fee for connecting to the Internet.

Discovering what's there

The World Wide Web. The area of the Internet that gets the most publicity is the World Wide Web, which is growing exponentially by millions of pages. Information on the Web is organized and displayed as colorful sites, some with many "pages." You can move through pages in any sequence by clicking on highlighted or underlined words called *hyperlinks*. Never mind that the computer that originates the page might be thousands of miles away. Those pages show up on your screen in a matter of seconds or minutes, depending on the type of Internet connection you have.

Email (electronic mail). With a computer and modem, you can send email to anyone who's also connected to the Internet. Using email, you can send your message down the information highway almost instantly—no stamp or trip to the post office necessary. People in almost every country in the world can now receive email. Check to see if your school offers free email accounts for students.

Chat rooms. Chat rooms connect you with other people who share your interests. These services allow people to carry on instantaneous conversations in "real" time by typing messages to each other from their computers. Chat rooms exist on almost any subject.

Usenet (newsgroups). Computerized bulletin boards or newsgroups exist in an area of the Internet called Usenet. Here people post messages in public files. You can download these messages to your computer at any time and post a message of your own in response. As with chat rooms, newsgroups exist on countless subjects.

File transfer. On the Internet you can find thousands of files running the gamut from games to virus detectors and everything in between. You can copy or download such files from a remote computer to your computer—usually for free.

 The Internet is changing daily. For updates to this article, visit Houghton Mifflin's College Survival/Becoming a Master Student web site: **http://collegesurvival.college. hmco.com/students.**

Finding what you want on

I magine a library with millions of books—a place where anyone can bring in materials and place them on any shelf or even toss them randomly on the floor. That's something like the way information accumulates on the Internet. Finding your way through this maze can be a challenge. But it's worth it. On the Internet and at your fingertips are articles on any subject you can imagine, created by individuals and organizations around the planet.

Determine up front what you want.
Before you touch a computer to find something you want on the Internet, know your purpose. You can frame this purpose as a question ("What were some factors leading to the collapse of the Berlin Wall?") or a statement ("I want to find the names and addresses of five schools that offer majors in forestry management").

Also consider the *type* of material you want. Perhaps you want statistics, data from a survey, an exact quotation, or the results of a scientific study. In other cases, finding a summary of an article or a feature story from a popular magazine might be all that's needed to meet your purpose.

Use URLs and hyperlinks.
Every document on the Web is identified by a string of letters and numbers called a *URL (Uniform or Universal Resource Locator)*. The URL functions as a site's address on the Web. If you have a specific URL on hand, you can type it into your browser and go directly to that document.

When you want to connect to a specific web site, remember to type the URL exactly. Including a stray character or extra space in a URL can send you to an irrelevant web site, just as reversing numbers in a street address can send a letter to the wrong house.

Once you're at the site you want, look for underlined words and phrases that are often in a different color than the rest of the text on the page. These are *hyperlinks* (also called *links*). Clicking on these will take you to related web sites.

Distinguish between directories and search engines.
When searching a nonfiction book for a specific idea or fact, you can use two basic tools. One is the table of contents, a brief ordered list of the major topics in each chapter. The other tool is the index, a detailed alphabetized list of topics and subtopics that appear on each page of the book. When searching the Internet—especially the World Wide Web—you can use similar tools.

Directories offer extensive lists of web pages, all grouped by topic. Think of directories as a table of contents for the Web. Human beings create and maintain these directories, just as librarians create and maintain catalogs of library materials.

Search engines are more like indexes. These tools send out "spiders"—computer programs that "crawl" the Web and other parts of the Internet to find sites that relate to a specific topic. These programs scan millions of web pages in the same way that a human indexer reviews hundreds of book pages.

You'll find sites on the Web that work as either directories or search engines or both. All of these will return a list of web sites that relate to a specific topic.

To use directories and search engines, look for a query box somewhere on the search tool's main page. Move your computer's cursor to that box and type in *keywords* that relate to the topic you're researching. Say that your purpose is to find a list of mutual funds that invest in bonds offered by the United States Treasury. Keywords relating to your search include *mutual funds, bonds, treasury,* and *United States.*

The challenge is to get a list of the sites that are most relevant to your purpose. Choosing specific keywords often helps. Whenever possible, use proper nouns and names instead of general concepts or categories.

Go to directories to start your research.
Since these sites are organized by subject, you can often get results that are relevant to your purpose. Go to a search engine later in your research, when you've narrowed down your topic and have more specific keywords.

Find a few search tools you like and use them consistently. That way you get to know each tool well and capitalize on its strengths.

the Internet

Use Boolean operators. Boolean operators offer you methods of combining keywords. (These methods were invented by a mathematician named George Boole.) Boolean operators perform a valuable service by helping you narrow your search so that you don't end up with a long list of irrelevant sites.

Boolean operators include the words *AND, OR,* and *NOT.* For example, if you type *portfolios AND résumés,* you'll get a list of web sites that refer to both portfolios and résumés. *Portfolios OR résumés* will give you sites that refer to either topic. *Portfolios NOT résumés* will give you sites that relate only to portfolios.

Use other searching tricks. Knowing some other nifty tricks can help you save even more research time:

- When using a search tool, look for a link that will take you to a page explaining options for doing a more advanced search.
- Restrict your search to a specific part of the Internet, such as newsgroups.
- Bookmark web sites that you frequently visit. (A bookmark is a way to store addresses of sites that you want to visit again.)

Persist. If you run into a dead end in your research, do at least one more search. Use a new set of keywords or a new search tool. Be persistent. The results you want might be just one click away.

Keep in mind that web sites appear and disappear with surprising frequency. Also, the site that you want might be deluged with more visitors than it can handle. If you can't connect to a site, double-check the URL you're using. Or try connecting again at a later time.

Play. When you have some time to spare, cultivate serendipity in your searching. Set aside a specific amount of time to surf web sites at random. Have fun. By accident you might stumble on a perfect site to use as a source for your next paper.

Go forth into the world. Much of the information and ideas created by human beings still doesn't appear on the Internet. This material is stored in academic libraries, public libraries, books, magazines, and newspapers. Some of the information you want might exist only in people's heads. During your research, take a break from the computer and go to the library. Then go into the real world and talk with people. Research is often best done face to face.

For updates to this article, visit Houghton Mifflin's College Survival/Becoming a Master Student web site: **http://collegesurvival.college.hmco.com/students.**

PRACTICING CRITICAL THINKING **#19**

On a separate sheet of paper, write down three possible scenarios describing how the Internet could affect the way you live and work in the year 2010. Choose a best-case scenario, a worst-case scenario, and a most probable case scenario.

Then focus on your most probable case scenario. What could change it into a best-case or worst-case scenario? Write down your answers on a separate sheet of paper.

Share your responses to this exercise on the World Wide Web and see what other students predict. Visit Houghton Mifflin's College Survival/Becoming a Master Student web site: **http://collegesurvival.college. hmco.com/students.**

WORKPLACE APPLICATIONS

In many workplace settings, email is as important as the telephone or fax machine. To get the most from this medium of communication, remember to:

Write an informative subject line. Along with your name, the subject line is what a recipient sees when your message shows up in his email box. Rather than writing a generic description, include a capsule summary of your message. "Report due next Tuesday" packs more information than "Report." If your message is urgent, include that word in the subject line as well.

Think short. Keep your subject line short, your paragraphs short, and your message as a whole short. Most people don't want to read long documents on a computer screen.

Provide context. If you're responding to a question from a previous email, quote that question in your response.

Minimize formatting. Many email programs don't display special formatting such as boldface, italics, and color. Stick to straight text.

Keep in mind that any message you send via the Internet is essentially a public document. Any competent hacker can intercept a private message. Before sending, ask yourself: What would be the costs if this information were made public?

Thinking critically about information on the Internet

Sources of information on the Internet range from the reputable (such as the Library of Congress) to the flamboyant (such as the *National Enquirer*). This fact underscores the need for thinking critically about every aspect of the Internet.

Long before the Internet, critical thinking was valuable in every form of communication. Typos, mistakes, rumors, and downright lies have crept into print and television throughout the ages. Newspaper, magazine, and book publishers often employ fact checkers, editors, and lawyers to screen out errors and questionable material before publication. But authors of web pages and other Internet sources might not have these resources.

Taking a few simple precautions when you surf the Internet can keep you from crashing onto the rocky shore of misinformation.

Look for overall quality.
Before thinking critically about a web site, step back and examine the features of that site in general. Note the clarity of the text and visuals. Also note how well the site is organized and whether you can navigate the site's features with ease. Look for the date that crucial information was posted, and determine how often the site is updated.

When viewing any web page, you can also evaluate the site's links to related web pages. Look for links to pages of reputable organizations. Click on a few of those links. If they lead you to dead ends, this might indicate a page that's not updated often—one that's not a reliable source for late-breaking information.

Look at the author.
Think about the credibility of the organization that posts a web site. Look for evidence of bias or special interest. Perhaps that organization wants you to buy a service, a product, or a point of view. If so, then determine whether this fact colors the ideas and information posted on the web site. The domain in the Uniform Resource Locator (URL) for a web site can give you significant clues about sources of information and possible bias. For example, distinguish between information from a for-profit enterprise (URL ending in .com), a nonprofit one (.org), a government agency (.gov), and a school, college, or university (.edu).

Distinguish between ideas and information.
To think more powerfully about what you find on the Internet, remember the difference between information and ideas. For example, consider the following sentence: *Nelson Mandela became president of South Africa in 1994.* That statement provides information about South Africa. In contrast, the following sentence states an idea: *Nelson Mandela's presidency means that apartheid has no future in South Africa.*

Information refers to facts that can be verified by independent observers. *Ideas* are interpretations or opinions based on facts. Several people with the same information might adopt different ideas based on that information.

People who speak of the Internet as the "information superhighway" often forget to make this distinction. Don't assume that an idea is reasonable or accurate just because you find it on the Internet.

Look for documentation.
When you encounter an assertion on a web page or other Internet resource, note the types and quality of the evidence offered. Look for credible examples, quotations from authorities in the field, documented statistics, or summaries of scientific studies. Also look for endnotes, bibliographies, or another way to find the original sources of information.

Set an example.
In the midst of the Internet's chaotic growth, you can light a path of rationality. Whether you're sending a short email message or building a massive web site, you can bring your own critical thinking skills into play. Every word and image you send down the wires to the Web can display the hallmarks of critical thinking—sound logic, credible evidence, and respect for your audience.

 You can find additional suggestions for thinking critically about information on the Internet at Houghton Mifflin's College Survival/Becoming a Master Student web site: **http://collegesurvival.college.hmco.com/students.**

Using computers to manage ideas and information

Computers can be a great tool to help you succeed in school. They can help you write and revise papers, create winning presentations, manipulate numbers, maintain mailing lists, and track your personal finances. They can also help you create calendars, store to-do lists, and send and receive faxes.

Research efficiently.
If you currently take notes for a research paper on 3×5 cards, consider using a computer instead. A single floppy disk can store the same amount of text as thousands of cards. With high-capacity Zip drives and CD-ROMs, you can store hundreds or thousands of times more information. Once they are stored in computer files, your notes can be reduced, rearranged, and rewritten with ease.

Outline your ideas.
Creating outlines can save you hours of writing time. An outline lays bare the structure of your thinking, helping you spot gaps in logic or holes in a story plot before you draft hundreds or even thousands of words. To be even more efficient, write your outline in complete sentences rather than single words or phrases.

Many word processing programs include an outlining feature. You can use this feature to write headings at various levels. In this article, for instance, the title "Using computers to manage ideas and information" is the major heading. "Outline your ideas" is a subheading that falls one level under the title. You could also think of the topic sentence of each paragraph in this article as a sub-subheading (a heading that falls under a subheading).

Outlining tools make it easy to rearrange headings, assign them to different levels, and insert sentences under each heading. You can also use outlining software to organize your notes on textbooks and lectures. Divide a chapter or lecture into sections, then write a heading to capture the main idea of each section. To save time when you review, just display the headlines and scan them as you would scan the headlines in a newspaper.

Revise your writing.
Many word processing programs offer editing features. These include spelling checkers and utilities for compiling indexes, tables of contents, endnotes, and bibliographies. In addition, these programs often include a computer-based dictionary and thesaurus. Your word processing program might even correct typos automatically and count the number of words in your paper. Cutting and pasting text is as simple as clicking your mouse.

Word processing software often includes ways for you to create maps, tables, charts, and other visuals and paste them into your documents. For creating more complex graphics or multimedia presentations, check out software such as *PowerPoint*.

Stay in contact via email.
When you're crunched for time and don't want to mail a long letter, just send a paragraph or two via email—much as you would a postcard. With email, you can send shorter notes, send them often, and stay in close touch with relatives, friends, and job contacts. These people can receive your notes almost instantaneously. Popular email software includes *Eudora* and *Outlook Express*.

Send and receive documents.
Check with your instructor about policies for submitting assignments electronically—via email, disk, or fax. You might be able to send a longer document as an attachment to an email message. Before you rely on this option, make sure your instructor can open up and read whatever files are sent in this way.

Stay informed—and keep others informed about you.
Computers offer an efficient way to keep up with the news. Using a web-based news site, you can scan the headlines of articles, read the lead paragraph of each article, or display the full text. Choose from a vast selection of online newsletters, newspapers, magazines, and journals.

Using software such as *Microsoft FrontPage* or *NetObjects Fusion,* you can also create your own web site—a personal home page with news about yourself that you can update at any time.

Crunch numbers and manage money.
Just about everybody can benefit from crunching numbers with spreadsheets such as *Excel.* This type of computer software allows you to create and alter budgets of any size. By plugging in numbers based on assumptions about the future, you can quickly create many scenarios for future income and expenses. *Quicken* and its related web site (www.quicken.com) include spreadsheets and other features that can help you manage your personal finances. The World Wide Web also offers sites that allow you to manage your bank account, get stock quotes, place classified ads for items you want to sell, book airline reservations, and buy almost anything.

Create new ideas and solve problems.
Problem Solver from Mind Link includes a series of writing exercises, sample analogies, and word association games designed to help you see new connections between ideas. *Inspiration,* published by Inspiration Software, helps you create diagrams, flow charts, project schedules, and outlines. Use these programs and others like them to create ideas in both verbal and visual forms.

Manage projects and detailed information.
Many computer applications can function as personal information managers and project managers. These products generally help you keep track of calendar items and to-do lists. Examples are *ClarisOrganizer, Day-Timer, Hallmark Connections, Microsoft Scheduler,* and *Now Up-to-Date & Contact.*

When you have a lot of information that's filed alphabetically or numerically—names, addresses, or lists of inventory—consider using database software such as *FileMaker Pro.*

The titles mentioned in this article are just a few examples of useful software. Many more are available from computer dealers, wholesalers, and software catalogs.

 For updates to this article, visit Houghton Mifflin's College Survival/Becoming a Master Student web site: **http://collegesurvival.college.hmco.com/students.**

Ways to waste time with a computer

To enjoy the full benefits of a computer, take a few precautions. Stay alert for the following computer-based time-wasters.

Trial-and-error learning. Flying by the seat of your pants as you learn the computer sometimes works well. In other cases, you can save hours by spending a few minutes reading the instructions or by taking a computer class.

Hours that evaporate while you play. When cruising the Internet or playing computer games, you might find that a whole morning, afternoon, or evening has disappeared into the digital void. If you start losing too much time to computer play, set a time to end the fun before you start.

Endless revising. Computers make it easy to revise your writing, and you might feel tempted to keep fiddling with a paper to the point that you miss your timeline. Experiment with dictating your revisions or marking them on hard copy with a red pencil.

Losing data. It's been said that the two most important words in using a computer are *backup* and *save.* This refers to the fact that power surges and loss of electricity can destroy data. Computer users tell stories about losing hours of work in a millisecond. To prevent this fate, take two simple but powerful steps: First, make backup copies of your work on separate disks. Then make a backup of your backup disks to store separately. This way you will still have what you might have spent days creating. Also save your work every few minutes. Your computer manual will explain how. (Some software does this automatically.)

Crashing and freezing. Your computer might *crash* or *freeze*—that is, suddenly quit or refuse to respond to anything that you type. Find out how to shut down and restart the computer if this happens.

Getting "spammed." *Spam* is the Internet equivalent of junk mail—unwanted messages that show up in your email inbox. To avoid spam, be selective in giving out your email address.

One more caution. Don't expect your grades to soar right after you buy a computer. Learning to become more productive can take several weeks. And there's always more to learn.

Computers can perform many tasks with dizzying speed. What they *don't* do is write papers, create ideas, read textbooks, or attend classes. For those tasks, human beings are irreplaceable.

Practice "netiquette"

Being kind while you're online

Netiquette is a collection of informal standards that apply to people who "talk" to each other through personal computers. Think of these standards as an etiquette code for the Internet.

Put out the flames.
"Flaming" takes place when someone sends an online message tinged with sarcasm or outright hostility. To create positive relationships when you're online, avoid sending such messages.

Some Internet users cut "flamers" a little slack. These users argue that an occasional outburst of anger is as appropriate when people are online as when they're face to face. But few advocate "flame wars"—a long series of insults and tirades exchanged among a few people. This kind of hostile dialogue can send the tone of an online community into the gutter.

Respect others' time and privacy.
People often turn to the Internet in the hope of saving time—not wasting it. You can accommodate their desires by typing concise messages. If you create your own web page, limit its download time by using simple, tasteful graphics. Update your page regularly and include your email address. Finally, if you have access to other people's computers, respect the privacy of their online documents.

Keep the medium in mind.
Communicating by computer eliminates nonverbal communication, including hand gestures and facial expressions. In face-to-face conversation, you rely on these subtle cues to decode another person's message. When your link to another person takes place only via words on a monitor, those cues vanish.

Use humor with caution. A joke that's funny when told in person might offend someone when written and sent via computer.

Use emoticons with care. Emoticons are combinations of keyboard characters that represent an emotion, such as :>). Emoticons are not appropriate for some communications, including exchanges with a prospective employer.

AVOID MESSAGES THAT APPEAR IN UPPERCASE LETTERS. They are the equivalent of shouting during a face-to-face conversation.

Remember—behind every computer is a person.
The cornerstone of netiquette is to remember that there is a human being on the receiving end of your communications. Whenever you're ready to send a message across the Internet, ask yourself one question: Would you say it to the person's face?

Staying up-to-date with technology

Computer technology is so dynamic that statements made about it can become outdated almost instantaneously. What once seemed like remote possibilities—such as web-based television and Internet connection via cable television lines—quickly became realities. To get the most value from emerging technology, adopt the following habits that can help you to stay up-to-date.

Read magazines and periodicals devoted to emerging technology.
For example, the *Chronicle of Higher Education* regularly includes articles about new technology and its implications for vocational schools, colleges, and universities. *Wired* magazine covers digital technology and popular culture.

Hang out with those who know.
Go to computer stores and browse the displays and new products. Talk with the salespeople and ask about what's new. Investigate computer clubs at your school or in the community. Seek out other people who seem technologically savvy.

Go to the Internet.
Search engines and directories often highlight web sites that cover the latest developments. Directories such as Yahoo! include tutorials and help screens that offer an overview of the Internet. These resources are updated regularly. Also check the *New York Times* Technology Section online at www.nytimes.com/pages/technology/index.html.

Look beyond personal computers.
Watch for other innovations in technology that could touch your life. Possibilities include DVDs, PDAs, cellular phones with an Internet connection, and watches and other small devices with computing and communication capabilities.

Go back to your purpose.
Technology can add value to your life and can also complicate it. Laptops, PDAs, and cell phones make it possible for people to work all the time, anywhere. Consider your purpose. That may not be what you want.

Library
The buried treasure

Books. That's what most of us imagine when we hear the word *library*. Books take up a lot of space in a library, and they are only one of the many resources that can be found there.

Most libraries have books. Many also have records, compact discs, works of art, maps, telephone directories for major cities, audiovisual equipment, newspapers, microfiche, microfilm, audio- and videocassettes, computers, CD-ROMs, magazines, dictionaries and encyclopedias of all varieties, research aids, government documents, pamphlets, and more.

Libraries range widely in size. Most have the same purpose. They exist to help you find facts and ideas.

Getting familiar with the library's resources and services will help you succeed in school. Knowing ways to unearth a library's treasures can enhance your reading skills, expand your vocabulary, increase your self-confidence, and save you time.

The best library resource

Libraries give you access to a resource that goes beyond the pages of a book or a site on the World Wide Web. That resource is a living person called a librarian whose job is to help you find what you want. Librarians are trained explorers. They know ways to find information in countless places. Ask for help.

Remember that librarians have different specialties. Most libraries have a reference librarian who can usually let you know whether the library has what you need. He might suggest a different library or direct you to another source, such as a business, community agency, or government office.

Any book you want

Most libraries can now provide nearly any book you could ever want—along with many nonprint materials—through interlibrary loans. This sharing of materials gives even the smallest library access to millions of books. Just ask your library to borrow the material you want from another library.

Periodicals

The type of magazines, trade journals, technical journals, and newspapers that a library carries depends mostly on the size, type, location, and purpose of the library. A neighborhood branch of a public library might have copies of the local paper and magazines right from the grocery store aisle. A library in a business school is more likely to have the *Wall Street Journal* and trade journals for accountants and business managers.

Reference materials in print

Books in Print is a list of most books currently available for sale in the United States. Like the library catalog, it is organized by subject, author, and title.

The Reader's Guide to Periodical Literature indexes articles found in many magazines. Searching by subject, you can find titles of articles. The magazine name, date, volume, and page numbers are listed. If you want an older magazine, many libraries require that you fill out a form requesting the magazine so it can be retrieved from storage in closed stacks.

Other guides to recent periodicals include: *New York Times Index, Business Periodicals Index, Applied Science and Technology Index, Social Sciences Index, Accountants' Index, General Science Index, Education Index, Humanities Index,* and *Art Index.* These indices help you find what you want in a hurry.

Abstracts are publications that summarize current findings in specific fields. You can review condensed versions of specialized articles by reading materials such as *Chemical Abstracts, Psychological Abstracts,* or *Sociological Abstracts.*

Pamphlets and clippings are usually stored in file cabinets organized by subject. This section contains information from the U.S. Government Printing Office and state and local governments, as well as newspaper and magazine clippings.

Facts about virtually anything you can imagine are waiting in almanacs and publications from government departments such as Labor, Commerce, and Agriculture.

The U.S. Government Printing Office is the largest publisher in the world. The *Monthly Catalog* of its printings takes up several feet of shelf space.

General and specialized encyclopedias are also found in the reference section. Specialized examples include: *Cyclopedia of World Authors, Grove's Dictionary of Music and Musicians, Encyclopedia of Religion and Ethics.*

Dictionaries of all sizes and specialties are also available in a library. Many disciplines (medicine, computer science, engineering) have their own dictionaries.

Of special value to your writing is the thesaurus. This is one place to check for synonyms—words that have a similar meaning to the word you look up. A thesaurus provides relief when you just can't think of the word you want. Many word processing programs for personal computers include an electronic thesaurus.

Computer-based resources

A library's catalog lists the materials available at that location. These listings used to be kept on cards, and in a few cases they still are. Today most libraries catalog their materials electronically on computers, and some even include listings for several libraries.

The catalog is an alphabetical listing that is cross-referenced by subject, author, and title. Each listing carries the author's name, the title, the publisher, the date of publication, the number of pages and illustrations, the Library of Congress or Dewey decimal system number (for locating materials), and sometimes a brief description of the material.

A computerized catalog gives you more flexibility in searching for materials. For example, you can type in a keyword or a phrase and ask the computer to search for all listings with that word.

Some of these systems will also allow you to see if the title is on the shelf or checked out. They might even allow you to put a hold on the materials you want.

Most libraries offer computers with Internet access. These computers are often available on a first-come, first-served basis, for free or for a nominal cost. Through the Internet, you can access materials from libraries across the world. You might also be able to find an online version of the printed reference materials mentioned above. Ask a librarian for help.

Many resources that were once found only in print are now available on CD-ROMs. Examples include encyclopedias, dictionaries, and thesauruses. While you're poking through the CD-ROM section, also look for specialized indices such as *Magazine Index, Business Index, Info'Trac, Newsbank,* and *Medline.* These sources provide the same information as the traditional print materials, yet many people find CD-ROMs quicker and easier to use.

Some materials on CD-ROM, such as the *Encyclopaedia Britannica,* allow you to do plain-English queries. Just type in the question you want answered.

Strategies for effective library research

To save research time, plan. Say that the purpose of your paper is to persuade students to use laptop computers in class. Begin by asking yourself typical questions that a reader might ask: What can a laptop computer really do for me? How much does one cost? Can I get along fine without one?

Next, choose what type of sources you want to consult and in what order. For help with this step, ask a librarian. Describe your subject, purpose, audience, and the questions you want to answer.

Start your research from home. If you have a computer with Internet access, do an initial search for materials before you go to the library. If your library doesn't have what you want, you can save yourself a trip. And if another library has what you want, you can request an interlibrary loan—sometimes right from your own personal computer.

Many libraries now have their own web sites. These might allow you to view an online catalog, reserve and renew materials, or query a librarian via email.

Check the front matter and back matter. Look in the front of printed reference materials for guidelines on how to use them. Often this section will tell you the meanings of abbreviations and how the entries in that volume were selected. Also use the index at the back of a book or the last volume of an encyclopedia set to save time when searching for information. When reading articles on CD-ROMs, look for links to Internet sites.

Look for the most specific items first. Start with specifics and then generalize, if needed. For example, if you are looking for a user's manual for a particular word processing program, look under the name of that program. If that doesn't work, then look under the more general category of "word processing."

Use libraries for purposes other than studying. Find tips for ways to finance your education, quit smoking, build bookshelves, or knit a sweater. You can also find product ratings that provide valuable information about major purchases, such as a car.

Attend an orientation session. Many libraries offer workshops about their materials and services. These workshops are usually free and offer a way to promote your success. The library exists for your benefit, waiting only for you to use it.

Risk being a fool

*A powerful person has the courage to take risks.
And taking risks means being willing to fail sometimes—
even to be a fool. This idea can work for you
because you already are a fool.*

Don't be upset. All of us are fools at one time or another. There are no exceptions. If you doubt it, think back to that stupid thing you did just a few days ago. You know the one. Yes . . . *that* one. It was embarrassing and you tried to hide it. You pretended you weren't a fool. This happens to everyone.

People who insist that they have never been fools are perhaps the biggest fools of all. We are all fallible human beings. Most of us, however, spend too much time and energy trying to hide our fool-hood. No one is really tricked by this—not even ourselves. And whenever we pretend to be something we're not, we miss part of life.

For example, many of us never dance because we don't want to risk looking ridiculous. We're not wrong. We probably would look ridiculous. That's the secret of risking being a fool.

It's OK to look ridiculous while dancing. It's all right to sound silly when singing to your kids. Sometimes it's OK to be absurd. It comes with taking risks.

Taking risks is not being foolhardy

Sometimes it's not OK to be absurd. This Power Process comes with a warning label: Taking risks does *not* mean we get to escape responsibility for our actions. "Risk being a fool" is not a suggestion to get drunk at a party and make a fool of yourself. It is not a suggestion to act the fool by disrupting class. It is not a suggestion to be foolhardy or to "fool around."

Taking risks and being a fool means recognizing that foolishness—along with dignity, courage, cowardice, grace, clumsiness, and other qualities—is a human characteristic. We all share it. You might as well risk being a fool because you already are one, and nothing in the world can change that. Why not enjoy it once in a while?

Consider the case of the person who won't dance because he's afraid he'll look foolish. This same person will spend an afternoon tripping over his feet on a basketball court. If you say that his jump shot from the top of the key looks like a circus accident, he might even agree.

"So what?" he might say. "I'm no Michael Jordan." He's right. On the basketball court, he is willing to risk looking like a fool in order to enjoy the game.

He is no Fred Astaire, either. For some reason, that bothers him. The result is that he misses the fun of dancing. (Dancing badly is as much fun as shooting baskets badly—and maybe a lot more fun.)

There's one sure-fire way to avoid any risk of being a fool, and that's to avoid life. The writer who never finishes a book will never have to worry about getting negative reviews. The center fielder who sits out every game is safe from making any errors. And the comedian who never performs in front of an audience is certain to avoid telling jokes that fall flat. The possibility of succeeding at any venture increases when we're comfortable with making mistakes—that is, with the risk of being a fool.

Look at courage in a new way

Again, remember the warning label. This Power Process does not suggest that the way to be happy in life is to do things badly. Courage involves the willingness to face danger and risk failure. Mediocrity is not the goal. The point is that mastery in most activities calls for willingness to do something new, to fail, to make corrections, to fail again, and so on. On the way to becoming a good writer, be willing to be a bad writer.

Consider these revised clichés: Anything worth doing is worth doing badly at first. Practice makes improvement. If at first you don't fail, try again.

Most artists and athletes have learned the secret of being foolish. Comedians are especially well versed in this art. All of us know how it feels to tell a joke and get complete silence. We truly look and feel like fools. Professional comedians risk feeling that way for a living. Being funny is not enough for success in the comedy business. A comedian must have the courage to face failure.

Courage is an old-fashioned word for an old-fashioned virtue. Traditionally, people have reserved that word for illustrious acts of exceptional people—the campaigns of generals and the missions of heroes.

This concept of courage is fine. At the same time, it can be limiting and can prevent us from seeing courage in everyday actions. Courage is the kindergartner who, with heart pounding, waves good-bye to his parents and boards the bus for his first day of school. Courage is the 40-year-old who registers for college courses after being away from the classroom for 20 years.

For a student, the willingness to take risks means the willingness to experiment with new skills, to achieve personal growth, and sometimes to fail. The rewards of risk taking include expanded creativity, more satisfying self-expression, and more joy.

An experiment for you

Here's an experiment you can conduct to experience the joys of risk taking. The next time you take a risk and end up doing something silly or stupid, allow yourself to be totally aware of your reaction. Don't deny it. Don't cover it up. Notice everything about the feeling, including the physical sensations and thoughts that come with it. Acknowledge the foolishness. Be exactly who you are. Explore all of the emotions, images, and sensations surrounding your experience.

Also remember that we can act independently of our feelings. Courage is not the absence of fear but the willingness to take risks even when we feel fear. We can be keenly homesick and still register for classes. We can tremble at the thought of speaking in public yet still walk up to the microphone.

When we fully experience it, the fear of taking risks loses its power. Then we have the freedom to expand and grow.

master student
CESAR CHAVEZ

(1927–1993) leader of the United Farm Workers (UFW), organized strikes, boycotts, and fasts to improve conditions for migrant workers.

A *few men and women have engraved their names* in the annals of change through nonviolence, but none have experienced the grinding childhood poverty that Chavez did after the Depression-struck family farm on the Gila River was foreclosed in 1937.

Chavez was 10. His parents and the five children took to the picking fields as migrant workers.

Chavez's faith sustained him, but it is likely that it was both knowing and witnessing poverty and the sheer drudgery and helplessness of the migrant life that drove him.

He never lost the outreach that he had learned from his mother, who, despite the family's poverty, told her children to invite any hungry people in the area home to share what rice, beans and tortillas the family had.

He left school to work. He attended 65 elementary schools but never graduated from high school. Always moving on with the season, his extended family hunger, fatigue, illness, and the excruciating pain that can come from hours of backbreaking tasks. . . .

It was in the fields, in the 1950s, that Chavez met his wife, Helen. The couple and their eight children gave much to "La Huelga," the strike call that became the UFW trademark, from their eventual permanent home near Bakersfield. Chavez did not own the home . . . but paid rent out of his $900 a month as a union official.

Yet, in the fields in the 1930s, something happened that changed Chavez's life. He was 12 when a Congress of Industrial Organizations union began organizing dried-fruit industry workers, including his father and uncle. The young boy learned about strikes, pickets and organizing.

For two years during World War II, Chavez served in the U.S. Navy; then it was back to the fields and organizing. There were other movements gaining strength in the United States during those years, including community organizing.

From 1952 to 1962, Chavez was active outside the fields, in voter registration drives and in challenging police and immigration abuse of Mexicans and Mexican-Americans.

At first, in the 1960s, only one movement had a noticeable symbol: the peace movement. By the time the decade ended, the United Farm Workers, originally established as the National Farm Workers Association, gave history a second flag: the black Aztec eagle on the red background.

In eight years, a migrant worker son of migrants helped change a nation's perception through nonviolent resistance. It took courage, imagination, the ability to withstand physical and other abuse.

The facts are well-known now. During the 1968 grape boycott, farmers and growers fought him, but Chavez stood firm. Shoppers hesitated, then pushed their carts past grape counters without buying.

The growers were forced to negotiate.

The UFW as a Mexican-American civil rights movement in time might outweigh the achievements of the UFW as a labor movement, for Chavez also represented something equally powerful to urban Mexican-Americans and immigrants—a nonviolent leader who had achieved great change from the most humble beginnings.

Yet, through the UFW, Chavez and his colleagues brought Americans face-to-face with the true costs, the human costs, of the food on their tables and brought Mexican-Americans into the political arena and helped keep them there. . . .

Word of Chavez's death spread to the union halls decorated with the Virgin of Guadalupe and UFW flag, to the fields, to the small towns and larger cities. And stories about the short, compact man with the ready smile, the iron determination, the genuine humility and the deep faith were being told amid the tears.

From Arthur Jones, "Millions Reaped What Cesar Chavez Sowed," National Catholic Reporter, *Reprinted by permission of the* National Catholic Reporter, *Kansas City, MO 64111*

For more biographical information on Cesar Chavez, visit Houghton Mifflin's College Survival/ Becoming a Master Student web site:
http://collegesurvival.college.hmco.com/students.

1 List three campus resources and three community resources that could help you succeed in school.

 2 Name at least three methods for decreasing expenses that you could apply immediately.

 3 Summarize the concept of financial independence as explained in this chapter.

4 Name at least five ways to find money for school.

5 According to the text, most money problems have a single source. Explain that source and a basic strategy for solving it.

 6 Explain at least three strategies for finding what you want on the Internet.

  7 Describe three criteria to consider when buying a computer.

Quiz
CONTINUED

 8 In general, you can assume that information you find on the Internet is more current and accurate than information you find in print materials. True or False? Explain your answer.

 9 Explain the distinction between *ideas* and *information* as described in the text and how this distinction applies to thinking critically about the Internet.

 10 Describe three strategies for doing library research more effectively.

JOURNAL ENTRY

#50

Discovery/Intention Statement

Review what you learned in this chapter about the way you manage money or use technology.

I discovered that I ...

_____

_____

_____

Choose one money- or technology-related behavior you want to change. Describe when you intend to make this change.

I intend to ...

_____

_____

_____

LEARNING STYLES APPLICATION   CHAPTER 10

Mode 4 *After carrying out your plan, consider how well it worked for you. Which resources do you intend to continue on a regular basis? List those resources.*

Mode 1 *Describe a problem you are experiencing right now that you might be able to solve by using a service on your campus or in your community. For example, you might want tutoring in a specific subject or help in resolving a conflict with an instructor.*

Mode 3 *Create an action plan for using the resources you listed for Mode 2. Write five Intention Statements and set a date for taking each action.*

Mode 2 *List five resources mentioned in this chapter that could help you solve the problem you just described.*

BIBLIOGRAPHY

INTERNET RESOURCES

ENDNOTE

1 Joe Dominguez and Vicki Robin, *Your Money or Your Life: Transforming Your Relationship with Money and Achieving Financial Independence* (New York: Viking, 1992).

ADDITIONAL READING

Anthony, Jason, and Karl Cluck. *Debt-Free by 30.* New York: Plume, 2001.

Elgin, Duane. *Voluntary Simplicity.* New York: Morrow, 1993.

Manning, Robert. *Credit Card Nation: The Consequences of America's Addiction to Credit.* New York: Basic Books, 2000.

Orman, Suze. *The Road to Wealth.* New York: Riverhead, 2001.

Pejsa, Jack. *Success in College Using the Internet.* Boston: Houghton Mifflin, 1998.

U.S. Department of Education. *The Student Guide.* Published yearly. (Federal Student Aid Information Center, P.O. Box 84, Washington, DC 20044-0084, 1-800-4-FED-AID)

Financial Aid Information Page
www.finaid.org

Library Spot
www.libraryspot.com

Netiquette
http://www.albion.com/netiquette/index.html

Student Guide (Financial Aid)
www.ed.gov/prog_info/SFA/StudentGuide/

WeMedia—Products and services for people with disabilities
www.wemedia.com/

Wired Magazine
www.wired.com

CHAPTER 11 | Health

To be somebody you must last.
RUTH GORDON

Emotion, which is suffering, ceases to be suffering as soon as we have a clear picture of it.
BARUCH SPINOZA

IN THIS CHAPTER . . . Maintain physical and mental energy by treating your body as an incredible machine—one that deserves at least as much attention as your car. Choose ways to fuel, move, rest, observe, and protect your machine. Also develop self-esteem, deal with emotional pain, and consider the truth about drugs. To support all of these techniques, see surrender as a path to satisfaction instead of defeat.

Thinking about health

If you want to experience greater health, then start by exercising some tissue that lies between your ears—the organ called your brain. Often the path to greater health starts not with new food or aerobic activity but with a change in thinking.

Consider the power of beliefs. Some of them erect barriers to higher levels of health: "Your health is programmed by your heredity." "Some people are just low on energy." "Healthful food doesn't taste very good." "Over the long run, people just don't change."

Add to this some basic confusion about what the word *health* means. Ask 20 different people for a definition, and you'll probably get 20 different answers—10 of them variations on "I don't know." That's amazing, given the fact that bookstores stock hundreds of titles about health and popular magazines feature the topic every month.

To think clearly about health, start with language. The word *health* is similar in origin to *whole, hale, hardy,* and even *holy*. Implied in this list are qualities that most of us associate with healthy people: alertness, vitality, and vigor. Healthy people meet the demands of daily life with energy to spare. Illness or stress might slow them down for a while, and then they bounce back. They are complete, sound in body, mind, and spirit.

To open up your inquiry into health—and to open up new possibilities for your life—consider two ideas.

First, health is a continuum. On one end of that continuum is a death that comes too early. On the other end is a long life filled with satisfying work and fulfilling relationships. Many of us exist between those extremes at a point we might call average. Most of the time we're not sick. And most of the time we're not truly thriving, either.

Second, health changes. Health is not a fixed state. In fact, health fluctuates from year to year, day to day, and moment to moment. Those changes can occur by chance. Or they can occur by choice, as we take conscious control of our thinking and behavior.

Perhaps *health* is one of those rich, multilayered concepts that we can never define completely. That's okay. We can still clear our mental decks of beliefs that undermine us. We can also adopt habits that lengthen life and sustain our well-being.

JOURNAL ENTRY

#51

Discovery Statement

On a separate sheet of paper, make a quick list of your activities during the last 48 hours, including the foods you ate at each meal. Circle any activities on your list that promoted your health. Underline any activities that could detract from your health. Sum up your discoveries below.

I discovered that I . . .

_____

_____

_____

_____

_____

_____

Next, scan this chapter for any strategies you can use immediately to sustain your health-promoting behaviors or change any health-defeating behaviors. List three strategies you want to read about in more detail.

_____

_____

_____

_____

_____

_____

You don't have to accept these two ideas just because they're printed here. Test them as you would any other idea in this book. Ultimately, your definition of health comes from your own experience. The proof lies not on the page but in your life—in the level of health that you create, starting now.

TAKE CARE OF YOUR MACHINE

Some people are offended by the notion that the human body is a machine.

This analogy is made with great respect for our bodies and with the understanding that we are more than our bodies. We have a mind and a soul that are certainly separate from our bodies, even though they are connected. And in order to house our mind and soul, we have a body—a fantastic machine.

Our machines are truly incredible. They often continue to operate despite abuse. We pollute them, dent them, run them too hard, let them sit idle for years, even wreck them. At times we try to fuel our machines with junk food. We pollute them with empty calories and expose them to unnecessary risks of illnesses or accidents. And still our incredible machines continue to run—most of the time. Ironically, we can also take excellent care of our machines, only to have them quit on us just when we need them most.

To an extent greater than most of us imagine, we choose our level of health. We can promote our health by taking definite steps.

When we buy a car or a new appliance, we generally look at the owner's manual. We study it to find out just how this new machine works. We make sure we understand all of its features and what is needed to properly maintain it. For example, we know that people can prevent damage to their cars by performing simple maintenance procedures, such as regular oil changes and tune-ups.

It's amazing that many of us take better care of our cars, dishwashers, air conditioners, and furnaces than we do of our bodies. We can change this. We can spend at least as much time learning about our own health as we do reading the owner's manual for a new car.

It would be easier if each of us received an owner's manual for our bodies at the moment of birth. Unfortunately, no such manual exists. Our challenge is to create a personal guidebook to health based on our own observations, studies, and experiences.

The suggestions on the next several pages are accepted by almost all experts on health. Study them as if they were an owner's manual for a priceless machine—one that can't be replaced, one that your life depends on. That machine is your body.

Your machine:
Fuel it

It is a cliché, but it's true: You are what you eat. The brain needs nutrients to function properly. What you eat can have immediate and long-term effects on your performance as a student. That giant jelly donut can make you drowsy within minutes, and a steady diet of them can affect the amount of energy you have available to meet and juggle the demands of classes, family members, jobs, extracurricular activities, and other commitments.

There have been hundreds of books written about nutrition. One says don't drink milk. Another says buy a cow. Some say load up on 5,000 milligrams of vitamin C a day. Others say avoid oranges. This debate can be confusing. There is, however, some agreement among nutritional scientists. A list of dietary guidelines was developed by a committee of experts and published by the U.S. Senate (see page [333]) Though you might find a healthier diet, you can do well by following these guidelines.

If you are overweight, you can avoid people, groups, and dietary proponents who make claims about a quick fix. Even if that "Lose 20 pounds in 20 days!" diet works, you're likely to gain the weight back in a few weeks—plus a few extra pounds.

The formula for weight loss is simple: Eat better food, eat less food, and exercise regularly. And to maintain your health, avoid losing more than two pounds per week. Though the formula is simple, using it is sometimes not so simple. Local newspapers and the Yellow Pages list classes, support groups, and professionally run programs that can help you reach and then maintain your ideal weight.

There are two eating disorders that affect many students. *Bulimia* is a serious illness that involves cycles of excessive eating and forced purges. A person with this disorder might gorge on a large pizza, a dozen donuts, and a gallon of ice cream, and then force herself to vomit. Or she might compensate for overeating by using excessive laxatives, enemas, or diuretics. *Anorexia nervosa* is a potentially fatal illness characterized by self-starvation, either through extended fasts or by eating only one food for weeks at a time. People suffering from this condition—males as well as females—often have distorted self-images and imagine that they are overweight, even as their weight plummets. Another characteristic of this disorder is a fear of the future and the unknown. By controlling their weight, whether consciously or subconsciously, anorexics strive to exert some measure of control over their lives.

Both of these disorders call for treatment. If you're worried about having an eating disorder, go to your medical health care professional (doctor, nurse practitioner, or physician's assistant), campus health service, or local public health clinic. If you see signs of an eating disorder in someone else, express your concern with "I" messages as explained in the Communicating chapter. Also contact the organizations below for help.

National Association of Anorexia Nervosa and Associated Disorders **(847) 831-3438** or **www.anad.org.**
Anorexia Nervosa and Related Eating Disorders, Inc. **(541) 344-1144** or **www.anred.com.**

EXERCISE

#31

Setting your bio-alarm

Sometimes, after only a few hours of sleep, we wake up feeling miserable. Other times, we bounce out of bed feeling terrific. How we feel in the morning can depend on how we program our bio-alarm clock the night before.

After a long night of studying, you might go to bed thinking, "I shouldn't have stayed up so late. I'll be exhausted tomorrow. I hope I hear the alarm in the morning." The next morning, you oversleep and miss class.

To wake up refreshed, try this. Before going to bed, decide what time you want to get up in the morning. Then say out loud, "I am going to get up at 7 a.m." (or whatever time you choose).

Next, lie in bed and allow your body to relax. Imagine feeling heavy and sinking into the bed. Softly say (out loud if possible), "I will wake naturally at 7 a.m. feeling refreshed, rested, and ready to start my day."

You will probably wake up feeling great—at exactly the time you chose.

Your machine:
Move it

Regular exercise can improve your performance in school. Your brain usually functions best if the rest of your body is in shape, and the right kind of exercise is an effective way to dissipate the tension that builds up when you are hunched over a keyboard, hammering out a term paper.

Our bodies need to be exercised. The world ran on muscle power back in the era when we had to hunt down a woolly mammoth every few weeks and drag it back to the cave. Now we can grab a burger at a drive-up window. It's convenient, but it doesn't do much for our deltoids, quadriceps, and other muscles. According to the Centers for Disease Control, obesity among Americans increased 60 percent from 1991 to 1999. (For most people, obesity means being at least 30 pounds overweight.) The heart is a muscle that can get fat, too. A fat belly might be unattractive. A fat heart can be lethal. Lean muscles absorb nutrients more efficiently than muscles marbled with fat. The best reason to get in shape isn't to improve how you will look in designer jeans—it's to function better at whatever you do, whether it's mammoth hunting or boning up on math.

Sometimes people who are out of shape or overweight think that they cannot change. The human body *can* change. Inside even the most dilapidated body there is a trim, healthy, energized body that is waiting to emerge. Begin by taking a First Step. Tell the truth about the problem and declare your desire to change.

You can make real progress in a matter of weeks. Sticking to an exercise schedule for just three weeks can bring rewards. Remember, dieting alone doesn't create lean muscles and a strong heart. The only way to get lean is by moving.

You don't have to train for the Boston Marathon, however. It's not even smart, unless you're already in great shape. Do something you enjoy. Start by walking briskly 15 minutes every day. Increase that time gradually and add a little running.

Once you're in reasonable shape, you can stay there by doing three 20- to 30-minute sessions a week of aerobic activity—the kind that elevates your heart rate to a faster and steady pace.

School can be a great place to get in shape. Classes might be offered in aerobics, swimming, volleyball, basketball, golf, tennis, and other sports.

Before beginning any vigorous exercise program, consult a medical health care professional. This is critical if you are overweight, over age 60, in poor condition, or a heavy smoker, or if you have a history of health problems.

Student Voices

Staying in shape has always been important to me so including time in my schedule for exercise is something I always try to do. It started to be the one thing I wasn't accomplishing because I had reading or studying to prepare for class that I let take precedence. Then I signed up for a water aerobics course that met once a week. Having a fixed time when I knew I had to be at the specific class helped me keep it a priority.

— LUPE SANTIAGO

Your machine:
Rest it

In addition to requiring activity, human bodies need sufficient periods of rest. A severe lack of sleep can result in serious mental and physical illness.

As a student, you might be tempted to cut back drastically on your sleep once in a while. All-nighters to study for exams or catch up on a lengthy reading assignment can become common for some students. If you find you are indulging in them often, read the Time chapter for some time-management ideas. Depriving yourself of sleep is a choice you can avoid.

Sometimes, getting to sleep isn't easy, even when you feel tired. If you have trouble falling asleep, experiment with the following suggestions:

- Exercise daily. For many people, this promotes sounder sleep.
- Avoid naps during the daytime.
- Take a warm bath, not a shower, just before bed.
- Keep your sleeping room cool.
- Sleep in the same place each night. When you're there, your body gets the message "It's time to go to sleep."
- While lying in bed, practice relaxation techniques.
- If you can't fall asleep after 30 minutes, get up and study or do something else until you're tired.
- If sleeplessness persists, see a medical health care professional.

How much sleep is enough? Your body knows when it's tired. Also look for signs of depression, irritability, and other emotional problems. Lack of sleep can interfere with your memory, your concentration, and your ability to stay awake in class. The solution is a good night's sleep.

You can sleep 12 hours a day and still not get enough rest if you are not effectively managing stress. School environments can be especially stressful, so it is important that you know ways to relax.

Stress is not always harmful. It can result from pleasant experiences as well as unpleasant ones. The excitement of a new term—new classes, new instructors, new classmates—can be fun and stressful at the same time. Oddly enough, your body perceives excitement in almost the same way that it perceives fear. Both emotions produce rapid heart rates, increased adrenaline flow, and muscle contractions. Both emotions produce stress.

Stress, at appropriate times and at manageable levels, is normal and useful. It can sharpen our awareness and boost our energy just when we need it the most. When stress persists or becomes excessive, it is harmful.

Chances are, your stress level is too high if you consistently experience any of the following symptoms: irritability; depression; low productivity; strained relationships at work or home; health problems such as an upset stomach, frequent colds, and a low energy level; a pattern of avoiding tasks; difficulty falling asleep or staying asleep; feeling burned out at home or at work; feeling tense, nervous, or fearful.

Stress has both mental and physical components. The mental components include thoughts and worries; the physical components include illnesses and muscle tension. The fact that stress has these two elements points to two broad strategies for managing it.

One powerful way to deal with stressful thoughts is to manage our self-talk. We can notice and regulate the little voice in the back of our minds that is constantly giving us messages. Exercises that help us mentally rehearse success and visualize positive outcomes increase the odds for positive results.

Methods of dealing with the physical element of stress include breathing exercises, relaxation techniques such as body scans and guided imageries, massage, and aerobic exercise. Some schools offer training in these techniques.

Also read this book. It includes a number of relaxation and breathing exercises. Many of the Power Processes and the techniques for letting go of test anxiety can help you manage stress.

If these techniques don't work within a few weeks, get help. There are trained relaxation therapists in most cities. Ask a medical health care professional, counselor, or college dean for a referral. Also check with the student health service or counseling center at your school. Stress management is a well-researched field. There is no need to continue to have a pain in your neck, a knot in your stomach, cold feet, or other symptoms of tension. Relax.

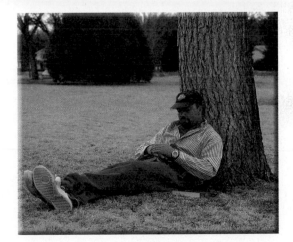

Your machine:
Observe it

Like a skilled mechanic, you are an expert on your body. You are more likely to notice changes before anyone else does. Pay attention to these changes. They are often your first clue about the need for medical treatment or intervention.

Watch for the following signs:

- Weight loss of more than 10 pounds in 10 weeks with no apparent cause.
- A sore, scab, or ulcer that does not heal in three weeks.
- A skin blemish or mole that bleeds, itches, or changes size, shape, or color.
- Persistent or severe headaches.
- Sudden vomiting that is not preceded by nausea.
- Fainting spells.
- Double vision.
- Difficulty swallowing.
- Persistent hoarseness or a nagging cough.
- Blood that is coughed up or vomited.
- Shortness of breath for no apparent reason.
- Persistent indigestion or abdominal pain.
- A big change in normal bowel habits, such as alternating diarrhea and constipation.
- Black and tarry bowel movements.
- Rectal bleeding.
- Pink, red, or unusually cloudy urine.
- Discomfort or difficulty when urinating or during sexual intercourse.
- Lumps or thickening in a breast.
- Vaginal bleeding between menstrual periods or after menopause.

If you are experiencing any of these symptoms, get help. Even if you think it might not be serious, check it out. Without timely and proper treatment, a minor illness or injury can lead to serious problems. Begin with your medical health care professional or school health service.

JOURNAL ENTRY #52

Intention Statement

For three minutes, brainstorm things you can do during the next month to improve your health. Use a separate sheet of paper for your brainstorm.

Next, pick three of your ideas that you can begin to use or practice this week. Finally, write an Intention Statement below about how and when you intend to use these ideas.

I intend to …

_____
_____
_____
_____
_____
_____
_____
_____
_____
_____

JOURNAL ENTRY #53

Intention Statement

Choose one habit related to your health that you would like to change immediately. Below write an Intention Statement about changing this habit so that your body can begin experiencing greater health today.

I intend to …

_____
_____
_____
_____
_____
_____
_____
_____

Your machine:
Protect it

Protect against sexually transmitted diseases.

Choices about sex can be life altering. Sex is a basic human drive, and it can be wonderful. Sex can also be hazardous to your physical and psychological health. It pays to be clear about the pitfalls. These include sexually transmitted diseases and unwanted pregnancies.

Technically, anyone who has sex is at risk of getting a sexually transmitted disease (STD). Without treatment, some of these diseases can lead to blindness, infertility, cancer, heart disease, or even death. Sometimes there are no signs or symptoms of an STD; the only way to tell if you're infected is to be tested by a health care professional.

STDs are often spread through body fluids that are exchanged during sex—semen, vaginal secretions, and blood. Some STDs, such as herpes and genital warts, are spread by direct contact with infected skin. Human immunodeficiency virus (HIV) can be spread in other ways, also.

There are more than 25 kinds of STDs, including chlamydia, gonorrhea ("clap"), syphilis, genital warts, genital herpes, and trichomoniasis. STDs are the most common contagious diseases in the United States.

Consider these facts from the Centers for Disease Control:

- In the United States, more than 12 million new cases of sexually transmitted diseases (STDs) occur each year—at least three million of them among teenagers.

- Of the top 10 reportable diseases in the United States in 1995, four were STDs (chlamydial infection, gonorrhea, AIDS, and syphilis).

- About two-thirds of those who get STDs in the United States are younger than 25.

- Health problems from STDs tend to be more frequent and severe for women than for men.

HIV is one of the most serious STDs, and it is different from the others in several respects. HIV is the virus that causes acquired immune deficiency syndrome (AIDS). AIDS is the last stage of HIV infection. A person with AIDS has an immune system that is weakened to the point of having difficulty in fighting off many kinds of infections and cancers.

Someone infected with HIV might feel no symptoms for months—sometimes years. Many times, those who are spreading HIV don't even know that they have it.

HIV/AIDS is not transmitted just through unprotected sexual contact. It can be transmitted by shared needles or equipment used to inject drugs. The virus can also be passed from an infected pregnant woman to her fetus during pregnancy or delivery, or through breastfeeding after delivery. Before 1985, HIV was sometimes spread through contaminated blood transfusions. Since March 1985, blood supplies have been screened for HIV, and blood transfusion is no longer considered a means of HIV infection.

Although the disease was initially prevalent in this country among male homosexuals, HIV/AIDS is becoming increasingly common among heterosexuals. HIV/AIDS cases among women have been rising steadily, and it is predicted to become one of the five leading causes of death among women.

Public hysteria and misinformation about HIV/AIDS still flourish. You cannot get HIV/AIDS from touching, kissing, hugging, food, coughs, mosquitoes, toilet seats, hot tubs, or swimming pools.

Being infected with HIV is not a death sentence. There are medical treatments that can slow down the rate at which HIV weakens the immune system. Some of the illnesses associated with AIDS can be prevented or treated, although AIDS itself is not curable. Some people live with HIV for years without developing AIDS, and people with AIDS may live for years after developing the condition. As with other chronic illnesses, early detection and early entry into medical care offers more options for treatment and a longer life.

STDs other than AIDS and herpes can be cured, if treated early. Prevention is better. The only way to be absolutely safe from STDs is to abstain from sex or to have sex exclusively with one person who is free of infection and has no other sex partners. Also avoid injecting illegal drugs. Sharing needles or other paraphernalia with other drug users is a high-risk behavior.

The more people you have sex with, the greater your risk. You are at risk even if you have sex only once with one person who is infected. If you have sex with several different people, get checked for STDs twice each year. Do this even if you have no symptoms.

If you choose to have sex with more than one partner, then protect yourself and others from STDs by practicing "safer sex." (The term *safe sex* is no longer used, since the choice to have multiple sex partners always poses a risk of infection.) Safer sex refers to a variety of methods that prevent the exchange of body fluids such as semen, vaginal secretions, and blood.

One such method is using male condoms—thin membranes stretched over the penis prior to intercourse. Condoms prevent semen from entering the vagina. Both women and men can carry them and insist that they be used.

For added protection, use a birth control foam, jelly, or cream along with condoms. Make sure these include a spermicide, preferably nonoxynol 9. When used with condoms, nonoxynol 9 can provide protection against HIV infection.

While the use of condoms with spermicides can be effective, they are not guaranteed to be 100 percent effective. Condoms can break, leak, or slip off.

If you think you have an STD, call your medical health care professional, campus health service, or local public health clinic. If you think you might be infected with HIV or any STD, then avoid infecting others. Seek counseling and further testing to find out if you are really infected. Early entry into treatment for HIV or any STDs can prevent serious health problems.

Protect against unwanted pregnancy.

Following is some information that can help you and your partner avoid unwanted pregnancy. This is not a complete list of options, so supplement it with information from your medical health care professional.

Abstinence is choosing not to have intercourse. Contrary to popular belief, many people exist happily without sexual intercourse. You might feel pressured to change your mind about this choice. If so, remember that abstinence as a means of birth control is guaranteed only when it is practiced without exception.

The *"pill"* is a synthetic hormone that "tells" a woman's body not to produce eggs. To be effective, it must be taken every day for 21 days a month. Birth control pills must be prescribed by a medical health care professional; the type of pill and the dose needed vary from one woman to the next. Side effects sometimes include slight nausea, breast tenderness, weight gain from water retention, and moodiness.

Some women choose not to take the pill due to health risks. Women who smoke and those with a history of blood clots or breast or endometrial cancer might be advised against taking the pill. The pill might contribute to cardiovascular disease, including high blood pressure and blocked arteries. Consult your medical health care professional.

Depo-Provera is injected by a doctor or nurse into the buttocks or arm muscle every three months. This hormone prevents pregnancy by decreasing ovulation, preventing sperm from reaching the egg, and preventing a fertilized egg from implanting in the uterus. Unlike the pill, this method requires little effort: Women simply need an injection every three months. Side effects can include irregular periods, weight gain, and breast tenderness.

The *Norplant* device is a small contraceptive implanted under the skin of a woman's upper arm. This device releases a steady stream of the hormone progestin (one of the hormones in the pill). Side effects can include inflammation or infection at the site of the implant, menstrual cycle changes, weight gain, and breast tenderness.

An *intrauterine device* (IUD) is a small metal or plastic device that is inserted in the uterus and left there for one to 10 years. It prevents fertilized eggs from developing. Side effects might include heavier menstrual flow, anemia, pelvic infection, perforation of the cervix or uterus, or septic abortion.

One brand of IUD—the Dalkon Shield—was taken off the market in 1975 after it was associated with pelvic infection, infertility, and some deaths. Today, IUDs rarely lead to serious complications. Possible side effects include increased risk of pelvic inflammatory disease, perforation of the uterus, abnormal bleeding, and cramps.

A *diaphragm* is a shallow rubber dome that is covered with a spermicide (sperm-killing cream) and inserted in the vagina. It fits over the cervix, which is the opening of the uterus, and prevents sperm from getting to the egg. A trained medical health care professional must measure and fit the diaphragm. It must be inserted before intercourse and left in place for six to eight hours after intercourse. It is more than 80 percent effective.

The *cervical cap* is a soft rubber cup that fits snugly around the cervix. Available by prescription only, it is also used with spermicide. Wearing it for more than 48 hours is not recommended due to a low risk of toxic shock syndrome. A *sponge* works something like a diaphragm. It is effective for 24 hours. The sponge has been unavailable since 1995 when its only producer stopped making it. However, the sponge still has federal approval and might be marketed in the future.

Foams, creams, tablets, suppositories, and *jellies* are chemicals that are placed in the vagina before intercourse and prevent sperm from getting to the egg.

When used carefully and consistently, *male condoms* offer a safe method of birth control. Latex condoms work the best for reducing the risk of STDs. Do not use male condoms with oil-based lubricants such as petroleum jelly, lotions, or baby oil, all of which can lead to breakage.

The *female condom* is a sheath of lubricated polyurethane with a ring on each end that is inserted into the vagina. This is a relatively new form of contraceptive device, and not many studies exist to document its effectiveness. Ask your medical health care professional for the latest information.

Natural family planning is based on looking for specific signs of fertility in a woman. (This is not to be confused with the rhythm method.) There are no side effects with natural family planning, and this method is gaining acceptance. Before you consider it, however, talk to a qualified instructor.

The *rhythm method* involves avoiding intercourse during ovulation. The problem with this method is that it is difficult to know for sure when a woman is ovulating.

Douching is flushing the vagina with water or another liquid after intercourse. Do not use it for birth control. Even if a woman douches immediately after intercourse, this method is ineffective. Sperm are quicker than humans.

Withdrawal is the act of removing the penis before ejaculation occurs. This is also ineffective, since sperm can be present in pre-ejaculation fluid.

Sterilization is a permanent form of birth control, and one to avoid if you still want to have children.

These methods vary in effectiveness. Of course, abstinence is 100 percent effective in preventing pregnancy when practiced faithfully, and sterilization is nearly 100 percent effective. Methods that deliver extra hormones to a woman—through pills, injections, or implants—are typically rated 95 to 99 percent effective, along with the IUD. Condoms for both women and men are less effective—around 80 percent.

However, effectiveness rates can only be estimated. The actual effectiveness of most contraceptive methods depends on many factors—for example, the health of the people using them, the number of sexual partners, and the frequency of sexual activity. Effectiveness also depends on how carefully and consistently the methods are used.

Protect yourself against rape.

Rape and other forms of sexual assault are all too common at vocational schools, colleges, and universities. People often hesitate to report rape for many reasons, such as fear, embarrassment, and lack of credibility. Both women and men can take steps to prevent rape from occurring in the first place. For example:

• Get together with a group of people and take a tour of the school grounds. Make a special note of danger spots, such as unlighted paths and unguarded buildings. Also note that rape can occur during daylight and in well-lit places.

• Ask if your school has escort services for people taking evening classes. These might include personal escorts, car escorts, or both. If you do take an evening class, ask if there are security officers on duty before and after the class.

• Take a course or seminar on self-defense and rape prevention. To find out where these courses are being held, check with your student counseling service, community education center, or local library.

• If you are raped, get to the nearest rape crisis center, hospital, student health service, or police station as soon as you can. It's wise to report the crime even if you decide not to press charges. Also arrange for follow-up counseling.

Date rape—the act of forcing sex on a date—is the most common form of rape among college students. Date rape is rape. It is a crime. It is particularly dangerous when neither the victim nor the perpetrator realizes that a crime has taken place. A person who has been raped by a date might become depressed, feel guilty, have difficulty in school, lose a sense of trust, have sexual problems, or experience self-blame.

You can take steps to protect yourself by communicating clearly what you want and don't want. That means being assertive. It also pays to be cautious about using alcohol or drugs, and to be wary of dates who get drunk or high. You might also provide your own transportation on dates and avoid going to secluded places with people you don't know well.

It is never all right to force someone to have sex—on a date or anywhere else. You have the right to refuse to have sex with anyone, including dates. You also have the right to refuse sex with your partner, fiancé(e), or spouse.

Protect yourself against accidents.

In North America, more than four million disabling injuries occur every year in the haven called the home, and more than 27,000 people die of accidents in their homes. Almost twice that many die in their cars. Following are ways you can greatly reduce the odds of this happening to you:

• Don't drive after drinking alcohol or using psychoactive drugs.

- Drive with the realization that other drivers are possibly preoccupied, intoxicated, or careless.

- Put poisons out of reach of children, and label poison clearly. Poisoning takes a larger toll on people aged 15 to 45 than on children.

- Keep stairs, halls, doorways, and other pathways clear of shoes, toys, newspapers, and other debris.

- Don't smoke in bed.

- Don't let candles burn unattended.

- Keep children away from hot stoves, and turn pot handles inward.

- Check electrical cords for fraying, loose connections, or breaks in insulation. Don't overload extension cords.

- Keep a fire extinguisher handy.

- Watch for ways that an infant or a toddler could suffocate or choke: small objects that can be swallowed, old refrigerators or freezers that can act as air-tight prisons, unattended or unfenced swimming pools, kerosene heaters in tightly closed rooms, and plastic kitchen or clothing bags.

- Install smoke detectors where you live and work. Most of these run on batteries that need occasional replacement. Follow the manufacturer's guidelines.

WORKPLACE APPLICATIONS

Under certain conditions, people who work continually at computers can experience health problems that range from eyestrain and lower back pain to numbness in the arms and wrists.

The field of study called *ergonomics* focuses on ways to prevent such problems. You can even consult specialists in ergonomics to redesign your workspace. That costs money. You can use the following suggestions for free:

- To prevent eyestrain caused by staring too long at a computer screen, rest your eyes from time to time. Looking out a window or at another object that is closer or farther away can help by forcing your eyes to readjust their focus. Also set up your computer away from windows so you can avoid squinting as you look at the screen.

- Take breaks. Get away from the computer. Stretch. Move. Walk, jog, or run.

- Avoid lower back problems by paying attention to your posture as you sit at the computer. Adjust your chair so that you can sit comfortably, with your back relaxed and your spine erect. It might help to place a pillow or small cushion behind your lower back.

- Type with the keyboard in your lap. This allows your hands to be lower than your elbows and minimizes the tension in your shoulders.

The whole idea is to position yourself to remain alert *and* relaxed while you're at the computer. Taking some simple precautions now can help you avoid feeling like a pretzel in a few years.

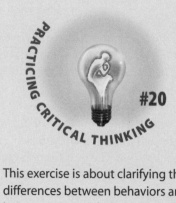

PRACTICING CRITICAL THINKING #20

This exercise is about clarifying the differences between behaviors and interpretations. A behavior is factual and observable, while an interpretation is subjective and often based on observed behaviors.

For instance, arriving 10 minutes after a lecture starts or pulling a dog's tail are both observable behaviors. In contrast, an interpretation is a conclusion we draw on the basis of the observed behavior: "She's either too rude or too irresponsible to get to a lecture on time." "She hates animals; just look at how she pulled that dog's tail." Keep in mind that other interpretations are possible. Perhaps the person's car broke down on the way to the lecture, or maybe the owner of the dog is playing a game that her pet enjoys.

Consider another example. "She shouted at me, left the room, and slammed the door" is a statement that describes behaviors. "She was angry" is one interpretation of the social significance or meaning of the observed behavior.

With this distinction in mind, brainstorm a list of behaviors you have seen in others when they were in conflict with you. On a separate sheet of paper, list your observations. Afterward, review your list to see if some of the behaviors you noted are actually interpretations.

The experts recommend
Seven dietary guidelines

1 Eat a variety of foods. Include fruits, vegetables, whole grains, breads, cereals, milk, cheese, yogurt, meats, poultry, fish, and eggs in your diet.

2 Maintain healthy weight. Overweight people tend to develop high blood pressure, heart disease, strokes, common diabetes, and certain cancers. To lose weight, eat less sugar and fat, avoid alcohol, serve smaller portions, refrain from second helpings, and eat slowly, chewing food thoroughly. These dietary measures combined with a regular exercise program will help maintain a healthy weight.

3 Choose a diet low in fat, saturated fat, and cholesterol. This is a good idea even if you are not overweight. High blood cholesterol is a health risk. Lean meat, fish, poultry, dried beans, and peas are low-cholesterol sources of protein. Limit your intake of eggs, organ meats, butter, cream, shortening, and oil. Broil, bake, or boil rather than fry. Cut off excess fat before cooking meat.

4 Choose a diet with plenty of vegetables, fruits, and grain products. Include at least three servings of vegetables, two servings of fruit, and six servings of grain (preferably whole grain) products daily. For those who eat little meat, combining whole grains with legumes (dried beans and soy products) will provide important proteins.

5 Use sugars in moderation. Obesity, impaired circulation, tooth decay, and other problems relate to excess sugar in the diet. Many prepared foods contain immoderate amounts of sugar. Do not select foods if sugar is listed as the first, second, or third ingredient on the label. Sometimes sugar is called corn syrup, dextrose, fructose, glucose, maltose, sucrose, honey, or molasses.

6 Use salt and sodium in moderation. Your body does need sodium chloride (salt). However, you need much less than most people eat, and reduction will benefit those people whose blood pressure rises with salt intake. Use table salt sparingly, if at all, in food preparation or at meals. Limit your intake of salty foods such as pretzels, potato chips, cheese, salted nuts, pickles, and popcorn.

7 If you drink alcoholic beverages, do so in moderation. Moderate drinking is no more than one drink in one day for a woman or two drinks for a man. Some people should not drink at all. Too much alcohol might cause cirrhosis of the liver, inflammation of the pancreas, damage to the heart and brain, high blood pressure, hemorrhagic stroke, increased risk for many cancers, and alcoholism. Do not drink and drive.

Discovery Statement

If you look and feel healthy, a greater understanding of your body can help you be aware of what you're doing right. If you are not content with your present physical or emotional health, you might discover some ways to adjust your personal habits and increase your sense of well-being.

This exercise is a structured Discovery Statement that allows you to look closely at your health. As with the Discovery Wheel exercise in Chapter One, the usefulness of this exercise will be determined by your honesty and courage.

1. On a separate sheet of paper, draw a simple outline of your body. You might have positive and negative feelings about various internal and external parts of your body. Label the parts and include a short description of the attributes you like or dislike. For example: straight teeth, fat thighs, clear lungs, double chin, straight posture, etc.

2. The body you drew substantially reflects your past health practices. To discover how well you take care of your body, complete the following sentences on a separate sheet of paper.

EATING

1. The truth about what I eat is …

2. What I know about the way I eat is …

3. What I would most like to change about my diet is …

4. My eating habits lead me to be …

EXERCISE

1. The way I usually exercise is …

2. The last time I did 20 minutes or more of heart/lung (aerobic) exercise was …

3. As a result of my physical conditioning I feel …

4. And I look …

5. It would be easier for me to work out regularly if I …

6. The most important benefit for me in exercising more is …

HARMFUL SUBSTANCES

1. My history of cigarette smoking is …

2. An objective observer would say my use of alcohol is …

3. In the last 10 days the number of alcoholic drinks I have had is …

4. I would describe my use of coffee, colas, and other caffeinated drinks as …

5. I have used the following illegal drugs in the past week:

6. When it comes to drugs, what I am sometimes concerned about is …

7. I take the following prescription drugs:

RELATIONSHIPS

1. Someone who knows me fairly well would say I am emotionally …

2. The way I look and feel has affected my relationships by …

3. My use of drugs or alcohol has been an issue with …

4. The best thing I could do for myself and my relationships would be to …

SLEEP

1. The number of hours I sleep each night is …

2. On weekends I normally sleep …

3. I have trouble sleeping when …

4. Last night I …

5. The night before last I …

6. The quality of my sleep is usually …

What concerns me more than anything else about my health is …

Crazed glazed donut runs amok

Editor's note: For those of you who think this article might be a bit cutesy, please understand the theoretical and pedagogical rationale for its inclusion, which incorporated the purpose of puncturing the pretentiousness of pundits' puritanical prattle. This article is here to lighten up a subject that is so often approached with guilt and the solemnity of a final exam.

By Bill Harlan

PANCREAS CITY, IOWA—

A glazed donut, apparently out of control, caused a multisugar pileup here early yesterday.

The entire state is reeling in lethargy, and the governor has called in extra fatty tissue.

The pileup occurred shortly after 9 a.m., when assistant brain cells in Hypothalamusville noticed an energy shortage. They telephoned the state procurement office in Right Hand with a request for a glazed donut.

Procurement officers delivered the donut to Mouth, two miles north of Throat, at 9:04 a.m. "We were only following orders," one said.

When the donut reached Stomach, the town was nearly deserted. "No one had been here since dinner the night before," a witness said. The donut raced straight through Duodenum Gap and into Intestine County.

Records indicate that the energy level throughout the state did rise for more than a half-hour. However, about 45 minutes after the donut was delivered, residents in Eyelid noticed what one witness described as "a sort of drooping effect." Within 90 minutes the whole state was in a frenzy. Energy levels dropped. Tremors were reported in Hand. A suspicious "growl" was heard near Stomach.

By that time, confusion reigned in Pancreas. Officials there later claimed the donut was pure glucose, the kind of sugar that causes an immediate but short-lived energy boost. The glazed perpetrator apparently burned itself out in a metabolic rampage. Soon, only the smoking traces of burned glucose remained.

Minutes later, terror-stricken cells near Stomach began screaming, "Send down a candy bar." The cry was taken up throughout the state, as cells everywhere begged for more sugar.

For the rest of the day, the state reeled under an assault of caffeine and sugar. Three candy bars. Four soft drinks. Pie and coffee.

By evening, the governor's office had called up alcohol reserves.

"We've been recommending complex carbohydrates and small amounts of protein since Tuesday," said a highly placed source, who was reached on vacation at the Isle of Langerhans in Lake Pancreas. "Carbohydrates and proteins burn energy gradually, all day. An egg, some cereal, a piece of fruit, and this tragedy could have been avoided. Heck, a burger would have been better. This donut thing has got to stop."

This morning, a saddened state lies under a layer of fat. "I'm guessing it will take a hard 10-mile run to get this mess cleaned up," an administrative assistant in Cerebellum said.

Officials in Legs could not be reached.

Developing self-esteem

Self-esteem refers to how we "grade" ourselves and measure our own worth. The challenge of higher education often puts self-esteem at risk. The rigors of class work, financial pressures, and new social settings can test our ability to adapt and change.

Our self-esteem can erode in ways that are imperceptible to us. Over time, we can gradually buy into a reduced sense of our own possibilities in life. This orientation makes it less likely that we'll take risks, create a vision for the future, and accomplish our goals.

There is always another option. We can form a clear intention to maintain our self-esteem and then take specific steps to ensure that we do so.

Consider the possibility that strong self-esteem is a habit that we can develop. Maybe we fall into a habitual

way of thinking about ourselves. If this is true, then like other habits, the way we think about ourselves can be changed.

One process for change is explained in the article "Ways to change a habit" in the Time chapter. Focus on three of the suggestions: commit, set up a feedback system, and practice without reproach. You can apply each suggestion toward developing self-esteem.

Commit.
Declare that you are going to start generating higher self-esteem. Tell every important person in your life about your new intention.

To make your commitment more solid, list the ways that higher self-esteem will benefit all areas of your life. Write Intention Statements that detail exactly what you will do to promote your self-esteem. Some suggestions follow.

Release unrealistic standards.
Consider for a moment the characters in popular television shows and films. Notice the models in advertisements, both in print and on television. Everywhere we see people who seem to have better looks, more money, and more sex appeal than we do. Naturally, we wonder if we'll ever be good enough, smart enough, handsome or pretty enough, or rich enough.

Remember that common images of success are contrived and artificial. Those "perfect" characters are conceived by scriptwriters. Those stunning models are often carefully crafted by plastic surgeons and makeup artists. We can begin developing our self-esteem by refusing to measure ourselves against the arbitrary and unrealistic standards set up by our mass media.

Change the conversation about yourself.
Monitor what you say and think about yourself. Remember that this self-talk might be so habitual that you don't even notice it. Whether you are fully aware of them or not, your thoughts do affect you.

Pay close attention and notice when you speak or think negatively about yourself. Telling the truth about your weaknesses is one thing. Consistently underrating yourself is another.

In the conversation about yourself, go for balance. Spend more time writing, speaking, and thinking about what works well in your life. Soak in the acknowledgments of others. Instead of deflecting compliments ("It was nothing"), fully receive the positive things that others say about you ("Thank you"). Also take responsibility for your successes. "Well, I was just lucky" can change to "I worked hard to achieve that goal."

Trust your own choices.
Asking for advice can sometimes undermine your ability to create your own solutions to problems. An alternative is to start trusting your own choices and acting on your most powerful thinking.

When you're faced with a problem, you can ask for coaching rather than advice. An effective coach—whether a friend, family member, instructor, or counselor—does more listening than talking. This person creates an environment in which you can freely explore a problem and invent your own solutions. You're more likely to act on those solutions than on even the best advice from other people.

Compare yourself to yourself.
Our own failures are often more dramatic to us than the failures of others, and our own successes are often more invisible. When we're unsure of ourselves, we can look in any direction and see people who seem more competent and more confident than we do. When we start the comparison game, we open the door to self-doubt.

There is a way to play the comparison game and win: Instead of comparing yourself to others, compare yourself to yourself. Take time to note any progress you've made toward your goals over time. Write Discovery Statements about that progress. Celebrate your success in any area of life, no matter how small that success might seem.

Volunteer to help others.
Volunteering allows you to experience the value of making a difference in the world and enhances self-esteem. Teach someone else about something that you enjoy and do well. Consider your skills in all areas, not just sports or academics. Maybe you're good at gardening, cooking, putting on makeup, or training dogs. All of us are good at several things. Celebrate what you're good at by sharing it with others.

Set up winning situations.
Set yourself up for success by breaking a big project down into small tasks. Then complete just one task. This accomplishment can help you move onto the next task with higher self-esteem. Success breeds more success.

Set up a feedback system.
As you adopt the new habit of developing self-esteem, build some feedback into the process. Give yourself a daily score on how well you practice this habit. You might use grades such as A, B, C, or D to track how consistently you act on your intentions. Or you could assign a number from −3 to +3.

Remember that other people can provide valuable feedback. Ask them to tell you when they see or hear you display low self-esteem. For example, they can point out when you discount your achievements or when you criticize your appearance. They can do this with a positive message rather than a criticism. For example, others could say "You're great" as a reminder that you just spoke poorly of yourself.

Practice without reproach.
However you practice your new habit of self-esteem, remember to do it without reproach. As with other new habits, you might forget to practice it, especially at first. When developing self-esteem, be gentle with yourself.

Suicide

Suicide is one of the leading causes of death among students. While preparing for and entering higher education, people typically face major changes. The stress that they feel can lead to an increase in depression, anxiety, and attempted suicide.

Recognize danger signals

Talking about suicide. People who attempt suicide often talk about it. They might say, "I just don't want to live anymore." Or "I want you to know that no matter what happens, I've always loved you." Or "Tomorrow night at 7:30 I'm going to end it all with a gun."

Planning for it. People planning suicide will sometimes put their affairs in order. They might close bank accounts, give away or sell precious possessions, or make or update a will. They might even develop specific plans on how to kill themselves.

Having a history of previous attempts. Some estimates suggest that up to 50 percent of the people who kill themselves have attempted suicide at least once before.

Dwelling on problems. Expressing extreme helplessness or hopelessness about solving problems can indicate that someone might be considering suicide.

Feeling depressed. Although not everyone who is depressed attempts suicide, almost everyone who attempts suicide feels depressed.

Take prompt action

Most often, suicide can be prevented. If you suspect that someone you know is considering suicide, do whatever it takes to ensure the person's safety. Let this person know that you will persist until you are certain that she's safe. Any of the following actions can help.

Take it seriously. Taking suicidal comments seriously is especially important when you hear them from young adults. Suicide threats are more common in this age group and might be dismissed as "normal." Err on the side of being too careful rather than on the side of being negligent.

Listen fully. Encourage the person at risk to express thoughts and feelings appropriately. If she claims that she doesn't want to talk, be inviting, be assertive, and be persistent. Be totally committed to listening.

Speak powerfully. Let the person at risk know that you care. Trying to talk someone out of suicide or minimizing problems is generally useless. Acknowledge that problems are serious *and* that they can be solved. Point out that suicide is a permanent solution to a temporary problem—and that help is available.

Get professional help. Suggest that the person see a mental health professional. If she resists help, offer to schedule the appointment for her and to take her to it. If this fails, get others involved, including the depressed person's family or school personnel.

Remove access to firearms. Most suicides are attempted with guns. Get rid of any that might be around. Also remove dangerous drugs and razors.

Ask the person to sign a "no-suicide contract." Get a promise, in writing, that the person will not hurt herself before speaking to you. A written promise can provide the "excuse" she needs not to take action.

Handle an emergency. If a situation becomes a crisis, do not leave the person alone. Call a crisis hot line, 911, or a social service agency. If necessary, take the person to the nearest hospital emergency room, clinic, or police station.

Follow up. Someone in danger of attempting suicide might resist further help even if your first intervention succeeds. Ask this person if she's keeping counseling appointments and taking prescribed medication. Help this person apply strategies for solving problems. Stay in touch.

Take care of yourself

If you ever begin to think about committing suicide, remember that you can apply any of the above suggestions to yourself. For example, look for warning signs and take them seriously. Seek out someone you trust and tell this person how you feel. If necessary, make an appointment to see a counselor and ask someone to accompany you. When you're at risk, you deserve the same compassion that you'd willingly extend to another person.

Find out more on this topic from the American Foundation for Suicide Prevention at **1-888-333-AFSP** or **www.afsp.org**.

Emotional pain is not a sickness

Emotional pain has gotten a bad name. This type of slander is undeserved. There is nothing wrong with feeling bad. It's OK to feel miserable, depressed, sad, upset, angry, dejected, gloomy, or unhappy.

It might not be pleasant to feel bad, but it can be good for you. Often, the appropriate way to feel is bad. When you leave a place you love, sadness is natural. When you lose a friend or lover, misery might be in order. When someone treats you badly, it is probably appropriate to feel angry.

Unless you are suicidally depressed, it is almost impossible to feel too bad. Feeling bad for too long can be a problem. If depression, sadness, or anger persists, get help. Otherwise, allow yourself to experience these emotions. They're usually appropriate and necessary for personal growth.

When a loved one dies, it is necessary to grieve. The grief might appear in the form of depression, sadness, or anger. There is nothing wrong with extreme emotional pain. It is natural, and it doesn't have to be fixed.

When feeling bad becomes a problem, it is usually because you didn't allow yourself to feel bad at the outset. So the next time you feel rotten, go ahead and feel rotten. It will pass, and it will probably pass more quickly if you don't fight it or try to ignore it.

Allowing yourself to feel bad might even help you get smart. Harvey Jackins, a psychotherapist, bases his work on this premise.[1] Jackins believes that when people fully experience and release their emotions, they also remove blocks to their thinking and clear a path for profound personal insights. And Daniel Goleman, author of *Emotional Intelligence,* asserts that being attuned to feelings can lead to sounder personal decisions.[2]

Following are some good ways to feel bad

Don't worry about reasons. Sometimes we allow ourselves to feel bad if we have a good reason. For example: "Well, I feel very sad, but that is because I just found out my best friend is moving to Europe." It's all right to know the reason why you are sad, and it is fine *not* to know. You can feel bad for no apparent reason. The reason doesn't matter.

Set a time limit. If you are concerned about feeling bad, if you are worried that you need to "fix it," give yourself a little time. Before you force yourself not to feel the way you feel, set a time limit. Say to yourself, "I am going to give myself until Monday at noon, and if I don't feel better by then, I am going to try to fix myself." Sometimes it is appropriate to fix a bad feeling. There might be a problem that needs a solution. You can use feeling bad as your motivation to solve the problem. And sometimes it helps just to feel bad for a while.

Reassure others. Sometimes other people—friends or family members, for example—have a hard time letting you feel bad. They might be worried that they did something wrong and want to make it better. They want you to quit feeling bad. Tell them you will. Assure them that you will feel good again but that for now, you just want to feel bad.

This is no joke. Sometimes students think that this whole idea of allowing yourself to feel bad is a joke, reverse psychology, or something else. It isn't. This suggestion is based on the notion that good mental health is possible only if you allow yourself to feel the full range of your emotions.

Alcohol, tobacco & drugs

The truth is that getting high can be fun. In our culture, and especially in our media, getting high has become synonymous with having a good time. Even if you don't smoke, drink, or take drugs, you are certain to come in contact with people who do.

For centuries, human beings have devised ways to change their feelings and thoughts by altering their body chemistry. The Chinese were using marijuana five thousand years ago. Herodotus, the ancient Greek historian, wrote about a group of people in Eastern Europe who threw marijuana on hot stones and inhaled the vapors. More recently, during the American Civil War, customers could buy opium and morphine across the counter of their neighborhood store. A few decades later, Americans were able to buy soft drinks that contained coca—the plant from which cocaine is derived.

Today we are still a drug-using society. Drugs (legal and illegal), alcohol, tobacco, and caffeine are accepted and sought-after answers to practically any problem anyone has. Do you have a headache? Take a drug. Is it hard for you to fall asleep? Take a drug. Is it hard to stay awake? Take a drug. Are you depressed? Are you hyperactive? Are you nervous? Are you too skinny? Too fat? The often-heard response is "Take something." There is a brand of alcohol, a certain cigarette, or a faster-acting drug that can help.

We live in times when reaching for instant comfort via chemicals is not only condoned—it is approved. If you're bored, tense, or anxious, you can drink a can of beer, down a glass of wine, or light up a cigarette. And these are only the legal drugs. If you're willing to take risks, you can pick from a large selection of illegal street drugs.

There is a big payoff in using alcohol, tobacco, caffeine, prescription drugs, cocaine, and heroin—or people wouldn't do it. The payoff can be direct, as when people experience relaxation, self-confidence, comfort, excitement, pleasure. At times, the payoff is not so obvious, as when people seek to avoid rejection, mask emotional pain, attain peer group acceptance, or reject authority.

Perhaps drugs have a timeless appeal because human beings face two perennial problems: how to cope with unpleasant moods, and how to deal with life's most difficult circumstances, such as pain, sickness, poverty, and death. When faced with either problem, people often find it tempting to bypass suffering with a chemical fix.

In addition to the payoffs, there are costs. For most people, the cost is much greater than the payoff. Yet they continue to use and abuse alcohol and other drugs. And sometimes these people become addicted. That cost goes beyond money. If cocaine, heroin, and other drugs don't make you broke, they can make you crazy. This is not necessarily the kind of crazy where you dress up like Napoleon. Rather, it is the kind where you care about little else except finding more drugs—friends, school, work, and family be damned.

Those are just some of the costs. With addiction comes the danger of overdose, infection, and lowered immunity to disease—all of which can be fatal. Long-term excessive drinking damages every organ system in the human body. People have died of heart attacks induced by amphetamines. And each year, almost 400,000 people die from the effects of cigarette smoking.

Lectures about why to avoid alcohol and drug abuse can be pointless. Ultimately, we don't take care of our bodies because someone says we should. We might take care of ourselves when we see that the costs of using a substance outweigh the benefits. You choose. It's your body. On the facing page are some facts—the truth—that can help you make choices about what to put into your body.

Acknowledging that alcohol, tobacco, and other drugs can be fun infuriates a lot of people who might assume that this is the same as condoning their use. The point is this: People are more likely to abstain when they're convinced that using these substances leads to more pain than pleasure over the long run.

Some facts...

Among preventable health problems in the United States, substance abuse and addiction result in the highest costs to society. Consider the following:

- The consequences of excessive drinking include drunk driving, cancer, strokes, falls, liver disease, and other health risks. These risks lead to at least 100,000 deaths each year.

- More than one-third of AIDS deaths have occurred among people who inject illegal drugs themselves and among the sexual partners of injection drug users.

- At least half of the adults arrested for a major crime test positive for drugs at the time of their arrest.

- More than 23 million Americans need treatment for alcohol and other drug abuse; less than one-fourth of them get it. Only 18 percent of the federal drug control budget goes to fund treatment.

- Forty-four percent of college students have had at least one episode of binge drinking.

Sources: Schneider Institute for Health Policy at Brandeis University, Substance Abuse: The Nation's Number One Health Problem *(Robert Wood Johnson Foundation, 2001). H. Wechsler, J. E. Lee, M. Kuo, and H. Lee, "College Binge Drinking in the 1990s: A Continuing Problem— Results of the Harvard School of Public Health 1999 College Alcohol Study,"* Journal of American College Health 48, *no. 10 (2000): 199–210.*

 For current statistics on addiction and fact sheets on various drugs, visit the National Institute of Drug Abuse at **www.nida.nih.gov.**

#32

Addiction, how do I know ...

People who have problems with drugs and alcohol are great at hiding that fact from themselves and from others. It is also hard to admit that a friend or loved one might have a problem.

The purpose of this exercise is to give you an objective way to look at your relationship with drugs or alcohol. This exercise can also help you determine if a friend might be addicted. Addiction can be emotional as well as physical. There are signals that indicate when drug or alcohol use has become abusive.

Answer the following questions quickly and honestly with "yes," "no," or "n/a" (not applicable). If you are concerned about someone else, then apply the following questions to that person by replacing each "you" with the person's name.

_____ Are you uncomfortable discussing drug abuse or alcoholism?

_____ Are you worried about your drug or alcohol use?

_____ Are any of your friends worried about your drug or alcohol use?

_____ Have you ever hidden from a friend, spouse, employer, or coworker the fact that you were drinking? (Pretended you were sober? Covered up alcohol breath?)

_____ Do you sometimes use alcohol or drugs to escape lows rather than to produce highs?

_____ Have you ever gotten angry when confronted about your use?

_____ Do you brag about how much you consume? ("I drank her under the table.")

_____ Do you think about or do drugs when you are alone?

_____ Do you store up alcohol, drugs, cigarettes, or caffeine (in coffee or soft drinks) so you are sure you won't run out?

_____ Does having a party almost always include alcohol or drugs?

_____ Do you try to control your drinking so that it won't be a problem? ("I drink only on weekends now." "I never drink before 5 p.m." "I drink only beer.")

_____ Do you often explain to other people why you are drinking? ("It's my birthday." "It's my friend's birthday." "It's Veterans Day." "It sure is a hot day.")

(continued on the next page)

_____ Have you changed friends to accommodate your drinking? ("She's OK, but she isn't excited about getting high.")

_____ Has your behavior changed in the last several months? (Grades down? Lack of interest in a hobby? Change of values or what you think is moral?)

_____ Do you drink to relieve tension? ("What a day! I need a drink.")

_____ Do you have medical problems (stomach trouble, malnutrition, liver problems, anemia) that could be related to drinking?

_____ Have you ever decided to quit drugs or alcohol and then changed your mind?

_____ Have you had any fights, accidents, or similar incidents related to drinking or drugs in the last year?

_____ Has your drinking or drug use ever caused a problem at home?

_____ Do you envy people who go overboard with alcohol or drugs?

_____ Have you ever told yourself you can quit at any time?

_____ Have you ever been in trouble with the police after or while you were drinking?

_____ Have you ever missed school or work because you had a hangover?

_____ Have you ever had a blackout (a period you can't remember) after drinking?

_____ Do you wish that people would mind their own business when it comes to your use of alcohol or drugs?

_____ Is the cost of alcohol or other drugs taxing your budget or resulting in financial stress?

_____ Do you need increasing amounts of the drug to produce the desired effect?

_____ When you stop taking the drug, do you experience withdrawal?

_____ Do you spend a great deal of time obtaining and using alcohol or other drugs?

_____ Have you used alcohol or another drug when it was physically dangerous to do so (such as when driving a car or working with machines)?

_____ Have you been arrested or had other legal problems resulting from the use of a substance?

Now count the number of questions you answered "yes." If you answered "yes" five or more times, talk with a professional. Five "yes" answers does not mean that you are an alcoholic or that you have a serious problem. It does point out that drugs and/or alcohol are adversely affecting your life. It is important that you talk to someone with alcohol- and drug-abuse training. Do not rely on the opinion of anyone who lacks such training.

If you answered this questionnaire about another person and you answered "yes" five or more times, your friend might need help. You probably can't provide that help alone. Seek out a counselor or a support group such as Al-Anon. Call the local Alcoholics Anonymous chapter to find out about an Al-Anon meeting near you.

Seeing the full scope of addiction

Substance abuse—the compulsive use of a chemical in alcohol or drugs—is only part of the picture. People can also abuse food, gambling, sugar, money, sex, personal relationships, and even work. Sometimes people can't stop their self-defeating behaviors unless they get help. That's addiction.

Here are some guidelines that can help you decide if addiction is a barrier for you right now. Most addictions share some key features, such as the following:

- A loss of control over the substance or activity—continued use or activity in spite of adverse consequences.

- A pattern of relapse—vowing to quit or limit the activity or substance and continually failing to do so.

- Tolerance—a need to take increased amounts of a substance to produce the desired effect.

- Withdrawal—signs and symptoms of physical and mental discomfort or illness when the substance is taken away.[3]

The same basic features can be present in anything from cocaine use to compulsive gambling. All of this can add up to a continuous cycle of abuse or addiction. These common features prompt many people to call some forms of addiction a disease. The American Medical Association formally recognized alcoholism as a disease in 1956.

Some people do not agree that alcoholism is a disease or that all addictions can be labeled with that term. You don't have to wait until this question is settled before examining your own life.

If you have a problem with addiction, consider getting help. The problem might be your own addiction or perhaps the behavior of someone you love. In any case, consider acting on several of these suggestions.

Admit the problem. People with active addictions are a varied group—rich and poor, young and old, successful and unsuccessful. Often these people do have one thing in common: They are masters of denial. They deny that they are unhappy. They deny that they have hurt anyone. They are convinced that they can quit any time they want. They sometimes become so adept at hiding the problem from themselves that they die.

When you use, pay attention. If you do use a substance compulsively or behave in compulsive ways, do so with awareness. Then pay attention to the consequences. Act with deliberate decision rather than out of habit or under pressure from others.

Look at the costs. There is always a tradeoff. Drinking 10 beers might result in a temporary high, and you will probably remember that feeling. No one feels great the morning after consuming 10 beers, but it seems easier to forget pain. Often people don't notice how bad alcoholism, drug addiction, or other forms of substance abuse make them feel.

Instead of blaming yourself, take responsibility for recovery. Nobody plans to become an addict. If you have pneumonia, you can recover without guilt or shame. Approach an addiction in yourself or others in the same way. You can take responsibility for your recovery without blame, shame, or guilt.

Get help. Many people find that they cannot treat addiction on their own. Addictive behaviors are often symptoms of an illness that needs treatment.

Two broad options exist for getting help with addiction. One is the growing self-help movement. The other is formal treatment. People recovering from addiction often combine the two.

Many self-help groups are modeled after Alcoholics Anonymous. AA is made up of recovering alcoholics and addicts. These people understand the problems of abuse firsthand, and they follow a systematic, 12-step approach to living without it. This is one of the oldest and most successful self-help programs in the world. Chapters of AA welcome people from all walks of life, and you don't have to be an alcoholic to attend most meetings. Programs based on AA principles exist for many other forms of addiction as well.

Some people feel uncomfortable with the AA approach. Other resources exist for these people, including private therapy and group therapy. Also investigate organizations such as Women for Sobriety, the Secular Organizations for Sobriety, and Rational Recovery Systems. Use what works for you.

Treatment programs are available in almost every community. They might be residential (you live there for weeks or months at a time) or outpatient (you visit several hours a day). Find out where these treatment centers are located by calling a doctor, a mental health professional, or a local hospital.

Alcohol and drug treatments are now covered by many health insurance programs. If you don't have insurance, it is usually possible to arrange some other payment program. Cost is no reason to avoid treatment.

Get help for a friend or family member.
You might know someone who uses alcohol or other drugs in a way that can lead to serious and sustained negative consequences. If so, you have every right to express your concern to that person. Wait until the person is clear-headed and then mention specific incidents. For example: "Last night you drank five beers when we were at my apartment, and then you wanted to drive home. When I offered to call a cab for you instead, you refused." Also be prepared to offer a source of help, such as the phone number of a local treatment center.

Where to turn for more information on recovery

Begin with your doctor or school health care center. You can also contact:

Alcoholics Anonymous World Services
1-212-870-3400
www.alcoholics-anonymous.org

National Institute for Drug Abuse
1-800-662-4357
www.nida.nih.gov

National Black Alcoholism and Addictions Council
1-315-732-3739
www.borg.com/~nbac

National Alliance for Hispanic Health
1-202-387-5000
www.cossmho.org

Rational Recovery
1-800-303-2873
rational.org/recovery

Women for Sobriety
1-215-536-8026
www.womenforsobriety.org

PRACTICING CRITICAL THINKING #21

The advice about health that we receive in the popular press often seems contradictory. For example, one expert might claim that running is an ideal form of exercise. Another authority might warn about the dangers of injury from jogging and recommend walking instead.

Choose one health topic on which you see diverging viewpoints. Explain each point of view, then see if you can construct a viewpoint that reconciles the conflicting opinions—or at least clarifies the nature of the disagreement.

Summarize your viewpoint on a separate sheet of paper. Upon closer examination, you might conclude that the experts might not really be in disagreement, considering the ways that they qualify their opinions.

Warning: Advertising can be dangerous to your health

The average American is exposed to hundreds of advertising messages per day. Unless you are stranded on a desert island, you are affected by commercial messages.

Advertising serves a useful function. It helps us make choices about how we spend our money. We can choose among cars, kitchen appliances, health clubs, books, plants, groceries, home builders, dog groomers, piano tuners, vacation spots, locksmiths, movies, amusement parks—the list is endless. Advertising makes us aware of the options.

Advertising space is also expensive, and the messages are carefully crafted. They can play on our emotions and be dangerously manipulative. For example, consider the messages that advertising conveys about your health. Advertising alcohol, tobacco, and pain relievers is a big business. Newspapers, magazines, radio, television, and web sites depend on advertising these products for much of their revenue.

Ads for alcohol glorify drinking. One of their aims is to convince heavy drinkers that the amount they drink is normal. Advertisers imply that daily drinking is the norm, pleasant experiences are enhanced by drinking, holidays naturally include alcohol, parties are a flop without it, relationships are more romantic over cocktails, and everybody drinks. Each of these implications is questionable.

Advertising can affect our self-image. A typical advertising message is "You are not OK unless you buy our product." These messages are painstakingly programmed to get us to buy clothes, makeup, and hair products to make us look OK; drugs, alcohol, and food to make us feel OK; perfumes, toothpaste, and deodorants to make us smell OK. Advertising also promotes the idea that buying the right product is essential to having valuable relationships in our lives.

Advertising affects what we eat. Multimedia advertisers portray the primary staples of our diets as sugary breakfast cereals, candy bars, and soft drinks. The least nutritious foods receive the most advertising money.

Another problem with advertising is the image of women that is commonly portrayed. The basic message has been that women love to spend hours discussing floor wax, deodorants, tampons, and laundry detergent—and that they think constantly about losing weight and looking sexy. In some ads, women handle everything from kitchen to bedroom to boardroom—these women are Superwomen.

Images such as these are demeaning to women and damaging to men. Women lose when they allow their self-image to be influenced by ads. Men lose when they expect real-life women to look and act like the women on television and in magazines. Advertising photography creates illusions. The next time you're in a crowd, notice how few people look like those in the media.

Though advertising is making progress in representing racial diversity, it still frequently excludes people of color. If our perceptions were based solely on advertising, we would be hard pressed to know that our society is racially and ethnically diverse. See how many examples of cultural stereotypes you can find in the ads you encounter this week.

Use advertising as a continual opportunity to develop the qualities of a critical thinker. Be aware of how a multibillion-dollar industry threatens your health and well-being.

JOURNAL ENTRY

#55

Discovery Statement

Think of a time when after seeing an advertisement or a commercial, you craved a certain food or drink or you really wanted to buy something. On a separate sheet of paper, describe in detail how the advertising influenced you.

POWER PROCESS

Surrender

Life can be magnificent and satisfying. It can also be devastating. Sometimes there is too much pain or confusion. Problems can be too big and too numerous. Life can bring us to our knees in a pitiful, helpless, and hopeless state. A broken relationship with a loved one, a sudden diagnosis of cancer, total frustration with a child's behavior problem, or even the prospect of several long years of school are situations that can leave us feeling overwhelmed—powerless.

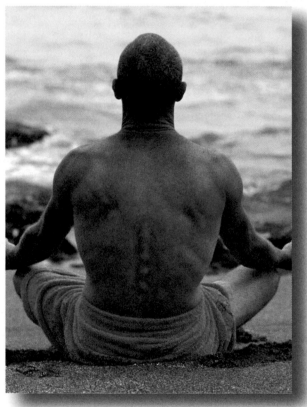

In these troubling situations, the first thing we can do is to admit that we don't have the resources to handle the problem. No matter how hard we try and no matter what skills we bring to bear, some problems remain out of our control. When this is the case, we can tell the truth: "It's too big and too mean. I can't handle it."

Releasing control, receiving help

Desperately struggling to control a problem can easily result in the problem's controlling you. Surrender is letting go of being the master in order to avoid becoming the slave.

Once you have acknowledged your lack of control, all that remains is to surrender. Many traditions make note of this. Western religions speak of surrendering to God. Hindus say surrender to the Self. Members of Alcoholics Anonymous talk about turning their lives over to a Higher Power. Agnostics might suggest surrendering to the ultimate source of power. Others might speak of

following their intuition, their inner guide, or their conscience. William James wrote about surrender as a part of the conversion experience.[4]

In any case, surrender means being receptive to help. Once we admit that we're at the end of our rope, we open ourselves up to receiving help. We learn that we don't have to go it alone. We find out that other people have faced similar problems and survived. We give up our old habits of thinking and behaving as if we have to be in control of everything. We stop acting as general manager of the universe. We surrender. And that creates a space for something new in our lives.

Surrender works

Surrender works for life's major barriers as well as for its insignificant hassles.

You might say, as you struggle to remember someone's name, "It's on the tip of my tongue." Then you surrender. You give up trying and say, "Oh well, it will come to me later." Then the name pops into your mind.

An alcoholic admits that he just can't control his drinking. This becomes the key that allows him to seek treatment.

A person with multiple sclerosis admits that she's gradually losing the ability to walk. She tells others about this fact. Now the people around her can understand, be supportive, and explore ways to help.

A man is devastated when his girlfriend abandons him. He is a "basket case," unable to work for days. Instead of struggling against this fact, he simply admits the full extent of his pain. In that moment, he is able to trust. He trusts that help will come and that one day he will be OK again. He trusts in his ability to learn and to create a new life. He trusts that new opportunities for love will come his way.

After trying unsuccessfully for years to have a baby, a couple finally surrenders and considers adoption. The woman then conceives in a few months.

After finding out she has terminal cancer, a woman shifts between panic and depression. Nothing seems to console her. Finally, she accepts the truth and stops fighting her tragedy. She surrenders. Now at peace, she invests her remaining years in meaningful moments with the people she loves.

A writer is tackling the first chapter of his novel, feeling totally in control. He has painstakingly outlined the whole plot, recording each character's actions on individual 3×5 cards. Three sentences into his first draft, he finds that he's spending most of his time shuffling cards instead of putting words on paper. Finally, he puts the cards aside, forgets about the outline, and just tells the story. The words start to flow effortlessly, and he loses himself in the act of writing.

In each of these cases, the people involved learned the power of surrendering.

What surrender is not

Surrender is not resignation. It is not a suggestion to quit and do nothing about your problems. You have many skills and resources. Use them. You can apply all of your energy to handling a situation and surrender at the same time. Surrender includes doing whatever you can in a positive, trusting spirit. Giving up is fatalistic and accomplishes nothing. So let go, keep going, and know that the true source of control lies beyond you.

This Power Process says, in effect, don't fight the current. Imagine a person rafting down a flowing river with a rapid current. She's likely to do fine if she surrenders control and lets the raft flow with the current. After all, the current always goes around the rocks. If she tries to fight the current, she could end up in an argument with a rock about where the current is going—and lose.

Detachment helps us surrender

Watching yourself with detachment can help your ability to surrender. Pretend that you are floating away from your body, and then watch what's going on from a distance.

Objectively witness the drama of your life unfolding as if you were watching a play. When you see yourself as part of a much broader perspective, surrender seems obvious and natural.

"Surrender" might seem inconsistent with the Power Process "I create it all." An old parable says that the Garden of Truth, the grand place everyone wants to enter, is guarded by two monsters—Fear and Paradox. Most of us can see how fear keeps us from getting what we want. The role of paradox might not be as clear.

The word *paradox* refers to a seemingly contradictory statement that might nonetheless be true. It is our difficulty in holding seemingly contradictory thoughts that sometimes keeps us out of the Garden of Truth. If we suspend the sovereignty of logic, then we might discover that ideas that seem contradictory can actually coexist. With application, we can see that both "Surrender" and "I create it all" are valuable tools.

JOURNAL ENTRY

#56

Discovery Statement

Review the Power Process "Employ your word" in the Communicating chapter. Below list one problem in your life and explain how it could be related to broken agreements.

I discovered that I …

_____

_____

_____

_____

_____

_____

_____

_____

master student
CHRISTOPHER REEVE

well-known actor, was left paralyzed after a horseback-riding accident and today is an advocate for people with disabilities.

Soon I realized that I'd have to leave Kessler [hospital] at some point. A tentative date was set for sometime between Thanksgiving and mid-December. I thought: God, I've totally given up on breathing. So what am I going to do, stay on a ventilator for the rest of my life?. . .

I announced that on the first Monday of November, I was going to try again to breathe on my own. At 3:30 in the afternoon of November 2, Bill Carroll, Dr. Kirshblum, Dr. Finley, and Erica met me in the PT room. And I remember thinking: This is it. I've *got* to do something, I have simply *got* to. I don't know where it's going to come from, but I've got to produce some air from someplace.

Dr. Finley said, "We're going to take you off the ventilator. I want you to try to take ten breaths. If you can only do three, then that's the way it is, but I want you to try for ten. And I'm going to measure how much air you move with each breath, and let's just see where you are. Okay?"

And I took ten breaths. I was lying on my back on the mat. My head moved as I struggled to draw in air; I wasn't able to move my diaphragm at all, just my chest, neck, and shoulder muscles in an intense effort to bring some air into my lungs. I was only able to draw in an average of 50 cc's with each attempt. But at least it was something. I had moved the dial.

We came back the next day, and now I was really motivated. I prepared myself mentally by imagining my chest as a huge bellows that I could open and close at will. I told myself over and over again that I was going home soon and that I couldn't leave without making some real progress. Dr. Finley asked me to take another ten breaths for a comparison with yesterday's numbers. I took the ten breaths, and my average for each one was 450 cc's.

They couldn't believe it. I thought to myself: All right. Now we're getting somewhere.

At 3:30 the next day I was in place and ready to begin. . . . Finally I was really taking charge. When Dr. Finley arrived once again he asked me to take ten breaths. This time the average was 560 cc's per breath. A cheer broke out in the room. . . .

After that Erica and I worked alone. Every day we would breathe. I went from seven minutes to twelve to fifteen. Just before I left Kessler on the thirteenth of December, I gave it everything I had, and I breathed for thirty minutes. . . . The previous summer, still adjusting to my new circumstances, I had given up. But by November I had the motivation to go forward. . . .

Juice had often told me, "You've been to the grave two times this year, brother. You're not going there again. You are here for a reason." He thought my injury had meaning, had a purpose. I believed, and still do, that my injury was simply an accident. But maybe Juice and I are both right, because I have the opportunity now to make sense of this accident. I believe that it's what you do after an accident that can give it meaning.

I began to face my new life. On Thanksgiving in 1995, I went home to Bedford to spend the day with my family. In the driveway, when I saw our home again, I wept. Dana held me. At the dinner table, when each of us in turn spoke a few words about what we were thankful for, Will said, "Dad."

From Still Me *by Christopher Reeve. Copyright ©1998 by Cambria Productions, Inc. Reprinted by permission of Random House, Inc.*

For more biographical information on Christopher Reeve, visit Houghton Mifflin's College Survival/Becoming a Master Student web site: **http://collegesurvival.college. hmco.com/students.**

1 Explain three ways you can respond effectively if someone you know threatens to commit suicide.

 2 The strategies suggested for dealing with stress do *not* include:
  (A) Manage self-talk.
  (B) Practice relaxation techniques.
  (C) Cut back on exercising.
  (D) Mentally rehearse success and visualize positive events.
  (E) Check with the student health service.

 3 How is the Power Process "Surrender" different from giving up?

 4 A person infected with HIV may have no symptoms for months—sometimes years. True or False? Explain your answer.

 5 Define *date rape* and describe at least two ways to prevent it.

 6 List at least three dietary guidelines that can contribute to your health.

 7 One of the suggestions for dealing with addiction is "When you use, pay attention." This implies that it's OK to use drugs, as long as you do so with full awareness. True or False? Explain your answer.

Quiz

 8 Name at least three methods for preventing unwanted pregnancy.

 9 The article "Emotional pain is not a sickness" advises that sometimes it helps to allow yourself to feel bad for a while. What is the point behind this idea?

 10 Explain two ways that an uncritical response to advertising can undermine your health.

JOURNAL ENTRY

#57

Discovery/Intention Statement

Describe what you learned in this chapter about the way you take care of your "machine."

I discovered that I ...

_____

_____

_____

Now choose one health-related behavior that you want to change. Describe when and how you will make this change.

I intend to ...

_____

_____

_____

LEARNING STYLES APPLICATION   CHAPTER 11

Mode 4 *After carrying out your plan, consider how well it worked for you. Which actions do you intend to continue on a regular basis? Are there any new actions you intend to take or any changes you want to make in your action plan? Write answers to both of these questions.*

Mode 1 *Name one specific health benefit you'd like to gain. Possibilities include less stress, weight loss, or an increased energy level.*

Mode 3 *Create an action plan for using the ideas you listed for Mode 2. Write five Intention Statements and set a date for taking each action.*

Mode 2 *List five ideas from this chapter that can help you gain the benefit you just listed.*

 BIBLIOGRAPHY

 INTERNET RESOURCES

ENDNOTES

1 Harvey Jackins, *The Benign Reality* (Seattle: Rational Island, 1991).

2 Daniel Goleman, *Emotional Intelligence* (New York: Bantam, 1997).

3 American Psychological Association, *Diagnostic and Statistical Manual of Psychoactive Substance Abuse Disorders* (Washington, DC: American Psychological Association, 1994).

4 William James, *The Varieties of Religious Experience: A Study in Human Nature* (New York: Scribner, 1997).

ADDITIONAL READING

Boston Women's Health Book Collective. *The New Our Bodies, Ourselves.* New York: Simon & Schuster, 1996.

Fletcher, Anne. *Sober for Good.* Boston: Houghton Mifflin, 2001.

Robbins, John. *Diet for a New America.* New York: H J Kramer, 1998.

Schlosser, Eric. *Fast Food Nation.* Boston: Houghton Mifflin, 2001.

Weil, Andrew. *Health and Healing.* Boston: Houghton Mifflin, 1995.

Weil, Andrew. *Natural Health, Natural Medicine.* Boston: Houghton Mifflin, 1998.

Eating Disorders
www.anred.com

IntelliHealth
www.intelihealth.com

Violence Against Women
www.ojp.usdoj.gov/vawo/

CHAPTER 12

What Next?

Think wrongly if you please, but in all cases think for yourself.
DORIS LESSING

Live as if you were to die tomorrow. Learn as if you were to live forever.
GANDHI

Learning is not a task or a problem—it is a way to be in the world. Man learns as he pursues goals and projects that have meaning for him.
SIDNEY JOURARD

NOW THAT YOU'RE DONE . . . Begin again. Choose your favorite techniques from this course and start using them for the rest of your life. Support your choices with attitudes, affirmations, and visualizations. Begin career planning, and choose ways to contribute through the art of selfishness. Document your continuing success with a portfolio and make the world your classroom with distance learning. And at any time, use a process that enhances any technique—"Be it."

Now that you're done—begin

If you used this book, if you actively participated in reading the contents, writing the journals, doing the exercises, practicing critical thinking, completing the learning styles applications, and applying the suggestions, then you have had quite a journey. You are on a path of growth toward becoming a master student. Now what? What's the next step?

The world is packed with opportunities for master students. If you excel in adventure, exploration, discovery, and creativity, you will never lack for possibilities. If you want to continue to grow and to continue to learn how to learn, the choices are endless.

You are on the edge of a universe so miraculous and full of wonder that your imagination at its most creative moment cannot encompass it. Paths are open to lead you to worlds beyond your wildest dreams.

If this sounds like a pitch for the latest recreational drug, it might be. The drug is adrenaline, and it is automatically generated by your body when you are growing, risking, and discovering new worlds inside and outside your skin.

This book has started the process of discovery and intention, a powerful tool that can assist you in getting exactly what you want out of life. Following are several ways to reinforce the discovery and intention process.

Student Voices

After reading this book, my professor challenged our class to come up with a list of how we could apply the strategies we learned to promote our success in the workplace. In reviewing the table of contents, I discovered that almost every skill could be turned into an applicable career tool. I intend to discuss these master student qualities in an upcoming job interview.

—SEAN CUDDY

JOURNAL ENTRY #58

Discovery Statement

Complete the following sentences with the first thoughts that come to mind.

From this chapter, I want …

_____
_____
_____
_____
_____
_____
_____
_____
_____
_____
_____

From my life, I want …

_____
_____
_____
_____
_____
_____
_____
_____
_____
_____
_____

"...use the following suggestions to continue..."

Discovery Statements and Intention Statements that you learned in this book. For more ideas, see "Taking notes on your journey: The art of journal writing" in the Notes chapter.

Take a workshop.
Schooling doesn't have to stop at graduation, and it doesn't have to take place on a campus. In most cities, there are a variety of organizations that sponsor ongoing workshops, covering topics from cosmetology to cosmology. Use workshops to learn skills, understand the world, and discover yourself. You can be trained in cardiopulmonary resuscitation (CPR), attend a lecture on developing nations, or take a course on assertiveness training.

Read, watch, and listen.
Publications related to the topic of becoming a master student are recommended in the bibliographies at the end of each chapter in this book. Ask friends and instructors what they are reading. Sample a variety of newspapers and magazines. None of them has all of the truth; most of them have a piece of it.

In addition to books, many bookstores and publishing houses offer audio- and videotapes on personal growth topics. Record your most exciting discoveries in an idea file.

Take an unrelated class.
Sign up for a class that is totally unrelated to your major. If you are studying to be a secretary, take a physics course. If you are going to be a doctor, take a bookkeeping course.

You can discover a lot about yourself and your intended future when you step out of old patterns. In addition to formal courses offered at your school, check

Keep a journal.
Psychotherapist Ira Progoff based his Intensive Journal System on the idea that regular journaling can be a path to life-changing insights.[1]

To begin journaling, consider buying a bound notebook in which to record your private reflections and dreams for the future. Get one that will be worthy of your personal discoveries and intentions. Write in this journal daily. Record what you are learning about yourself and the world.

Write about your hopes, wishes, and goals. Keep a record of significant events. Consider using the format of

Student Voices

I believe the concept of a master student is more about a journey than a destination. It's not about straight A's or graduating at the top of the class, even though those are worthwhile goals. It doesn't end with getting a degree, either. It's more a philosophy of life, and a true master student never stops learning and growing. My journey to become a master student is just beginning.

— CATHY FREDERICK

into local community education courses. These offer a low-cost alternative that poses no threat to your grade point average.

Travel.
See the world. Visit new neighborhoods. Travel to other countries. Explore. Find out what it looks like inside buildings that you normally have no reason to enter, museums that you never found interesting before, cities that are out of the way, forests and mountains that lie beyond your old boundaries, and far-off places that require planning and saving to reach.

Get counseling.
Solving emotional problems is not the only reason to visit a counselor, therapist, or psychologist. These people are excellent resources for personal growth. You can use counseling to look at and talk about yourself in ways that might be uncomfortable for anyone except a trained professional. Counseling offers a chance to focus exclusively on yourself, something that is usually not possible in normal social settings.

Form a support group.
Just as a well-organized study group can promote your success in school, an organized support group can help you reach goals in other areas of your life.

Today, people in support groups help one another lose weight, stay sober, cope with chronic illness, recover from emotional trauma, and overcome drug addiction.

Groups can also brainstorm possibilities for job hunting, career planning, parenting, solving problems in relationships, promoting spiritual growth—for reaching almost any goal you choose.

Find a mentor—or become one.
Seek the counsel of experienced people you respect and admire. Use them as role models. If they are willing, ask them to be sounding boards for your plans and ideas. Many people are flattered to be asked.

You can also become a mentor. If you want to perfect your skills as a master student, teach them to someone else. Offer to coach another student in study skills in exchange for childcare, free lunches, or something else you value. A mentor relationship can bridge the boundaries of age, race, or culture.

Redo this book.
Start by redoing one chapter or maybe just one exercise. If you didn't get everything you wanted from this book, it's not too late.

You can also redo portions that you found valuable. Redo the quizzes to test your ability to recall certain information. Redo the exercises that were particularly effective for you. They can work again. Many of the exercises in this book can produce a different result after a few months. You are changing, and your responses change, too.

The Discovery Wheel can be useful in revealing techniques you have actually put into practice. Redo the Journal Entries. If you keep your own journal, refer to it as you rewrite the Journal Entries in this book.

As you redo this book or any part of it, reconsider techniques that you skimmed over or skipped before. They might work for you now. Modify the suggestions or add new ones. Redoing this book can refresh and fine-tune your study habits.

Another way to redo this book is to retake your student success course. People who do this will often say that the second time is much different from the first. They pick up ideas and techniques that they missed the first time and gain deeper insight into things they already know.

EXERCISE

#33

Do something you can't

You can accomplish much more than you might think you can. Few significant accomplishments result when people stick to the familiar. Risk yourself.

Pick something that you don't know how to do and do it. Choose something that you think you can't do and do it.

Be smart. Don't pick something that will hurt you physically, such as flying from a third-floor window.

This exercise has three parts.

Part 1 Select something that you have never done before, that you don't know how to do, that you are fearful of doing, or that you think you probably can't do. On a separate sheet of paper, describe the thing you have chosen.

Part 2 Do it. Of course, this is easier to say than to do. This exercise is not about easy. It is about discovering capabilities that stretch your self-image.

In order to accomplish something that is bigger than your self-perceived abilities, use all of the tools you have. Develop a plan. Divide and conquer. Be willing to take a risk. Stay focused. Use all available outside resources. Let go of self-destructive thoughts.

Part 3 Write about the results of this exercise in your journal, if you choose to start one.

Attitudes, affirmations & visualizations

I'M A GREAT STUDENT!

"I have a bad attitude." Some of us say this as if we were talking about having the flu. An attitude is certainly as strong as the flu, but it isn't something we have to succumb to or accept.

Some of us see our attitudes the way we see our height or eye color: "I might not like it, but I might as well accept it."

Acceptance is certainly a worthwhile approach to things we cannot change. When it comes to attitudes, acceptance is not necessary—attitudes *can* change. We don't have to live our lives with an attitude that doesn't work.

Attitudes are powerful; they create behavior. If your attitude is that you're not very interesting at a party, then your behavior will probably match your attitude, and you might act like a bore. If your attitude is that you are fun at a party, then your behavior is more likely to be playful. Soon you are the life of the party. All that has to change is attitude.

You can change your attitudes through regular practice with affirmations and visualizations.

I AM AWESOME

Affirm it. An affirmation is a statement describing what you want. The most effective affirmations are personal, positive, and written in the present tense.

Affirmations have an almost magical power. They are used successfully by athletes and actors, executives and ballerinas, and tens of thousands of people who have succeeded in their lives. Affirmations can change your attitudes and behaviors.

To use affirmations, first determine what you want, then describe yourself as if you already have it. For example, if you decide you want a wonderful job, you might write, "I, Susan Webster, have a wonderful job. I respect and love my colleagues, and they feel the same way about me. I look forward to going to work each day."

Or if money is your desire, you might write, "I, John Henderson, am rich. I have more money than I can spend. I have everything I want, including a six-bedroom house, a new sports car, a 200-watt sound system, and a large-screen television with a satellite dish receiver."

What makes the affirmation work is detail. Use brand names, people's names, and your own name. Involve all of your senses—sight, sound, smell, taste, touch. Take a positive approach. Instead of saying, "I am not fat," say, "I am slender."

Once you have written the affirmation, repeat it. Practice saying it out loud several times a day. This works best if you say it at a regular time, such as just before you go to sleep or just after you wake up.

Sit in a chair in a relaxed position. Take a few deep and relaxing breaths, and then repeat your affirmation with emotion. It's also effective to look in a mirror while saying the affirmation. Keep looking and repeating until you are saying your affirmation with conviction.

Visualize it. It would be difficult to grow up in our culture without hearing the maxim that practice improves performance. The problem is that most of us limit what we consider to be practice. Effective practice can occur when we are not moving a muscle.

You can improve a golf game, a tennis serve, or your skiing ability when lying in bed. You can become a better driver, speaker, or cook while sitting silently in a chair. In line at the grocery store, you can improve your ability to type or to take tests. This is all possible through visualization—the technique of seeing yourself be successful.

Here's one way to begin: Decide what you want to improve, and write down what it would look like, sound like, and feel like to have that improvement in your life. If you are learning to play the piano, write down briefly what you would see, hear, and feel if you were playing skillfully. If you want to improve your relationships with your children, write down what you would see, hear, and feel if you were communicating successfully.

A powerful visualization includes not only seeing but other senses as well. Feel the physical sensations. Hear the sounds. Note any smells, tastes, textures, or qualities of light that accompany the scene in your mind.

Once you have a sketch of what it would be like to be successful, practice it in your imagination—successfully. Rehearse in your mind. Include as many details as you can. Always have your practices be successes. Each time you toss the basketball, it will swish through the net. Every time you invite someone out, the person will say yes. Every test will have an A on the top. Practice at least once per day.

You can also use visualizations to replay errors. When you make a mistake, replay it in your imagination. After a bad golf shot, stop and replay it in your head. Imagine yourself making that same shot again, this time very successfully. If you just had a discussion with your lover that turned into a fight, replay it successfully. Get all of your senses involved. See yourselves calmly talking it over together. Hear the words, and feel the pleasure of a successful interaction.

Visualizations and affirmations can restructure your attitudes and behaviors. Be clear about what you want—and then practice.

I am a loving Parent!

Attitude replacements

You can use affirmations to replace a negative attitude with a positive one. There are no limitations, other than your imagination and your willingness to practice. Here are some sample affirmations. Modify them to suit your individual hopes and dreams, and then practice them. The article "Attitudes, affirmations & visualizations" explains ways to use these attitude replacements.

I, *Rowena* am healthy.
I, *Rowena*, have abundant energy and vitality throughout the day.
I, *Rowena*, exercise regularly.
I, *Rowena*, work effectively with many different kinds of people.
I, *Rowena*, eat wisely.
I, *Rowena*, plan my days and use time wisely.
I, _____, have a powerful memory.
I, _____, take tests calmly and confidently.
I, _____, have a sense of self-worth that is independent of my test scores.
I, _____, am a great speller.
I, *Rowena*, fall asleep quickly and sleep soundly.
I, *Rowena*, am smart.
I, _____, learn quickly.
I, *Rowena*, am creative.
I, *Rowena*, am aware of and sensitive to other people's moods.
I, *Rowena*, have relationships that are mutually satisfying.
I, *Rowena*, work hard and contribute to other people through my job.
I, *Rowena*, am wealthy.
I, *Rowena*, know ways to play and have fun.
I, *Rowena*, am attractive.
I, *Rowena*, focus my attention easily.
I, *Rowena*, like myself.
I, *Rowena*, am liked by other people.
I, *Rowena*, am a worthwhile person even though I am *not flawless*.
I, *Rowena*, have a slim and attractive body.
I, _____, am relaxed in all situations, including _____.
I, *Rowena*, make profitable financial investments.
I, _____, have an income that far exceeds my expenses.
I, *Rowena*, live a life of abundance and prosperity.
I, *Rowena*, always live my life in positive ways for the highest good of all people.

To hear an online version of these affirmations, visit Houghton Mifflin's College Survival/Becoming a Master Student web site:
http://collegesurvival.college.hmco.com/students.

√ due next time?

EXERCISE

#34

Reprogram your attitude

Affirmations and visualizations can be used to successfully reprogram your attitudes and behaviors. Use this exercise to change your approach to any situation in your life.

Step 1

Pick something in your life that you would like to change. It can be related to anything—relationships, work, money, or personal skills. Below, write a brief description of what you choose to change.

Step 2

Add more details about the change you described in Step 1. Write down how you would like the change to come about. Be outlandish. Imagine that you are about to ask your fairy godmother for a wish you know she will grant. Be detailed in your description of your wish.

Step 3

Here comes the fairy godmother. Use affirmations and visualizations to start yourself on the path to creating exactly what you wrote about in Step 2. Below, write at least two affirmations that describe your dream wish. Also, briefly outline a visualization that you can use to picture your wish. Be specific, detailed, and positive.

Step 4

Put your new attitudes to work. Set up a schedule to practice them. Let the first time be right now. Then set up at least five other times and places that you intend to practice your affirmations and visualizations.

I intend to relax and practice my affirmations and visualizations for at least five minutes on the following dates and at the times and place(s) given.

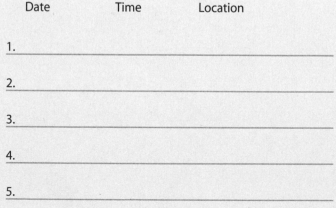

	Date	Time	Location
1.			
2.			
3.			
4.			
5.			

#35

This book shouts, "Use me!"

Becoming a Master Student is designed to be used for years. The success strategies presented here are not likely to become habits overnight. There are more suggestions than can be put into action immediately. Some of what is discussed might not apply to your life right now, but might be just what you could use in a few months.

Plan to keep this book and use it again. Imagine that your book has a mouth. (Visualize the mouth.) That it has arms and legs. (Visualize them.)

Now picture your book sitting on a shelf or table that you see every day. Imagine a time when you are having trouble in school and struggling to be successful as a student. Visualize your book jumping up and down shouting, "Use me! Read me! I might have the solution to your problem, and I know I can help you solve it."

This is a memory technique to remind you to use a resource. Sometimes when you are stuck, all you need is a small push or a list of possible actions. At those times, hear your book shout, "Use me!"

Other ideas for getting lasting value from *Becoming a Master Student* include:

- Keep it on the coffee table, in the kitchen, or in the bathroom.
- Keep it near your bedroom nightstand.
- Loan the book to someone else, then talk about it with that person.
- Teach your favorite suggestions from this book to your friends and family members.
- Tear out specific articles and share them with family members or friends.
- In your calendar or appointment book, schedule periodic times to review *Becoming a Master Student*.

WORKPLACE APPLICATIONS

Even the most brilliant people can fall flat when predicting trends in business and the workplace. Case in point: Thomas Watson, founder of IBM, said, "I think there's a world market for about five computers."

Still, you can benefit from keeping up-to-date with breaking changes in your career field. That's easier to do than ever before, thanks to resources mentioned throughout this book:

The Internet. Use your skills in searching the Internet to find web sites devoted to your field. Start by keying your job title into a search engine such as Google. Also search for list servers—programs that distribute email messages to groups of people with similar interests.

Periodicals. Read the business sections of the *New York Times* and the *Wall Street Journal*, for example. Many newspapers also have online editions; so do general interest magazines such as *Time* and *Business Week*.

Professional associations. People in similar jobs like to band together and give each other a heads up on emerging trends—one reason for professional associations. These range from the American Medical Association to the Society of Actuaries. There's bound to be one for people in your field. Ask colleagues and search the Internet. *Note:* Many associations post web sites and publish trade magazines.

Conferences and conventions. Many professional associations sponsor annual meetings. Here's where you can meet people face-to-face and use your networking skills. Print and online publications are powerful sources of news, but sometimes nothing beats plain old schmoozing.

[Source for Watson quote: Charles Hard Townes, in Martin Moskovits (Ed.), *Science and Society, the John C. Polanyi Nobel Laureates Lectures*, Anansi Press, Concord, Ontario, 1995, p. 8., listed on *A Dictionary of Scientific Quotations*, http://naturalscience.com/dsqhome.html, accessed 2-6-02]

Changing schools

Transferring to a different school involves making a decision that will have a major impact on your education. This is true at many points in higher education—such as when you're transferring from a two-year to a four-year school, or when you're choosing a graduate school.

Selecting a school for the next step in your higher education is much like choosing a career. First, you define the profile of an ideal prospective school, much as you would that of an ideal job. Next, you create a profile of yourself—your skills, background, experience, learning style, and other preferences. Then you seek a reasonable fit between yourself and your ideal school, just as you seek a fit between yourself and your ideal job.

The following suggestions can assist you in making this important decision.

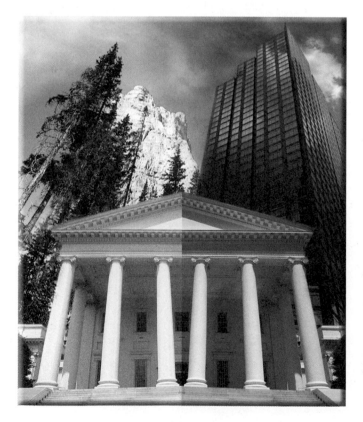

Know key terms

As you begin researching schools, take a few minutes to review some key terms.

Transfer is an official term for changing schools.

Course equivalents are courses you've already taken that another school will accept as meeting its requirements. Since no two schools offer the same curriculum, determining course equivalents is often a matter of interpretation. In some cases, you might be able to persuade a registrar or an admissions office to accept some of your previous courses.

Articulation agreements are official documents that spell out the course equivalents a school accepts.

Prerequisites are courses or skills that a school requires students to complete or have before they enter or graduate.

Learn about the different types of schools

Schools differ in countless dimensions. Start by digging up key facts in the following ten areas about each school you're considering.

1. Number of students. The largest state universities can have a student body numbering 50,000 or more. Small private schools and vocational schools might have fewer than 1,000 students. The student bodies of many schools lie between these extremes.

2. Class sizes. Large schools might enroll 1,000 in a general education course. At smaller schools, your largest class might number between 20 and 30 people. You might enroll in seminars with a handful of students or take an individualized, guided reading course. Even within a single school, class sizes can vary between course levels and departments.

3. Contact with instructors. Some schools employ faculty members who are dedicated to teaching. You could take most of your classes from associate or full professors. In other schools, graduate assistants teach lower-level courses, and professors focus mainly on graduate students, publishing, or research. If you value close contact with your instructors, this is a crucial factor to investigate.

4. *Admissions criteria.* Some schools are highly competitive, admitting only a small percentage of the students who apply each year. Other schools are relatively open, admitting most students with high school diplomas.

5. *Availability of degrees.* Community colleges and vocational-technical schools commonly offer associate in arts (A.A.) degrees, also called two-year degrees. Public and private colleges and universities generally offer four-year degrees, such as the bachelor of arts (B.A.) or bachelor of science (B.S.). Because their schedules vary so greatly, students might find that these degrees take longer than two or four years to complete. Many larger schools also offer graduate programs, leading to master's and doctoral degrees or specialized degrees in law, medicine, dentistry, or the ministry. If you want to make only one transfer, then the availability of such degrees can have an impact on your decision.

6. *Costs.* Schools that receive public funding generally have lower tuition than private schools. Even so, tuition is only one of the costs of attending school. Others include books, materials, residence hall fees, and laboratory fees. If you plan to live off campus, factor in the cost of living in the surrounding community.

7. *Mission.* Schools that emphasize liberal education could have fewer courses that prepare students for specific careers. In contrast, many community colleges and vocational schools offer degrees geared toward a specific job field, such as dental assistance, real estate, or auto mechanics. Some schools have a reputation for their teacher education programs, while others excel in research or offer outstanding graduate programs.

8. *Location.* The school you choose might be nestled in an idyllic rural setting or thrive in the heart of a large city. The differences can greatly color your experience of higher education. Also consider the school's distance from your current home.

9. *Religious affiliation.* You might value contact with students who share your sense of spirituality. Or perhaps you want a school attended by people of many spiritual perspectives. Schools differ greatly along this continuum.

10. *Diversity.* This term can apply to faculty members as well as students. Some schools primarily serve women or people of color, while others enroll a highly diverse student body. Also consider the mix between full-time and part-time students, students who live at the school and those who commute, and graduate and undergraduate students.

Dig up other key facts

Before you transfer to any school or choose a graduate program, gather the facts about your current academic profile. This includes grades, courses completed, degrees attained, and grade point average (GPA). Standardized test scores are also important, such as those for the Scholastic Aptitude Test (SAT), the American College Test (ACT), the Graduate Record Exam (GRE), and any advanced placement tests you've taken. Also keep a folder of syllabuses from your courses; they can be useful when transferring credits.

List each school's course requirements. Note all prerequisites, including those required for general education or your proposed major, and any other courses required for graduation. Check the availability of courses in your major, including any graduate courses and advanced degrees, if you're planning on graduate work.

With your requirements in hand, begin creating a list of course equivalents. Most schools will have specific worksheets for this purpose. The school's registrar or admissions office can answer your questions about how to complete these forms.

After totaling the costs of attending a school, check on the financial aid that would be available at this school. For more specific ideas, see the Resources chapter.

Resources such as a counseling center, career planning center, or job placement office can be critical to your success in school. Check out the availability of these services at each school you consider.

Turn to three basic sources

So far this article has suggested what to ask about when you research a school. How to find this information is a

Student Voices

In the beginning I wasn't sure that I had made the right decision by moving from a two-year community college to a four-year university. But it turned out to be just what I needed to move toward my career goals. My academic advisor at the university helped me to have all of my credits transferred to my new school. I'm only three semesters away from applying for a graduate program in my field of study.

—Anthony LaRosa

separate question. Basically, you can turn to three sources: materials, people, and your own experience.

Materials include print sources, such as school catalogs. Also check more general guides, such as *Barron's Profiles of American Colleges, Peterson's National College Data Bank,* or the *Directory of Special Programs for Minority Group Members.*

In addition, many schools have sites on the World Wide Web. To find them, go to a search tool such as Yahoo! (www.yahoo.com) or Google (www.google.com) and key in the name of the school you want to investigate.

People include instructors, academic advisors, counselors, and other school staff members. Also seek out current students at a school, as well as former students who are now working in your chosen field.

Your own experience includes a visit to the two or three schools on the top of your list. Take a thorough tour of the facilities—the library, laboratories, residence halls, bookstores, cafeterias, and student center. Also ask about sources of entertainment, such as restaurants, theaters, galleries, and concert halls. When you're done with the "official" tours, just walk around and observe the school grounds. Your direct experience of a school can be more intensive if you work in the surrounding community for a summer or take a course at the school before you transfer.

Put this choice in context

Crucial to this process is the larger context that shapes your choice. To begin with, consider the needs and wishes of your family members. Ask for their guidance and support. If you involve them in the decision, they can have more stake in your success.

Then broaden the context even more. Consider the purposes, values, and long-term goals you've generated through exercises and Journal Entries in this book, such as the lifeline exercise. All of these can have a bearing on the school you select.

Your experience of a school goes well beyond the facts listed in the catalog. After you gather facts, let them simmer in your subconscious. Then pay attention to your instincts and intuition—your attraction to one school or feelings of hesitation about another.

Finally, just choose. There is no one "right" school for you, and you could probably thrive at many schools (perhaps even your current one). Use the suggestions in this book to practice self-responsibility and take charge of your education—no matter what school you attend.

no

PRACTICING CRITICAL THINKING #22

Imagine that you are about to teach a student success course. Analyze the topic of student success and then create a brief outline or syllabus for the course. Choose the main subtopics you will cover, any texts or other materials you will use, and any guest speakers you will invite. Write down your ideas in the space below.

_____
_____
_____
_____
_____
_____
_____
_____
_____
_____
_____

Now reflect on what you just wrote. What results did you want students to achieve in this course? What other ways could you, as a teacher, help them achieve these results?

_____
_____
_____
_____
_____
_____
_____
_____
_____
_____
_____

Getting the most from distance learning

You can use technology to transcend the limits of time and space while learning anything from astrology to zoology. Through distance learning, students and instructors literally enter a classroom without walls.

Distance learning takes place when teachers and learners are separated geographically and communicate by means of the Internet or other technology.

In former days, the term *distance learning* often referred to correspondence courses in which teachers and students exchanged materials by old-fashioned "snail mail." Now, participants in distance learning stay in touch through fax, email, web sites, and teleconferencing.

In addition to exchanging print materials, students and instructors often share computer disks, videotapes, audiotapes, and other audiovisual materials. Sometimes distance learning involves traveling across the state or across the country for in-person interactions with instructors.

Distance learning is unlikely to completely replace the traditional classroom. Yet it is growing in popularity and provides a wonderful alternative for many students.

Consider the benefits.
Through distance learning, students with limited mobility—such as those with physical disabilities—gain access to higher education. So do older students with full-time jobs and busy family lives.

Distance learning can link you to experts in your field, even if those experts are thousands of miles away. And within some reasonable limits set by the instructor, distance learning allows you to complete assignments on your own schedule, at your own pace.

Choose carefully.
Before signing up for a distance learning course, consider whether this medium fits your learning style. If you like to work independently, it could be ideal. If you thrive on face-to-face interaction with peers and instructors, then distance learning might not work for you.

Besides removing the chance to meet regularly with other people, some forms of distance learning erase the nonverbal signals that you pick up by watching an instructor lecture. Often those signals relay important information—such as clues about what will be covered on the next test.

When considering whether to register for a distance learning course, do some research up front. Contact the instructor ahead of time. Ask to review the course materials before you sign up. See if you can talk with someone who's already taken the course. Get a sense of whether distance learning will be a fit for you.

Also consider the credibility of any organization offering distance learning programs. These programs vary in quality, so shop carefully.

Manage your time.
Without a regular schedule of in-person classes and face-to-face meetings with an instructor, some students act as if they have all the time in the world to complete their distance learning assignments. These students can run into a last-minute crunch at the end of the course. Even conscientious students might neglect a distance

learning course that seems "invisible" compared to their traditional courses.

To succeed at distance learning, front-load your efforts. Early in the term, create a detailed timeline with a due date for each assignment. Break big assignments into smaller steps and schedule a due date for each step. If possible, submit assignments early. Review the antiprocrastination strategies in the Time chapter, as without weekly class meetings, there is often a tendency to put off work on distance learning courses. Staying ahead of the game will help you avoid an all-nighter during finals week.

Prepare. Find out whether the equipment you'll need for distance learning—computer, phone, modem, fax machine—is available through your school. The instructor might expect you to supply this equipment on your own. Learn to use the technology before the course starts. When it does start, you can then focus on content instead of fumbling with equipment.

Distance learning can test your patience. Sending images and sound over the Internet might create delays in transmission, and connections can be maddeningly slow.

Distance learning can also test your ability to communicate effectively and efficiently. When you communicate with others in real time during a teleconference or chat room session, speak or write concisely. Let other students have the "floor" when it's their turn. In a virtual classroom in which no one sees anyone else, etiquette takes on a whole new meaning.

Ask for feedback. To get the most from distance learning, request frequent and detailed feedback from your instructor. Ask for regular conferences by phone and find out whether a toll-free number is available for this purpose. Other options for contact include email, chat rooms, and fax.

The instructor for your course might teach at your school and have an office there. If so, that's great. Call to schedule at least one meeting in person.

Contact other students.

Make personal contact with another student in your class. Meet with this person to share notes, quiz each other, critique papers, and do other cooperative learning tasks. Finding a buddy in your distance learning course can help you stay on task, get some face-to-face contact, and promote your success. Even interacting with a fellow student in cyberspace (through the Internet) can help.

Know the technological ground rules for assignments.

Find out how the instructor wants you to submit your work. If you can do this via email or fax, you might be able to send papers and other assignments on the same day that they're due. If you need to use the regular mail or an overnight service, allow enough time for delivery.

Some instructors will let you send papers and reports as attachments to an email message. People who use computers with different operating systems might find that they can't exchange files in this way. File translation software exists to help solve this problem. Before you count on this software to submit an assignment, do a trial run to see if it really works.

Remember that no technology works perfectly at all times. Sometimes a power surge or other mishap sends computer messages into the digital void. Keep backup copies of all the assignments you submit. Be prepared to send duplicates if one is lost in the mail or during data transmission.

Take responsibility. All learning, especially distance learning, relies on your initiative. When it comes to doing required reading, completing assignments, and preparing for teleconferences, you are largely on your own.

Don't rely on a distance learning instructor to motivate you. Instead, manufacture your own motivation. Be clear about what you'll gain by doing well in the course. Connect the course content to your personal goals. Don't wait to be contacted by your classmates and instructor. Initiate that contact on your own—right at the beginning of the course.

Reflect on your learning.

Classroom discussion often provides the opportunity to connect theory and practice. In response to your questions, an instructor can give examples that relate a concept to your daily experience.

To succeed at distance learning, go beyond memorizing facts and dates by rote. Reflect on those facts. Write Discovery and Intention Statements to explore other viewpoints on an issue and state how you'll apply what you've learned.

After completing your distance learning course, take the time to evaluate. Write about what you liked and what you'd do differently next time. Go beyond the technology and focus on the outcomes. When you invent ways to make distance education work, you gain another option for lifelong learning.

Career Planning

BEGIN NOW

A satisfying and lucrative career is often the goal of education. It pays to define clearly both your career goal and your strategy for reaching that goal. Then you can plan your education effectively.

Career planning is an adventure that involves exploration. There are dozens of effective paths to planning your career. *Career Planning,* a supplement to this text, offers many suggestions on this subject and guides you to more.

You can begin your career-planning adventure now by remembering the following ideas.

1 *You already know a lot about your career plan.*

When people learn study skills and life skills, they usually start with finding out things they don't know. That means discovering new strategies for taking notes, reading, writing, managing time, and the other subjects covered in this book.

Career planning is different. You can begin by realizing how much you know right now. You've already made many decisions about your career. This is true for young people who say, "I don't have any idea what I want to be when I grow up." It's also true for mid-life career changers.

Consider the student who can't decide if he wants to be a cost accountant or a tax accountant and then jumps to the conclusion that he is totally lost when it comes to career planning. It's the same with the student who doesn't know if he wants to be a veterinary assistant or a nurse.

These people forget that they already know a lot about their career choices. The person who couldn't decide between veterinary assistance and nursing had already ruled out becoming a lawyer, computer programmer, or teacher. He just didn't know yet whether he had the right bedside manner for horses or for people. The person who was debating tax accounting versus cost accounting already knew he didn't want to be a doctor, playwright, or taxicab driver. He did know he liked working with numbers and balancing books. In each case, these people have already narrowed their list of career choices to a number of jobs in the same field—jobs that draw on the same core skills. In general, they already know what they want to be when they grow up.

Find a long list of occupations. (One source is *The Dictionary of Occupational Titles*, a government publication available at many libraries.) Using a stack of 3×5 cards, write down about 100 randomly selected job titles, one title per card. Sort through the cards and divide them into two piles. Label one pile "Careers I've Definitely Ruled Out for Now." Label the other pile "Possibilities I'm Willing to Consider."

It's common for people to go through a stack of 100 such cards and end up with 95 in the "definitely ruled out" pile and five in the "possibilities" pile. This demonstrates that they already have a career in mind.

2 Career planning is a choice, not a discovery.
Many people approach career planning as if they were panning for gold. They keep sifting through the dirt, clearing the dust, and throwing out the rocks. They are hoping to strike it rich and discover the perfect career.

Other people believe that they'll wake up one morning, see the heavens part, and suddenly know what they're supposed to do. Many of them are still waiting for that magical day to dawn.

We can approach career planning in a different way. Career planning can be the bridge between our dreams and the reality of our future. Instead of seeing a career as something we discover, we can see it as something we choose. We don't find the right career. We create it.

There's a big difference between these two approaches. Thinking that there's only one "correct" choice for your career can lead to a lot of anxiety: Did I choose the right one? What if I made a mistake?

Viewing your career as your creation helps you relax. Instead of anguishing over finding the right career, you can stay open to possibilities. You can choose one career today, knowing that you can choose again later.

Suppose that you've narrowed your list of possible careers to five, and you still can't decide. Then just choose one. Any one. Many people will have five careers in a

lifetime anyway. You might be able to do all of your careers, and you can do any one of them first. The important thing is to choose.

One caution is in order. Choosing your career is not something to do in an information vacuum. Rather, choose after you've done a lot of research. That includes research into yourself—your skills and interests—and a thorough knowledge of what careers are available.

Career-planning materials and counselors can help you on both counts. You can take skills assessments to find out more about what you like doing. You can take career-planning courses and read books about careers. You can contact people who are actually doing the job you're researching and ask them what it's like (an *information interview*). You can also choose an internship, summer job, or volunteer position in a field that interests you. There's no end to resources for gathering information about yourself and the job market.

After all of the data has been gathered, there's only one person who can choose your career: you. This choice does not have to be a weighty one. In fact, it can be like going into your favorite restaurant and choosing from a menu that includes all of your favorite dishes. At this point, it's difficult to make a mistake. Whatever you choose, you can enjoy it.

3 Name names.
One key to making your career plan real and to ensuring that you can act on it is naming. Go back over your plan to see that you include specific names whenever they're called for.

Name your job. Take the skills you enjoy using and find out which jobs use them. What are those jobs called? List them. Note that the same job might have different names.

Name your company—the agency or organization you want to work for. If you want to be self-employed or start your own business, name the product or service you'd sell. Also list some possible names for your business. If you plan to work for others, name the organizations or agencies that are high on your list.

Name your contacts. Take the list of organizations you just compiled. What people in these organizations are responsible for hiring? List those people and contact them directly. If you choose self-employment, list the names of possible customers or clients. All of these people are job contacts.

Expand your list of contacts by brainstorming with your family and friends. Come up with a list of names—anyone who can help you with career planning and job hunting. Write each of these names on a 3×5 card or Rolodex card. You can also use a spiral-bound notebook or computer.

Next, call the key people on your list. After you speak with them, make brief notes about what you discussed. Also jot down any actions you agreed to take, such as a follow-up call.

Consider everyone you meet a potential member of your job network, and be prepared to talk about what you do. Develop a "pitch"—a short statement of your career goal that you can easily share with your contacts. For example: "After I graduate, I plan to work in the travel business. I'm looking for an internship in a travel agency for next summer. Do you know of any that take interns?"

Name your location. Ask if your career choices are consistent with your preferences about where to live and work. For example, someone who wants to make a living as a studio musician might consider living in a large city such as New York or Toronto. This contrasts with the freelance graphic artist who conducts his business mainly by phone, fax, and email. He might be able to live anywhere and still pursue his career.

Cruising for jobs on the Internet

New technology could change the way that you plan your career and find jobs in the future. On the World Wide Web, you can research companies you'd like to work for, read lists of job openings, and post your résumé. Through faxes, overnight deliveries, cellular phones, and email, you can stay in continual contact with potential employers. Perhaps one day you'll even do a long-distance job interview through a videoconference or a chat room on the Internet.

According to one estimate, about two million people go online every month to hunt for jobs. That's a testament to the potential power of the digital medium and to some of its pitfalls as well. When you're looking for a job, the strength of the Internet—the sheer density of data—can also lead to frustration:

- The haphazard organization of the Internet makes it hard for potential employers to find your résumé when you post it online. The organizations you most want to work for might avoid using the Internet to find job applicants.

- Job openings listed on the Internet can be heavily skewed to certain fields, such as jobs for computer professionals or people in other technical fields.

- Across all fields, the majority of job openings are not listed on the Internet (or in newspaper want ads, for that matter).

This is not meant to disparage the Internet as a tool for job hunters and career planners. The point is that posting a résumé on a web site will not automatically lead to an email in-basket that's bursting to the digital seams with job offers. For an effective job search, view the Internet as just one resource. The article "Career planning: Begin now" explains many others.

With this caveat in mind, you might choose to post your résumé online and scan Internet job ads. If you do, begin with sites such as *JobBank USA* at www.jobbankusa.com, which links to over 20 search engines for finding job openings. Also check *Career Path* at www.careerpath.com for want ads from major U.S. newspapers, updated weekly.

When responding to ads and posting résumés online, avoid some common mistakes. One is to use word processing software to create lots of fancy formatting for your résumé and then attach it to an email message. Many web sites are not powerful enough to handle such formatting and will garble your attachments. Instead, skip the word processing and paste your résumé right into an email message. Proofread it one more time before you hit the "send" button.

Some people create personal web pages to highlight their accomplishments and entice employers. If you go this route, keep your page simple and easy to download. Some web hosts will want to run banner ads on your page. These ads are widely seen as tacky. Avoid them.

Even if you don't choose to post a digital résumé or web page, you can access many career-planning resources on the Internet. Begin with "gateway" sites that offer organized links to many career-related pages on the World Wide Web. For instance, *The Riley Guide* at www.dbm.com/jobguide gives an overview of job hunting on the Internet.

Also check www.jobhuntersbible.com, a site maintained by Richard Bolles, author of *What Color Is Your Parachute?* This site focuses on effective ways to use the Internet. And for some revealing figures, visit sites such as Salary.com to find out the current pay scales of typical jobs in your field.

One way in which the Internet can really help you is in researching organizations before you contact them. Chances are that the company you're interested in has a web site. Go to the site to gather information, discover the names of key players, and view financial data. Doing so will show potential employers that you've done your homework. That can make a favorable impression and even land you a job.

4 Get back to your purpose. When we're deep into the details of planning, it's easy to lose sight of the big picture. Listing skills, researching jobs, writing résumés—all this is necessary and useful. At the same time, attending to these tasks can obscure our broadest goals. To get perspective, we can go back to the basics—a life purpose.

Your deepest desire might be to see that hungry children are fed, to make sure that beautiful music keeps getting heard, or to help alcoholics become sober. When such a large purpose is clear, smaller decisions about what to do are often easier.

A life purpose makes a career plan simpler and more powerful. It cuts through the stacks of job data and employment figures. Your life purpose is like the guidance system for a rocket. It keeps the plan on target while revealing a path for soaring to the heights.

5 Change your mind when appropriate. Career planning is not a once-and-for-all proposition. Rather, career plans are made to be changed and refined as you gain new information about yourself and the world. Career planning never ends. If your present career no longer feels right, you can choose again—no matter what stage of life you're in. The process is the same, whether you're choosing your first career or your fifth.

6 Conduct a more effective job hunt by rethinking typical strategies. The logical outcome of your career plan is a focused job hunt. Mention the words *job hunting,* and many people envision someone poring through the help wanted sections in newspapers or on web sites, sending out hundreds of résumés, or enlisting the services of employment agencies to find job openings and set up interviews.

Richard Bolles, author of *What Color Is Your Parachute?,* points out a shortcoming of these job-hunting strategies: Many employers turn to help wanted listings, résumés, and employment agencies only as a last resort. When jobs open up, they prefer instead to hire people they know—friends and colleagues—or people who walk through the door and prove that they're excellent candidates for available jobs.

With this in mind, Bolles recommends the following steps in career planning and job hunting:[2]

- Discover which skills you want to use in your career.
- Discover which jobs draw on the skills you want to use.
- Interview people who are doing the kind of jobs you'd want to do.

- Research companies you'd like to work for and find out what kinds of problems they face on a daily basis.
- Identify your contacts—a person at each one of these companies who has the power to hire you.
- Arrange an interview with that person.

7 Use résumés to get interviews. A résumé is a piece of persuasive writing, not a dry recitation of facts or laundry list of previous jobs. It has a basic purpose—to get you to the next step in the hiring process, usually an interview.

Begin your résumé with your name, address, phone number, and email address. Then name your desired job, often called an "objective" or "goal." Follow with the body of your résumé—your skills, work experience, and education. In fact, you can use those last three topics as major headings printed in bold in a larger font.

Write your résumé so that the facts leap off the page. Describe your work experiences in short phrases that start with active verbs: "*Supervised* three people." "*Wrote* two annual reports." "*Set up* sales calls." Also leave reasonable margins and space between paragraphs. The person who scans your résumé will sigh with relief when she sees a piece of paper that's not crammed full of ink.

As you draft your résumé, remember that every organization has problems to solve. Factories grapple with employee turnover. Software developers struggle to get their products out faster than the competition. Publishers seek ways to make their books, periodicals, and web sites capture consumer attention.

Show in your résumé that you know about those problems and can offer your skills as solutions. Whenever you can, give evidence that you used those skills to get measurable results. For example: "Our program reduced the average training time for newly hired people by 25 percent."

8 Use interviews to "hire" an employer. You might think of job interviews as a time when a potential employer sizes you up and possibly screens you out. Consider another viewpoint—that interviews offer you a chance to size up potential employers and possibly screen *them* out.

This attitude is easier to take on when you've already done your homework by completing the previous steps mentioned in this article. Those steps can lead you to a strong list of contacts, along with specific ideas about *what* job skills you want to use and *where* you want to use them. By the time you get to a job interview, you'll be able to see if the job is something that you really want. By interviewing, you're "hiring" yourself an employer.

To get the most from your interviews, learn everything you can about each organization that interests you. Get a feel for its strong points and know about its successes in the marketplace. Also find out what challenges the organization faces. As in a résumé, use interviews to present your skills as unique solutions for those challenges.

Job interviewers have many standard questions. Most of them boil down to a few major concerns:

- How did you find out about us?

- Would we be comfortable working with you?

- How can you help us?

- Will you learn this job quickly?

- What makes you different from other applicants?

Before your interview, prepare some answers to these questions. After you've presented those answers and hit it off with a potential employer, you can talk money.

You can make thousands of dollars in just a few minutes—the minutes devoted to negotiating your salary. Salaries for many jobs are flexible. Employers usually have a range in mind, and their first offer will often be at the low end of that range. Remember that you don't have to accept that first offer. Before the interview, find out typical salaries for jobs in your field. Also think about how much money you need to maintain your chosen standard of living. Add at least 10 percent to give yourself room to negotiate.

If you get turned down for the job after your interview, don't take it personally. Every interview is a source of feedback about what works—and what doesn't work—in contacting employers. Use that feedback to interview more effectively next time.

9 Counter bias and discrimination.

During your job hunt, you might worry about discrimination based on your race, ethnic background, or gender preference. Remember that Title VII of the Civil Rights Acts bans discrimination in virtually all aspects of the workplace, from hiring to firing. Congress set up the Equal Employment Opportunity Commission (EEOC) to enforce this act. You can contact this agency at 1-800-669-4000 and through its web site at www.eeoc.gov. Many companies also have internal policies that deal with discrimination, and some employ equal employment officers.

To help prevent discrimination, keep records of your performance at every job you get. Log your achievements. Also ask for copies of your performance evaluations and make sure they're accurate. These documents will bolster your confidence at every step of the job-hunting process. They will also furnish key documentation if you ever file a grievance or take legal action.

10 Be prepared to act like a free agent.

International competition, corporate downsizing, and new technology could make the typical job as we know it a thing of the past. The workplace of the future might be organized around projects done by flexible teams of free agents instead of employees who spend years with a single company.

If this happens, you can prosper by seeing yourself as self-employed—even if you have a "regular" job. Think like a freelance or contract employee who's hired to complete a specific project. Demonstrate your value in each project, continually revise your job goals, expand your contacts, and constantly update your skills. Continuous career planning will help you prosper, no matter what direction the economy takes.

Dave Ellis, Stan Lankowitz, Ed Stupka, and Doug Toft, Career Planning, *Second Edition Copyright © 1997 by Houghton Mifflin Company. Reprinted by Permission.*

JOURNAL ENTRY

#59

Intention Statement

Even if you are not sure of your career preference, write a career plan right now. Include three elements: a career goal, a list of steps you can take to prepare for that career, and a timeline for reaching that career goal.

Your plan might be incomplete or tentative. No problem. You can change this plan later—even throw it out and start over. Career planning is a continual cycle of discovery, intention, and feedback.

The point is to dive into the process and make career planning a lifelong habit. This habit can radically affect the quality of your life.

You can plan now, with no further research. Go ahead. There's nothing to lose and lots of space to write in. Make an outline, do a mind map—use any format you like. Discover what you already know.

Mind map, outline, or write down your career plan on a separate sheet of paper. You can also use a computer for this purpose.

EXERCISE

#36

Discovery Wheel— coming full circle

This book doesn't work. It is worthless. Only you can work. Only you can make a difference and use this book to become a more effective student.

The purpose of this book is to give you the opportunity to change your behavior. The fact that something seems like a good idea doesn't necessarily mean that you will put it into practice. This exercise gives you a chance to see what behaviors you have changed on your journey toward becoming a master student.

Answer each question quickly and honestly. Record your results on the Discovery Wheel on this page and then compare it with the one you produced in Chapter One.

The scores on this Discovery Wheel indicate your current strengths and weaknesses in becoming a master student. The last Journal Entries in this chapter provide opportunities to write about how you intend to change. As you complete this self-evaluation, ask yourself how you want to change. Your commitment to change allows you to become a master student.

Note: Your scores might be lower here than on your earlier Discovery Wheel. That's OK. Lower scores might result from increased self-awareness and honesty—valuable assets.

 An online version of this exercise is available on Houghton Mifflin's College Survival/Becoming a Master Student website: **http://collegesurvival.college.hmco. com/students.**

The wheel sections, clockwise from top: (1) MOTIVATION, (2) TIME, (3) MEMORY, (4) READING, (5) NOTES, (6) TESTS, (7) THINKING, (8) COMMUNICATING, (9) DIVERSITY, (10) RESOURCES, (11) HEALTH, (12) PURPOSE. Scale marks at 10, 20, 30.

5 points
This statement is always or almost always true of me.

4 points
This statement is often true of me.

3 points
This statement is true of me about half the time.

2 points
This statement is seldom true of me.

1 point
This statement is never or almost never true of me.

1. _____ I start courses highly motivated and I stay that way.

2. _____ I have adequate support from teachers and administrators to succeed in higher education.

3. _____ I enjoy learning.

4. _____ I study even when distracted by activities of lower priority.

5. _____ I am satisfied with how I progress toward achieving goals.

6. _____ I use knowledge of learning styles to support my success in school.

7. _____ I am excited about courses I take.

8. _____ I have a clear idea of the benefits I expect to get from my education.

_____ Total score (1) *Motivation*

1. _____ I set long-term goals and periodically review them.
2. _____ I set short-term goals to support my long-term goals.
3. _____ I write a plan for each day and each week.
4. _____ I assign priorities to what I choose to do each day.
5. _____ I plan review time so I don't have to cram before tests.
6. _____ I plan regular recreation time.
7. _____ I adjust my study time to meet the demands of individual courses.
8. _____ I have adequate time each day to accomplish what I plan.

_____ Total score (2) *Time*

1. _____ I am confident of my ability to remember.
2. _____ I remember people's names.
3. _____ At the end of a lecture, I can summarize what was presented.
4. _____ I apply techniques that enhance my memory skills.
5. _____ I can recall information when I'm under pressure.
6. _____ I remember important information clearly and easily.
7. _____ I can jog my memory when I have difficulty recalling.
8. _____ I can relate new information to what I've already learned.

_____ Total score (3) *Memory*

1. _____ I preview and review reading assignments.
2. _____ When reading, I ask myself questions about the material.
3. _____ I underline or highlight important passages when reading.
4. _____ When I read textbooks, I am alert and awake.
5. _____ I relate what I read to my life.
6. _____ I select a reading strategy to fit the type of material I'm reading.
7. _____ I take effective notes when I read.
8. _____ When I don't understand what I'm reading, I note my questions and find answers.

_____ Total score (4) *Reading*

1. _____ When I am in class, I focus my attention.
2. _____ I take notes in class.
3. _____ I am aware of various methods for taking notes and choose those that work best for me.
4. _____ I distinguish important material and note key phrases in a lecture.
5. _____ I copy down material that the instructor writes on the chalkboard or overhead projector.
6. _____ I can put important concepts into my own words.
7. _____ My notes are valuable for review.
8. _____ I review class notes within 24 hours.

_____ Total score (5) *Notes*

1. _____ I feel confident and calm during an exam.
2. _____ I manage my time during exams and am able to complete them.
3. _____ I am able to predict test questions.
4. _____ I adapt my test-taking strategy to the kind of test I'm taking.
5. _____ I understand what essay questions ask and can answer them completely and accurately.
6. _____ I start reviewing for tests at the beginning of the term.
7. _____ I continue reviewing for tests throughout the term.
8. _____ My sense of personal worth is independent of my test scores.

_____ Total score (6) *Tests*

1. _____ I have flashes of insight and often think of solutions to problems at unusual times.
2. _____ I use brainstorming to generate solutions to a variety of problems.
3. _____ When I get stuck on a creative project, I use specific methods to get unstuck.
4. _____ I see problems and tough decisions as opportunities for learning and personal growth.
5. _____ I am willing to consider different points of view and alternative solutions.
6. _____ I can state the assumptions that underlie a series of assertions.
7. _____ I can detect common errors in logic.
8. _____ I approach courses in mathematics and science with confidence.

_____ Total score (7) *Thinking*

1. _____ I am candid with others about who I am, what I feel, and what I want.
2. _____ Other people tell me that I am a good listener.
3. _____ I can communicate my upset and anger without blaming others.
4. _____ I have the ability to make friends and create valuable relationships in a new setting.
5. _____ I am open to being with people I don't especially like in order to learn from them.
6. _____ I can effectively plan and research a large writing assignment.
7. _____ I create first drafts without criticizing my writing, then edit later for clarity, accuracy, and coherence.
8. _____ I know ways to prepare and deliver effective speeches.

_____ Total score (8) *Communicating*

1. _____ I am aware of my biases and am open to understanding people from other cultures, races, and ethnic groups.
2. _____ I build rewarding relationships with people from other backgrounds.
3. _____ I can point out examples of discrimination and sexual harassment and effectively respond to them.
4. _____ I am learning ways to thrive with diversity—attitudes and behaviors that will support my career success.
5. _____ I can effectively resolve conflict with people from other cultures.
6. _____ My writing and speaking are free of sexist expressions.
7. _____ I can recognize bias and discrimination in the media.
8. _____ I am aware of and interested in the changing demographics in my country and community.

_____ Total score (9) *Diversity*

1. _____ I use school-based services to support my success.
2. _____ I know where to get help in my community for a variety of problems.
3. _____ I am involved in extracurricular activities that align with my long-term goals and support my success in school.
4. _____ I am confident that I will have enough money to complete the education that I want.
5. _____ I minimize debt and repay my existing debts on time.
6. _____ I can efficiently find information on the Internet that is useful and accurate.
7. _____ I stay up-to-date with technology and use computers in specific ways to support my success.
8. _____ I can effectively use libraries to find the resources and information I want.

_____ Total score (10) *Resources*

1. _____ I have enough energy to study and still fully enjoy other areas of my life.
2. _____ If the situation calls for it, I have enough reserve energy to put in a long day.
3. _____ The food I eat supports my long-term health.
4. _____ The way I eat is independent of my feelings of self-worth.
5. _____ I exercise regularly to maintain a healthful weight.
6. _____ My emotional health supports my ability to learn.
7. _____ I notice changes in my physical condition and respond effectively.
8. _____ I am in control of any alcohol or other drugs I put into my body.

_____ Total score (11) *Health*

1. _____ I see learning as a lifelong process.
2. _____ I relate school to what I plan to do for the rest of my life.
3. _____ I learn by contributing to others.
4. _____ I revise my plans as I learn, change, and grow.
5. _____ I am clear about my purpose in life.
6. _____ I know that I am responsible for my own education.
7. _____ I take responsibility for the quality of my life.
8. _____ I am willing to accept challenges even when I'm not sure how to meet them.

_____ Total score (12) *Purpose*

Filling in your Discovery Wheel

Using the total score from each category, shade in each section of the Discovery Wheel. Use different colors, if you want. For example, you could use green to denote areas you want to work on. When you have finished, complete the following Journal Entries.

Name _____ Date ____/____/____ ✓

JOURNAL ENTRY

#60

Discovery/Intention Statement

The purpose of this Journal Entry is to 1) review both of the Discovery Wheels you completed in this book, 2) summarize your insights from doing them, and 3) declare how you will use these insights to promote your continued success in school.

In addition, your instructor might like to know the collective experience of your class. With that purpose in mind, your instructor can collect this first page of your Discovery Wheel summary and keep it as a record of the changes made by all the students in the class.

Begin by tearing out the blank sheet of paper that follows this page, then list your scores for the Discovery Wheel in Chapter One (pages 14–16) and in this chapter (pages 370–372). Again, a lower score on the second Discovery Wheel does not necessarily indicate decreased personal effectiveness. Instead, the lower score could result from increased honesty and greater self-awareness.

	Chapter 1	Chapter 12
Motivation	_____	_____
Time	_____	_____
Memory	_____	_____
Reading	_____	_____
Notes	_____	_____
Tests	_____	_____
Thinking	_____	_____
Communicating	_____	_____
Diversity	_____	_____
Resources	_____	_____
Health	_____	_____
Purpose	_____	_____

Comparing the Discovery Wheel in this chapter with the Discovery Wheel in Chapter One, I learned that I . . .

_____

_____

_____

In the next six months, I intend to review the following articles from this book for additional suggestions I could use:

_____

_____

_____

_____

This page intentionally left blank.

Remove this sheet before completing Journal Entry #60.

This page is inserted to ensure that the other writing you do in this book doesn't show through on the following page.

**Remove this sheet before completing
Journal Entry #60.**

*This page is inserted to ensure that the other writing you do in this book doesn't show
through on the following page.*

This page intentionally left blank.

JOURNAL ENTRY

#60

Discovery/Intention Statement

The purpose of this Journal Entry is to 1) review both of the Discovery Wheels you completed in this book, 2) summarize your insights from doing them, and 3) declare how you will use these insights to promote your continued success in school.

In addition, your instructor might like to know the collective experience of your class. With that purpose in mind, your instructor can collect this first page of your Discovery Wheel summary and keep it as a record of the changes made by all the students in the class.

Begin by tearing out the blank sheet of paper that follows this page, then list your scores for the Discovery Wheel in Chapter One (pages 14–16) and in this chapter (pages 370–372). Again, a lower score on the second Discovery Wheel does not necessarily indicate decreased personal effectiveness. Instead, the lower score could result from increased honesty and greater self-awareness.

	Chapter 1	Chapter 12
Motivation	_____	_____
Time	_____	_____
Memory	_____	_____
Reading	_____	_____
Notes	_____	_____
Tests	_____	_____
Thinking	_____	_____
Communicating	_____	_____
Diversity	_____	_____
Resources	_____	_____
Health	_____	_____
Purpose	_____	_____

Comparing the Discovery Wheel in this chapter with the Discovery Wheel in Chapter One, I learned that I . . .

_____

_____

_____

In the next six months, I intend to review the following articles from this book for additional suggestions I could use:

_____

_____

_____

_____

Job skills for the new millennium

In the early 1990s, the U.S. Department of Labor began issuing reports created by the Secretary's Commission on Achieving Necessary Skills (SCANS). This series of documents—called the *SCANS reports*—lists skills to promote success for workers as they enter this new century. You can use these influential documents to develop your résumé, plan your career, and link your school experiences to the world of work. The SCANS reports identify three foundations (basic skills, thinking skills, and personal qualities) and five core competencies (resources, interpersonal skills, information, systems, and technology). More details about each of these follow.

As a student, you are already developing many of the skills listed in the SCANS reports. Remember that employers might hire you for demonstrated evidence of these skills—even more than for years of experience in your chosen field.

Three foundations

Basic skills

- Reading to locate, understand, and interpret written information.
- Writing to communicate ideas and information.
- Using arithmetic to perform basic computations and solve problems.
- Listening to interpret and respond to verbal messages and other cues.

Thinking skills

- Speaking to inform and persuade others.
- Creative thinking to generate new ideas.
- Decision making to set and meet goals.
- Problem solving to identify challenges and implement action plans.
- Seeing things in the mind's eye to interpret and create symbols, pictures, graphs, and other visual tools.
- Knowing how to learn.

Personal qualities

- Responsibility to exert high effort and persist in meeting goals.

- Self-esteem to maintain a positive view of your abilities.
- Social skills that demonstrate adaptability and empathy.
- Self-management to assess yourself accurately, set personal goals, and monitor personal progress.

Five core competencies

Resources

- Allocating time for goal-relevant activities.
- Allocating money to prepare budgets and meet them.
- Allocating materials and facilities.
- Allocating human resources to assign tasks effectively and provide others with feedback.

Interpersonal skills

- Participating as a member of a team.
- Teaching others.
- Serving clients and customers.
- Exercising leadership.
- Negotiating to reach agreements.
- Working with diversity.

Information

- Acquiring and evaluating information.
- Organizing and maintaining information.
- Interpreting and communicating information in oral, written, and visual forms.
- Using computers to process information.

Systems

- Understanding how social and technological systems operate.
- Monitoring and correcting performance.
- Improving or designing systems.

Technology

- Selecting appropriate technology.
- Applying technology to tasks.
- Maintaining and troubleshooting technology.

Adapted from U.S. Department of Labor, *Skills and Tasks for Jobs: A SCANS Report for America 2000.* 1992. Access it online at **wdr.doleta.gov/SCANS/whatwork/whatwork.html.**

Link to the world of work

The suggestions in *Becoming a Master Student* are geared toward promoting your success in school. Nearly all of the suggestions in this book can promote your success on the job as well.

Staying current in the job market means continually expanding your knowledge and skills. Frequent career changes are common among today's workers, and these trends call for continuous learning. As a master student, you can gain favor with employers by getting up to speed quickly on new jobs and new projects. Apply the techniques and tools you've gained from this course to any learning situation—on or off the job.

Start now. Redo this book with a new mental filter in place. Ask yourself: How can I use this idea to meet my career goals? How can I apply this technique to my current job?

For starters, review the workplace applications scattered throughout this book. Also consider the examples that follow, which are tied to each chapter. Then invent applications of your own. There's no limit to the possibilities.

First Steps—Chapter One.
Keep using the Discovery and Intention Journal Entry system while you're in the workforce. Write Discovery Statements to note your current strengths in job skills as well as areas for improvement. Also use Discovery Statements to stay in touch with what you want from your career.

Follow up with Intention Statements to align your activities with your career plan. Use Intention Statements to list actions you can take today to meet your short-term and long-term job goals.

Breakdowns happen at every work site. People miss due dates. Valued employees choose to quit. Expenses go over budget or profits take a plunge. When events such as these occur, take a First Step. Tell the truth about what's not working in your workplace. An atmosphere of truth telling shines a light on the source of any problem and points to solutions.

Remember that every time you find a way to apply a suggestion from this book to your career, you're using the Power Process "Ideas are tools."

Time—Chapter Two.
Use the Time Monitor/Time Plan process to become conscious of the way you currently use your time at work. With this awareness, you can minimize downtime and boost your productivity.

The article "25 ways to get the most out of now" is packed with ideas you can transfer to the workplace. For example, tackle difficult tasks first in the day, or at any other time when your energy peaks. Also find five-minute tasks that you can complete while waiting for a meeting to start.

With strategies for long-term planning, you can create long-term goals for your organization. In addition, strategies for scheduling can help you complete short-term goals that align with that mission.

Procrastination is as widespread in the workplace as on any campus. Review "The seven-day antiprocrastination plan" and related suggestions for ways to remove this obstacle to your success.

Memory—Chapter Three.
Techniques for remembering names can help as you meet people during your job search and get introduced to new coworkers. The 20 memory techniques offered in this chapter will also come in handy as you learn the policies and procedures for a new job.

For occasional inspiration, review the "Notable failures" in this chapter. Some of them involve work-related snafus. And to transform failure into success, review the Power Process "Love your problems."

Reading—Chapter Four.
Use Muscle Reading to keep up with journals and books in your field. This set of techniques can also help you scan web sites for the information you want, keep up with ever increasing volumes of email, and reduce mountains of interoffice memos to manageable proportions.

Notes—Chapter Five.

Experiment with different formats for taking notes during a meeting—mind maps, concept maps, the Cornell format, and more.

In addition, notice the times that you expose your handwriting to colleagues—for example, when filling out expense reports and time sheets or scrawling your comments on the draft of a proposal or report. If your penmanship does not present you in the best light, turn to "Improving your handwriting" for help.

Tests—Chapter Six.

Adapt the ideas mentioned in "Cooperative learning: Study with people" to cooperate more effectively with members of a project team. Also use suggestions for test taking when you take licensing exams, certification exams, and other tests in your field. Finally, see if you can use suggestions from "Have some FUN" to cultivate enjoyment at work. You're more likely to excel professionally when you're having a blast at your job.

Thinking—Chapter Seven.

Strategies for creating and evaluating new ideas can assist you in developing new services. Critical thinking skills, such as uncovering assumptions and faulty logic, being willing to change your mind, and examining problems from different points of view, can be of benefit when it comes time to make a job-related decision or to solve a workplace problem.

Communicating—Chapter Eight.

Your "soft" skills—including the ability to get along with colleagues—can be as important to your work success as your technical skills. Ideas for managing conflict and stating "I" messages can help you defuse tensions among coworkers. The ability to separate sending from receiving can improve your relationships with both supervisors and employees.

Use interpersonal skills to preserve contact with coworkers as they change jobs and move to new companies. These people could be in a position to hire you some day.

Writing techniques can assist you in preparing memos, writing reports, composing email, and creating text for a web site. With ideas from "Writing and delivering speeches," you can craft presentations to persuade your supervisor to increase your department budget—or give you a raise.

Diversity—Chapter Nine.

With tools for responding to diversity, you can relate more effectively to coworkers from many cultures. The suggestions for adapting to the culture of higher education can also assist you in adapting to the culture of a new job. Each company, large or small, develops its own culture—a set of shared values and basic assumptions. Even if you are self-employed, you can benefit by discovering and adapting to a client's corporate culture.

Resources—Chapter Ten.

Running any business—from a sole proprietorship to a multinational corporation—calls for money management skills. Chief financial officers deal with many of the same basic issues that individuals do—increasing money in and decreasing money out. Turn to this chapter for ideas when preparing project budgets and setting financial goals. And for fun, see if you can modify the "Education by the hour" exercise to calculate what it costs you to attend a one-hour business meeting.

In this chapter are useful ideas for locating what you want on the Internet and thinking critically about the information that you find there. Whether you're connecting to cyberspace from a campus or from a work cubicle, this information can be helpful.

Health—Chapter Eleven.

Suggestions for managing your health can help you achieve the mental and physical energy needed to work to your full capacity. Also keep in mind the toll that addiction to alcohol and other drugs takes on business. Employees who show up to work hung over or "under the influence" are, at the very least, unproductive. If they drive or operate machinery, they are downright dangerous. Use your understanding of addiction to speak candidly with a colleague about his drinking or drug use problem and offer help.

What Next?—Chapter Twelve.

Use ideas from this chapter to define your personal values, to align your job with those values, and to create projects that contribute to others. With the suggestions for career planning, you can start now to envision the jobs you want to have in five years, 10 years, and 20 or more years into the future.

Creating and using portfolios

In medieval times, artisans who wished to join a guild presented samples of their work. Furniture makers showed cabinets and chairs to their potential mentors. Painters presented samples of their sketches and portraits. Centuries later, people still value a purposeful collection of work samples. It is called a portfolio.

Martin Kimeldorf, author of *Portfolio Power,* notes that the word *portfolio* derives from two Latin terms: *port,* which means "to move," and *folio,* which means "papers" or "artifacts." True to these ancient meanings, portfolios are movable collections of papers and artifacts.

Portfolios differ from résumés. A résumé lists facts, including your interests, skills, work history, and accomplishments. Although a portfolio might include these facts, it can also include tangible objects to verify the facts—anything from transcripts of your grades to a videotape that you produced. Résumés offer facts; portfolios provide artifacts.

Photographers, contractors, and designers regularly show portfolios filled with samples of their work. Today, employers and educators increasingly see the portfolio as a tool that's useful for everyone. Some schools require students to create them, and some employers expect to see a portfolio before they'll hire a job applicant.

Enjoy the benefits—academic, professional, and personal. A well-done portfolio benefits its intended audience. To an instructor, your portfolio gives a rich, detailed picture of what you did to create value from a class. To a potential employer, your portfolio gives observable evidence of your skills and achievements. In both cases, a portfolio also documents something more intangible—your levels of energy, passion, and creativity.

Portfolios benefit you in specific ways. When you create a portfolio to document what you learned during a class, you review the content of the entire course. When you're creating a portfolio related to your career, you think about the skills you want to develop and ways to showcase those skills. And when you're applying for work, creating a portfolio prepares you for job interviews. Your portfolio can stand out from stacks of letters and résumés and distinguish you from other applicants.

By creating and using portfolios, you also position yourself for the workplace of the future. People such as William Bridges, author of *Jobshift*, have predicted a "jobless economy."[3] In such an economy, work will be done by teams assembled for specific projects instead of by employees in permanent positions. Workers will move from team to team, company to company, and career to career far more often than they do today. If these changes take place on a wide scale, then listing your job titles on a résumé will be less useful than documenting your skills in a vivid, detailed way. Creating and using portfolios is a wonderful way to provide that documentation.

In a more general sense, creating a portfolio helps you reflect on your life as a whole. When selecting artifacts to include in your portfolio, you celebrate your accomplishments. You discover key themes in your experience. You clarify what's important to you and create goals for the future. Portfolios promote the cycle of discovery, intention, and action presented in the Journal Entries and exercises included throughout this text. To create a portfolio, experiment with a four-step process: Collect and catalog artifacts. Plan your portfolio. Assemble your portfolio. Present your portfolio.

Collect and catalog artifacts.
An artifact is any object that's important to you and that reveals something about yourself. Examples include photographs, awards, recommendation letters, job descriptions for positions you've held, newspaper articles about projects you've done, lists of grants or scholarships you've received, programs from performances you've given, transcripts of your grades, or models you've constructed.

Taken together, your artifacts form a large and visible "database" that gives a picture of you—what you value, what you've done, and what skills you have. You can add to this database during every year of your life. From this constantly evolving collection of artifacts, you can create many portfolios for different purposes and different audiences.

Start collecting now. Write down the kinds of artifacts you'd like to save. Think about what

Artifacts for your portfolio

When looking for items to include in a portfolio, start with the following checklist. Then brainstorm your own list of added possibilities.

❏ Brochures describing a product or service you created, or workshops you attended

❏ Certificates, licenses, and awards

❏ Computer disks with sample publications, databases, or computer programs you've created

❏ Course descriptions and syllabi from classes you've taken or taught

❏ Formal evaluations of your work

❏ Job descriptions from positions you've held

❏ Letters of recommendation

❏ Lists of grants, scholarships, clients, customers, and organizations you've joined

❏ Newspaper and magazine articles about projects you participated in

❏ Objects you've created or received—anything from badges to jewelry

❏ Plans—lists of personal and professional values, goals, action plans, completed tasks, project timelines, and lifelines

❏ Printouts of email and web pages (including your personal web page)

❏ Programs from artistic performances or exhibitions

❏ Résumés or a curriculum vitae

❏ Sheet music or scores

❏ Tapes (video or audio), compact discs, or CD-ROMs

❏ Transcripts of grades, test scores, vocational aptitude tests, or learning styles inventories

❏ Visual art, including drawings, photographs, collages, and computer graphics

❏ Writing samples, such as class reports, workplace memos, proposals, policy and mission statements, bids, manuscripts for articles and books, and published pieces or bibliographies of published writing will be most useful to you in creating portfolios for your courses and your job search. In some cases, collecting artifacts requires follow-up. You might call former instructors or employers to request letters of recommendation. Or you might track down newspaper articles about a service learning project you did. Your responses to the Journal Entries and exercises in this book can also become part of your portfolio.

To save hours when you create your next portfolio, start documenting your artifacts. On a 3×5 card, record the "five W's" about each artifact: *who* was involved with it, *what* you did with it, *when* it was created, *where* it was created, and *why* the artifact is important to you. File these cards and update them as you collect new artifacts. Another option is to manage this information with a computer, using word processing or database software.

Plan your portfolio.

When you're ready to create a portfolio for a specific audience, allow some time for planning. Begin with your purpose for creating the portfolio—for example, to demonstrate your learning or to document your work experience as you prepare for a job interview.

Also list some specifics about your audience. Write a description of anyone who will see your portfolio. List what each person already knows about you and predict what else these people will want to know. Answer their questions in your portfolio.

Being aware of your purpose and audience will serve you at every step of creating a portfolio. Screen artifacts with these two factors in mind. If a beautiful artifact fails to meet your purpose or fit your audience, then leave it out for now. Save the artifact for a future portfolio.

When you plan your portfolio, also think about how to order and arrange your artifacts. One basic option is a chronological organization. For example, start with work samples from your earliest jobs and work up to the present.

Another option is to structure your portfolio around key themes, such as your values or work skills. When preparing this type of portfolio, you can define *work* to include any time you used a job-related skill, whether or not you got paid.

Assemble your portfolio.

With a collection of artifacts and a written plan, you're ready to assemble your portfolio. Arranging artifacts according to your design is a big part of this process. Also include elements to orient your audience members and guide them through your portfolio. Such elements can include:

- a table of contents.
- an overview or summary of the portfolio.
- titles and captions for each artifact.
- an index to your artifacts.

Although many portfolios take their final form as a collection of papers, remember that this is just one possibility. You can also create a bulletin board, a display, or a case that contains your artifacts. You could even create a videotape or a digital portfolio in the form of a personal web site.

You might find it useful to combine your résumé and portfolio into one document. In other cases, you can mention in your résumé that a separate portfolio is available on request.

Present your portfolio.

Your audience might ask you to present your portfolio as part of an interview or oral exam. If that's the case, then rehearse your portfolio presentation the way you would rehearse a speech. Write down questions that people might ask about your portfolio. Prepare some answers. Then do a dry run: Present your portfolio to friends and people in your career field, and request their feedback.

That feedback will give you plenty of ideas about ways to revise your portfolio. Any portfolio is a living document. Change it as you acquire new perspectives and skills.

 For more ideas on portfolios, go to Houghton Mifflin's College Survival/Becoming a Master Student web site: **http://collegesurvival.college.hmco.com/students.**

Also see Eve Evans Walden, *Portfolio to Accompany Becoming a Master Student* (Boston: Houghton Mifflin, 2000).

Contributing:
The art of selfishness

This book is about contributing to yourself—about taking care of yourself, being selfish, and fulfilling your own needs. The techniques and suggestions in these pages focus on ways to get what you want out of school and out of life.

One of the results of all this successful selfishness is the capacity for contributing, for giving to others. Contributing is what's left to do when you're satisfied, when your needs are fulfilled—and it completes the process.

People who are satisfied with life can share that satisfaction with others. It is not easy to contribute to another person's joy until you experience joy yourself. The same is true for love. When people are filled with love, they can more easily contribute love to others.

Our interdependence calls for contributing.
Every day we depend on contributing. We stake our lives on the compassion of other people. When you drive, you depend on others for your life. If a driver in an oncoming lane should cross into your own lane, you might die. You also depend upon the sensibilities of world leaders for your safety.

People everywhere are growing more interdependent. A plunge in the U.S. stock market reverberates in markets across the planet. A decrease in oil prices gives businesses everywhere a shot in the arm. A nuclear war would ignore national boundaries and devastate life on the planet. Successful arms negotiations allow all people to sleep a little easier.

In this interdependent world, there is no such thing as win/lose. If others lose, their loss directly affects us. If we lose, it is more difficult to contribute to others.

The only way to win and to get what we want in life is for others to win, also.

A caution.
The idea of contributing is not the same as knowing what is best for other people. We can't know. There are people, of course, who go around "fixing" others: "I know what you need. Here, do it my way." That is not contributing. It often causes more harm than good and can result in dependence on the part of the person we are "helping."

True contributing occurs only after you find out what another person wants or needs and then determine that you can lovingly support his having it.

How you can begin contributing.
The world will welcome your gifts of time, money, and talent. The advantages of contributing are clear. When we contribute, the whole human family benefits in a tangible way. Close to home, contributing often means getting involved with other people. This is one way to "break the ice" in a new community and meet people with interests similar to your own.

When you've made the decision to contribute, the next step is knowing how. There are ways to contribute in your immediate surroundings. Visit a neighbor, take a family member to a movie, or offer to tutor a roommate. Look for ways you can contribute by volunteering. An additional benefit of volunteer work is that it offers a way to explore possible career choices. Consider the following organizations, for starters.

Big Brothers and Big Sisters provide friendship and guidance to children who might have only one parent. Girls Club, Boys Club, Girl Scouts, and Boy Scouts of America all need large numbers of volunteers.

Sierra Club, Greenpeace, Audubon Society, World Wildlife Fund, and similar organizations are dedicated to protecting the environment and endangered species.

Amnesty International investigates human rights violations. It assists people who are imprisoned or tortured for peacefully expressing their points of view. You can participate in letter-writing campaigns.

Museums and art galleries need interested people to conduct tours and provide supervision. Performing arts organizations, such as local theater groups or ballet companies, are always in need of volunteers for everything from set decoration to ticket sales.

Hospitals and hospice programs often depend on volunteer help to supplement patient care provided by the professional staff. Nursing homes welcome visitors who are willing to spend time listening and talking with residents.

Political parties, candidates, and special interest groups need volunteers to stuff envelopes, gather petition signatures, and distribute literature. The American Red Cross provides disaster relief. Local community care centers use volunteers to help feed homeless people.

Service organizations like Cosmopolitan, Zonta, Jaycees, Altrusa, Kiwanis, Lions, American Association of University Women, Sertoma, Business and Professional Women, and Rotary want members who are willing to serve others.

Tutoring centers offer opportunities for competent students to help non-English-speaking people, grade school and high school students, and illiterate adults. Churches of all denominations want volunteers to assist with projects for the community and the world. World hunger groups want you to help feed starving people and to inform all of us about the problems of malnutrition, food spoilage, and starvation. These groups include Oxfam America, CARE, and The Hunger Project.

Considering the full scope of our international problems reminds us that there are plenty of opportunities for contributing. For instance, there are still enough nuclear warheads on the planet to end human life. According to the Food and Development Organization of the United Nations, 800 million people in the developing world do not have enough to eat. In the industrialized countries, another 34 million experience chronic food insecurity. Also, the World Bank reports that 1.2 billion people live on less than one dollar per day, and nearly 10 million children under age 5 died in 1999—most of them from preventable diseases.

If they remain unused, the techniques and strategies in this book make no difference in all this. However, you can make a difference. You can use these techniques to work with others and choose a new future for our planet.

JOURNAL ENTRY

#61

Discovery Statement

Recall a time when you contributed—for example, when you volunteered your time for an important cause or a worthy group. On a separate sheet of paper, write down details of the contribution you made and how you felt afterward.

JOURNAL ENTRY

#62

Intention Statement

Review the organizations mentioned in the article "Contributing: The art of selfishness." Choose one or two that interest you. Also, think about people in your life to whom you could give time, money, or something of yourself.

Make a commitment to contribute, and consider doing it through service learning. Make this commitment detailed and time-specific.

I intend to …

_____

_____

_____

_____

_____

_____

_____

_____

_____

_____

_____

_____

_____

_____

_____

Service learning
The art of learning from contributing

As part of a service learning project for a sociology course, students volunteer at a community center for older adults. For another service learning project, history students interview people in veterans' hospitals about their war experiences. These students plan to share their interview results with a psychiatrist on the hospital staff.

Meanwhile, business students provide free tax-preparation help at a center for low-income people. Students in graphic arts classes create free promotional materials for charities. Other students staff a food cooperative and community credit union.

These examples of actual projects from the National Service-Learning Clearinghouse demonstrate the working premise of service learning—that volunteer work and other forms of contributing can become a vehicle for higher education.

Service learning generally includes three elements: meaningful community service, a formal academic curriculum, and time for students to reflect on what they learn from service. That reflection can include speeches, journal writing, and research papers.

Service learning creates a win/win scenario. For one thing, students gain the satisfaction of contributing. They also gain experiences that can guide their career choices and help them develop job skills.

At the same time, service learning adds a valuable resource to the community with a handsome return on investment. For example, participants in the Learn and Serve program (administered by the Corporation for National Service) provided community services valued at four times the program cost.

When you design a service learning project, consider these suggestions:

- Work with a community agency that has experience with students. Make sure that the agency has liability insurance to cover volunteers.
- Handle logistics. Integrating service learning into your schedule can call for detailed planning. If your volunteer work takes place off campus, arrange for transportation and allow for travel time.
- Reflect on your service learning project with a tool you've used throughout this book—the Discovery and Intention Journal Entry system explained in Chapter

One. Write Discovery Statements about what you want to gain from service learning and how you feel about what you're doing. Follow up with Intention Statements about what you'll do differently for your next volunteer experience.

- Include ways to evaluate and improve your project. From your Intention Statements, create action goals and outcome goals. *Action goals* state what you plan to do and how many people you intend to serve, for instance, "We plan to provide 100 hours of literacy tutoring to 10 people in the community." *Outcome goals* describe the actual impact that your project will have: "At the end of our project, 60 percent of the people we tutor will be able to write a résumé and fill out a job application." Build numbers into your goals whenever possible. That makes it easier to evaluate your project.
- Create a way to build long-term impact into your project. One potential pitfall of service learning is that the programs are often short lived. Programs can die after the students pack up and return to campus. To avoid this fate, make sure that other students or community members are willing to step in and take over for you when the semester ends.
- Celebrate mistakes. If your project fails to meet its goals, have a party. State—in writing—the obstacles you encountered and ways to overcome them. The solutions you offer will be worth gold to the people who follow in your footsteps. Sharing the lessons learned from your mistakes is an act of service in itself.

Student Voices

I first began working with a local environmental organization in our community during my freshman year. It was intended partly as a way to be more social in a strange, new town, but after a year of service, we now have a university-supported recycling program that services both the students and the local residents.

—MANDY WISCONSIN

Be it

All of the techniques in this book are enhanced by this Power Process. To tap into its full benefits, consider that most of our choices fall into three categories. We can:

- *Increase our material wealth (what we have).*
- *Improve our skills (what we do).*
- *Develop our "being" (who we are).*

Many people devote their entire lifetime to the first two categories. They act as if they are "human havings" instead of human beings. For them, the quality of life hinges on what they have. They devote most of their waking hours to getting more—more clothes, more cars, more relationships, more degrees, more trophies. "Human havings" define themselves by looking at the circumstances in their lives—what they have.

Some people escape this materialist trap by adding another dimension to their identities. In addition to living as "human havings," they also live as "human doings." They thrive on working hard and doing everything well. They define themselves by how efficiently they do their jobs, how effectively they raise their children, and how actively they participate in clubs and organizations. Their thoughts are constantly about methods, techniques, and skills.

Look beyond doing and having

In addition to focusing on what we have and what we do, we can also focus on our being. Of course, it is impossible to live our lives without having things and doing things. This Power Process suggests that we balance our lives and give lots of attention to who we are—an aspect of our lives that goes beyond having and doing. Call it soul, passion,

purpose, or values. Call it being. This word describes how we see ourselves—our deepest commitments, the ground from which our actions spring.

The realm of being is profound and subtle. It is also difficult to capture in words, though philosophers have tried for centuries. Christian theologian Paul Tillich described this realm when he defined faith as "ultimate commitment" and the "ground of being." In the New Testament, Jesus talked about being when he asked his followers to love God with all of their heart, soul, and mind. An ancient Hindu text also touches on being: "You are what your deep, driving desire is."

If all this seems far removed from taking notes or answering test questions, then read on. Consider an example of how "Be it" can assist in career choices. In a letter to her father, a young woman wrote:

We just went to see the Dance Theatre of Harlem. It was great!!! After the last number, I decided that I want to dance more than anything. I have a great passion to do it, more than anything else I can think or dream of. Dancing is what will make me happy and feel like I can leave this earth when my time comes. It is what I must do. I think that if I never fulfill this passion, I will never feel complete or satisfied with what I have done with my life.

In her heart, this woman *is* a dancer now, even before her formal training is complete. From her passion, desire, commitment, and self-image (her *being*) comes her willingness to take classes and rehearse (*doing*). And from her doing she might eventually *have* a job with a professional dance company.

Picture the result as you begin

The example of the dancer illustrates that once you have a clear picture of what you want to *be*, the things you *do* and *have* fall more naturally into place.

The idea is this: Getting where you want to be by what you do or by what you have is like swimming against the current. Have → do → be is a tough journey. It's much easier to go in the other direction: be → do → have.

Usually, we work against nature by trying to have something or do something before being it. That's hard. All of your deeds (what you do) might not get you where you want to be. Getting all of the right things (what you have) might not get you there either.

Take the person who values athletics and wants to master tennis. He buys an expensive racket and a stylish tennis wardrobe. Yet he still can't return a serve. Merely having the right things doesn't deliver what he values.

Suppose that this person takes a year's worth of tennis lessons. Week after week, he practices doing everything "right." Still, his game doesn't quite make it.

What goes wrong is hard to detect. "He lost the match even though he played a good game," people say. "Something seemed to be wrong. His technique was fine, but each swing was just a little off." Perhaps the source of his problem is that he cannot see himself as ever mastering the game. What he has and what he does are at war with his mental picture of himself. You can see this happen in other areas of life. Two people tell the same joke in what seems to be the same way. Yet one person brings a smile, while the other person has you laughing so hard your muscles hurt. The difference in how they do the joke is imperceptible. When the successful comedian tells a joke, he does it from his experience of already being funny.

To have and do what you want, be it. Picture the result as you begin. If you can first visualize where you want to be, if you can go there in your imagination, if you can be it today, then you set yourself up to succeed.

Be a master student now

Now relate this Power Process to succeeding in school. All of the techniques in this book can be worthless if you operate with the idea that you are an ineffective student. You might do almost everything this book suggests. Yet you are likely to subtly sabotage your success and never have the success in school that you desire.

For example, if you believe you are stupid in math, then you are likely to fail at math. If you believe that you are not skilled at remembering, then all of the memory techniques in the world might not improve your recall. Generally we don't outperform our self-concept.

If you value success in school, then picture yourself as a master student right now. Through higher education you are gaining knowledge and skills that reflect and reinforce this view of yourself.

This principle works in other areas of life. For example, if you value a fulfilling career, then picture yourself as already being on a path to a job you love. Use affirmations and visualizations to plant this idea firmly in your mind. Change the way you see yourself, and watch your actions and results shift as if by magic.

Define your values, align your actions

One key way to use this Power Process is to define your values. Values are the things in life that you want for their own sake. Values influence and guide your choices, including your moment by moment choices of what to do and what to have. Your values define who you want to be.

Some people are guided by values that they automatically adopt from others or by values that remain largely unconscious. These people could be missing the opportunity to live a life that's truly of their own choosing.

Investing time and energy to define your values is a pivotal suggestion in this book. As you begin to do this, consider those who have gone before you. In creeds, scriptures, philosophies, myths, and sacred stories, the human race has left a vast and varied record of values. Be willing to look everywhere, including sources that are close to home. The creed of your local church or temple might eloquently describe some of your values—so might the mission statement of your school, company, or club. Another way to define your values is to describe the qualities of people you admire.

Also translate your values into behavior. Though defining your values is powerful, it doesn't guarantee any results. To actually get what you want, take action in ways that align with your values.

And while you're at it, remember that this Power Process is not positive thinking or mental cheerleading. "Be it" works well when you take a First Step—when you tell the truth about your current abilities.

In summary, define your values. Align your actions. Then watch your circumstances change. Flow with the natural current of be → do → have.

If you want it, be it.

One set of values

Following is a sample list of values. Don't read them with the idea that they are the "right" set of values for you. Instead, use this list as a point of departure in creating your own list.

Value: Be accountable

This means being:

- Honest
- Reliable
- Trustworthy
- Dependable
- Responsible

Being accountable includes making and keeping agreements—operating with integrity.

Value: Be loving

This means being:

- Affectionate
- Dedicated
- Devoted
- Equitable
- Accepting

Being loving includes appreciating ourselves and others—being gentle, considerate, forgiving, respectful, friendly, and courteous. It also includes being nonantagonistic, nonresistant, inclusive, understanding, compassionate, fair, and ethical.

Value: Be self-generating

This means being:

- Self-responsible
- The creator of our internal experiences—regardless of our external circumstances

Being self-generating includes not being a victim and not blaming others. Instead, we choose how to interpret and respond to all stimuli.

Value: Be promotive

This means being:

- Nurturing
- Contributing—charitable; thrifty; generous with time, money, and possessions

- Frugal—achieving the best results with the fewest possible dollars
- Helpful
- Encouraging
- Reasonable
- Judicious
- Cooperative—working as a member of a team or a community
- Appreciative

Value: Be candid

This means being:

- Honest
- Authentic
- Genuine
- Self-expressed
- Frank
- Outspoken
- Spontaneous
- Sincere
- Free of deceit
- Able to avoid false modesty without arrogance
- Self-disclosing
- Open about strengths and weaknesses

Value: Be detached

This means being:

- Impartial
- Unbiased
- Experimental
- Satisfied
- Patient (not resigned)
- Open-minded
- Without distress
- Adaptable
- Trusting
- Tolerant
- Willing to surrender
- Joyful—fun-loving, humorous, lighthearted, and happy

Detachment includes being separate from but aware of thoughts, emotions, body, health, accomplishments, relationships, desires, commitments, possessions, values, opinions, roles, and expectations. The opposite of detachment is being addicted (physically or emotionally), dogmatic, bigoted, absolutely certain, prejudiced, anxious, grave, or somber.

Value: Be aware of the possible

This means being:

- Creative
- Imaginative
- Resourceful
- Inventive
- Foresighted
- Holistic
- Visionary
- Inquisitive
- Audacious
- Exploring

Being aware of the possible means expecting great things of ourselves and others.

Value: Be involved

This means being:

- Committed
- Participative
- Focused—precise and attentive to detail
- Enthusiastic—having intense or eager interest
- Enduring—persistent, persevering
- Courageous—vulnerable, willing to take risks, trusting
- Energetic—displaying the capacity for action or accomplishment; being vigorous, robust, hardy, rugged, and strong
- Productive—putting ourselves at risk, operating with something at stake, pursuing excellence, acting with a sense of urgency yet without panic, and allowing projects to matter

#37

Define your values

One way to define your values is to finish this sentence: "I value being…." Complete the sentence with a single word or phrase that describes one of your deepest commitments. To gain further clarity, list synonyms for that word or phrase. For suggestions, see the article titled "One set of values."

Write about several of your own values below.

I value being …

_____

_____

_____

_____

_____

_____

_____

_____

_____

_____

_____

_____

_____

_____

_____

EXERCISE

#38

no

Master mind map (part two)

On a separate sheet of paper, create a mind map of Chapters Seven through Twelve of this book. If you did not read all of these chapters, then make a mind map of the ones you did read. Do this without reviewing the chapters first. After creating your mind map, go back through the text and scan each chapter, spending no more than 10 minutes per chapter. Then revise your mind map on the basis of this review.

master student
GOLDA MEIR

(1898–1978) a pioneer in the creation of Israel, was elected its fourth prime minister.

I *started school in a huge, fortress like building on Fourth* street near Milwaukee's famous Schlitz beer factory, and I loved it. I can't remember how long it took me to learn English (at home, of course, we spoke Yiddish, and luckily, so did almost everyone else on Walnut Street), but I have no recollection of the language ever being a real problem for me, so I must have picked it up quickly. I made friends quickly, too. Two of those early first- or second-grade friends remained friends all my life, and both live in Israel now. One was Regina Hamburger (today Medzini), who lived on our street and who was to leave America when I did; the other was Sarah Feder, who became one of the leaders of Labor Zionism in the United States. . . .

More than fifty years later—when I was seventy-one and a prime minister—I went back to that school for a few hours. It had not changed very much in all those years except that the vast majority of its pupils were now black, not Jewish, as in 1906. They welcomed me as though I were a queen. Standing in rows on the creaky old stage I remembered so

well, freshly scrubbed and neat as pins, they serenaded me with Yiddish and Hebrew songs and raised their voices to peal out the Israeli anthem "Hatikvah" which made my eyes fill with tears. Each one of the classrooms had been beautifully decorated with posters about Israel and signs reading SHALOM (one of the children thought it was my family name), and when I entered the school, two little girls wearing headbands with Stars of David on them solemnly presented me with an enormous white rose made of tissue paper and pipe cleaners, which I wore all day and carefully carried back to Israel with me.

Another of the gifts I got that day in 1971 from the Fourth Street School was a record of my grades for one of the years I had spent there: 95 in reading, 90 in spelling, 95 in arithmetic, 85 in music, and a mysterious 90 in something called manual arts, which I cannot remember at all. But when the children asked me to talk to them for a few minutes, it was not about book learning that I chose to speak. I had learned a lot more than fractions or how to spell at Fourth Street, and I decided to tell those eager, attentive children—born, as I myself had been, into a minority and living, as I myself had lived, without much extravagance (to put it mildly)—what the gist of that learning had been. "It isn't really important to decide when you are

very young just exactly what you want to become when you grow up," I told them. "It is much more important to decide on the way you want to live. If you are going to get involved with causes which are good for others, not only for yourselves, then it seems to me that that is sufficient, and maybe what you will be is only a matter of chance." I had a feeling that they understood me.

From My Life *by Golda Meir, published by Weidenfeld & Nicholson Ltd. Permission granted by the Orion Publishing Group Ltd.*

For more biographical information on Golda Meir, visit Houghton Mifflin's College Survival/Becoming a Master Student web site: **http://collegesurvival.college.hmco.com/ students.**

PRACTICING CRITICAL THINKING

#23

Review the master student profiles included throughout this book. Focus on one person and explain how she or he displays qualities of a critical thinker. Summarize your conclusions on a separate piece of paper.

Name _____ Date _____/_____/_____

 1 Briefly discuss the meaning of "Now that you're done—begin."

 2 Which of the following affirmations does *not* follow the suggestions for an effective affirmation?
- (A) I have a healthy, enjoyable, respectful relationship with my in-laws.
- (B) I am an artistic person.
- (C) I will stop putting off math assignments.
- (D) I speak clearly and concisely.
- (E) All of the above are effective affirmations.

 3 Explain how career planning can be a process of choosing instead of a process of discovery.

 4 What are three responses given in this chapter for the argument that making the wrong career choice will waste time?

Define the three main types of choices explained in the Power Process "Be it."

 6 Using the Power Process "Be it" eliminates the need to take action. True or False? Explain your answer.

 7 If your scores are lower on the Discovery Wheel the second time you finish it, that means your study skills have not improved. True or False? Explain your answer.

Quiz

C O N T I N U E D

8 Contributing to others does *not* involve:
  - (A) Telling people the best way for them to change.
  - (B) Finding out what people want or need.
  - (C) Determining if you can help people get what they want.
  - (D) Giving your time, talent, or money.
  - (E) Making sure that you experience satisfaction, also.

9 List three factors to consider before you sign up for a distance learning course.

10 List at least four ways that you can continue on your path of becoming a master student after completing this book.

JOURNAL ENTRY

#63

Discovery/Intention Statement

Consider the benefits of doing this book one year from now. Imagine what you could gain by rereading the material, rewriting the Journal Entries, and redoing the exercises. Also consider the costs of redoing the book. You would spend hours reading, writing, and experimenting. You might even feel uncomfortable looking at some aspects of yourself or discovering that you created your circumstances.

Once you have thought about the potential costs and benefits of redoing this book, write your intention below, including a specific time frame.

I intend to ...

_____

_____

_____

_____

_____

_____

_____

388   Chapter Twelve   **WHAT NEXT?**

LEARNING STYLES APPLICATION   CHAPTER 12

Mode 4 *Imagine that you are going to teach your own student success course next term. Consider how you will design the course. What topics will you cover? What specific ideas and suggestions will you offer on each topic? Write a rough draft of your course outline.*

Mode 1 *Consider your experience with this book and your student success class. Which of your attitudes or actions changed as a result of this experience? In what ways are you meeting with more success in school?*

Mode 3 *Now list some suggestions that you would like to apply but have not yet acted upon. Write Intention Statements describing how you will implement these suggestions.*

Mode 2 *On a separate sheet of paper, brainstorm a list of the suggestions from this book that you've already applied. Rate each suggestion for its effectiveness on a scale of 1 to 5 (1 is most effective, 5 is least effective).*

BIBLIOGRAPHY

ENDNOTES

1 Ira Progoff, *At a Journal Workshop* (New York: Dialogue House, 1975).

2 Richard Nelson Bolles, *What Color Is Your Parachute?* (Berkeley, CA: Ten Speed Press, updated annually).

3 William Bridges, *Jobshift: How to Prosper in a Workplace Without Jobs* (New York: Perseus, 1995).

ADDITIONAL READING

Bandler, Richard, and John Grinder. *Frogs into Princes: Neuro-Linguistic Programming.* Moab, UT: Real People, 1979.

Ellis, Dave. *Creating Your Future: Five Steps to the Life of Your Dreams.* Boston: Houghton Mifflin, 1998.

Ellis, Dave, and Stan Lankowitz. *Human Being: A Manual for Happiness, Health, Love and Wealth.* Rapid City, SD: Breakthrough Enterprises, 1995.

Ellis, Dave, Stan Lankowitz, Ed Stupka, and Doug Toft. *Career Planning.* Boston: Houghton Mifflin, 1997.

Gawain, Shakti. *Creative Visualization.* New York: New World Library, 1998.

Golas, Thaddeus. *The Lazy Man's Guide to Enlightenment.* New York: Bantam, 1993.

Keyes, Ken, Jr. *Handbook to Higher Consciousness.* Berkeley, CA: Living Love, 1974.

Lathrop, Richard. *Who's Hiring Who?* Berkeley, CA: Ten Speed, 1989.

Rajneesh, Bhagwan S. *Journey Toward the Heart.* New York: Harper and Row, 1980.

INTERNET RESOURCES

College Search Engine
www.collegeboard.com

National Service-Learning Clearinghouse
www.servicelearning.org

Portfolio Power
www.publishingonline.com

Resources for Distance Education
http://ccc.commnet.edu/HP/pages/darling/distance.htm

U.S. News College Rankings
www.usnews.com/usnews/edu/college/cohome.htm

PHOTO AND ILLUSTRATION CREDITS

© Keith Brofsky/PhotoDisc/PictureQuest: page 291; © Ron Chapple/Thinkstock/PictureQuest pages 322, 346; Lee Christiansen: pages 34, 80, 108, 132, 160, 190, 220, 254, 282, 318, 348, 386; © Comstock IMAGES pages 84, 164; © Corbis Images/PictureQuest pages 286, 306, 379; Corbis/Royalty Free: pages 104, 112, 157, 258, 316; © DigitalVision (logging) page 217; © elektraVision: AG/PictureQuest page 6; Eyewire pages 75, 188; © 1999 Image Ideas, Inc. page 352; Walter Kopec: pages 138, 141, 146, 336, 337; © S. Meltzer/PhotoLink/ PhotoDisc/PictureQuest: pages 288, 289; PhotoDisc © 2002: pages 8, 30, 31, 38, 74, 75, 86, 87, 88, 90, 121, 130, 132, 136, 150, 175, 183, 186, 194, 212, 214, 217 (seedling), 241, 265, 271, 260, 268, 277, 279, 294, 296, 299, 305, 308, 311, 324, 325, 326, 327, 328, 329, 333, 338–339, 341, 354, 360, 363, 365, 376, 382; Stockbyte pages 74, 224. Collage on page 61 created digitally by Walter Kopec, using images from the following sources: Woman's face, Clock, Trash Can © 2002 PhotoDisc; Gears, Eight Ball, "Rush" stamp © ComstockKlips. Collage on page 62 created digitally by Walter Kopec, using images from the following sources: Woman's face, Clock, Folders © 2002 PhotoDisc; Gears, "Stop" sign © ComstockKlips; Hammock © Artville. Collages on pages 114–119 created digitally by Walter Kopec, using images © 2002 PhotoDisc. Collages on pages 262–264 created digitally by Walter Kopec, using images © 2002 PhotoDisc. Collage on page 273 created digitally using references from the following sources: Francis Marion, Clara Barton, Queen Elizabeth I, Dictionary of American Portraits, published by Dover Publications, Inc. © 1967; Thomas Jefferson, Dictionary of American Portraits, published by Dover Publications, Inc. © 1967, courtesy of Bowdoin College; American Horse, Dictionary of American Portraits, published by Dover Publications, Inc. © 1967, courtesy of Smithsonian Institute; Joseph Hayne Rainey, Dictionary of American Portraits, published by Dover Publications, Inc. © 1967, courtesy of National Archives, Brady Collection; Dwight D. Eisenhower, Dictionary of American Portraits, published by Dover Publications, Inc. © 1967, Library of Congress photo; Abraham Lincoln, Dictionary of American Portraits, published by Dover Publications, Inc. © 1967, engraving by H.B. Hall's Sons; George Washington, Hillary Rodham Clinton, Barbara Bush, © Library of Congress; astronaut image Copyright © 2002 PhotoDisc.

INDEX

MONDAY ___/___/___			TUESDAY ___/___/___			WEDNESDAY ___/___/___	
MONITOR	PLAN		MONITOR	PLAN		MONITOR	PLAN
7:00	7:00		7:00	7:00		7:00	7:00
	7:15			7:15			7:15
	7:30			7:30			7:30
	7:45			7:45			7:45
8:00	8:00		8:00	8:00		8:00	8:00
	8:15			8:15			8:15
	8:30			8:30			8:30
	8:45			8:45			8:45
9:00	9:00		9:00	9:00		9:00	9:00
	9:15			9:15			9:15
	9:30			9:30			9:30
	9:45			9:45			9:45
10:00	10:00		10:00	10:00		10:00	10:00
	10:15			10:15			10:15
	10:30			10:30			10:30
	10:45			10:45			10:45
11:00	11:00		11:00	11:00		11:00	11:00
	11:15			11:15			11:15
	11:30			11:30			11:30
	11:45			11:45			11:45
12:00	12:00		12:00	12:00		12:00	12:00
	12:15			12:15			12:15
	12:30			12:30			12:30
	12:45			12:45			12:45
1:00	1:00		1:00	1:00		1:00	1:00
	1:15			1:15			1:15
	1:30			1:30			1:30
	1:45			1:45			1:45
2:00	2:00		2:00	2:00		2:00	2:00
	2:15			2:15			2:15
	2:30			2:30			2:30
	2:45			2:45			2:45
3:00	3:00		3:00	3:00		3:00	3:00
	3:15			3:15			3:15
	3:30			3:30			3:30
	3:45			3:45			3:45
4:00	4:00		4:00	4:00		4:00	4:00
	4:15			4:15			4:15
	4:30			4:30			4:30
	4:45			4:45			4:45
5:00	5:00		5:00	5:00		5:00	5:00
	5:15			5:15			5:15
	5:30			5:30			5:30
	5:45			5:45			5:45
6:00	6:00		6:00	6:00		6:00	6:00
	6:15			6:15			6:15
	6:30			6:30			6:30
	6:45			6:45			6:45
7:00	7:00		7:00	7:00		7:00	7:00
	7:15			7:15			7:15
	7:30			7:30			7:30
	7:45			7:45			7:45
8:00	8:00		8:00	8:00		8:00	8:00
	8:15			8:15			8:15
	8:30			8:30			8:30
	8:45			8:45			8:45
9:00	9:00		9:00	9:00		9:00	9:00
	9:15			9:15			9:15
	9:30			9:30			9:30
	9:45			9:45			9:45
10:00	10:00		10:00	10:00		10:00	10:00
	10:15			10:15			10:15
	10:30			10:30			10:30
	10:45			10:45			10:45
11:00	11:00		11:00	11:00		11:00	11:00
	11:15			11:15			11:15
	11:30			11:30			11:30
	11:45			11:45			11:45
12:00	12:00		12:00	12:00		12:00	12:00

THURSDAY ___/___/___

MONITOR	PLAN
7:00	7:00
	7:15
	7:30
	7:45
8:00	8:00
	8:15
	8:30
	8:45
9:00	9:00
	9:15
	9:30
	9:45
10:00	10:00
	10:15
	10:30
	10:45
11:00	11:00
	11:15
	11:30
	11:45
12:00	12:00
	12:15
	12:30
	12:45
1:00	1:00
	1:15
	1:30
	1:45
2:00	2:00
	2:15
	2:30
	2:45
3:00	3:00
	3:15
	3:30
	3:45
4:00	4:00
	4:15
	4:30
	4:45
5:00	5:00
	5:15
	5:30
	5:45
6:00	6:00
	6:15
	6:30
	6:45
7:00	7:00
	7:15
	7:30
	7:45
8:00	8:00
	8:15
	8:30
	8:45
9:00	9:00
	9:15
	9:30
	9:45
10:00	10:00
	10:15
	10:30
	10:45
11:00	11:00
	11:15
	11:30
	11:45
12:00	12:00

FRIDAY ___/___/___

MONITOR	PLAN
7:00	7:00
	7:15
	7:30
	7:45
8:00	8:00
	8:15
	8:30
	8:45
9:00	9:00
	9:15
	9:30
	9:45
10:00	10:00
	10:15
	10:30
	10:45
11:00	11:00
	11:15
	11:30
	11:45
12:00	12:00
	12:15
	12:30
	12:45
1:00	1:00
	1:15
	1:30
	1:45
2:00	2:00
	2:15
	2:30
	2:45
3:00	3:00
	3:15
	3:30
	3:45
4:00	4:00
	4:15
	4:30
	4:45
5:00	5:00
	5:15
	5:30
	5:45
6:00	6:00
	6:15
	6:30
	6:45
7:00	7:00
	7:15
	7:30
	7:45
8:00	8:00
	8:15
	8:30
	8:45
9:00	9:00
	9:15
	9:30
	9:45
10:00	10:00
	10:15
	10:30
	10:45
11:00	11:00
	11:15
	11:30
	11:45
12:00	12:00

SATURDAY ___/___/___

MONITOR	PLAN

SUNDAY ___/___/___

MONITOR	PLAN

Monday	Tuesday	Wednesday	Thursday	Friday	Saturday	Sunday

Name _____

Month _____

Name ———————

Month ———————

Monday	Tuesday	Wednesday	Thursday	Friday	Saturday	Sunday